Family
in
Transition

Family
in
Transition
Ninth Edition

Arlene S. Skolnick
University of California, Berkeley

Jerome H. Skolnick
University of California, Berkeley

 LONGMAN

An imprint of Addison Wesley Longman, Inc.

New York • Reading, Massachusetts • Menlo Park, California • Harlow, England
Don Mills, Ontario • Sydney • Mexico City • Madrid • Amsterdam

Executive Editor: Alan McClare
Project Coordination, Text and Art Design,
     and Electronic Page Makeup: Thompson Steele Production Services
Supplements Editor: Tom Kulesa
Cover Designer: Kay Petronio
Electronic Production Manager: Eric Jorgensen
Manufacturing Manager: Hilda Koparanian
Printer and Binder: RR Donnelley & Sons Co.
Cover Printer: Phoenix Color Corp.

Library of Congress Cataloging-in-Publication Data

Family in transition / [edited by] Arlene S. Skolnick, Jerome H.
  Skolnick. — 9th ed.
     p. cm.
    Includes bibliographical references.
    ISBN 0–673–52512–0
    1. Family.   I. Skolnick, Arlene S., 1933– .   II. Skolnick,
  Jerome H.
    HQ518.F336 1997
    306.85—dc20   96–24488
                                                    CIP

0-673-52512-0

12345678910—DOC—99989796

Contents

Preface   xi

Introduction: Family in Transition   1

Part One   The Changing Family   17

Chapter 1   Families Present and Past   21

READING 1   *Dennis A. Ahlburg* and *Carol J. De Vita* / "New Realities of the American Family"   21

Census Bureau data on American families reveals dramatic change, but no evidence that the family is a disappearing institution.

READING 2   *Tamara K. Hareven* / "Continuity and Change in American Family Life"   29

Over the past two centuries what has been lost is not the mythical "great extended family," but the flexibility that enabled households to expand.

READING 3   *Arlene Skolnick* / "The Life Course Revolution"   37

Changes in mortality rates have had profound, yet little-appreciated, effects on family life.

READING 4   *Stephanie Coontz* / "The Way We Wish We Were"   46

Nostalgia not only clouds our understanding of the family in past times, but leads to distorted impressions of the present.

Chapter 2   The Meaning(s) of "Family"   58

READING 5   *Marjorie L. DeVault* / "Constructing the Family"   58

The meaning of "Family" is enacted in daily life as mealtimes bring family members together.

READING 6   *David M. Rosen* / "What Is a Family? Nature, Culture, and the Law"   70

As the traditional nuclear family declines, the law grapples uneasily with redefining the meaning of "family."

READING 7   *James Davison Hunter* / "The Family and the Culture War"   81

In America's culture wars, there is no conflict more embattled than that over the definition of the family.

Part Two   The Sexes   93

Chapter 3   Gender   99

READING 8   *Jessie Bernard* / "The Good-Provider Role: Its Rise and Fall"   99

The dilution of the male good-provider role is an important social change, marking the decline of sharp definitions that link gender with work.

READING 9   *William J. Goode* / "Why Men Resist"   119

Although men still struggle against losing their advantages, prospects for equality never looked better.

Chapter 4   Sexuality   132

READING 10   *Robert T. Michael, John H. Gagnon, Edward D. Laumann,* and *Gina Kolata* / "Finding a Partner"   132

Most people still find mates the old-fashioned way—in their own social networks of friends and family.

READING 11   *Lillian B. Rubin* / "The Culture of Adolescent Sexuality"   148

The most striking evidence of the sexual revolution is to be found in the new sexual norms among teenagers.

Chapter 5   Marriage, Divorce, Remarriage   156

READING 12   *John Gottman* / "Marriage Styles: The Good, the Bad, and the Volatile"   156

Happy families are not all alike—there are several styles of successful marriage.

READING 13   *Frances Klagsbrun* / "Long-Term Marriages"   169

There's no formula for marital success, but long-term couples share identifiable characteristics.

READING 14   *E. Mavis Hetherington, Tracy C. Law,* and *Thomas G. O'Connor* / "Divorce: Challenges, Changes, and New Chances"   176

Divorce is not a single event, with the same effects on all the children and adults who experience it. It is a long complicated process, with varying outcomes.

READING 15   *Constance R. Ahrons* and *Roy H. Rodgers* / "The Remarriage Transition"   185

Although divorce ends marriage, complex family relationships often develop.

Part Three   Parents and Children   197

Chapter 6   Parenthood   201

READING 16   *Carolyn P. Cowan* and *Phillip A. Cowan* / "Becoming a Parent"   201

Parenthood in America is usually a difficult period of transition.

READING 17   *Reed Larson* and *Maryse H. Richards* / "Healthy Families: Toward Convergent Realities"   214

Family members spend most of their days in different worlds; it's possible for them to share their separate realities.

READING 18   *Frank F. Furstenberg, Jr.* / "Good Dads–Bad Dads: Two Faces of Fatherhood"   221

Some men are becoming nurturant, involved, "Cosby" style dads, while others are shirking their parental responsibilities.

READING 19   *Elizabeth Bartholet* / "Adoption and Stigma"   242

Even though adoptive families have existed since time immemorial, many people still feel that biological families are somehow more "real."

Chapter 7   Childhood   256

READING 20   *Donald Hernandez*, with *David E. Myers* / "Revolutions in
Children's Lives"   256

Over the past 200 years, the lives of American children have
been transformed several times by changes in the economy,
society, and family life.

READING 21   *Frank F. Furstenberg* and *Andrew J. Cherlin* / "Children's
Adjustment to Divorce"   267

For most children, divorce is painful, but most do not suffer
long-lasting problems. The key factor in children's adjustment: the relationship with the custodial parent.

READING 22   *Phillip W. Davis* / "The Changing Meanings of
Spanking"   278

To spank or not to spank? Some people feel it's an essential
part of child-rearing, others feel it's a form of child abuse.

Part Four   Families in Society   291

Chapter 8   Work and Family   297

READING 23   *Lillian B. Rubin* / "Families on the Fault Line"   297

"Downsizing," corporate moves, and other workplace
changes have undermined the security of working-class families—no matter what their race or ethnic group.

READING 24   *Maxine Baca Zinn* / "Family, Race, and Poverty"   316

The "underclass" is caused by massive economic transformations that moved opportunity out of the inner cities, not by a
"breakdown in family values."

READING 25   *Arlie Hochschild*, with *Anne Machung* / "The Second Shift:
Working Parents and the Revolution at Home"   330

Men who do not share the work of the home may be harm-
ing their marriages.

Chapter 9   Family Diversity   338

READING 26   *Paulette Moore Hines, Nydia Garcia-Preto, Monica McGoldrick,
Rhea Almeida*, and *Susan Weltman* / "Intergenerational
Relationships Across Cultures"   338

The rules governing relations between parents and their adult
children vary across ethnic groups.

READING 27   *Laura Benkov* / "Reinventing the Family"   356

Lesbian and gay parents are creating a variety of family types that challenge the traditional meaning of family structure.

READING 28   *Catherine Street Chilman* / "Hispanic Families in the United States: Research Perspectives"   380

Hispanic families are not all alike; they come from a diverse array of national cultures.

READING 29   *William P. O'Hare, Kelvin M. Pollard, Taynia L. Mann*, and *Mary M. Kent* / "African-Americans in the 1990s"   395

African-American family life has been affected by a variety of forces—persisting racial discrimination, increasing opportunity for the educated, increasing unemployment and poverty for those left behind in the inner-city ghetto.

Chapter 10   The Age Revolution   407

READING 30   *Matilda White Riley* / "The Family in an Aging Society: A Matrix of Latent Relationships"   407

Unprecedented increases in longevity will have profound consequences on the norms and quality of family and kin relationships.

READING 31   *Andrew J. Cherlin* and *Frank F. Furstenberg, Jr.* / "The Modernization of Grandparenthood"   419

Grandparenthood as a distinct and nearly universal part of family life is a relatively new phenomenon, appearing in the decades since World War II.

Chapter 11   Trouble in the Family   426

READING 32   *Kristin Luker* / "Dubious Conceptions: The Controversy Over Teen Pregnancy"   426

Teen pregnancy is less about sex than about restricted horizons, hope, and opportunity.

READING 33   *Katherine S. Newman* / "The Downwardly Mobile Family"   439

Family bonds may be strained to the breaking point when a breadwinner father loses his job.

READING 34   *Richard J. Gelles* and *Murray A. Straus* / "Profiling Violent Families"   445

No single factor predicts family violence; it arises from stresses, frustrations, and power differences that are experienced by many families.

Preface

"May you live in interesting times" is said to be an ancient Chinese curse. The two decades we have been editing this book have certainly been interesting times to be studying the family. Family life has changed dramatically, and the meaning of these changes is fiercely debated, both in the field of family studies and in the public arena. Fears over the "breakdown of the family" have become a national obsession and a central issue in American politics. As a result, the importance of having basic knowledge about the family is more than academic.

As in previous editions, we have had three aims in this version. First, we have tried to describe current trends in family life, and place them in historical context. Second, we have tried to include articles representing the cutting edge of family scholarship, and yet balance them with excellent older ones. Third, we have tried to select articles that are scholarly, and yet understandable to an audience of undergraduates.

The 15 new readings include the following:

- Dennis Ahlburg and Carol De Vita's analysis and interpretation, based on Census Bureau data, of "the new realities of the American family."
- Findings from two innovative research projects on family life close up and in real time: John Gottman's observational studies of married couples in face-to-face interaction; and Reed Larson's and Maryse Richards's tracking, via beeper, of family members as they move through their separate worlds of work and school, and come together at the end of the day.
- Donald Hernandez's demographic analysis of the revolutions in American children's lives over the past two hundred years.
- A selection from *Families on the Fault Line*, Lillian Rubin's new study of working class families facing hard new economic realities and heightened ethnic and racial tensions.

In addition to the new articles, the book has been reorganized in the interests of clarity and coherence.

A test bank, providing multiple choice, true/false, and essay questions for each reading has been developed by Russell Craig, of Ashland University.

Finally, a word of thanks to all the people over the years who have helped us with suggestions for this book. Thanks also to Rosanna Santana, whose literature searches and general helpfulness made this edition possible. As usual, Rod Watanabe and the staff of the Center for the Study of Law and Society at the University of California helped in many ways. We are also grateful to Jordana Pestrong of the Sociology Department at New York University for locating several articles we needed as well as for her many valuable suggestions.

Last but not least, thanks to the following reviewers who offered many good ideas for this edition:

Alice M. Hines, PhD	San Jose State University
Michael C. Hoover, PhD	Missouri Western State College
Mary Jo Huth, PhD	University of Dayton
Sally K. Gallagher, PhD	Oregon State University
Elise Lake, PhD	University of Mississippi
Joan D. Lynch, PhD	Villanova University
Chandra Muller, PhD	University of Texas, Austin
Charles K. O'Connor, PhD	Bemidji State University

Arlene Skolnick
Jerome H. Skolnick

INTRODUCTION: FAMILY IN TRANSITION

It was one of the oddest episodes in America's political history—a debate between the vice president of the United States and a fictional television character. During the 1992 election campaign, former Vice President Dan Quayle set off a firestorm of debate with a remark denouncing a fictional television character for choosing to give birth out of wedlock. The *Murphy Brown* show, according to Quayle, was "mocking the importance of fathers." It reflected the "poverty of values" that was responsible for the nation's ills. From the talk shows to the front pages of newspapers to dinner tables across the nation, arguments broke out about the meaning of the vice president's remarks.

Comedians found Quayle's battle with a TV character good for laughs. But others saw serious issues being raised. Many people saw Quayle's comments as a stab at single mothers and working women. Some saw them as an important statement about the decline of family values and the importance of the two-parent family. In the opening show of the fall season, *Murphy Brown* fought back by poking fun at Quayle and telling the audience that families come in many different shapes and sizes. After the election, the debate seemed to fade away. It flared up again in the spring of 1993, after the *Atlantic Monthly* featured a cover story entitled "Dan Quayle was Right."

Why did a brief remark in a political speech set off such a heated and long lasting debate? The Dan Quayle–Murphy Brown affair struck a nerve because it touched on a central predicament in American society: the gap between the everyday realities of family life and our cultural images of how families ought to be. Contrary to the widespread notion that some flaw in American character or culture is to blame for these trends, comparable shifts are found throughout the industrialized world. All advanced modern countries have experienced shifts in

1

women's roles, rising divorce rates, lower marriage and birth rates, and an increase in single-parent families. In no other country, however, has family change been so traumatic and divisive as ours.

The transformation of family life has been so dramatic that to many Americans it has seemed as if "an earthquake had shuddered through the American family" (Preston, 1984). Divorce rates first skyrocketed, then stabilized at historically high levels. Women have surged into the workplace. Birth rates have declined. The women's movement has changed the way men and women think and act toward one another, both inside the home and in the world at large. Furthermore, social and sexual rules that once seemed carved in stone have crumbled away: unmarried couples can live together openly; unmarried mothers can keep their babies. Abortion has become legal. Remaining single and remaining childless, thought to be highly deviant once (though not illegal), have both become acceptable lifestyle options.

Today most people live in ways that do not conform to the cultural ideal that prevailed in the 1950s. The traditional breadwinner/housewife family with minor children today represents only a small minority of families. The "typical" American family in the last two decades of the twentieth century is likely to be one of four other kinds: the two-wage-earner family, the single-parent family, the "blended" family of remarriage, or the "empty nest" couple whose children have grown up and moved out. Indeed, in 1984 fully half of American families had no children under age 18 (Norton and Glick, 1986, p. 9). Apart from these variations, large numbers of people will spend part of their lives living apart from their families—as single young adults, as divorced singles, as older people who have lost a spouse.

The changes of recent decades have affected more than the forms of family life; they have been psychological as well. A major study of American attitudes over two decades revealed a profound shift in how people think about family life, work, and themselves (Veroff, Douvan, and Kulka, 1981). In 1957 four-fifths of respondents thought that a man or woman who did not want to marry was sick, immoral, and selfish. By 1976 only one-fourth of respondents thought that choice was bad. Two-thirds were neutral, and one-seventh viewed the choice as good. Summing up many complex findings, the authors conclude that America underwent a "psychological revolution" in the two decades between surveys. Twenty years earlier, people defined their satisfaction and problems—and indeed themselves—in terms of how well they lived up to traditional work and family roles. More recently, people have become more introspective, more attentive to inner experience. Fulfillment has come to mean finding intimacy, meaning, and self-definition, rather than satisfactory performance of traditional roles.

A DYING INSTITUTION?

All of these changes, occurring as they did in a relatively short period of time, gave rise to fears about the decline of the family. Since the early 1970s anyone watching television or reading newspapers and magazines would hear again and again that the family is breaking down, falling apart, disintegrating, and even becoming "an endangered species." There also began a great nostalgia for the "good old days" when Mom was in the kitchen, families were strong and stable, and life was uncomplicated. This mood of nostalgia mixed with anxiety contributed to the rise of the conservative New Right and helped to propel Ronald Reagan into the White House.

In the early 1980s, heady with victory, the conservative movement hoped that by dismantling the welfare state and overturning the Supreme Court's abortion decision, the clock could be turned back and the "traditional" family restored. As the 1990s began, it became clear that such hopes had failed. Women had not returned to full-time homemaking; divorce rates had not returned to the levels of the 1950s. The "liberated" sexuality of the 1960s and 1970s had given way to greater restraint, largely due to fear of AIDS, although the norms of the 1950s did not return.

Despite all the changes, however, the family in America is "here to stay" (Bane, 1976). The vast majority of Americans—at least 90 percent—marry and have children, and surveys repeatedly show that family is central to the lives of most Americans. They find family ties their deepest source of satisfaction and meaning, as well as the source of their greatest worries (Mellman, Lazarus, and Rivlin, 1990). In sum, family life in America is a complex mixture of both continuity and change.

While the transformations of the past three decades do not mean the end of family life, they have brought a number of new difficulties. For example, most families now depend on the earnings of wives and mothers, but the rest of society has not caught up to the new realities. There is still an earnings gap between men and women. Employed wives and mothers still bear most of workload in the home. For both men and women, the demands of the job are often at odds with family needs. Debates about whether or not the family is "in decline" do little to solve these dilemmas.

During the same years in which the family was becoming the object of public anxiety and political debate, a torrent of new research on the family was pouring forth. The study of the family had come to excite the interest of scholars in a range of disciplines—history, demography, economics, law, psychology. As a result of this research, we now have much more information available about the family than ever before. Ironically, much of the new scholarship is at odds with the widespread assumption that the family had a long, stable history until hit by the social "earthquake" of the 1960s and 1970s. We have learned from historians that the "lost" golden age of family happiness and stability we yearn for never actually existed.

Because of the continuing stream of new family scholarship, as well as shifts in public attitudes toward the family, each edition of *Family in Transition* has been different from the one before it. When we put together the first edition of this book in the early 1970s, the first rumblings of change were beginning to be felt. The youth movements of the 1960s and the emerging women's movement were challenging many of the assumptions on which conventional marriage and family patterns had been based. The mass media were regularly presenting stories that also challenged in one way or another traditional views on sex, marriage, and family. There was talk, for example, of "the population explosion" and of the desirability of "zero population growth." There was a growing perception that the ideal of the three-, four-, or five-child family of the 1950s was not necessarily good for the country as a whole, or for every couple.

Meanwhile, Hollywood movies were presenting a new and cynical view of marriage. It was almost taken for granted that marriages were unhappy, particularly if the spouses were middle class, middle aged, or affluent. Many people were openly defying conventional standards of behavior: College girls were beginning to live openly with young men, unwed movie actresses were publicizing rather than hiding their pregnancies, and homosexuals were beginning openly to protest persecution and discrimination.

It seemed as if something was happening to family life in America, even if there were no sharp changes in the major statistical indicators. People seemed to be looking at sex, marriage, parenthood, and family life in new ways, even if behavior on a mass scale was not changing very noticeably. John Gagnon and William Simon (1970) had observed that the moment of change may be when new forms of behavior seem "plausible." For example, even though there was no evidence that the homosexual population had grown, homosexuality had become more plausible. Because someone was a homosexual did not mean that he or she was automatically to be defined as a moral pariah.

In putting together the readings for that first edition of *Family in Transition*, we found that the professional literature of the time seemed to deny that change was possible in family structure, the relations between the sexes, and parenthood. An extreme version of this view was the statement by an anthropologist that the nuclear family (mother, father, and children) "is a biological phenomenon . . . as rooted in organs and physiological structures as insect societies" (LaBarre, 1954, p. 104). Any changes in the basic structure of family roles or in child rearing were assumed to be unworkable, if not unthinkable.

The family in modern society was portrayed as a streamlined, more highly evolved version of a universal family. According to the sociological theorist Talcott Parsons and his followers (1951, 1954), the modern family had become more specialized. It transferred work and educational roles to other agencies and specialized in child rearing and emotional support. No less important for having relinquished certain tasks, the modern family was now the only part of society to carry out such functions.

The family theories of the postwar era were descriptively correct insofar as they portrayed the ideal middle-class family patterns of a particular society at a particular historical period. But they went astray in elevating the status quo to the level of a timeless necessity. In addition, the theories did not acknowledge the great diversity among families that has always existed in America. For example, the working-mother or single-parent family could be seen only as deviant. Ethnic differences also received very little attention, or were considered undesirable variations from the mainstream, middle-class norm.

Still another flaw in the dominant view was its neglect of internal strains within the family, even when it was presumably functioning as it was supposed to. Paradoxically, these strains were vividly described by the very theorists who idealized the role of the family in modern society. Parsons, for example, observed that when home no longer functioned as an economic unit, women, children, and old people were placed in an ambiguous position. They became dependent on the male breadwinner and were cut off from society's major source of achievement and status.

Parsons saw women's roles as particularly difficult: Being a housewife was not a real occupation; it was vaguely defined, highly demanding, yet not considered real work in a society that measures achievement by the size of one's paycheck. The combination of existing strains and the demystifying effects of the challenges to the family status quo seems to have provided, as Judith Blake (1978, p. 11) points out, a classic set of conditions for social change.

A TIME OF TROUBLES

Major changes in the family would have been unsettling even if other social conditions had remained stable, but everything else was also changing quickly. Despite assassinations and turmoil in the streets, the 1960s was an optimistic period. Both dissidents and the establishment agreed that progress was possible, that problems could be solved. Both sides believed in limitless economic growth.

No one foresaw that the late 1970s would dramatically reverse this optimism and the social and economic conditions that had sustained it. Rather than hearing of an end to scarcity and poverty, we began to hear of lowered expectations, survival, and lifeboat ethics. For the first time in history, Americans had to confront the possibility that their children and their children's children might not lead better lives. A popular country and western song expressed the national mood when it asked, "Are the good times really over for good?" (Haggard, 1982).

The "malaise" of the late 1970s, followed by the conservative renewal of the 1980s, once again changed the terms in which family issues were discussed and debated. Among family scholars and other social commentators, the terms of the debate about the family were also changed by shifts in feminist thinking. Some of the most vocal feminists of the 1960s had criticized the family as the major source of the oppression of women. By the 1970s, however, many feminists had articulated a new emphasis on nurturance, care, and intimacy. In fact, one of the surprising themes to emerge in that era was the celebration of family in the name of social criticism.

Some radical attacks on the modern world and its ways seem consonant with traditional conservative arguments. Historian Christopher Lasch (1978) argued that while the family once provided a haven of love and decency in a heartless world, it no longer does so. In his view the family has been "invaded" by outside forces—advertising, the media, experts, and family professionals—and stripped of its functions and authority. Corporate capitalism, with its need for limitless consumption, has created a "culture of narcissism" in which nobody cares about anybody else. Other scholars insisted that the family remains a vital and resilient institution.

THE STATE OF THE CONTEMPORARY FAMILY

Part of the confusion surrounding the current status of the family arises from the fact that the family is a surprisingly problematic area of study; there are few if any self-evident facts, even statistical ones. Researchers have found, for example, that when the statistics of family life are plotted for the entire twentieth century, or back into the nineteenth century, a surprising finding emerges: Today's young people—with their low marriage, high divorce, and low fertility rates—appear to be behaving in ways consistent with long-term historical trends (Cherlin, 1981; Masnick and Bane, 1980). The recent changes in family life only appear deviant when compared to what people were doing in the 1940s and 1950s. But it was the postwar generation that married young, moved to the suburbs, and had three, four, or more children that departed from twentieth-century trends. As one study put it, "Had the 1940s and 1950s not happened, today's young adults would appear to be behaving normally" (Masnick and Bane, 1980, p. 2).

Thus, the meaning of change in a particular indicator of family life depends on the time frame in which it is placed. If we look at trends over too short a period of time—say ten or twenty years—we may think we are seeing a marked change, when, in fact, an older pattern may be reemerging. For some issues, even discerning what the trends are can be a problem. Whether or not we conclude that there is an "epidemic" of teenage pregnancy depends on how we define adolescence and what measure of illegitimacy we use. Contrary to the popular notion of skyrocketing teenage pregnancy, teenaged childbearing has actually been on the decline during the past two decades (Luker, this volume). It is possible for the *ratio* of illegitimate births to all births to go up at the same time as there are declines in the *absolute number* of births and in the likelihood that an individual will bear an illegitimate child. This is not to say that concern about teenage pregnancy is unwarranted; but the reality is much more complex than the simple and scary notion an "epidemic" implies.

Given the complexities of interpreting data on the family, it is little wonder that, as Joseph Featherstone observes (1979, p. 37), the family is a "great intellectual Rorschach blot." One's conclusions about the current state of the family often derive from deeper values and assumptions one holds in the first place about the definition and role of the family in society. We noted earlier that the family theories of the postwar era were largely discredited within sociology itself (Blake, 1978; Elder, 1978). Yet many of the assumptions of those theories continue to influence discussions of the family in both popular and scholarly writings. Let us look in more detail at these persistent assumptions.

1. The Myth of the Universal Nuclear Family

To say that the family is the same everywhere is in some sense true. Yet families vary in organization, membership, life cycles, emotional environments, ideologies, social and kinship networks, and economic and other functions. Although anthropologists have tried to come up with a single definition of family that would hold across time and place, they generally have concluded that doing so is not useful (Geertz, 1965; Stephens, 1963).

Biologically, of course, a woman and a man must unite sexually to produce a child—even if only sperm and egg meet in a test tube. But no social kinship ties or living arrangements flow inevitably from biological union. Indeed, the definition of marriage is not the same across cultures. Although some cultures have weddings and notions of monogamy and permanence, many cultures lack one or more of these attributes. In some cultures, the majority of people mate and have children without legal marriage and often without living together. In other societies, husbands, wives, and children do not live together under the same roof.

In our own society, the assumption of universality has usually defined what is normal and natural both for research and therapy and has subtly influenced our thinking to regard deviations from the nuclear family as sick or perverse or immoral. As Suzanne Keller (1971) points out:

> The fallacy of universality has done students of behavior a great disservice. By leading us to seek and hence to find a single pattern, it has blinded us to historical precedents for multiple legitimate family arrangements.

An example of this disservice is the treatment of illegitimacy. For decades the so-called principle of legitimacy, set forth by Malinowski (1930), was taken as evidence for the universality of the nuclear family. The principle stated that in every society a child must have a socially recognized father to give the child a status in the community. Malinowski's principle naturally leads to the assumption that illegitimacy is a sign of social breakdown.

Although the principle usually has been treated by social scientists as if it were a natural law, in fact it is based on certain prior assumptions about society (Goode, 1960; Blake, 1978). Chiefly, it assumes that children inherit their status from their father or from family origin rather than achieving it themselves. The traditional societies that anthropologists study are, of course, societies that do ascribe status in this way. In modern, democratic societies, such as the United States, a child's future is not supposed to be determined solely by who its father happens to be. The Malinowski principle, however compelling in understanding traditional societies, has decreasing relevance for modern ones. Current legal changes that blur the distinction between legitimate and illegitimate births may be seen as a way of bringing social practice in line with national ideals.

2. The Myth of Family Harmony

To question the idea of the happy family is not to say that love and joy are not found in family life or that many people do not find their deepest satisfactions in their families. Rather, the happy family assumption omits important, if unpleasant, aspects of family life. Western society has not always assumed such a sentimental model of the family. From the Bible to the fairy tale, from Sophocles to Shakespeare, from Eugene O'Neill to the soap opera, there is a tragic tradition of portraying the family as a high-voltage emotional setting, charged with love and hate, tenderness and spite, even incest and murder.

There is also a low-comedy tradition. George Orwell once pointed out that the world of henpecked husbands and tyrannical mothers-in-law is as much a part of the Western cultural heritage as is Greek drama. Although the comic tradition tends to portray men's discontents rather than women's, it scarcely views the family as a setting for ideal happiness.

Social theorists have not always portrayed the family as harmoniously fulfilling the needs of its members and society. Around the turn of the century, the founders of sociology took for granted that conflict was a basic part of social life and that individuals, classes, and social institutions would struggle to promote their own interests and values. They argued that intimate relations inevitably involve antagonism as well as love. This mixture of strong positive and negative feelings sets close relationships apart from less intimate ones.

In recent years, family scholars have been studying family violence such as child abuse and wife beating to understand better the realistic strains of family life. Long-known facts about family violence have recently been incorporated into a general analysis of the family. More police officers are killed and injured dealing with family fights than in dealing with any other kind of situation; of all the relationships between murderers and their victims, the family relationship is most common (Steinmetz and Straus, 1974). Studies of family violence reveal that it is much more widespread than had been assumed, cannot easily be attributed to mental illness, and is not confined to the lower classes. Family violence seems to be a product of psychological tensions and external stresses that can affect all families at all social levels.

The study of family interaction has also undermined the traditional image of the happy, harmonious family. About two decades ago, researchers and therapists began to bring mental patients and their families together to watch how they behaved with one another. Oddly, whole family groups had not been systematically studied before.

At first the family interactions were interpreted as pathogenic: a parent expressing affection in words but showing nonverbal hostility; alliances being made between different family members; families having secrets; one family member being singled out as a scapegoat to be blamed for the family's troubles. As more and more families were studied, such patterns were found in many families, not just in those families with a schizophrenic child. Although this line of research did not uncover the cause of schizophrenia, it made an important discovery about family life: So-called normal families can often be, in the words of one study, "difficult environments for interaction."

3. The Myth of Parental Determinism

The kind of family a child grows up in leaves a profound, lifelong impact. But a large body of recent research shows that early family experience is not the all-powerful, irreversible influence it has sometimes been thought to be. An unfortunate childhood does not doom a person to an unhappy adulthood. Nor does a happy childhood guarantee a similarly blessed future (Macfarlane, 1964; Emde and Harmon, 1984; Rubin, 1996).

There are several flaws in the notion that early relations with parents are the primary determinants of a child's social and psychological future. First, children come into this world with their own temperamental and other individual characteristics. As parents have long known, child rearing is not like molding clay or writing on a blank slate. Rather, although parents are far more powerful, it's a two-way process in which both parent and child try to shape each other. Further, children are active perceivers and interpreters of the world. Finally, parents and children do not live in a social vacuum; children are also influenced by the world around them and the people in it—the kin group, the neighborhood, other children, the school, the media.

4. The Myth of a Stable, Harmonious Past

Laments about the current state of decay of the family imply some earlier era when the family was more stable and harmonious. But unless we can agree what earlier time should be chosen as a baseline and what characteristics of the family should be specified, it makes little sense to speak of family decline. Historians have not, in fact, located a golden age of the family.

Recent historical studies of family life also cast doubt on the reality of family tranquillity. Historians have found that premarital sexuality, illegitimacy, generational conflict, and even infanticide can best be studied as a part of family life itself rather than as separate categories of deviation. For example, William Kessen (1965), in his history of the field of child study, observes:

> Perhaps the most persistent single note in the history of the child is the reluctance of mothers to suckle their babies. The running war between the mother, who does not want to nurse, and the philosopher-psychologists, who insist she must, stretches over two thousand years (pp. 1–2).

The most shocking finding of the recent wave of historical studies is the prevalence of infanticide throughout European history. Infanticide has long been attributed to primitive peoples or assumed to be the desperate act of an unwed mother. It now appears that infanticide provided a major means of population control in all societies lacking reliable contraception, Europe included, and that it was practiced by families on legitimate children. Historians now believe that increases and decreases in recorded birth rates may actually reflect variations in infanticide rates.

Rather than being an instinctive trait, having tender feelings toward infants—regarding a baby as a precious individual—seems to emerge only when infants have a decent chance of surviving and adults experience enough security to avoid feeling that children are competing with them in a struggle for survival. Throughout many centuries of European history, both of these conditions were lacking.

Another myth about the family is that of changelessness—the belief that the family has been essentially the same over the centuries, until recently, when it began to come apart. Family life has always been in flux; when the world around them changes, families change in response. At periods when a whole society undergoes some major transformation, family change may be especially rapid and dislocating.

In many ways, the era we are living through today resembles two earlier periods of family crisis and transformation in American history (see Skolnick, 1991). The first occurred the early nineteenth century, when the growth of industry and commerce moved work out of the home. Briefly, the separation of home and work disrupted existing patterns of daily family life, opening a gap between the way people actually lived and the cultural blueprints for proper gender and generational roles (Ryan, 1981). In the older pattern, when most people worked on farms, a father was not just the head of the household, but also boss of the family enterprise. Mother and children and hired hands worked under his supervision. But when work moved out, father—along with older sons and daughters—went with it, leaving behind mother and the younger children. These dislocations in the functions and meaning of family life unleashed an era of personal stress and cultural confusion.

Eventually, a new model of family emerged that not only reflected the new separation of work and family, but glorified it. No longer a workplace, the household now became idealized as "home sweet home," an emotional and spiritual shelter from the heartless world outside. Although father remained the head of the family, mother was now the central figure in the home. The new model celebrated the "true woman's" purity, virtue, and selflessness. Many of our culture's most basic ideas about the family in American culture, such as "women's place is in the home," were formed at this time. In short, the family pattern we now think of as traditional was in fact the first version of the modern family.

Historians label this model of the family "Victorian" because it became influential in England and Western Europe as well as in the United States during the reign of Queen Victoria. It reflected, in idealized form, the nineteenth-century middle-class family. However, the Victorian model became the prevailing cultural definition of family. Few families could live up to the ideal in all its particulars; working-class, black, and ethnic families, for example, could not get by without the economic contributions of wives, mothers, and daughters. And even for middle-class families, the Victorian idea prescribed a standard of perfection that was virtually impossible to fulfill (Demos, 1986).

Eventually, however, social change overtook the Victorian model. Beginning around the 1880s, another period of rapid economic, social, and cultural change unsettled Victorian family patterns, especially their gender arrangements. Several generations of so-called new women challenged Victorian notions of femininity. They became educated, pursued careers, became involved in political causes—including their own—and created the first wave of feminism. This ferment culminated in the victory of the women's suffrage movement. It was followed by the 1920s' jazz age era of flappers and flaming youth—the first, and probably the major, sexual revolution of the twentieth century.

To many observers at the time, it appeared that the family and morality had broken down. Another cultural crisis ensued, until a new cultural blueprint emerged—the companionate model of marriage and the family. The new model was a revised, more relaxed version of the Victorian family; companionship and sexual intimacy were now defined as central to marriage.

This highly abbreviated history of family and cultural change forms the necessary backdrop for understanding the family upheavals of the late twentieth century. As in earlier times, major changes in the economy and society have destabilized an existing model of family life and the everyday patterns and practices that have sustained it. We have experienced a triple revolution: first, the move toward a postindustrial service and information economy; second, a life course revolution brought about the reductions in mortality and fertility; and third, a psychological transformation rooted mainly in rising educational levels.

Although these shifts have profound implications for everyone in contemporary society, women have been the pacesetters of change. Most women's lives and expectations over the past three decades, inside and outside the family, have departed drastically from those of their own mothers. Men's lives today also are different from their fathers' generation, but to a much lesser extent.

THE TRIPLE REVOLUTION

The Postindustrial Family

The most obvious way the new economy affects the family is in its drawing women, especially married women, into the workplace. A service and information economy produces large numbers of jobs that, unlike factory work, seem suitable for women. Yet as Jessie Bernard (1982) once observed, the transformation of a housewife into a paid worker outside the home sends tremors through every family relationship. It creates a more "symmetrical" family, undoing the sharp contrast between men's and women's roles that marks the breadwinner/housewife pattern. It also reduces women's economic dependence on men, thereby making it easier for women to leave unhappy marriages.

Beyond drawing women into the workplace, shifts in the nature of work and a rapidly changing globalized economy have unsettled the lives of individuals and families at all class levels. The well-paying industrial jobs that once enabled a blue-collar worker to own a home and support a family are no longer available. The once secure jobs that sustained the "organization men" and their families in the 1950s and 1960s have been made shaky by downsizing, an unstable economy, corporate takeovers, and a rapid pace of technological change.

The new economic climate has also made the transition to adulthood increasingly problematic. The reduction in job opportunities is in part responsible for young adults' lower fertility rates and for women flooding into the workplace. Further, the family formation patterns of the 1950s are out of step with the increased educational demands of today's postindustrial society. In the postwar years, particularly in the United States, young people entered adulthood in one giant step—going to work, marrying young and moving to a separate household from their parents, and having children quickly. Today, few young adults can afford to marry and have children in their late teens or early twenties. In an economy where a college degree is necessary to earn a living wage, early marriage impedes education for both men and women.

Those who do not go on to college have little access to jobs that can sustain a family. Particularly in the inner cities of the United States, growing numbers of young people have come to see no future for themselves at all in the ordinary world of work. In middle-class families, a narrowing opportunity structure has increased anxieties about downward mobility for offspring, and parents as well.

The "Hamlet syndrome" or the "incompletely launched young adult syndrome" has become common: Young adults deviate from their parents' expectations by failing to launch careers and become successfully independent adults, and may even come home to crowd their parents' empty nest (Schnaiberg and Goldenberg, 1989).

The Life Course Revolution

The demographic transformations of the twentieth century are no less significant than the economic ones. We cannot hope to understand current predicaments of family life without understanding how radically the demographic and social circumstances of twentieth-century Americans have changed. In earlier times, mortality rates were highest among infants, and the possibility of death from tuberculosis, pneumonia, or other infectious diseases was an ever-present threat to young and middle-aged adults. Before the turn of this century, only 40 percent of women lived through all the stages of a normal life course—growing up, marrying, having children, and surviving with a spouse to the age of 50 (Uhlenberg, 1974).

Demographic and economic change has had a profound effect on women's lives. Women today are living longer and having fewer children. When infant and child mortality rates fall, women no longer have to have five or seven or nine children to make sure that two or three will survive to adulthood. After rearing children, the average woman can look forward to three or four decades without maternal responsibilities. Since traditional assumptions about women are based on the notion that they are constantly involved with pregnancy, child rearing, and related domestic concerns, the current ferment about women's roles may be seen as a way of bringing cultural attitudes in line with existing social realities.

As people live longer, they can stay married longer. Actually, the biggest change in twentieth-century marriage is not the proportion of marriages disrupted through divorce, but the potential length of marriage and the number of years spent without children in the home. By the 1970s the statistically average couple would spend only 18 percent of their married lives raising young children, compared with 54 percent a century ago (Bane, 1976). As a result, marriage is becoming defined less as a union between parents raising a brood of children and more as a personal relationship between two individuals.

A Psychological Revolution

The third major transformation is a set of psychocultural changes that might be described as "psychological gentrification" (Skolnick, 1991). That is, cultural advantages once enjoyed only by the upper classes—in particular, education—have been extended to those lower down on the socioeconomic scale. Psychological gentrification also involves greater leisure time, travel, and exposure to information, as well as a general rise in the standard of living. Despite the persistence of poverty, unemployment, and economic insecurity in the industrialized world, far less of the population than in the historical past is living at the level of sheer subsistence.

Throughout Western society, rising levels of education and related changes have been linked to a complex set of shifts in personal and political attitudes. One of these is a more psychological approach to life—greater introspectiveness and a yearning for warmth and intimacy in family and other relationships (Veroff, Douvan, and Kulka, 1981). There is also evidence of an increasing preference on the part of both men and women for a more companionate ideal of marriage and a more democratic family. More broadly, these changes in attitude have been described as a shift to "postmaterialist values," emphasizing self-expression, tolerance, equality, and a concern for the quality of life (Inglehart, 1990).

The multiple social transformations of our era have brought both costs and benefits: Family relations have become both more fragile and more emotionally rich; mass longevity has brought us a host of problems as well as the gift of extended life. Although change has brought greater opportunities for women, persisting gender inequality means women have borne a large share of the costs of these gains. But we cannot turn the clock back to the family models of the past.

Paradoxically, after all the upheavals of recent decades, the emotional and cultural significance of the family persists. Family remains the center of most people's lives and, as numerous surveys show, a cherished value. While marriage has become more fragile, the parent-child relationship—especially the mother-child relationship—remains a core attachment across the life course (Rossi and Rossi, 1990). The family, however, can be both "here to stay" and beset with difficulties. There is widespread recognition that the massive social and economic changes we have lived through call for public and private sector policies in support of families. Most European countries have recognized for some time that governments must play a role in supplying an array of supports to families—health care, children's allowances, housing subsidies, support for working parents and children (such as child care, parental leave, and shorter work days for parents), as well as an array of services for the elderly.

Each country's response to these changes, as we've noted earlier, has been shaped by its own political and cultural traditions. The United States remains embroiled in a cultural war over the family; many social commentators and political leaders have promised to reverse the recent trends and restore the "traditional" family. In contrast, other Western nations, including Canada and the other English-speaking countries, have responded to family change by establishing policies aimed at mitigating the problems brought about by economic and social changes. As a result of these policies, these countries have been spared much of the poverty and social disintegration that has plagued the United States in the last decade (Edgar, 1993; Smeeding, 1992).

Looking Ahead

The world at the end of the twentieth century is vastly different from what it was at the beginning, or even the middle. Families are struggling to adapt to new realities. The countries that have been at the leading edge of family change still find themselves caught between yesterday's norms, today's new realities, and an uncertain future. As we have seen, changes in women's lives have been a pivotal factor in recent family trends. In many countries there is a considerable difference between men's and women's attitudes and expectations of one another. Even where both partners accept a more equal division of labor in the home, there is often a gap between attitudes and behavior. In no country have employers, the government, or men fully caught up to the changes in women's lives.

But a knowledge of family history reveals that the solution to contemporary problems will not be found in some lost golden age. Families have always struggled with outside circumstances and inner conflict. Our current troubles inside and outside the family are genuine, but we should never forget that many of the most vexing issues confronting us derive from benefits of modernization few of us would be willing to give up—for example, longer, healthier lives, and the ability to choose how many children to have and when to have them. There was no problem of the aged in the past, because most people never aged; they died before they got old. Nor was adolescence a difficult stage of the life cycle when children worked, education was a privilege of the rich, and a person's place in society was determined by heredity rather than choice. And when most people were hungry illiterates, only aristocrats could worry about sexual satisfaction and self-fulfillment.

In short, there is no point in giving in to the lure of nostalgia. There is no golden age of the family to long for, nor even some past pattern of behavior and belief that would guarantee us harmony and stability if only we had the will to return to it. Family life is bound up with the social, economic, and ideological circumstances of particular times and places. We are no longer peasants, Puritans, pioneers, or even suburbanites circa 1955. We face conditions unknown to our ancestors, and we must find new ways to cope with them.

A Note on "the Family"

Some family scholars have suggested that we drop the term "the family" and replace it with "families" or "family life." The problem with "the family" is that it calls to mind the stereotyped image of the Ozzie and Harriet kind of family— two parents and their two or three minor children. But those other terms don't always work. In our own writing we use the term "the family" in much the same way we use "the economy"—as an abstract term that refers to a mosaic of forms and practices in the real world.

REFERENCES

Bane, M. J. 1976. *Here to Stay*. New York: Basic Books.

Bernard, J. 1982. *The Future of Marriage*. New York: Bantam.

Blake, J. 1978. Structural differentiation and the family: A quiet revolution. Presented at American Sociology Association, San Francisco.

Cherlin, A. J. 1981. *Marriage, Divorce, Remarriage*. Cambridge, Mass.: Harvard University Press.

Demos, John. 1986. *Past, Present, and Personal.* New York: Oxford University Press.

Emde, R. N., and R. J. Harmon, eds. 1984. *Continuities and Discontinuities in Development.* New York: Plenum Press.

Featherstone, J. 1979. Family matters. *Harvard Educational Review* 49, no. 1: 20–52.

Gagnon, J. H., and W. Simon. 1970. *The Sexual Scene.* Chicago: Aldine/Transaction.

Geertz, G. 1965. The impact of the concept of culture on the concept of man. In *New Views of the Nature of Man,* edited by J. R. Platt. Chicago: University of Chicago Press.

Haggard, M. 1982. Are the Good Times Really Over for Good? Song copyright 1982.

Inglehart, Ronald. 1990. *Culture Shift.* New Jersey: Princeton University Press.

Keller, S. 1971. Does the family have a future? *Journal of Comparative Studies* Spring.

Kessen, E. W. 1965. *The Child.* New York: John Wiley.

LaBarre, W. 1954. *The Human Animal.* Chicago: University of Chicago Press.

Lasch, C. 1978. *Haven in a Heartless World.* New York: Basic Books.

Macfarlane, J. W. 1964. Perspectives on personality consistency and change from the guidance study. *Vita Humana* 7: 115–126.

Malinowski, B. 1930. Parenthood, the basis of the social order. In *The New Generation,* edited by Calverton and Schmalhousen, New York: Macauley Company.

Masnick, G., and M. J. Bane. 1980. *The Nation's Families: 1960–1990.* Boston: Auburn House.

Mellman, A., E. Lazarus, and A. Rivlin. 1990. Family time, family values. In *Rebuilding the Nest,* edited by D. Blankenhorn, S. Bayme, and J. Elshtain. Milwaukee: Family Service America.

Norton, A. J., and P. C. Glick. 1986. One-parent families: A social and economic profile. *Family Relations* 35: 9–17.

Parsons, T. 1951. *The Social System.* Glencoe, Ill.: Free Press.

Parsons, T. 1954. The kinship system of the contemporary United States. In *Essays in Sociological Theory.* Glencoe, Ill.: Free Press.

Preston, S. H. 1984. Presidential address to the Population Association of America. Quoted in *Family and Nation* by D. P. Moynihan (1986). San Diego: Harcourt Brace Jovanovich.

Rossi, A. S., and P. H. Rossi. 1990. *Of Human Bonding: Parent-Child Relations Across the Life Course.* Hawthorne, New York: Aldine de Gruyter.

Rubin, L. 1996. *The Transcendent Child.* New York: Basic Books.

Ryan, M. 1981. *The Cradle of the Middle Class.* New York: Cambridge University Press.

Schnaiberg, A., and S. Goldenberg. 1989. From empty nest to crowded nest: The dynamics of incompletely launched young adults. *Social Problems* 36, no. 3 (June) 251–69.

Skolnick, A. 1991. *Embattled Paradise: The American Family in an Age of Uncertainty.* New York: Basic Books.

Steinmetz, D., and M. A. Straus, eds. 1974. *Violence in the Family.* New York: Dodd, Mead Co.

Stephens, W. N. 1963. *The Family in Cross-Cultural Perspective*. New York: World.

Uhlenberg, P. 1980. Death and the family. *Journal of Family History* 5, no. 3: 313–20.

Veroff, J., E. Douvan, and R. A. Kulka. 1981. *The Inner American: A Self-Portrait from 1957 to 1976*. New York: Basic Books.

◈

PART ONE

THE
CHANGING
FAMILY

◈

INTRODUCTION

The study of the family does not fit neatly within the boundaries of any single scholarly field; genetics, physiology, archaeology, history, anthropology, sociology, psychology, and economics all touch upon it. Religious and ethical authorities claim a stake in the family, and troubled individuals and families generate therapeutic demands on family scholarship. In short, the study of the family is interdisciplinary, controversial, and necessary for the formulation of social policy and practices. Interdisciplinary subjects demand competence in more than one field. At a time when competent scholars find it difficult to master even one corner of a field, intellectual demands on students of the family become vast. Although writers on the family confront many issues, their professional competence is usually limited. Thus a biologist may cite articles in psychology to support a position without comprehending the tentativeness with which psychologists regard the researcher and his work. Similarly, a psychologist or sociologist may draw upon controversial biological studies. Professional competence means more than the ability to read technical journals; it includes informal knowledge—being "tuned in" to verbal understandings and evaluations of research validity. Usually a major theory or line of research is viewed more critically in its own field than outsiders realize.

Interdisciplinary subjects present characteristic problems. Each discipline has its own assumptions and views of the world, which may not directly transfer into another field. Some biologists and physically oriented anthropologists, for example, analyze human affairs in terms of individual motives and instincts; for them, society is a shadowy presence, serving mainly as the setting for biologically motivated individual action. Many sociologists and cultural anthropologists, in contrast, perceive the individual as an actor playing a role written by culture and society. According to this view, the individual has no wholly autonomous thoughts and impulses. One important school of psychology sees people neither as passive recipients of social pressures nor as creatures driven by powerful lusts, but as information processors trying to make sense of their environment. There is no easy way to reconcile such perspectives. Scientific paradigms—characteristic ways of looking at the world—determine not only what answers will be found, but what questions will be asked. This fact has perhaps created special confusion in the study of the family.

"We speak of families," R. D. Laing has observed, "as though we know what families are. We identify, as families, networks of people who live together over time, who have ties of marriage or kinship to one another" (Laing, 1971, p. 3).

There is the assumption that family life, so familiar a part of everyday experience, is easily understood. But familiarity may breed a sense of destiny—what we experience is transformed into the "natural":

> One difficulty in the psychological sciences lies in the familiarity of the phenomena with which they deal. A certain intellectual effort is required to see how such phenomena can pose serious problems or call for intricate explanatory theories. One is inclined to take them for granted as necessary or somehow "natural." (Chomsky, 1968, p. 21)

The selections in Part One examine the myths, realities, and meanings of "family." Chapter One examines current trends in American family life and places them in historical perspective. Dennis Ahlburg and Carol De Vita use Census Bureau data to describe recent trends in marriage, divorce, single parenthood, and living arrangements. Despite the dramatic changes, there is continuity as well—married couples with children remain a prominent family pattern.

Tamara Hareven's historical examination of the American family also reveals both continuity and change. She shows how family forms and relationships are shaped by economic opportunity and family needs. In contrast to nostalgic images of families in the past, Hareven finds that earlier generations were no freer of problems and dilemmas than families today. Arlene Skolnick's article reveals the profound and disturbing impact death used to have on family life and how some of our new problems arise from the lengthening of the life span over the course of the twentieth century.

Stephanie Coontz's article points to further flaws in nostalgic assumptions about the family in the past. What comes to mind when you think of "the traditional family"? Many people conjure up a mixture of characteristics that never existed at any one time. Nostalgia, she argues, not only distorts the past but also leads to mistaken ideas about the present.

The selections in Chapter Two deal with the meaning of family in today's culture. What makes a family distinct from other groups? How should we define the term "family"? Marjorie DeVault shows how the planning and cooking of meals are more than work—they are the means by which family life is constructed. In feeding the family, women try to create family togetherness, and at the same time, take account of the individuality of family members.

In recent years, the definition of family has been a problem facing our nation's legal system, as well as a hot political issue. Single mothers with children, single fathers with children, a grandparent and grandchildren, unmarried couples, gay couples—all are increasingly common domestic arrangements. And all raise questions about the legal definition of family. David Rosen's article discusses how courts have struggled with these issues. More broadly, James Davison Hunter argues that the definition of the family has become the central battleground in the culture war over family values.

REFERENCES

Chomsky, N. 1968. *Language and Mind*. New York: Harcourt, Brace and World.
Laing, R. D. 1971. *The Politics of the Family*. New York: Random House.

CHAPTER 1

◈

FAMILIES PRESENT
AND PAST

R E A D I N G

1

New Realities of the American Family

Dennis A. Ahlburg and Carol J. De Vita

The family has changed so much in just a few decades that it is difficult for individuals and social institutions to keep up. Men and women who were raised in the 1950s and 1960s when television programs such as *Ozzie and Harriet* and *Father Knows Best* epitomized the image of the American family are now likely to find themselves in family situations that look and function very differently. Families today most likely have two or fewer children; there is a good chance that the mother is employed outside the home; and the odds of divorce before the children are grown are about 50–50.

The breadwinner-homemaker model with husband and wife raising their own biological (or adopted) children was once the dominant pattern. Today, many family forms are common: single-parent families (resulting either from unmarried parenthood or divorce), remarried couples, unmarried couples, stepfamilies, foster families, extended or multigenerational families, and the doubling up of two families within the same home. Women are just as likely to be full- or part-time workers as full-time homemakers.

If ordinary people sometimes find themselves puzzled about how to respond to (or interpret) the new family patterns, so are the experts. Family patterns are so fluid that the U.S. Census Bureau has difficulty measuring family trends.

From Dennis A. Ahlburg and Carol J. De Vita, "New Realities of the American Family." *Population Bulletin*, 47, no. 2 (August 1992).

Most large-scale, nationally representative surveys cannot readily tell us what proportion of husband-wife families are stepfamilies; how adopted or foster-care children are faring; distinguish roommates from couples who are living together as unmarried partners; or measure the extent of family support networks for elderly persons who live alone.

Workplace policies often lag behind the new family arrangements, as the movement to pass "parental leave" or "family leave" policies suggests. Family health insurance, which is often provided through the workplace, may cover only married husband-wife partners and their off-spring, not cohabiting couples. Gay and lesbian advocates have questioned the fairness of these restrictions based on the premise that the living arrangements of gays and lesbians function much the same way as married-couple families. Stepfamilies may encounter a maze of bureaucratic red tape in trying to establish whose children are covered by which insurance policy. Family law—particularly the advent of no-fault divorce law, joint child custody, and inheritance and estate planning—has slowly evolved to try to accommodate the new fluidity of marital and family arrangements.

As a consequence, few social institutions have received as much attention and scrutiny as the American family. The family unit forms the cornerstone for U.S. social policy, and the economic well-being of the family often serves as a barometer for measuring the well-being of the nation. Given the importance of the family, it is not surprising that current statistics on the formation and structure of American families have been viewed with alarm:

The marriage rate fell almost 30 percent between 1970 and 1990;

The divorce rate increased by nearly 40 percent during this same period;

Over one-quarter of all births in 1990 were to unmarried mothers, compared with one in ten in 1970; and

About half of all children today are expected to spend some part of their childhood in a single-parent home.

Demographic trends are key to this evolution. Marriage, divorce, widowhood, remarriage, and childbearing patterns have changed dramatically since the 1950s and have radically altered the size and composition of the American family. Young people are marrying at older ages and more are foregoing marriage altogether. Marriage is less permanent. People are more likely to divorce, although remarriage rates are high. Women are having fewer children and generally waiting until older ages to have them. But more births are occurring outside of marriage, and more children are being raised in single-parent homes. Intertwined with demographic factors are economic changes—the stagnation of men's wages, the loss of manufacturing jobs, increased competition in global markets—that have contributed to the difficulties of raising and sustaining families.

This report will discuss the social and demographic trends that contribute to the changing composition and economic status of the American family. It will describe the various types of families that are prevalent today and project their numbers into the future.

The United States is not alone in experiencing such far-reaching demographic change. Family patterns in the United States reflect broad social and demographic trends that are occurring in most industrialized countries around the world. Low marriage and fertility rates and high divorce and nonmarital birth rates are seen in many other industrialized nations. Although every country has its own social and political traditions, Americans can learn important lessons by studying how other nations are responding to these changes.

DEFINING HOUSEHOLDS AND FAMILIES

The U.S. Bureau of the Census carefully distinguishes between a *household* and a *family*. Households are defined as all persons who occupy a housing unit such as a house, apartment, single room, or other space intended to be living quarters. A household may consist of one person who lives alone or several people who share a dwelling. A family, on the other hand, is two or more persons related by birth, marriage, or adoption who reside together. This definition does not measure family ties that extend beyond the immediate housing unit. Yet, family members who live outside the home often help older people, young couples, and single parents maintain their independence and meet family responsibilities.

While all families form households, not all households are families under Census Bureau definitions. Indeed, the growth of the nonfamily household (that is, persons who live alone or with unrelated individuals) is one of the most dramatic changes to occur during the past 30 years. In 1960, 15 percent of all households were nonfamily households; by 1991, 30 percent were nonfamily units, and by the year 2000, 31 percent may be nonfamily households. Nonfamily households are a diverse group. They may consist of elderly individuals who live alone, college-age youth who share an apartment, cohabiting couples, individuals who delay or forego marriage, or those who are "between marriages." While these individuals may not reside within an officially designated family unit, most have family ties beyond their immediate household. What is more, given the aging of the U.S. population and current patterns of marriage, divorce, childbearing, and widowhood, nonfamily households are expected to account for a growing share of the housing market well into the twenty-first century.

TYPES OF FAMILIES

While the share of family households has declined in the past 30 years, the structure of American families has grown more complex. A popular image of the American family is a married couple with two or more children in which the husband is the sole source of family income and the wife stays at home to attend to family matters. The demographic reality is that in 1991 just over one-third of all families (37 percent) consisted of a married couple with children—regardless of the number of children or the labor force status of the wife—and only one in five married couples with children fits the popular stereotype described above.

Although 70 percent of households contain a family unit, family composition is quite diverse. They include: married couples with children, married couples without children, single-parent families headed by a woman, single-parent families headed by a man, and other family units, such as siblings living together, an unmarried daughter living with her aging mother, or grandparents raising grandchildren. Just under half of all families have children, but there is considerable variation in these family arrangements.

Married Couples with Children

Despite our changing lifestyles, married couples with children continue to be a prominent family pattern. But even within this model there are two distinct types: the intact biological family and the stepfamily or blended family that may include adopted children. Most married-couple families with children are intact biological families (77 percent in 1985, the last available estimate), but 19 percent had one or more stepchildren, and 2 percent had one or more adopted children.[1] Although over 80 percent of stepfamilies are white, the odds of being in a stepfamily are twice as great for African-Americans as for whites. Thirty-five percent of all black married-couple families in 1985 were stepfamilies, compared with 18 percent for whites. The vast majority of stepchildren in married-couple families live with their biological mother and stepfather. Demographer Paul Glick estimates that one out of every three Americans is now a stepparent, a stepchild, a stepsibling, or some other member of a stepfamily. If current trends continue, the share will rise to nearly half by the year 2000.[2]

Combining and blending families is not always easy and does not necessarily mitigate differences between family types. Compared with stepfamilies, intact biological families tend to involve marriages of longer duration, have more children, are somewhat more likely to have only one parent in the labor force, and have higher family income.[3] Blended families may also generate conflict and tension, particularly for children, which is sometimes seen as a factor in the high divorce rates among remarriages.

Married Couples without Children

Forty-two percent of all families in 1991 consisted of married couples without children. But again, there are distinct differences within this category. Some of these couples might be called *preparents* (those who have not yet had children); others may be *empty nesters* whose children are grown and have left the family home; while others may be *nonparents* either by choice or because of infertility problems. Among married couples without children in 1991, about 15 percent of the women were under age 35, suggesting a possible delay in childbearing. Indeed, over half of all married women younger than 35 who were childless in 1990 reported that they expected to have a child at some point in the future.[4] This figure rises to over 80 percent for married women in their twenties. On the other hand, half of all married couples without children had a woman age 55 or older. Many women of this age group are the mothers of the post–World War II baby-boom generation and probably have adult children who live elsewhere.

The aging of the baby-boom generation (born 1946–1964) will affect the growth of families without children. While many younger baby boomers (born 1957–1964) are still in the preparent stage of family life and are likely to become parents in the not-too-distant future, older baby boomers (born 1946–1956) who currently have children at home will soon be entering the empty nest phase. Projections by Decision Demographics show that married couples without children are likely to represent 43 percent of all families in 2000 if current trends in family formation remain unchanged.

Single-Parent Families

Nearly one in eight families was headed by a single parent in 1991, double the proportion in 1970. Women were five times more likely than men to be raising a family alone in 1991, and African-Americans were almost three times more likely than whites to be single parents. Single-parent families represented one in five white families with children, one in three Hispanic families with children, and six in ten black families with children. Changing patterns of marriage, divorce, remarriage, and the rise in births to unmarried women have contributed to the growth of single-parent families. "About half of today's young children will spend some time in a single-parent family, most as a consequence of divorce . . ." writes demographer Larry Bumpass. "Furthermore, this is not just simply a transitional phase between a first and second marriage. The majority will reside in a mother-only family for the remainder of their childhood."[5]

LIVING ARRANGEMENTS OF CHILDREN, YOUNG ADULTS, AND ELDERLY

The growing diversity of U.S. family life in the 1990s is most apparent in the living arrangements of children, young adults, and older persons. These groups have experienced the most dramatic change.

Children

One-quarter of all children (or 16.6 million children) in 1991 lived with only one parent—double the percentage of 1970 and almost triple that of 1960. Minority children were most affected by this change. In 1960, two-thirds of African-American children lived in two-parent homes; by 1980, less than half (42 percent) did so, and by 1991, only one-third (36 percent) were in a two-parent family. The number of Hispanic children in one-parent homes almost doubled between 1980 and 1991, reaching 2.2 million (or 30 percent) of all Hispanic children. High divorce rates and out-of-wedlock childbearing contributed to this trend.

But difficult economic times have also resulted in more families "doubling up," that is, sharing a common household together. Since 1970, the share of children who live in their grandparents' home has risen from 3 percent to 5 percent in 1991. These data reflect children (and their parents) who live in the home of the grandparent, not arrangements whereby grandparents move in with their adult children and grandchildren. About 3.3 million children lived in their grandparents' home in 1991. African-American children are three times more likely than white children to live with grandparents (12 percent versus 4 percent, respectively). About 6 percent of Hispanic children live with grandparents.

In most cases, one or both parents are present in the household. For half of these households, only the mother is present; in 17 percent, both parents are present. The "doubling up" of two-parent families within the grandparents' home increased during the 1980s (13 percent in 1980) as families responded to difficult economic conditions. In 28 percent of these households, neither parent is present, however, and grandparents are solely responsible for their grandchild.

Young Adults

The transition from being a dependent in the parental home to establishing an independent household has become increasingly complex and diverse. Compared with the 1970s, more young adults (ages 18 to 24) are living at home with their parents, more are living alone or with roommates, and fewer are maintaining married-couple family households of their own. Over half (54 percent) of all 18- to 24-year-olds lived with their parents in 1991—up from 47 percent in 1970. Some of these young adults never left the home after completing high school; others are college students who live at home at least part of the year. Even by ages 25 to 34, about 12 percent of young adults in this age group were at home with their parents—up from just 8 percent in 1970. Inflationary pressures, the rising cost of housing, slower wage growth, the increased cost of higher education, and the repayment of student loans are seen as important factors that have kept young adults at home with their parents. Less than half (48 percent) of adults under age 35 were the head (or spouse of the head) of a separate family household in 1991.

For those who can afford it, living alone or with roommates has also become increasingly common. So, too, has cohabitation—that is, living with someone in a sexual union without a formal marriage. Three million households in 1991 had cohabiting couples, nearly 60 percent of whom were under age 35. Cohabitation has increased sixfold since 1970 when only 500,000 households had cohabiting couples. Only opposite-sex couples are counted in these figures, so these data underestimate the extent of cohabitation in the United States today.[6]

About one-third of all cohabiting, opposite-sex couples in 1991 had children under age 15 present in their homes, but far more cohabiting couples are parents. By one estimate, almost half of cohabiting couples have children either living with them or living elsewhere with a custodial parent.[7]

Cohabitation is often seen as a prelude to marriage. Although only 5 percent of women ages 15 to 44 were cohabiting with a male partner in 1988, one-third had done so at some time in the past.[8] One-quarter of white women, one-quarter of Hispanic women, and nearly one-third of black women had lived with their first (or only) husband before marriage. Among single persons who plan to cohabit in the future, more than 80 percent said that cohabiting allows couples to make sure they are compatible before getting married. At least one of the partners expects the arrangement to result in marriage in 90 percent of cohabitations.[9] Respondents may be overly optimistic, however: 55 percent of first cohabiting unions of white women and 42 percent of those of black women resulted in marriage.[10]

It is important to note that the rise in cohabitation has helped to offset much, although not all, of the fall in marriage rates.[11] If we expand our notion of "marriage" to include legal marriage *and* cohabitation, there has been little decline in the institution of marriage in the United States.

Elderly

Often overlooked in the discussion of families is the living arrangements of older persons. The majority (54 percent in 1991) of persons age 65 and older are in married-couple households. But this fact masks considerable differences in living arrangements by the age and sex of the older person. It also masks the role that the extended family network plays in the support and care of older individuals.

Three out of four men ages 65 and older lived with their wife in 1991, whereas less than half (40 percent) of older women lived with their husband. Because women tend to live longer than men, there are more older women than older men. Most older women live alone, particularly after age 75. This is likely to increase the need for assistance from family, friends, or social agencies as failing health or chronic disabilities rob older individuals of their independence. In general, older women are twice as likely as older men to live with other family members, although by age 85, the difference narrows somewhat. About 5 percent of all persons age 65 and older were living in institutions, such as nursing homes, in 1990.

OUTLOOK FOR THE AMERICAN FAMILY

The American family is like a patchwork quilt—composed of many patterns yet durable and enduring even when it becomes frayed around the edges. Despite the diversity and fragmentation of family patterns that have emerged over the past 40 years, most Americans continue to regard the family as a central component of their life. They may no longer live in the seemingly well-ordered family world of the 1950s, but they are struggling to understand and adapt to the new realities of family life.

Making predictions about the future course of the American family is a hazardous business. The scope and magnitude of change in our marriage, divorce, and childbearing patterns have been enormous, making a total reversal of these trends seem unlikely. Yet assuming that future change will continue at the same rapid pace witnessed over the past 20 or 30 years is also an unlikely scenario. While most people will marry and continue to regard the two-parent family as the preferred norm, considerable variation will exist, depending on social and economic conditions.

In the short run, demographic factors suggest a slower pace of change in family patterns during the 1990s. The baby-boom generation, the largest generation in U.S. history, is in the prime childbearing/child-rearing ages. For the next ten years, there is likely to be little change in the overall share of families with children. But the composition of those families—whether single-parent, blended, multigenerational, or intact nuclear families—is likely to shift and change with time. Although we know that single-parent families are at greatest risk of living in disadvantaged situations, we have relatively little knowledge of the stepfamily or blended-family model. Because divorce and remarriage rates continue to be at relatively high levels, these reconstituted families are (and will continue to be) a dominant force in the life of many children. What is more, we need to understand how these families function in regard to older relatives: will members of stepfamilies feel the same sense of responsibility and obligation toward assisting older relatives as individuals who grew up in intact nuclear families? The answer to this question is likely to shape our public policy options and strategies.

In the long run, as we move into the twenty-first century, two demographic trends will strongly influence the structure of American family life. First, the aging of the population—that is, the continued growth in the size and share of the older population—will increase both the number of households without children and the number of persons who live alone. This trend may raise concern over public commitment toward school bond referenda or other public expenditures for children's programs. On the other hand, an increasing number of frail elderly who live alone will require more supportive services in an era when adult daughters hold jobs and are not as readily available as earlier generations to be caregivers. The political struggle over the allocation of scarce resources will almost inevitably be seen in terms of generational conflict and trade-offs. But a better understanding of the mutual supports and interdependencies that extend beyond the nuclear family will be a key part of meeting this challenge.

Second, the U.S. minority population is large and growing, and this fact places a special spotlight on children in need. By the year 2000, one in three school-age children will be from a minority population, compared with about one in four today. Child poverty rates, however, are two to three times higher for minority children than for non-Hispanic whites, and minority children are at greater risk of growing up in disadvantaged circumstances. Neglecting the needs of the next generation can only undercut America's investment in its own economic future.

Valuing the family should not be confused with valuing a particular family form. Indeed, family life in the 1990s will be marked by its diversity. As blended families become the norm, the responsibilities of family members become more complex, more ambiguous, and more open to dispute. Social legislation (or "pro-family" policies) narrowly designed to reinforce only one model of the American family is likely to be shortsighted and have the unintended consequence of weakening, rather than strengthening, family ties. Recognizing the diversity of American families and addressing the complexity of their needs must lie at the heart of the policy debates on family issues.

NOTES

1. Louisa F. Miller and Jeanne E. Moorman, "Married-Couple Families with Children," *Current Population Reports* P-23, no. 162 (1989): table B.

2. See Jan Larson, "Understanding Stepfamilies," *American Demographics* (July 1992): 36–40.

3. Jeanne E. Moorman and Donald J. Hernandez, "Married-Couple Families with Step, Adopted, and Biological Children," *Demography* 26, no. 2 (May 1989): 267–277.

4. Martin O'Connell, "Late Expectations: Childbearing Patterns of American Women for the 1990's," Studies in American Fertility, *Current Population Reports* P-23, no. 176 (1991): table H.

5. Larry L. Bumpass, "What's Happening to the Family? Interactions Between Demographic and Institutional Change," *Demography* 27, no. 4 (1990): 485.

6. U.S. Bureau of the Census, "Marital Status and Living Arrangements: March 1991." *Current Population Reports* P-20, no. 461 (1992): table 8.

7. Larry L. Bumpass, James A. Sweet, and Andrew Cherlin, "The Role of Cohabitation in Declining Rates of Marriage," *Journal of Marriage and the Family* 53, no. 4 (November 1991): 913–927.

8. See Kathryn A. London, "Cohabitation, Marriage, Marital Dissolution, and Remarriage: United States, 1988," *Advance Data from Vital and Health Statistics*, no. 194 (Hyattsville, MD: National Center for Health Statistics, 1991): 1–3.

9. Bumpass, "What's Happening to the Family?" p. 487.

10. London, "Cohabitation," p. 2.

11. Bumpass, "What's Happening to the Family?" p. 488.

R E A D I N G

2

Continuity and Change in American Family Life

Tamara K. Hareven

. . . Recent research on the family in colonial American society has dispelled the myths about the existence of ideal three-generational families in the American past. The historical evidence now shows that there never has been in American society an era when coresidence of three generations in the same household was the dominant pattern. The "great extended families" that became part of the folklore of modern industrial society were rarely in existence. Early American

From Leudtke, L.S. (editor). 1992. *Making America: The Society and Culture of the U.S.* Chapel Hill and London: The University of North Carolina Press.

households and families were simple in their structure and not drastically different in their organization from contemporary families. The most typical residential family unit was nuclear—consisting of parents and their children, not extended kin. Three generations seldom lived together in the same household. Given the high mortality rate in preindustrial societies, most parents could not have expected to overlap with their grandchildren. It would thus be futile to argue that industrialization destroyed the great extended family of the past. In reality, such a family type rarely existed.

Family arrangements in the colonial period differed, however, from those in our times. Even though they did not contain extended kin, these households did include unrelated individuals, boarders, lodgers, apprentices, or servants. In this respect the composition of the household in the colonial period was significantly different from that in contemporary society. The tendency of families to include nonrelatives in the household was connected with an entirely different concept of family life. In contrast to the current emphasis on the family home as a private retreat, the household of the past was the site of a broad array of functions and activities that transcended the more restricted circle of the nuclear family. The household was a place of production and served as an abode for servants, apprentices, and dependent members of the community, such as orphaned children and old men or women without relatives.

A considerable number of urban families continued to take in nonrelatives as boarders as late as the 1920s. The practice of young people boarding with other families thus continued even after the practice of masters having apprentices reside in their households had disappeared. Through the nineteenth and into the early twentieth century about one-fourth to one-third of the population either had lived in someone's household as a boarder or had taken boarders or lodgers at some point in their lives. Boarding or lodging with urban families was an important form of exchange between generations. It enabled young men and women in their late teens and twenties who had left their parents' households or who had migrated from other communities to live as boarders in the households of older people whose own children had left home. This practice enabled young people to stay in surrogate family arrangements; at the same time it provided old people with the opportunity to continue heading their own households without being isolated. Boarding and lodging also fulfilled a critical function in providing continuity in urban life and helping new migrants and immigrants adapt to urban living. Its existence suggests great flexibility in families and households, a flexibility that has been lost over the past half century.

Increasing availability of housing since the 1920s and the rise of values of privacy in family life have led to the phasing out of boarding and lodging, except among black families. The practice has virtually disappeared from the larger society. With its disappearance the family has lost some of its major sources of resilience in adapting to urban living. Thus, the most important change in American family life has not been the breakdown of a three-generational family but rather the retreat of the family into its private household and the withdrawal of nonrelatives from the family's abode. Since the beginning of this century the home has become identified as a retreat from the outside world, and the presence of nonrelatives has been considered threatening to the privacy of the family.

Because of the decline in boarding and lodging, the number of households containing only one member has been increasing steadily since the 1920s. While in the nineteenth century solitary residence was almost unheard of, now a major portion of the population resides alone. The disquieting aspect of this pattern is the high percentage of aging widows living by themselves. For a large part of the population, living alone is not a matter of free choice but rather an unavoidable and often painful arrangement. What has been lost over the past two centuries is not the great extended family, but the flexibility of the family that enabled households to expand when necessary and to take people in to live in surrogate family settings rather than in isolation.

KIN RELATIONS

Another pervasive myth about family life in the past has been the assumption that industrialization broke up traditional kinship ties and destroyed the organic interdependence between the family and the community. Once again historical research has shown that industrialization, rather than breaking up traditional family structures, has led to the redefinition of family functions. In industrial communities the family continued to function as a work unit. Relatives acted as recruitment, migration, and housing agents for industrial laborers, helping each other to shift from rural to industrial life and work patterns. Families migrated in groups to industrial centers, and relatives were active in the recruitment of workers into the factory system. Often several family members, even distant kin, continued to work in the same place and fulfilled valuable functions in providing mutual assistance and support in the workplace. Migration to industrial communities did not break up traditional kinship ties; rather, families used these ties to facilitate their own transitions into industrial life and to adapt to new living conditions and life-styles.

During the periods of adjustment to migration, to settlement in new places, and to industrial work, reliance on kin persisted as the most basic resource for assistance. Following the early period of industrialization, kin in rural and urban areas continued to engage in mutual assistance and in reciprocal services. Kin performed a crucial role in initiating and organizing migration from rural areas to factory towns locally, and from rural communities abroad to industrial communities in the United States. Thus, although the majority of families lived in nuclear household arrangements, they were still enmeshed in kinship networks outside the household and depended heavily on mutual assistance.

Even in the late nineteenth and early twentieth centuries, workers who migrated from rural areas to the cities in most industrializing communities carried parts of their kinship ties and family traditions into new settings. Young unmarried sons and daughters of working age, or young married couples without their children, tended to migrate first. After they found jobs and housing, they sent for their relatives. Chain migration thus helped maintain ties and continuities between family members in their new communities of settlement.

In factories and other places of employment, newly arrived workers utilized the connections established by relatives who were already working there to facilitate their hiring and adaptation to work. Hiring and placement through kin often continued even in large-scale modern factories. Kinship networks infiltrated formal, bureaucratized industrial organizations and clustered within them. Even when they worked in different locales, kin made collective decisions about each other's work careers.

Kinship networks also formed an important part of the fiber of urban neighborhoods. Relatives tended to settle in proximity to each other, and as immigrants arrived in American cities, they preferred to live close to their kin whenever possible. So kinship ties brought both coherence and mutual support to the urban neighborhood. This pattern has persisted to some extent among ethnic groups but has gradually weakened in the remainder of the population. While major portions of the American population are still in close contact with their kin, the interdependence that was typical of earlier times has eroded considerably as a result of the continuing redefinition of individualism, as well as patterns of migration and the development of mass transportation. Kin have ceased to be the major source of social security, and some of the functions of mutual assistance formerly found among kin have been replaced by public programs.

Even if industrialization did not bring about major changes in the structure of the family, it did produce changes in the functions of the family and in the values governing family life. Since the early nineteenth century the family gradually has surrendered to other social institutions functions previously concentrated within it.

CHANGING FAMILY FUNCTIONS AND VALUES

During the preindustrial period the family not only reared children but also served as a workshop, a school, a church, and a welfare agency. Preindustrial families meshed closely with the community and carried a variety of public responsibilities within the larger society. "Family and community," John Demos writes, "private and public life, formed part of the same moral equation. The one supported the other and they became in a sense indistinguishable." In preindustrial society most of the work took place in the household. Roles of parenting were therefore congruent with social and economic roles. Children were considered members of the work force and were seen as economic assets. Childhood was treated as a brief preparatory period terminated by apprenticeship and the commencement of work, generally before puberty. Adolescence was virtually unknown as a distinct stage of life. Family members were integrated into common economic activities. The segregation of roles in the family along gender and age lines that characterizes middle-class family life in modern society had not yet appeared. As long as the household functioned as a workshop as well as a family home, family life was not clearly separated from work life.

Even though preindustrial families contained large numbers of children, women invested relatively less time in motherhood than their successors in the nineteenth century and in our time did and still do. Child care was part of a general effort of household production rather than a woman's exclusive preoccupation; children were viewed not merely as objects of nature but as productive members of the family from an early age on. The tasks of child rearing did not fall exclusively on mothers; other relatives living nearby also participated in this function.

The integration of family and work in preindustrial society allowed for an intensive sharing of labor between husbands and wives and between parents and children that was later diminished in industrial society. Housework was inseparable from domestic industries or agricultural work, and it was valued, therefore, as an economic asset. Since children constituted part of the labor force, motherhood, too, was valued for its economic contributions and not only for its nurturing tasks.

Under the impact of industrialization many of these functions were transferred to agencies and institutions outside the family. The workplace was separated from the home, and functions of social welfare were transferred from the family to asylums and reformatories. "The family has become *a more specialized agency than before*," wrote Talcott Parsons, "probably more specialized than it has been in any previously known society . . . but not in any general sense less important, because the society is dependent *more* exclusively on it for the performance of *certain* of its vital functions." These vital functions include childbearing, child rearing, and socialization. The family has ceased to be a work unit and has limited its economic activities primarily to consumption and child care.

The transformation of the household from a busy workplace and social center to a private family abode involved the withdrawal of strangers, such as business associates, partners, journeymen, apprentices, and boarders and lodgers, from the household; it also involved a more rigorous separation of husbands from wives and fathers from children in the course of the workday. Specialization in work schedules significantly altered the daily lives of family members in urban society, since the majority of men worked outside the home while women stayed at home and children went to school. In working-class families this specialization was even more far-reaching, since women also worked outside the home, but often on different schedules than the men in their households.

Under the impact of industrialization, in middle-class families housework lost its economic and productive value. Since it was not paid for, and since it no longer led to the production of visible goods, it lost its place in the occupational hierarchy. Housework continued to be governed by nonstandardized time schedules, thus remaining through the nineteenth century a nonindustrial occupation. This is another reason (in addition to economic ones) why housework has been devalued in modern society—where achievement is measured not only by products but also by systematic time and production schedules.

These changes brought about in family life by industrialization were gradual and varied significantly from class to class as well as among different ethnic groups. While scholars have sometimes generalized for an entire society on the basis of the middle-class experience, it is now becoming clear that preindustrial family patterns persisted over longer time periods in rural and in urban working-class families. Since the process of industrialization was gradual, domestic industries and a variety of small family enterprises were carried over into the industrial system. In most working-class families work was still considered a family enterprise, even when their members were employed in different enterprises and the work did not take place in the home. In such families the work of wives, sons, and daughters was carefully regulated by the collective strategies of the family unit. Much of what we perceive today as individual vocational activity was actually considered in earlier times part of a collective family effort.

With the growth of industrial child labor in the nineteenth century, working-class families continued to recognize the economic value of motherhood, as they had in rural society. Segregation along age groups within working-class families was almost nonexistent. Children were socialized for industrial work from an early age and began to contribute to the family's work effort at a younger age than specified by law. They were considered assets, both for their contribution to the family's economy during their youth and for the prospect of their support during their parents' old age. Parents viewed their efforts in child rearing as investments in future social security.

In working-class families, even though the process of industrialization offered women opportunities for independent work outside their homes, women continued to function as an integral part of the family's productive effort. Even when they worked in factories, single working women were bound by family obligations and contributed most of their earnings to their parents. A woman's work was considered part of the family's economic effort, not an independent career. During periods of large-scale industrial development families continued to function as collective economic units in which husbands, wives, and children were all responsible for the well-being of the family.

THE ROLE OF WOMEN

This continuity in the function of the family as a collaborative economic unit is significant for understanding the changes in the roles of women that industrialization introduced into working-class life. By introducing changes in the modes of production as well as in the nature and pace of work, industrialization offered women the opportunity to become wage earners outside the household. Industrialization did not, however, bring about immediate changes in the family's corporate identity in the working class—at least not during the early stages of industrialization. Among middle-class families, on the other hand, industrialization had a more dramatic impact on gender roles: the separation between the home and the workplace that followed in the wake of industrialization led to the glorification of the home as a domestic retreat from the outside world. The new ideology of domesticity that developed in the first half of the nineteenth century relegated women to the home and glorified their role as homemakers and mothers.

The emergence of the ideology of domesticity and of full-time motherhood was closely connected with the decline in the average number of children a woman had and with the new attitudes toward childhood that were emerging in the nineteenth century. One of these major changes was the recognition of childhood as a distinct stage of life among urban middle-class families. Children began to be treated as objects of nurture rather than as working members of the family. Stripped of the multiplicity of functions that had been previously concentrated in the family, urban middle-class families developed into private, domestic, and child-centered retreats from the world of work and politics. Children were no longer expected to join the work force until their late teens, a major indication of the growing recognition of childhood as a distinct stage of development. Instead of considering children as potential working members of the family group, parents began to view them as dependent objects of tender nurture and protection.

This marked the emergence of the domestic middle-class family as we know it today. The glorification of motherhood as a full-time career served both to enshrine the family as a domestic retreat from the world of work and to make families child centered. The gradual separation of the home from the workplace that had started with industrialization reached its peak in the designation of the home as a therapeutic refuge from the outside world. As custodians of this retreat, women were expected to concentrate on making the home a perfect place and on child rearing, rather than on being economic partners in the family. Tenderness, gentleness, affection, sweetness, and a comforting demeanor began to emerge as a central value at the base of family relationships.

The ideology of domesticity and the new view of childhood combined to revise expectations of parenthood. The roles of husbands and wives became gradually more separate; a clear division of labor replaced the old economic cooperation, and the wife's efforts concentrated on homemaking and child rearing. With men leaving the home to work elsewhere, time invested in fatherhood was concentrated primarily on leisure hours. Thus the separation of husbands from wives and parents from children for major parts of the day came about. These patterns, which emerged in the early nineteenth century, formed the base of relations characteristic of the contemporary American family. Some of these patterns persist to the present day and are the root of problems and crises in the family.

The cult of domesticity that emerged in the nineteenth century as a major part of the ideology of family life in America has dominated perceptions of women's roles until very recently and has shaped prevailing assumptions governing family life. One of its consequences was the insistence that confinement of women's main activities to the domestic sphere and the misguided assumption that mothers' work in the labor market would be harmful to the family and to society. Only over the past few decades have these values been criticized and partly rejected. Since the prejudices against mothers' labor force participation persevered as long as they did in American society, and have handicapped women's pursuit of occupations outside the home, it is important to understand their origin in the nineteenth-century cult of domesticity.

Although the ideology of domesticity originated in urban middle-class families, it was gradually adopted as the dominant model for family life in the entire society. Second- and third-generation immigrant families, who originally held a more integrated view of the family as a corporate unit, and who had earlier accepted the wife's work outside the home, began to embrace the ideology of domesticity as part of their "Americanization" process. The ideals of urban middle-class life subsequently handicapped the role of women as workers outside the home. As immigrants became "Americanized" in the early part of the twentieth century, they internalized the values of domesticity and began to view women's labor force participation as demeaning, as carrying low status, or as compromising for the husband and dangerous for the children. Consequently, married women entered the labor force only when driven by economic necessity.

Despite the impact of the ideal of domesticity in American culture, working-class and ethnic families to a significant degree continued to adhere to the earlier ways of life and maintained a collective view of the family and its economy. In contrast to the values of individualism that govern much of family life today, traditional values of family collectivity have persisted among various ethnic groups and, to some extent, among black families. In working-class and ethnic families the relationships between husbands and wives, parents and children, and other kin were based upon reciprocal assistance and support. Such relations, often defined as "instrumental," drew their strength from the assumption that family members were all engaged in mutual obligations and in reciprocity. Although obligations were not specifically defined by contract, they rested on the accepted social values as to what family members owed to each other. In the period preceding the welfare state instrumental relationships among family members and more distant kin provided important supports to individuals and families, particularly during critical life situations.

A collective view of familial obligations was the very basis of survival in earlier time periods. From such a perspective marriage and parenthood were not merely love relationships but partnerships governed by family economic and social needs. In this respect the experience of working-class families in the nineteenth century and of ethnic families in the more recent past was drastically different from that of middle-class families, in which sentimentality emerged as the dominant base of family relationships. Among traditional families sentiment was secondary to family needs and survival strategies. Under such conditions childbearing and work were not governed by individual decisions. Mate selection and the timing of marriage were regulated in accordance with collective family considerations rather than directed by strictly individual whim. The transfer of property and work were not regulated strictly according to individual decisions. At times collective family "plans" took priority over individual preferences. For example, parents often tried to delay the marriage of the last child in the household, commonly a daughter, in order to secure continued economic support, especially in later life when they were withdrawing from the labor force.

Thus, the major historical change in family values has been one from a collective view of the family to one of individualization and sentiment. Over the past several decades American families have been experiencing an increasing emphasis on individual priorities and preferences over collective family needs. This individualization of family relations has also led to an exaggerated emphasis on emotional nurture, intimacy, and privacy as the major base of family relations. It has contributed considerably to the liberation of individuals, but it has also eroded the resilience of the family and its ability to withstand crises. Moreover, it has contributed to a greater separation among family members and especially to the isolation of older people. . . .

R E A D I N G

3

The Life Course Revolution

Arlene Skolnick

Many of us, in moments of nostalgia, imagine the past as a kind of Disneyland— a quaint setting we might step back into with our sense of ourselves intact, yet free of the stresses of modern life. But in yearning for the golden past we imagine we have lost, we are unaware of what we have escaped.

In our time, for example, dying before reaching old age has become a rare event; about three-quarters of all people die after their sixty-fifth birthday. It is hard for us to appreciate what a novelty this is in human experience. In 1850, only 2 percent of the population lived past sixty-five. "We place dying in what we take to be its logical position," observes the social historian Ronald Blythe, "which is at the close of a long life, whereas our ancestors accepted the futility of placing it in any position at all. In the midst of life we are in death, they said, and they meant it. To them it was a fact; to us it is a metaphor."

This longevity revolution is largely a twentieth-century phenomenon. Astonishingly, two-thirds of the total increase in human longevity since prehistoric times has taken place since 1900—and a good deal of that increase has occurred in recent decades. Mortality rates in previous centuries were several times higher than today, and death commonly struck at any age. Infancy was particularly hazardous; "it took two babies to make one adult," as one demographer put it. A white baby girl today has a greater chance of living to be sixty than her counterpart born in 1870 would have had of reaching her first birthday. And after infancy, death still hovered as an ever-present possibility. It was not unusual for young and middle-aged adults to die of tuberculosis, pneumonia, or other infection diseases. (Keats died at twenty-five, Schubert at thirty-one, Mozart at thirty-five.)

These simple changes in mortality have had profound, yet little-appreciated effects on family life; they have encouraged stronger emotional bonds between

Excerpt "Unheralded Revolutions," from *Embattled Paradise* by Arlene Skolnick. Copyright © 1991 by Arlene Skolnick. Reprinted by permission of Basic Books, a division of HarperCollins Publishers, Inc.

parents and children, lengthened the duration of marriage and parent-child relationships, made grandparenthood an expectable stage of the life course, and increased the number of grandparents whom children actually know. More and more families have four or even five generations alive at the same time. And for the first time in history, the average couple has more parents living than it has children. It is also the first era when most of the parent-child relationship takes place after the child becomes an adult.

In a paper entitled "Death and the Family," the demographer Peter Uhlenberg has examined some of these repercussions by contrasting conditions in 1900 with those in 1976. In 1900, for example, half of all parents would have experienced the death of a child; by 1976 only 6 percent would. And more than half of all children who lived to the age of fifteen in 1900 would have experienced the death of a parent or sibling, compared with less than 9 percent in 1976. Another outcome of the lower death rates was a decline in the number of orphans and orphanages. Current discussions of divorce rarely take into account the almost constant family disruption children experienced in "the good old days." In 1900, 1 out of 4 children under the age of fifteen lost a parent; 1 out of 62 lost both. The corresponding figures for 1976 are, respectively, 1 out of 20 and 1 out of 1,800.

Because being orphaned used to be so common, the chances of a child's not living with either parent was much greater at the turn of the century than it is now. Indeed, some of the current growth in single-parent families is offset by a decline in the number of children raised in institutions, in foster homes, or by relatives. This fact does not diminish the stresses of divorce and other serious family problems of today, but it does help correct the tendency to contrast the terrible Present with an idealized Past.

Today's children rarely experience the death of a close relative, except for elderly grandparents. And it is possible to grow into adulthood without experiencing even that loss. "We never had any deaths in my family," a friend recently told me, explaining that none of her relatives had died until she was in her twenties. In earlier times, children were made aware of the constant possibility of death, attended deathbed scenes, and were even encouraged to examine the decaying corpses of family members.

One psychological result of our escape from the daily presence of death is that we are ill prepared for it when it comes. For most of us, the first time we feel a heightened concern with our own mortality is in our thirties and forties when we realize that the years we have already lived outnumber those we have left.

Another result is that the death of a child is no longer a sad but normal hazard of parenthood. Rather, it has become a devastating, life-shattering loss from which a parent may never fully recover. The intense emotional bonding between parents and infants that we see as a sociobiological given did not become the norm until the eighteenth and nineteenth centuries. The privileged classes created the concept of the "emotionally priceless" child, a powerful ideal that gradually filtered down through the rest of society.

The high infant mortality rates of premodern times were partly due to neglect, and often to lethal child-rearing practices such as sending infants off to a wet nurse* or, worse, infanticide. It now appears that in all societies lacking reliable contraception, the careless treatment and neglect of unwanted children acted as a major form of birth control. This does not necessarily imply that parents were uncaring toward all their children; rather, they seem to have practiced "selective neglect" of sickly infants in favor of sturdy ones, or of later children in favor of earlier ones.† In 1801 a writer observed of Bavarian peasants:

> The peasant has joy when his wife brings forth the first fruit of their love, he has joy with the second and third as well, but not with the fourth. . . . He sees all children coming thereafter as hostile creatures, which take the bread from his mouth and the mouths of his family. Even the heart of the most gentle mother becomes cold with the birth of the fifth child, and the sixth, she unashamedly wishes death, that the child should pass to heaven.

Declining fertility rates are another major result of falling death rates. Until the baby boom of the 1940s and 1950s, fertility rates had been dropping continuously since the eighteenth century. By taking away parents' fear that some of their children would not survive to adulthood, lowered early-childhood mortality rates encouraged careful planning of births and smaller families. The combination of longer lives and fewer, more closely spaced children created a still-lengthening empty-nest stage in the family. This in turn has encouraged the companionate style of marriage, since husband and wife can expect to live together for many years after their children have moved out.

Many demographers have suggested that falling mortality rates are directly linked to rising divorce rates. In 1891 W. F. Willcox of Cornell University made one of the most accurate social science predictions ever. Looking at the high and steadily rising divorce rates of the time, along with falling mortality rates, he predicted that around 1980, the two curves would cross and the number of marriages ended by divorce would equal those ended by death. In the late 1970s, it all happened as Willcox had predicted. Then divorce rates continued to increase before leveling off in the 1980s, while mortality rates continued to

---

*Wet-nursing—the breastfeeding of an infant by a woman other than the mother—was widely practiced in premodern Europe and colonial America. Writing of a two-thousand-year-old "war of the breast," the developmental psychologist William Kessen notes that the most persistent theme in the history of childhood is the reluctance of mothers to suckle their babies, and the urgings of philosophers and physicians that they do so. Infants were typically sent away from home for a year and a half or two years to be raised by poor country women, in squalid conditions. When they took in more babies than they had milk enough to suckle, the babies would die of malnutrition.

The reluctance to breast-feed may not have reflected maternal indifference so much as other demands in premodern, precontraceptive times—the need to take part in the family economy, the unwillingness of husbands to abstain from sex for a year and a half or two. (Her milk would dry up if a mother became pregnant.) Although in France and elsewhere the custom persisted into the twentieth century, large-scale wet-nursing symbolizes the gulf between modern and premodern sensibilities about infants and their care.

†The anthropologist Nancy Scheper-Hughes describes how impoverished mothers in northeastern Brazil select which infants to nurture.

decline. As a result, a couple marrying today is more likely to celebrate a fortieth wedding anniversary than were couples around the turn of the century.

In statistical terms, then, it looks as if divorce has restored a level of instability to marriage that had existed earlier due to the high mortality rate. But as Lawrence Stone observes, "it would be rash to claim that the psychological effects of the termination of marriage by divorce, that is by an act of will, bear a close resemblance to its termination by the inexorable accident of death."

THE NEW STAGES OF LIFE

In recent years it has become clear that the stages of life we usually think of as built into human development are, to a large degree, social and cultural inventions. Although people everywhere may pass through infancy, childhood, adulthood, and old age, the facts of nature are "doctored," as Ruth Benedict once put it, in different ways by different cultures.

The Favorite Age

In 1962 Phillipe Ariès made the startling claim that "in medieval society, the idea of childhood did not exist." Ariès argued not that parents then neglected their children, but that they did not think of children as having a special nature that required special treatment; after the age of around five to seven, children simply joined the adult world of work and play. This "small adult" conception of childhood has been observed by many anthropologists in preindustrial societies. In Europe, according to Ariès and others, childhood was discovered, or invented, in the seventeenth and nineteenth centuries, with the emergence of the private, domestic, companionate family and formal schooling. These institutions created distinct roles for children, enabling childhood to emerge as a distinct stage of life.

Despite challenges to Ariès's work, the bulk of historical and cross-cultural evidence supports the contention that childhood as we know it today is a relatively recent cultural invention; our ideas about children, child-rearing practices, and the conditions of children's lives are dramatically different from those of earlier centuries. The same is true of adolescence. Teenagers, such a conspicuous and noisy presence in modern life, and their stage of life, known for its turmoil and soul searching, are not universal features of life in other times and places.

Of course, the physical changes of puberty—sexual maturation and spurt in growth—happen to everyone everywhere. Yet, even here, there is cultural and historical variation. In the past hundred years, the age of first menstruation has declined from the mid-teens to twelve, and the age young men reach their full height has declined from twenty-five to under twenty. Both changes are believed to be due to improvements in nutrition and health care, and these average ages are not expected to continue dropping.

Some societies have puberty rites, but they bring about a transition from childhood not to adolescence but to adulthood. Other societies take no note at all of the changes, and the transition from childhood to adulthood takes place simply and without social recognition. Adolescence as we know it today appears to have evolved late in the nineteenth century; there is virtual consensus among social scientists that it is "a creature of the industrial revolution and it continues to be shaped by the forces which defined that revolution: industrialization, specialization, urbanization . . . and bureaucratization of human organizations and institutions, and continuing technological development."

In America before the second half of the nineteenth century, youth was an ill-defined category. Puberty did not mark any new status or life experience. For the majority of young people who lived on farms, work life began early, at seven or eight years old or even younger. As they grew older, their responsibility would increase, and they would gradually move toward maturity. Adults were not ignorant of the differences between children and adults, but distinctions of age meant relatively little. As had been the practice in Europe, young people could be sent away to become apprentices or servants in other households. As late as the early years of this century, working-class children went to work at the age of ten or twelve.

A second condition leading to a distinct stage of adolescence was the founding of mass education systems, particularly the large public high school. Compulsory education helped define adolescence by setting a precise age for it; high schools brought large numbers of teenagers together to create their own society for a good part of their daily lives. So the complete set of conditions for adolescence on a mass scale did not exist until the end of the nineteenth century.

The changed family situations of late-nineteenth- and early-twentieth-century youth also helped make this life stage more psychologically problematic. Along with the increasing array of options to choose from, rapid social change was making one generation's experience increasingly different from that of the next. Among the immigrants who were flooding into the country at around the time adolescence was emerging, the generation gap was particularly acute. But no parents were immune to the rapid shifts in society and culture that were transforming America in the decades around the turn of the century.

Further, the structure and emotional atmosphere of middle-class family life was changing also, creating a more intimate and emotionally intense family life. Contrary to the view that industrialization had weakened parent-child relations, the evidence is that family ties between parents and adolescents intensified at this time: adolescents lived at home until they married, and depended more completely, and for a longer time, on their parents than in the past. Demographic change had cut family size in half over the course of the century. Mothers were encouraged to devote themselves to the careful nurturing of fewer children.

This more intensive family life seems likely to have increased the emotional strain of adolescence. Smaller households and a more nurturing style of child rearing, combined with the increased contact between parents, especially mothers, and adolescent children, may have created a kind of " 'Oedipal family' in middle class America."

The young person's awakening sexuality, particularly the young male's is likely to have been more disturbing to both himself and his parents than during the era when young men commonly lived away from home. . . . There is evidence that during the Victorian era, fears of adolescent male sexuality, and of masturbation in particular, were remarkably intense and widespread.

Family conflict in general may have been intensified by the peculiar combination of teenagers' increased dependence on parents and increased autonomy in making their own life choices. Despite its tensions, the new emotionally intense middle-class home made it more difficult than ever for adolescents to leave home for the heartless, indifferent world outside.

By the end of the nineteenth century, conceptions of adolescence took on modern form, and by the first decades of the twentieth century, *adolescence* had become a household word. As articulated forcefully by the psychologist G. Stanley Hall in his 1904 treatise, adolescence was a biological process—not simply the onset of sexual maturity but a turbulent, transitional stage in the evolution of the human species: "some ancient period of storm and stress when old moorings were broken and a higher level attained."

Hall seemed to provide the answers to questions people were asking about the troublesome young. His public influence eventually faded, but his conception of adolescence as a time of storm and stress lived on. Adolescence continued to be seen as a period of both great promise and great peril: "every step of the upward way is strewn with the wreckage of body, mind and morals." The youth problem—whether the lower-class problem of delinquency, or the identity crises and other psychological problems of middle-class youth—has continued to haunt America, and other modern societies, ever since.

Ironically, then, the institutions that had developed to organize and control a problematic age ended by heightening adolescent self-awareness, isolating youth from the rest of society, and creating a youth culture, making the transition to adulthood still more problematic and risky. Institutional recognition in turn made adolescents a more distinct part of the population, and being adolescent a more distinct and self-conscious experience. As it became part of the social structure of modern society, adolescence also became an important stage of the individual's biography—an indeterminate period of being neither child nor adult that created its own problems. Any society that excludes youth from adult work, and offers them what Erikson calls a "moratorium"—time and space to try out identities and lifestyles—and at the same time demands extended schooling as the route to success is likely to turn adolescence into a "struggle for self." It is also likely to run the risk of increasing numbers of mixed-up, rebellious youth.

But, in fact, the classic picture of adolescent storm and stress is not universal. Studies of adolescents in America and other industrialized societies suggest that extreme rebellion and rejection of parents, flamboyant behavior, and psychological turmoil do not describe most adolescents, even today. Media images of the youth of the 1980s and 1990s as a deeply troubled, lost generation beset by crime, drug abuse, and teenage pregnancy are also largely mistaken.

Although sexual activity and experimenting with drugs and alcohol have become common among middle-class young people, drug use has actually declined in recent years. Disturbing as these practices are for parents and other adults, they apparently do not interfere with normal development for most adolescents. Nevertheless, for a significant minority, sex and drugs add complications to a period of development during which a young person's life can easily go awry—temporarily or for good.

More typically, for most young people, the teen years are marked by mild rebelliousness and moodiness—enough to make it a difficult period for parents but not one of a profound parent-child generation gap or of deep alienation from conventional values. These ordinary tensions of family living through adolescence are exacerbated in times of rapid social change, when the world adolescents confront is vastly different from the one in which their parents came of age. Always at the forefront of social change, adolescents in industrial societies inevitably bring discomfort to their elders, who "wish to see their children's adolescence as an enactment of the retrospectively distorted memory of their own. . . . But such intergenerational continuity can occur only in the rapidly disappearing isolation of the desert or the rain forest."

If adolescence is a creation of modern culture, that culture has also been shaped by adolescence. Adolescents, with their music, fads, fashions, and conflicts, not only are conspicuous, but reflect a state of mind that often extends beyond the years designated for them. The adolescent mode of experience—accessible to people of any age—is marked by "exploration, becoming, growth, and pain."

Since the nineteenth century, for example, the coming-of-age novel has become a familiar literary genre. Patricia Spacks observes that while Victorian authors looked back at adolescence from the perspective of adulthood, twentieth-century novelists since James Joyce and D. H. Lawrence have become more intensely identified with their young heroes, writing not from a distance but from "deep inside the adolescence experience." The novelist's use of the adolescent to symbolize the artist as romantic outsider mirrors a more general cultural tendency. As Phillipe Ariès observes, "Our society has passed from a period which was ignorant of adolescence to a period in which adolescence is the favorite age. We now want to come to it early and linger in it as long as possible."

The Discovery of Adulthood

Middle age is the latest life stage to be discovered, and the notion of mid-life crisis recapitulates the storm-and-stress conception of adolescence. Over the course of the twentieth century, especially during the years after World War II, a developmental conception of childhood became institutionalized in public thought. Parents took it for granted that children passed through ages, stages, and phases: the terrible twos, the teenage rebel. In recent years the idea of development has been increasingly applied to adults, as new stages of adult life are discovered. Indeed much of the psychological revolution of recent years—the tendency to look at life through psychological lenses—can be understood in part as the extension of the developmental approach to adulthood.

In 1976 Gail Sheehy's best-selling *Passages* popularized the concept of mid-life crisis. Sheehy argued that every individual must pass through such a watershed, a time when we reevaluate our sense of self, undergo a crisis, and emerge with a new identity. Failure to do so, she warned, can have dire consequences. The book was the most influential popular attempt to apply to adults the ages-and-stages approach to development that had long been applied to children. Ironically, this came about just as historians were raising questions about the universality of those stages.

Despite its popularity, Sheehy's book, and the research she reported in it, have come under increasing criticism. "Is the mid-life crisis, if it exists, more than a warmed-over identity crisis?" asked one review of the research literature on mid-life. In fact, there is little or no evidence for the notion that adults pass through a series of sharply defined stages, or a series of crises that must be resolved before passing from one stage to the next.

Nevertheless, the notion of a mid-life crisis caught on because it reflected shifts in adult experience across the life course. Most people's decisions about marriage and work are no longer irrevocably made at one fateful turning point on the brink of adulthood. The choices made at twenty-one may no longer fit at forty or fifty—the world has changed; parents, children, and spouses have changed; working life has changed. The kind of issue that makes adolescence problematic—the array of choices and the need to fashion a coherent, continuous sense of self in the midst of all this change—recurs throughout adulthood. As a Jules Feiffer cartoon concludes, "Maturity is a phase, but adolescence is forever."

Like the identity crisis of adolescence, the concept of mid-life crisis appears to reflect the experience of the more educated and advantaged. Those with more options in life are more likely to engage in the kind of introspection and reappraisal of previous choices that make up the core of the mid-life crisis. Such people realize that they will never fulfill their earlier dreams, or that they have gotten what they wanted and find they are still not happy. But as the Berkeley longitudinal data show, even in that segment of the population, mid-life crisis is far from the norm. People who have experienced fewer choices in the past, and have fewer options for charting new directions in the future, are less likely to encounter a mid-life crisis. Among middle Americans, life is dominated by making ends meet, coping with everyday events, and managing unexpected crises.

While there may be no fixed series of stages or crises adults must pass through, middle age or mid-life in our time does have some unique features that make it an unsettled time, different from other periods in the life course as well as from mid-life in earlier eras. First, as we saw earlier, middle age is the first period in which most people today confront death, illness, and physical decline. It is also an uneasy age because of the increased importance of sexuality in modern life. Sexuality has come to be seen as the core of our sense of self, and sexual fulfillment as the center of the couple relationship. In mid-life, people confront the decline of their physical attractiveness, if not of their sexuality.

There is more than a passing resemblance between the identity problems of adolescence and the issues that fall under the rubric of "mid-life crisis." In a list of themes recurring in the literature on the experience of identity crisis, particularly in adolescence, the psychologist Roy Baumeister includes: feelings of emptiness, feelings of vagueness, generalized malaise, anxiety, self-consciousness. These symptoms describe not only adolescent and mid-life crises but what Erikson has labeled identity problems—or what has, of late, been considered narcissism.

Consider, for example, Heinz Kohut's description of patients suffering from what he calls narcissistic personality disorders. They come to the analyst with vague symptoms, but eventually focus on feelings about the self—emptiness, vague depression, being drained of energy, having no "zest" for work or anything else, shifts in self-esteem, heightened sensitivity to the opinions and reactions of others, feeling unfulfilled, a sense of uncertainty and purposelessness. "It seems on the face of it," observes the literary critic Steven Marcus, "as if these people are actually suffering from what was once called unhappiness."

The New Aging

Because of the extraordinary revolution in longevity, the proportion of elderly people in modern industrial societies is higher than it has ever been. This little-noticed but profound transformation affects not just the old but families, an individual's life course, and society as a whole. We have no cultural precedents for the mass of the population reaching old age. Further, the meaning of *old age* has changed—indeed, it is a life stage still in process, its boundaries unclear. When he came into office at the age of sixty-four, George Bush did not seem like an old man. Yet when Franklin Roosevelt died at the same age, he did seem to be "old."

President Bush illustrates why gerontologists in recent years have had to revise the meaning of "old." He is a good example of what they have termed the "young old" or the "new elders"; the social historian Peter Laslett uses the term "the third age." Whatever it is called, it represents a new stage of life created by the extension of the life course in industrialized countries. Recent decades have witnessed the first generations of people who live past sixty-five and remain healthy, vigorous, alert, and, mostly due to retirement plans, financially independent. These people are "pioneers on the frontier of age," observed the journalist Frances Fitzgerald, in her study of Sun City, a retirement community near Tampa, Florida, "people for whom society had as yet no set of expectations and no vision."

The meaning of the later stages of life remains unsettled. Just after gerontologists had marked off the "young old"—people who seemed more middle-aged than old—they had to devise a third category, the "oldest old," to describe the fastest-growing group in the population, people over eighty-five. Many if not most of these people are like Tithonus, the mythical figure who asked the gods for eternal life but forgot to ask for eternal youth as well. For them, the gift of long life has come at the cost of chronic disease and disability.

The psychological impact of this unheralded longevity revolution has largely been ignored, except when misconstrued. The fear of age, according to Christopher Lasch, is one of the chief symptoms of this culture's alleged narcissism. But when people expected to die in their forties or fifties, they didn't have to face the problem of aging. Alzheimer's disease, for example, now approaching epidemic proportions, is an ironic by-product of the extension of the average life span. When living to seventy or eighty is a realistic prospect, it makes sense to diet and exercise, to eat healthy foods, and to make other "narcissistic" investments in the self.

Further "the gift of mass longevity," the anthropologist David Plath argues, has been so recent, dramatic, and rapid that it has become profoundly unsettling in all postindustrial societies: "If the essential cultural nightmare of the nineteenth century was to be in poverty, perhaps ours is to be old and alone or afflicted with terminal disease."

Many people thus find themselves in life stages for which cultural scripts have not yet been written; family members face one another in relationships for which tradition provides little guidance. "We are stuck with awkward-sounding terms like 'adult children' and . . . 'grandson-in-law.' " And when cultural rules are ambiguous, emotional relationships can become tense or at least ambivalent.

A study of five-generation families in Germany reveals the confusion and strain that result when children and parents are both in advanced old age—for example, a great-great-grandmother and her daughter, who is herself a great-grandmother. Who has the right to be old? Who should take care of whom? Similarly, Plath, who has studied the problems of mass longevity in Japan, finds that even in that familistic society the traditional meaning of family roles has been put into question by the stretching out of the life span. In the United States, some observers note that people moving into retirement communities sometimes bring their parents to live with them. Said one disappointed retiree: "I want to enjoy my grandchildren; I never expected that when I was a grandparent I'd have to look after my parents."

READING

4

The Way We Wish We Were

Stephanie Coontz

When I begin teaching a course on family history, I often ask my students to write down ideas that spring to mind when they think of the "traditional family." Their lists always include several images. One is of extended families in which all members worked together, grandparents were an integral part of family life,

From *The Way We Never Were: American Families and the Nostalgia Trap* by Stephanie Coontz. Copyright © 1992 by Basic Books. Reprinted by permission of Basic Books, a division of HarperCollins Publishers, Inc.

children learned responsibility and the work ethic from their elders, and there were clear lines of authority based on respect for age. Another is of nuclear families in which nurturing mothers sheltered children from premature exposure to sex, financial worries, or other adult concerns, while fathers taught adolescents not to sacrifice their education by going to work too early. Still another image gives pride of place to the couple relationship. In traditional families, my students write—half derisively, half wistfully—men and women remained chaste until marriage, at which time they extricated themselves from competing obligations to kin and neighbors and committed themselves wholly to the marital relationship, experiencing an all-encompassing intimacy that our more crowded modern life seems to preclude. As one freshman wrote: "They truly respected the marriage vowels"; I assume she meant *I-O-U*.

Such visions of past family life exert a powerful emotional pull on most Americans, and with good reason, given the fragility of many modern commitments. The problem is not only that these visions bear a suspicious resemblance to reruns of old television series, but also that the scripts of different shows have been mixed up: June Cleaver suddenly has a Grandpa Walton dispensing advice in her kitchen; Donna Stone, vacuuming the living room in her inevitable pearls and high heels, is no longer married to a busy modern pediatrician but to a small-town sheriff who, like Andy Taylor of *The Andy Griffith Show*, solves community problems through informal, old-fashioned common sense.

Like most visions of a "golden age," the "traditional family" my students describe evaporates on closer examination. It is an ahistorical amalgam of structures, values, and behaviors that never coexisted in the same time and place. The notion that traditional families fostered intense intimacy between husbands and wives while creating mothers who were totally available to their children, for example, is an idea that combines some characteristics of the white, middle-class family in the mid-nineteenth century and some of a rival family ideal first articulated in the 1920s. The first family revolved emotionally around the mother-child axis, leaving the husband-wife relationship stilted and formal. The second focused on an eroticized couple relationship, demanding that mothers curb emotional "overinvestment" in their children. The hybrid idea that a woman can be fully absorbed with her youngsters while simultaneously maintaining passionate sexual excitement with her husband was a 1950s invention that drove thousands of women to thearapists, tranquilizers, or alcohol when they actually tried to live up to it.

Similarly, an extended family in which all members work together under the top-down authority of the household elder operates very differently from a nuclear family in which husband and wife are envisioned as friends who patiently devise ways to let the children learn by trial and error. Children who worked in family enterprises seldom had time for the extracurricular activities that Wally and the Beaver recounted to their parents over the dinner table; often, they did not even go to school full-time. Mothers who did home production generally relegated child care to older children or servants; they did not suspend work to savor a baby's first steps or discuss with their husband how to facilitate a grade-schooler's "self-esteem." Such families emphasized formality, obedience to authority, and "the way it's always been" in their childrearing.

Nuclear families, by contrast, have tended to pride themselves on the "modernity" of parent-child relations, diluting the authority of grandparents, denigrating "old-fashioned" ideas about childraising, and resisting the "interference" of relatives. It is difficult to imagine the Cleavers or the college-educated title figure of *Father Knows Best* letting grandparents, maiden aunts, or in-laws have a major voice in childrearing decisions. Indeed, the kind of family exemplified by the Cleavers . . . represented a conscious *rejection* of the Waltons' model.

THE ELUSIVE TRADITIONAL FAMILY

Whenever people propose that we go back to the traditional family, I always suggest that they pick a ballpark date for the family they have in mind. Once pinned down, they are invariably unwilling to accept the package deal that comes with their chosen model. Some people, for example, admire the discipline of colonial families, which were certainly not much troubled by divorce or fragmenting individualism. But colonial families were hardly stable: High mortality rates meant that the average length of marriage was less than a dozen years. One-third to one-half of all children lost at least one parent before the age of twenty-one; in the South, more than half of all children aged thirteen or under had lost at least one parent.

While there are a few modern Americans who would like to return to the strict patriarchal authority of colonial days, in which disobedience by women and children was considered a small form of treason, these individuals would doubtless be horrified by other aspects of colonial families, such as their failure to protect children from knowledge of sexuality. Eighteenth-century spelling and grammar books routinely used *fornication* as an example of four-syllable word, and preachers detailed sexual offenses in astonishingly explicit terms. Sexual conversations between men and women, even in front of children, were remarkably frank. It is worth contrasting this colonial candor to the climate in 1991, when the Department of Health and Human Services was forced to cancel a proposed survey of teenagers' sexual practices after some groups charged that such knowledge might "inadvertently" encourage more sex.

Other people searching for an ideal traditional family might pick the more sentimental and gentle Victorian family, which arose in the 1830s and 1840s as household production gave way to wage work and professional occupations outside the home. A new division of labor by age and sex emerged among the middle class. Women's roles were redefined in terms of domesticity rather than production, men were labeled "breadwinners" (a masculine identity unheard of in colonial days), children were said to need time to play, and gentle maternal guidance supplanted the patriarchal authoritarianism of the past.

But the middle-class Victorian family depended for its existence on the multiplication of other families who were too poor and powerless to retreat into their own little oases and who therefore had to provision the oases of others. Childhood was prolonged for the nineteenth-century middle class only because it was drastically foreshortened for other sectors of the population. The spread of textile mills, for example, freed middle-class women from the most time-consuming of their former chores, making cloth. But the raw materials for these mills were produced by slave labor. Slave children were not exempt from field labor unless they were infants, and even then their mothers were not allowed time off to nurture them. Frederick Douglass could not remember seeing his mother until he was seven.

Domesticity was also not an option for the white families who worked twelve hours a day in Northern factories and workshops transforming slave-picked cotton into ready-made clothing. By 1820, "half the workers in many factories were boys and girls who had not reached their eleventh birthday." Rhode Island investigators found "little half-clothed children" making their way to the textile mills before dawn. In 1845, shoemaking families and makers of artificial flowers worked fifteen to eighteen hours a day, according to the *New York Daily Tribune*.

Within the home, prior to the diffusion of household technology at the end of the century, house cleaning and food preparation remained mammoth tasks. Middle-class women were able to shift more time into childbearing in this period only by hiring domestic help. Between 1800 and 1850, the proportion of servants to white households doubled, to about one in nine. Some servants were poverty-stricken mothers who had to board or bind out their own children. Employers found such workers tended to be "distracted," however; they usually preferred young girls. In his study of Buffalo, New York, in the 1850s, historian Lawrence Glasco found that Irish and German girls often went into service at the age of eleven or twelve.

For every nineteenth-century middle-class family that protected its wife and child within the family circle, then, there was an Irish or a German girl scrubbing floors in that middle-class home, a Welsh boy mining coal to keep the home-baked goodies warm, a black girl doing the family laundry, a black mother and child picking cotton to be made into clothes for the family, and a Jewish or an Italian daughter in a sweatshop making "ladies" dresses or artificial flowers for the family to purchase.

Furthermore, people who lived in these periods were seldom as enamored of their family arrangements as modern nostalgia might suggest. Colonial Americans lamented "the great neglect in many parents and masters in training up their children" and expressed the "greatest trouble and grief about the rising generation." No sooner did Victorian middle-class families begin to withdraw their children from the work world than observers began to worry that children were becoming *too* sheltered. By 1851, the Reverend Horace Bushnell spoke for many in bemoaning the passing of the traditional days of household production, when the whole family was "harnessed, all together, into the producing process, young and old, male and females, from the boy who rode the plough-horse to the grandmother knitting under her spectacles."

The late nineteenth century saw a modest but significant growth of extended families and a substantial increase in the number of families who were "harnessed" together in household production. Extended families have never been the norm in America; the highest figure for extended-family households ever recorded in American history is 20 percent. Contrary to the popular myth that industrialization destroyed "traditional" extended families, this high point occurred between 1850 and 1885, during the most intensive period of early industrialization. Many of these extended families, and most "producing" families of the time, depended on the labor of children; they were held together by dire necessity and sometimes by brute force.

There was a significant increase in child labor during the last third of the nineteenth century. Some children worked at home in crowded tenement sweatshops that produced cigars or women's clothing. Reformer Helen Campbell found one house where "nearly thirty children of all ages and sizes, babies predominating, rolled in the tobacco which covered the floor and was piled in every direction." Many producing households resembled the one described by Mary Van Kleeck of the Russell Sage Foundation in 1913:

> In a tenement on MacDougal Street lives a family of seven—grandmother, father, mother and four children aged four years, three years, two years and one month respectively. All excepting the father and the two babies make violets. The three year old girl picks apart the petals; her sister, aged four years, separates the stems, dipping an end of each into paste spread on a piece of board on the kitchen table; and the mother and grandmother slip the petals up the stems.

Where children worked outside the home, conditions were no better. In 1900, 120,000 children worked in Pennsylvania mines and factories; most of them had started work by age eleven. In Scranton, a third of the girls between the ages of thirteen and sixteen worked in the silk mills in 1904. In New York, Boston, and Chicago, teenagers worked long hours in textile factories and frequently died in fires or industrial accidents. Children made up 23.7 percent of the 36,415 workers in southern textile mills around the turn of the century. When reformer Marie VanVorse took a job at one in 1903, she found children as young as six or seven working twelve-hour shifts. At the end of the day, she reported: "They are usually beyond speech. They fall asleep at the tables, on the stairs; they are carried to bed and there laid down as they are, unwashed, undressed; and the inanimate bundles of rags so lie until the mill summons them with its imperious cry before sunrise."

By the end of the nineteenth century, shocked by the conditions in urban tenements and by the sight of young children working full-time at home or earning money out on the streets, middle-class reformers put aside nostalgia for "harnessed" family production and elevated the antebellum model once more, blaming immigrants for introducing such "un-American" family values as child labor. Reformers advocated adoption of a "true American" family—a restricted, exclusive nuclear unit in which women and children were divorced from the world of work.

In the late 1920s and early 1930s, however, the wheel turned yet again, as social theorists noted the independence and isolation of the nuclear family with renewed anxiety. The influential Chicago School of sociology believed that immigration and urbanization had weakened the traditional family by destroying kinship and community networks. Although sociologists welcomed the increased democracy of "companionate marriage," they worried about the rootlessness of nuclear families and the breakdown of older solidarities. By the time of the Great Depression, some observers even saw a silver lining in economic hardship, since it revived the economic functions and social importance of kin and family ties. With housing starts down by more than 90 percent, approximately one-sixth of urban families had to "double up" in apartments. The incidence of three-generation households increased, while recreational interactions outside the home were cut back or confined to the kinship network. One newspaper opined: "Many a family that has lost its car has found its soul."

Depression families evoke nostalgia in some contemporary observers, because they tended to create "dependability and domestic inclination" among girls and "maturity in the management of money" among boys. But, in many cases, such responsibility was inseparable from "a corrosive and disabling poverty that shattered the hopes and dreams of . . . young parents and twisted the lives of those who were 'stuck together' in it." Men withdrew from family life or turned violent; women exhausted themselves trying to "take up the slack" both financially and emotionally, or they belittled their husbands as failures; and children gave up their dreams of education to work at dead-end jobs.

From the hardships of the Great Depression and the Second World War and the euphoria of the postwar economic recovery came a new kind of family ideal that still enters our homes in *Leave It to Beaver* and *Donna Reed* reruns. . . . [T]he 1950s were no more a "golden age" of the family than any other period in American history. . . . [O]ur recurring search for a traditional family model denies the diversity of family life, both past and present, and leads to false generalizations about the past as well as wildly exaggerated claims about the present and the future.

THE COMPLEXITIES OF ASSESSING FAMILY TRENDS

If it is hard to find a satisfactory model of the traditional family, it is also hard to make global judgments about how families have changed and whether they are getting better or worse. Some generalizations about the past are pure myth. Whatever the merit of recurring complaints about the "rootlessness" of modern life, for instance, families are *not* more mobile and transient than they used to be. In most nineteenth-century cities, both large and small, more than 50 percent—and often up to 75 percent—of the residents in any given year were no longer there ten years later. People born in the twentieth century are much more likely to live near their birthplace than were people born in the nineteenth century.

This is not to say, of course, that mobility did not have different effects then than it does now. In the nineteenth century, claims historian Thomas Bender, people moved from community to community, taking advantage . . . of nonfamiliar networks and institutions that integrated them into new work and social relations. In the late twentieth century, people move from job to job, following a career path that shuffles them from one single-family home to another and does not link them to neighborly networks beyond the family. But this change is in our community ties, not in our family ones.

A related myth is that modern Americans have lost touch with extended-kinship networks or have let parent-child bonds lapse. In fact, more Americans than ever before have grandparents alive, and there is good evidence that ties between grandparents and grandchildren have become stronger over the past fifty years. In the late 1970s, researchers returned to the "Middletown" studied by sociologist Robert and Helen Lynd in the 1920s and found that most people there maintained closer extended-family networks than in earlier times. There had been some decline in the family's control over the daily lives of youth, especially females, but "the expressive/emotional function of the family" was "more important for Middletown students of 1977 than it was in 1924." More recent research shows that visits with relatives did *not* decline between the 1950s and the late 1980s.

Today 54 percent of adults see a parent, and 68 percent talk on the phone with a parent, at least once a week. Fully 90 percent of Americans describe their relationship with their mother as close, and 78 percent say their relationship with their grandparents is close. And for all the family disruption of divorce, most modern children live with at least *one* parent. As late as 1940, 10 percent of American children did not live with either parent, compared to only one in twenty-five today.

What about the supposed eclipse of marriage? Neither the rising age of those who marry nor the frequency of divorce necessarily means that marriage is becoming a less prominent institution than it was in earlier days. Ninety percent of men and women eventually marry, more than 70 percent of divorced men and women remarry, and fewer people remain single for their entire lives today than at the turn of the century. One author even suggests that the availability of divorce in the second half of the twentieth century has allowed some women to try marriage who would formerly have remained single all their lives. Others argue that the rate of hidden marital separation in the late nineteenth century was not much less than the rate of visible separation today.

Studies of marital satisfaction reveal that more couples reported their marriages to be happy in the late 1970s than did so in 1957, while couples in their second marriages believe them to be much happier than their first ones. Some commentators conclude that marriage is becoming less permanent but more satisfying. Others wonder, however, whether there is a vicious circle in our country, where no one even tries to sustain a relationship. Between the late 1970s and late 1980s, moreover, reported marital happiness did decline slightly in the United States. Some authors see this as reflecting our decreasing appreciation of marriage, although others suggest that it reflects unrealistically high expectations of love in a culture that denies people safe, culturally approved ways of getting used to marriage or cultivating other relationships to meet some of the needs that we currently load onto the couple alone.

Part of the problem in making simple generalizations about what is happening to marriage is that there has been a polarization of experiences. Marriages are much more likely to be ended by divorce today, but marriages that do last are described by their participants as happier than those in the past and are far more likely to confer such happiness over many years. It is important to remember that the 50 percent divorce rate estimates are calculated in terms of a forty-year period and that many marriages in the past were terminated well before that date by the death of one partner. Historian Lawrence Stone suggests that divorce has become "a functional substitute for death" in the modern world. At the end of the 1970s, the rise in divorce rates seemed to overtake the fall in death rates, but the slight decline in divorce rates since then means that "a couple marrying today is more likely to celebrate a fortieth wedding anniversary than were couples around the turn of the century."

A similar polarization allows some observers to argue that fathers are deserting their children, while others celebrate the new commitment of fathers to childrearing. Both viewpoints are right. Sociologist Frank Furstenberg comments on the emergence of a "good dad–bad dad complex": Many fathers spend more time with their children than ever before and feel more free to be affectionate with them; others, however, feel more free simply to walk out on their families. According to 1981 statistics, 42 percent of the children whose father had left the marriage had not seen him in the past year. Yet studies show steadily increasing involvement of fathers with their children as long as they are in the home.

These kinds of ambiguities should make us leery of hard-and-fast pronouncements about what's happening to the American family. In many cases, we simply don't know precisely what our figures actually mean. For example, the proportion of youngsters receiving psychological assistance rose by 80 percent between 1981 and 1988. Does that mean they are getting more sick or receiving more help, or is it some complex combination of the two? Child abuse reports increased by 225 percent between 1976 and 1987. Does this represent an actual increase in rates of abuse or a heightened consciousness about the problem? During the same period, parents' self-reports about very severe violence toward their children declined 47 percent. Does this represent a real improvement in their behavior or a decreasing willingness to admit to such acts?

Assessing the direction of family change is further complicated because many contemporary trends represent a reversal of developments that were themselves rather recent. The expectation that the family should be the main source of personal fulfillment, for example, was not traditional in the eighteenth and nineteenth centuries. . . . Prior to the 1900s, the family festivities that now fill us with such nostalgia for "the good old days" (and cause such heartbreak when they go poorly) were "relatively undeveloped." Civic festivals and Fourth of July parades were more important occasions for celebration and strong emotion than family holidays such as Thanksgiving. Christmas "seems to have been more a time for attending parties and dances than for celebrating family solidarity." Only in the twentieth century did the family come to be the center of festive attention and emotional intensity.

Today, such emotional investment in the family may be waning again. This could be interpreted as a reestablishment of balance between family life and other social ties; on the other hand, such a trend may have different results today than in earlier times, because in many cases the extrafamilial institutions and customs that used to socialize individuals and provide them with a range of emotional alternatives to family life no longer exist.

In other cases, analysis of statistics showing a deterioration in family well-being supposedly caused by abandonment of tradition suggests a more complicated train of events. Children's health, for example, improved dramatically in the 1960s and 1970s, a period of extensive family transformation. It ceased to improve and even slid backward, in the 1980s, when innovative social programs designed to relieve families of some "traditional" responsibilities were repealed. While infant mortality rates fell by 4.7 percent a year during the 1970s, the rate of decline decreased in the 1980s, and in both 1988 and 1989, infant mortality rates did not show a statistically significant decline. Similarly, the proportion of low-birth-weight babies fell during the 1970s but stayed steady during the 1980s and had even increased slightly as of 1988. Child poverty is lower today than it was in the "traditional" 1950s but much higher than it was in the nontraditional late 1960s.

WILD CLAIMS AND PHONY FORECASTS

Lack of perspective on where families have come from and how their evolution connects to other social trends tends to encourage contradictory claims and wild exaggerations about where families are going. One category of generalizations seems to be a product of wishful thinking. As of 1988, nearly half of all families with children had both parents in the work force. The two-parent family in which only the father worked for wages represented just 25 percent of all families with children, down from 44 percent in 1975. For people overwhelmed by the difficulties of adjusting work and schools to the realities of working moms, it has been tempting to discern a "return to tradition" and hope the problems will go away. Thus in 1991, we saw a flurry of media reports that the number of women in the work force was headed down: "More Choose to Stay Home with Children" proclaimed the headlines; "More Women Opting for Chance to Watch Their Children Grow."

The cause of all this commotion? The percentage of women aged twenty-five to thirty-four who were employed dropped from 74 percent to 72.8 percent between January 1990 and January 1991. However, there was an exactly equal decline in the percentage of men in the work force during the same period, and for both genders the explanation was the same. "The dip is the recession," explained Judy Waldrop, research editor at *American Demographics* magazine, to anyone who bothered to listen. In fact, the proportion of *mothers* who worked increased slightly during the same period.

This is not to say that parents, especially mothers, are happy with the pressures of balancing work and family life. Poll after poll reveals that both men and women feel starved for time. The percentage of women who say they would prefer to stay home with their children if they could afford to do so rose from 33 percent in 1986 to 56 percent in 1990. Other polls show that even larger majorities of women would trade a day's pay for an extra day off. But, above all, what these polls reveal is women's growing dissatisfaction with the failure of employers, schools, and government to pioneer arrangements that make it possible to combine work and family life. They do not suggest that women are actually going to stop working, or that this would be women's preferred solution to their stresses. The polls did not ask, for example, how *long* women would like to take off work, and failed to take account of the large majority of mothers who report that they would miss their work if they did manage to take time off. Working mothers are here to stay, and we will not meet the challenge this poses for family life by inventing an imaginary trend to define the problem out of existence.

At another extreme is the kind of generalization that taps into our worst fears. One example of this is found in the almost daily reporting of cases of child molestation or kidnapping by sexual predators. The highlighting of such cases, drawn from every corner of the country, helps disguise how rare these cases actually are when compared to crimes committed within the family.

A well-publicized instance of the cataclysmic predictions that get made when family trends are taken out of historical context is the famous *Newsweek* contention that a single woman of forty has a better chance of being killed by a terrorist than of finding a husband. It is true that the proportion of never-married women under age forty has increased substantially since the 1950s, but it is also true that the proportion has *decreased* dramatically among women over that age. A woman over thirty-five has a *better* chance to marry today than she did in the 1950s. In the past twelve years, first-time marriages have increased almost 40 percent for women aged thirty-five to thirty-nine. A single woman aged forty to forty-four still has a 24 percent probability of marriage, while 15 percent of women in their late forties will marry. These figures would undoubtedly be higher if many women over forty did not simply pass up opportunities that a more desperate generation might have snatched.

Yet another example of the exaggeration that pervades many analyses of modern families is the widely quoted contention that "parents today spend 40 percent less time with their children than did parents in 1965." Again, of course, part of the problem is where researchers are measuring from. A comparative study of Muncie, Indiana, for example, found that parents spent much more time with their children in the mid-1970s than did parents in the mid-1920s. But another problem is keeping the categories consistent. Trying to track down the source of the 40 percent decline figure, I called demographer John P. Robinson, whose studies on time formed the basis of this claim. Robinson's data, however, show that parents today spend about the same amount of time caring for children as they did in 1965. If the total amount of time devoted to children is less, he suggested, I might want to check how many fewer children there are today. In 1970, the average family had 1.34 children under the age of eighteen; in 1990, the average family had only .96 children under age eighteen—a decrease of 28.4 percent. In other words, most of the decline in the total amount of time parents spend with children is because of the decline in the number of children they have to spend time with!

Now I am not trying to say that the residual amount of decrease is not serious, or that it may not become worse, given the trends in women's employment. Robinson's data show that working mothers spend substantially less time in primary child-care activities than do nonemployed mothers (though they also tend to have fewer children); more than 40 percent of working mothers report feeling "trapped" by their daily routines; many routinely sacrifice sleep in order to meet the demands of work and family. Even so, a majority believe they are *not* giving enough time to their children. It is also true that children may benefit merely from having their parents available, even though the parents may not be spending time with them.

But there is no reason to assume the worst. Americans have actually gained free time since 1965, despite an increase in work hours, largely as a result of a decline in housework and an increasing tendency to fit some personal requirements and errands into the work day. And according to a recent Gallup poll, most modern mothers think they are doing a better job of communicating with their children (though a worse job of house cleaning) than did their own mothers and that they put a higher value on spending time with their family than did their mothers. . . .

NEGOTIATING THROUGH THE EXTREMES

Most people react to these conflicting claims and contradictory trends with understandable confusion. They know that family ties remain central to their own lives, but they are constantly hearing about people who seem to have *no* family feeling. Thus, at the same time as Americans report high levels of satisfaction with their *own* families, they express a pervasive fear that other people's families are falling apart.

In a typical recent poll, for example, 71 percent of respondents said they were "very satisfied" with their own family life, but more than half rated the overall quality of family life as negative: "I'm okay; you're not."

This seemingly schizophrenic approach does not reflect an essentially intolerant attitude. People worry about families, and to the extent that they associate modern social ills with changes in family life, they are ambivalent about innovations. Voters often defeat measures to grant unmarried couples, whether heterosexual or homosexual, the same rights as married ones. In polls, however, most Americans support tolerance for gay and lesbian relationships. Although two-thirds of respondents to one national poll said they wanted "more traditional standards of family life," the same percentage rejected the idea that "women should return to their traditional role." Still larger majorities support women's right to work, including their right to use child care, even when they worry about relying on day-care centers too much. In a 1990 *Newsweek* poll, 42 percent predicted that the family would be worse in ten years and exactly the same percentage predicted that it would be better. Although 87 percent of people polled in 1987 said they had "old-fashioned ideas about family and marriage," only 22 percent of the people polled in 1989 defined a family solely in terms of blood, marriage, or adoption. Seventy-four percent declared, instead, that family is any group whose members love and care for one another.

These conflicted responses do not mean that people are hopelessly confused. Instead, they reflect people's gut-level understanding that the "crisis of the family" is more complex than is often asserted by political demagogues or others with an ax to grind. In popular commentary the received wisdom is to "keep it simple." I know one television reporter who refuses to air an interview with anyone who uses the phrase "on the other hand." But my experience in discussing these issues with both the general public and specialists in the field is that people are hungry to get beyond oversimplifications. They don't want to be told that everything is fine in families or that if the economy improved and the government mandated parental leave, everything would be fine. But they don't believe that every hard-won victory for women's rights and personal liberty has been destructive of social bonds and that the only way to find a sense of community is to go back to some sketchily defined "traditional" family that clearly involves denying the validity of any alternative familial and personal choices.

Americans understand that along with welcome changes have come difficult new problems; uneasy with simplistic answers, they are willing to consider more nuanced analyses of family gains and losses during the past few decades. Indeed, argues political reporter E. J. Dionne, they are *desperate* to engage in such analyses. Few Americans are satisfied with liberal and feminist accounts that blame all modern family dilemmas on structural inequalities, ignoring the moral crisis of commitment and obligation in our society. Yet neither are they convinced that "in the final analysis," as David Blankenhorn of the Institute for American Values puts it, "the problem is not the system. The problem is us."

Despite humane intentions, an overemphasis on personal responsibility for strengthening family values encourages a way of thinking that leads to moralizing rather than mobilizing for concrete reforms. While values are important to Americans, most do not support the sort of scapegoating that occurs when all family problems are blamed on "bad values." Most of us are painfully aware that there is no clear way of separating "family values" from "the system." Our values may make a difference in the way we respond to the challenges posed by economic and political institutions, but those institutions also reinforce certain values and extinguish others. The problem is not to berate people for abandoning past family values, nor to exhort them to adopt better values in the future—the problem is to build the institutions and social support networks that allow people to act on their best values rather than on their worst ones. We need to get past abstract nostalgia for traditional family values and develop a clearer sense of how past families actually worked and what the different consequences of various family behaviors and values have been. Good history and responsible social policy should help people incorporate the full complexity and the tradeoffs of family change into their analysis and thus into action. Mythmaking does not accomplish this end.

CHAPTER 2

◈

THE MEANING(S)
OF "FAMILY"

R E A D I N G
5

Constructing the Family

Marjorie L. DeVault

The form of family found in modern Western societies has developed over time. As productive work moved out of the home, the family began to be thought of as a bounded unit, "associated with property, self-sufficiency, with affect and a sphere 'inside' the home" (Collier, Rosaldo, and Yanagisako 1982:32). As this kind of family developed, its day-to-day construction came to be part of the work to be done within a household, and as the physical tasks of maintenance have become less arduous, the work of constructing a particular type of household life has received increasing emphasis. Leonore Davidoff, in an analysis of middle- and upper-class households in nineteenth-century England, points out that we can see this activity emerging clearly in those households where servants did the routine work of maintenance and wives could devote themselves to supervising the construction of a special sort of place:

The ultimate nineteenth-century ideal became the creation of a perfectly orderly setting of punctually served and elaborate meals, clean and tidy and warmed rooms, clean pressed and aired clothes and bed linen . . . there was to be a complete absence of all disturbing or threatening interruptions to orderly existence which could be caused either by the intractability, and ultimate disintegration, of things or by the emotional disturbance of people. (1976:130)

Obviously, such standards could be met in only a very few households. Still, they served to define a model which was becoming the basis for a developing form of family life. Davidoff's analysis led her to define housework as a project of "boundary maintenance":

Housework is concerned with creating and maintaining order in the immediate environment, making meaningful patterns of activities, people and materials. (1976:124)

The ideals have changed—hardly any contemporary wives or mothers even aim for "perfect order"—but housework is still a project of "making meaningful patterns." Feeding the family is work that makes use of food to organize people and activities. It is work that negotiates a balance between the sociability of group life and the concern for individuality that we have come to associate with modern family life.

SOCIABILITY

Meals are social events. They can provide occasions when household members come together as a group, but they do not do this "naturally" or automatically. If household members are to come together for dinner, someone must organize the meal so that it becomes a part of several different sequences of events. Family members are involved in various individual activities throughout the day, mostly outside the household. Their paths do not necessarily cross, and points of intersection must be planned. Since routines are often customary, they seem natural, like "what everybody does." But those who organize meals work at developing these patterns, and understand that they have significance for family relations; they talk about their choices as pieces of a consciously crafted structure of family life. The times of coming together that result are thought of— though not entirely consciously—as making a family.

The intentional quality in the plans that produce these activities, apparently so simple and natural, can be seen in women's accounts of the details of their everyday routines. Susan, a white woman whose husband is a construction worker, quit her job as a nurse when her two-year-old daughter was born; now she works at taking care of her child and house. Though she has been married for five years, her daughter's relatively recent arrival signaled the beginning of a new kind of family. When I asked how the mealtime routines had changed, she explained:

Our mealtimes are at a certain time. And I have an idea of what I'm going to have. Whereas before, it was, whatever, it was very casual. We didn't have the responsibility.

The responsibility she speaks of is not merely responsibility for providing food. As she elaborates, we can see that she organizes the mealtime routine so that the three individuals in her household will come together "as a family." She said:

> I'll pull her high chair up so that she can be part of the family . . . I think she was six months old when she started eating as part of the family—breakfast, lunch and dinner. We adjusted our schedule a little bit to her schedule. And it worked out really well. Now, everything is as a family.

Part of the intention behind producing the meal is to produce "home" and "family." In a study of mealtimes in Welsh workingclass families, Anne Murcott (1983) found that women thought of the evening meal as a kind of marker for their husbands, signifying the end of work and return to the family. They talked of a "cooked dinner" in terms of associations with home and well-being. But the significance of the meal is not just that it represents, or is associated with the idea of family; indeed, the meal comes to be thought of in this way because it involves household members in the actual day-to-day activities that constitute family relations over time. Furthermore, the linkage between food and family depends on women's work. Susan spoke of how she produces a homecoming for her husband:

> If it's real ugly outside and I know that my husband's going to want a hot meal— which is all the time—and I want the house to warm up and smell good, I'll make stew. Or I'll bake a cake.

As she thinks ahead toward the evening meal, she plans to produce an experience: the return to a warm and pleasant house.

Susan's comments also show how activities like baking can be fit into a larger scheme for producing a particular kind of everyday life. When she spoke of baking a cake, she added:

> I usually end up freezing half of it, because we don't usually eat that much of it. It's just something to do. Or now that my daughter's helpful, we bake a cake. And we make cookies. That's an all-day affair.

Cooking is a way that she and her daughter can spend time together, and a way that her two-year-old learns, through participation, the special work of producing home and family, anticipating a dinner together.

Scheduling a meal requires attention to the various schedules of individuals in the family, and a process of adjustment that reconciles family events with their separate needs and projects. For Susan, this process is relatively simple: her husband's work schedule is fixed, and she must adapt to it; and she has developed a schedule for her daughter; but her own activities are quite flexible. She uses this flexibility to preserve the routines of others. For example, she explained:

> Routine is really good for kids. They know what's expected of them . . . I don't like to stray too much from my routine. Because then she's going to get confused.
>
> But dinner time, though, I can probably stretch, if my husband's going to be home late, or whatever. I can stretch within an hour. But if it looks like too much, I'll feed her, first. But she likes to be part of the family supper.

Susan is the one who keeps track of the activities of other family members. When her husband takes more time than usual coming home, she must consider the consequences of this change for her daughter, and for the "family supper." Part of her work is to monitor schedules, and eventually, to make a judgment as to whether it will be possible to have a meal together. In order to make it possible, she changes her own activities, "stretching" the dinner hour as far as she can.

Susan adapts to her daughter's schedule throughout the day as well. She explained that she can easily complete her household chores by noon, and added, "Then I have the rest of the day to spend with her." She has observed that her daughter is especially cranky while she is preparing dinner, and she organizes her work routine to minimize this time:

> Usually what I try to do, if I know what I'm going to prepare, and it's going to take time away from her—a lot of time, like chopping vegetables or whatever—I'll do it while she's sleeping, her nap. And I'll have everything ready. If it's something like breaded pork chops, I'll bread them before, put them in a pan, and put them in the refrigerator. So all I have to do is put them in the oven. Or even like a salad, I'll put everything in but the tomatoes. And I'll do it when she's not around, so she doesn't feel rejected.

Again, Susan considers the consequences of different ways of organizing her work. She plans her work activities to produce a particular kind of everyday household life for her child.

Susan likes the way she does things, and seems to do them easily. She explained that she is a very disciplined person, and that she thinks about organizing her household work as part of an overall strategy for managing her home. She is "big on rules," and explained that, "It's just a lot easier if you're organized. If you know where to put things, you know where to find them." The work of adaptation and reconciliation that produces Susan's family is relatively easy; she has fewer material constraints and competing demands than most women. The family is small, and Susan's daughter is too young to be involved in independent activities. Though Susan enjoyed working as a nurse before her daughter was born, she has decided since then that she is "more needed at home." She does not need to work outside the home because her husband's wage is adequate for the family's support. She has plenty of time to devote to the work of constructing a family life.

For other women, the work of scheduling is much more complicated and difficult. But the process is similar: the task is one of adjustment and reconciliation in order to create points of intersection among diverse sets of activities. Jean, for example, is a white woman who works as a legal secretary, whose husband works at night as a security officer. Her two children are in elementary school. She must plan meals to fit with several different schedules outside the home, and she has little time to plan and prepare meals. Like Susan, though, she works at combining different schedules, and using the resources she has, to produce points of intersection among diverging paths. The process can be seen in her detailed account as she thinks out loud about how she will manage one evening meal, which she must prepare and serve in the time between her own arrival home and her husband's departure for work an hour later. She explained:

> Tonight has to be a real rushed dinner, because the kids are going ice-skating and they're getting picked up at 6:00, so there's a package of smoky links in the refrigerator and they're going to have that. And David will probably either have that, or—

well, we had friends over last night, actually I did, because he was gone—and it was a potluck dinner, but I was lucky because since it was at my house I got all the left-overs. So tonight—this isn't a good night to ask about, but—so the kids will—it'll be three different things. The kids'll probably have the smoky links, and David will probably have—well, see there's still a little hunk of ham left, and there's still—what's the other thing? We have something else left over, plus we have the things from last night.

I asked what the children would have with their smoky links:

They'll have—if I have time, I'll make macaroni and cheese to go with it, because that's one of their favorite dinners. They'll have that. And if I can get them to, they'll probably have an apple, for dessert, or I think I'll get them to eat a tomato, I don't know. It won't be real balanced.

And her husband?

Given the choice, given the fact that—I don't know what he'll have. I tend to think he'll have the very last bit of that ham that's left. I could be wrong, he might have smoky links. I don't think he'll have what we had for dinner last night because I think it's something he doesn't like.

If he has the smoky links he'll probably just have it in a sandwich, because he doesn't like macaroni and cheese—see he's not big on pasta, he doesn't like spaghetti either. He would probably just have a sandwich. I might be able to get him to eat some sliced tomatoes too, but that would probably be it.

If he has the ham, he'll probably slice it up, and I would imagine that it'll be fried with some eggs, or I'll make an omelette for him, something like that.

And if I have the leftovers, I'll have the leftovers and probably a sliced tomato. That'll be it. There are some brownies left, I'm sure I'll have a brownie (laughing).

The meal that Jean imagines will be produced at the intersection of several sequences of events. She has to keep interrupting herself in order to explain to me why she has various things on hand, and as she thinks prospectively toward the meal, she can see that much depends on her husband's choice among the several options she will offer him, so that she must think of several alternative plans. The previous days' meals, the children's plans for the evening, and the preferences and choices of family members (which I will say more about later)—all these are part of the reasoning behind the choices she makes. With all of these things in mind, in the time that is available, Jean will provide a meal that fits into her husband's and children's lives. When she thinks of having a brownie at the end of it all, one cannot help feeling that she will certainly deserve it.

Jean must organize her family's eating in the context of a very difficult set of schedules. She works all day; she has only the evening with her children, and only an hour or so before her husband must leave for work. Still, like Susan, when she organizes her time and work, she aims at producing the kind of house-hold life she wants for her family. She explained:

So much of the way I manage my time is affected by my children . . . Really that whole chunk of time, from 5:30 or 6 at night until bedtime, is theirs.

During that chunk of time of course I do make dinner. And sometimes do the dishes. Usually I wait and do the dishes—I mean I really have this worked out into some sort of weird system of my own. I watch the news, you know, at 10:00. And when the sports comes on, I really could care less about sports, I go back to the kitchen and I do my dishes. And then depending on what I have left to do . . . It's all just sandwiched in.

Jean gets everyone in her family fed, but she is not usually able to produce the kind of regular dinners that Susan talked about. Jean worries that her family rarely sits down together and talks, because she believes that such encounters constitute "quality family time":

> If you have a real discussion at the dinner table, like we used to have when I was a kid, you can give a person a chance to let you in on their life. What they were doing all day when they weren't with you. You can find out more about that person.

When she was a child, she explained:

> We'd sit down and everybody would tell what they had done that day. And my father, when the main meal was over, you know, like if there was dessert or something, that was time for Daddy to give us quizzes on world capitals or something like that.

Jean works at creating such family times, seizing the few opportunities available in her busy weeks. For some time, she made a special effort to get the family together for Saturday night dinner. On those evenings, she explained:

> There were some rules for that. I mean, there were self-imposed rules. That it be a good meal, not—not hamburger, not hot dogs, but something decent. You know, a really nice meal that I really took some time to create and prepare. The kids would set the table. Yeah, there would be rules about what would be served and how it would be served and it would be a more formal thing.

These attempts were frustrating, though, partly because she did not get the help she needed from her husband, who doesn't share her ideas about "family time." She reported:

> Lately what's been happening—we hardly ever all eat together—but lately David gets up and leaves before the rest of us, and that really makes me angry. Because I think that's a rotten example he's setting.

Part of Jean's work, then, is to struggle with her husband (she called it "hammering away") about the activities that constitute family life. He seems not to share her understanding of how specific activities contribute to the construction of a group life. His reluctance makes her efforts to produce "family times" stand out in sharp relief.

> He said, "What do you want me to do?" And I said, "You've got to give us at least two Saturdays a month, that are just ours."
>
> So this Saturday, we'll see, we're supposed to go bowling. And while we're bowling, I'm supposed to have something cooking so that when we're done we can come home and eat it together.

This kind of event is conceived as a time for being together, when family members can share a pleasurable activity. But there is work involved in producing such an event. Jean, like most women, is the worker behind the scenes, as well as a guest at the party. Somehow, while they are bowling, she is to "have something cooking." It is her work that brings their time together into being.

Both Susan and Jean are doing more than just cooking. In addition to producing meals, they organize their cooking so as to produce a group life for their families. They adjust to work and school schedules, and as they make decisions about managing their work, they weave together the paths of household members. Their efforts are directed toward creating patterns of joint activity out of the otherwise separate lives of family members.

INDIVIDUALITY

Feeding the individuals who live in a household makes them a group, as shown above, by reconciling their different activities in order to produce a common life; but feeding is also done so as to produce a particular kind of group, one that is intimate and personal. The work involves special attention to the individuality of each household member. To some extent, this kind of attention to preference is necessary: children, especially, may not eat at all if they dislike what is served, and in many households, individuals have health problems that require special diets. However, the personal attention that is part of feeding work has a family character that goes beyond necessity. The family is a place where people expect to be treated in a unique, personally specific way instead of anonymously, as they are often treated outside. Part of the work of feeding is to give this kind of individual attention, and doing so constitutes a particular household group as the kind of place we expect a "family" to be.

All of the women I talked with reported planning meals around the tastes of family members. They select and serve foods that will be eaten enthusiastically. But the personal service I refer to here is more meaningful than this feature of planning suggests. It involves attention to the specific, often ideosyncratic tastes of individuals within the family group, and decisions about which of these desires will be satisfied and which not. Often, it involves making distinctions among individuals in the family, and personalizing their meals. Distinctions can be quite simple or rather elaborate. For example, a Puerto Rican woman whose second husband is from Guatemala does extra cooking almost every night in order to satisfy his different tastes. Her mother cooks a standard meal for the rest of the family, and she adapts it for her husband. She gave some examples:

> If I know that she's making, say, rice and black beans and steak in a sauce with a lots of onions and green pepper, then I know that for that day what I'll do is I'll take the black beans and I'll mash them in a special little machine that I have and then I'll refry them, because that's what he likes, the refried beans. So that the rest of us will eat the beans whole and he'll eat them refried.
>
> For the next day, if there's steak left over then what I do is I chop it up real fine, and I'll buy the large Mexican green peppers that are hot, and I stuff them with this and then I beat eggs and I fry those peppers for him. And I'll use some canned

stewed tomatoes for a sauce over it. So that this way I'm kind of satisfying both tastes.

In other cases, adjustments are much simpler. For example, I watched while Ed served his family a dinner that was standard for the household: beans and rice. But I saw that each of the two children had a unique way of eating this standard meal. As he served one son, Ed asked him, "Now do you want your beans right next to your rice?" And as he served the other only rice, "You're going to have your beans later, right?" Each boy had established his own routine. Their father had learned to take these preferences into account, as a small but important part of the negotiation required to insure that each child would eat his meal.

This kind of personal attention is unique to feeding at home. When we eat with friends, we usually take what is offered (though friends often care for special guests by serving favorite foods). When we eat in restaurants, we can choose what to eat, but only from a standard set of foods (though the most expensive restaurants may offer customized service, and some wives continue to attend to husbands by helping them order their meals). In most settings outside the home, then, we learn not to expect meals tailored to our individual tastes; we select from the items that are offered. Consider, for example, a family's dinner in a fast-food restaurant: I watched a father ask his son what he wanted, and heard the boy answer, "Double cheese, large fry, large Coke." A pause, and then, "No—medium Coke." Clearly, this child knew the categories, and could use them. At home, however, there is no standard set of categories, and family members can be quite picky.

The women I talked with take many individual preferences into account as they work at feeding their families, but they do not think of themselves as controlled by individuals' whims. Rather, they understand that preferences are part of what constitutes individuality. They pay attention to preferences and they consider how best to satisfy divergent tastes. As they do so, they evaluate the boundaries of legitimate preference, and make decisions that simultaneously define both arenas for the self-assertion of family members and also the women's own roles as caretakers.

Most analysts of housework point out that women's decisions are often influenced by husbands' preferences (Oakley 1974; Murcott 1983; Charles and Kerr 1988). Studies consistently demonstrate that husbands' needs dominate, and that women's own needs generally come last. Meg Luxton (1980:50), while noting this pattern, also suggests that women are not "powerless," and that a woman will often "get him to do things her way." These writers sometimes imply that the issue is a rather straightforward one of autonomy versus constraint. I would argue that the phenomenon is somewhat more complex. Certainly, the behavior of many women suggests a trained unwillingness to be forthright about their own needs. But my informants' accounts show that personal attention is only partially the result of pressure from others; it also makes sense to these women. It is part of the logic organizing their work, a way of caring for others well that is central to the social contribution they make through their work.

The women I talked with did not think of themselves as "catering" to family members. They distinguished themselves from others who they think do "unreasonable" amounts of work. Still, they insist that some attention to personal taste—quite a lot in some cases—is "reasonable," and, in a quite straightforward way, part of the craft of feeding. Janice, for example, told about her complex shopping routine: she buys special foods for her adult children, who are vegetarians, and particular cuts of meat and brands of canned foods for her husband. Then she added:

> It's not a hassle. I mean, I don't think it's outrageous. It's not—there's nothing eccentric about it. I mean, you know, everybody has food preferences.

She is aware that some would criticize her care with the shopping as unnecessarily burdensome, and she responds to the possible criticism in my questions about the influence of individuals' tastes. She begins by asserting that what she does is no "hassle"; then, apparently not quite comfortable with that statement, she starts again and explains what she means: attending to preference is a normal part of the work, and she expects to do it.

"Everybody has food preferences": the statement provides an understanding of human nature that sets conditions for the work of feeding. Part of the work is to understand the character of taste, and how it operates for the individuals in a particular household. When women talk about taking account of special requests, they rely on rudimentary theories about eating, which they develop partly from the knowledge of their own food preferences. For example:

> I'm sure—I remember quite clearly as a child, and even to a certain extent now— texture of food is very important as to how you like it. And I would assume she does not like the texture of rice, because she likes noodles, and they slide down.

Again, her understanding makes this preference a "reasonable" pickiness.

The issue, then, is not whether, but which special tastes should be allowed. Laurel, whose children are young, reported that she does not do much catering to their preferences, but then added:

> I'm sure there'll be a time when that'll be necessary. Just because of legitimate taste differences.

Ultimately, women must decide which of their family's requests are "legitimate." As they make these decisions about what they will and will not do, they operationalize unspoken conceptions of the family, and the extent to which individuality will be accepted as legitimate within it. Some foods, for example, are defined as beyond the bounds of family life. Susan reported:

> He really likes lobster. But he'll never see it here. We go out for stuff like that. I mean, certain things I don't make, because I know I can't compete with the restaurant. He can take me out for it if he wants it.

In the same way, family members must be made to understand that they cannot always have what they particularly want. Annie explained that she sometimes mixes corn with rice; her boyfriend likes the combination, but her son does not:

> He'll eat it, though. Because I tell him, if he doesn't eat that, he's not eating anything. But sometimes he'll ask, if I'll leave the corn out. And sometimes I do. But I tell him, if I do it that way just for him, he'll think he's in a restaurant.

Her account not only shows that she is in charge of deciding how often to satisfy the tastes of each family member; in addition, her own language draws on the contrast between family eating and the abstracted provision of service in a restaurant setting. Family members cannot be independent, as they would be outside the home, but must adjust their demands to allow for the needs of others.

Women's comments about whose needs they would attend to also reveal strong connections between feeding and family life, and can often be understood as indicators of the boundaries of their concepts of family. People were ambivalent, for example, about pets. Janice, who does quite a lot of special shopping for her family, explained that she refuses to do that kind of shopping for the dog, which belongs to her husband and son:

> Sometimes I'll buy a couple of cans of food to tide them over, but I'm not going to go about the business of hauling home a bag of food, I'm not going to spend a lot of time and energy buying dog food.

Another woman finished her account of special tastes by reporting wryly, "We don't do a lot of special shopping for the dog." And then added, "But when we were overseas, that did figure into the shopping, we had to get horse meat for the dog and make dog food."

The connection between special cooking and the boundaries of family life can be seen even more clearly in households that do not conform to their members' ideas of what a family should be. For example, Phyllis, a white single mother, cooks only to please her daughter, and not for her male friend who lives with them. She explained:

> I usually cook a real dinner. But only for Marilyn. Because when Marilyn isn't home, if I know it ahead of time, I won't cook at all . . . I only make it for her, really, so anything she doesn't like I wouldn't make.

When I asked if she considered her friend's tastes, she laughed and answered, "He's lucky to get what he gets."

Margaret, another white single mother, was living with her children in her parents' household when I interviewed her. She was recently separated, as was her sister, also living in the house, and their parents were considering a separation as well. Margaret's job was to cook for the young children; she would also do special cooking for her father, and she would cook for her brother and sisters as well, but only if they got to dinner on time:

> If they're here, they're here. If they eat, they eat, if they don't eat, they don't eat. I'm not cooking later on. Except I'll cook for my dad when he gets home, around 11:00.

Margaret defined her stay in her parents' home as a temporary one. She explained that, because of the disruptions in all of their lives, things were "on edge," and that "nobody really does for each other as they should." The members of this household did not make up what she thought of as a proper family. When I asked if people's preferences had much influence on her cooking, she replied:

> With my father, I more or less know that he won't eat tomatoey stuff and spicy stuff, because he's got an ulcer, it disagrees. And that's what it does to me, so I kind of

remember that way. Then with my brother, the only vegetable he likes is corn, so that's easy to remember. And you know, stuff like, if I was to make chicken soup, I'd know he wouldn't eat it, because he's fourteen years old, he's more into hot dogs and corn and stuff like that. But I don't really get into it so much because I won't be here that long. So except for cereal, I stick with—I don't really go deep into it.

She has decided on a minimal level of attention to individuality in this transitory situation; she doesn't "go deep into it" as she might in a family she defined as more legitimate.

The family, then, is a setting in which wives and mothers learn to attend to quite particular needs, and others learn to expect such attention. Women contribute to this expectation when they organize their work to provide personal attention. However, there are boundaries to the kinds of attention considered appropriate. As women do the work of feeding, they make decisions about what they will and will not do, and these decisions are based on a conception of "family" defined in terms of a balance between group life and individuality. As they act in accord with such a conception, these women constitute particular household groups as personal "family" spaces for household members.

FEEDING PRODUCES "FAMILY"

An analysis of family work from the standpoint of those who do it shows that the work joins material and interpersonal tasks: the organization of maintenance work emerges from a conception of family life, and the ongoing accomplishment of the work, day by day, produces interpersonal relations through specific activities. Feeding work, for example, reconciles the diverse schedules and projects of individuals so as to produce points of intersection when they come together for group events. Within the group that this kind of scheduling creates, attention to individual needs and preferences establishes the family as a social space that is personalized.

These household activities are organized through shared understandings of family life, communicated in a variety of ways. As women talk about their work, they refer to the practices of mothers. They also reason about the needs of family members, and how to manage the work with the time and resources available. They talk with friends about how to feed their families better, or more easily. This strategizing has an ideological component: women, mothers, friends, and family members have all learned about feeding and family life partly from literature and the media, from advertising, and from professionals in social services and health care. As they do the work of feeding, these women draw from a discourse with a history, which both reflects and organizes concepts of "family." They apologize . . . for not producing a "Walton family breakfast." But they integrate such media images with more idiosyncratic, largely unarticulated ideas that develop from their own experience. From a variety of sources, then, these women develop routines appropriate for particular household groups. Through day-to-day activities, each produces a version of "family" in a particular local setting: adjusting, filling in, and repairing social relations to produce— quite literally—this form of household life. The households they live in rarely fit the pattern of some ideal "family." Instead, households are quite varied, homes for motley groups of actual individuals with their particular quirks and idiosyncrasies. Both inclination and necessity produce variation in daily activities within and among households. But the work of "feeding the family" tends to collect these unruly individuals and tame their centrifugal moves, cajoling them into some version of the activity that constitutes family. Because this work of social construction is largely visible, such efforts simultaneously produce the illusion that this form of life is a "natural" one.

REFERENCES

Charles, Nickie, and Marion Kerr. 1988. *Women, Food, and Families.* Manchester: Manchester University Press.

Collier, Jane, Michelle Z. Rosaldo, and Sylvia Yanagisako. 1982. Is There a New Family? New Anthropological Views. In Barrie Thorne with Marilyn Yalon, eds., *Rethinking the Family,* 25–39. New York: Longman.

Davidoff, Leonore. 1976. The Rationalization of Housework. In Diana L. Barker and Sheila Allen, eds., *Dependence and Exploitation in Work and Marriage,* 121–51. London: Longman Group.

Luxton, Meg. 1980. *More Than a Labour of Love: Three Generations of Women's Work in the Home.* Toronto: The Women's Press.

Murcott, Anne. 1983. "It's a Pleasure to Cook for Him": Food, Mealtimes and Gender in some South Wales Households. In Eva Garmarnikow, David H. J. Morgan, Jane Purvis, and Daphne Taylorson, eds., *The Public and the Private,* 78–90. London: Heinemann.

Oakley, Ann. 1974. *The Sociology of Housework.* New York: Pantheon Books.

R E A D I N G

6

What Is a Family? Nature, Culture, and the Law

David M. Rosen

Throughout the United States, courts are grappling with the problem of how to define family and kinship relationships. Until recently, this appeared to be a relatively straightforward issue. The only family relationships given legal or jural recognition were those based upon blood ties, marriage, or adoption. But the emergence of new forms of domestic relationships, especially domestic relationships between gay and lesbian partners, has forced courts to decide whether traditional legal concepts of family relations should be extended to include new relationships that otherwise have no basis in law. In this article, I argue that deeply-rooted concepts of kinship underlie legal decision-making in this area, and define the boundaries of judicial discretion to modify the basic concepts of family law.[1]

To demonstrate this I analyze three recent cases in which New York courts have adopted three distinct strategies for meeting the legal challenges of new families. These strategies are:

1. The outright application of traditional family law concepts to new family arrangements.
2. The rejection of family law concepts as applicable to new family arrangements.
3. The rejection of the application of family law concepts to new families, coupled with the substitution of non-family-law legal concepts so as to provide judicial relief to the parties involved.

FIRST LEGAL STRATEGY: APPLICATION OF FAMILY LAW TO NEW FAMILY ARRANGEMENTS

An example of the first strategy is found in the New York case of *Braschi* v. *Stahl Associates Co.* (1989) in which the New York State Court of Appeals ruled that the term "family" applied to a gay couple who had lived together for ten years. The

From *Marriage and Family Review*, vol. 17, No. 112. © 1991 by The Haworth Press, Inc. All rights reserved.

practical issue involved was whether under New York law the survivor of a long-term domestic relationship had the right to possession of a rent-controlled apartment which the couple shared. In New York, this is a significant property right. The court, in upholding the right of the surviving partner, declared that protection against eviction "should find its foundation in the reality of family life. In the context of eviction, a . . . realistic, and certainly valid, view of a family includes two adult life-time partners whose relationship is long-term and characterized by an emotional and financial commitment and interdependence."

This decision of the court prompted the New York Division of Housing and Renewal to redefine the concept of family to include long-term gay and lesbian relationships. Although lesbian and gay couples will benefit greatly by these actions, the greatest beneficiaries are expected to be a wide range of non-traditional families, especially families of the poor.

SECOND LEGAL STRATEGY: REJECTION OF FAMILY LAW CONCEPTS IN REFERENCE TO NEW FAMILY ARRANGEMENTS

The second strategy is exemplified by the case of *Alison D. v. Virginia M.* (1990) in which a New York Appellate Division ruled that the term "parent" applied solely to biological relationships, and denied a former lesbian partner visitation rights to a child she and the biological mother of the child had parented together. In this case, the two women began living with each other in 1978. In 1980, they decided to raise a family, and Virginia M. was artificially inseminated. A boy was born, and the two women shared in the care of the child and jointly assumed all parenting responsibilities. In 1983, the relationship between the women ended, and Alison D. moved out of their home. Initially, she enjoyed regular visitation, but her former partner cut off all visitation in 1987. The Court's decision of May 1990 left Alison D. without any legal rights to see the child.

THIRD LEGAL STRATEGY: DENIAL OF THE FAMILY-LAW MODEL, BUT APPLICATION OF OTHER LEGAL THEORIES TO PROVIDE RELIEF TO THE PARTIES

An example of the third strategy lies in the case titled *The Estate of Steven Szabo* (1990) decided in July 1990. Here a New York Surrogate's Court determined that the term "spouse" did not apply to a gay life-partner, and denied the partner any inheritance rights in his deceased partner's estate. In this case, the two men had lived together for eighteen years before Mr. Szabo died. After his death, a will was probated. The will predated the relationship between the parties, and made no mention of the surviving partner.

Under New York law, a spouse cannot be disinherited, and if the spouse is unnamed in a will, he or she can by law obtain up to one half of the deceased's estate. In this case, had the surviving partner been deemed a "spouse" he would have been able to obtain a large share of the estate. Of particular importance was the cooperative apartment in which the couple had lived, but to which the deceased partner held title. The Court rejected the plaintiff's claim that he was a spouse, but it was willing to entertain his claims to the estate based upon proof of the financial arrangements between the partners during their lifetime together.

These instances show that these three terms in American kinship and law—family, parent, and spouse—have been treated in markedly different ways by New York Courts. While the decisions in all these cases involve complex legal reasoning, underlying these decisions are key concepts of American kinship, especially the concepts of "nature" and "culture." In brief, I argue that when "new" family relationships are modeled on traditional relationships grounded in "nature," the law is less likely to recognize the "new" relationship. Conversely, the more a "new" family relationship is modeled on a traditional relationship grounded in culture, the more likely it is that the law will legally recognize the new relationship. Consequently, kin terms such as "parent," "mother" or "father," which in American kinship are understood as involving cultural and legal recognition of an existing biological fact, are not readily transferred to new family relationships. A term like "family," which incorporates multiple relationships grounded in both nature and culture, is more easily applied to new family relationships. Finally, terms such as "spouse," "husband" or "wife," straddle the boundaries between nature and culture, and evoke a hybrid response from the courts.

THE ORDER OF NATURE, THE ORDER OF CULTURE AND THE ORDER OF LAW

Kinship terms are cultural constructs which derive their meaning from their relationships with other concepts. In American kinship, as Schneider (1980) has pointed out, the world of relatives is constructed out of deeply felt assumptions about nature and culture.[2] Schneider has termed the distinction between nature and culture as the "order of nature" and the "order of law." Both of these orders are culturally constructed; that is, what is considered "nature" is itself culturally defined. Schneider's usage of the order of nature refers to the belief that some persons are considered relatives because they share a common heredity or blood. They are biogenetically connected. Schneider uses the "order of law" to refer to the belief that other persons are relatives because they are bound together by law or custom. For the purpose of this article, I distinguish between the order of nature, the order of culture and the order of law. All of these orders are culturally constructed, but they refer to specific ways in which human experience is symbolized.[3]

By the "order of nature" I mean that system of symbols that tends to define certain human characteristics as inherent. The symbolism of nature may describe the make up of persons, relations, or even sentiments, to the extent that these are perceived as arising from "nature."

By the "order of culture," I mean a system of symbols that stands for the world of customary beliefs, codes of conduct, and traditions created and imposed by human beings to serve as guidelines for action. The "order of law" is defined as a symbolic subdomain of the order of culture, which refers specifically to those codes of conduct created by judges, courts, legislatures and other law-making bodies in society.

In American kinship, the primary use of natural symbolism is found in the belief that some relatives are natural relatives because they share in a common substance: blood or heredity. But it is also the case that social actions and social relationships can be symbolized as more or less natural. For example, former United States Supreme Court Justice Burger, in his concurring opinion in the case of *Bowers* v. *Hardwick* (1985), resurrected with approval the commentaries of the eighteenth century English jurist Blackstone, that sodomy is "a crime against nature . . . the very mention of which is a disgrace to human nature" (p. 197). With this rhetorical flourish, a Georgia statute criminalizing homosexual relations was upheld as constitutional, and homosexuality was banished from the world of nature to the world of deviant culture.

Though Supreme Court Justices may see the distinction between nature and culture as relatively fixed, anthropologists have usually been of the mind that these categories are far more elastic. Some time ago, Ortner (1974) pointed out that the dichotomy between nature and culture was frequently used to define the relationship between male and female. Similarly, Barnes (1977) has demonstrated that the kin category of "mother" is usually more closely identi-fied with nature than is the category of "father," even though both father and mother are equal participants in the genetic make-up of the child. All this suggests that the symbolism of nature and culture enters into human experience in a variety of predictable and unpredictable ways.

The orders of nature, culture and law combine to create American ideas of kinship. The primary elements are the combination of the order of nature and the order of culture. The combination of these two creates the world of relatives as these are understood in American kinship. The order of law may or may not recognize these relatives. That is, the relationships as they exist in nature, culture, or some combination thereof may or may not have any legally defined rights or obligations. [Figure 6.1] illustrates how the world of kinship is created through the intersection of nature and culture.

NATURE		CULTURE	
sperm donors	father	husband	fictive kin
"illegitimate" children	mother	wife	adopted children
	parent		

FIGURE 6.1 "Nature" and "culture" as components of family relationships.

At the far left side of the chart are relatives that exist primarily in the order of nature and may include so-called "illegitimate children," as well as the offspring of sperm donors. These are relatives to whom an individual may be related "by blood," but for whom no significant relationship in culture or in law exists.

At the far right of the chart are relatives who exist by virtue of culture alone. These include all the various fictive kin relationships that exist in American culture. Fictive aunts and uncles, brothers and sisters, and adopted children. These may exist only in culture, as in the case of fictive "brothers" and "sisters," or they may exist in both culture and in law, as in the case of adopted children.

Finally, in the middle are two categories of relatives that exist in both nature and culture. These are relatives for whom the order of nature appears to be reified by the order of culture. Relatives such as father and mother exist both in nature and in culture because the code of conduct expressed in culture is understood as a symbolic reenactment or replication of inherent ties. Thus for Americans, much of what is called kinship is symbolized as a cultural recognition of biological or natural facts. Many of these relationships, (e.g., mother and father) also exist in the order of law, in that law-making bodies have created a special symbolic code for governing these relationships. Other relationships, such as the relationships between second or third cousins, do not necessarily exist in the order of law. These are relatives solely in nature and culture. In this paper, I place the husband and wife relationship in the orders of nature and culture. Obviously, husbands and wives are not usually "blood" relatives, but in American culture, the relationship is seen as arising out of the nature of male-female relationships and the natural desire of men and women to mate and reproduce. In addition, it is sometimes remarked that the husband-wife relationship involves an exchange of fluids (i.e., semen) which gives this relationship a natural quality mimicking that of blood. Moreover, one practically universal basis for the annulment of marriage in American law is the failure of this exchange of fluids to take place. An annulment is conceptually different from a divorce, in that while divorce terminates a marriage, an annulment decrees that a marriage never existed. Thus the essence of a marital relationship is a blend of nature and culture.

In addition, there is tension between nature and culture which pervades American thinking about kinship. For example, the literature on step-parenting indicates that stepmothers have far more difficulty in integrating themselves into reconstituted families than do stepfathers, because of the cultural perception that relationships between mothers and children are more deeply imbedded in nature than in culture. Stepfathers seem to more easily assume the more culturally defined father role (Johnson, Klee and Smith, 1988).

The tension between nature and culture is even more apparent in adoption. By law, adoption severs all the rights of the biological mother and father to the child. All these rights and duties are transferred to the adopting parents. Yet nature looms as an ever-present danger to the adopting parents, and a host of devices exist to keep nature at bay. In the not-so-distant past, the fact of adoption was kept a secret, to be withheld from a child until he or she was "old enough to know"; that is old enough so that the cultural definition of the parent could resist the "pull" of the biological parent. The fear that someday the biological mother might come to successfully reclaim the love and loyalty linked to blood is not far from the minds of many adoptive parents, even though this fearsome scenario rarely occurs in fact.

Adopting parents also use geographic and cultural distance as ways of keeping nature at bay. Children are frequently adopted from foreign countries or distant states. Language also plays a role in the process. In current adoption jargon, the biological mother is now called the "birth mother" while the adopting mother is now "the mother." Adoption literature is also careful to spell out that a child "was" adopted, rather than "is" adopted, so as to signify that adoption is a way of coming into a family rather than an eternal condition. And, a pregnant woman seeking to find an adoptive family for her baby is termed a "situation," a term that clearly distances the adopting parents from the compelling fact of biological kinship.

Finally, the innumerable personal and procedural barriers placed in the way of so-called "open" adoptions are clearly linked to the fears of adopting parents and the law of the powerful claim of the biological mother. At the root of these feelings lies the primordial fear that culture cannot triumph over nature.

The Law Grapples with Redefining Family Relationships

A more detailed look at the legal decisions described above will illustrate how the tensions between nature and culture manifest themselves in legal decision-making. It is important to note that in all these cases, none of the kin or family terms are defined by statute or regulation. It fell to the courts to provide the definitions.[4]

What Is a Family? In the case of *Braschi* v. *Stahl Associates Co.* (1989), the question was whether Miguel Braschi would be able to remain as a tenant in the apartment he had shared with his domestic partner Leslie Blanchard for more than ten years. At issue was the Court's interpretation of New York City Rent and Eviction regulations which provided that upon the death of a tenant in a rent controlled apartment, the landlord may not dispossess "either the surviving spouse of the deceased tenant or some other family member of the deceased tenant's *family* who has been living with the tenant" (p. 206). The Court of Appeals specifically focused upon the meaning of the term "family." It did not address the issue of the term "spouse."

The Court rejected the idea that the term "family member" should be construed consistently with New York's intestacy laws, which regulate the inheritance of property, to mean relationships of blood, consanguinity, or adoption (p. 209). Instead, the Court argued that the non-eviction provisions are not designed to govern succession to property, but to protect certain occupants from the loss of their homes. In light of this, the Court argued that the term "family" should not be "rigidly restricted to those people who have formalized their relationship by obtaining, for instance, a marriage certificate or adoption order. The intended protection against sudden eviction should not rest on fictitious legal distinctions or genetic history, but instead should find its foundation in the reality of family life" (p. 211). The Court proceeded to provide a distinctly cultural view of family as "a group of people united by certain convictions or common affiliation" or as a "collective body of persons who live in one house under one head or management." Finally, the Court added that in using the term "family" the legislature had "intended to extend protection to those who reside in households having all of the normal familial characteristics" (p. 211). Indeed, the Court went on at length to describe how much the relationship between Braschi and Blanchard fit the facts of family life. As the Court put it:

> Appellant and Blanchard lived together as permanent life partners for more than 10 years. They regarded one another, and were regarded by friends and family, as spouses. The two men's families were aware of the nature of the relationship, and they regularly visited each other's families and attended family functions together, as a couple. Even today, appellant continues to maintain a relationship with Blanchard's niece, who considers him an uncle. (p. 213)

It is of considerable significance that the Court characterized the relationship between the parties as factually equivalent to a spousal relationship. Yet the issue of whether the parties were spouses to each other was apparently never raised or addressed. By resting his case on a cultural definition of family, Mr. Braschi obtained a favorable decision. Exactly how he would have fared had he relied on the idea that he was Blanchard's spouse cannot be ascertained from this case. However, the next case, *The Estate of Steven Szabo*, suggests that he would have had a more difficult time.

What Is a Spouse?   In the *Estate of Steven Szabo* (1990), the plaintiff presented a number of theories under which he should prevail. Each was predicated on the same set of facts, namely, that he and the deceased were gay life partners since 1970, and that they had agreed from the outset of their relationship to share living expenses and quarters, although they had signed no written agreement. According to the surviving partner, the financial arrangements between them were that he would give his entire monthly paycheck to Szabo, who then subtracted the cost of monthly household expenses, including the maintenance of the cooperative apartment that they shared. The balance of the money was placed in a savings account, and Szabo gave the plaintiff an allowance for weekly personal expenses. As seen earlier, when Szabo died, a will was probated, which predated the relationship and did not mention the plaintiff. In addition, there were no joint bank accounts, nor was the surviving partner the beneficiary of any life insurance policy. Title to the cooperative apartment in which they had lived together was also apparently held solely in the name of Szabo (p. 31).

It is easy to see, from the plaintiff's point of view, that this was a long-term relationship, like a marriage, in which the surviving partner was about to be evicted from the cooperative apartment he shared with the deceased without any of the money they had saved together for nearly twenty years. The plaintiff's most novel theory was that a gay life-partner is equivalent to a spouse. As previously stated, under New York law, a surviving spouse who is unnamed in a will is entitled to up to one-half of the net estate of the deceased partner. Therefore, if he were declared a spouse, he could obtain a substantial share of the estate solely by virtue of his spousal relationship and without having to prove any of the facts about their financial relationship.

However, the Court rejected this claim. Instead, the Court held that, by definition, a spouse means the person to whom one is legally married, and that the law made no provision for a marriage between persons of the same sex. "Marriage," the Court stated, "is and always has been a contract between a man and a woman" (p. 31). Here, of course the Court is emphasizing that marriage is a creation of both nature and culture. On the one hand, marriage is a contract, a cultural construction or transaction consisting of a series of mutual promises. On the other hand, it is grounded in nature, in that the only persons entitled to enter into such a contract are those persons who are heterosexual.

But the Court is able to separate the natural and cultural elements. For while nature and culture must come together in the creation of a marriage, and while the issue of inheritance flows from the natural side of the marriage, the financial relationships between the parties lie primarily in the world of culture. As a result, the Court allowed the plaintiff to proceed on two alternative theories; first on a claim for "money had and received," and old Common Law theory, which asserts that Szabo, and now his estate, received money that in equity and good conscience belong to the plaintiff; second, on the claim of "constructive trust," namely, that the estate has legal title to property in violation of some essential principal of equity. Under this theory the plaintiff would be permitted to show that the parties, by reason of their close relationship, were fiduciaries to each other, and that Szabo (and now, his estate) had a duty to act for his partner's benefit in connection with the money he had saved for him. These alternative theories find their bases in the world of business and commerce. They belong primarily to the world of culture. They derive from transactions into which all people, regardless of their natural connection to each other, can freely choose to enter.

What Is a Parent?   In *Alison D.* v. *Virginia M.* (1990) the Court was called upon to define the meaning of parent under New York's Domestic Relations law. At issue in this case was whether Alison D. had visitation rights to a child she and her former lesbian lover had parented together. Her basic claim was that she stood *in loco parentis* to the child, namely that the relationship the partners created gave her all the rights, duties, and responsibilities of a parent. As in the previous cases, the language of the law does not specifically define the term parent. Thus, the Court was asked to adopt the concept of parent as one standing *in loco parentis* (p. 23).

The Court saw no connection between the issues in *Braschi* v. *Stahl Associates Co.* and this case, but did not detail any reason why. The Court admitted that Alison D. and the child had a close and loving relationship, but it framed the entire dispute as one between a parent and a non-parent with respect to visitation of the child. Pronouncing Alison D. a "biological stranger," it chose to follow a line of cases which grants rights to non-parents only under extraordinary circumstances such as the unfitness of the biological parent.

Justice Kooper, who dissented in this case rejected the Court's reliance upon biology. She argued for a cultural definition of parenthood. In particular, she asserted that like the term "family," the term "parent" should be subject to a "frank inquiry into the realities of the relationship involved" (p. 24).

Interestingly, in this case the Court could have solved the problem by adopting the theory of equitable estoppel. Equitable estoppel is a vague legal concept which allows the Court to do justice by preventing a person from asserting a right he or she might otherwise have had. It is often used when the voluntary conduct of one party induces another to act in such a way that it is unjust for the party who does the misleading to assert his or her legal rights. Thus, in this case, the Court could have accepted the view that Virginia M. induced Alison D. into a long-term parental relationship and as a result, she should be barred from asserting the legal claim that Alison D. was not a parent. In this way, the Court would have done justice without actually having to redefine the concept of parent.

Significantly, this doctrine has sometimes been used to suppress biological claim to kinship. The classic example is where a woman becomes pregnant as a result of an adulterous relationship. Should she and her husband ultimately divorce, she will ordinarily be prevented from proving that the husband was not the biological father of their child. The doctrine of equitable estoppel creates the unrebuttable legal fiction that the child of a lawful marriage is the child of the husband and wife.

It might also be argued that adoption provides another model upon which the decision could have been based. After all, once adoption takes place, the issue of nature becomes legally irrelevant. Adoption could stand for the principle that a cultural-legal relationship can override a natural relationship even in parent-child relationships. A similar principle could be applied to lesbian and gay life-partner situations. This scenario is unlikely in the immediate future, since adoption was created through legislative action, rather than through judicial interpretation.

It is also clear that, adoption aside, parent-child relationships are one of the most difficult to redefine in the order of culture. Denmark, for example, allows for marriage-like unions for gay and lesbian couples which involve virtually all the rights and duties of marriage, but does not grant such couples the right to adopt or obtain joint custody of a child (Rule, 1989). The limited legal recognition of domestic partnerships in cities such as New York and San Francisco cannot deal with the issue of children.

The tension between the order of nature and the order of culture will continue to inform the domain of American family law. That the categories are undergoing constant revision is clear. In a recent surrogate mother case, a California Superior Court awarded full custody of the child to her genetic parents, and denied any rights to the surrogate mother, in whom a fertilized egg had been implanted after in-vitro fertilization. Whereas the New York Court dubbed Alison D. a "biological stranger," the California Court declared the surrogate mother a "genetic stranger." In making the decision, the Court was eventually forced to define the womb and the umbilical connection between the surrogate mother and the child as culture, analogizing it to a "fosterparent" relationship and a "home" for the embryo (Mydans, 1990).

CONCLUSION

Beginning in the 1930's, American law began to develop around the theory of legal realism. Legal realism was not as much a philosophical theory as it was an attitude. It called for an instrumental utilitarian use of law which rejected legal fictions. Law was a social tool (Friedman, 1985). In this light, it has sometimes been noted that family law has historically been the least amenable to legal realism and has been the most preoccupied with conscious creation of the symbolism of family life (Melton, 1987; Melton and Wilcox, 1989).

Certainly, the cases discussed in this article show some attempt to develop a more "realistic" view of family relationships. Nevertheless, it is clear that "realism," in the context of family law, requires a fundamental reordering of rather basic concepts of American kinship. This may be harder to accomplish than in other areas of law, where realism has triumphed. As this article has shown, the categories of nature and culture remain prime symbolic vehicles through which issues of family and kinship are addressed. "Adjudication," as Fiss puts it, "is interpretation . . . it is neither wholly discretionary nor . . . wholly mechanical" (Fiss, 1988). Judges will continue to bend and shape these categories, but they are not so easily abandoned. Judges will continue to make use of the cultural tools at hand to craft legal decisions.

NOTES

1. By family law, I mean the entire body of law which defines the rights and duties of kin. These laws may fall under the gloss of family law, domestic relations law, estate law, the law of wills, etc.

2. The following paragraphs constitute an extended dialogue with Schneider's text.

3. My use of the term symbol follows that of Clifford Geertz (1973). As to the specific issue of the symbolism of law, I take the view that law makes use of ideas and concepts that cut across all forms of social action, although in some societies law also makes use of a rather specialized vocabulary. For a fuller discussion of these issues see Geertz (1983) and Rosen (1989).

4. It is important to note that legal proceedings in the United States are shaped primarily by the parties to the issue and not the Court. Each side, plaintiff and defendant, comes to court with various theories as to why he or she should prevail. The theories must be offered by the parties themselves and the court will usually not substitute its own theories for those of the litigants. Moreover, litigants may present alternative and even inconsistent theories. The litigants usually try to present as many theories as possible under which their side could prevail. The Court will normally have the opportunity to choose among a variety of legal justifications for its decision.

REFERENCES

Barnes, J. A. (1977). "Genetrix:genitor::nature:culture?", in J. Goody (Ed.), *The character of kinship*, Cambridge: Cambridge University Press.

Fiss, Owen (1988). "Objectivity and interpretation," in S. Levinson & S. Maillauz (Eds.) *Interpreting law and literature* (pp. 229–249) Evanston: Northwestern University Press.

Friedman, Lawrence (1985). *A history of American law* (pp. 688–89). New York: Simon and Schuster.

Geertz, Clifford (1973). *The interpretation of culture.* New York: Basic Books.

Geertz, Clifford (1983). Local knowledge: fact and law in comparative perspective, in his *Local Knowledge* (pp. 167–234). New York: Basic Books.

Johnson, C. E., Klee, L., and Schmidt, C. (1988). Conceptions of parenthood and kinship among children of divorce. *American Anthropologist*, 90:136–144.

Melton, Gary B. (1987). The clashing of symbols: prelude to child and family policy, *American Psychologist*, 42:345–54.

Melton, Gary B. and Wilcox, Brian (1989). Changes in family law and family life, *American Psychologist* 44:1213–1216.

Mydans, Seth. Surrogate denied custody of child. (1990, October 23) *New York Times* p. A-14.

Ortner, Sherry (1974). Is female to male as nature is to culture?, in M. Rosaido and L. Lamphere (Eds.), *Women, culture and society*, Stanford: Stanford University Press.

Rosen, Lawrence (1989). *The anthropology of justice.* Cambridge: Cambridge University Press.

Rule, Sheila. Rights for gay couples in Denmark. (1989, October 2) *New York Times* p. A-19.

Schneider, David (1980). *American kinship: a cultural account.* Chicago: University of Chicago Press.

LIST OF CASES

In re *Alison D.* v. *Virginia M.*, (1990, March 9) *New York Law Journal*, p. 21

Bowers v. *Hardwick*, 478 U.S. 186, 197 (1985)

Braschi v. *Stahl Associates Co.*, 74 N.Y. 2d 201 (1989)

The Estate of Steven Szabo, (1990, July 16) *New York Law Journal*, p. 31

READING

7

The Family and the Culture War

James Davison Hunter

In many ways, the family is the most conspicuous field of conflict in the culture war. Some would argue that it is the decisive battleground. The public debate over the status and role of women, the moral legitimacy of abortion, the legal and social status of homosexuals, the increase in family violence, the rise of illegitimacy particularly among black teenagers and young adults, the growing demand for adequate day care, and so on, prominently fill the headlines of the nation's newspapers, magazines, and intellectual journals. Marches and rallies, speeches and pronouncements for or against any one of these issues mark the significant events of our generation's political history. One might be tempted, then, to say that this field of conflict is the beginning and end of the contemporary culture war, for the issues contested in the area of family policy touch upon and may even spill over into other fields of conflict—education, the arts, law, and politics. In the final analysis there may be much more to the contemporary culture war than the struggle for the family, yet there is little doubt that the issues contested in the realm of family life are central to the larger struggle and are perhaps fateful for other battles being waged.

Most who observe the contest over the family, however, tend to grasp the controversy as a disagreement over the relative strength of this institution. One observer, for example, has described the controversy as one between optimists and pessimists. Both sides, he argued, agree that the family is changing yet they disagree sharply over the scope, meaning, and consequences of those changes. The pessimists view rising trends in divorce, single-parent families, dual-income couples, couples living out of wedlock, secular day care, and the like, as symptoms of the decline of a social institution. The optimists, on the other hand, regard the changes as positive at best and benign at worst and, therefore, they believe that social policy should reflect and accommodate the new realities. The American family is not disintegrating, the optimists say, but is adapting to new social conditions. The resilience of the family, therefore, signals that the family is "here to stay."

Observations such as these provide interesting perspective and insight on the matter, forcing us to consider the concrete social and economic circumstances of family life. But they miss what is really at stake. The contest over the family, in fact, reflects fundamental differences in the assumptions and world views of the antagonists. The issue, then, is not whether the family is failing or surviving. Rather, the contest is over *what constitutes the family* in the first place. If the symbolic significance of the family is that it is a microcosm of the larger society, . . . then the task of defining what the American family *is* becomes integral to the very task of defining America itself. For this reason it is also a task that is, on its own terms, intrinsically prone to intense political contention.

DEFINING THE FAMILY

But what is new in all of this? The family, as many have observed, has long been a social problem that has engendered heated political debate. One can observe, for example, profound anxiety about the well-being of the family in America and fears of its impending decline well into the nineteenth century. This was a time when industrialization was considered to threaten the cohesiveness of the family by severing its traditional ties to extended kinship, community, and church networks; when urbanization was viewed as threatening the moral development of the young and as brutalizing the integrity of family bonds. As a report to the National Congregational Council put it in 1892, "Much of the very mechanism of our modern life . . . is destructive of the family."

Yet, as tangible as these problems were, there was still a general cultural agreement about what exactly it was that was being threatened and, therefore, what it was that needed defending. The nature and contours of the family were never publicly in doubt. Not so anymore: as with so many other aspects of American life, the nineteenth-century consensus about the character and structure of family life has collapsed, leaving the very viability of the institution *as traditionally conceived* in question. The divisive issue now is in what form or forms contemporary families will remain viable.

Signs that the family would become an explicit public policy issue subject to polemical controversy appeared before the 1980s. The social science establishment began to raise the issue as a subject of national policy concern as early as the mid-1960s. Research and writing on the problem expanded through the 1970s. The abstract rhetoric of intellectual discourse, however, soon translated into the push and pull of real political debate. In 1973, for example, the United States Senate held hearings on "American Families: Trends and Pressures." "Family experts" offered their views of problems faced by the family and suggested how the government might deal with them. Then in 1977, the Carnegie Council on Children (founded in 1972) published a report recommending that "the nation develop a family policy as comprehensive as its defense policy." In the words of the report, "Our nation's professed belief in the importance of the family has not been matched by actions designed to protect the family's integrity and vitality. Although the sanctity of the family is a favorite subject for Fourth of July orators, legislators rarely address the question of how best to support family life or child development." The call for concerted policy action would soon be answered.

Within the policy establishment itself, there were a wide range of perspectives about what problems actually plagued the family as well as how they should best be addressed. Among these "experts," a consensus was emerging that there was no one family type to which a national policy would be oriented. Rather than viewing families that were not nuclear, patriarchal, or self-sustaining as somehow deviant—families that were caught in what Daniel Patrick Moynihan called, in 1965, a "tangle of pathology"—public policy would now have to recognize a diversity of families. It was generally recognized that families differed in size, economic status, national origin and custom, and, not least, structure and composition.

During the 1980 White House Conference on Families, the quandary over how to define the American family was elevated to a permanent component of the national family policy debate. Indeed, in the early stages of organization and preparation the conference title itself was changed from the singular "family" to the plural "families" because the organizers could not agree on what the American family was supposed to be.

The conference, promised by President Carter during his 1976 presidential campaign, pledged the power and prestige of the White House to explore the ways in which public policy might strengthen U.S. families. Its outcome was mixed. That the conference succeeded in becoming an event of national scope there is little doubt. Statewide hearings and conferences took place in all fifty states, along with five national hearings, culminating in three White House conferences—in Baltimore, Minneapolis, and Los Angeles. But instead of generating a coherent set of policy recommendations serving to strengthen American families, the primary substantive accomplishment was to further crystallize and politicize, on a national scale, differences of opinion over the nature, structure, and composition of the family. . . .

THE FATE OF THE TRADITIONAL FAMILY

The White House Conference on Families was an important event in the history of the family policy debate in its own right; however, its story is recounted here because it displays the level and intensity of discord over how Americans define the family. Obviously, more is at stake than a dictionary definition of "the family." The debate actually takes form as a political judgment about the fate of *one particular conception of the family and family life*. The rhetoric of the activists, however, misses the mark. Leaders within the orthodox alliance call it the "traditional" family, by which they mean persons living together who are related either by blood, marriage, or adoption. But the family type they envision is "traditional" only in a limited sense. What is in fact at stake is a certain *idealized* form of the nineteenth-century middle-class family: a male-dominated nuclear family that both sentimentalized childhood and motherhood and, at the same time, celebrated domestic life as a utopian retreat from the harsh realities of industrial society. Although such bourgeois families were central in many ways to the flourishing of the early modern society, their fate is now in serious doubt. The political debate asks whether this family type should be preserved or abandoned. . . .

POLICY BRAWLS

The struggle to define the American family—whether public policy should embrace or reject the nineteenth-century middle-class family ideal—is practically enjoined not in its totality but in terms of its component parts. The clash, in other words, takes shape over specific concepts that underlie various policy proposals under debate—components that together make up a definition of the American family.

Authority

Families, however they are practically imagined, are a social unit that cooperates to carry out collective tasks—providing for the members' basic material and emotional needs, nurturing children to acceptable levels of social and moral responsibility, and so on. But who is responsible for these tasks and who will have the final say when difficult decisions need to be made? The issue here is one of *authority*. Should it rest with husband and father, as the orthodox and their culturally conservative allies prefer? Or should authority and responsibility be shared on egalitarian principles, as progressives and their liberal allies favor?

The issue of authority is implicit within several policy debates. Perhaps the most important, because it has been debated for the better part of the twentieth century, has been the Equal Rights Amendment (ERA). This amendment to the Constitution initially was introduced in Congress in 1923 through the efforts of the National Women's party. It finally was passed by Congress in 1972, yet it failed to be ratified by a sufficient number of state legislatures by a 1982 deadline. Reintroduced in 1983, the proposal lay largely dormant through the 1980s and early 1990s. Even so, the goal of the ERA has remained a central aspiration of the women's movement and of political progressives in general.

Advocates argue that the amendment guarantees equal protection under the law without regard for a person's gender. Conservatives claim that such protections are already guaranteed under the Constitution and that an amendment would be redundant. The deeper significance of the amendment, however, is symbolic. For progressivists, the Equal Rights Amendment symbolizes the formal recognition by the state (through the instrumentality of law) that women are autonomous from and therefore economically and politically equal to men. For those on the orthodox side, the amendment symbolizes a forsaking of the inherited structure of social relationships in the family and society as a whole. The ERA, claimed one conservative Illinois legislator, was "really an attack on the home. It [was] an attack on motherhood. It says that for a woman to have to be a mother and have to be a housewife is somehow degrading."

Moreover, many activists with orthodox commitments may also have mobilized against the ERA because it was viewed as way of "smuggling" legal protection of homosexual rights into a Constitutional amendment. One Fundamentalist opponent to the amendment put it this way: "If effective laws to help women are already on the books, who needs the ERA? Not women as a sex but lesbians and homosexuals need the ERA; and believe me, that's what it's really all about! Homosexuals and lesbians, who number perhaps 6 percent of the population, recognize their unpopular status. They decided early that the feminist movement and the ERA provided them with a handy vehicle to ride piggyback upon 'women's rights' and achieve homosexual rights. Fortunately, citizens who suddenly realized how close we were to the city limits of Sodom and Gomorrah successfully resisted the ERA." Other symbolic issues were at stake as well, such as the role of women in the military and the fate of single-sex institutions (such as Catholic seminaries and Orthodox Jewish schools) which discriminate according to gender for religious reasons. These issues remain key symbolic landmarks on both sides of the cultural divide.

The ERA is, of course, only one of the ways in which the issue of authority in family and society is played out in public policy. The identical arguments emerge in policy debates over such ideas as an "Equal Rights Act" and "comparable worth" or "pay equity." Though the latter issue technically deals with gender bias in wage setting, the symbolic meaning of the proposal is clear. Its advocates contend that the issue involves more than "just money," it involves "the esteem of half our population." Opponents insist that, among other things, pay equity "requires us to close our eyes to innate sexual differences which affect job preferences." The matter of authority is also contested in our very language. Language is not challenged at the level of federal law, although it is disputed at the level of organizational etiquette. This conflict focuses on the use of gender-specific language, as in the generic use of masculine pronouns (he, him, his) or the generic use of masculine titles (chairman, repairman, garbageman). What for traditionalists is the proper use of the English language is, for progressives, a pattern of speech that denigrates women and linguistically validates male domination. On both sides of the cultural divide, language itself—the ordering of symbols in our society—has become a politicized dimension of the culture war. This reality begins in the conflict over authority but it extends to the issue of abortion, homosexuality, euthanasia, and so on. The battle will be nearly over when the linguistic preferences of one side of the cultural divide become the conventions of society as a whole. . . .

Obligation

Another concept crucial to family life (however it is defined) is that of *obligation*. Of course, in a family there is a mutual obligation to care for and nurture each other. But to whom are we bound in this way? To what extent are we bound and for how long are we bound in this way? The answers to these questions reveal positions on matters of personal autonomy. No matter how tight the family is as a social unit, the family is made up of individuals who have needs and desires apart from the family. So, in addition to the questions surrounding obligation, a further question asks how the need for individual autonomy is to be balanced against the requirement of family obligation. Should the need for autonomy (the obligation to the self) take priority over the needs of the family (our obligation to others) or should personal needs be subordinated to the will and interests of the family?

Consider the matter of abortion. The sociologist Kristin Luker has argued cogently that the struggle over abortion is ultimately a struggle over the concept of motherhood. For pro-life activists, motherhood tends to be viewed as the most important and satisfying role open to a woman. Abortion, therefore, represents an attack on the very activity that gives life meaning. For pro-choice activists, motherhood is simply one role among many, and yet when defined as the only role, it is almost always a hardship. Abortion in this context is a means of liberating women from the burden of unplanned or unwanted childbearing and childrearing.

Luker's argument is certainly true as far as it goes, but beyond the concept of motherhood, abortion also raises issues of obligation and autonomy. Those holding to the orthodox vision tend to believe that family obligation extends not only to the born and living but to the unborn as well. Pro-life activists contend that the unborn have rights that must be protected by others, since they cannot defend those rights themselves. Because historically and religiously, the duty of motherhood is commonly viewed as the protection of children, legalized abortion represents an assault on the mother's principal obligation and her source of identity. Progressivists reject this idea and wonder how we can be obligated to what are, at best, "potential persons." The legal right to an abortion is seen as ensuring that women maintain their individual autonomy from men who might compete with them in the workplace or husbands who wish to restrict wives' freedom by keeping them in the realm of domestic travail. In this view, legislation that restricts access to abortion would, in the words of a statement from the National Abortion Rights Action League, "threaten the core of a woman's constitutionally valued autonomy . . . by violating the principle of bodily integrity that underlies much of the [Constitution's] promise of liberty . . . and by plac[ing] severe constraints on women's employment opportunities and . . . their ability to support themselves and their families."

The same issue of obligation underlies the policy debates over child care. With an increasing number of women in the work force and an increasing number of working women with young children, it is not surprising that child care would become politicized. The question is not really who has the obligation to care for young children. Everyone would agree that it is the parents or those acting as parents. The real question is, what are the legitimate ways that parents or guardians can meet those obligations? Two different understandings of parental responsibility have taken shape. Within the progressivist vision, parental responsibility is principally achieved in meeting the growing economic requirements of raising children at the end of the twentieth century. Besides meeting basic needs, this means making sure that children have the opportunities to develop their full potentials as human beings. As for moral and social development, progressivists tend to believe that the children of dual-career families do not necessarily suffer if some child care is given by someone other than a parent or family member. What matters is the *quality* of time spent with children. But the consensus among cultural conservatives is that children do suffer when others besides family members participate in child care. Parents, they claim, are the ones best suited to socializing the young, particularly when it comes to passing on a moral and religious heritage. "The education and upbringing of children is the primary responsibility of parents. Selfishly or ignorantly surrendering this role would be a grave disservice to our youth as well as our free society. The family must cling to its God-ordained roles or future generations will suffer the consequences."

These opposing views lead to predictable positions on public policy concerning child care. Policies promoting government-sponsored child care for dual-career families are seen as a way to give economic assistance to a growing number of women who have small children and must work, or as an abdication of the parental obligation to provide care and moral instruction to children. In the Act for Better Child Care, for example, we can see virtually all of the dimensions of the culture war.... [T]he act was supported by, among others, the National Organization for Women, *Ms.* Magazine, the Union of American Hebrew Congregations, and the United Methodist Board of Church and Society. The act was opposed by such orthodox groups as Concerned Women for America, the American Council of Christian Churches (and criticized by its Fundamentalist News Service), and James Dobson's Focus on the Family periodical *Citizen.* The bill assumed, according to its critics, that "the federal government is more capable than the parents to determine what is best for the child." Catholic constitutional lawyer William Bentley Ball said that the bill "reads flat out as a secularist prescription for the care of American children."

It is the sense that family obligations are being willfully abandoned that is behind the conservative complaint about the liberalization of divorce law (as in the idea and practice of "no fault divorce") and the concomitant rise in the rate of divorce as well. For many holding to a progressivist vision of moral life, the liberalization of divorce law is simply a means of guaranteeing individual autonomy when the obligations of marriage or of family life become burdensome and oppressive.

Sexuality: The Challenge of Homosexuality

Sexuality, of course, is also at the heart of family life. It is the family more than any other institution that establishes the rules for sexual intimacy—the codes that define the persons with whom, the time when, and the conditions under which sexual intimacy is acceptable. How the family enacts these rules also implies a judgment upon what "nature" will allow or should allow. But what is "natural" in matters of sexuality? The answer goes right to the heart of assumptions about the moral order: what is good, what is right, what is appropriate. Family life, however, is also a "school of virtue," for it bears the responsibility, as no other institution can, for socializing children—raising them as decent and moral people, passing on the morals of a community to the next generation. How parents view nature in matters of sexuality, therefore, is reflected in the ways they teach children about right and wrong. How the actors in the contemporary culture war view nature in matters of sexuality, in turn, will be reflected in their different ideals of how the moral order of a society will take shape in the future.

Perhaps with the exception of abortion, few issues in the contemporary culture war generate more raw emotion than the issue of homosexuality. The reason is plain: few other issues challenge the traditional assumptions of what nature will allow, the boundaries of the moral order, and finally the ideals of middle-class family life more radically. Homosexuality symbolizes either an absolute and fundamental perversion of nature, of the social order, and of American family life, or it is simply another way in which nature can evolve and be expressed, another way of ordering society, and an alternative way of conducting family life.

Both sides of the contemporary cultural divide understand the critical importance of homosexuality for the larger culture war. One apologist for gay and lesbian interests put it this way: "We should see anti-gay fear and hatred as part of a cultural offensive against liberal egalitarian social principles generally. Homophobia is a vehicle for the conservative ideology that links the defense of the patriarchal family with the maintenance of class, race, and gender hierarchy throughout society." To be gay, then, is to share the ordeal of other marginalized people in the nation; to be public about it places one in solidarity with the oppressed and their agenda of social change. Clearly, this is why major gay rights organizations participate in and often officially co-sponsor activism on behalf of abortion rights, women's rights, the homeless, and so on. As literature from the National Gay and Lesbian Task Force put it, they are "committed to ending systems of oppression in all forms."

The hostility to gay rights activism on the other side of the cultural divide follows much the same line as presented by Chuck McIlhenny or Rabbi Levin, for whom homosexuality represents an assault on biblical truths. Republican Congressman William Dannemeyer from California, for example, is quoted as saying that the homosexual movement represents "the most vicious attack on traditional family values that our society has seen in the history of our republic." Some in the orthodox alliance have argued that "the family is the fundamental unit of society, for it is the principle of permanence. For most persons it furnishes the primary experience of stability, continuity and fidelity. In this respect, and in many others, it is a school for citizenship. But it can maintain its function over the long run only if we accord it preferential status over alternative sexual arrangements and liaisons." The homosexual movement, therefore, is "destructive of the family and . . . a potent threat to society."

The rejoinder to this orthodox contention is an explicit affirmation of the aim to redefine the family—to proclaim "a new vision of family life." The response of the National Gay and Lesbian Task Force is that "lesbians and gay men are not a threat to families, but are an essential thread in the fabric of American family life." Ours, they contend, "is a vision of diverse family life that is directly opposed to the once-upon-a-time myth promoted by the right wing. Our vision is inclusive, not discriminatory. It is functional, rather than legalistic." Therefore, "threats to the American family do not come from the desire of gay men and lesbians to create loving relationships," but rather "from the right wing's manipulation of ignorance, bigotry and economic injustice. These threats to *our* families must be met with outrage . . . action . . . and resources."

And indeed the gay community has responded in this way within several areas of public policy. Perhaps the most important area over which the issue of the legitimacy of the "gay alternative" is concretely contested is the matter of marriage rights for homosexual couples. Let's be very clear about this: more is at stake here than the emotional rewards of formalizing a shared commitment in a relationship. The practical benefits of marriage are of tangible and often crucial importance to the lives of individuals: marriage partners may take part in the spouse's health plan and pension programs, share the rights of inheritance and community property, make a claim upon a spouse's rent-controlled apartment, and file joint tax returns. These legal and economic advantages were all designed to encourage the economic independence and interdependence of the traditional family unit and indeed, couples in traditional heterosexual marriages have long benefited from them. By the same token they have been denied to homosexual couples, heterosexual couples living out of wedlock, and living arrangements involving long-term platonic roommates—all of which may involve the same degree of economic and emotional dependence that occurs within a traditional family.

As the contemporary culture war has intensified, the general ambition of gay rights activists has been to push for the legal recognition of homosexual relationships as legitimate marriages or at least as "domestic partners" in order to ultimately secure these economic benefits. . . . While the fifty states have been reluctant to recognize the legality or legal rights of homosexual marriages, a handful of cities such as Los Angeles; New York; Madison, Wisconsin; and Takoma Park, Maryland, do provide bereavement leave for domestic partners who are municipal workers. A few others, such as Berkeley, Santa Cruz, and West Hollywood, offer health benefits for the same. This push has continued in still other cities around the country where laws prohibiting discrimination on the basis of marital status are being examined to see whether they extend to the living arrangements of homosexual couples.

Needless to say, such proposals pose a serious challenge to the traditional conception of marriage and family. The very idea is a "serious blow to our society's historic commitment to supporting marriage and family life," stated the archbishop of San Francisco in response to the domestic partners referendum in that city. Yet even in the gay community there is disagreement about this goal—not because it shares the archbishop's views, but because the legislation does not go far enough. The campaign for domestic partnership or gay marriage is misdirected, argued one lesbian activist, because it tries to adopt traditional heterosexual institutions for gays rather then encourage tolerance for divergent life-styles. "Marriage, as it exists today, is antithetical to my liberation as a lesbian and as a woman, because it mainstreams my life and voice."

The issues of bigotry and discrimination, in the view of homosexuals and of many activists for the progressivist vision, have gone beyond disputes over marriage rights or domestic partners to other areas of policy concern. For example, bigotry has been seen in the battles to either perpetuate or repeal "sodomy laws," as in the 1986 Supreme Court decision *Bowers* v. *Hardwick*, which upheld Georgia's sodomy law. Such laws (which still exist in twenty-four states), according to gay activists, "define our sexual lives as criminal, unnatural, perverse and repulsive." The perpetuation of these laws they feel, "gives the government's stamp of approval on individual people's homophobia, in much the same way that Jim Crow laws institutionalized racism and the segregation of black people in the American South." The struggle over the passage, in 1990, of the Hate Crime Statistics Act, requiring the federal government to collect statistics on crimes motivated by prejudice based on race, ethnicity, religion, or "sexual orientation" brought gay issues to the fore when Congress passed an amendment to this bill stating that "American family life is the foundation of American society" and "nothing in this act shall be construed" to "promote or encourage homosexuality." The symbolic significance of that amendment was not missed by the gay rights activists, even as they celebrated the bill's passage. Direct mail from the National Gay and Lesbian Task Force called the act "the most significant lesbian and gay rights victory in the history of the U.S. Congress!" Bigotry and discrimination in economic issues such as employment and housing have been sharply contested in policy debates over the Civil Rights Amendments Act. The original Civil Rights Act of 1964 prohibited discrimination on the basis of race, color, religion, or national origin; the new amendment (originally proposed in 1975) would extend the existing act to include the prohibition of discrimination relating to sexual orientation. In each of these policy areas, what is at stake is a tacit recognition on the part of the government that homosexuality is an authentic manner of life, social relationship, family, and community.

Interestingly, the stakes of recognition and legitimacy are raised to perhaps their highest symbolic level in those cases where the source of "discrimination and bigotry" is the military establishment itself. The military, of course, is an American institution that has long been defined by a rigid organizational hierarchy and by traditional notions of manliness: bravery, platonic bonding, emphatic heterosexuality, and the like. The contrast between U.S. military culture and a subculture that is defined by an intimacy among members of the same sex could not be more stark. The tensions are inevitable. A Naval cadet near the top of his class was expelled just two months before his graduation from the Annapolis Naval Academy after announcing to his friends that he was gay; fourteen lesbians at Parris Island boot camp were discharged from the Marine Corps in 1988; and twelve noncommissioned officers in the Air Force were discharged in 1989 for homosexual activity. These occurrences are not uncommon, for according to Department of Defense figures, an average of about 1,400 gay men and women are expelled from the armed forces every year. Legal challenges to incidents such as these, and to military policy that requires dismissal of gay officers in training from ROTC programs at universities (where the military often acquires more than half of its new officers) point to an intensification of the conflict that will be decisive for the larger controversy.

The other pivotal institutions in which the legitimacy of homosexuality has been contested are the churches. One might imagine that the deep and long-standing hostility of the Judeo-Christian faiths toward homosexuality would encourage homosexual men and lesbians to leave their faiths altogether. But for those who continue to identify with a particular religious tradition, there appears to be little desire to leave. . . . Said one priest, "My Catholicism is a deep part of my identity, as is my sexuality. I do not plan to give up either." Others have echoed this sentiment, "As members of Dignity we are a gay presence in the Church and a Christian presence within the gay community. We are proud that we can bring Christian values and beliefs to the gay community and equally proud that we can bring our gayness before the Church." One lesbian nun spoke for many others of every religious confession when she described herself as "very much of a prophet among my own sisters." The objective is not to be changed by the church but to change the church from the inside. The sense that they are succeeding in this was captured in the words of one layman who lamented, "What in 1963 was regarded as an offense against basic morality and a betrayal of solemn vows is today, alas, too often regarded as a legitimate 'sexual prefer-ence,' a 'human right,' and a 'progressive cause.'. . . [Today] those who still think that homosexual acts are sinful are accused of being 'homophobic,' while active homosexuals boldly proclaim their own moral superiority. . . ."

As the strongest institutional bulwarks of traditionalist ideals of gender roles and sexuality, the military establishment and the churches are barometers of how the conflict over homosexuality fares in the larger social order. As the armed forces and the churches go on this issue, so may go the rest of American society.

What intensifies the struggle over the homosexuality issue is the AIDS crisis in the gay community. The quest for public recognition and legitimacy has become a matter of life and death because along with recognition and legitimacy comes the ability to credibly argue for and expect both public sympathy and increased public expenditure for medical research and health care. Cultural conservatives recognize this as well, many believing that "homosexuals and liberals are using the AIDS crisis to force our children to be taught their ultra-liberal views on sexuality and morality." A measure of the desperation that gays feel is seen in the practice of "outing"—intentional exposure of secret and usually prominent homosexuals (politicians, religious leaders, and the like) by other homosexuals. The rationale is that the gay rights movement needs all the support it can muster. These public figures could be helping the cause but either have chosen silence or have openly worked against the cause in order to protect their careers. They deserve "outing" for their "malicious hypocrisy on matters of life and death."

In Sum

The disputes over the nature and structure of authority, the moral obligations of parenting and marital commitment, the natural and legitimate boundaries of sexual experience, and so on, are all part of the struggle to define the family in its totality. In this struggle, it is important to point out that progressive activists have faced a difficult time shaking the image of being anti-family and anti-chil-dren. "Its enthusiasm for abortion and for day care," one observer remarked, "has strengthened this impression, suggesting that here are people who want to prevent children from being born . . . and failing this, to dump children so that mothers can pursue their selfish programs of self-realization." Progressive activists vehemently deny that their agenda is anti-family. They maintain that they desire a much more "inclusive vision of family life . . . of people who love and care for one another." Their insistence on this serves to confirm the argument made here, that each side of the cultural divide simply operates with a different conception of what the family is, how it behaves, and what its place and role should be. Which side is finally tarred with the label "anti-family" will depend on which model of the family finally prevails in public policy. . . .

PART TWO

◈

THE
SEXES

◈

INTRODUCTION

American society has experienced both a sexual revolution and a sex-role revolution. The first has liberalized attitudes toward erotic behavior and expression; the second has changed the roles and status of women and men in the direction of greater equality. Both revolutions have been brought about by the rapid social changes in recent years, and both revolutions have challenged traditional conceptions of marriage.

The conventional idea of sexuality defines sex as a powerful biological drive continually struggling for gratification against restraints imposed by civilization. The notion of sexual instincts also implies a kind of innate knowledge: A person intuitively knows his or her own identity as male or female, he or she knows how to act accordingly, and he or she is attracted to the "proper" sex object—a person of the opposite gender. In other words, the view of sex as biological drive pure and simple implies "that sexuality has a magical ability, possessed by no other capacity, that allows biological drives to be expressed directly in psychological and social behaviors" (Gagnon and Simon, 1970, p. 24).

The whole issue of the relative importance of biological versus psychological and social factors in sexuality and sex differences has been obscured by polemics. On the one hand, there are the strict biological determinists who declare that anatomy is destiny. On the other hand, there are those who argue that all aspects of sexuality and sex-role differences are matters of learning and social construction.

There are two essential points to be made about the nature-versus-nurture argument. By the 1970s, scientists understood that extreme positions overlook the connection between biology and experience:

> In the theory of psychosexual differentiation, it is now outmoded to oppose or juxtapose nature vs. nurture, the genetic vs. psychological, or the instinctive vs. the environmental, the innate vs. the acquired, the biological vs. the psychological, or the instinctive vs. the learned. Modern genetic theory avoids these antiquated dichotomies. (Money and Ehrhardt, 1972, p. 1)

A second and related point concerns a misconception about how biological forces work. Both biological determinists and their opponents assume that if a biological force exists, it must be overwhelmingly strong. But the most sophisticated evidence concerning both gender development *and* erotic arousal suggests that physiological forces are gentle rather than powerful. Acknowledging the possible effects of prenatal sex hormones on the brains of human infants, Robert Stoller (1972) thus warned against "biologizing":

> While the newborn presents a most malleable central nervous system upon which the environment writes, we cannot say that the central nervous system is neutral or neuter. Rather, we can say that the effects of these biological systems, organized prenatally in a masculine or feminine direction, are almost always . . . too gentle in humans to withstand the more powerful forces in human development, the first and most powerful of which is mothering. (p. 211)

Research into the development of sex differences thus suggests not an opposition between genetics and environment but an interaction. Gender identity as a child and occupation as an adult are primarily the product of social learning rather than anatomy and physiology.

In terms of scholarship, the main effect of the sex-role and sexual revolutions has been on awareness and consciousness. For example, much early social science writing was revealed to have been based on sexist assumptions. Many sociologists and psychologists took it for granted that women's roles and functions in society reflect universal physiological and temperamental traits. Since in practically every society women were subordinate to men, inequality was interpreted as an inescapable necessity of organized social life. Such analysis suffered from the same intellectual flaw as the idea that discrimination against nonwhites implies their innate inferiority. All such explanations failed to analyze the social institutions and forces producing and supporting the observed differences. In approaching the study of either the physical or the social relations between the sexes, it is therefore important to understand how traditional stereotypes have influenced both popular and professional concepts of sexuality and sex differences.

Jessie Bernard's and William J. Goode's articles on male and female sex roles develop this theme in different ways, but generally examine how stereotyping influences and sets limits on male and female socialization. These limits rob both men and women of a broader potential—for example, gentleness for men, achievement for women. Stereotyping thus diminishes the capacity of both women and men to fulfill a broader potential than conventional sex roles dictate.

As gender and family roles have shifted, so have ideas about sexual norms and behavior. Prior to the 1960s, men and women were, ideally, to remain chaste before marriage. Nevertheless, premarital male sexual behavior was winked at, if not condoned. But nowhere, as Lillian Rubin asserts, do we find the effects of the sexual revolution more graphically illustrated and played out than in the sexual behavior—and sense of entitlement to sex—of today's teenagers. This represents a profound change, especially for girls.

Despite all the changes, however, one tradition persists: As Robert Michael and his colleagues show in their selection, most people find partners for love and marriage in the old-fashioned way, through their own social networks of friends, family, and acquaintances. Though some couples meet as strangers "across a crowded room," surprisingly few lasting relationships begin that way.

To many people, the current state of marriage seems to provide the clearest evidence that the family is falling apart. In the past three decades, marriage rates have declined, divorce rates have risen, and increasing numbers of couples have come to live together without being married. Yet these changes do not necessarily mean that people no longer want long-term commitments or that they are psychologically incapable of forming deep attachments. Rather, they reflect the fact that in the modern world marriage is increasingly a personal relationship between two people. Over time, fewer and fewer reasons tie couples to unsatisfactory relationships. As the standards for emotional fulfillment in marriage have risen, so have the levels of discontent.

In the preindustrial past, the least important aspect of marriage was the emotional relationship between husband and wife. A marriage was an exchange between kin groups, a unit of economic production, and a means of replenishing populations with high death rates. In traditional societies, parents often selected their children's mates. Parents were more interested in the practical consequences of choice than in romantic considerations.

By contrast, people are supposed to marry for "love" in our modern society. They may marry for practical reasons or for money; nevertheless, they often follow their culture's rules and decide they are "in love." People may also decide they are in love and want to live together but do not care to have their union licensed by the state or blessed by the clergy.

Couple relationships are thus influenced by the new fluidity and openness with regard to social norms in general and sexual behavior in particular. At one time, a relationship between a man and a woman could be easily categorized: It was either "honorable" or "dishonorable." An "honorable" relationship went through several distinct stages: dating, keeping company, going steady, agreeing to be married, announcing the engagement, and finally getting married, presumably for life. Divorce was regarded as a personal tragedy and social disgrace. Sexual relations before marriage were also shameful, especially for the woman, although the shame decreased as the marriage drew nearer. Today the system of courtship has yielded to a new pattern of couple relationships—less permanent, more flexible, more experimental.

Couples still marry with the ideal of "till death do us part"; few brides and grooms expect that they will end up divorced. Why then do so many marriages break down? In his article, John Gottman describes the processes that can put couples on the road to divorce. Based on in-depth observations of marital interaction, Gottman finds that the key to the success of a marriage is how the partners deal with the conflicts that are inevitable in any close relationship. Gottman finds several different types of successful marriage, including a "volatile" style in which the couple quarrels a lot. The patterns of behavior that lead to divorce, however, involve emotional withdrawal, blaming, and contempt, as expressed in insults and put-downs. Using a different research approach, Frances Klagsbrun also addresses the question of what makes for a happy and lasting marriage. Based on interviews with long-married couples, she concludes that eight factors, including an ability to change and to tolerate change, contribute to staying together.

As in Gottman's selection, the article by Mavis Hetherington and colleagues also shows how divorce is not a single event, but a long process. It is a complex chain of events and life experiences that begins long before the divorce itself and continues long after. Although divorce is an emotionally wrenching process for all concerned, it's difficult to make blanket statements about its long-term effects. Divorce tends to be a different experience for men, women, and children; and individual reactions to it vary enormously.

One frequent outcome of a divorce is remarriage by one or both spouses. Such remarriages generate interesting and problematic kinship structures and relationships that have scarcely been studied and for which we may not even have names. We know something about stepparents and stepchildren, but is there a difference between the way a father acts with his own children of his first marriage who live part of the time with his first wife, and the children of his second marriage who live full-time with him and his second wife? What of half-brothers and -sisters? What of the relationship between a father's first-marriage children, his second wife's first-marriage children, and the children of the second marriage? The selection by Constance R. Ahrons and Roy H. Rodgers discusses the family complexities generated by divorce and modern remarriage.

Despite all its difficulties, marriage is not likely to go out of style in the near future. Ultimately we agree with Jessie Bernard (1982), who, after a devastating critique of marriage from the point of view of a sociologist who is also a feminist, said this:

> The future of marriage is as assured as any social form can be. . . . For men and women will continue to want intimacy, they will continue to want to celebrate their mutuality, to experience the mystic unity which once led the church to consider marriage a sacrament. . . . There is hardly any probability such commitments will disappear or that all relationships between them will become merely casual or transient. (p. 301)

REFERENCES

Bernard, Jessie. 1982. *The Future of Marriage*. New York: World.

Gagnon, J. H., and W. Simon. 1970. *The Sexual Scene*. Chicago: Aldine/ Transaction.

Money, J., and A. A. Ehrhardt. 1972. *Man and Woman, Boy and Girl*. Baltimore: Johns Hopkins University Press.

Stroller, R. J. 1972. The bedrock of masculinity and femininity: Bisexuality. *Archives of General Psychiatry* 26: 207–212.

CHAPTER 3

❖

GENDER

R E A D I N G

8

The Good-Provider Role:
Its Rise and Fall

Jessie Bernard

ABSTRACT

The general structure of the "traditional" American family, in which the husband-father is the provider and the wife-mother is the housewife, began to take shape early in the 19th century. This structure lasted about 150 years, from the 1830s to 1980, when the U.S. Census no longer automatically denominated the male as head of the household. As "providing" became increasingly mediated by cash derived from participation in the labor force or from commercial enterprises, the powers and prerogatives of the provider role augmented, and those of the housewife, who lacked a cash income, declined. Gender identity became associated with the work site as well as with work. As affluence spread, the provider role became more and more competitive and escalated into the good-provider role. There were always defectors from the good-provider role, and in recent years expressed dissatisfaction with it increased. As more and more married women entered the labor force and thus assumed a share of the provider role, the powers and prerogatives of the good-

---

From *American Psychologist*, Vol. 36, No. 1, January 1981, pp. 1–12. Copyright © 1981 by the American Psychological Association. Reprinted by permission.

provider role became diluted. At the present time a process that Ralph Smith calls "the subtle revolution" is realigning family roles. A host of social-psychological obstacles related to gender identity have to be overcome before a new social-psychological structure can be achieved.

The Lord is my shepherd, I shall not want. He sets a table for me in the very sight of my enemies; my cup runs over (23rd Psalm). And when the Israelites were complaining about how hungry they were on their way from Egypt to Canaan, God told Moses to rest assured: There would be meat for dinner and bread for breakfast the next morning. And, indeed, there were quails that very night, enough to cover the camp, and in the morning the ground was covered with dew that proved to be bread (Exodus 16:12–13). In fact, in this role of good provider, God is sometimes almost synonymous with Providence. Many people, like Micawber, still wait for him, or Providence, to provide.

Granted, then, that the first great provider for the human species was God the Father, surely the second great provider for the human species was Mother, the gatherer, planter, and general factotum. Boulding (1976), citing Lee and deVore, tells us that in hunting and gathering societies, males contribute about one fifth of the food of the clan, females the other four fifths (p. 96). She also concludes that by 12,000 B.C. in the early agricultural villages, females provided four fifths of human subsistence (p. 97). Not until large trading towns arose did the female contribution to human subsistence decline to equality with that of the male. And with the beginning of true cities, the provisioning work of women tended to become invisible. Still, in today's world it remains substantial.

Whatever the date of the virtuous woman described in the Old Testament (Proverbs 31:10–27), she was the very model of a good provider. She was, in fact, a highly productive conglomerate. She woke up in the middle of the night to tend to her business; she oversaw a multiple-industry household; *her* candles did not go out at night; there was a ready market for the high-quality linen girdles she made and sold to the merchants in town; and she kept track of the real estate market and bought good land when it became available, cultivating vineyards quite profitably. All this time her husband sat at the gate talking with his cronies.

A recent counterpart to the virtuous woman was the busy and industrious shtetl woman:

> The earnings of a livelihood is sexless, and the large majority of women . . . participate in some gainful occupation if they do not carry the chief burden of support. The wife of a "perennial student" is very apt to be the sole support of the family. The problem of managing both a business and a home is so common that no one recognizes it as special. . . . To bustle about in search of a livelihood is merely another form of bustling about managing a home; both are aspects of . . . health and livelihood. (Zborowski & Herzog, 1952, p. 131)

In a subsistence economy in which husbands and wives ran farms, shops, or businesses together, a man might be a good, steady worker, but the idea that he was *the* provider would hardly ring true. Even the youth in the folk song who listed all the gifts he would bestow on his love if she would marry him—a golden comb, a paper of pins, and all the rest—was not necessarily promising to be a good provider.

I have not searched the literature to determine when the concept of the good provider entered our thinking. The term *provider* entered the English language in 1532, but was not yet male sex typed, as the older term *purveyor* already was in 1442. Webster's second edition defines the good provider as "one who provides, especially, colloq., one who provides food, clothing, etc. for his family; as, he is a good or an adequate provider." More simply, he could be defined as a man whose wife did not have to enter the labor force. The counterpart to the good provider was the housewife. However the term is defined, the role itself delineated relationships within a marriage and family in a way that added to the legal, religious, and other advantages men had over women.

Thus, under the common law, although the husband was legally head of the household and as such had the responsibility of providing for his wife and children, this provision was often made with help from the wife's personal property and earnings, to which he was entitled:

> He owned his wife's and children's services, and had the sole right to collect wages for their work outside the home. He owned his wife's personal property outright, and had the right to manage and control all of his wife's real property during marriage, which included the right to use or lease property, and to keep any rents and profits from it. (Babcock, Freedman, Norton, & Ross, 1975, p. 561)

So even when she was the actual provider, the legal recognition was granted the husband. Therefore, whatever the husband's legal responsibilities for support may have been, he was not necessarily a good provider in the way the term came to be understood. The wife may have been performing that role.

In our country in Colonial times women were still viewed as performing a providing role, and they pursued a variety of occupations. Abigail Adams managed the family estate, which provided the wherewithal for John to spend so much time in Philadelphia. In the 18th century "many women were active in business and professional pursuits. They ran inns and taverns; they managed a wide variety of stores and shops; and, at least occasionally, they worked in careers like publishing, journalism and medicine" (Demos, 1974, p. 430). Women sometimes even "joined the menfolk for work in the fields" (p. 430). Like the household of the proverbial virtuous woman, the Colonial household was a little factory that produced clothing, furniture, bedding, candles, and other accessories, and again, as in the case of the virtuous woman, the female role was central. It was taken for granted that women provided for the family along with men.

The good provider as a specialized male role seems to have arisen in the transition from subsistence to market—especially money—economies that accelerated with the industrial revolution. The good-provider role for males emerged in this country roughly, say, from the 1830s, when de Tocqueville was observing it, to the late 1970s, when the 1980 census declared that a male was not automatically to be assumed to be head of household. This gives the role a life span of about a century and a half. Although relatively short-lived, while it lasted the role was a seemingly rock-like feature of the national landscape.

As a psychological and sociological phenomenon, the good-provider role had wide ramifications for all of our thinking about families. It marked a new kind of marriage. It did not have good effects on women: The role deprived them of many chips by placing them in a peculiarly vulnerable position. Because she was not reimbursed for her contribution to the family in either products or services, a wife was stripped to a considerable extent of her access to cash-mediated markets. By discouraging labor force participation, it deprived many women, especially affluent ones, of opportunities to achieve strength and competence. It deterred young women from acquiring productive skills. They dedicated themselves instead to winning a good provider who would "take care of" them. The wife of a more successful provider became for all intents and purposes a parasite, with little to do except indulge or pamper herself. The psychology of such dependence could become all but crippling. There were other concomitants of the good-provider role.

EXPRESSIVITY AND THE GOOD-PROVIDER ROLE

The new industrial order that produced the good provider changed not so much the division of labor between the sexes as it did the site of the work they engaged in. Only two of the concomitants of this change in work site are selected for comment here, namely, (a) the identification of gender with work site as well as with work itself and (b) the reduction of time for personal interaction and intimacy within the family.

It is not so much the specific kinds of work men and women do—they have always varied from time to time and place to place—but the simple fact that the sexes do different kinds of work, whatever it is, which is in and of itself important. The division of labor by sex means that the work group becomes also a sex group. The very nature of maleness and femaleness becomes embedded in the sexual division of labor. One's sex and one's work are part of one another. One's work defines one's gender.

Any division of labor implies that people doing different kinds of work will occupy different work sites. When the division is based on sex, men and women will necessarily have different work sites. Even within the home itself, men and women had different work spaces. The woman's spinning wheel occupied a different area from the man's anvil. When the factory took over much of the work formerly done in the house, the separation of work space became especially marked. Not only did the separation of the sexes become spatially extended, but it came to relate work and gender in a special way. The work site as well as the work itself became associated with gender; each sex had its own turf. This sexual "territoriality" has had complicating effects on efforts to change any sexual division of labor. The good provider worked primarily in the outside male world of business and industry. The homemaker worked primarily in the home.

Spatial separation of the sexes not only identifies gender with work site and work but also reduces the amount of time available for spontaneous emotional give-and-take between husbands and wives. When men and women work in an economy based in the home, there are frequent occasions for interaction.

(Consider, for example, the suggestive allusions made today to the rise in the birth rate nine months after a blackout.) When men and women are in close proximity, there is always the possibility of reassuring glances, the comfort of simple physical presence. But when the division of labor removes the man from the family dwelling for most of the day, intimate relationships become less feasible. De Tocqueville was one of the first to call our attention to this. In 1840 he noted that

> almost all men in democracies are engaged in public or professional life; and . . . the limited extent of common income obliges a wife to confine herself to the house, in order to watch in person and very closely over the details of domestic economy. All these distinct and compulsory occupations are so many natural barriers, which, by keeping the two sexes asunder, render the solicitations of the one less frequent and less ardent—the resistance of the other more easy. (de Tocqueville, 1840, p. 212)

Not directly related to the spatial constraints on emotional expression by men, but nevertheless a concomitant of the new industrial order with the same effect, was the enormous drive for achievement, for success, for "making it" that escalated the provider role into the good-provider role. De Tocqueville (1840) is again our source:

> The tumultuous and constantly harassed life which equality makes men lead [becoming good providers] not only distracts from the passions of love, by denying them time to indulge in it, but it diverts them from it by another more secret but more certain road. All men who live in democratic ages more or less contract ways of thinking of the manufacturing and trading classes. (p. 221)

As a result of this male concentration on jobs and careers, much abnegation and "a constant sacrifice of her pleasures to her duties" (de Tocqueville, 1840, p. 212) were demanded by the American woman. The good-provider role, as it came to be shaped by this ambience, was thus restricted in what it was called upon to provide. Emotional expressivity was not included in that role. One of the things a parent might say about a man to persuade a daughter to marry him, or a daughter might say to explain to her parents why she wanted to, was not that he was a gentle, loving, or tender man but that he was a good provider. He might have many other qualities, good or bad, but if a man was a good provider, everything else was either gravy or the price one had to pay for a good provider.

Lack of expressivity did not imply neglect of the family. The good provider was a "family man." He set a good table, provided a decent home, paid the mortgage, bought the shoes, and kept his children warmly clothed. He might, with the help of the children's part-time jobs, have been able to finance their educations through high school, and, sometimes, even college. There might even have been a little left over for an occasional celebration in most families. The good provider made a decent contribution to the church. His work might have been demanding, but he expected it to be. If in addition to being a good provider, a man was kind, gentle, generous, and not a heavy drinker or gambler, that was all frosting on the cake. Loving attention and emotional involvement in the family were not part of a woman's implicit bargain with the good provider.

By the time de Tocqueville published his observations in 1840, the general outlines of the good-provider role had taken shape. It called for a hard-working man who spent most of his time at his work. In the traditional conception of the role, a man's chief responsibility is his job, so that "by definition any family behaviors must be subordinate to it in terms of significance and [the job] has priority in the event of a clash" (Scanzoni, 1975, p. 38). This was the classic form of the good-provider role, which remained a powerful component of our societal structure until well into the present century.

COSTS AND REWARDS OF THE GOOD-PROVIDER ROLE FOR MEN

There were both costs and rewards for those men attached to the good-provider role. The most serious cost was perhaps the identification of maleness not only with the work site but especially with success in the role. "The American male looks to his breadwinning role to confirm his manliness" (Brenton, 1966, p. 194).[1] To be a man one had to be not only a provider but a *good* provider. Success in the good-provider role came in time to define masculinity itself. The good provider had to achieve, to win, to succeed, to dominate. He was a bread*winner*. He had to show "strength, cunning, inventiveness, endurance—a whole range of traits henceforth defined as exclusively 'masculine' " (Demos, 1974, p. 436). Men were judged as men by the level of living they provided. They were judged by the myth "that endows a money-making man with sexiness and virility, and is based on man's dominance, strength, and ability to provide for and care for 'his' woman" (Gould, 1974, p. 97). The good provider became a player in the male competitive macho game. What one man provided for his family in the way of luxury and display had to be equaled or topped by what another could provide. Families became display cases for the success of the good provider.

The psychic costs could be high:

> By depending so heavily on his breadwinning role to validate his sense of himself as a man, instead of also letting his roles as husband, father, and citizen of the community count as validating sources, the American male treads on psychically dangerous ground. It's always dangerous to put all one's psychic eggs into one basket. (Brenton 1966, p. 194)

The good-provider role not only put all of a man's gender-identifying eggs into one psychic basket, but it also put all the family-providing eggs into one basket. One individual became responsible for the support of the whole family. Countless stories portrayed the humiliation families underwent to keep wives and especially mothers out of the labor force, a circumstance that would admit to the world the male head's failure in the good-provider role. If a married woman had to enter the labor force at all, that was bad enough. If she made a good salary, however, she was "co-opting the man's passport to masculinity"

---

[1]Rainwater and Yancy (1967), critiquing current welfare policies, note that they "have robbed men of their manhood, women of their husbands, and children of their fathers. To create a stable monogamous family we need to provide men with the opportunity to be men, and that involves enabling them to perform occupationally" (p. 235).

(Gould, 1974, p. 89) and he was effectively castrated. A wife's earning capacity diminished a man's position as head of the household (Gould, 1974, p. 99).

Failure in the role of good provider, which employment of wives evidenced, could produce deep frustration. As Komarovsky (1940, p. 20) explains, this is "because in his own estimation he is failing to fulfill what is the central duty of his life, the very touchstone of his manhood—the role of family provider."

But just as there was punishment for failure in the good-provider role, so also were there rewards for successful performance. A man "derived strength from his role as provider" (Komarovsky, 1940, p. 205). He achieved a good deal of satisfaction from his ability to support his family. It won kudos. Being a good provider led to status in both the family and the community. Within the family it gave him the power of the purse and the right to decide about expenditures, standards of living, and what constituted good providing. "Every purchase of the family—the radio, his wife's new hat, the children's skates, the meals set before him—all were symbols of their dependence upon him" (Komarovsky, 1940, pp. 74–75). Such dependence gave him a "profound sense of stability" (p. 74). It was a strong counterpoise vis-à-vis a wife with a stronger personality. "Whether he had considerable authority within the family and was recognized as its head, or whether the wife's stronger personality . . . dominated the family, he nevertheless derived strength from his role as a provider" (Komarovsky, 1940, p. 75). As recently as 1975, in a sample of 3,100 husbands and wives in 10 cities, Scanzoni found that despite increasing egalitarian norms, the good provider still had "considerable power in ultimate decision-making" and as "unique provider" had the right "to organize his life and the lives of other family members around his occupation" (p. 38).

A man who was successful in the good-provider role might be freed from other obligations to the family. But the flip side of this dispensation was that he could not make up for poor performances by excellence in other family roles. Since everything depended on his success as provider, everything was at stake. The good provider played an all-or-nothing game.

DIFFERENT WAYS OF PERFORMING THE GOOD-PROVIDER ROLE

Although the legal specifications for the role were laid out in the common law, in legislation, in legal precedents, in court decisions, and, most importantly, in custom and convention, in real-life situations the social and social-psychological specifications were set by the husband or, perhaps more accurately, by the community, alias the Joneses, and there were many ways to perform it.

Some men resented the burdens the role forced them to bear. A man could easily vent such resentment toward his family by keeping complete control over all expenditures, dispensing the money for household maintenance, and complaining about bills as though it were his wife's fault that shoes cost so much. He could, in effect, punish his family for his having to perform the role. Since the money he earned belonged to him—was "his"—he could do with it what he pleased. Through extreme parsimony he could dole out his money in a mean, humiliating way, forcing his wife to come begging for pennies. By his reluctance and resentment he could make his family pay emotionally for the provisioning he supplied.

At the other extreme were the highly competitive men who were so involved in outdoing the Joneses that the fur coat became more important than the affectionate hug. They "bought off" their families. They sometimes succeeded so well in their extravagance that they sacrificed the family they were presumably providing for to the achievements that made it possible (Keniston, 1965).[2]

The Depression of the 1930s revealed in harsh detail what the loss of the role could mean both to the good provider and to his family, not only in the loss of income itself—which could be supplied by welfare agencies or even by other family members, including wives—but also and especially in the loss of face.

The Great Depression did not mark the demise of the good-provider role. But it did teach us what a slender thread the family hung on. It stimulated a whole array of programs designed to strengthen that thread, to ensure that it would never again be similarly threatened. Unemployment insurance was incorporated into the Social Security Act of 1935, for example, and a Full Employment Act was passed in 1946. But there proved to be many other ways in which the good-provider role could be subverted.

ROLE REJECTORS AND ROLE OVERPERFORMERS

Recent research in psychology, anthropology, and sociology has familiarized us with the tremendous power of roles. But we also know that one of the fundamental principles of role behavior is that conformity to role norms is not universal. Not everyone lives up to the specifications of roles, either in the psychological or in the sociological definition of the concept. Two extremes have attracted research attention: (a) the men who could not live up to the norms of the good-provider role or did not want to, at one extreme, and (b) the men who overperformed the role, as the other. For the wide range in between, from blue-collar workers to professionals, there was fairly consistent acceptance of the role, however well or poorly, however grumblingly or willingly, performed.

First the nonconformists. Even in Colonial times, desertion and divorce occurred:

---

[2]Several years ago 1 presented a critique of what I called "extreme sex role specialization," including "work-intoxicated fathers." I noted that making success in the provider role the only test for real manliness was putting a lot of eggs into one basket. At both the blue-collar and the managerial levels, it was dysfunctional for families. I referred to the several attempts being made even then to correct the excesses of extreme sex role specialization: rural and urban communes, leaving jobs to take up small-scale enterprises that allowed more contact with families, and a rebellion against overtime in industry (Bernard, 1975, pp. 217–239).

Women may have deserted because, say, their husbands beat them; husbands, on the other hand, may have deserted because they were unable or unwilling to provide for their usually large families in the face of the wives' demands to do so. These demands were, of course, backed by community norms making the husband's financial support a sacred duty. (Scanzoni, 1979, pp. 24–25)

Fiedler (1962) has traced the theme of male escape from domestic responsibilities in the American novel from the time of Rip Van Winkle to the present:

The figure of Rip Van Winkle presides over the birth of the American imagination; and it is fitting that our first successful home-grown legend should memorialize, however playfully, the flight of the dreamer from the shrew—into the mountains and out of time, away from the drab duties of home . . . anywhere to avoid . . . marriage and responsibility. One of the factors that determine theme and form in our great books is this strategy of evasion, this retreat to nature and childhood which makes our literature (and life) so charmingly and infuriatingly "boyish." (pp. xx–xxi)

Among the men who pulled up stakes and departed for the West or went down to the sea in ships, there must have been a certain proportion who, like their mythic prototype, were fleeing the good-provider role.

The work of Demos (1974), a historian, offers considerable support for Fiedler's thesis. He tells us that the burdens thrust on men in the 19th century by the new patterns of work began to show their effects in the family. When "the [spatial] separation of the work lives of husbands and wives made communication so problematic," he asks, "what was the likelihood of meaningful communication?" (Demos, 1974, p. 438). The answer is, relatively little. Divorce and separation increased, either formally or by tacit consent—or simply by default, as in the case of a variety of defaulters—tramps, bums, hoboes— among them.

In this connection, "the development of the notorious 'tramp' phenomenon is worth noticing," Demos (1974, p. 438) tells us. The tramp was a man who just gave up, who dropped out of the role entirely. He preferred not to work, but he would do small chores or other small-scale work for a handout if he had to. He was not above begging the housewife for a meal, hoping she would not find work for him to do in repayment. Demos (1974) describes the type:

Demoralized and destitute wanderers, their numbers mounting into the hundreds of thousands, tramps can be fairly characterized as men who had run away from their wives. . . . Their presence was mute testimony to the strains that tugged at the very core of American family life. . . . Many observers noted that the tramps had created a virtual society of their own [a kind of counterculture] based on a principle of single-sex companionship. (p. 438)

A considerable number of them came to be described as "homeless men" and, as the country became more urbanized, landed ultimately on skid row. A large part of the task of social workers for almost a century was the care of the "evaded" women they left behind.[3] When the tramp became wholly demoralized, a chronic alcoholic, almost unreachable, he fell into a category of his own—he was a bum.

Quite a different kettle of fish was the hobo, the migratory worker who spent several months harvesting wheat and other large crops and the rest of the year in cities. Many were the so-called Wobblies, or Industrial Workers of the World, who repudiated the good-provider role on principle. They had contempt for the men who accepted it and could be called conscientious objectors to the role. "In some IWW circles, wives were regarded as the 'ball and chain.' In the West, IWW literature proclaimed that the migratory worker, usually a young, unmarried male, was 'the first specimen of American manhood . . . the leaven of the revolutionary labor movement' " (Foner, 1979, p. 400). Exemplars of the Wobblies were the nomadic workers of the West. They were free men. The migratory worker, "unlike the factory slave of the Atlantic seaboard and the central states, . . . was most emphatically 'not afraid of losing his job.' No wife and family cumbered him. The worker of the East, oppressed by the fear of want for wife and babies, dared not venture much" (Foner, 1979, p. 400). The reference to fear of loss of job was well taken; employers preferred married men, disciplined into the good-provider role, who had given hostages to fortune and were therefore more tractable.

Just on the verge between the area of conformity to the good-provider role—at whatever level—and the area of complete nonconformity to it was the non–good provider, the marginal group of workers usually made up of "the under-educated, the under-trained, the under-employed, or part-time employed, as well as the under paid, and of course the unemployed" (Snyder, 1979, p. 597). These included men who wanted—sometimes desperately—to perform the good-provider role but who for one reason or another were unable to do so. Liebow (1966) has discussed the ramifications of failure among the black men of Tally's corner: The black man is

> under legal and social constraints to provide for them [their families], to be a husband to his wife and a father to his children. The chances are, however, that he is failing to provide for them, and failure in this primary function contaminates his performance as father in other aspects as well. (p. 86)

---

[3]In one department of a South Carolina cotton mill early in the century, "every worker was a grass widow" (Smuts, 1959, p. 54). Many women worked "because their husbands refused to provide for their families. There is no reason to think that husbands abandoned their duties more often than today, but the woman who was burdened by an irresponsible husband in 189 usually had no recourse save taking on his responsibilities herself. If he deserted, the law-enforcement agencies of the time afforded little chance of finding and compelling him to provide support" (Smuts, 1959, p. 54). The situation is not greatly improved today. In divo child support is allotted in only a small number of cases and enforced in even fewer. "Roughly half of all families with an absent parent don't have awards at all. . . . Where awards do exist they are usually for small amounts, typically ranging from $7 to $18 per child" (Jones, 1976, abstract). A summary of all the studies available concludes that "approximately 20 percent of all divorced and separated mothers receive child support regularly, with an additional 7 percent receiving it 'sometimes': 8 percent of all divorced and separated women receive alimony regularly or sometimes" (Jones, 1976, p. 23

In some cases, leaving the family entirely was the best substitute a man could supply. The community was left to take over.[4]

At the other extreme was the overperformer. De Tocqueville, quoted earlier, was already describing him as he manifested in the 1830s. And as late as 1955 Warner and Ablegglen were adding to the considerable literature on industrial leaders and tycoons, referring to their "driving concentration" on their careers and their "intense focusing" on interests, energies, and skills on these careers, "even limiting their sexual activity" (pp. 48–49). They came to be known as workaholics or work-intoxicated men. Their preoccupation with their work even at the expense of their families was, as I have already noted, quite acceptable in our society.

Poorly or well performed, the good-provider role lingered on. World War II initiated a challenge, this time in the form of attracting more and more married women into the labor force, but the challenge was papered over in the 1950s with an "age of togetherness" that all but apotheosized the good provider, his house in the suburbs, his homebody wife, and his third, fourth, even fifth, child. As late as the 1960s most housewives (87%) still saw breadwinning as their husband's primary role (Lopata, 1971, p. 91).[5]

INTRINSIC CONFLICT IN THE GOOD-PROVIDER ROLE

Since the good-provider role involved both family and work roles, most people believed that there was no incompatibility between them or at least that there should not be. But in the 1960s and 1970s evidence began to mount that maybe something was amiss.

De Tocqueville had documented the implicit conflict in the American businessman's devotion to his work at the expense of his family in the early years of the 19th century; the Industrial Workers of the World had proclaimed that the good-provider role which tied a man to his family was an impediment to the great revolution at the beginning of the 20th century; Fiedler (1962) had noted that throughout our history, in the male fantasy world, there was freedom from the responsibilities of this role; about 50 years ago Freud (1930/1958) had analyzed the intrinsic conflict between the demands of women and the family on one side and the demands of men's work on the other:

> Women represented the interests of the family and sexual life, the work of civilization has become more and more men's business; it confronts them with ever harder tasks, compels them to subliminations of instinct which women are not easily able to achieve. Since man has not an unlimited amount of mental energy at his disposal, he must accomplish his tasks by distributing his libido to the best advantage. What he

---

[4]Even though the annals of social work agencies are filled with cases of runaway husbands, in 1976 only 12.6% of all women were in the status of divorce and separation, and at least some of them were still being "provided for." Most men were at least trying to fulfill the good-provider role.

[5]Although all the women in Lopata's (1971) sample saw breadwinning as important, fewer employed women (54%) than either nonemployed urban (63%) or suburban (64%) women assigned it first place (p. 91).

employs for cultural [occupational] purposes he withdraws to a great extent from women, and his sexual life; his constant association with men and his dependence on his relations with them even estrange him from his duties as husband and father. Woman finds herself thus forced into the background by the claims of culture [work] and she adapts an inimical attitude towards it. (pp. 50–51)

In the last two decades, researchers have been raising questions relevant to Freud's statement of the problem. They have been asking people about the relative satisfactions they derive from these conflicting values—family and work. Among the earliest studies comparing family–work values was a Gallup poll in 1940 in which both men and women chose a happy home over an interesting job or wealth as a major life value. Since then there have been a number of such polls, and a considerable body of results has not accumulated. Pleck and Lang (1979) and Hesselbart (Note 1) have summarized the findings of these surveys. All agree that there is a clear bias in the direction of the family. Pleck and Lang conclude that "men's family role is far more psychologically significant to them than is their work role" (p. 29), and Hesselbart—however critical she is of the studies she summarizes—believes they should not be dismissed lightly and concludes that they certainly "challenge the idea that family is a 'secondary' valued role" (p. 14).[6] Douvan (Note 2) also found in a 1976 replication of a 1957 survey that family values retained priority over work: "Family roles almost uniformly rate higher in value production than the job role does" (p. 16).[7]

The very fact that researchers have asked such questions is itself interesting. Somehow or other both the researchers and the informants seem to be saying that all this complaining about the male neglect of the family, about the lack of family involvement by men, just is not warranted. Neither de Tocqueville nor Freud was right. Men do value family life more than they value their work. They do derive their major life satisfactions from their families rather than from their work.

It may well be true that men derive the greatest satisfaction from their family roles, but this does not necessarily mean they are willing to pay for the

---

[6]Pleck and Lang (1979) found only one serious study contradicting their own conclusions: "Using data from the 1973 NORC (National Opinion Research Center) General Social Survey, Harry analyzed the bivariate relationship of job and family satisfaction to life happiness in men classified by family life cycle stage. In three of the five groups of husbands . . . job satisfaction had a stronger association than family satisfaction to life happiness" (pp. 5–6).

[7]In 1978, a Yankelovich survey on "The New Work Psychology" suggested that leisure is now becoming a strict competitor for both family and work as a source of life satisfactions: "Family and work have grown less important than leisure; a majority of 60 percent say that although they enjoy their work, it is not their major source of satisfaction" (p. 46). A 1977 survey of Swedish men aged 18 to 35 found that the proportion saying that the family was the main source of meaning in their lives declined from 45% in 1955 to 41% in 1977; the proportion indicating work as the main source of satisfaction dropped from 33% to 17%. The earlier tendency for men to identify themselves through their work is less marked these days. In the new value system, the individual says, in effect, "I am more than my role. I am myself" (Yankelovich, 1978). Is the increasing concern with leisure a way to escape the dissatisfaction with both the alienating relations found on the work site and the demands for increased involvement with the family?

benefit. In any event, great attitudinal changes took place in the 1960s and 1970s.

Douvan (Note 2), on the basis of surveys in 1957 and 1976, found, for example, a considerable increase in the proportion of both men and women who found marriage and parenthood burdensome and restrictive. Almost three fifths (57%) of both married men and married women in 1976 saw marriages as "all burdens and restrictions," as compared with only 42% and 47%, respectively, in 1957. And almost half (45%) also viewed children as "all burdens and restrictions" in 1976, as compared with only 28% and 33% for married men and married women, respectively, in 1957. The proportion of working men with a positive attitude toward marriage dropped drastically over this period, from 68% to 39%. Working women, who made up a fairly small number of all married women in 1957, hardly changed attitudes at all, dropping only from 43% to 42%. The proportion of working men who found marriage and children burdensome and restrictive more than doubled, from 25% to 56% and from 25% to 58%, respectively. Although some of these changes reflected greater willingness in 1976 than in 1957 to admit negative attitudes toward marriage and parenthood—itself significant—profound changes were clearly in process. More and more men and women were experiencing disaffection with family life.[8]

"ALL BURDENS AND RESTRICTIONS"

Apparently, the benefits of the good-provider role were greater than the costs for most men. Despite the legend of the flight of the American male (Fiedler, 1962), despite the defectors and dropouts, despite the tavern habitués "ball and chain" cliché, men seemed to know that the good-provider role, if they could succeed in it, was good for them. But Douvan's (Note 2) findings suggest that recently their complaints have become serious, bone-deep. The family they have been providing for is not the same family it was in the past.

Smith (1979) calls the great trek of married women into the labor force a subtle revolution—revolutionary not in the sense of one class overthrowing a status quo and substituting its own regime, but revolutionary in its impact on both the family and the work roles of men and women. It diluted the prerogatives of the good-provider role. It increased the demands made on the good provider, especially in the form of more emotional investment in the family, more sharing of household responsibilities. The role became even more burdensome.

However men may now feel about the burdens and restrictions imposed on them by the good-provider role, most have, at least ostensibly, accepted them.

---

[8]Men seem to be having problems with both work and family roles. Veroff (Note 3), for example, reports an increased "sense of dissatisfaction with the social relations in the wok setting" and a "dissatisfaction with the affiliative nature of work" (p. 47). This dissatisfaction may be one of the factors that leads men to seek affiliative-need satisfaction in marriage, just as in the 19th century they looked to the home as shelter from the jungle of the outside world.

The tramp and the bum had "voted with their feet" against the role; the hobo or Wobbly had rejected it on the basis of a revolutionary ideology that saw it as enslaving men to the corporation; tavern humor had glossed the resentment habitués felt against its demands. Now the "burdens-and-restrictions" motif has surfaced both in research reports and, more blatantly, in the male liberation movement. From time to time it has also appeared in the clinicians' notes.

Sometimes the resentment of the good provider takes the form of simply wanting more appreciation for the life-style he provides. All he does for his family seems to be taken for granted. Thus, for example, Goldberg (1976), a psychiatrist, recounts the case of a successful businessman:

> He's feeling a deepening sense of bitterness and frustration about his wife and family. He doesn't feel appreciated. It angers him the way they seem to take the things his earnings purchase for granted. They've come to expect it as their due. It particularly enrages him when his children put him down for his "materialistic middle-class trip." He'd like to tell them to get someone else to support them but he holds himself back. (p. 124)

Brenton (1966) quotes a social worker who describes an upper-middle-class woman: She has "gotten hold of a man who'll drive himself mad to get money, and [is] denigrating him for being too interested in money, and not interested in music, or the arts, or in spending time with the children. But at the same time she's subtly driving him—and doesn't know it" (p. 226). What seems significant about such cases is not that men feel resentful about the lack of appreciation but that they are willing to justify their resentment. They are no longer willing to grin and bear it.

Sometimes there is even more than expressed resentment; there is an actual repudiation of the role. In the past, only a few men like the hobo or Wobbly were likely to give up. Today, Goldberg (1976) believes, more are ready to renounce the role, not on theoretical revolutionary grounds, however, but on purely selfish ones:

> Male growth will stem from openly avowed, unashamed, self-oriented motivation. . . . Guilt-oriented "should" behavior will be rejected because it is always at the price of a hidden build-up of resentment and frustration and alienation from others and is, therefore, counterproductive. (p. 184)

The disaffection of the good provider is directed to both sides of his role. With respect to work, Lefkowitz (1979) has described men among whom the good-provider role is neither being completely rejected nor repudiated, but diluted. These men began their working lives in the conventional style, hopeful and ambitious. They found a job, married, raised a family, and "achieved a measure of economic security and earned the respect of . . . colleagues and neighbors" (Lefkowitz, 1979, p. 31). In brief, they successfully performed the good-provider role. But unlike their historical predecessors, they in time became disillusioned with their jobs—not jobs on assembly lines, not jobs usually characterized as alienating, but fairly prestigious jobs such as aeronautics engineer and government economist. They daydreamed about other interests. "The common theme which surfaced again and again in their histories, was the need to find a new social connection—to reassert control over their lives, to gain some sense of freedom" (Lefkowitz, 1979, p. 31). These men felt "entitled to freedom and independence." Middle-class, educated, self-assured, articulate, and for the most part white, they knew they could talk themselves into a job if they had to. Most of them did not want to desert their families. Indeed, most of them "wanted to rejoin the intimate circle they felt they had neglected in their years of work" (p. 31).

Though some of the men Lefkowitz studied sought closer ties with their families, in the case of those studied by Sarason (1977), a psychologist, career changes involved lower income and had a negative impact on families. Sarason's subjects were also men in high-level professions, the very men least likely to find marriage and parenthood burdensome and restrictive. Still, since career change often involved a reduction in pay, some wives were unwilling to accept it, with the result that the marriage deteriorated (p. 178). Sometimes it looked like a no-win game. The husband's earlier career brought him feelings of emptiness and alienation, but it also brought financial rewards for the family. Greater work satisfaction for him in lower paying work meant reduced satisfaction with lifestyle. These findings lead Sarason to raise a number of points with respect to the good-provider role. "How much," he asks, "does an individual or a family need in order to maintain a satisfactory existence? Is an individual being responsible to himself or to his family if he provides them with little more than the bare essentials of living?" (p. 178). These [are] questions about the good-provider role that few men raised in the past.

Lefkowitz (1979) wonders how his downwardly mobile men lived when they left their jobs. "They put together a basic economic package which consisted of government assistance, contributions from family members who had not worked before and some bartering of goods and services" (p. 31). Especially interesting in this list of income sources are the "contributions from family members who had not worked before" (p. 31). Surely not mothers and sisters. Who, of course, but wives?

WOMEN AND THE PROVIDER ROLE

The present discussion began with the woman's part in the provider role. We saw how as more and more of the provisioning of the family came to be by way of monetary exchange, the woman's part shrank. A woman could still provide services, but could furnish little in the way of food, clothing, and shelter. But now that she is entering the labor force in large numbers, she can once more resume her ancient role, this time, like her male counterpart the provider, by way of a monetary contribution. More and more women are doing just this.

The assault on the good-provider role in the Depression was traumatic. But a modified version began to appear in the 1970s as a single income became inadequate for more and more families. Husbands have remained the major providers, but in an increasing number of cases the wife has begun to share this role. Thus, the proportion of married women aged 15 to 54 (living with their husbands) in the labor force more than doubled between 1950 and 1978, from

25.2% to 55.4%. The proportion for 1990 is estimated to reach 66.7% (Smith, 1979, p. 14). Fewer women are now full-time housewives.

For some men the relief from the strain of sole responsibility for the provider role has been welcome. But for others the feeling of degradation resembles the feeling reported 40 years earlier in the Great Depression. It is not that they are no longer providing for the family but that the role-sharing wife now feels justified in making demands on them. The good-provider role with all its prerogatives and perquisites has undergone profound changes. It will never be the same again.[9] Its death knell was sounded when, as noted above, the 1980 census no longer automatically assumed that the male member of the household was its head.

THE CURRENT SCENE

Among the new demands being made on the good-provider role, two deserve special consideration, namely, (1) more intimacy, expressivity, and nurturance—specifications never included in it as it originally took shape—and (2) more sharing of household responsibilities and child care.

As the pampered wife in an affluent household came often to be an economic parasite, so also the good provider was often, in a way, a kind of emotional parasite. Implicit in the definition of the role was that he provided goods and material things. Tender loving care was not one of the requirements. Emotional ministrations from the family were his right; providing them was not a corresponding obligation. Therefore, as de Tocqueville had already noted by 1840, women suffered a kind of emotional deprivation labeled by Robert Weiss "relational deficit" (cited in Bernard, 1976). Only recently has this male rejection of emotional expression come to be challenged. Today, even blue-collar women are imposing "a host of new role expectations upon their husbands or lovers. . . . A new role set asks the blue-collar male to strive for . . . deep-coursing intimacy" (Shostak, Note 4, p. 75). It was not only vis-à-vis his family that the good provider was lacking in expressivity. This lack was built into the whole male role script. Today not only women but also men are beginning to protest the repudiation of expressivity prescribed in male roles (David & Brannon, 1976; Farrell, 1974; Fasteau, 1974; Pleck & Sawyer 1974).

Is there any relationship between the "imposing" on men of "deep-coursing intimacy" by women on one side and the increasing proportion of men who find marriage burdensome and restrictive on the other? Are men seeing the new emotional involvement being asked of them as "all burdens and restrictions"? Are they responding to the new involvements under duress? Are they feeling oppressed by them? Fearful of them?

---

[9]Among the indices of the waning of the good-provider role are the increasing number of married women in the labor fore; the growth in the number of female-headed families; the growing trend toward egalitarian norms in marriage; the need for two earners in so many middle-class families; and the recognition of these trends in the abandonment of the identification of head of household as a male.

From the standpoint of high-level pure-science research there may be something bizarre, if not even slightly absurd, in the growing corpus of serious research on how much or how little husbands of employed wives contribute to household chores and child care. Yet it is serious enough that all over the industrialized world such research is going on. Time studies in a dozen countries—communist as well as capitalist—trace the slow and bungling process by which marriage accommodates to changing conditions and by which women struggle to mold the changing conditions in their behalf. For everywhere the same picture shows up in research: an image of women sharing the provider role and at the same time retaining responsibility for the household. Until recently such a topic would have been judged unworthy of serious attention. It was a subject that might be worth a good laugh, for instance, as when an all-thumbs man in a cartoon burns the potatoes or finds himself bumbling awkwardly over a diaper, demonstrating his—proud—male ineptness at such female work. But it is no longer funny.

The "politics of housework" (Mainardi, 1970) proves to be more profound than originally believed. It has to do not only with tasks but also with gender—and perhaps more with the site of the tasks than with their intrinsic nature. A man can cook magnificently if he does it on a hunting or fishing trip; he can wield a skillful needle if he does it mending a tent or a fishing net; he can even feed and clean a toddler on a camping trip. Few of the skills of the homemaker are beyond his reach so long as they are practiced in a suitably male environment. It is not only women's work in and of itself that is degrading but any work on female turf. It may be true, as Brenton (1966) says, that "the secure man can wash a dish, diaper a baby, and throw the dirty clothes into the washing machine—or do anything else women used to do exclusively—without thinking twice about it" (p. 211), but not all men are that secure. To a great many men such chores are demasculinizing. The apron is shameful on a man in the kitchen; it is all right at the carpenter's bench.

The male world may look upon the man who shares household responsibilities as, in effect, a scab. One informant tells the interviewer about a conversation on the job: "What, are you crazy?" his hard-hat fellow workers ask him when he speaks of helping his wife. "The guys want to kill me. 'You son of a bitch! You are getting us in trouble.' . . . The men get really mad" (Lein, 1979, p. 492). Something more than persiflage is involved here. We are fairly familiar with the trauma associated with the invasion by women of the male work turf, the hazing women can be subjected to, and the male resentment of admitting them except into their own segregated areas. The corresponding entrance of men into the traditional turf of women—the kitchen or the nursery—has analogous but not identical concomitants.

Pleck and Lang (1979) tell us that men are now beginning to change in the direction of greater involvement in family life. "Men's family behavior is beginning to change, becoming increasingly congruent with the long-standing psychological significance of the family in their lives" (p. 1). They measure this greater involvement by way of the help they offer with homemaking chores. Scanzoni (1975), on the basis of a survey of over 3,000 husbands and wives, concludes that at least in households in which wives are in the labor force, there is the "possibility of a different pattern in which responsibility for households would unequivocally fall equally on husbands as well as wives" (p. 38). A brave new world indeed. Still, when we look at the reality around us, the pace seems intolerably slow. The responsibilities of the old good-provider role have attenuated far faster than have its prerogatives and privileges.

A considerable amount of thought has been devoted to studying the effects of the large influx of women into the work force. An equally interesting question is what the effect will be if a large number of men actually do increase their participation in the family and the household. Will men find the apron shameful? What if we were to ask fathers to alternate with mothers in being in the home when youngsters come home from school? Would fighting adolescent drug abuse be more successful if fathers and mothers were equally engaged in it? If the school could confer with fathers as often as with mothers? If the father accompanied children when they went shopping for clothes? If fathers spent as much time with children as do mothers?

Even as husbands, let alone as fathers, the new pattern is not without trauma. Hall and Hall (1979), in their study of two-career couples, report that the most serious fights among such couples occur not in the bedroom, but in the kitchen, between couples who profess a commitment to equality but who find actually implementing it difficult. A young professional reports that he is philosophically committed to egalitarianism in marriage and tries hard to practice it, but it does not work. He even feels guilty about this. The stresses involved in reworking roles may have an impact on health. A study of engineers and accountants finds poorer health among those with employed wives than among those with nonemployed wives (Burke & Wier, 1976). The processes involved in role change have been compared with those involved in deprogramming a cult member. Are they part of the increasing sense of marriage and parenthood as "all burdens and restrictions"?

The demise of the good-provider role also calls for consideration of other questions: What does the demotion of the good provider to the status of senior provider or even more coprovider do to him? To marriage? To gender identity? What does expanding the role of housewife to that of junior provider or even coprovider do to her? To marriage? To gender identity? Much will of course depend on the social and psychological ambience in which changes take place.

A PARABLE

I began this essay with a proverbial woman. I close it with a modern parable by William H. Chafe (Note 5), a historian who also keeps his eye on the current scene. Jack and Jill, both planning professional careers, he as doctor, she as lawyer, marry at age 24. She works to put him through medical school in the expectation that he will then finance her through law school. A child is born during the husband's internship, as planned. But in order for him to support her through professional training as planned, he will have to take time out from his career. After two years they decide that both will continue their training on a part-time basis, sharing household responsibilities and using day-care services. Both find part-time positions and work out flexible work schedules that leave both of them time for child care and companionship with one another. They live happily ever after.

That's the end? you ask incredulously. Well, not exactly. For, as Chafe (Note 5) points out, as usual the personal is also political:

> Obviously such a scenario presumes a radical transformation of the personal values that today's young people bring to their relationships as well as a readiness on the part of social and economic institutions to encourage, or at least make possible, the development of equality between men and women. (p. 28)

The good-provider role may be on its way out, but its legitimate successor has not yet appeared on the scene.

NOTES

1. Hesselbart, S. *Some Underemphasized Issues About Men, Women, and Work.* Unpublished manuscript, 1978.

2. Douvan, E. *Family Roles in a Twenty-year Perspective.* Paper presented at the Radcliffe Pre-Centennial Conference. Cambridge, Massachusetts, April 2–4, 1978.

3. Veroff, J. *Psychological Orientations to the Work Role: 1957–1976.* Unpublished manuscript, 1978.

4. Shostak, A. *Working-class Americans at Home: Changing Expectations of Manhood.* Unpublished manuscript, 1973.

5. Chafe, W. *The Challenge of Sex Equality: A New Culture or Old Values Revisited?* Paper presented at the Radcliffe Pre-Centennial Conference. Cambridge, Massachusetts, April 2–4, 1978.

REFERENCES

Babcock, B., Freedman, A. E., Norton, E. H., & Ross, S. C. *Sex Discrimination and the Law: Causes and Remedies.* Boston: Little, Brown, 1975.

Bernard, J. *Women, Wives, Mothers.* Chicago: Aldine, 1975.

Bernard, J. Homosociality and female depression. *Journal of Social Issues,* 1976, *32,* 207–224.

Boulding, E. Familial constraints on women's work roles. *SIGNS: Journal of Women in Culture and Society.* 1976, *1,* 95–118.

Brenton, M. *The American Male.* New York: Coward-McCann, 1966.

Burke, R., & Weir, T. Relationships of wives' employment status to husband, wife and pair satisfaction and performance. *Journal of Marriage and the Family,* 1976, *38,* 279–287.

David, D. S. & Brannon, R. (Eds.). *The Forty-nine Percent Majority: The Male Sex Role.* Reading, Mass.: Addison-Wesley, 1976.

Demos, J. The American family in past time. *American Scholar*, 1974, *43*, 422–446.

Farrell, W. *The Liberated Man.* New York: Random House, 1974.

Fasteau, M. F. *The Male Machine.* New York: McGraw-Hill, 1974.

Fiedler, L. *Love and Death in the American Novel.* New York: Meredith, 1962.

Foner, P. S. *Women and the American Labor Movement.* New York: Free Press, 1979.

Freud, S. *Civilization and its Discontents.* New York: Doubleday-Anchor, 1958. (Originally published, 1930.)

Goldberg, H. *The Hazards of Being Male.* New York: New American Library, 1976.

Gould, R. E. Measuring masculinity by the size of a paycheck. In J. E. Pleck & J. Sawyer (Eds.), *Men and Masculinity.* Englewood Cliffs, N. J.: Prentice-Hall, 1974. (Also published in *Ms.,* June 1973, pp. 18ff.)

Hall, D., & Hall, F. *The Two-career Couple.* Reading, Mass.: Addison-Wesley, 1979.

Jones, C. A. *A Review of Child Support Payment Performance.* Washington, D.C.: Urban Institute, 1976.

Keniston, K. *The Uncommitted: Alienated Youth in American Society.* New York: Harcourt, Brace & World, 1965.

Komarovsky, M. *The Unemployed Man and His Family.* New York: Dryden Press, 1940.

Lefkowitz, B. Life without work. *Newsweek,* May 14, 1979, p. 31.

Lein, L. Responsibility in the allocation of tasks. *Family Coordinator,* 1979, *28,* 489–496.

Liebow, E. *Tally's Corner.* Boston: Little, Brown, 1966.

Lopata, H. *Occupational Housewife.* New York: Oxford University Press, 1971.

Mainardi, P. The politics of housework. In R. Morgan (Ed.), *Sisterhood is Powerful.* New York: Vintage Books, 1970.

Pleck, J. H., & Lang, L. Men's family work: Three perspectives and some new data. *Family Coordinator,* 1979, *28,* 481–488.

Pleck, J. H., & Sawyer, J. (Eds.), *Men and Masculinity.* Englewood Cliffs, N.J.: Prentice-Hall, 1974.

Rainwater, L., & Yancy, W. L. *The Moynihan Report and the Politics of Controversy.* Cambridge, Mass.: M.I.T. Press, 1967.

Sarason, S. B. *Work, Aging, and Social Change.* New York: Free Press, 1977.

Scanzoni, J. H. *Sex Roles, Life Styles, and Childbearing: Changing Patterns in Marriage and the Family.* New York: Free Press, 1975.

Scanzoni, J. H. An historical perspective on husband-wife bargaining power and marital dissolution. In G. Levinger & O. Moles (Eds.), *Divorce and Separation in America.* New York: Basic Books, 1979.

Smith, R. E. (Ed.), *The Subtle Revolution.* Washington, D.C.: Urban Institute, 1979.

Smuts, R. W. *Women and Work in America.* New York: Columbia University Press, 1959.

Snyder, L. The deserting, non-supporting father: Scapegoat of family non-policy. *Family Coordinator,* 1979, *38,* 594–598.

Tocqueville, A. de. *Democracy in America*. New York: J. & H. G. Hangley, 1840.

Warner, W. L., & Ablegglen, J. O. *Big Business Leaders in America*. New York: Harper, 1955.

Yankelovich, D. The new psychological contracts at work. *Psychology Today*, May, 1978, pp. 46–47, 49–50.

Zborowski, M., & Herzog, E. *Life is With People*. New York: Schocken Books, 1952.

R E A D I N G

9

Why Men Resist

William J. Goode

For many women, the very title of my essay is an exercise in banality, for there is no puzzle. To analyze the peculiar thoughtways of men seems unnecessary, since ultimately their resistance is that of dominant groups throughout history: they enjoy an exploitive position that yields them an unearned profit in money, power, and prestige. Why should they give it up?

That answer contains, of course, some parts of the truth, but we shall move more effectively toward equality only if we grasp much more of the truth than that bitter view reveals. If it were completely true, then the great power of men would have made all societies male-vanity cultures, in which women are kept behind blank walls and forced to work at productive tasks only with their sisters, while men laze away their hours in parasitic pleasure. In fact, one can observe that the position of women varies a good deal by class, by society, and over time, and no one has succeeded in proving that those variations are only the result of men's exploitation.

Indeed, there are inherent socioeconomic contradictions in any attempt by males to create a fully exploitative set of material advantages for all males. Moreover, there are inherent emotional contradictions in any effort to achieve full domination in that intimate sphere.

As to the first contradiction, women—and men, too, in the same situation, who are powerless, slavish, and ignorant are most easily exploitable, and thus

From *Rethinking the Family*, 1992. Barrie Thorne and Marilyn Valom (Eds.). Boston: Northeastern University Press.

there are always some male pressures to place them in that position. Unfortunately, such women (or men) do not yield much surplus product. In fact, they do not produce much at all. Women who are freer and are more in command of productive skills, as in hunting and gathering societies and increasingly in modern industrial ones, produce far more, but they are also more resistant to exploitation or domination. Without understanding that powerful relationship, men have moved throughout history toward one or the other of these great choices, with their built-in disadvantages and advantages.

As to emotional ties, men would like to be lords of their castle and to be loved absolutely—if successful, this is the cheapest exploitative system—but in real life this is less likely to happen unless one loves in return. In that case what happens is what happens in real life: men care about the joys and sorrows of the women to whom they are attached. Mutual caring reduces the degree to which men are willing to exploit their wives, mothers, and sisters. More interesting, their caring also takes the form of wanting to prevent other men from exploiting these women when they are in the outside world. That is, men as individuals know that they are to be trusted, and so should have great power, but other men cannot be trusted, and therefore the laws should restrain such fellows.

These large sets of contrary tensions have some effect on even those contemporary men who do not believe that the present relations between men and women are unjust. Both sets, moreover, support the present trend toward greater equality. In short, men do resist, but these and other tensions prevent them from resisting as fully as they might otherwise, and not so much as a cynical interpretation of their private attitudes would expect. On the other hand, they do resist somewhat more strenuously than we should predict from their public assertion in favor of, for example, equal pay, or slogans like "liberty and justice for all."

Why is that resistance so strenuous? My attempt here to answer that question is necessarily limited. Even to present the latest data on the supposed psychological traits of males would require more space than is available here. I shall try to avoid the temptation of simply describing men's reactions to the women's movement, although I do plan to inform you of men's attitudes toward some aspects of equality. I shall try to avoid defending men, except to the extent that explaining them may be a defense. And, as is already obvious, I shall not assert that we are on the brink of a profound, sudden change in sex-role allocations in the direction of equality, for we must never underestimate the cunning or the staying power of those in charge. Finally, because we are all observers of men, it is unlikely that can bring forward many findings that are entirely unknown to you. At best, I can suggest some fruitful, perhaps new, ways of looking at male roles. Within these limitations, I shall focus on the following themes:

1. As against the rather narrow definition of men's roles to be found in the current literature on the topic, I want to remind you of a much wider range of traditionally approved roles in this and other cultures.

2. As against the conspiracy theory of the oppression of women, I shall suggest a modest "sociology of the dominant group" to interpret men's behavior and

thinking about male roles and thus offer some robust hypotheses about why they resist.

3. I shall point to two central areas of role behavior, occupations and domestic tasks, where change seems glacial at present and men's resistance strong.

4. As against those who feel that if utopia does not arrive with the next full moon, we should all despair, I shall point to some processes now occurring that are different from any in recorded history and that will continue to press toward more fundamental changes in men's social positions and role in this as well as other countries of the world.

THE RANGE OF SEX ROLES

Let me begin by reminding you of the standard sociological view about the allocation of sex roles. First, although it is agreed that we can, with only small error, divide the population into males and females, the biological differences between the two that might affect the distribution of sex roles—which sex is supposed to do which social tasks, which should have which rights—are much too small to determine the large differences in sex-role allocation within any given society or to explain the curious doctrines that serve to uphold it. Second, even if some differences would give an advantage to men (or women) in some tasks or achievements, the overlap in talent is so great that a large minority of women (or men)—perhaps even a majority—could do any task as well as could members of the other sex. Third, the biological differences are too fixed in anatomy and physiology to account for the wide diversity of sex-role allocation we observe when we compare different societies over time and cultures.

Consequently, most of the sex-role allocation must be explained by how we rear children, by the sexual division of labor, by the cultural definitions of what is appropriate to the sexes, and by the social pressures we put on the two sexes to keep each in its place. Since human beings created these role assignments, they can also change them. On the other hand, these roles afford large advantages to men (e.g., opportunity, range of choices, mobility, payoffs for what is accomplished, cultivation of skills, authority, and prestige) in this and every other society we know. Consequently, men are likely to resist large alterations in roles. They will do so even though they understand that in exchange for their privileges, they have to pay high costs in morbidity, mortality, and failure.[1] As a consequence of this fact about men's position, it can be supposed that they will resist unless their ability to rig the system in their favor is somehow reduced. It is my belief that this capacity is in fact being undermined somewhat, though not at a rapid rate.

A first glance at descriptions of the male role, especially as described in the literature on mass media, social stereotypes, family roles, and personality attributes, suggests that the male role is definite, narrow, and agreed upon. Males, we are told, are pressed into a specific mold. For example, "the male role prescribes that men be active, aggressive, competitive, . . . while the female role prescribes that women should be nurturant, warm, altruistic . . . and the like."[2] The male role requires the suppression of emotion: "the male role, as personally and socially defined, requires men to appear tough, objective, striving, achieving, unsentimental. . . . If he weeps, if he shows weakness, he will likely be viewed as unmanly." Or: "Men are programmed to be strong and 'aggressive.' "[3] Those statements were published some time ago, but the flood of books since then has only elaborated that description.

We are so accustomed to reading such descriptions that we almost believe them, unless we stop to ask, first, how many men do we actually know who carry out these social prescriptions (i.e., how many are emotionally anesthetized, aggressive, physically tough and daring, unwilling or unable to give nurturance to a child)? Second, and this is the test of a social role, do they lose their membership cards in the male fraternity if they fail in these respects? If socialization and social pressures are so all-powerful, where are all the John Wayne types in our society? Or, to ask a more searching question, how seriously should we take such sex-role prescriptions if so few men live up to them? The recent creation of male groups chanting around a campfire, searching for the lost primitive hunter within each bosom, suggests that our generation can not even play the role anymore without a great deal of coaching.

The key fact is not that many men do not live up to such prescriptions; that is obvious. They never did. Rather, many other qualities and performances have always been viewed as acceptable or admirable, and this is true even among boys, who are often thought to be strong supporters of sex stereotypes. The macho boy is admired, but so is the one who edits the school newspaper, who draws cartoons, or who is simply a warm friend. There are at least a handful of ways of being an admired professor. Indeed, a common feminist complaint against the present system is that women are much more narrowly confined in the ways they are permitted to be professors, or members of any occupation.

But we can go further. A much more profound observation is that oppressed groups are *typically* given narrow ranges of social roles, while dominant groups afford their members a far wider set of behavior patterns, each qualitatively different but each still accepted or esteemed in varying degrees. One of the privileges granted, or simply assumed, by ruling groups, is that they can indulge in a variety of eccentricities while still demanding and getting a fair measure of authority or prestige. Consider in this connection, to cite only one spectacular example, the crotchets and quirks cultivated by the English upper classes over the centuries.

Moreover, if we enlarge our vision to encompass other times and places, the range becomes even greater. We are not surprised to observe Latin American men embrace one another, Arab or Indian boys walk together hand in hand, or seminary students being gentle. The male role prescriptions that commonly appear in the literature do not describe correctly the male ideal in Jewish culture, which embodies a love of music, learning, and literature; an avoidance of physical violence; an acceptance of tears and sentiment, nurturance, and a sensitivity to others feelings. In the South that I knew half a century ago, young rural boys were expected to nurture their younger siblings, and male-male relations were ideally expected to be tender, supporting, and expressed occasionally by embraces. Among my own kin, some fathers then kissed their school-age sons; among Greek Americans in New York City, that practice continues many decades later. Or, to consider England once more, let us remember the admired men of Elizabethan England. True enough, one ideal was the violent, daring Sir Francis Drake and the brawling poet Ben Jonson. But men also expressed themselves in kissing and embracing, writing love poems to one another, donning decorative (not to say gaudy and flamboyant) clothing, and studying flowers as well as the fiery heavens.

I assert, then, that men manage to be in charge of things in all societies but that their very control permits them to create a wide range of ideal male roles, with the consequence that large numbers of men, not just a few, can locate rewarding positions in the social structure. Thereby, too, they considerably narrow the options left for feminine sex roles. Feminists especially resent the narrowness of the feminine role in informal interaction, where they feel they are dealt with only as women, however this may be softened by personal warmth or affection. . . .

THE SOCIOLOGY OF SUPERORDINATES

That set of relationships is only part of the complex male view, and I want to continue with my sketch of the main elements in what may be called the "sociology of superordinates." That is, I believe there are some general principles or regularities to be found in the relationships between superordinates—here, the sex-class called males—and subordinates, in this instance women. Those regularities do not justify, but they do explain in some degree, the modern resistance of men to their social situation.[4] Here are some of them:

1. The observations made by either men or women about members of the other sex are limited and somewhat biased by what they are most interested in and by their lack of opportunity to observe behind the scenes of each others' lives.[5] However, far less of what men do is determined by women; what men do affects women much more. As a consequence, men are often simply less motivated to observe carefully many aspects of women's behavior and activity because women's behavior does not affect as much what men propose to do. By contrast, almost everything men do will affect what women *have* to do, and thus women are motivated to observe men's behavior as keenly as they can.

2. Since any given cohort of men know they did not create the system that gives them their advantages, they reject any charges that they conspired to dominate women.

3. Since men, like other dominants or superordinates, take for granted the system that gives them their status, they are not aware of how much the social structure, from attitude patterns to laws, pervasively yields small, cumulative, and eventually large advantages in most competitions. As a consequence, they assume that their greater accomplishments are actually

the result of inborn superiority. Dominants are never satisfied with their rule unless they can also justify it.

4. As a corollary to this male view, when men weigh their situation, they are more aware of the burdens and responsibilities they bear than of their unearned advantages.

5. Superiors, and thus men, do not easily notice the talents or accomplishments of subordinates, and men have not in the past seen much wisdom in giving women more opportunities for growth, for women, in their view, are not capable of much anyway, especially in the areas of men's special skills. As is obvious, this is a self-validating process. Thus, few women have embarrassed men in the past by becoming superior in those areas. When they did, their superiority was seen, and is often still seen, as an odd exception. As a consequence, men see their superior position as a just one.

6. Men view even small losses of deference, advantages, or opportunities as large threats and losses. Their own gains, or their maintenance of old advantages, are not noticed as much.[6]

Although the male view is similar to that of superordinates generally, as the foregoing principles suggest, one cannot simply equate the two. The structural position of males is different from that of superordinate groups, classes, ethnic populations, or castes. Males are, first, not a group, but a social segment or a statistical aggregate within the society. They share much of a common destiny, but they share few if any group or collective goals (within small groups they may be buddies, but not with all males). Second, males share with certain women whatever gain or loss they experience as members of high or low castes, ethnic groups, or classes. For example, women in a ruling stratum share with their men a high social rank deference from the lower orders, and so on; men in a lowly Indian caste share that rank with their women, too. In modern societies, men and women in the same family are on a more or less equal basis with respect to "inheritance, educational opportunity (at least undergraduate), personal consumption of goods, most rights before the law, and the love and responsibility of their children."[7] They are not fully equal, to be sure, but much more equal than are members of very different castes or social classes.

Moreover, from the male view, women also enjoy certain exemptions: "freedom from military conscription, whole or partial exemption from certain kinds of heavy work, preferential courtesies of various kinds." Indeed, men have generally believed, on the whole, that their own lot is the more difficult one.[8]

It is possible, however, that feminist cries of indignation have touched their hearts, and those of women too, in recent years. Without giving a breakdown by gender, Gallup announced "a remarkable shift of opinion" in 1989: almost half those polled asserted that men "have a better life" than women, compared with only 32 percent in 1975. Almost certainly many women have been convinced, since nearly two-thirds of younger women felt that way.[9] Fifty-nine percent of a 1990 *Times Mirror* sample of women aged eighteen to twenty-four agreed, but so did 65 percent of the men. . . .

DOMESTIC DUTIES AND JOBS

So far, the opinion data give some small cause for optimism. Nevertheless, all announcements of the imminent arrival of utopias are premature. Although men's approval of more equality for women has risen, the record in two major areas of men's roles—the spheres of home and occupation—gives some reason for optimism, but little for rejoicing. Here we can be brief, for though voluminous and complex data exist, the main conclusions can easily be summarized.[10] Changes have occurred, but they are not great if we consider the society as a whole and focus on changes in behavior. In short, men have gained great credit (in conformity with their higher ranking) for a few modest steps toward equality.

Let us consider first the domestic role of men. The many complex studies done during the past decade have at least shown how difficult it is to pin down the causes of the present division of labor in the home. Thus, a simple summary is not adequate, but I note some salient findings here.

Women who work full-time have reduced the hours they spend on household tasks—in some studies, by almost half, while the reduction is substantial even if only routine tasks are included.[11] Husbands do not do much more housework if their wives are employed full time; nevertheless, over time men have increased their contribution (especially in child care), although the increase must be measured by a few minutes per day. White men and men with high incomes are least likely to increase their contribution. About half of both husbands and wives believe they ought to share equally; four-fifths think this of child care.[12] This represents a substantial change among wives, since until the end of the 1970s only about one-fourth of wives stated that they thought their husbands should work more, while the vanguard of opinion was led by the young, the educated, and African Americans.[13]

I have sometimes suggested that men generally decide if they must contribute more equally to housework, then they begin to feel the seduction of doing it in a quicker, more slovenly fashion. One study of a highly educated sample suggests this relationship: both spouses at least express more satisfaction when the division is equal, but the two want different things. The man wants to spend only a few hours in household work, while the women wants the traditional chores (laundry, shopping, cooking) to be shared.[14] In the United States, as in other countries, men are quicker to express support for equality in that sphere than actually to practice it. They may be wise in doing so, for that is surely less costly, at least for the present.

Of course, there are some differences. If a child two years or younger is in the house, the father does more, especially in child care. Better-educated husbands do a bit more, and so do younger husbands. But the indisputable fact is that men's domestic contribution does not change much whether or not they work, and whether or not their wives work.

With reference to the second large area of men's roles, holding jobs, we observe two further general principles of the relations between superordinates and those at lesser ranks. One is that men do not, in general, feel threatened by competition from women if they believe that the competition is fair and that women do not have an inside track. (To be sure, against overwhelming evidence, many do believe women enjoy that preference, while many whites believe that Blacks also have the inside track.) Men still feel that they are superior and will do better if given the chance. Since no society has actually tried the radical notion of genuinely fair competition, they have little reason to fear as yet. Except in a few occupations, they have lost very little ground. Women's position (by some measures) did improve during the 1970s, but changed very little in the 1980s.[15]

The second general principle of superordination noted here is that those who hold advantaged positions in the social structure (men, in this case) can perceive or observe that they are being flooded by people they consider their inferiors—women, Blacks, or the lower classes—while the massive statistical fact is that only a few such people are rising by much. There are several causes of this seeming paradox.

First, the new arrivals are more visible, by being different from those who have held the jobs up to this time. The second cause is our perception of relative numbers. Since there are far fewer positions at higher job levels, only a few new arrivals constitute a fair-size minority of the total at that level. Third, the mass media emphasize the hiring of women in jobs that seem not to be traditional for them, for that is considered news. Men's structural position, then, causes them to perceive radical change here even when little has taken place, and they resist it.

Nevertheless, the general conclusion does not change much. There is progress, but it is not at all clear-cut. After all, as long as the entrance of a few women into good jobs is news, the reality is less rosy than one might hope. Here are a few details:

The number of businesses owned by women increased by 63 percent between 1982 and 1987.[16]

The percentage of physicians who were women rose to 20 percent by 1988, an increase of two-thirds from 1980.

Women made almost no inroads into the skilled crafts.

Women made up almost one-half of all bakers, but nearly all simply put the dough through the final process in retail stores.

As buyers and as administrators or managers in education, auditing, personnel, and training, women occupied about one-half of the jobs by 1988. However, they made up only about 3 percent of the top executives in large U.S. companies by 1991, almost no change from 1980. In general, their earnings in this group of managerial jobs were about two-thirds of male salaries.[17]

As bus drivers and bartenders, women had almost half of the jobs.

Over the decade, women's salaries rose; instead of making two-thirds of men's wages, they were making 72 percent.

The strongest variable that determines the lower wages of women is occupational segregation by sex, and that changed very little in the 1980s.[18] The blunt fact is that women have been able to enter a given occupation easily only if men longer defend that territory. Or, more dramatically, the common pattern of "feminization" in most occupations is simple: They are rising on an elevator in a crumbling building. The job itself is being downgraded. They get better wages than other women, perhaps, but lower wages than men once made in those occupations.

Although the mass figures are correct, we need not discount all our daily observation either. We do see women entering formerly masculine jobs, from garbage collecting to corporate management. That helps undermine sex stereotypes and thereby becomes a force against inequality. Although occupational segregation continues to be strong, it did decline in most professions (e.g., engineering, dentistry, science, law, medicine). That is, the percentage of women in those professions did rise. Generally they doubled or trebled in the period 1970–88.[19] Of course, the absolute percentages of women in such professions remain modest (4–22 percent), because in occupations where almost everyone was once male, it is not possible to recruit, train, and hire enough women to achieve equality within even a generation. Still, the trend seems clear.

A secondary effect of these increasing numbers should be noted. Percentages are important, but so are absolute numbers. When women lawyers increase from about seven thousand to more than a hundred thousand, they become a much larger social force, even though they still form no more than about 22 percent of the total occupation. When women medical students, while remaining a minority in their classes, increase in number so that they can form committees, petition administrators, or give solidarity to one another against any traditional masculine badgering and disesteem, they greatly increase their influence on discriminatory attitudes and behavior. That is, as their rise in numbers permits the formation of real groups in any occupation, their power mounts faster (except at the very start) than the numbers or the percentages. Thus, changes occur even when the percentage of the occupation made up of women is not really large.

BASES OF PRESENT CHANGES

Most large-scale, objective measures of men's roles show little change over the past decade, but men do feel now and then that their position is in question, and their security somewhat fragile. I believe they are right, for they sense a set of forces that lie deeper and are more powerful than the day-to-day negotiation and renegotiation of advantage among individual husbands and wives, fathers and children, or bosses and those who work for them. Men are troubled by this new situation.

The conditions we live in are different from those of any earlier civilization, and they give less support to men's claims of superiority than perhaps any other historical era. When these conditions weaken that support, men can rely only on previous tradition, on power, or on their attempts to socialize their children to shore up their faltering advantages. Such rhetoric is not likely to be successful against the new objective conditions and the claims of aggrieved women. Thus, men are correct when they feel they are losing some of their privileges, even if many continue to smile at the rhetoric of the women's liberation movement.

The new conditions can be listed concretely, but I shall also give you a theoretical formulation of the process. Concretely, because of the increased use of various mechanical gadgets and devices, fewer tasks require much strength. As to those that still require strength, most men cannot do them either. Women can now do more household tasks that men once felt only they could do, and still more tasks are done by repair specialists called in to do them. With the development of modern warfare, there are few if any important combat activities that only men can do. Even now, their "auxiliary" tasks take them in and around battle zones as a matter of course. Women are much better educated than before.

With each passing year, psychological and sociological research reduces the areas in which men are reported to excel over women and discloses far more overlap in talents, so that even when males still seem to have an advantage, it is but slight. It is also becoming more widely understood that the top posts in government and business are not best filled by the stereotypical aggressive male but by the people, male or female, who are sensitive to others' needs, adept at obtaining cooperation, and skilled in social relations. Indeed, had male management in a number of U.S. industries followed that truth over the past decade, their failure to meet Japanese competition would surely have been less. Finally, in one sphere after another, the number of women who try to achieve rises, and so does the number who succeed.

Although the pressure of new laws has its direct effect on these conditions, the laws themselves arise from an awareness of the foregoing forces. Phrased in more theoretical terms, the underlying shift is toward the decreasing marginal utility of males, and this I suspect is the main source of men's resistance to women's liberation. That is, fewer people believe that what the male does is indispensable, is nonsubstitutable, or adds such a special value to any endeavor that it justifies his extra "price" or reward. In past wars, for example, males enjoyed a very high value not only because it was felt that they could do the job better than women but also because they might well make the key or marginal difference between being conquered and remaining free. In many societies, their marginal utility came from their contribution of animal protein through hunting. As revolutionary heroes, explorers, hunters, warriors, and daring capitalist entrepreneurs, men felt, and doubtless their women did too, that their contribution was beyond anything women could do. Without question, this would not be true of all men, but it would have been true of men as a distinct group. Men thereby earned extra privileges of rank, authority, and creature services.

It is not then as individuals, as persons, that males will be deemed less worthy in the future or their contributions less needed. Rather, they will be seen as having no claims to extra rewards solely because they are members of the male sex-class. This is part of a still broader trend of our generation, which will also increasingly deny that being white or upper-class produces a marginally superior result and thus justifies extra privileges.

The relations of individuals are subject to continuous renegotiation as people try to gain or keep advantages or cast off burdens. They fail or succeed in part because one or the other person has special resources or deficits that are unique to that individual. Over the long run, however, the outcome of those negotiations depends on the deeper social forces I have been describing, which ultimately determine which qualities or performances are more or less valued.

Men now perceive that they may be losing some of their advantages and that more aspects of their social roles are subject to public challenge and renegotiation than in the past. They resist these changes, and we can suppose they will continue to do so. In all such changes, there are gains and losses. Commonly, when people at lower social ranks gain freedom, those at higher ranks lose some power or centrality. When those at the lower ranks also lose some protection, some support, those at the higher ranks lose some of the burden of responsibility. It is also true that the care or help given by any dominant group in the past was never as much as their members believed, and their loss in political power or economic rule was never as great as they feared.

On the other hand, I know of no instance when a group or social stratum gained its freedom or moved toward more respect and then its members decided that they did not want it. Therefore, although men will not joyfully give up their rank, in spite of its burdens, neither will women decide that they would like to get back the older feminine privileges, accompanied by the lack of respect and material rewards that went with those courtesies.

I believe that men perceive their roles as being under threat in a world that is different from any in the past. No society has yet come even close to equality between the sexes, but the modern social forces described here did not exist before, either. At the most cautious, we must concede that the conditions favoring a trend toward more equality are more favorable than at any previous time in history. If we have little reason to conclude that equality is at hand, let us at least rejoice that we are still marching in the right direction.

NOTES

1. Herbert Goldberg, *The Hazards of Being Male* (New York: Nash, 1976), and Patricia C. Sexton, *The Feminized Male: Classrooms, White Collars, and the Decline of Manliness* (New York: Random House, 1969). On the recognition of disadvantages, see J. S. Chafetz, *Masculine/Feminine or Human?* (Itasca, Ill.: Peacock, 1974), 56 ff.

2. Joseph H. Pleck, "The Psychology of Sex Roles: Traditional and New Views," in *Women and Men: Changing Roles, Relationships, and Perceptions*, ed. Libby A. Cater and Anne F. Scott (New York: Aspen Institute for Humanistic Studies, 1976), 182. Pleck has carried out the most extensive research on male roles, and I am indebted to him for special help in this inquiry.

3. Sidney M. Jourard, "Some Lethal Aspects of the Male Role," in *Men and Masculinity*, ed. Joseph H. Pleck and Jack Sawyer (Englewood Cliffs, N.J.: Prentice-Hall, 1974), 22, and Irving London, "Frigidity, Sensitivity, and Sexual Roles," in *Men and Masculinity*, ed. Pleck and Sawyer, 42. See also the summary of such traits in I. K. Braverman et al., "Sex-Role Stereotypes: A Current Appraisal," in *Women and Achievement*, ed. Martha T. S. Mednick, S. S. Tangri, and Lois W. Hoffman (New York: Wiley, 1974), 32–47.

4. Robert Bierstedt's "The Sociology of the Majority," in his *Power and Progress* (New York: McGraw-Hill, 1974), 199–220, does not state these principles, but I was led to them by thinking about his analysis.

5. Robert K. Merton, in "The Perspectives of Insiders and Outsiders," in his *The Sociology of Science* (Chicago: University of Chicago Press, 1973), 99–136, has analyzed this view in some detail.

6. This general pattern is noted at various points in my monograph *The Celebration of Heroes: Prestige as a Social Control System* (Berkeley and Los Angeles: University of California Press, 1979).

7. Erving Goffman, "The Arrangement between the Sexes," *Theory and Society* 4 (1977): 307.

8. Hazel Erskine, "The Polls: Women's Roles," *Public Opinion Quarterly 35* (Summer 1971).

9. Linda DeStefano and Diane Colasanto, Gallup Organization press release, 5 February 1989. For the *Times Mirror* sample, see Times Mirror Center for the People and the Press, press release, September 1990, 5.

10. By now, the research data on household tasks are voluminous, their conclusions complex, and by the time they are published they may be somewhat dated. For comparison with other countries, see Jonathan Gershuny and John P. Robinson, "Historic Changes in the Household Division of Labor," *Demography* 25 (1988): 537–52. See also Linda Thompson and Alexis J. Walker, "Gender in Families: Women and Men in Marriage, Work, and Parenthood," *Journal of Marriage and the Family* 51 (1989): 845–71; Mary H. Benin and Joan Agostinelli, "Husbands' and Wives' Satisfaction with the Division of Labor," *Journal of Marriage and the Family* 50 (1988): 349–61; and Beth A. Shelton, "The Distribution of Household Tasks," *Journal of Family Issues* 11 (1990): 115–35. Joseph Pleck was a leader in these studies during the 1970s and 1980s.

11. Shelton, "Distribution of Household Tasks," table 2, p. 124; Gershuny and Robinson, "Historical Changes," 550.

12. Thompson and Walker, "Gender in Families," 857.

13. Arland Thornton and Deborah S. Freedman, "Changes in the Sex Role Attitudes of Women, 1962–1977," *American Sociological Review* 44 (1979): 833.

14. Benin and Agostinelli, "Husbands' and Wives' Satisfaction," 360.

15. For an excellent analysis of the many complex processes involved in these changes, see Barbara F. Reskin and Patricia A. Roos, *Job Queues, Gender Queues* (Philadelphia: Temple University Press, 1990).

16. U.S. Department of Commerce, Bureau of the Census, *Statistical Abstract of the United States, 1991* (Washington, D.C.: GPO, 1992).

17. These and other related data were published in *U.S. News and World Report*, 17 June 1991, from a study of the "glass ceiling" conducted for the Department of Labor but not officially issued.

18. Reskin and Roos, *Job Queues, Gender Queues*, tables 1.7, 1.8. See especially the case studies of changes in occupational segregation in ibid., part 2. In the usual case of "desegregation," women move into men's jobs (bartending, in-store baking, bus driving, banking) when those jobs are downgraded, usually technologically, so that the wages no longer attract men. Most of the expansion of women's jobs has occurred in "female" jobs, service jobs at lower levels.

19. Ibid., 19. On the earlier period, see also Victor R. Fuchs, "A Note on Sex Segregation in Professional Occupations," *Explorations in Economic Research* 2, no. 1 (Winter 1975): 105–11.

CHAPTER 4

⬦

SEXUALITY

READING

10

Finding a Partner

Robert T. Michael, John H. Gagnon, Edward D. Laumann, and Gina Kolata

At one time or another, almost everyone has felt excluded from the world of loving couples. Almost everyone has watched young lovers walk hand in hand through a park on a balmy spring afternoon or noticed how many women, young and old, beautiful and not so beautiful, sport wedding rings, or how many men, attractive or not, prominently display pictures of their wife and family in their office. And almost everyone has asked: How do people meet their mates?

We like to believe that we will know immediately when we meet Mr. or Ms. Right. We believe we will fall in love in an irrational way, that falling in love involves physical chemistry, an affair of the heart, an experience that is out of our control. Most Americans abhor the idea of an arranged marriage and take umbrage when well-meaning friends and family members try to butt into their personal lives.

It's an old image: Cupid with his bow. Jane Eyre. Cinderella. Famous lines from centuries past. "No sooner met but they looked; no sooner looked but they loved," Shakespeare wrote in *As You Like It*.

This is the image conveyed by the familiar song from the musical *South Pacific:* "Some enchanted evening, you will see a stranger . . . across a crowded room." We have the classic books, like Daphne du Maurier's ever-popular *Rebecca*, in which the heroine is a poor girl, working as a paid companion to a rich older woman, when the fabulously rich Max de Winter notices her, immediately marries her, and whisks her away to his mansion. We have the movie *Pretty Woman* in which the rich young man falls in love with the poor prostitute.

Yet when people tell how they met the people they married, their stories can sound almost boring, all too mundane—meeting at school, being introduced by friends. The stories scarcely vary, whether the meetings took place decades ago or last month. Rare indeed are the stories of the alluring and mysterious stranger, so totally different from oneself, found in a chance encounter.

Hillary Rodham Clinton and Bill Clinton met when they both were law students at Yale, two bright students on their way up and very much alike—both white, both Protestant, both ambitious. Francis Collins, a doctor and scientist who directs the Human Genome Project, said he married the first girl he ever kissed, his high-school sweetheart. The two began dating when they were fifteen years old and married when they were nineteen.

Ordinary everyday Americans tell the same sort of stories. Martha Bari, a forty-year-old graduate student in art history at the University of Maryland, was introduced to Mike DiPirro, a physicist at Goddard Space Center, by her friend and fellow graduate student, whose husband was Mike's friend and colleague at work. The two fell in love and married a year later.

Kathy, a music student, met Todd, a rhetoric student, in college in Indiana. Three years later they were both members of a friend's wedding and, after that, they began to date. Their friendship turned to love.

On the night before Labor Day in 1974, Paul Monette, a writer, went to a dinner party in Boston. There he met Roger Horwitz, a lawyer, who became not just his best friend but the love of his life.

We wanted to know how people who married met and, just as important, how people met their sexual partners. Do you meet the people you marry in different ways from those you have sex with, but do not marry? Knowing who chooses whom and why can help individuals to understand how they can find a partner if they are looking for one. And understanding partner selection also can help us understand the spread of AIDS and other sexually transmitted diseases. To be at risk for these diseases, you first have to have a partner who is infectious.

Our hunch was that people's choices of sexual and marriage partners are severely constrained but also greatly facilitated by their social networks. It's not that you never see a stranger across a crowded room and fall instantly in love. It's more that that stranger you notice will look just like you. This stranger will be of your race, educational status, social class, and probably religion, too. The single biggest reason why, of course, is that most of the people in that crowded room are preselected to be alike. The social world is organized so that you will meet people like yourself.

At the same time, we learn to be most open to new relationships when we meet people we think are like us and to be wary of total strangers who come to us with no social context.

Tom Byrne, the chairman of the New Jersey Democratic Party, met his wife, Barbara, at a New York club for people from Ivy League colleges. He really did spot her across a crowded room. Barbara, an investment banker, was "a beautiful classy woman," Byrne says. Later, he asked her: what would she have said if he had approached her on a New York subway with the same pickup line? She would have snubbed him, she replied.

Our data support our suspicions. We find that most couples met in the most conventional ways—they were introduced by family members or friends. They met at work. They met at a party.

Despite the mushrooming business in personal ads and singles bars, despite even the emergence of erotic e-mail, where people sit at their computer terminals and type messages to strangers, social networks reign supreme in bringing couples together. In fact, we find, selecting a sexual partner is actually governed by many of the same factors that govern the ways we choose colleges or jobs or cars. And, just as we often choose a college, job, or car after consulting with our families, friends, and other advisers, so we rely on our personal social networks when we choose sexual partners.

Very few people met sexual partners by going outside their networks—through a personal ad in the paper or at a bar or on a Club Med vacation. Moreover, we find, those couples who did venture outside their network were more likely to have short sexual relationships that never blossomed into anything more. Those who stayed together, like Harry and Sally in the movie *When Harry Met Sally . . .* , were more likely to have gotten to know each other as friends first and then became lovers.

We also find that one group of Americans can be hard put to find any sex partners at all, no matter how hard they look. These are the older women, and for them the partner problem is not just hypothetical—it is starkly real. Our data combined with another national sample dramatically show that the older a single woman is, the less likely it is that she will find a sexual partner.

To capture the social factors that determine who meets whom and who chooses whom, we analyzed the answers to two questions that we asked of our respondents: Who introduced you to each of your sexual partners? Where did you meet? By knowing who introduced people to their partners, we can see how strongly family and social networks influence our choices. By knowing where people met, we can see where and with whom there are opportunities to find a partner. It also shows the successful strategies for finding a partner.

In addition to those who are married and cohabiting, our sample included 1,743 sexual relationships that took place in the last year among people who were neither married nor living with a sexual partner. About half of these people had only one sexual partner in the past year.

Most couples were introduced by families or friends or introduced themselves, usually in situations where others in the room were already preselected— they were at a party given by a mutual friend or they were at a social organization or club. And the more stable the relationship, the more likely people were to have met through their social networks.

As the pie charts in Figure 10.1 illustrate, people are most likely to meet individuals that they will have sex with when they are introduced by someone they know well. In Panel C, for example, 55 percent of the unmarried dating couples who had been together for more than a month were introduced by someone who knew both of them. The observation that friends and family members are such important brokers, that they are so likely to introduce us to our sexual partners, shows how and why people end up with partners who are so like themselves.

Married people are even more likely to have been introduced by family and friends, coworkers, classmates, and neighbors. Sixty-three percent of them were introduced in this way, nearly all by family members and friends.

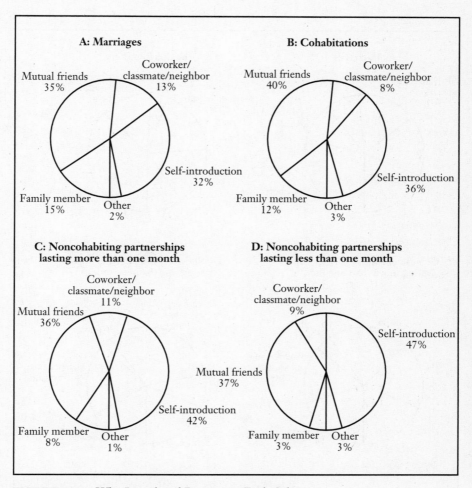

FIGURE 10.1   Who Introduced Partners to Each Other

We suspect that many of the self-introductions also took place in circumstances where the potential partners were already chosen to fit in well with the person's social network. Like Tom Byrne's introduction to Barbara, people tend to introduce themselves to people they see at a club for people like themselves or in a classroom. Some people undoubtedly introduced themselves to people they saw in a subway or on the street or at a bar, but, as the next figure shows, this was not a very common way to meet.

These effects of social networks also showed up when we asked where people met their partners. As Figure 10.2 illustrates, we found that 50 to 60 percent of couples in all four types of partnerships met at school, work, a private party, or church. These are social settings in which you are likely to meet someone much like yourself, as contrasted with finding someone through a personal ad or on a vacation.

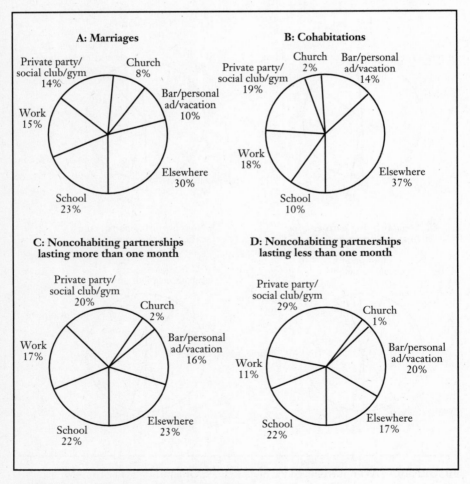

FIGURE 10.2   Where the Partners First Met

Those who married were much more likely to meet at church—8 percent of them did so—than those who had a short-term sexual partnership—just 1 percent of them met at church.

Another way of looking at the data is to ask how often people meet each other in ways that are independent of their social networks. These include, for example, occasions when a man introduces himself to a good-looking woman at a bar, or when a women meets a man through a personal ad. And, we might assume, these are more likely to be relationships that were intended from the start to be short-term, sexual ones. If you just want a passionate partner for the night, why would you want to meet that partner through your social network? Why should your brother or your best friend introduce you to someone you do not intend to see again? It would only lead to misunderstandings and hurt feelings. It might be easier to pick up someone at a bar.

And that is what we find, as Figure 10.2 shows. Only 10 percent of those who married met in a bar or on vacation or through a personal ad, while 20 percent of those who were short-term, noncohabiting partners met that way.

Of course, just because something is unlikely does not mean it will never happen. A New York doctor in her forties, who had never married and had all but given up on men, finally answered a personal ad, more out of desperation than any expectation that the man would even be presentable. But she met and, within a year, married a college professor who was just as lonely as she was.

The message, however, is that this sort of strategy really is a long shot. And, as our data show, people you meet in these unlikely ways are much more likely to end up as your short-term sexual partners than as your long-term lovers and friends.

The findings suggest that some paths are much more likely than others to lead to a lover. And, they say, there is more to finding someone than trying to lose ten pounds or buying a new wardrobe or frequenting places like a café attached to a bookstore, where you think attractive and unattached people might drift by.

Some people have intuitively grasped this reality. Geri Thoma, a literary agent, offered her friends a prize if they could introduce her to someone she married. Thoma explained her reasoning to a *New York Times* reporter: "It's amazing to me how many single people sit around waiting for the miraculous to happen. They really believe you're going to meet someone in a Laundromat, which means that you're limiting yourself to guys who hang out in Laundromats."

So Thoma proposed her award to her friends at her book club. She says she told them, "The person who sets me up with the greatest number of dates in the next year gets a ten-speed bike, and if you set me up with someone I end up marrying, you get the grand prize. I'll send you on a vacation." Within a few months, however, a friend from outside the book club introduced Thoma to a man she dated, then married. Although the friend did not know of the award, Thoma gave it to him anyway: two tickets to the Caribbean.

Other people thank their matchmakers more subtly. Martha Bari and Mike Di Pirro's matron of honor and best man at their wedding were the friends who introduced them.

The vast popularity of school and work as meeting places is part of the social game, whereby the firm hand of society inevitably guides us toward people that we and our stakeholders would view as acceptable sex partners. One reason why so many people met their partners at school or at work is that most people spend so much time there, going to school for years and then working for decades. The total time spent in school and at work far overshadows the time spent in such places as a bar or on vacation or in a health club.

Another reason, however, is the setting. School and work are far more conducive to meeting someone your friends and family will approve of, someone with interests like yours and a background like yours. They are, in fact, places where your friends and family are likely to introduce you to a partner.

We also can see the importance of social networks in establishing sexual partnerships when we look at the relationship between how a couple met, how long their partnership lasted, and how long they knew each other, as acquaintances or friends, before having sex. People who chose partners within their social network are more likely to have known their partners for some time and to be confident that their partners fit in well with their family and friends. Like Kathy and Todd, a man and woman might first get to know each other at school before starting to date. A gay man may have known another man at work for years before the friendship evolves into love.

The most permanent sexual relationships are marriages, and so, we might expect, people who marry knew their partners longer before having sex with them than people who have short-term sexual relationships. And that is what our data show.

To read Figure 10.3, look at the upper left-hand set of bar graphs. They show that for the partnerships that are formal marriages, 10 percent of these couples who were introduced by a family member had sex less than a month after meeting each other. Once again, this does not necessarily mean that the remaining 90 percent dated for more than a month before having sex—although they might have. It means that they knew each other, as friends, as classmates, as neighbors, as colleagues at work, for more than a month before having sex. About 55 percent of that same group of married couples introduced by a family member knew each other for more than a year before having sex. Each of the bar graphs in this figure can be read in the same way—the black portion showing the percentage of the group who had sex less than a month after meeting, the gray portion at the top showing the percentage who first had sex a year or more after meeting, and the white middle section showing the percentage of the group that had sex some time between one month and one year after meeting.

The upper right-hand set of bar graphs shows the pattern for partnerships that are cohabitations. A much larger portion—35 percent on average—of these cohabiting couples had sex less than a month after they first met, than was the case for the married couples. You can see that at a glance by noticing the much larger portion of the bar graph that is the black section. Correspondingly, a much smaller portion of these cohabiting couples waited a year or more after they met before first having sex, as seen by the smaller portion of the bar graph that is gray.

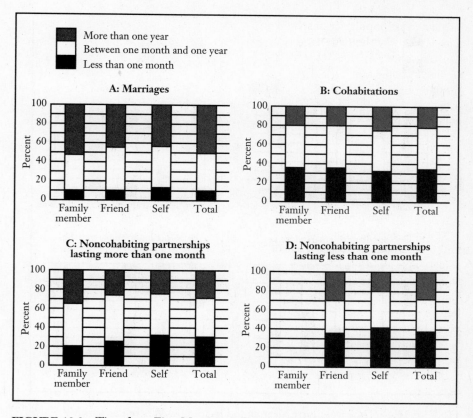

FIGURE 10.3   Time from First Meeting to First Sex, by Who Introduced Partners

For the noncohabiting partnerships, shown in the bottom panels of Figure 10.3, we see that once again more of these couples, in both the long-term and short-term relationships, began having sex within a month of meeting than did the married couples. And fewer of them waited as long as a year.

Figure 10.4 tells us how the amount of time before having sex differed by where the couple met.

Those who met in a bar are a lot more likely to have sex quickly. Up to half of those who met in bars and are casual sex partners met less than a month before they first had sex. Apparently, there is also some love at first sight, or more accurately, sex at first sight, on the job, since 41 percent of those who met at work and had only short-term liaisons had sex within a month of first meeting.

The top, gray portion of each bar graph in Figure 10.4 shows the other end of the spectrum—those who did not have sex within a year of having met each other. There we see the mirror image of the story told by the bottom, black portion of each bar graph. Those who met in bars do not typically have sex with each other if they have not done so within a year of first meeting—only one in five do so after so long a time. But then one in five of those who met in bars and

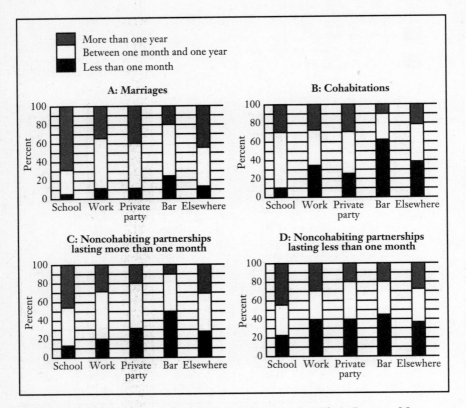

FIGURE 10.4   Time from First Meeting to First Sex, by Where Partners Met

subsequently married did know each other for a year before marrying, the table tells us. More than two-thirds of those who met in school and subsequently married did not have sex within the first year of knowing each other. So the classic love story of getting to know your partner gradually, as a friend, going slowly and finally having sex and then marrying is abundantly evident in our data. (For technical reasons, this table, but this table only, has just the married couples who married within the past decade.)

In Figure 10.3, the type of introduction matters less than the nature of a relationship—like marriage or cohabitation. That is, the different heights of the bar graph in Figure 10.3 vary more from panel to panel than they vary within a panel. That is not the case for Figure 10.4, however. There, the location of the meeting—in a bar versus a school, for example—has a much bigger effect on how soon sex occurs after a meeting than does the nature of the meeting —in a bar versus a school, for example—has a much bigger effect on how soon sex occurs after a meeting than does the nature of the relationship that is formed.

We think that what happens is that people often understand, even at the beginning of an encounter, whether the new acquaintance is potentially suitable for marriage. Consciously or not, they judge whether the person is part of their social network or has the same social background. If the potential isn't there for a long-term partnership, the relationship is unlikely to proceed as if it were anything but a casual sexual one.

That's what happened when Lisa, a working-class Italian girl, met Pete, a rich man from Boston, at a swimming pool in Maryland. Their first date was dinner at a modest restaurant, with red-checkered tablecloths and pasta. On their next date, they saw a movie. By the third date, they were spending the night together at Pete's apartment, making love.

Lisa told herself that this relationship really could last, and even though she knew that Pete was all but engaged to Janet, a woman from Pete's social background, back in Boston, she thought that she could lure him away. But Pete never intended to stay with Lisa, and, without ever explicitly saying so or perhaps without ever even admitting it to himself, Pete decided from the start that Lisa was never going to be anything more than a sex partner for the summer. Deeply hurt, Lisa blamed herself when Pete left her to go back to Janet in the fall and thought that she must not be pretty enough or smart enough to keep him.

It's not that Lisa did anything wrong—it's more that she was a victim of the romantic myths we tell ourselves. But because she was not part of Pete's social network, Lisa had a very different relationship with Pete from the start.

If your potential partner shares your social network, you will be cautious about moving too quickly toward sex, because any misunderstandings can have a personal cost to you. If your partner is of the same social background, he or she is unlikely to define the relationship as a short-term sexual one. You also are more likely to know your partner in another context, as a classmate or colleague at work, and you may well be friends already. This means that it will be harder for either of you simply to have sex and then forget the other person.

So before the relationship even gets under way, there are greater investments and greater costs than you would have if you found someone outside your network or social class and dated him or her. This means that we can't simply look at the paltry number of one-night stands that our respondents reported and decide that people just do not want casual sex. The number of one-night stands is also a reflection of the opportunity for such encounters. If you simply want sex, you must find your partners within a context that makes them appropriate for a relationship that is only defined by the desire for sex.

Our survey shows that only 1.4 percent of married couples had sex within the first two days of meeting each other. Nearly ten times as many couples, or 13.7 percent in short-term partnerships of a month or less, had sex so soon after they met. Some of these couples may eventually marry—we got just a snapshot of relationships when we asked about couples who were dating. But we believe that a general pattern is clear.

In fact, even these people who had sex in the first month are unlikely to have sex immediately after meeting, showing, once again, how far from reality is the Hollywood picture of romance, where couples routinely have intercourse within hours after they meet. It also indicates that the Mr. Goodbar type of pickup sex is highly unusual. Moreover, students who met their partners in school are unlikely to have sex within the first month of meeting each other, suggesting that the popular fear that college students are hopping from partner to partner is largely unfounded.

One consequence of the social networks that we use to find partners is that our pool of potential sexual partners is actually very small. We have no way of meeting most Americans, even if we wanted to.

For some people, that is a constant frustration, a slamming shut of the door to a more exciting life. While it has challenged a few to find ways around the barriers of geography and social class, many feel they are trapped by their life circumstances.

One woman, who liked having sex with professional basketball players, said part of the thrill was simply finding a way to meet them. The idea, she said, that a man like Michael Jordan, who seems so unreal, like a god, could actually come to know her was almost unimaginable. These players seemed to inhabit another universe. She quickly realized that her beauty was not enough, nor was dressing provocatively and going to games or to bars after the games. So many other young women had that idea that the odds were against Jordan or any other player noticing her. So she figured out ingenious ways to attract a player's attention, like sending mysterious messages in Federal Express packages to the player she was after. She succeeded in some cases, but her relationships never lasted—which should be no surprise according to the social network theory that we discussed in the previous chapter.

Her story reveals a quiet truth. Unless we do something unusual, like this woman's campaign to meet basketball stars, we simply cannot associate with some people because we do not live near them and they are not in our office or school.

There may be no blacks in a white suburban neighborhood, for example, or no Jews in a small farm town in the Midwest. We cannot know any California girls because we live in New York. We cannot get to know the Rockefellers or the Kennedys because we do not go to the right schools or live in Palm Beach or on Park Avenue.

Even in high schools, where social classes mix, studies have shown that students divide up into homogeneous cliques. The jocks, the intellectuals, the drug users, the Christian right. And these cliques clearly are stratified by social class and race. Classes are segregated according to academic aspirations, which often translate into social class. The college-bound group seldom interacts with the (usually poorer) group of teenagers whose education will end with high school. And, as with any other people looking for sexual partners, teenagers are acutely aware of whom they can bring home to meet their parents.

Teenagers, like adults, are likely to have partners of the same race, not necessarily because they refuse to date people of other races but because they are unlikely to meet many of them. Their parents, for example, may live in the suburbs, so already, deliberately or not, they usually have prescreened their teenager's friends for race.

Although we give lip service to racial equality and although federal fair housing laws might seem to have insured that people can live anywhere they can afford to, many studies have shown that most Americans do not want to live in racially integrated neighborhoods. One way that whites separate themselves from blacks is to live in suburbs. The end result is that Americans live in a segregated society, by any sort of measure of separateness, with blacks and whites in distinct worlds.*

Well before they become sexually active, American adolescents are traveling in social circles with people just like themselves. Adults, too, screen their partners, staying within their social network with organizations like church groups that help newly divorced people find mates who are like themselves. Others find partners because they are part of the same social group. They may be students at the same college or associates in the same law firm or may both be working as trainers at a health club, for example.

Of course, if it were not advantageous for us to pick partners who are like us, we might be less willing to pick partners from within our social networks. And if those social networks were not so well organized, we would not be as successful in finding partners who are so similar to us.

Yet even though we usually restrict our partner search to our own social networks, the system is highly effective in bringing like people together. The problem, however, occurs when people grow older. Many single women have complained that the older they are, the more difficult it can seem to find a man. And older men have said it's not so easy for them, either.

The question of whether there really is a man shortage has prompted countless newspaper and magazine articles, and served as the focus for numerous radio and television talk shows. It became a feminist issue, with some saying that the notion of a man shortage was just a way to put women in their place, to tell them that if they persisted in delaying marriage to start their careers they would suffer in the end: no man would want them.

One way to decide if there are enough men is simply to divide the number of suitable men for any particular woman by the number of suitable women for these men. If there are 100 single men in a town who wish to marry, regardless of any other of their attributes, and 200 women who wish to marry, again disregarding any other attributes of these women, then the ratio is 1:2. That means that half the women will not find men in this lottery.

We can make the calculation a little more realistic if, as we assume, most people choose marriage partners whose age is within five years of their own. Using data from the *Statistical Abstract of the U.S.*, 1992 edition, we then can determine how many men there are for every woman at various ages. The conclusion, as illustrated in the table below, shows that even if we ignore any other social factors, the age factor alone will force many interested women to be bereft of marital partners.

As Table 10.1 illustrates, the only time when there are more men than women is when people are in their twenties, when most people are marrying or living with a partner. But by their forties, men are already starting to die off disproportionately, so that by age forty to forty-four, there are already too few men for the number of women. With every year that passes thereafter, more

---

*Douglas Massey and Nancy Denton, *American Apartheid* (Chicago: University of Chicago Press, 1993).

Table 10.1

Age 20–24:	105 men per 100 women
Age 40–44:	98 men per 100 women
Age 60–64:	88 men per 100 women
Age 75+:	55 men per 100 women

men than women die. By the time a woman reaches the age of seventy-five or over, there are nearly twice as many women as men her age in the population. The situation for the widowed women in the older age groups is actually worse than the figures suggest because many of the men and the women are, in fact, married, and thus the unmarried women end up with even fewer men to choose from.

So it is no surprise that there is a man shortage for older women.

But a simple proportion is not a sufficient answer. It does not tell who is a suitable partner for whom. More realistically, most people include four criteria in their definition of "suitable." The first is age. Most women want to marry a man who is older than they are, while most men want a woman who is younger. Next is race. Most people want to marry someone of the same race. Then comes marital status. People who are already married usually are not interested in seriously looking for new spouses, and most people who are unmarried do not want to go after a married person. The fourth criterion is education. People tend to marry people with as much education as they have.

People often think of these restrictions, imposed by our culture, as personal preferences, but they are only partially so. The restrictions have become socially structured and they operate to reduce the number of suitable men, especially for women with better educations and women who are older.

The sexual marketplace is entirely different for the single forty-year-old man than it is for the single forty-year-old woman. It turns out that quite conventional men, who do not have great wealth or power to offer, find it much easier to remarry in their later years.

As a newly divorced man in his forties looks around, he discovers that the vast majority of women his own age, race, and education are already spoken for. It can be a sobering experience for him, looking in such a market. Chances are that the last time he was unattached, he was in his twenties and virtually every woman he met was also unattached. Even though the divorce rate is high, these divorces do not all occur at any one age, and at any given moment only a small number of people of any age group are separated, widowed, or divorced. This small number is subdivided into even smaller markets according to such things as race, religion, education, and social class. And the pool of eligible people is constantly shifting as people remarry, with men remarrying much faster than women.

The new marketplace leaves this man with three choices. He can search for one of the few unattached women of his own age, hoping that she will fit in with his social group and that he will be attracted to her. That option leaves the man with very few women to choose from and a slim chance that he will actually end up with a new mate.

A second option is to go after a married woman of his own age. That choice is fraught with even more severe difficulties. To get a married woman, he has to separate her from her husband and family, a process whose social costs are high. Surveys have consistently shown that nearly 80 percent of Americans strongly disapprove of extramarital sex. It's almost certain that the man's friends and family and the married woman's friends and family will censure any attempt by the man to woo this married woman. In fact, most Americans find marital infidelity so unacceptable that we expect illicit lovers to keep their relationship a secret.

So highly charged are these secrets that one man tried to sue the New York Times Company when one of its papers printed a picture of him walking down the street holding hands with a young woman. The picture was supposed to illustrate love in bloom in the springtime. The problem was that the man and the woman were married—to other people. (He had to drop the suit because the law says that the street is a public place where people do not have to give their permission to be photographed.)

Wary of even getting started with a married woman, many men turn to the third option—to look for a woman where women are still available. That means widening the age range where he looks and even dating younger women, in their twenties, who are not yet spoken for. The older man may have something to offer the young woman—his relative prosperity and lack of encumbrances.

Even a balding, paunchy, sixty-eight-year-old New York taxi driver with bad teeth can find it possible to attract younger women, said Susan Jacoby, a writer who lives in New York. This cabby told Jacoby that he had no trouble finding women in their forties to date.

"I asked him if he ever went out with women his own age," Jacoby wrote. The driver, she added, replied, "Never. You think that's unfair, right? Well, it is unfair, I don't want to go out with women in their sixties. I'll tell you why—their bodies are just as flabby as mine. And, see, I don't have to settle for that. I've got a good pension from twenty-five years in the fire department on top of what I make driving a cab. Gives me something to offer a younger woman. Oh, I know they aren't going out with me because I'm so sexy looking. A woman my age is in a tougher spot. See, she looks just as old as I look but most of the time she's got no money and no job. The way I figure it, you've got to have something else to offer when the body starts falling apart."

The story is very different for most older women. A recently divorced woman in her forties looks around her and, like the man her age, finds that there is almost no one available. Almost all the men her age are spoken for, involved in marriages. She faces the same disincentives as the man faces if she tries to pull a man away from an established relationship with another woman. She can look for a younger man, but, unlike the man in his forties, she is likely to have little independent wealth or power to offer. She is likely to have children, an encumbrance the younger man does not want. And she is past her most fertile period, so the younger man cannot look forward to having his own family with her.

Not all relationships between older women and younger men end badly, of course, but older women are at a profound disadvantage when they try to use wealth and power to lure a man because the generally accepted rules of who is suitable for whom virtually guarantee that the match will be disapproved by both the woman's and the man's stakeholders.

The demographic data show that the older men get, within limits, the better their odds because there are more women who are younger, as well as or less educated, single, and of the same race.

A group of demographers has calculated that for every 100 white college-educated women between the ages of thirty-five and thirty-nine, there are only thirty-nine men available who are white, unmarried, as old as or older than the women, and who are also college educated. But white college-educated men aged thirty-five to thirty-nine have the odds in their favor in the sexual market-place. There are 200 women for every 100 men who fulfill these suitability criteria.

The analysis is actually more complex because there are even more restrictions on the availability of marriage partners; some people are out of the pool of potential partners because they do not want to marry. Others are not interested in sex with people of the opposite gender.

Every problem that white women have is exacerbated for well-educated black women, who are at a much greater disadvantage than white women at every age because fewer black men finish high school and go on to college. Their pool of suitable men is shrunk from the beginning. In contrast, educated black men at every age have a much better chance of finding a suitable partner than do black women. That's one reason why black women often say they are enraged when they see a professional black man with a white woman.

The following graph shows what happens to a woman's chance of finding a partner as she grows older. The graph combines our data, which go to age fifty-nine, with data from the General Social Survey, which agree with ours up to age fifty-nine but continue to age eighty-nine. By age fifty, women are significantly more likely than men to have had no sexual partner in the past year—22 percent of the women versus 8 percent of the men. But the discrepancies only grow from there. By ages sixty to sixty-four, 45 percent of the women have no partners and 15 percent of the men have no partners. (The respondents in the General Social Survey are noninstutionalized, so they exclude unhealthy elderly who are in hospitals or nursing homes.)

Given data like these, it is no surprise that women have so much trouble finding men.

Of course, men, too, often have problems finding partners as they grow older. Even though they can draw from a larger pool of women, most women in the population still are married or living with a partner, making them essentially inaccessible. And older men, like older women, often have trouble even finding potential partners since the extensive social structures, like schools and youth groups, that help teenagers and young adults are not available to them.

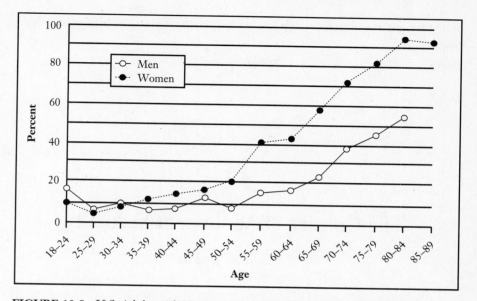

FIGURE 10.5   U.S. Adults with No Sexual Partner in the Past Twelve Months

Reflecting the hard time many older people have, male as well as female writers have poured out tens of thousands of words over the years on the painful search for someone to share their bed.

Men who divorced and had to look for new mates complained that it was much harder the second time around. Roderick Thorp, a fiction writer in Los Angeles, said he found himself alone much of the time, "and sometimes it's depressing. Other people have told me it's much the same for them."

Charles Simmons, a novelist, lamented that as an older man, he has become invisible to women. The grocery store clerks, he said, used to flirt with him. Now, he wrote, "There comes a time when, like the boy putting groceries in your cart, she doesn't see you. She sees the cold cuts and the beer, the half a loaf of bread, and that's all." He concludes: "You are being screened out."

But the problem for women is deeper and more stubbornly resistant to any obvious solutions. The facts are so bleak that they make the sort of pat advice dispensed to women look silly. The Saturday before Valentine's Day in 1994, when every radio show, television show, and newspaper was casting about for something fresh and new to say about love, a talk radio show in Philadelphia, "Voices in the Family," featured a psychologist who said she was an expert on love and sex between older people. A woman called the show to ask what an older woman can do if she is unable to find a man. The psychologist replied that women have three options. One is to masturbate. Another is to find a female lover. And the third is to find a younger man.

In fact, there are no easy answers for older women who have not found a man. The one consolation, as we will discuss later, is that all of our evidence argues against the theory that a woman without a partner is a sexually thwarted creature. Instead, we find, women—and men—who have no partners think less about sex and report having what often are very happy and fulfilling lives without it.

R E A D I N G

11

The Culture of Adolescent Sexuality

Lillian B. Rubin

If there are two words that describe the sexual sensibility of today's youth, they are "tolerance" and "entitlement." *Nowhere are the effects of the sexual revolution more dramatically evident than in teenagers' sense of entitlement to make their own choices about sex and in their tolerance of all kinds of sexual behaviors, so long as they meet the current peer norms.* A sharp contrast to the young of earlier generations, among whom tolerance was limited and entitlement almost nonexistent.

It's the language of love and romance, not commitment and marriage, that defines the boundaries of sexuality for most teenagers today. No promises made, given or implied. "We love each other, so there's no reason why we shouldn't be making love," said 16-year-old Emily from Columbus, Ohio, her dark eyes fixing me with an intent gaze.

"Does that mean you've made a long-term commitment to each other?"

She hesitated and looked doubtful, then finally spoke: "I don't know what you mean by that. Do you mean are we going to get married? The answer is no. Or will we be together next year? I don't know about that; that's a long time from now. Most kids don't stay together such a long time. But we won't date anybody else as long as we're together. That's a commitment, isn't it? Just because we don't expect to get married doesn't mean we're not in love, does it?"

Data on teenage sexual activity are inexact, to say the least. But most experts in the field agree that somewhere over 60 percent of American teenagers have had sexual intercourse by the time they finish high school. A Harris poll in 1986 found that 57 percent of the nation's 17-years-olds, 46 percent of the 16-year-olds and 29 percent of the 15-year-olds had had sexual intercourse. In a finely tuned analysis of the national data, demographer Sandra Hofferth estimates

---

From Lillian B. Rubin, *Erotic Wars: What Happened to the Sexual Revolution?* 1990. New York: Harper-Collins. References have been deleted.

conservatively that 66 percent are sexually experienced by the time they reach their nineteenth birthday. Planned Parenthood puts the figure at 75 percent. And all agree that the age at which adolescents make their sexual debut continues to decline. A recent survey of eighth-grade students—that is, 14-year-olds—from three rural counties in Maryland revealed that 58 percent of the boys and 47 percent of the girls had experienced coitus.

Even among teenagers brought up in conservative Christian families, the proportion who are sexually experienced is very high. In mid-1987, eight evangelical denominations in the central and southern states conducted a study of teen sexual behavior. The findings could have given little comfort to the advocates of sexual abstinence in the teenage world. Forty-three percent of the young people surveyed, all of whom attended church regularly, had had sexual intercourse before their eighteenth birthday, and an almost equal number had experimented with sexual behaviors short of actual coitus. Equally unsettling for their parents and ministers, well over one-third of these students refused to brand sex outside marriage as morally unacceptable.

These impressive statistics speak to important changes in the culture of adolescent sexuality—changes that are especially profound for girls, since boys and men have always had more sexual leeway than girls and women. For boys, the big difference now is that, for the first time ever, their sexual exploration and activity need not be confined to "bad" girls only. No small change, it's true, but insignificant when compared with the shift for girls, who now have permission to be sexually active outside the context of love, marriage and commitment.

Still, there's something more to be said about the statistics we commonly cite about teenage sex. For while statistics may not lie, they often leave us with a distorted version of the truth. It isn't that the findings of the studies are wrong, but that, by the very nature of large-scale statistical surveys, they can get at only a small corner of reality. In the matter of adolescent sexual behavior, these studies ask such questions as: Have you ever had sexual intercourse? A yes puts the respondent into the sexually active category, a no into its opposite. But these are labels that tell us little about the reality of a young person's sexual experience, especially among the girls, even about whether they are sexually active or not.

Two-thirds of the teenagers I met had had sexual intercourse. Yet among those "sexually active" young people were several girls who, after trying it out once, decided to put the whole issue on hold. "It was with my boyfriend, who I'd been going out with for about seven or eight months," explained a 16-year-old Oakland girl, who looked around uncomfortably as she spoke. "We talked about it a lot, and we both decided we wanted to and, like, the time was right. It was the first time for both of us, and we decided we wanted to have sex for the first time with each other."

"And how did you feel about it afterwards?"

"It didn't affect me in the way I thought it would. I mean, I didn't sit around afterwards thinking: 'Gosh, I took this great, huge step.' I think I expected everything in the world to change, but the world just kept going on the next day just like it did the day before. But I do feel it was an important experience that maybe I should have done when I was older. I'm not sure. I don't have any regrets, but it wasn't exactly what I expected. I mean, it wasn't that bad, but it wasn't like it felt real good or anything. I'm glad the first time was with him, but I don't feel like rushing out and doing it again with him or anyone else, not in the near future anyway."

There are others who also would come up positive in the sexually active column yet who, on closer examination, turned out to have been abstinent for as long as a year or two at the time of our meeting. Seventeen-year-old Joanne, a high-school senior from Richmond, Virginia, had her first sexual experience about six months after her fourteenth birthday. "We had been together for four months, and he asked me to have sex. He didn't push me; he was very understanding. But we were really in love, and it felt like, why shouldn't we?"

"How was it for you?"

"It was fine. Everyone was saying, 'You'll be really scared the first time,' but I wasn't. I knew I really loved him a lot, and I knew he felt the same way about me. So it didn't bother me at all. I felt really close to him and I liked that, and I could tell he really felt close to me, too. It felt really nice. We went together for a year and a half, and since then I haven't had sex with anyone else."

"Do you want to?"

"No, not really, not now anyway. If I fall in love with someone, I'm sure I will— want to, I mean. But I haven't yet, and it's been over a year since we broke up."

Finally, there are those who had been quite sexually active, girls who at 14 or 15 had had more than one sexual experience, sometimes with several different partners, and in the process seemed to have scared themselves into celibacy. "I go to this Christian school, and a lot of the kids are into stuff they shouldn't be doing, you know, sex and drugs and things like that," said a 17-year-old New York suburbanite, the words rushing from her as if in a confessional. "It's not as bad as the public school in this town, but there's a lot of that stuff in my school, too. Anyway, I met this boy there who became my boyfriend for a little while. That was the first time I had sex.

"At the time, my parents and I weren't getting along, and I was rebelling against them. So sex and drugs and all that was a good way to do it. But I always felt guilty and stuff; I'd wake up the next morning and feel miserable. Then the headmaster of the school found out about what the kids were doing, and they really cleaned house and expelled a whole bunch of kids. I was so terrified that they'd get me, too, but I was one of the lucky ones."

Interrupting the flow of words for a moment, she planted her elbows on the table, cupped her face in her hands and said quietly, "I was so relieved. I was getting more and more scared, like I didn't know what was happening to me, or why I was doing what I was doing. It seemed like I was trying to find a way to stop but didn't know how. I found out that sex without marriage is more physically enjoyable than it is mentally. So now I'm saving myself for when I get married. Maybe that's why I'm looking forward to marriage so much."

"What do you mean when you say sex was more physically than mentally enjoyable?"

"You know, it was nice; it feels good; it's nice to be close like that to someone you care about. But then you have all the guilt."

"Did you have orgasms?"

"Not at first, but after we were doing it for a while, I did—not all the time, but a lot of times."

Just as the words "sexually active" do not define the experience of such young people, so it is a travesty to describe most of the rest as "not sexually active" simply because they have not had sexual intercourse. Among the teenagers I met, just over one-third would fall into the "not sexually active" category of most large-scale surveys. Yet only seven had never engaged in any sexual play at all—all of them 13–15 year olds.

Ironically, our historic and obsessive concern with virginity, which discourages sexual intercourse, unintentionally fosters behaviors no one thought to prohibit. Thus, most of those who had not yet had coitus engaged in all kinds of sexual practices, from genital fondling to mutual masturbation to oral sex. And the older they were, the more sophisticated the level of exploration and experimentation became. Indeed, by the time these "not sexually active" young people were finishing high school, fellatio and cunnilingus had become a significant part of sexual activity for close to half of them. "I don't mind giving a guy a blow job if he comes fast," said a Houston 17-year-old, fingering her long golden-highlighted brown hair as she spoke. "But with some guys it takes them a while to come, and my jaws lock, and that's not the most enjoyable thing in the world."

Anal sex, behavior that was almost unheard of among heterosexuals a couple of decades ago, also is part of the sexual discourse now, something kids talk about as a possibility, although only a few of them, whether they had had coitus or not, had tried it out before the end of high school. "I think whatever a couple does is their business; it's up to them," said 16-year-old Sara from Louisville. "There are things I won't do, like anal sex. My last boyfriend started to do it, and it hurt. It's terrible; I made him stop. But my best friend says she likes it, and if that's what she wants, that's okay. I don't think anyone has a right to judge what people do. It's nobody's business as long as the couple both agree."

Even the most conservative of the young people I met were firm in their belief ✗ that the choice about being sexual belongs to the individual alone. They make no judgments of others, and expect none to be made of them. "I have friends who are sexually active, and I think that's great for them," said 15-year-old Ying, a San Franciscan. "As far as I'm concerned, I think each person has to make their own decision about what they're going to do. If they're mature enough to handle it, that's fine; it's up to them. I can respect their decision, and I want people to respect mine. For me, I know I'm not ready, and I think it would be kind of dumb to do something I don't really want to do. But I don't know how I'll feel next year. If I meet somebody I really care about and it seems right, then I'd have sex."

"Do people respect your decision not be sexual now?"

"Yeah, mostly. I mean, if you go to a dance or a party, there's always some boy who'll try. But I don't go to those things a lot. And my real friends, they'd never pressure me about something like that. People mostly figure it's your business, and you'll do what you want."

The question of peer pressure is not quite so simple, of course. But generally it also is not the kind of direct, one-on-one pressure the adult world so often envisions. Instead, the pressure resides largely in the atmosphere itself—pressure that permeates all facts of teenage life, whether the style of dress, the language used, the music listened to or the initiation into sexual activity. The need to belong, to feel one with the world in which we live, is common to all of us, adolescents and adults. Why else do fashions sweep the country, influencing not just the clothes we buy and the books we read, but personal habits of health and leisure? If everybody's wearing it, reading it, listening to it, doing it, the temptation to conform, to share in the experiences of those around us, is almost irresistible.

For adolescents who are struggling to separate from the family, to find a self-in-the-world that's uniquely theirs, a reference group against which to judge and measure themselves is a must. The peer group is the place where the possibilities of a self-yet-to-become can find expression. But like the family before it, this new group has its own needs for conformity among its members and its own requirements for acceptance. Paradoxically, then, the very group that facilitates the separation from the family and its restrictions becomes another arbiter of behavior in equally powerful ways.

When it comes to sex, it's not just the need to belong that exerts pressure, it's the need to know as well. A member of the peer group is the first to take the plunge and talk about it. It's news; it's consequential. For those who have not yet had the experience, it's riveting. Someone close has actually done it, can describe it, can say what it feels like. The veil of silence is pierced. But for the uninitiated, the mystery deepens; the pressure to know grows.

Undoubtedly there are instances when peer pressure is more direct and specific. The girl who is the first among her friends to have sexual intercourse may need to convince others to join her in order to assuage whatever guilt or anxiety may accompany her behavior. "I have to admit I was glad when a couple of my friends did it, too. It made me feel better that I wasn't the only one," said Lorie, now 18, as she recalled her feelings when she had her first experience at 15. "I didn't exactly try to talk them into it, but I didn't not try either. I mean, I talked about it a lot, and maybe I even made it better than I really thought it was so they'd get jealous and do it."

Some adolescents are able to resist all such persuasions. Most of these boys and girls stand outside the mainstream of peer culture and identify themselves—sometimes with pain, sometimes with pride—as "not in with the popular kids at school." A few, however, manage to withstand the pressure, whether around sex, drugs or alcohol, while still sustaining an identification with friends and peers whose behavior differs from their own. These generally are young people who exhibit a kind of personal magnetism that's unusual at any stage of life and who also have serious commitments to career or sports—a boy who's a committed runner and bicyclist, a girl who expects a college basketball scholarship, another who not only knows she's going on to college, but already has chosen a career path that requires an advanced degree. Their personal charm helps them to maintain status in the peer group, while their special interests enable them to keep enough distance to oppose its pressures.

Once in a while, there's someone for whom the example of friends and peers inspires restraint rather than the kind of titillation that seeks mimicry.

"Whatever I do, I do in moderation; I know my limits," said 16-year-old Valerie, a Los Angeles girl, who spoke in a quiet, firm voice that matched the controlled, poised manner she exhibited throughout the interview. "A lot of people feel like when they get to high school, they have to become 'unvirgined.' I have no hang-ups about that. I'm not sexually active yet. I figure when the time comes, it comes, and I'll know it. I watch some of my friends and see the trouble they're getting into—you know, they get pregnant, or they're doing so bad in school that they'll never be able to get into a decent college. A couple of kids I know even dropped out of school. It's not at all appealing to me."

But these are the rare ones. For the rest, even though they may never have a conscious awareness of the pressure, it's clear that the peer culture in which they live and with which they identify is a powerful influence in their decision making about sex.

Boys have always felt the urgency to be one of the guys, whether in doing sex or talking about it. For them, the difference between the present and the past is only in the timing. The age at which they come under pressure to conform sexually is substantially younger today than it was a few decades ago. "I was 15 the first time I had sex, and before that I lied about it, told people I did it when I didn't," said a 17-year-old Chapel Hill boy, the discomfort on his face contradicting the words that seemed to come so easily.

"Why did you feel you had to lie?"

"There was always a lot of pressure from the other guys to join in the action, and I didn't want them to think I was a wimp or a nerd. You know, they were always talking about it, whether this girl or that one is a good lay, or about some girl who's got great tits, or somebody who likes it in the ass. And you want to be a part of it all, so you lie."

Girls, too, have always lied to accommodate peer norms. But in earlier generations, the sexually active girl played the role of the native innocent. Today the innocent pretends to be the sexual sophisticate. "I haven't found someone I feel comfortable with, so I haven't felt the need to have sex yet," said Hannah, a 15-year-old from suburban Chicago. "I don't see the point in rushing anything; I'm young; I have time. But only my very best friend knows the truth. The other kids don't know because I lie and say I'm doing things I'm not. As long as you say what they want to hear, nobody bothers you. It's when you're different that they don't like it."

According to the standards of today's adolescent culture, both boys and girls are expected to have sex with only one person at a time and to be true to the relationship. For most sexually active teenagers, therefore, serial monogamy is the rule. The definition of relationship, however, can be very loose. "A relationship is when two people decide they're going together, even if it's only for a weekend," explained 15-year-old Rick.

Most relationships probably last more than a weekend, but a month is a long time, and a year an eternity. To the adult mind, this seems shocking. But to the 15-year-old, for whom a year is such a significant proportion of conscious life, it is a very long time indeed.

Ideally, the norm calling for serial monogamy applied to all, regardless of gender. But, as is the case in any complex part of life, change and stability live alongside each other, sometimes easily, sometimes not. Therefore, there's a great distance between their ideal statements and the reality with which these young people live. In the real world, the double standard of sexuality that has for so long defined our sexual consciousness has been wounded, but is not yet dead. Consequently, a boy still has very wide latitude before he's criticized or censured, while a girl who is involved with more than one boy at a time will soon acquire a "bad rep." For her, the word is "slut"—a term in common use in high schools and colleges all across the land and one of unequivocal derogation. In a rather dramatic shift from the past, however, the girls are no longer so quick to be the enforcers of the sexual rules. In fact, they're far less likely to do the censuring now than they were in the fifties.

I don't mean to suggest that adolescent girls no longer render judgments on their peers or that a girl won't use the word "slut" to describe the behavior of another. But to the degree that they do, the standards by which those judgments are made are likely to be far more diverse than they were in the past and, more important, not so totally derived from the ideals of sexual conduct that, historically, have been decreased by those in power.

Obviously, no one is immune to the impact of those edicts. Adolescent girls, like their adult sisters and mothers, know quite well that men retain at least some of their ancient power to name women's behavior, to define what is worthy and acceptable and what is not. But most girls and women no longer accept such labeling without question or contention. This, in fact, is one of the unheralded gains of the feminist movement. The changes it has wrought in women's conception of self—in their belief in their right to define themselves and, at the very least, to participate in setting their own behavioral standards—have been so deeply internalized by now that they seem natural to the adolescents of this generation, as if it were ever thus. Consequently, teenage girls today not only are tolerant of an extraordinarily wide range of sexual behaviors, they also believe that, just as their own behavior is no one else's business, so it is with another's.

As with any of us, belief and behavior don't always match, of course. But many of the girls I met are conscious of the conflict between the two and persist in trying to reduce the dissonance. Even when they can't or don't, however, the girl who offends group norms usually isn't turned into a pariah and thrown into exile as she was in the fifties. "You know, it doesn't seem right that a girl gets a bad name; the guys sleep around all the time, and nobody calls them anything," said a 16-year-old small-town Texas girl angrily.

"Well, how do you feel about girls who sleep around?"

"I don't believe in it, and I don't really think anybody should do it. But, I don't know, I guess it's not my business, and I don't think it should be theirs either," she concluded emphatically.

For most men, however, the power to name and label is not given up lightly. Here again, I'm not suggesting that a man consciously sets out to control female sexual behavior or that any given man is aware that he's doing it. Rather, I'm saying that it's so deeply ingrained a part of the social fabric that it seems almost as natural as breathing. "A guy's got to know what he's getting into when he starts up with a girl," cautioned a 17-year-old Pittsburgh boy, straightening himself in his chair as if to make sure that his body language matched the certainty in his voice. "If you're looking for a girlfriend, not just some quick and dirty sex, you don't want to get involved with a slut, you know, one of those girls who goes out with more than one guy at a time, or a girl who goes for those one-nighters. You want her to be one of the nice girls, you know, the kind of girl who only has sex with her boyfriend, and she makes sure he's her boyfriend before she does it."

While male condemnation of girls who violate the norm of monogamy is ubiquitous, I never heard anyone speak about a boy with equal disparagement. Indeed, if they wanted to, they would have had a hard time finding a way to express their feelings, since there are no words in the lexicon of teenage life that would give evidence that any serious stigma attaches to a sexually promiscuous male. For him, the favored term is "stud," a word that traditionally has carried far more approbation than opprobrium. But here, too, there are subtle changes to suggest that girls are taking to themselves some of the power to name and label. Thus, when a girl uses the word "stud" now, it often is said sarcastically, carrying negative connotations and designed to warn other girls to beware. Among boys, however, the word still has the power to evoke images of masculinity and feelings of envy.

Certainly there are plenty of boys today who are sensitive to relationship issues, who say they only really enjoy sex when it's with someone they care about, who wouldn't be proud to be called a stud. But the same boys also find themselves envious of the guy who has such a reputation, even though his behavior may be distasteful to them. "There's these guys at school who are real studs, and sometimes I look at them and wonder: 'How do they do it?' " said a 16-year-old Cincinnati boy with reluctant admiration. "I don't know, I guess you can't help envying guys who can always get any girl. I mean, I don't like the idea of degrading girls or anything like that, but, well, I don't know, it seems that those guys are the ones who get the prettiest girls in school."

Change and stability, coexisting together, living side by side so peacefully that most of the time we don't even notice the contradictions involved. The changes in the world of adolescent sex, especially for girls, are massive and real: A teenage girl can now be fully sexually active without risk to her reputation and, therefore, to her sense of self. But some things remain doggedly, intransigently, the same: The power to determine the limits of her behavior, to legislate who's fit to be girlfriend, wife, mother, remains in the hands of men. Courts still declare a woman an "unfit" mother and take custody of her children from her because of her sexual behavior. Who ever heard of the phrase "unfit father"? And what is it that would make him "unfit"? Certainly not the fact that he's having a sexual relationship with a woman.

CHAPTER 5

❖

MARRIAGE,
DIVORCE,
REMARRIAGE

READING

12

Marriage Styles: The Good, the Bad,
and the Volatile

John Gottman

Late at night, countless TV sets around the nation still tune in to watch Ralph and Alice go at it on reruns of *The Honeymooners*. His take-no-prisoners attacks and her smart-alecky comebacks have reduced generations of Americans to belly laughs. There's something about the marital explosions that detonate in their sparse Brooklyn living room that so many of us find endearing and entertaining.

You probably know of at least one couple like the Cramdens. These high-decibel twosomes often entertain their unfortunate neighbors with ear-shattering discussions about whether to buy solid or chunk-style tuna, or put 60- or

---

From *Why Marriages Succeed or Fail*. Copyright © 1994 by John Gottman. Reprinted by permission of Simon and Schuster. pp. 32–50

75-watt bulbs above the medicine cabinet. Most psychologists would probably call such frequent verbal sniping dysfunctional, even pathological. For years, marriage counselors have tried to steer couples away from this sort of bickering, convinced that it poisons a marriage.

It's certainly true that few people would aspire to a union fraught with so much tension and strife—but here's the surprise: there are couples whose fights are as deafening as the Honeymooners' yet who have long-lasting, happy marriages. If you had made that claim to me before I began my research I would have found it unlikely. But after years of tracking married couples of all sorts I have discovered that what makes a relationship work, or fall apart, is far from obvious. Some of our traditional notions of marital stability may be misguided. To see this for yourself, try your hand at predicting which of the following three newly married couples I studied remained happily married some four years later.

COUPLE NUMBER ONE

Bert and Betty Oliver, both thirty, met at a friend's wedding. For a year they sustained a long-distance romance complete with frequent plane trips and multipage phone bills. Eventually Betty moved from Cincinnati to Chicago to be with Bert and they married six months later. Bert works long, grueling hours as manager of a printing plant, a circumstance that puts some stress on their marriage. Both said they came from families where the parents weren't very communicative or intimate. Bert and Betty were determined to learn from their parents' mistake and made communication a priority in their relationship. Although they squabbled occasionally, they usually addressed their differences before the anger boiled over. Rather than shouting matches, they dealt with disagreements by having "conferences" in which each person aired his or her perspective. They tried to be understanding of each other's point of view and usually were able to arrive at a compromise. Married only two years when first interviewed, Betty expressed delight that she had been able to find that elusive creature: "a truly nice man." Bert still considered himself lucky that someone as lovely as Betty was interested in him.

COUPLE NUMBER TWO

Max Connell, forty, and Anita Gallo, twenty-five, were also married about two years when first interviewed. Max, a carpenter, met Anita on the job—he was doing repairs at a home where she was working as a nanny. In the beginning, Max was concerned that Anita would consider him too old, but she said his age was one of the things that initially attracted her. What immediately caught Max's eye was Anita's expressiveness—whatever she was feeling, she let him know. "If I try to put something off that's bothering me for maybe two days, there will be a major explosion," Anita explained. "Instead, I have to deal with it right away." Both admitted that they quarreled far more than the average couple. Their engagement was marked by so many turf wars that twice they came close to calling off the wedding. Even after marrying, they tended to interrupt each other and defend their own viewpoint rather than listen to what their partner was expressing. Eventually, however, they would reach some sort of accord. Despite their frequent tension, they seemed to take much delight in each other. They spent far more of their time together laughing, joking, and being physically affectionate than they did squabbling. Both considered passion and independence crucial factors in their lives together. They acknowledged that they had their problems, but like Bert and Betty, considered themselves happily married.

COUPLE NUMBER THREE

The Nelsons, Joe, twenty-nine, and Sheila, twenty-seven, seemed as closely paired as matching bookends. Both grew up in the suburbs of St. Louis, went to private schools, considered church-going a major focus of their lives, and were devoted to horseback riding. They said they thought alike about most everything and felt an "instant comfort" from the start. The Nelsons spent a good deal of time apart—he in his basement workshop and she in her sewing room where she devoted herself to cross-stitching. Still, they enjoyed each other's company and fought very rarely. "Not that we always agree," Sheila explained, "but we're not into conflict." When tension did arise, both considered a solo jogging session around the local country club more helpful in soothing the waters than talking things out or arguing. Asked about their major areas of tension, they gave a short list of relatively trivial concerns such as Sheila's tardiness or Joe's lack of interest in weekend chores when a Cardinals game was on TV. Sheila also mentioned as if in passing that Joe wanted to have sex far more frequently than she did, a situation that remained unresolved. In all, Joe and Sheila were proud of how well they got along. They knew that in some marriages opposites attract—"We have friends that are like that and it does work," said Sheila. "But that's not for us," Joe added.

If you guessed that couple number one, Betty and Bert Oliver, were still happily married four years later, you are right. If you guessed the same for couple number two, Anita and Max, or number three, the Nelsons, you are right again and again. If you thought only Bert and Betty were going to make it, then you're probably a clinical psychologist or have read plenty of books and articles on what makes a marriage work. Marriages like theirs, which emphasize communication and compromise, have long been held up as the ideal. Yet, after tracking the fate of so many couples over the years, I have had to reject the notion that there is only one type of successful marriage. Rather, I believe that marriages settle into one of five different styles over time. While two of these types do lead to marital dissolution, there are three very different styles that are quite stable. Bert and Betty, Anita and Max, and Joe and Sheila are examples of these three successful marital adaptations. In other words, each represents a very specific kind of marriage that our research has linked to long term stability and happiness. The closer a marriage comes to settling into one of these three adaptations, the better its chances for permanency seem to be.

One important way we identify what type of marriage a couple has is by how they fight. Although there are other dimensions that are telling about a union, the intensity of argument seems to bring out a marriage's true colors. To classify a marriage, we look at the frequency of fights, the facial expressions and physiological responses (such as pulse rate and amount of sweating) of both partners during the confrontation, as well as what they say to each other and their tone of voice. Using these observations as our guideposts, we have named the three types of stable marriages based on their style of combat: validating, volatile, or avoidant.

BETTY AND BERT: VALIDATING

There are good reasons why Bert and Betty are close to a marriage counselor's ideal: they are virtuosos at communication. Even when discussing a hot topic, they display a lot of ease and calm. Most of all they have a keen ability to listen to and understand the other's point of view and emotions. That's why I call couples like Betty and Bert *validators:* in the midst of disagreement they still let their partner know that they consider his or her opinions and emotions valid, even if they don't agree with them. For example, here's what happened when Betty confronted Bert with a problem.

Betty: There's one thing that's bugging me. It seems like we never do anything on the weekends. It's been so long since we've gotten together with friends, or just gone to a movie or something.

Bert: You wish we went out more often.

Betty: Yeah. Sometimes by the end of the week I'm crawling the walls. And I just want to go out and have a good time. But then you get home Friday night and you're tired and all you want to do is watch TV and go to sleep.

Bert: Uh-huh.

Betty: And then on Saturday and Sunday you fill up the time with chores and then you don't want to go out.

Bert: Well, you know, for me . . . I'm at the plant every day, with long hours. And when I get home I just want to be home!

Betty: Yeah, home at last!

Bert: Right. I just want no demands, no pressures, just to hang out.

Betty: I see.

When Betty first brought up her complaint that she wanted to go out more, there were a number of ways Bert could have responded. He could have pooh-poohed her concern, denied there was a problem, gotten angry, or immediately jumped in with his opinion. Instead, he listened to her point of view, even reflecting back to her what he heard her saying. When validating couples air their differences you tend to hear a lot of "Mmm-hmms" and "I sees." Often, the listener will also mirror the speaker's facial expressions of worry and distress. But this validation doesn't necessarily mean the partner agrees. Rather, the listener is saying, "Okay, go on. I'm interested and listening to your feelings. I may have my own point of view on this issue, but I want to hear yours." Betty offers Bert the same courtesy. Once she's said her piece, she supports him while he gives his point of view—that he's just too tired to want to go out.

This expression of mutual respect tends to limit the number of arguments couples need to have. Validator couples, we've found, tend to pick their battles carefully. Those flare-ups that do occur end up sounding more like a problem-solving discussion than a hostile call to arms.

Although not every validator argument follows a similar script, these couples do tend to display a particular pattern during their conflicts, whatever the topic. In fact, this pattern is one of the identifying characteristics of a validating couple. Usually they begin by listening as each other says their piece, as Betty and Bert did. Once they both feel they have fully aired their opinions, they move to phase two: attempting to persuade each other of the rightness of their position.

> Betty: But wouldn't it be relaxing to go out to a nice dinner, just the two of us? Or see a movie? You used to think so.
>
> Bert: I just don't feel like it anymore. Maybe because I'm under so much pressure, it's most relaxing just to, you know . . .
>
> Betty: Relax.
>
> Bert: Yeah. Don't you think so?
>
> Betty: (*Laughs*) No way!

Though they still don't see eye to eye, their attempts to convince each other are good-natured. There is no arm-twisting or insistence that their perspective alone is valid.

Finally, in the third phase, they negotiate a compromise both like or can at least live with.

> Bert: Okay, so what do you suggest?
>
> Betty: Well, I think we should go out sometimes. But what happens is that I feel bad asking you 'cause you look so tired. And if I do say something you'll get angry.
>
> Bert: Yeah. Well, you know. I'm afraid you're gonna jump on me all the time. That if I walk in the door with a big smile, you'll think I'm ready to go party and we'll be going out every night.
>
> Betty: So you think if you don't act really tired then I'm gonna constantly be pressuring you to go out?
>
> Bert: Yeah, I guess I do.
>
> Betty: But I don't have to go out every weekend. It's just that right now we're not going out at all!
>
> Bert: Okay. Well, how 'bout you agree that we won't go out more than, say, four times a month?
>
> Betty: For now.
>
> Bert: Right.
>
> Betty: And then we'll definitely go out those four times.
>
> Bert: Yeah, as long as you want to.
>
> Betty: You've got a deal.

As part of resolving the issue in a way that satisfied both of them, Bert and Betty got at the fundamental cause of the conflict: that Bert feared if he didn't fend off Betty by emphasizing how tired he was, they would go out far more often than he felt comfortable with. As a consequence, he acted so exhausted that they didn't go out at all. Although this sort of psychological insight is not always a part of conflict resolution in a validating couple, it is common.

In studying validating couples we have found that they tend to share other characteristics as well as the *validation/persuasion/compromise* sequence of argument. Research by Mary Anne Fitzpatrick of the University of Wisconsin on couples very similar to validators found that there is a fair amount of stereotypical sex roles in these marriages. In other words, each spouse has a separate sphere of influence. The wife is usually in charge of the home and children. The husband is usually the final decision maker. While he tends to see himself as analytical, dominant, and assertive, she views herself as nurturing, warm, and expressive. Validating couples seem to be good friends who value the "we-ness" of their marriage over their individual goals and values. It's not uncommon for them to finish each other's sentences. Among the qualities they value highly in their relationship are communication, verbal openness, being in love, displaying affection, sharing their time, activities, and interests with each other. These couples tend to consider "what's mine is yours." In their homes, they rarely have off-limit zones or a great need for privacy.

Of course, validating couples don't necessarily have marriages made in heaven. Even happy unions have their share of problems. I suspect the risk for validating couples is that they may turn their marriage into a passionless arrangement in which romance and selfhood are sacrificed for friendship and togetherness. In such a scenario they may end up forgoing personal development in favor of keeping their bond strong. I have noticed that when these couples do argue, the topic often has to do with balancing individual desires with the shared needs of the marriage. For example, one husband wanted to spend more time painting and acting, but his wife worried that his creative pursuits would squeeze out his time with her and the children. In another couple, the wife felt guilty if she spent a night out with her friends who her husband didn't like. Even though he assured her that he didn't mind, she remained unconvinced.

Still, a validating marriage appears likely to be a solid one. And that probably shouldn't be surprising. After all, when both partners feel their grievances get a sympathetic hearing, compromise is a lot easier.

MAX AND ANITA: VOLATILE

Anita: I think that everything that we talk about, in every aspect of our relationship practically, we're always competing. Like if I say I had a hard day, you say you had a worse day.

Max: No I don't.

Anita: Yes you do. You do that with everything. If I say my leg hurts, you say your knee and your elbow hurts.

Max: Well, what I'm saying is that I can relate to your pain because I'm feeling some pain right now myself.

Anita: You don't say that as a way to outdo me?

Max: No.

Anita: 'Cause it's like, I say, "Oh, I had a really hard day." And you say, "Well you should have my job. You could never handle doing what I do everyday." I don't think that's being sympathetic.

Max: I don't say that when you say you had a really hard day.
Anita: Yes you do.

Anita and Max certainly take a different approach to squabbling than do Bert and Betty. If you were a fly on the wall of their house you would hear a lot of *Coke* vs. *Pepsi* bickering: Who is a better cook? Is the drive from New York to Boston four hours or five? Whose mother is a bigger snoop? The content of their arguments is so minor, it's hard to imagine a couple like Bert and Betty wasting time on it. How can people like Max and Anita who seem to thrive on skirmishes live happily together? The truth is that not every couple who fights this frequently has a stable marriage. But we call those who do *volatile*. Such couples fight on a grand scale and have an even grander time making up. An uninvolved or withdrawn partner does not exist in a volatile marriage. These relationships are marked by a high level of engagement during discussions.

As you can see from the above dialogue, volatile couples like Max and Anita have little interest in hearing each other's point of view in the heat of argument— and I do mean heat! In essence, volatile couples simply skip the validator's first phase of discussing a delicate issue: they don't try to understand and empathize with their partner. Instead, they jump right into part two: trying to persuade. While validators tend to spend little time in the persuasion mode, for volatile couples, winning is what it's all about. That's why Anita and Max's discussion is littered with "yes you do," and "no I don't" rather than "mm-hmm" and "I see."

Here's how another volatile couple we studied "discussed" their differences over financial matters:

Rebecca: I'm worried that we're not saving enough money. We seem to live hand to mouth.
John: I don't agree. We do not have a problem with finances. You're wrong.
Rebecca: No, you're wrong. I would feel more secure if we had some savings.

For the sake of contrast, let me reconstruct the above dialogue to show how a validating couple might discuss the same issue:

Wife: I'm worried that we're not saving enough money. We seem to live hand to mouth.
Husband: Uh huh. So you'd like to save more. Well I don't think we have a problem with finances.
Wife: I see.
Husband: I think you're wrong about our finances.
Wife: Um hmm. I just would feel more secure if we had some savings.
Husband: I see.

And I'm sure *you* see the difference too. While arguing à la John and Rebecca or Max and Anita may seem like a sure route to marital disaster, my research has found otherwise. It turns out that these couples' volcanic arguments are just a small part of an otherwise warm and loving marriage. The passion and relish with which they fight seems to fuel their positive interactions even more. Not only do they express more anger but they laugh and are more affectionate than the average validating couple. They express more negative *and* more positive emotions. These couples certainly do not find making up hard to do—they are masters at it. As intense as their battles may be, their good times are that much better.

Despite the vitriol, volatile couples are able to move to phase three: resolving their differences. For example, Max and Anita were able to navigate their way through the flashpoint in their marriage they discussed above—her belief that he always tries to outdo her complaints rather than be sympathetic. Max says he thinks Anita misinterprets his comments—that he is being supportive, but she doesn't hear it. She says it is his responsibility to express himself in a way that she will understand. He rejects the notion that this is solely his obligation:

Max: Well, I don't think I should have to carry all the responsibility for whether we're getting along or not.
Anita: How else is it gonna work?
Max: If something I say bothers you, you should say to me: "Is this really what you're saying?" before you get emotionally involved.
Anita: But I'm automatically going to have an emotional reaction to what you say!
Max: (*Laughs*) But usually it's an emotion about something I *didn't* say. Sometimes you interpret what I say to be something like your dad would say, so you have a pat reaction that's not accurate to what *I've* actually said.
Anita: So you think I should repeat what you said back to you.
Max: Well, not always. But when you do repeat it, if I tell you that's *not* what I meant I want you to believe me.
Anita: All right.
Max: That's what I'd like.
Anita: Okay.
Max: I think that's the problem most of the time for me.
Anita: That I don't believe you?
Max: You just, yeah, stay with your biased, misconstrued reaction.
Anita: Okay.

Just as validators tend to have certain qualities in common, volatile-like couples also share psychological characteristics. More than the other types, they see themselves as equals. They are independent sorts who believe that marriage should emphasize and strengthen individuality. While validating couples tend to finish each other's sentences, volatiles are more likely to interrupt each other with questions. At home they tend to have separate personal spaces and respect each other's privacy. They both consider themselves analytical. He also sees himself as nurturing: she as expressive. Indeed, they are very open with each other about their feelings—both positive and negative. The ease with which they disclose their innermost thoughts and emotions fuels both their battles and their romance. These marriages tend to be passionate and exciting, as if the marital punch has been spiked with danger.

Perhaps even more than the validating style, a volatile marriage has plenty of potential pitfalls. If the couple loses sight of the boundaries, they could slide from the stability of a volatile marriage into a style far more likely to destroy their bond. The overall danger is that their constant quarreling and bickering will consume the marriage, overwhelming their happy times together. If this occurs, even violence is possible in extreme cases. Of course, at that point we would no longer consider them to have a volatile marriage, but a highly unstable one.

Volatile couples seem to enjoy playfully teasing one another, but this brand of humor is also risky. Sometimes the playful teasing can hit a tender area and inadvertently lead to hurt feelings.

Also, because volatile couples tend to believe strongly that honesty in all matters is very important in a marriage, they censor very few of their thoughts. Their relentless commitment to honesty at whatever cost can be exhilarating and brave, but it can also be terrifying since it leaves no hurt unstated. It's easy to see how some hurts could arise that are difficult to heal and that therefore endanger the high levels of positivity that keep their marriage afloat. One exchange we videotaped of a volatile couple, Tom and Judy, showed how dangerously close to the edge this penchant for openness and self-disclosure can take a couple. In the course of discussing their sexual relationship, Judy suddenly confessed, "Sometimes I think I could have sex with a perfect stranger . . . and just have no strings attached to it. That would be enjoyable. Because [between us] there are a whole lot of other things that get in the way, if I'm a little peeved with you about something."

This led Tom, a professor, to recall earlier in their marriage when he spent time "admiring the fit of those jeans" on women walking by him on campus. He tells Judy, "I remember that there were periods when I felt that way, and we'd get into a fight or something and one of us would say something like, 'if you're going to be that way about it, then we'll have to separate,' or something like that."

Suddenly, through their confessions the couple find themselves discussing the issue of breaking up. Now, Tom says he would "entertain the possibility" again in light of his wife's admission, but decides, "I don't like the feeling."

Judy agrees, "Oh freedom sounds good, but there are other aspects that are just too unsettling." Although these concluding comments restate their commitment to one another, there is a tentativeness to this affirmation of togetherness—a result of taking the confessions too far. At the end of the discussion they display an uneasiness that wasn't present when they first sat down.

The goal for volatile couples like Tom and Judy is to keep steady amidst the high winds of their passion. That can require quite a balancing act considering the frequent storms these couples subject themselves to. But as long as they hold on tight, I think they are likely to experience many years of joy and positive intensity.

JOE AND SHEILA: AVOIDANT

Moving from a volatile to an avoidant style marriage is like leaving the tumult of a hurricane for the placid waters of a summer lake. Not much seems to happen between husband and wife in this type of marriage. A more accurate name for them is probably *conflict minimizers* because they make light of their differences rather than resolving them. Like Joe and Sheila, these couples will claim that they have disagreements, but when you actually explore what they mean by *conflict* you realize that they conspire to dodge and hedge. We've seen that validators listen to each other's point of view before trying to persuade, while volatile couples jump right in, advocating for their opinion. But when avoidant couples air their differences very little gets settled. The phrase that comes up time and again when you speak with these couples about their marriage is that they end their friction by "agreeing to disagree." By this they usually mean that they avoid discussions they know will result in a deadlock.

Consider Sheila and Joe. In my view, their major conflict was a common—and potentially calamitous—one for a marriage. Namely, he wanted to have sex far more frequently than she did. She didn't enjoy sex with him, she said, because he was not as affectionate as she wanted at other times. He agreed that this was a problem and attributed it to his stress at work. Over time, she responded by becoming detached when they made love. It's not hard to imagine a conflict of this magnitude having serious consequences for a marriage. Yet, from their conversation it was clear that Sheila and Joe considered the issued "resolved":

Interviewer: How do you each feel? Are you comfortable? Is it frustrating?

Joe: No, it's more of an ideological dispute in some ways than frustrating emotionally or physically.

Sheila: I think I've come to feeling resigned about it. It's one thing I'm pretty sure is just not gonna be any different for us. . . . Sometimes I think we don't talk about things that we probably should, or that would be better if we did.

Joe: Well, you know, neither of us come from families that have very much physical contact.

Sheila: We kids always did with my mother.

Joe: Well, we never did.

Sheila: I don't know. It doesn't bother me. I mean, people make a big deal about having sex, sexual compatibility, and so on, but I think in the long run it's probably more important that we have our other compatibilities.

Joe: Yeah.

Sheila: If our sex life was wonderful and we disagreed about everything else, we'd probably be considering divorce.

Though it is clear that Joe and Sheila disagreed on what frequency of physical contact felt right to them, neither attempted to persuade the other. Nor did they reach a compromise. They just concluded jointly that the conflict wasn't a big enough deal to work through. Each person stated his or her case, and that was the end of it. They felt that the common ground and values they shared overwhelmed the disagreement, making the conflict unimportant.

In a sense, conversations like Joe and Sheila's are standoffs. They reach some understanding that they disagree but do not explore the precise emotional nature of their differences. In these relationships, solving a problem usually means ignoring the difference, one partner agreeing to act more like the other (for example, if there is a dispute over disciplining children), or most often just letting time take its course. And yet, if you ask these couples whether they ever argue, many will readily say they do. And in a sense their reply is accurate: they do air their conflicts, but they follow up with only minimum attempts to convince each other of their point. They resolve their issues by avoiding or minimizing them.

Rather than resolve conflicts, avoidant couples appeal to their basic shared philosophy of marriage. They reaffirm what they love and value in the marriage, accentuate the positive, and accept the rest. In this way, they often end an unresolved discussion still feeling good about one another.

This type of successful coupling flies in the face of conventional wisdom that links marital stability to skillful "talking things out." So it seems a marriage *can* work even if a couple does not resolve their disputes. In contrast to the validating style, an avoidant style leads to a different sense of "we-ness":—it's as if the couple knows their bond is so strong they can overlook their disagreements. Yet there is a low level of companionship and sharing in the marriage. They value separateness and maintain autonomy in their use of space. These couples tend to live calm, pleasant lives. Though they display little of the intense passion of a volatile couple and less even than a validating couple, they face little of the risk that comes from testing their marriage as the other two types do.

One potentially problematic quality of the avoidant style, however, is that it leaves husband and wife very unschooled in how to address a conflict should they someday be forced to do so. If an issue develops that is too overwhelming to be handled through "agreeing to disagree," their marriage could end up like a fish washed up on shore, flailing about outside of its element. The result could be that negativity overwhelms their interaction and the marriage falls apart.

Another hazard of this type of marriage is that it can become lonely. These marriages are marked by a low degree of introspection or psychological sophistication. As a consequence, husband and/or wife may eventually feel that the other doesn't really know or understand them. This can occur when neither spouse is deeply aware of the real emotional bases of their upsets. In essence, they keep missing each other. If this becomes extreme, an avoidant marriage can get off course.

One couple we studied, Bill and Jane, are prime examples of this lack of introspection during arguments, although they remain happily married. The major source of strife in their marriage at the time they were interviewed was the hassle involved in building a new house. Jane's father was financing the project— and insisting on controlling even minor details of the construction. He was on the site regularly, informing the construction crew that he didn't think a light was needed over the kitchen counter, and so on. To an outside observer it was pretty obvious that the main source of tension between Jane and Bill was his resentment of her father's excessive involvement in the project and Jane's sense of divided loyalty between her husband and father. But in their arguments, neither Bill nor Jane ever raised either of these issues! Their exchanges didn't contain a single comment like, "I feel caught between you and my Dad," or, "I wish your Dad would just let us do it our way." Instead, they picked smaller, "safer" arguments such as whether a newspaper had advertised a paint sale at a local store, or whether Bill had talked to a workman on a particular day. These conflicts were easily resolved, leaving the couple with a renewed sense of unity, although they never actually addressed their underlying problem.

Clearly, though, there are drawbacks to an avoidant marriage just as there are to a volatile or validating one. It may well be that these different types of couples could glean a lot from each other's approach—for example, the volatile couple learning to ignore some conflicts and the avoidant one learning how to compromise. No matter how well suited husband and wife are, they may still need to work on their union to keep the balance intact and the love alive. . . . But the prognosis for these types of marriages is quite positive. In fact, I believe a successful marriage generally evolves into one of these three types—they are each healthy adaptations to living intimately with another human being.

The three types of stable couples will each say that they discuss feelings fully in their marriage and resolve issues. But they differ vastly on these dimensions and on what feels like a satisfying resolution. What is far more important than actually solving the issue or problem is feeling good about the interaction itself, and each of these types of couples has its own way to do that. Here, for example, is how each kind of couple might deal with the identical problem. First, the validating couple:

Husband: You've never been to church with me. I wish you'd come some time.
Wife: You know I don't believe in organized religion.
Husband: I'm not asking you to believe.
Wife: What then?
Husband: I get lonely without you.
Wife: You're saying you miss me?
Husband: Yeah, I am.
Wife: You're not trying to convert?
Husband: Maybe a little, but no. I just wish we'd be together as a family.
Wife: I kind of miss you too on Sunday morning.
Husband: I also think it's good for the kids.
Wife: I agree.
Husband: What about coming some time?
Wife: No pressure?
Husband: No pressure.
Wife: I'll think about it.
Husband: Fair enough.

Here's how the conversation about church might have sounded if a volatile couple had been having it:

Husband: You've never been to church with me. I wish you'd come some time.
Wife: You know I don't believe in organized religion.
Husband: I want to get Jason baptized.
Wife: (*Raising her voice*) Why? So he doesn't go to purgatory for original sin if he dies?
Husband: Because I feel it says that he has a spiritual life, that he's part of a religious community.
Wife: You got that from the priest.
Husband: Well, he said it quite well.
Wife: (*Sarcastically*) You're a lawyer and you can't put it in your own words?
Husband: God's got too good a case.

Wife: (*Laughs*) Yeah, we don't want to fight God.
Husband: (*Laughs*) Since you don't believe in any of it, why not go along with what I want?

This is what the conversation about going to church might have sounded like if the couple were conflict avoiders:

Husband: You've never been to church with me.
Wife: Um-hmm, that's true.
Husband: I wish you'd come some time.
Wife: I prefer the time alone.
Husband: Well, okay. It's not real important to me actually.
Wife: We have a lot else going for us, you know.
Husband: Oh I think ours is a great marriage. Yeah, my sister and Jeff go all the time and they fight like cats and dogs. Religion doesn't do much for them. I just thought I'd ask.
Wife: I'm glad you brought it up. But you know I could put in the time on our remodeling. We're so close to getting started with the plans.
Husband: That'd be more important, really, than your going with me to church. Go ahead.
Wife: You don't mind?
Husband: No. It's no big deal. It's not an issue.
Wife: I'll come to the picnics.
Husband: Fine. That'd be fine.
Wife: You don't mind?
Husband: Not really.
Wife: Good.

NEGOTIATING A TYPE OF STABLE MARRIAGE

Every couple probably goes through a negotiation starting early in their relationship for what style they will have. Partners often differ in the level of emotional intensity they are most comfortable with, and in their preferred way of handling emotional strife. It may seem unlikely that someone who would be most comfortable in an avoidant marriage would select someone who would be most comfortable in a volatile marriage, but I have seen it happen. Opposites do attract, at least sometimes. For example, I know a very emotionally controlled man who married a very expressive woman. She loved his stability and he loved her fire. After a while, though, he wished that she would be less explosive, more rational, and show more emotional control, and she wished he would be more spontaneous, responsive, and expressive. He wanted more privacy, psychological space, and autonomy than she found comfortable. They had trouble negotiating a marital style with which they could each live.

This negotiation is a hard task, but essential if you are to find stability. I think it may be possible to borrow from each marital style and create a viable mixed style. Being aware of the styles available to you may help in finding your own balance. . . .

READING

13

Long-Term Marriages

Frances Klagsbrun

What are the characteristics of long, satisfying, happy marriages? . . . [T]here is no formula, no single recipe that when used in the right proportions will produce the perfect marriage, or even a working one. Rather, there are certain abilities and outlooks that couples in strong marriages have, not all of them at all times, but a large proportion a good part of the time. They fall, it seems to me, into eight categories:

1. AN ABILITY TO CHANGE AND TOLERATE CHANGE

Change is inevitable in marriage as in life. Partners become involved in work and pull back from work; children are born, go to school, leave home; spouses age, get sick, drop old interests, take on new ones, make new friends, live through the sorrows of old ones; parents get old and die; couples move from apartments to houses and back to apartments, from one town to another. Changes bring anxieties and disequilibrium. Yet in the strongest marriages, each partner is able to make "midcourse corrections, almost like astronauts," as one psychiatrist put it. That is, they are able both to adapt to the change that is happening in the marriage or in the other partner and, when called for, to change themselves. . . .

In the marriages that have remained strong and viable, partners have had the flexibility to pick up what was useful to them from the barrage of slogans and confusions of "facts," and change their marriages and themselves to incorporate new ideals that made sense to them. Even the marriages that have kept the most traditional forms, as many have, have had to make concessions to the mood of the times, if not within the marriage itself then in the couple's outlook and their attitudes toward their children. The Flahertys, one of the most conventional couples interviewed, maintained that Peggy Flaherty's place was in her home, and her work the work of running the family finances and caring for her husband. Yet they strongly encouraged their two daughters to develop occupations—one is a dental technician, the other a nurse—and to continue working after they had families of their own. (True, these are typically "women's" occupations, but the very idea of a married woman working had once been anathema to Tom Flaherty.) Although practicing Catholics themselves, they have succored and supported one daughter who is divorced, recognizing, they said, that she had a right to rid herself of a bad marriage and seek her own happiness.

Much greater changes have taken place in the couples who have shifted their life patterns as social values have shifted. The women who have gone to work or back to school years into their marriages have come to see themselves as different beings than they were in their earlier days. They have not discarded their old selves; they have developed a different part of them. But in doing so they have changed their marriages. Their husbands have accommodated to those changes—some more willingly than others—and in doing so, many have changed themselves. They have changed the way they behave by taking on household tasks they would not have dreamed of touching when they first married, and by rearranging their schedules to make room for their wives' schedules. More important, they have changed inwardly, many of them, truly acknowledging their wives' strivings, ambitions and accomplishments outside their homes. One tiny manifestation of these changes in long marriages are the numbers of no-longer-young men I see at dinner parties automatically getting up to clear the table or serve a course while their wives sit and chat with guests. They are not self-consciously carrying out some carefully formulated contract. They have incorporated this domestic behavior into their way of being. For them, such acts are not merely gestures; they represent an inner change.

But there is an attitude toward change in long marriages that goes far beyond the social issues. There is this: People who stay happily married see themselves not as victims of fate, but as free agents who make choices in life. Although, like everyone else, they are influenced by their own family backgrounds, for the most part they do not allow their lives together to be dominated by their earlier family lives apart. Because they choose to be married to one another, a choice they make again and again, they are open to changing themselves, pulling away from what *was* in order to make what *is* alive and vital. In other words, as much as they are able to, they try to control their lives, rather than drifting along as the patsies of destiny. . . .

2. AN ABILITY TO LIVE WITH THE UNCHANGEABLE

[This] means to live with unresolved conflict when necessary. The simultaneous acceptance of change and of lack of change in long marriages is summed up by the words of a shopkeeper, married thirty-eight years: "You have to know when to holler and you have to know when to look away."

A statement made by many couples when asked about the "secrets" of their happy marriage was, "We don't expect perfection," or some variation thereof. They would go on to explain that their marriage had areas that were far from perfect, qualities in one another that they wish could have changed but they have come to recognize as qualities that will never change. Still, they live with those unchangeable, and sometimes disturbing, qualities, because, as one woman said,

"The payoff is so great in other areas." We have been so bombarded with advice books and articles about "solving" problems and "overcoming" adversity, about "improving" our marriages and becoming "ideal" mates that we often forget that it is possible also just to let things be, without solution or improvement.

On a superficial level, I think of a woman who described her misery early in her second marriage because of her husband's unbelievably ear-shattering snores. Night after night she lay awake listening to his nasal roars and wondering how she was going to survive this marriage. For a while she tried slipping out of bed in the middle of the night to sleep in the living room. But she didn't sleep well there, and, anyhow, she wanted to be in bed with her husband. Then she prevailed upon him to seek medical help to control the snoring. The doctors had nothing to offer, and the night sounds continued unabated. Finally, she stopped complaining and bought some ear plugs. They do not block out the noise completely, but they help. The snoring problem, she has decided, will never be solved, the plugs make it possible for her to live with it as best she can, and that is as much as she can do.

On a more serious level, long-married couples accept the knowledge that there are some deep-seated conflicts—about personality differences, habits, styles of dealing with things—that will never be solved. In the best of situations, they stop fighting about those issues and go about their lives instead of wasting their energies on a constant, fruitless struggle to settle differences "once and for all." Not long ago, at a time when marriage was under perpetual attack, this very quality of marriage, its imperfectability, was at the crux of the arguments against it. People spoke of marriage as a form of "settling" for something less than ideal, as "compromising" with what one wanted from life. Yet this ability to live with the imperfect is, it seems to me, the essence of maturity. Mature people are able to accept the limitations life places on them and work around them. And in the "working around," in finding ways to live with difficulties, they may experience some of the most creative moments of living. . . .

3. AN ASSUMPTION OF PERMANENCE

Most marriages, first, second or later, begin with the hope and expectation that they will last forever. In the marriages that do last, "forever" is not only a hope, but an ongoing philosophy. The mates do not seriously think about divorce as a viable option. Certainly there are "divorce periods," times of distancing and anger, but even if divorce itself crosses the minds of the couple, it is not held out as an escape from difficulties. One can argue that couples who got married more than fifteen or twenty years ago don't think about divorce because it was not as prevalent a part of our culture in earlier days as it is now. But that's not the complete story. Many couples married during those earlier days have divorced, and for many younger couples permanence is a built-in component of marriage, as it had been for their parents.

This attitude that a marriage will last, *must* last (not because some religious authority or family member says so, but because the marriage is that important to the couple), tempers a husband's and a wife's approach to conflicts and imperfections. They *see* the marriage as an entity in itself that must be protected. Or as family therapist Salvador Minuchin said, "A marriage is more than the sum of its parts. In marriage, one plus one doesn't equal two; it forms something different, something that is much more than two." And for the sake of that "something" that is the marriage, these couples are willing to make compromises and sacrifices when necessary. In today's terminology, they are committed to the marriage as well as to one another. . . .

4. TRUST

This is a word used again and again by couples, and it means many things. It means love, although people tend to use the word "trust" more often than they use "love." In part this is because "love" is an overused word, and one whose romantic meanings have overshadowed the deeper, more profound meaning of the love that binds married people. In larger part it is because feelings of love may wax and wane in the course of a marriage—in times of anger, for example, few people can keep in touch with those feelings—but trust is a constant; without it there is no true marriage. Trust also implies intimacy, or, rather, it forms the base for the closeness that couples in good marriages have established. But couples use the word "trust" more readily than "intimacy" or "love." And I believe they do because "trust" sums up much of the dynamic of a marriage, the back-and-forth interaction from which everything else grows. Trust in marriage allows for the sense of security and comfort that mark long and satisfying unions. Trust also makes possible the freedom marriage provides, the freedom and "right," in the words of psychiatrist Aaron Stein, "people have to be themselves and have their own feelings." Each partner trusts the other with his or her core self, trusts that that self will not be ridiculed or violated, trusts that it will be nurtured and protected—safe. And in that safety lies a special kind of freedom.

Intimacy, as I have said, is built around the trust partners allow themselves to have in one another. Once that trust exists, there is no set form intimacy must assume. I cannot say that every couple in a strong marriage communicate with one another as openly as the much-publicized communication ideals of our society would have them. Some do. Some are open and loose with one another, ventilating feelings and sensations freely. In other families, one partner, or both, may be more closed off, less able or willing to pour out heartsounds. But these marriages have their own ways of being intimate, which grow from the trust between partners. It may be that one partner is the expansive one while the second is more silent, relying on the other for emotional expressiveness. Or it may be that both act somewhat restrained in revealing sensitivities, yet they understand one another and feel comfortable with the more limited interchanges they have. I found many styles of relating among long-married couples, and no one seemed better than another as long as each couple was satisfied with their own style.

The trust that lies at the heart of happy marriages is also the foundation for sexual enjoyment among partners. When mates spoke about sexual loving, they almost always spoke about trusting feelings that had expanded over the years. "Sex is richer and deeper for us," said one woman. "We trust each other and we're not ashamed to get pleasure." Trust is also the reason invariably given for a commitment to monogamy, as in "I may be tempted, but I wouldn't want to violate our trust." When a partner has had a fling or brief affair, trust is the reason most often offered for having ended it or for avoiding further extramarital involvements. In short, trust is regarded by many couples as the linchpin of their marriage.

5. A BALANCE OF DEPENDENCIES

[This] is another way of saying a balance of power. I prefer "dependency," even though "power" is a sexier word, with its implied comparison between marriage and politics. I prefer "dependency" because it better conveys the way couples see and regard one another. They speak of needing each other and depending on each other, and in doing so, they are not speaking about the weaknesses of marriage, but about its strengths. In the best of marriages, partners are mutually dependent; interdependent is another way of saying that. They are aware of their dependencies and not ashamed to cater to them, acknowledging openly their debt to one another. . . .

Dependency, it needs to be added quickly, does not mean an obliteration of self. One thing I consistently became aware of was that no matter how close or how interdependent a couple, each spouse retained an individuality, a sense of self. If one or the other had lost that individuality and become completely submerged or exploited by the other, one or both partners usually expressed deep unhappiness in the marriage. Again, even in the most traditional marriages, where a woman's social identity may be tied to her husband's occupation or profession, the women who spoke most convincingly about the satisfactions of their marriages were women who viewed themselves as individuals, and who did not rely on their husbands to make them feel worthy. . . .

6. AN ENJOYMENT OF EACH OTHER

Wives and husbands in satisfying long marriages like one another, enjoy being together and enjoy talking to each other. Although they may spend evenings quietly together in a room, the silence that surrounds them is the comfortable silence of two people who know they do not *have* to talk to feel close. But mostly they do talk. For many couples conversations go on continually, whether the gossip of everyday living or discussions of broader events. And they listen to one another. I watched the faces of people I interviewed and watched each listening while the other spoke. They might argue, become irritated or jump in to correct each other, but they are engaged, and rarely bored.

They enjoy each other physically also, and sexual pleasures infuse many marriages for years and years. I could sense a sexual electricity between some partners. A different kind of warmth emanated from others, a feeling of closeness and affection. They held hands, they touched, they smiled and they spoke of sex as "warm and loving," as one woman said, "maybe not the wildness of our early marriage, but very pleasing."

They laugh at each other's jokes. Humor is the universal salve and salvation, easing tensions and marriage fatigue. "If you can laugh about it," everyone said, "you know it will be all right." And for them it is.

They find each other interesting, but they do not necessarily have the same interests. And that was a surprise. Far fewer couples than I expected spoke about sharing interests or hobbies. . . .

But if sharing interests is not a prerequisite for a rewarding marriage, sharing *values* is. Values refer to the things people believe in, the things they hold dear and worthy. The philosopher Bertrand Russell explained their importance in marriage well when he wrote, "It is fatal . . . if one values only money and the other values only good works." Such a couple will have trouble getting along, let alone enjoying one another's interests or ideas.

Mates who feel well-matched share a common base of values even when they disagree about other things. One couple described having their biggest arguments about money. He loves to spend whatever they have on clothes, records and the theater; she watches every cent, wearing the same dress again and again. Yet they had an instant meeting of minds when it came time to buy a cello for their musically gifted daughter. They bought the best they could afford, even using a good part of their savings, because they both valued their child's music education above anything else money could buy. Another couple, who love antique Oriental ceramics, think nothing of living in a dingy, run-down apartment while they spend their modest earnings on beautiful ceramic vases that they track down and buy together.

For some couples, religion is the value that informs everything else in life. Those couples were in a minority among the families I interviewed, as they are a minority in our secular society. But those who did value religion considered it the strongest bond in their lives, and many attributed the happiness and stability of their marriages to that bond. I found it interesting that marriages in which both partners valued religion, even if the partners were of different faiths, had fewer conflicts over religious issues than same-faith marriages, in which only one felt as religious commitment, especially if the other partner was disdainful of religion.

For all marriages, sharing values enhances the intimacy and mutual respect spouses feel, adding to their enjoyment of one another.

7. A SHARED HISTORY THAT IS CHERISHED

Every couple has a story, and couples in long marriages respect their own stories. They are connected to each other through those stories, and even the sadnesses they shared are a valued part of their history. "Our life is like a patchwork," one woman said. "We pull in red threads from here and blue threads from there and make them into one piece. Sometimes the threads barely hold, but you pull hard at them and they come together, and the patchwork remains whole."

The attachment couples have to their histories is not necessarily a senti-mental or nostalgic attachment, but an affectionate one that sees significance in the past and in all the times spent together. George Gilbert said it nicely. His marriage, with one of the most troubled histories of all, had been filled with the traumas of manic-depressive illness and alcoholism until some years ago when he made himself stop drinking and his illness was brought under control by medication. "You know," he said, "you talk about this and you talk about that, and it sounds so chaotic, the alcohol and the rest. But still, in the midst of it all there were great moments. Once, at the height of my drinking, we went to Cape Cod with our three sons and we got an acre of land. We put out a camper and we rented a canoe and we had a glorious time. Sure, when you reflect you think of the bad things—the flashing lights and the arms wrapped around the porcelain in the bathroom when you're hung over and sick. But there was so much else, even then. There was still a lot of fun, still a lot of humor, still a lot of good loving for both of us." . . .

People in long marriages value their joint history. When their ties in the present get raggedy, they are able to look to the past to find the good that they shared, rather than give in to the disillusionments of the moment. Their sense of history also gives them a respect for time. They know, by looking backward, that changes take time and that angers vanish with time, and they know that there is time ahead for new understandings and new adventures.

8. LUCK

It has to be said, because everyone said it. With it all, the history and the trust, the willingness to change and to live without change, people need a little bit of luck to keep a marriage going.

You need luck, first of all, in choosing a partner who has the capacity to change and trust and love. In their book *Marriage and Personal Development*, psychiatrists Rubin Blanck and Gertrude Blanck make the case that marriages work best when both partners have reached a level of maturity before marriage that makes them ready for marriage. They are quite right. The only difficulty with their case is that few people are terribly mature when they marry, certainly not people in first marriages who marry young, and not even many people in second marriages. Yet many marriages work because partners mature together, over the years of matrimony. So, you need a little luck in choosing someone who will mature and grow while you, too, mature.

And you need a little luck in the family you come from and the friends that you have. A horrendous family background in which parents abuse their chil-dren or offer no love can set up almost insurmountable obstacles to the ability to sustain a marital relationship. Yet there are couples in long, happy marriages who did have devastating backgrounds. Often they were able to break the patterns they had known because of the encouragement of an aunt or an uncle, a grandparent, a teacher, a friend. They were lucky in finding the support they needed.

Then, you need a little luck with life. A marriage might move along happily and smoothly enough until a series of unexpected events rain down on it. A combination of illnesses or job losses, family feuds or personal failures might push the marriage off-course, when without these blows, it could have succeeded. Every marriage needs some luck in holding back forces that could crush it.

These aspects of luck may be out of our power to control. But the good thing about luck is that it is not all out of our control. Many people who considered themselves happy in marriage also spoke about themselves as being lucky. Since they seemed to have the same share of problems and difficulties as anyone else, sometimes even more than their share, I came to think that luck in marriage, as in life, is as much a matter of attitude as of chance. Couples who regard themselves as lucky are the ones who seize luck when they are able to. Instead of looking outside their marriage and assuming the luck is all there, in other people's homes, they look inside their marriage and find the blessings there. They are not blind to the soft spots of their marriages—nobody denied difficulties; they just consider the positives more important. So they knock wood and say they are lucky. And I guess they are. They have grabbed luck by the tail and have twisted it to their own purposes.

R E A D I N G

14

Divorce: Challenges, Changes, and New Chances

E. Mavis Hetherington, Tracy C. Law, and Thomas G. O'Connor

Studies of the effects of divorce on family members traditionally have centered around the development of problem behaviors subsequent to marital dissolution. Recent findings, however, have emphasized the wide variation in responses to stressful experiences and life transitions, including divorce and remarriage (e.g., Rutter, 1987; Werner, 1987; Hetherington, 1991a). Although debate still exists over the question of the magnitude and duration of the effects of parental divorce on children, work in the past 10 years has converged in suggesting that the interaction among individual differences in personal and familial character-

---

istics and extrafamilial factors that support or undermine coping efforts by family members must be examined in order to understand the spectrum of responses to divorce. This spectrum can range from enhanced competence to clinical levels of problem behavior (Hetherington, 1989, 1991a; Stolberg, Camplair, Currier, & Wells, 1987).

In addition, it is becoming increasingly apparent that divorce should be viewed not as a discrete event but as part of a series of family transitions and changes in family relationships. The response to any family transition will depend both on what precedes and follows it. The response to divorce and life in a single-parent household will be influenced by individual adjustment and the quality of family relationships before the divorce as well as circumstances surrounding and following the divorce. In many families, divorce may trigger a series of adverse transactional factors such as economic decline, parenting stress, and physical and psychological dysfunction in family members. For others, it may present an escape from conflict and an unsatisfying marital relationship, a chance to form more gratifying and harmonious relationships, and an opportunity for personal growth and individuation (Gore & Eckenroade, 1992; Hetherington, 1989).

The recognition that divorce is part of a chain of marital transitions and shifting life experiences, and that individual responses to these experiences demonstrate marked variability, has been a powerful influence on recent theoretical models developed to explain children's adjustment to parental divorce. In understanding these findings, many researchers have adopted a developmental contextual framework (Gore & Eckenroade, 1992; Nock, 1982; Hetherington & Clingempeel, 1992; Hetherington & Martin, 1986). This approach examines adjustment across time, and on multiple levels, including interactions among the overarching social and historical context, changing dynamics within the family system, individual ontogenic characteristics of child and parent, and influences external to the family such as the extended family, peer relationships, and the educational, occupational, mental health, legal, religious, and welfare systems.

The purpose of this chapter is not to present a comprehensive review of research and clinical findings concerning the adjustment to divorce. Selected recent research examples and a developmental, contextual, interactive model will be used as an organizational framework in which to examine factors that contribute to individual differences in the way family members negotiate the changes and challenges associated with divorce. Many of the research findings will be drawn from the longitudinal studies of Hetherington and her colleagues. Before discussing the factors implicated in a developmental, contextual, interactive approach, it is important to place the findings in the larger context of demographic and social changes that have occurred in the last 20 years.

THE CHANGING WORLD OF THE FAMILY: DEMOGRAPHIC AND SOCIAL FORCES

Although the divorce rate doubled between 1960 and 1980, it has leveled off and even declined slightly in the past decade (Glick, 1988). Currently, it is estimated that half of all marriages will end in divorce and that approximately 60% of these dissolutions will involve children. Although the percentage of marriages ending in divorce has not changed appreciably since the early 1980's, the number of children affected by parental divorce, as well as the number of children from divorced families now of marriageable age themselves, has continued to increase (Bumpass, 1984). It has been estimated that 38% of white children and 75% of African-American children born to married parents in the United States will experience their parents' divorce before their 16th birthday (Bumpass, 1984). In addition, African-Americans not only have a higher rate of divorce than whites, they are also more likely to separate but not go through a legal divorce procedure, to experience a longer time-lag between time of separation and divorce, and are less likely to remarry (Glick, 1988; Teachman, Polonko, & Scanzoni, 1987). Although families who are poor, African-American, and suffering multiple life stresses are more likely to divorce, the rise in economic independence for well-educated women also has led to a greater likelihood that these women will divorce compared to their less-educated peers. Furthermore, since most divorced men and women remarry, and since the rate of divorce in second marriages is even higher than in first marriages (61% of men and 54% of women go through a second divorce), many children and parents encounter a series of marital transitions and reorganizations in family roles and relationships (Glick, 1988; Chase-Lansdale & Hetherington, 1990). These statistics indicate that divorce, once considered an atypical family event, is now a "normative," even if not a "normal," experience in the life cycle of many contemporary American families (Emery & Forehand, 1992).

Shifting social and historical factors affect patterns of both marriage and divorce (Cherlin, 1981; Teachman et al., 1987; Glick, 1988). Wars, whether the Civil War, World War II, the Korean War, or the Vietnam War, have been associated with hasty marriages followed by increased rates of divorce (Glick, 1988). Current high rates of divorce have also been attributed to greater labor force participation and economic independence of women, improved contraception, the emergence of the welfare system, an increase in the proportion of marriages involving premarital births, changing ideologies associated with the women's movement, and the liberalization of divorce laws. The family is being reshaped in response to transformations in social values and roles. Greater diversity in attitudes and accepted behaviors are found not only in family and gender roles but also in other social systems—in law, politics, religion, education, and the workplace. Divorce and the concomitant experiences of family members are only one reflection of the need for social institutions, such as the family, to adapt to historical and social change.

WHY MARRIAGES FAIL: THE PRECURSORS OF DIVORCE

Neither marital satisfaction nor sheer frequency of disagreements is a good predictor of divorce. Instead, styles of conflict resolution involving disengagement, stonewalling, contempt, denial, and blaming are likely to be associated with divorce (Gottman, 1994; Hetherington, 1989). One of the most common patterns of marital relations leading to divorce is a conflict-confronting, conflict-avoiding pattern where one spouse, usually the wife, confronts areas of concern and disagreements in the marriage and expresses her feelings about these problems, while the other spouse responds with defensiveness, avoidance, withdrawal, whining, and, if prodded, with resentment and anger. A second common marital pattern associated with later divorce is one in which couples have little overt conflict, but have different expectations and perceptions about family life, marriage and their children, and have few shared interests, activities, or friends (Hetherington & Tryon, 1989; Notarius & Vanzetti, 1983).

These patterns of relating in dysfunctional couples means that many children before the divorce are likely to have been exposed to unresolved disagreements, resentment, anger, and ineffective marital problem solving. Prospective studies indicate that troubled marital relations and interparental tension accompanied by unsupportive parenting and high rates of behavior problems in children occur years before the dissolution of the marriage (Block, Block, & Gjerde, 1986, 1988; Cherlin et al., 1991). The inept parenting and behavior disorders usually attributed to divorce and life in a one-parent household may, to some extent, be a continuation of predivorce functioning and be associated with disrupted processes in the nuclear family. Although the popular interpretation of these findings is that marital tension, alienation and conflict cause inept parenting and behavior problems in children, it may be that the stress of dealing with a difficult, noncompliant, antisocial child helps to undermine an already fragile marriage and precipitates divorce.

Recently, another explanation, based on the findings of twin studies, has been proposed. It suggests that divorce and problem behaviors in children are genetically linked, and that this may help to explain the slightly higher rates of divorce found in offspring of divorced parents (McGue & Lykken, in press). Irritable, antisocial behavior in parents may provoke marital problems and be genetically associated with behavior problems in children, with the subsequent marital difficulties of adult offspring of divorced parents, and with the intergenerational transmission of divorce. Whatever the reasons may be for the dysfunctional precursors of divorce, it is against a background of disrupted family relationships and disordered behavior in parents and children that family members move into the changes and challenges associated with separation, divorce, and life in a one-parent household.

CHANGES IN THE LIVING SITUATION

An established family system can be viewed as a mechanism for identifying and framing the roles, activities, and daily life of each family member. When a divorce occurs, it means not only the loss of patterns of everyday family interaction and a family member, but loss of a way of life. Pervasive alterations in expectations, life experiences, and the sense of self in parents and children are associated with the uncertainty, found not only in divorce, but also in other transitions, such as loss of a family member through death (Silverman, 1988) or even with the addition of a family member through remarriage (Hetherington, in press).

Immediately following divorce, household routines and roles break down and parents experience task overload as a single parent attempts to perform the tasks usually assumed by two parents. In such situations, children, especially daughters, in divorced families are often asked to assume responsibility for household chores and care of younger siblings. Many of the interactions between custodial mothers and their children, are instrumental in nature and occur in the context of shared tasks. The problems of overwhelming responsibility for parent and child are often exacerbated when divorced mothers must begin working or increase their workload because of economic necessity (Duncan & Hoffman, 1985).

In the first year following divorce, the average family income of women decreases by almost 40%. Although income relative to needs gradually increases, even 5 years after divorce, the income of divorced mothers remains at 94% of their predivorced income, in contrast to 130% for divorced fathers and 125% for remarried women (Duncan & Hoffman, 1985). This is the result, in part, of partial or intermittent payment, or nonpayment, of child support by 70% of divorced noncustodial fathers. This loss of income following martial dissolution often determines where families live, where children go to school, the quality of neighborhoods and peer groups, and the accessibility of jobs, health care, and support networks. Although income level or loss explains only a small amount of the variance related to children's adjustment following divorce, poverty does increase the probability of encountering these other transactional factors associated with the ability of parents and children to manage stress successfully and with developmental outcomes for children. Negative life stresses are most marked for members of divorced families in the first 2 years following divorce and gradually decline with time; however, they always remain higher than those in nondivorced families (Forgatch, Patterson, & Ray, in press; Hetherington, Cox, & Cox, 1985). An unexpected bill, illness, or a school closing may present a greater emergency for a divorced mother than for parents in a two-parent household with mutual support and greater resources.

In spite of the difficulties encountered by divorced women, by 2 years after divorce, whether or not they initiated the divorce, the vast majority of women report being more satisfied with their family situation than they had been in the last year of their marriage. Furthermore, although divorced mothers report more child-rearing stress than do nondivorced mothers, they also say that parenting is easier without a nonsupportive spouse who undermines or disagrees with their parenting practices. The balance between increased risk and stressors and positive life changes must be considered in examining the response to divorce (Hetherington, in press).

CUSTODY, CONTACT, AND CO-PARENTAL RELATIONS

In the vast majority of divorces, the mother is awarded custody of children; only 13% of fathers are awarded sole custody of their children at the time of divorce (Emery, 1988). In these cases, it is often because mothers are deemed incompetent, do not want custody of their children, or because male or adolescent children are involved. In spite of the overt or covert legal preference for mothers as custodians under the guise of best interests of the child or primary caregivers guidelines, there is no consistent evidence that fathers who seek custody are less competent parents than mothers (Warshak, 1992). In fact, by 2 years after divorce, custodial fathers report better family relations and fewer problems with their children than do custodial mothers (Furstenberg, 1988). This may be because custodial fathers, in contrast to custodial mothers, have higher incomes, more available supports, and are more likely to be caring for older children. In addition, fathers may be less sensitive and responsive than mothers to family dysfunction and behavior problems in children. However, reluctant fathers who assent to assume custody because of their wives' inability or disinclination to care for their children are less involved and able parents. A finding relevant to decisions involving custody is that, although there is some continuity in the pre- and postdivorce quality of parenting for mothers, there is little for fathers (Hetherington, Cox, & Cox, 1982). Some custodial fathers seem to exhibit a *Kramer vs. Kramer* response and develop an involvement and parenting skills they had not had before the divorce, but some intensely attached noncustodial fathers find intermittent parenting painful and withdraw from their children. On the other hand, a substantial number of noncustodial fathers report that their relationship with their children improves after divorce.

On the average, noncustodial fathers become increasingly less available to their children. In the most recent national study using a probability sample, mothers reported that, following divorce, only one-quarter of children see their fathers once a week or more, and over a third do not see their father at all or see them only a few times a year (Seltzer, 1991). Physical distance in residence, low socioeconomic status, remarriage, and having only female rather than male children are associated with less visitation by noncustodial fathers. Noncustodial mothers are more likely to maintain contact with their children than are noncustodial fathers (Furstenberg, 1988; Zill, 1988). This leads to the rather intriguing issue as to whether differences found in children in a mother's custody, and a father's custody are attributable to the relationship with the custodial parent or to differences in the child's contact with the noncustodial parent and additional support in childrearing for custodial fathers provided by noncustodial mothers.

The move toward facilitating visitation and joint custody has been based on the premises that continued contact with both parents is desirable and that noncustodial parents with joint custody will be more likely to maintain contact and financial support. The response to the first premise must be that it depends on who is doing the visiting and on the relationship between the parents. If the noncustodial parent is reasonably well-adjusted, competent in parenting, and has a close relationship with the child, and if the child is not exposed to conflict between the two parents, continued contact can have a salutary effect on the child's adjustment. However, it takes an exceptionally close relationship with a noncustodial parent to buffer a child from the deleterious effects of a conflictual, nonsupportive relationship with a custodial parent (Hetherington et al., 1982). If there is high conflict between the parents, joint custody and continued contact can have adverse effects on the child (Maccoby, Depner, & Mnookin, 1988; Wallerstein & Blakeslee, 1989). Furthermore, there is some evidence that, after remarriage, although continued involvement of the noncustodial father with the child does not interfere with family functioning in the stepfamily, frequent visits by the noncustodial mother may be associated with negative relations between children, especially daughters, and their stepmothers (Brand, Clingempeel, & Bowen-Woodward, 1988).

Although cooperative, consensual coparenting following divorce is the ideal relationship (Camara & Resnick, 1988), in most cases the best that can be attained is one of independent but noninterfering parental relations. In a substantial group of families, conflict is sustained or accelerates following divorce (Hetherington et al., 1982; Kline, Johnston, & Tschan, 1991; Maccoby, Depner, & Mnookin, 1990). Interparental conflict in the long run is related to diminished contact and fewer child support payments by noncustodial fathers (Seltzer, 1991). In addition, in such conflicted relationships, children may feel caught in the middle as they are sometimes asked to carry messages between parents, to inform each parent of the other's activities, to defend one parent against the other's disparaging remarks, or to justify wanting to spend time with the other parent (Buchanon, Maccoby, & Dombusch, 1991; Hetherington, in press). Being "caught in the middle," rather than divorce per se, or loss of contact with a noncustodial parent, has the most adverse effect on children's behavior and psychological well-being. Parental conflict provides children with an opportunity to exploit parents and play one off against the other, and when they are older, to escape careful monitoring of their activities. However children, especially older children, are able to function well over time in independent, noninterfering households. As long as they are not involved in parental conflict, children are able to cope well even if these households have different rules and expectations. Children are able to learn the differing role demands and constraints required in relating to diverse people in a variety of social situations such as in the peer group, church, the classroom, on the playing field, or at grandmother's house. In view of children's adaptability and differentiated responses to a broad range of social situations, the resistance to recognizing that children can cope with two different home situations is remarkable. Problems in joint custody come when parents interfere in each other's childrearing, and when children don't want to leave their friends, neighborhoods, or regular routines. In the rare cases where joint custody requires shifts between schools, this too may become a burden. Difficulty in visitation under any custody arrangement may emerge as children grow older and want to spend more time with their peers and less with parents.

Joint custody does tend to promote greater contact and financial support by noncustodial parents (Maccoby et al., 1988). Noncustodial fathers or fathers with joint custody are more likely to support children when they feel they have power in decisions relating to their children's life circumstances and activities. However, under conditions of high conflict, the increased contact associated with joint custody can be detrimental to the well-being of the child. Under conditions of low or encapsulated conflict, or emotional distancing between the parents, the effects of contact will be positive or at least neutral. Most children want to maintain contact with both parents and are more satisfied with continued contact. However, if the custodial parent has formed a hostile alliance with the child against the noncustodial parent, if the child feels caught in the middle of the parental conflict, or if the noncustodial parent has been extremely dysfunctional (e.g., abusive), children may seek to limit their contact with the nonresidential parent.

ADJUSTMENT OF DIVORCED PARENTS

Separation and divorce place both men and women at risk for psychological and physical dysfunction (Chase-Lansdale & Hetherington, 1990). In the immediate aftermath of marital dissolution, both men and women often exhibit extreme emotional lability, anger, depression, anxiety, and impulsive, and antisocial behavior, but for most this is gone by 2 years following divorce. However, even in the long run, alcoholism, drug abuse, psychosomatic problems, accidents, depression, and antisocial behavior are more common in divorced than nondivorced adults (Bloom, Asher, & White, 1978). Furthermore, recent research suggests that marital disruption alters the immune system, making divorced persons more vulnerable to disease, infection, chronic and acute medical problems, and even death (Kiecolt-Glaser et al., 1987). Some of these postdivorce symptoms in adults, such as depression and antisocial behavior, seem likely to have been present before divorce and even to have contributed to a distressed marriage and to marital dissolution. Depression and antisocial behavior are related to irritable, conflictual marital interactions. Adults exhibiting antisocial behavior are more likely to have disordered social relationships, to encounter negative life events, and to undergo multiple marital transitions (Forgatch et al., in press). Our own work, examining couples who later divorced, suggests that, especially for women in distant or hostile, conflicted marriages, depression is likely to decline following divorce, whereas antisocial behavior is likely to remain constant or to increase. Continued attachment to the ex-spouse is associated both with health problems and depression (Kiecolt-Glaser et al., 1987). This connection, however, declines with repartnering and the formation of a close meaningful relationship (Hetherington et al., 1982; Forgatch et al., in press).

We spoke earlier of divorce, like death of a spouse, involving loss of a way of life. It also involves loss of aspects of the self sustained by that way of life (Silverman, 1988). Because of this, the early years of separation and divorce offer great opportunity for positive and negative change. In this early phase, separated and divorced men and women often complain of being disoriented, of not knowing who they are or who they want to be, and of behaving in ego alien ways. They speak of having "not me experiences" where previously rational, self-controlled individuals report such things as smearing dog feces on their ex-spouse's face, following them and peering into their bedroom windows, defacing their property, fantasizing and sometimes acting out violent impulses, or whining and begging for reconciliation. "I can't believe I did that" or "That wasn't really me" is repeatedly heard in interviews with divorcing adults. Many noncustodial fathers feel rootless, disoriented, shut out of regular contact with their children and nurture unrealistic fantasies of reconciliation. Others throw themselves into a frenzy of social activity and try to develop a more open, free-living persona.

Conventional women have more problems in adapting to their new life situation than do less conventional, more internally controlled, androgynous, or working women. Nonemployed women in traditional marriages have often organized their identities around the achievements of their husbands and children. One said, "I used to be Mrs. John Jones, the bank manager's wife. Now I'm Mary Jones! Who is Mary Jones?" In spite of the problems with income, housing, inadequate childcare, loneliness, and limited resources and support encountered by many divorced women, our work shows that about 70% in the long run, prefer their new life to an unsatisfying marriage. Most think that divorce and raising children alone have provided an experience of personal growth, albeit sometimes painful growth. Some of these women were competent, autonomous women before the divorce. Others, in coping with the demands of their new situation, discovered strengths, developed skills, and attained levels of individuation that might never have emerged if they had remained in the constraints of a dysfunctional marriage. It should be noted however, that in comparison to married women, divorced women are overrepresented at both extremes of competence and adjustment. Some are found in a group with high self-esteem and few psychological problems who function ably in social situations, in the workplace, and in the family. Others seem permanently overwhelmed by the losses and changes in their lives, show little adequate coping behavior, and exhibit low self-esteem and multiple problems such as depression, antisocial behavior, substance abuse, and repeated, unsuccessful intimate relationships. Job training, continued education, and professional enhancement play important roles not only in the economic, but also the psychological, well-being of women. Adequate childcare is critical in facilitating these activities (Burns, 1992). Although work satisfaction plays an important role in the self-esteem of divorced adults, most custodial mothers and fathers restrict their social, and to some extent, work activities, and organize their lives around providing and caring for their children. Adequacy in these roles is central to their self-esteem.

Repartnering is the single factor that contributes most to the life satisfaction of divorced men and women; however, it seems more critical to men. Divorced fathers are less likely than divorced mothers to show marked personal growth and individuation while they are single. Men show more positive development in the security of a marriage.

The significance for children of these psychological, emotional, and physical changes in parents is that, in the early years following divorce, children are encountering an altered parent at a time when they need stability in a rapidly changing life situation. A physically ill, emotionally disturbed, or preoccupied parent and a distressed, demanding, angry child may have difficulty giving each other support or solace. Over time, the well-being of the child is associated with the adjustment of the custodial parent, and this is largely an indirect path mediated by parenting behaviors. If parent distress, low self-esteem, depression, or antisocial behavior results in disrupted parenting, behavior problems in children increase (Hetherington & Clingempeel, 1992; Patterson & Bank, 1989; Forgatch et al., in press). If a disturbed parent is able to maintain authoritative qualities, such as responsiveness, warmth, firm control, monitoring, and communication, adverse effects on children are less likely to occur.

R E A D I N G

15

The Remarriage Transition

Constance R. Ahrons and Roy H. Rodgers

The family change process set in motion by one marital disruption boggles one's mind. It frequently requires complex computation to chart and understand the kinship relationships. Even though the current remarriage rates show a continuing decline . . . , the vast majority of divorced families will move through the series of stressful transitions and structural changes brought about by the expansion of the family postdivorce. The structural changes in remarriage give rise to a host of disruptions in roles and relationships, and each transition may be mastered with varying amounts of stress and turmoil.

Projections from the current trends indicate that between 40 and 50 percent of the children born in the 1970s will spend some portion of their minor years in a one-parent household. Given the current remarriage rates it is also projected that approximately 25 to 30 percent of American children will live for some period of time in a remarried household. Although we do not have as adequate cohabitation information as we would like, we can assume that many of these children will also live for some period of time in a cohabiting household, which may or may not become a remarriage household. This means that at least 25 to 30 percent of the children will have more than two adults who function simultaneously as parents. Rates of redivorce are also increasing, resulting in even more complex kinship structures.

Consider the following case example of the Spicer/Tyler/Henry binuclear family. . . .

When Ellen was eight and David ten, their parents separated. They continued to live with their mother, Nancy, spending weekends and vacations with their father, Jim. Two years after the divorce their father married Elaine, who was the custodial parent of her daughter, Jamie, aged six. Ellen and David lived in a one-parent household with their mother for three years, at which time their mother remarried. Their new stepfather, Craig, also had been divorced, and he was the joint-custodial parent of two daughters, aged six and 11. His daughters spent about ten days each month living in his household. Within the next four years, Ellen and David's father and stepmother had two children of their own, a son and a daughter.

When Ellen and David are 15 and 17, their family looks like this: They have two biological parents, two stepparents, three stepsisters, a half-brother and a half-sister. Their extended family has expanded as well: They have two sets of step-grandparents, two sets of biological grandparents, and a large network of aunts, uncles, and cousins. In addition to this complex network of kin, they have two households of "family. . . ."

BINUCLEAR FAMILY REORGANIZATION THROUGH EXPANSION: AN OVERVIEW

The expansion of the binuclear family through remarriage involves the addition of new family members in all three generations. The recoupling of one of the formation spouses requires another reorganization of the former spouse subsystem and each of the parent-child subsystems; a recoupling of the other former spouse requires still another reorganization of the whole system. Each of these transitions has the potential of being highly stressful for family members. The way in which the family reorganizes itself will determine whether the binuclear family emerges as a functional or dysfunctional system. . . .

We are very much hindered by the inadequacy of current language in our discussion of the binuclear family in remarriage. For most of the relationships between family members in this expanded system there are no formal labels or role titles. What does one call one's former mate's new spouse? Or the children or parents of the new mate who have a relationship with one's child? Even the former spouse relationship has no current title, which requires that we continue to speak of it as a past relationship. Although ex-spouses with children may refer to each other as "my daughter's (or son's) father (or mother)," this does not capture the ongoing nonparental relationship between the divorced couple. So, of necessity, as we struggle to analyze some of the components of this complex system, our language suffers from being cumbersome and we will occasionally resort to inadequate terms that have emerged in the process of studying these families.

Former Spouse Subsystem

The former spouse relationship, with its many possible relational variations, becomes even more complex when one or both partners remarry. The timing of the remarriage further complicates the dynamics of this highly ambiguous post-divorce relationship. In McCubbin and Patterson's theoretical formulation of the pathways and mediating factors leading from stress to crisis, accumulating stressors, or "pileup," increase the potential for crisis. Consequently, if one of the ex-spouses remarries before the binuclear family has adequate time to establish new patterns for its reorganized structure, the potential for dysfunctional stress is high. Given the statistic that about 62 percent of men and 61 percent of women remarry within two years after divorce . . . , many families will experience the added stress of incorporating new family members in the midst of struggling with the complicated changes produced by the divorce.

Even if remarriage is delayed until the divorced family has had sufficient time to reorganize and stabilize, shifting of roles and relationships is necessary when a new member is introduced into the family system by remarriage. The family has to struggle with the role of the new family member while allegiances, loyalties and daily relationship patterns undergo transition. For many families, just as they are adjusting to one new member, the other ex-spouse remarries, which causes another transition requiring a shift in the family's tentative equilibrium. The length of time between one ex-spouse's remarriage and the second remarriage will influence the severity of stress experienced by all family members as they are required once again to cope with reorganization.

For the single ex-spouse, the remarriage of a former mate irrespective of the timing, may stimulate many of the feelings unresolved in the emotional divorce. If there are any lingering fantasies of reconciliation, the remarriage brings the sharp reality that reunion is no longer a possibility. It is not unusual for the single ex-spouse to feel a temporary loss of self-esteem as he or she makes comparisons to the new partner. Feelings of jealousy and envy are normal, even for those who thought they had worked through these feelings at the time of the divorce. Seeing an ex-spouse "in love" with someone else often rekindles the feelings of the early courtship and romantic phase of the first married relationship and a requestioning of the reasons for divorce. For a single ex-spouse who did not want the divorce, the remarriage has the potential of creating a personal crisis that closely resembles the experiences of the divorce. But even for those ex-spouses who may have initiated the divorce, the remarriage usually stimulates old feelings and resentments.

> Nancy: When Jim told me he was getting married I reacted with a cutting comment, saying I hoped she was better prepared for long evenings alone than I was. But what I was really scared about was that he would be different with her than he was with me. What if he had *really* changed? I realized that I wanted his marriage to fail. Then I would know that I was right in divorcing him.

Jim's remarriage resulted in Nancy's returning to therapy to work through many of the unresolved issues of the divorce. Jim's new wife was younger than

Nancy and had one child by a previous marriage. Nancy and Jim had become cooperative colleagues in their divorced parenting relationship and she was fearful that she would have to give up many of the conveniences of their shared parenting as Jim took on the responsibilities of a new family.

The remarriage of one or both of the former spouses might be expected to decrease the amount of coparenting between former spouses, since a person involved in a new relationship may have less time to spend, or interest in, relating to his or her former spouse, or may perhaps feel pressure from the new spouse to decrease his or her involvement with the first spouse. For Jim, the conflicts were many.

> Jim: When Elaine and I decided to get married I felt guilty and like I needed to tell Nancy immediately. I dreaded telling her. When I did tell her she didn't say much but I knew she was feeling upset. I wanted the kids to be part of the wedding and I knew Nancy was going to feel jealous and left out. I'd feel much better if she had someone else in her life. Elaine's relationship with her ex-husband is nothing like my relationship with Nancy and she didn't understand my wanting to ease Nancy's pain by not flaunting my new life at her.

Jim's marriage to Elaine initiates a complex cycle of changes for all participants. Nancy needs to adjust to Jim's sharing of his life with a new partner and a child, while both Jim and Elaine need to cope with two ex-spouses who will continue to be part of their future lives. Six months after Jim's marriage to Elaine, Nancy summarized it this way:

> Nancy: Things have changed a lot since Jim remarried. He's less willing to accommodate when I need to change plans around the kids. He always has to check with Elaine first. I really resent that—the kids should come first. I invited Jim to Ellen's birthday party but he couldn't come because of plans he had made with Elaine and her child. And I feel uncomfortable calling him at home about anything. Elaine usually answers the phone and I feel like she's listening the whole time. Jim has asked to take the kids on a week's vacation to visit Elaine's parents over Easter. I know it's his time with the kids but I think he should give them some special time and not make them spend it with Elaine's family.

For Nancy it is difficult for her to see her children's family extending to include more members not directly related to her. And in these early stages of his remarriage Jim is having difficulty coping with the conflicting demands that his increasing family membership causes.

> Jim: I knew Nancy would be upset about our plans for the Easter vacation. Sometimes I wish I could just go off with the kids skiing like we did the first year after the divorce, but I know Elaine wants to visit her parents. There's no way I can please everyone.

Nancy and Jim's relationship is in the process of undergoing considerable change. They talk less frequently and anger sparks up more often now as they try to make decisions about the kids. Jim feels more anger at Nancy now because she is "not understanding" his new responsibilities, and Nancy feels more anger as she has less access to Jim. They are traveling the bumpy road of this transition as they redefine their relationship again, dealing with the changes brought about by Elaine's entry into the family system.

In Ahrons' Binuclear Family Study a deterioration in coparental relations after remarriage did occur among the respondents. This was especially true if only the husband had remarried. For instance, the number and frequency of childrearing activities shared between the former spouses were highest where neither partner had remarried and lowest if only the husband had remarried. The amount of support in coparental interaction was highest and conflict lowest where neither partner had remarried, while conflict was highest and support lowest if only the husband had remarried. Also, if neither former spouse had remarried, they were most likely to spend time together with each other and their children, and least likely if only the husband had remarried. . . .

Remarried Couple Subsystem

The transition to remarriage after a divorce of one or both partners is markedly different from the transition to a first marriage. Not only do the new spouses bring their families of origin into their extended system, but they also have relationships with their first married families which need to be integrated in some way. Remarried couples overwhelmingly report that they are unprepared for the complexities of remarried life. Their model for remarriage is often based on a first marriage model. In contrast to the relatively impermeable boundary that surrounds a nuclear family, permeable boundaries are needed in households within the binuclear family system. These facilitate the exchange of children, money, and decision-making power. If one of the partners has not been previously married, he or she is particularly vulnerable to the dream of the ideal traditional family. . . .

When Elaine and Jim decided to get married, they talked about their divorce histories and their current relationships with their ex-spouses and brought their respective children together for brief periods of time. They fantasized about their plans for blending their family and perhaps adding a new child of their own to the picture. Although they were both aware of some potential problems, they felt able to cope because of the strong bond they had developed between themselves. But as they actually made the transition to remarriage many of the problems created more stress than they had anticipated.

> Elaine: When Jim and I decided to get married I was surprised by his feeling guilty about Nancy. I didn't have any of those feelings about my ex, Tom. When Tom remarried last year it didn't make much difference in my life. He hadn't seen much of Jamie anyway and he just saw her less after he remarried. It was a relief not to have much to do with him. So, after living alone with Jamie for three years, I was really excited to have a family again and give Jamie more of a dad. But it's not working out that way. Jamie is angry a lot about not having time alone with me, which ends up with Jim and me fighting a lot. Jim feels badly about not spending enough time with his kids and when the kids are together, it just seems to be everyone fighting over

Jim. And I feel resentful at not having enough time alone with Jim. Between every other weekend with his kids and the long hours we both work we never seem to have time alone together. Last Friday we were finally spending an evening all alone and, just as I was putting dinner on the table, Nancy called. Jim and I spent the next two hours talking about Nancy. It ended up spoiling our whole evening.

Elaine's feelings are not uncommon for second spouses within a complex binuclear family. The stresses of accommodating the existing bonds of first married relationships into the new stepfamily subsystem often turn the traditional "honeymoon stage" of marriage into an overwhelming cast of characters who share the marital bed. The reorganization required in moving from a one-parent household to a two-parent one often involves more adjustment than the single parent expected. Roles and relationships require realignment and the addition of a new person in some type of parent role is stressful for all the family participants. A frequent complaint in new remarriages is the lack of time and privacy for the newly remarried partners. Jim expressed his disillusionment this way:

Jim: Maybe we shouldn't have gotten married. When we were dating we made time for each other and spent many days and evenings enjoying things together. But after we got married Elaine felt guilty leaving Jamie with her mother or a babysitter very often. Jamie is very demanding—she always seems to want Elaine to do something for her. And Elaine can't seem to say no. Whenever I try to suggest to Elaine that Jamie should learn to play alone more, Elaine seems to get moody and quiet. Her resentment of the time I spend with my kids is hard for me to deal with. Sometimes I think she wishes I would stop seeing them or see them as little as Tom sees Jamie.

When the remarriage partners have been previously married, it is difficult for them not to compare their respective relationships with their ex-spouses. Their own former spouse relationship becomes the model for their new spouse's former spouse relationship. Elaine's expectation that Jim would have a similar relationship with Nancy as she had with Tom was shattered as she realized that Nancy was still very much a part of Jim's life.

The rise of dual-career marriages has resulted in a time problem for first marriages which is only exacerbated in the dual career remarriage. Add to this children and an ex-spouse or two and the issue of time becomes a very real problem. The usual marital issues of power and regulation of distance and intimacy are multiplied in the complex binuclear family. . . .

As with divorce, and with marriage as well, the first year of remarriage has the most potential for crisis. The rate for divorce after remarriage is even higher than that for divorce in first marriages. Glick calculates that 54 percent of women and 61 percent of men who remarry will divorce. The timing of redivorce also differs from that of a first divorce. Remarriages have a 50 percent greater probability of redivorce in the first five years than first marriages.

Current empirical work also suggests that remarriage satisfaction is highly dependent on stepparent-stepchild relationships. How the crises are handled by the remarriage pair will depend on many past experiences and will define the future functioning of the family. Over time, and perhaps with some professional help, Elaine and Jim may be able to find ways to cope with their overcrowded lives. They will need to devise ways to protect and nourish their relationship without damaging the existing parent-child bonds. This will require developing a new model of familying which includes more flexibility, compromise, and fluidity of boundaries than they may have expected originally. . . .

Sibling Subsystems: Step and Half

The child development literature notes the stresses of adding children to the family with its normalizing of "sibling rivalry." In the remarriage family with children of both partners, the joining of the new sibling subsystems is a difficult transition for the children—acquiring an "instant sibling" can pose a threat to even the most secure child. The new remarriage partners have their marriage at stake and, therefore, need their respective children to like each other. Given a host of factors, such as the age and temperament of the children, the blending of two households of unrelated children requires major adjustments. Few newly blended families resemble the "Brady Bunch," but many have this as their model for this transition!

The usual competitive struggles among siblings often become major battles in remarried families, as children must adapt to sharing household space and parental time with new siblings. . . . [T]he remarriage of Ellen and David's father included a new "kid sister" for them. That was followed a year later by their mother's remarriage, which included two more "kid sisters" who shared their home with them for one-third of every month. And, a few years down the line, they had to incorporate two half siblings when their father and stepmother had a son and a daughter. . . .

Empirical research on the effects of remarriage on children is not as easily summarized as the literature on the effects of divorce. Although research is steadily increasing, we still lack major longitudinal studies identifying the stresses and developmental phases of adding new members to the binuclear family. And sibling relationships in binuclear families have been a sadly neglected area of study. But it is our guess that for many children the transition to remarriage is more stressful than the transition to divorce. The addition of new family members can also mean more loss than gain for many children—if not permanent losses, then at least temporary relationship loss in the transition period. The changes children need to make when a parent inherits new children as part of his or her remarriage are numerous and difficult. And the newly remarried parent, who so frequently feels overwhelmed, may have her or his energies absorbed more in the new mate than in facilitating the child's transition.

Mother/Stepmother–Father/Stepfather Subsystems

Now we are faced with describing baffling relationships with a wordiness created by our current language deficits. We are hampered further in our efforts by the lack of clinical or empirical research on these relationships. Nevertheless, we will attempt here to describe some of the stressful aspects of these relationships, which form such an integral part of the remarriage transition.

In fact, these first and second spouses do have some bearing on each other's lives. For some second spouses, the "ghost" of the first spouse is ever present. For many, the first spouse can be an unwanted interloper, creating conflict between the remarriage pair. In other remarriage couples the first spouse is a uniting force on whom the new spouses place blame for all the problems of a dysfunctional family. This type of scapegoating is the subject of much humor and provides the basis for many of the prevalent negative stereotypes of this relationship.

Obviously, even in one family system, the relationships between current and former spouses can be quite different, depending on the type of relationship between the former spouse pairs and all the individual personalities. . . .

The possibilities and complexities in these types of relationships are vast, and our knowledge of them is almost nonexistent. But clearly the type of relationship style adopted by the former spouses is a major factor determining the relationship between first and second spouses. In many remarried binuclear systems the former spouse relationship is likely to diminish in importance over time, especially when there are no minor children to bind the parents together. As this happens the need for first and second spouses to relate also diminishes. . . .

Functional and Dysfunctional Remarriage Relationships

Our definition of functional and dysfunctional systems in remarriage is very similar to that of functional and dysfunctional divorces. . . . Developing new roles and relationships in remarriage which take into account the existence and losses of divorced family relationships is critical to enhancing remarried family functioning. The addition of new family members can result in dysfunctional binuclear family systems if prior kin relationships are severed. If remarriage subsystems try to model nuclear families—that is, if they insist upon "instant" family and try to establish traditional parenting roles—they will experience resistance and distress. A functional binuclear family system needs to have permeable boundaries which permit children and adults to continue prior family relationships while slowly integrating the new remarried subsystem. This, of necessity, causes transitory stresses and strains created by the conflict between new and old alliances. Remarriage is still another transition, with even more possibilities for stress than divorce.

As we emphasized in the divorce transition, the clear delineation of boundaries is critical to successful functioning. The remarried husband coparent, for example, must clarify his role vis-à-vis his biological and stepchildren, and his first and second spouses. He and his ex-spouse need to renegotiate what is appropriate and inappropriate in his continuing role as coparent. Coparenting agreements that may have been satisfactory prior to his remarriage are likely to have implications for his current spouse. For example, if it has been agreed that he needs to spend more time with his eight-year-old son, who wants and needs his father's attention, this takes time away from his marriage. His responsibilities as a parent and his spousal responsibilities come into conflict. This can be exacerbated by opinions expressed by his current partner that the "boy is spoiled and demanding and needs to learn that his father can't always be there." Or she may feel that the former spouse is using the child as a way of hanging on to her ex-husband. And, of course, she may also be concerned about the time taken away from her and the children she has brought to this new marriage. But the new partner must also be sensitive to the degree that expression of such thoughts violates important boundaries between the new marriage and the old.

While he will be wise not to pass these opinions of his new partner on to the former spouse (these are clearly outside the boundaries of the former spouse relationship), unless the husband coparent is able to deal effectively with his ex-spouse around these conflicting pressures, crisis may result. His former wife may see him as withdrawing from the coparental relationship they have agreed upon. And she, not having remarried, may have a renewed sense of abandonment resulting from the remarriage of her former spouse. Given their agreements concerning coparenting, she has legitimate call upon her former spouse. At the same time, the remarried spouse has equally legitimate expectations related to their marriage. Without explicit negotiation of arrangements and reasonable expectations from both sides, thus establishing clear boundaries for his actions in both subsystems, he is destined to fall short in both.

The single former spouse also may experience considerable distress in adjusting to the expanded system. Noncustodial parents will feel some resentment at losing some of their former responsibilities in both division of labor and decision-making. They may also feel that the new spouse interferes in their relationship with the former spouse and their children. A custodial parent, usually the mother, will often experience a loss of services when her former spouse remarries. She may no longer be able to call on him for help, as many of her demands—except as they are related to the coparenting relationship—begin to fall outside the legitimate boundaries of the former spouse relationship. Clearly, agreements and court orders with respect to financial child support are legitimate. However, expectations that the former husband will perform repairs or maintenance on the home of the former spouse may have to be rejected. This may be difficult, since that home is likely to be his former home, in which he may feel some residual investment, and in some cases may still retain some financial investment. However, resistance from the new partner to continuing such tasks is likely to severely restrict any such activity. All of this may be softened or made more difficult, depending upon the kind of postdivorce relationship style which has developed.

Remarriage restructures the division of labor developed in the postdivision reorganization. New spouses of custodial parents take on many of the day-to-day responsibilities for care of children and household tasks formerly handled alone by the custodial parent or carried out by one of the children from time to time. As we have seen, this may lead to some genuine friction, as children resent the new stepparent's "taking over" or displacing them in some valued responsibility. If the new spouse attempts to assume responsibilities which the noncustodial parent may have continued, this is another source of potential stress. The former spouse may resent it, the stepchildren may resent it, and even the new spouse may have difficulty in accepting it.

Decision-making and the power structure implications carry similar potential stress. This will be especially true around decisions concerning the stepchildren but may be true in other areas as well. If a new spouse has been used to having his or her former spouse participate and be involved in decisions concerning the children, the new spouse can easily be seen as "interfering," both by the other biological parent and the child. For example, as we have seen in the case presented this chapter, Nancy resented Elaine's parenting involvement.

The style of the postdivorce ex-spouse relationship may either ease these adjustments . . . or make them more difficult. . . . If former spouses are insecure and competitive about their parenting relationships with their children, . . . the addition of a new parent figure will intensify those feelings during the transition. An ex-spouse may feel threatened by the "new family" of the remarried spouse, anticipating that the children will prefer this new household to the one-parent household where they currently live.

When parents—both biological and step—are unclear about their roles, children are likely to use the ambiguity to manipulate the new stepparent, their custodial parent, and the noncustodial parent. During the early stages of the remarriage transition it is not unusual for children to play one parent off against another for some personal gain. For example, in the Spicer-Tyler-Henry family, Ellen, after spending a weekend at her father's house, might very well tell her mother that Elaine, her new stepmother, "lets me watch TV until 10 p.m." Ellen's hope, of course, is that her mother will respond by permitting her to stay up later than her usual bedtime. Sometimes, new stepparents will be more lenient with their stepchildren in the hopes of being liked and accepted by them. Consciously, or perhaps unconsciously, the new stepparent is competing with the other biological parent for the child's affections.

Although former spouses may have worked out consistent rules for discipline, etc., during the divorce transition, these are likely to need renegotiation when a new parent enters the family. Only now, the renegotiation is more complicated, as three parents become part of the process instead of the original two. And if another ex-spouse remarries, there may be a replay of some of the issues as the system accommodates to a fourth parent. As we noted earlier, however, this may be an easier transition. Not only are the parents familiar now with many of the problems of adjustment but the system itself is in better balance. There are now two stepfamily households, with each biological parent having an ally.

The remarried binuclear family faces a unique problem in controlling intimacy in the family. Incest taboos, which are assumed between blood kin in first marriage nuclear families (though, as is now being revealed, more often violated than many have known), become an important issue. The function of such taboos, of course, is to maintain unambiguous and appropriate intimate relationships in families. The potential for sexual feelings and possible abuse between non-blood parents and children, as well as between adolescent stepsiblings, is high. Therefore, establishment of clearly defined boundaries in this highly charged emotional area is essential.

A situation observed by one of the authors in family therapy illustrates how dysfunctional failure to establish such boundaries can be. In the course of the session, an adolescent stepdaughter revealed that she had been sexually involved with the son of her stepfather, i.e., her stepbrother. There were indications that this involvement was involuntary on her part. The mother of the young woman became very angry. At this point, the two biological daughters of the stepfather, who no longer lived in the household, confronted their stepmother with their sexual experiences some years before with her son—their stepbrother. They were extremely angry with the stepmother for not having the same reactions to their experiences, of which they believed the stepmother to be aware. These revelations, of course, provided some understanding of the kinds of conflicts in this stepfamily that had prompted the request for therapeutic treatment. The issues extended far beyond the matter of sexual abuse to include the entire range of emotional relationships which had developed in this remarried family over several prior years. Failure to have defined appropriate intimacy boundaries in the reorganization of this binuclear family had contributed to an extremely dysfunctional situation.

Relationships with extended kin find new stresses facing them upon the remarriage of one or both ex-spouses. Children may be particularly puzzled by suddenly finding their access to one set of grandparents or a favored aunt or uncle severely restricted or cut off. The nature of those relationships may also be changed, even if they are continued, by the inability of the extended kin to keep their feelings about the ex-spouse from contaminating their interactions with the children. Further, the introduction of new extended kin can also be confusing and stress-producing for children.

The new relationships with the spouse's extended family are not of the same character as those of first married couples. They often carry residual elements from the former marriage, particularly since these are not just in-laws, but also grandparents, uncles, and aunts. In addition, in many cases there are also associations to be worked out with the former spouse of the new partner. Until new relationships with extended family are established, they tend to be mediated through the new marital relationship.

CONCLUSION

The study of even one remarried subsystem alone presents sufficient complexities to cause many social scientists to return to studying individuals rather than family systems. Our lack of both language and analytic tools, as well as the difficulties in conceptualizing the totality of these complex systems, creates frustration in both the writer and the reader.

All of this brings into sharp relief the importance of developing a new set of meanings for the relationships between former spouses, with the new spouses, between former and current spouses, between stepparents and stepchildren, between step and half siblings, and with extended kin. If the expanded binuclear family structure is to survive and function in an effective manner, then all parties must develop clear understandings of what these meanings are in the new remarriage situation. These meanings are most likely to center on the coparenting responsibilities that the ex-spouses share, but they go well beyond this.

Clearly delineating a precise definition of functional and dysfunctional remarriage binuclear families is not possible, given our current lack of knowledge. Although we can comfortably conclude that remarriage subsystems must be open systems with permeable boundaries, we cannot say what degree of openness is optimal. Remarriage subsystems need to be able to develop their own sense of connectedness and independence, while simultaneously functioning as interdependent units. Stepparents have a confusing and difficult role. In most families they need to develop new parenting type roles that supplement, rather than replace, biological parents. And they need to do so expecting resistance and a long developmental process of integration. What is required is a new model of familying that encompasses an expanded network of extended and quasi-kin relationships.

PART THREE

❖

PARENTS
AND
CHILDREN

❖

INTRODUCTION

No aspect of childhood seems more natural, universal, and changeless than the relationship between parents and child. Yet historical and cross-cultural evidence reveals major changes in conceptions of childhood and adulthood and in the psychological relationships between children and parents. For example, the shift from an agrarian to an industrial society over the past 200 years has revolutionized parent-child relations and the conditions of child development.

Among the changes associated with this transformation of childhood are: the decline of agriculture as a way of life; the elimination of child labor; the fall in infant mortality; the spread of literacy and mass schooling; and a focus on childhood as a distinct and valuable stage of life. As a result of these changes, industrial-era parents bear fewer children, make greater emotional and economic investments in them, and expect less in return than their agrarian counterparts. Agrarian parents were not expected to emphasize emotional bonds or the value of children as unique individuals. Parents and children were bound together by economic necessity: children were an essential source of labor in the family economy and a source of support in an old age. Today, almost all children are economic liabilities. But they now have profound emotional significance.

Parents hope offspring will provide intimacy, even genetic immortality. Although today's children have become economically worthless, they have become emotionally "priceless" (Zelizer, 1985).

No matter how eagerly an emotionally priceless child is awaited, becoming a parent is usually experienced as one of life's major "normal" crises. In a classic article, Alice Rossi (1968) was one of the first to point out that the transition to parenthood is often one of life's difficult passages. Since Rossi's article first appeared over two decades ago, a large body of research literature has developed, most of which supports her view that the early years of parenting can be a period of stress and change as well as joy.

Parenthood itself has changed since Rossi wrote. As Carolyn and Philip Cowan observe, becoming a parent may be more difficult now than it used to be. The Cowans studied couples before and after the births of their first children. Because of the rapid and dramatic social changes of the past decades, young parents today are like pioneers in a new, uncharted territory. For example, the vast majority of today's couples come to parenthood with both husband and wife in the workforce, and most have expectations of a more egalitarian relationship than their own parents had. But the balance in their lives and their relationship has to shift dramatically after the baby is born. Most couples cannot afford the traditional pattern of the wife staying home full time; nor is this arrangement free of strain for those who try it. Young families thus face more burdens than in the past, yet supportive family policies such as visiting nurses, paid parental leave, and the like that exist in other countries are lacking in the United States.

Parents who successfully weather the early years often face another stressful period when their child becomes an adolescent. Reed Larson and Maryse Richards examine a sample of middle-class, two-parent families with a teenager in the home. Tracking the activities of family members throughout the day by means of beepers, they find that mothers, fathers, and children are pulled into separate worlds during the day. The fast-paced but different realities faced by each family member create a minefield of possible misunderstandings and conflict. Some families, however, manage to maintain warm and supporting relationships with one another; they don't get overstressed at work, and they keep "emotional brushfires" from flaring into emotional firestorms.

Mothers are still the principal nurturers and caretakers of their children, but the norms of parenthood have shifted—as the growing use of the term "parenting" suggests. Views of fatherhood in the research literature are changing along with the actual behavior of fathers and children in real life. Until recently, a father could feel he was fulfilling his parental obligations merely by supporting his family. He was expected to spend time with his children when his work schedule permitted, to generally oversee their upbringing, and to discipline them when necessary. Even scholars of the family and of child development tended to ignore the role of the father except as breadwinner and role model. His family participation did not call for direct involvement in the daily round of child rearing, especially when the children were babies. By contrast, scholars expressed the extreme importance of the mother and the dangers of maternal deprivation. Today, however, the role of father is beginning to demand much more active involvement in the life of the family, especially with regard to child rearing. Countering this trend, however, is the rising divorce rate of recent years, which for many children means a greatly reduced amount of life with father.

Frank Furstenberg examines these two faces of fatherhood in his article here. The old breadwinner model of fatherhood, he argues, has been replaced by two new models—the good father and the bad father. The good dad is like Bill Cosby—warm, nurturant, and "as adept at changing diapers as changing tires." The bad dads are the ones who duck out of their parental obligations—dropping out of their children's lives, failing to make support payments. Dads are more likely to be bad after divorce or when childbearing occurs outside of marriage. Furstenberg concludes that it is important for men to be involved in nurturing their children, and they should be encouraged do so in a variety of ways.

In these days of test-tube babies, surrogate mothers, and debates about fathers, it may seem surprising that adoption has become a newly controversial form of parenthood. But as Elizabeth Bartholet argues in her selection, adoption has acquired a bad name. It has always been considered a second-best solution for the childless, but in recent years it has come to be defined as unnatural and tragic for all concerned. An adoptive mother herself, Bartholet argues against these views.

Divorce too has become controversial in recent years, as it has become embroiled in the family values debate. Some commentators and politicians have called for making a divorce harder to get, or even outlawing it for parents with minor children. The justification for these proposals is the presumed devastating, lifelong effects of parental divorce on children.

In their article, Frank F. Furstenberg and Andrew J. Cherlin take a more detailed look at the effects of divorce on children's adjustment. They find that divorce is a long process, not a single event. Like Demo, they find that much of the negative impact of divorce on children stems from conflict between the parents. Indeed, there is evidence that children from divorcing families begin to have problems well before the parents separate. A key factor in children's well-being after divorce is the quality of the child's relationship with the custodial parent, usually the mother.

Finally, Phillip Davis addresses one of the oldest controversies in parent-child relations—spanking. He points out that there are deep divisions among parents, experts, and others about the meaning of spanking and other kinds of physical discipline. Is it a normal and natural part of parenting, or is it a form of child abuse and a violation of human rights?

REFERENCES

Rossi, A. 1968. Transition to parenthood. *Journal of Marriage and the Family* 30, 26–39.

Zelizer, V. A. 1985. *Pricing the Priceless Child.* New York: Basic Books.

CHAPTER 6

PARENTHOOD

READING
16

Becoming a Parent

Carolyn P. Cowan and Phillip A. Cowan

Sharon: I did a home pregnancy test. I felt really crummy that day, and stayed home from work. I set the container with the urine sample on a bookcase and managed to stay out of the room until the last few minutes. Finally, I walked in and it looked positive. And I went to check the information on the box and, sure enough, it *was* positive. I was so exited. Then I went back to look and see if maybe it has disappeared; you know, maybe the test was false. Then I just sat down on the sofa and kept thinking, "I'm pregnant. I'm really pregnant. I'm going to have a baby!"

Daniel: I knew she was pregnant. She didn't need the test as far as I was concerned. I was excited too, at first, but then I started to worry. I don't know how I'm going to handle being there at the birth, especially if anything goes wrong. And Sharon's going to quit work soon. I don't know when she's going to go back, and we're barely making it as it is.

Sharon: My mom never worked a day in her life for pay. She was home all the time, looking after *her* mother, and us, and cleaning the house. My dad left all of that to her. We're not going to do it that way. But I don't know how we're supposed to manage it all. Daniel promised that he's going to pitch in right along with me in taking care of the baby, but I don't know whether that's realistic. If he doesn't come through, I'm going to be a real bear about it. If

I put all my energy into Daniel and the marriage and something happens, then I'll have to start all over again and that scares the hell out of me.

Sharon is beginning the third trimester of her first pregnancy. If her grandmother were to listen in on our conversation with Sharon and her husband, Daniel, and try to make sense of it, given the experience of her own pregnancy fifty years ago, she would surely have a lot of questions. Home pregnancy tests? Why would a woman with a newborn infant *want* to work if she didn't have to? What husband would share the housework and care of the baby? Why would Sharon and Daniel worry about their marriage not surviving after they have a baby? Understandable questions for someone who made the transition to parenthood five decades ago, in a qualitatively different world. Unfortunately, the old trail maps are outmoded, and there are as yet no new ones to describe the final destination. They may not need covered wagons for their journey, but Sharon and Daniel are true pioneers.

Like many modern couples, they have two different fantasies about their journey. The first has them embarking on an exciting adventure to bring a new human being into the world, fill their lives with delight and wonder, and enrich their feeling of closeness as a couple. In the second, their path from couple to family is strewn with unexpected obstacles, hazardous conditions, and potential marital strife. Our work suggests that, like most fantasy scenarios, these represent extreme and somewhat exaggerated versions of what really happens when partners become parents. . . .

THE FIVE DOMAINS OF FAMILY LIFE

The responses of one couple to our interview questions offer a preview of how the five domains in our model capture the changes that most couples contend with as they make their transition to parenthood. Natalie and Victor have lived in the San Francisco Bay Area most of their lives. At the time of their initial interview, Natalie, age twenty-nine, is in her fifth month of pregnancy. Victor, her husband of six years, is thirty-four. When their daughter, Kim, is six months old, they visit us again for a follow-up interview. Arranged around each of the five domains, the following excerpts from our second interview reveal some universal themes of early parenthood.

Changes in Identity and Inner Life

After settling comfortably with cups of coffee and tea, we ask both Natalie and Victor whether they feel that their sense of self has shifted in any way since Kim was born. As would be typical in our interviews, Mother and Father focus on different aspects of personal change:

Natalie: There's not much "me" left to think about right now. Most of the time, even when I'm not nursing, I see myself as attached to this little being with only the milk flowing between us.

Victor: I've earned money since I was sixteen, but being a father means that I've become the family breadwinner. I've got this new sense of myself as having to go out there in the world to make sure that my wife and daughter are going to be safe and looked after. I mean, I'm concerned about advancing in my job—and we've even bought insurance policies for the first time! This "protector" role feels exciting *and* frightening.

Another change that often occurs in partners' inner lives during a major life transition is a shift in what C. Murray Parkes (1971) describes as our "assumptive world." Men's and women's assumptions about how the world works or how families operate sometimes change radically during the transition from couple to family.

> Natalie: I used to be completely apathetic about political things. I wasn't sure of my congressman's name. Now I'm writing him about once a month because I feel I need to help clean up some of the mess this country is in before Kim grows up.

> Victor: What's changed for me is what I think families and fathers are all about. When we were pregnant, I had these pictures of coming home each night as the tired warrior, playing with the baby for a little while and putting my feet up for the rest of the evening. It's not just that there's more work to do than I ever imagined, but I'm so much more a part of the action every night.

Clearly, Natalie and Victor are experiencing qualitatively different shifts in their sense of self and in how vulnerable or safe each feels in the world. These shifts are tied not only to their new life as parents but also to a new sense of their identities as providers and protectors. Even though most of these changes are positive, they can lead to moments when the couple's relationship feels a bit shaky.

Shifts in the Roles and Relationships within the Marriage

> Victor: After Kim was born, I noticed that something was bugging Natalie, and I kept saying, "What is bothering you?" Finally we went out to dinner without the baby and it came out. And it was because of small things that I never even think about. Like I always used to leave my running shorts in the bathroom . . .

> Natalie: He'd just undress and drop everything!

> Victor: . . . and Nat never made a fuss. In fact she *used* to just pick them up and put them in the hamper. And then that night at dinner she said, "When you leave your shorts there, or your wet towel, and don't pick them up—I get furious." At first I didn't believe what she was saying because it never used to bother her at all, but now I say, "OK, fine, no problem. I'll pick up the shorts and hang them up. I'll be very conscientious." And I have been trying.

> Natalie: You have, but you still don't quite get it. I think my quick trigger has something to do with my feeling so dependent on you and having the baby so dependent on me—and my being stuck here day in and day out. You at least get to go out to do your work, and you bring home a paycheck to show for it. I work here all day long and by the end of the day I feel that all I have to show for it is my exhaustion.

In addition to their distinctive inner changes, men's and women's roles change in very different ways when partners become parents. The division of labor in taking care of the baby, the household, the meals, the laundry, the shopping, calling parents and friends, and earning the money to keep the family fed, clothed, and sheltered is a hot topic for couples (C. Cowan and P. Cowan 1988; Hochschild 1989). It seems to come as a great surprise to most of them that changes in some of their major roles affect their feelings about their overall relationship.

In a domino effect, both partners have to make major adjustments of time and energy as individuals during a period when they are getting less sleep and fewer opportunities to be together. As with Natalie and Victor, they are apt to find that they have less patience with things that didn't seem annoying before. Their frustration often focuses on each other. For couples who thought that having a baby was going to bring them closer together, this is especially confusing and disappointing.

> Natalie: It's strange. I feel that we're much closer *and* more distant than we have ever been. I think we communicate more, because there's so much to work out, especially about Kim, but it doesn't always feel very good. And we're both so busy that we're not getting much snuggling or loving time.
>
> Victor: We're fighting more too. But I'm still not sure why.

Victor and Natalie are so involved in what is happening to them that even though they can identify some of the sources of their disenchantment, they cannot really make sense of all of it. They are playing out a scenario that was very common for the couples in our study during the first year of parenthood. Both men and women are experiencing a changing sense of self *and* a shift in the atmosphere in the relationship between them. The nurturance that partners might ordinarily get from one another is in very short supply. As if this were not enough to adjust to, almost all of the new parents in our study say that their other key relationships are shifting too.

Shifts in the Three-Generational Roles and Relationships

> Victor: It was really weird to see my father's reaction to Kim's birth. The week before Natalie's due date, my father all of a sudden decided that he was going to Seattle, and he took off with my mom and some other people. Well, the next day Natalie went into labor and we had the baby, and my mother kept calling, saying she wanted to get back here. But my dad seemed to be playing games and made it stretch out for two or three days. Finally, when they came back and the whole period was past, it turned out that my father was *jealous* of my mother's relationship with the baby. He didn't want my mother to take time away from him to be with Kim! He's gotten over it now. He holds Kim and plays with her, and doesn't want to go home after a visit. But my dad and me, we're still sort of recovering from what happened. And when things don't go well with me and Dad, Natalie sometimes gets it in the neck
>
> Natalie: I'll say.

For Victor's father, becoming a first-time grandfather is something that is happening *to* him. His son and daughter-in-law are having a baby and he is becoming grandfather, ready or not. Many men and women in Victor's parents' position have mixed feelings about becoming grandparents (Lowe 1991), but rarely know how to deal with them. As Victor searches for ways to become comfortable with his new identity as a father, like so many of the men we spoke to, he is desperately hoping that it will bring him closer to his father.

As father and son struggle with these separate inner changes, they feel a strain in the relationship between them, a strain they feel they cannot mention. Some of it spills over into the relationship between Victor and Natalie: After a visit with his parents, they realize, they are much more likely to get into a fight.

Changing Roles and Relationships Outside the Family

Natalie: While Victor has been dealing with his dad, I've been struggling with my boss. After a long set of negotiations on the phone, he reluctantly agreed to let me come back four days a week instead of full-time. I haven't gone back officially yet, but I dropped in to see him. He always used to have time for me, but this week, after just a few minutes of small talk, he told me that he had a meeting and practically bolted out of the room. He as much as said that he figured I wasn't serious about my job anymore.

Victor: Natalie's not getting much support from her friends, either. None of them have kids and they just don't seem to understand what she's going through. Who ever thought how lonely it can be to have a baby?

Although the burden of the shifts in roles and relationships outside the family affects both parents, it tends to fall more heavily on new mothers. It is women who tend to put their jobs and careers on hold, at least temporarily, after they have babies (Daniels and Weingarten 1982, 1988), and even though they may have more close friends than their husbands do, they find it difficult to make contact with them in the early months of new parenthood. It takes all of the energy new mothers have to cope with the ongoing care and feeding that a newborn requires and to replenish the energy spent undergoing labor or cesarean delivery. The unanticipated loss of support from friends and co-workers can leave new mothers feeling surprisingly isolated and vulnerable. New fathers' energies are on double duty too. Because they are the sole earners when their wives stop working or take maternity leave, men often work longer hours or take on extra jobs. Fatigue and limited availability means that fathers too get less support or comfort from co-workers or friends. This is one of many aspects of family life in which becoming a parent seems to involve more *loss* than either spouse anticipated—especially because they have been focused on the gain of the baby. Although it is not difficult for us to see how these shifts and losses might catch two tired parents off guard, most husbands and wives fail to recognize that these changes are affecting them as individuals and as a couple.

New Parenting Roles and Relationships

Natalie and Victor, unlike most of the other couples, had worked out a shared approach to household tasks from the time they moved in together. Whoever was available to do something would do it. And when Kim was born, they just continued that. During the week, Victor would get the baby up in the morning and then take over when he got home from work. Natalie put her to bed at night. During the weekends the responsibilities were reversed.

It was not surprising that Natalie and Victor expected their egalitarian system—a rare arrangement—to carry over to the care of their baby. What is surprising to us is that a majority of the couples predicted that they would share the care of their baby much more equally than they were sharing their housework and family tasks *before* they became parents. Even though they are unusually collaborative in their care of Kim, Natalie and Victor are not protected from the fact that, like most couples, their different ideas about what a baby needs create some conflict and disagreement:

Victor: I tend to be a little more . . . what would you say?
Natalie: Crazy.
Victor: A little more crazy with Kim. I like to put her on my bicycle and go for a ride real fast. I like the thought of the wind blowing on her and her eyes watering. I want her to feel the rain hitting her face. Natalie would cover her head, put a thick jacket on her, you know, make sure she's warm and dry.
Natalie: At the beginning, we argued a lot about things like that. More than we ever did. Some of them seemed trivial at the time. The argument wouldn't last more than a day. It would all build up, explode, and then be over. One night, though, Victor simply walked out. He took a long drive, and then came back. It was a bad day for both of us. We just had to get it out, regardless of the fact that it was three A.M.
Victor: I think it was at that point that I realized that couples who start off with a bad relationship would really be in trouble. As it was, it wasn't too pleasant for us, but we got through it.

Despite the fact that their emotional focus had been on the baby during pregnancy and the early months of parenthood, Victor and Natalie were not prepared for the way their relationship with the baby affected and was affected by the changes they had been experiencing all along as individuals, at work, in their marriage, and in their relationships with their parents, friends, and coworkers—the spillover effects. They sometimes have new and serious disagreements, but both of them convey a sense that they have the ability to prevent their occasional blowups from escalating into serious and long-lasting tensions.

As we follow them over time, Victor and Natalie describe periods in which their goodwill toward each other wears thin, but their down periods are typically followed by genuine ups. It seems that one of them always finds a way to come back to discuss the painful issues when they are not in so much distress. In subsequent visits, for example, the shorts-in-the-bathroom episode, retold with much laughter, becomes a shorthand symbol for the times when tensions erupt between them. They give themselves time to cool down, they come back to talk about what was so upsetting, and having heard each other out, they go on to find a solution to the problem that satisfies both of their needs. This, we know, is the key to a couple's stable and satisfying relationship (Gottman and Krokoff 1989).

Compared to the other couples, one of the unusual strengths in Natalie and Victor's life together is their ability to come back to problem issues after they have calmed down. Many couples are afraid to rock the boat once their heated feelings have cooled down. Even more unusual is their trust that they will both be listened to sympathetically when they try to sort out what happened. Because Natalie and Victor each dare to raise issues that concern them, they end up feeling that they are on the same side when it comes to the most important things in life (cf. Ball 1984). This is what makes it possible for them to engage in conflict and yet maintain their positive feelings about their relationship.

Most important, perhaps, for the long-term outcome of their journey to parenthood is that the good feeling between Victor and Natalie spills over to their daughter. Throughout Kim's preschool years and into her first year of kindergarten, we see the threesome as an active, involved family in which the members are fully engaged with one another in both serious and playful activities.

WHAT MAKES PARENTHOOD HARDER NOW

Natalie and Victor are charting new territory. They are trying to create a family based on the new, egalitarian ideology in which both of them work *and* share the tasks of managing the household and caring for their daughter. They have already embraced less traditional roles than most of the couples in our study. Although the world they live in has changed a great deal since they were children, it has not shifted sufficiently to support them in realizing their ideals easily. Their journey seems to require heroic effort.

Would a more traditional version of family life be less stressful? Couples who arrange things so that the woman tends the hearth and baby and the man provides the income to support them are also showing signs of strain. They struggle financially because it often takes more than one parent's income to maintain a family. They feel drained emotionally because they rely almost entirely on their relationship to satisfy most of their psychological needs. Contemporary parents find themselves in double jeopardy. Significant historical shifts in the family landscape of the last century, particularly of the last few decades, have created additional burdens for them. As couples set foot on the trails of this challenging journey, they become disoriented because society's map of the territory has been redrawn. Becoming a family today is more difficult than it used to be.

In recent decades there has been a steady ripple of revolutionary social change. Birth control technology has been transformed. Small nuclear families live more isolated lives in crowded cities, often feeling cut off from extended family and friends. Mothers of young children are entering the work force earlier and in ever larger numbers. Choices about how to create life as a family are much greater then they used to be. Men and women are having a difficult time regaining their balance as couples after they have babies, in part because the radical shifts in the circumstances surrounding family life in America demand new arrangements to accommodate the increasing demands on parents of young children. But new social arrangements and roles have simply not kept pace with these changes, leaving couples on their own to manage the demands of work and family.

More Choice

Compared with the experiences of their parents and grandparents, couples today have many more choices about whether and when to bring a child into their lives. New forms of birth control have given most couples the means to engage in an active sex life with some confidence, though no guarantee, that they can avoid unwanted pregnancy. In addition, despite recent challenges in American courts and legislatures, the 1973 Supreme Court decision legalizing abortion has given couples a second chance to decide whether to become parents if birth control fails or is not used.

But along with modern birth control techniques come reports of newly discovered hazards. We now know that using birth control pills, intrauterine devices, the cervical cap, the sponge, and even the diaphragm poses some risk to a woman's health. The decision to abort a fetus brings with it both public controversy and the private anguish of the physical, psychological, and moral consequences of ending a pregnancy (see Nathanson 1989). Men and women today may enjoy more choice about parenthood than any previous generation, but the couples in our studies are finding it quite difficult to navigate this new family-making terrain.

Sharon, who was eagerly awaiting the results of her home pregnancy test when we met her at the beginning of this reading, had not been nearly as eager to become a mother three years earlier.

> Sharon: Actually, we fought about it a lot. Daniel already had a child, Hallie, from his first marriage. "Let's have one of our own. It'll be easy," he said. And I said, "Yeah, and what happened before Hallie was two? You were out the door."
>
> Daniel: I told you, that had nothing to do with Hallie. She was great. It was my ex that was the problem. I just knew that for us a baby would be right.
>
> Sharon: I wasn't sure. What was I going to do about a career? What was going to do about me? I wasn't ready to put things on hold. I wasn't even convinced, then, that I wanted to become a mother. It wouldn't have been good for me, and it sure wouldn't have been good for the baby, to go ahead and give in to Daniel when I was feeling that way.

In past times, fewer choices meant less conflict between spouses, at least at the outset. Now, with each partner expecting to have a free choice in the matter, planning a family can become the occasion for sensitive and delicate treaty negotiations. First, couples who want to live together must decide whether they want to get married. One partner may be for it, the other not. Second, the timing of childbirth has changed. For couples married in 1950–54, the majority (60 percent) would have a baby within two years. Now, almost one-third of couples are marrying *after* having a child, and those who marry before becoming parents are marrying later in life. Only a minority of them have their first child within two years. Some delay parenthood for more than a decade (Teachman, Polonko, and Scanzoni 1987).

Couples are also having smaller families. The decline in fertility has for the first time reduced the birthrate below the replacement level of zero population growth—less than two children per family.* And because couples are having fewer children and having them later, more seems to be at stake in each decision about whether and when to have a child. What was once a natural progression has become a series of choice points, each with a potential for serious disagreement between the partners.

Alice is in the last trimester of her pregnancy. In our initial interview, she and Andy described a profound struggle between them that is not over yet.

> Alice: This pregnancy was a life and death issue for me. I'd already had two abortions with a man I'd lived with before, because it was very clear that we could not deal with raising a child. Although I'd known Andy for years, we had been together only four months when I became pregnant unexpectedly. I loved him, I was thirty-four years old, and I wasn't going to risk the possibility of another abortion and maybe never being able to have children. So when I became pregnant this time, I said, "I'm having this baby with you or without you. But I'd much rather have it with you."
>
> Andy: Well, I'm only twenty-seven and I haven't gotten on track with my own life. Alice was using a diaphragm and I thought it was safe. For months after she became pregnant, I was just pissed off that this was happening to me, to us, but I gradually calmed down. If it was just up to me, I'd wait for a number of years yet because I don't feel ready, but I want to be with her, and you can hear that she's determined to have this baby.

Clearly, more choice has not necessarily made life easier for couples who are becoming a family.

Isolation

The living environments of families with children have changed dramatically. In 1850, 75 percent of American families lived in rural settings. By 1970, 75 percent were living in urban or suburban environments, and the migration from farm to city is continuing.

We began our own family in Toronto, Canada, the city we had grown up in, with both sets of parents living nearby. Today we live some distance from our parents, relatives, and childhood friends, as do the majority of couples in North America. Increasingly, at least in the middle- and upper-income brackets, couples are living in unfamiliar surroundings, bringing newborns home to be reared in single-family apartments or houses, where their neighbors are strangers. Becoming a parent, then, can quickly result in social isolation, especially for the parent who stays at home with the baby.

John and Shannon are one of the younger couples in our study. He is twenty-four and she is twenty-three.

> John: My sister in Dallas lives down the block from our mother. Whenever she and her husband want a night out, they just call up and either they take the baby over to Mom's house or Mom comes right over to my sister's. Our friends help us out once in a while, but you have to reach out and ask them and a lot of times they aren't in a position to respond. Some of them don't have kids, so

---

*There are indications, however, that the birthrate in the United States is now on the rise.

they don't really understand what it's like for us. They keep calling us and suggesting that we go for a picnic or out for pizza, and we have to remind them that we have this baby to take care of.

Shannon: All the uncles, aunts, and cousins in my family used to get together every Sunday. Most of the time I don't miss that because they were intrusive and gossipy and into everybody else's business. But sometimes it would be nice to have someone to talk to who cares about me, and who lived through all the baby throw-up and ear infections and lack of sleep, and could just say, "Don't worry, Shannon, it's going to get better soon."

Women's Roles

Since we began our family thirty years ago, mothers have been joining the labor force in ever-increasing numbers, even when they have young babies. Women have always worked, but economic necessity in the middle as well as the working classes, and increased training and education among women, propelled them into the work force in record numbers. In 1960, 18 percent of mothers with children under six were working at least part-time outside the home. By 1970, that figure had grown to 30 percent, and by 1980 it was 45 percent. Today, the majority of women with children under *three* work at least part-time, and recent research suggests that this figure will soon extend to a majority of mothers of one-year-olds (Teachman, Polonko, and Scanzoni 1987).

With the enormous increase in women's choices and opportunities in the work world, many women are caught between traditional and modern conceptions of how they should be living their lives. It is a common refrain in our couples groups.

Joan: It's ironic. My mother knew that she was supposed to be a mom and not a career woman. But she suffered from that. She was a capable woman with more business sense than my dad, but she felt it was her job to stay home with us kids. And she was *very* depressed some of the time. But I'm *supposed* to be a career woman. I feel that I just need to stay home right now. I'm really happy with that decision, but I struggled with it for months.

Tanya: I know what Joan means, but it's the opposite for me. I'm doing what I want, going back to work, but it's driving me crazy. All day as I'm working, I'm wondering what's happening to Kevin. Is he OK, is he doing some new thing that I'm missing, is he getting enough individual attention? And when I get home, I'm tired, Jackson's tired, Kevin's tired. I have to get dinner on the table and Kevin ready for bed. And then I'm exhausted and Jackson's exhausted and I just hit the pillow and I'm out. We haven't made love in three months. I know Jackson's frustrated. *I'm* frustrated. I didn't know it was going to be like this.

News media accounts of family-oriented men imply that as mothers have taken on more of a role in the world of paid work, fathers have taken on a comparable load of family work. But this simply hasn't happened. As Arlie Hochschild (1989) demonstrates, working mothers are coming home to face a "second shift"—running the household and caring for the children. Although there are studies suggesting that fathers are taking on a little more housework and care of the children than they used to (Pleck 1985), mothers who are employed full-time still have far greater responsibility for managing the family work and child rearing than their husbands do (C. Cowan 1988). It is not simply that men's and women's roles are unequal that seems to be causing distress for couples, but rather that they are so clearly discrepant from what both spouses expected them to be.

Women are getting the short end of what Hochschild calls the "stalled revolution": Their work roles have changed but their family roles have not. Well-intentioned and confused husbands feel guilty, while their overburdened wives feel angry. It does not take much imagination to see how these emotions can fuel the fire of marital conflict.

Social Policy

The stress that Joan and Tanya talk about comes not only from internal conflict and from difficulties in coping with life inside the family but from factors outside the family as well. Joan might consider working part-time if she felt that she and her husband could get high-quality, affordable child care for their son. Tanya might consider working different shifts or part-time if her company had more flexible working arrangements for parents of young children. But few of the business and government policies that affect parents and children are supportive of anything beyond the most traditional family arrangements.

We see a few couples, like Natalie and Victor, who strike out on their own to make their ideology of more balanced roles a reality. These couples believe that they and their children will reap the rewards of their innovation, but they are exhausted from bucking the strong winds of opposition—from parents, from bosses, from co-workers. Six months after the birth of her daughter, Natalie mentioned receiving a lukewarm reception from her boss after negotiating a four-day work week.

Natalie: He made me feel terrible. I'm going to have to work *very* hard to make things go, but I think I can do it. What worries me, though, is that the people I used to supervise aren't very supportive either. They keep raising these issues, "Well, what if so-and-so happens, and you're not there?" Well, sometimes I wasn't there before because I was traveling for the company, and nobody got in a snit. Now that I've got a baby, somehow my being away from the office at a particular moment is a problem.

Victor: My boss is flexible about when I come in and when I leave, but he keeps asking me questions. He can't understand why I want to be at home with Kim some of the time that Natalie's at work.

It would seem to be in the interest of business and government to develop policies that are supportive of the family. Satisfied workers are more productive. Healthy families drain scarce economic resources less than unhealthy ones, and make more of a contribution to the welfare of society at large. Yet, the United States is the only country in the Western world without a semblance of explicit family policy. This lack is felt most severely by parents of young children. There are no resources to help new parents deal with their anxieties about child rearing (such as the visiting public health nurses in England), unless the situation is serious enough to warrant medical or psychiatric attention. If both parents want or need to work, they would be less conflicted if they could expect to have adequate parental leave when their babies are born (as in Sweden and other countries), flexible work hours to accommodate the needs of young children, and access to reasonably priced, competent child care. These policies and provisions are simply not available in most American businesses and communities (Catalyst 1988).

The absence of family policy also takes its toll on traditional family arrangements, which are not supported by income supplements or family allowances (as they are in Canada and Britain) as a financial cushion for the single-earner family. The lack of supportive policy and family-oriented resources results in increased stress on new parents just when their energies are needed to care for their children. It is almost inevitable that this kind of stress spills over into the couple's negotiations and conflicts about how they will divide the housework and care of the children.

The Need for New Role Models

Based on recent statistics, the modern family norm is neither the Norman Rockwell *Saturday Evening Post* cover family nor the "Leave It to Beaver" scenario with Dad going out to work and Mom staying at home to look after the children. Only about 6 percent of all American households today have a husband as the sole breadwinner and a wife and two or more children at home—"the typical American family" of earlier times. Patterns from earlier generations are often irrelevant to the challenges faced by dual-worker couples in today's marketplace.

After setting out on the family journey, partners often discover that they have conflicting values, needs, expectations, and plans for their destination. This may not be an altogether new phenomenon, but it creates additional strain for a couple.

James: My parents were old-school Swedes who settled in Minnesota on a farm. It was cold outside in the winters, but it was cold inside too. Nobody said anything unless they had to. My mom was home all the time. She worked hard to support my dad and keep the farm going, but she never really had anything of her own. I'm determined to support Cindy going back to school as soon as she's ready.

Cindy: My parents were as different from James's as any two parents could be. When they were home with us, they were all touchy-feely, but they were hardly ever around. During the days my mom and dad both worked. At night, they went out with their friends. I really don't want that to happen to Eddie. So, James and I are having a thing about it now. He wants me to go back to school. I don't want to. I'm working about ten hours a week, partly because he nags at me so much. If it were just up to me, I'd stay home until Eddie gets into first grade.

Cindy and James each feel that they have the freedom to do things differently than their parents did. The problem is that the things each of them wants to be different are on a collision course. James is trying to be supportive of Cindy's educational ambitions so his new family will feel different than the one he grew up in. Given her history, Cindy does not experience this as support. Her picture of the family she wanted to create and James's picture do not match. Like so many of the couples in our study, both partners are finding it difficult to establish a new pattern because the models from the families they grew up in are so different from the families they want to create.

Increased Emotional Burden

The historical changes we have been describing have increased the burden on both men and women with respect to the emotional side of married life. Not quite the equal sharers of breadwinning and family management they hoped to be, husbands and wives now expect to be each other's major suppliers of emotional warmth and support. Especially in the early months as a family, they look to their marriage as a "haven in a heartless world." Deprived of regular daily contact with extended family members and lifelong friends, wives and husbands look to each other to "be there" for them—to pick up the slack when energies flag, to work collaboratively on solving problems, to provide comfort when it is needed, and to share the highs and lows of life inside and outside the family. While this mutual expectation may sound reasonable to modern couples, it is very difficult to live up to in an intimate relationship that is already vulnerable to disappointment from within and pressure from without.

The greatest emotional pressure on the couple, we believe, comes from the culture's increasing emphasis on self-fulfillment and self-development (Bellah et al. 1985). The vocabulary of individualism, endemic to American society from its beginnings, has become even more pervasive in recent decades. It is increasingly difficult for two people to make a commitment to each other if they believe that ultimately they are alone, and that personal development and success in life must be achieved through individual efforts. As this individualistic vocabulary plays out within the family, it makes it even more difficult for partners to subordinate some of their personal interests to the common good of the relationship. When "my needs" and "your needs" appear to be in conflict, partners can wind up feeling more like adversaries than family collaborators.

The vocabulary of individualism also makes it likely that today's parents will be blamed for any disarray in American families. In the spirit of Ben Franklin and Horatio Alger, new parents feel that they ought to be able to make it on their own, without help. Couples are quick to blame themselves if something goes wrong. When the expectable tensions increase as partners become parents, their tendency is to blame each other for not doing a better job. We believe that pioneers will inevitably find themselves in difficulty at some points on a strenuous journey. If societal policies do not become more responsive to parents and children, many of them will lose their way.

READING

17

Healthy Families: Toward Convergent Realities

Reed Larson and Maryse H. Richards

In many ways the deck is stacked against contemporary families, including the comparatively privileged two-parent families we studied here. They must struggle to create internal vitality within a society that is massive, fragmented, and often pulls family members in different directions. When a couple gets married and has children, they enter a minefield of problems waiting to happen. Differences between the fast-paced daily realities lived by each family member create endless potential for misunderstanding and conflict.

Against this backdrop, our society has evolved a new ideal for family life: providing warm relationships and a personal haven for all members. Evidence shows that this new gold standard is one we should aspire to. When marital partners are caring toward each other, their well-being is greater, as is their children's. When relations between parent and child are warm, the child grows up to be a healthier adult. Our question has been, What can families do that would allow them to live up to this standard more consistently? How can families maintain internal warmth despite all the daily processes that pull them apart?

Certainly there are no easy answers. One woman said, "If you claim to have gotten through your child's adolescence without problems, you're lying." We have seen that the simplest interactions of daily life can lead family members into discord. Getting haircuts for the children, fixing the humidifier, a phone call between an adolescent and her boyfriend can create individual distress and collective disharmony.

Nonetheless, we feel it useful to look closely at the families in our study that were faring better. Despite the hazards of contemporary life, in some of these families the members usually got through most days feeling warm toward each other and good about themselves. Husbands and wives shared love and mutual respect, most of the time. Their children usually rebounded quickly from setbacks in their lives. Of course, all these families had moments of conflict, stress, and exchange of negative feelings—no one family had solved the Rubik's cube of domestic harmony. But in some families individual members were buoyant and their daily lives were coordinated most of the time.

In this concluding chapter we search for clues to what it was that was working in these healthier families: What daily patterns allowed them to surmount the many challenges of modern life? The conclusions we draw are limited to households sharing the cultural niche of those we studied: European-American, middle- and working-class, two-parent families. Even within this population, our conclusions are tempered by the fallibility of the measures we have used and the restricted size of our sample. Nevertheless, we think these families provide hints about a "wisdom" whereby some households function more smoothly.

DAILY PATTERNS OF HEALTHIER FAMILIES

Equilibrium Between Family and Public Spheres

We have already introduced some of the families that scored high on our index of family well-being: Del and Marlene, whose marital conflict was followed not by cycles of acrimony, but rather by creative thought about how to resolve the underlying source of their misunderstanding; Lorraine and her son, Luke, who appeared to maintain a healthy balance between their lives together and apart; Victor and his daughter, Vicki, who seemed to be more accepting of each other's feelings, including negative feelings, than most fathers and adolescents.

When we examine the daily patterns of these healthier families, a first finding that emerges concerns the equilibrium between the parents' lives at home and away from home. Throughout this book we have noted that both fathers and mothers typically experience an imbalance between these two spheres: men report high rates of distress at work and compensate for it by cultivating happier states at home; women are drained at home and depend on their job or interactions with friends for the happier part of their lives. These imbalances, we observed in the last chapter, make each spouse dependent on a particular part of his or her life for emotional sustenance and, as a result, promote distorted family relationships. In healthier families, however, we find that *fathers and mothers maintain emotional balance between their lives inside and outside the family*. They report comparable levels of emotion at home and away from home.

For fathers, this balance means that they less often burned themselves out at their jobs. Fathers in healthier families reported more favorable moods at their jobs than other fathers did: they were less likely to deplete themselves with frustration and anger. Possibly these fathers have deliberately chosen less stressful jobs. We mentioned one such father, John, who quit a high-pressure job because he was bringing home too much hostility and taking it out on his son. But our data also suggest that the fathers in healthier families took more breaks and paced themselves at work. We suspect they did more to regulate the intensity of their involvement, in order to avoid getting agitated. The important point is that these fathers were less likely to be emotional wrecks when they got home.

A good example of this balance is Erik Schaak, a father of four who worked in a factory as a forklift operator. This affable thirty-eight-year-old man experienced some pressure at work to move so many items a day, and events at the plant could anger him. At one point he got upset and cursed an "SOB." But he was usually able to regain his composure and keep himself from becoming overwrought. Because his wife, Judy, had a stable career, he did not feel as much obligation to be the breadwinning hero for the family as so many other fathers in our study did. The result of Erik's ability to keep stress in check at his job was that he arrived home with less of an emotional debt than many other fathers did and thus felt less need for immediate leisure when he came in the door.

For mothers as well, emotional balance means having sources of buoyancy both away from home and at home. While some mothers are solely invested in activities at home, many of the women in the healthier families in our study had rewarding outside activities: a job, school, volunteer work, or regular contact with friends. At home, they were engaged with their families but also gave themselves permission to relax and take care of their own needs: we found they had more leisure on weekends at home than other mothers did. They described pleasure in family recreation, reading a book by themselves, or taking a long bath, activities that restored their personal well-being.

Judy Schaak, a self-assured first-grade teacher, was a good example of this balance. She encountered stresses both at work and at home, but was able to keep them under control; she also found emotional rewards in both contexts, which she savored. Judy consistently reported looking forward to the next day, emphasizing the value of maintaining a "positive attitude." Because Erik shared responsibility for family work, she was able to disengage at home when she needed to, reporting time on her own for reading and embroidering. Because women in these healthier families had vital lives apart from their family activities, they were less likely to become overinvolved.

One result of this balance is that neither spouse felt like a victim at home. Neither brought home a personal agenda of unmet emotional needs. Each was less dependent on the family experience for emotional sustenance—and neither had to leave home to get needs met. Consequently, a couple like Judy and Erik are more flexible to accommodate to each other and negotiate each day according to whatever exigencies arise. When Judy heard on Friday that her job was threatened, she called and got support from Erik, just as he turned to her in other situations.

Another result of this balance is that they were more emotionally available as parents to deal with their children's needs. Fathers who are not preoccupied with work and mothers who have the perspective gained from outside involvements may be better able to provide this even, objective attention. Judy and Erik's sixth-grade son, Calvin, was sometimes angered by the discipline his parents imposed, but he also reported learning from the conversations he had with each of them around these disciplinary incidents. Through steady efforts, Calvin said, his father "finally made me realize that I lose my temper too much," for example. Because Erik's emotions were not continuously raw from events at work, he was better able to maintain an even-keeled dialogue with his son, resulting in an important victory of reason over adolescent passion.

The picturebook image of the happy family is one where everyone feels content when together. Our findings suggest that mothers' and fathers' feelings *away from* home may be nearly as important to a family's well-being. "Part of being a parent," the family educator Michael Popkin writes, "is taking care of the parent." And while this is a complicated topic, evidence throughout this book shows that maintaining a healthy family depends on how members run their lives across all their waking hours.

Containing Emotional Brushfires

We suspect this balance in parents' lives contributes to a second feature we find in healthier families. At various points we have seen that negative emotions can be contagious within families. Most often fathers affect other family members, but it can begin with others as well. In some families this contagion leads to cycles of runaway hostility, such as the quarrel between Jerry and Glenna that went on for three days. Healthier families, we find, show less evidence of this transmission of emotion and fewer of these sustained cycles. *One person's emotional states are less likely to be passed to another.*

The family therapist Robert Beavers reached a similar conclusion from his study of successful families. He found that in such families there are stronger "emotional boundaries" between members: it is easier to distinguish mothers', fathers', and children's feelings. Negative states were less often conveyed through blaming, attacking, or scapegoating.

Rather than spraying negative emotions, members of healthier families seem to find ways to process them. One father tried to get home from work early enough so he could go for a run before dinner to dissipate stress. A mother reported taking thirty minutes to pull herself together before leaving her office, because she knew she would be deluged with demands the minute she stepped in the door at home; and though this meant thirty minutes less with her daughter, she found that the restorative effect this time had on her mood made it worthwhile.

Certainly there were occasions in these families where negative emotions got expressed. Erik Schaak admitted that he was sometimes short-tempered after a hard day's work. But these families seemed to be able to respond to members' emotions without letting one person's emotions dictate or dominate another's, as was demonstrated one evening at the Schaaks'. Events on this evening began much like other conflagrations we have seen that rebounded out of control for hours. At 6:58 P.M. Erik and Judy Schaak both reported intense anger over Calvin's "mouthing off." By 8:52, however, all remaining trace of negative feeling was gone. What happened? First, both parents agreed that Calvin's behavior was unacceptable and presented a united front. They did not allow Calvin to play them off against each other as we have seen in some less healthy families. Second, in a kind of "bad cop, good cop" routine, Erik disciplines Calvin by sending him to his room with a clear explanation of why his behavior is unacceptable, then later, Judy went in and comforted Calvin and discussed what had happened. By communicating about the causes of their negative feelings and listening to each other, these families appeared to keep emotional brushfires from getting out of control. Later Calvin reported feeling respectful of how his parents handled the situation.

At heart, members of these families seemed to have greater understanding and acceptance of their own and each other's emotional patterns. Mothers, fathers, and even some adolescents were able to tell us that, yes, they got irritable in certain situations and those feelings could alter their behavior, but they realized it was a pattern they could work on. Parents of one eighth-grade girl characterized their daughter as emotional, but were aware that her emotions passed quickly. Thus rather than fixating and ruminating on her transgressions, they accepted that she was "a moody adolescent" and avoided being pulled in by her hour-to-hour emotional oscillations.

It was fathers in these healthier families who showed the biggest deviation from typical norms for their gender, more often shedding the cloak of patriarchal authority and relating to their wives and children as equals. They were more aware of their own feelings and thus were less likely to dump their negative emotions onto others. They also appeared less likely to withdraw from difficult situations: we found examples of these fathers sustaining engagement with their wives about marital issues and staying with their children even when emotions were painful.

While such attentiveness is customary for mothers, it is rare among fathers. Yet when it exists, it does much to stop the cycles of negative exchange and create a more favorable environment for all family members. Our findings suggest that the art of family life resides in all members being able to attend to, communicate, and contain negative emotions in ways that do not transmit and perpetuate them.

Averting the 6 O'Clock Crash

The volatility of many of the families in our study and the calm of others lie in what happens during the dicey period around six o'clock on weekday evenings. This is a time when lines are most often crossed, when negative emotions are frequently exchanged. It is during this period that we saw a mother's harsh words lead one girl to thoughts of suicide, an angry stepfather push his daughter against the wall, and a dispute between one husband and wife escalate into the husband being kicked out of the house.

Better-functioning families found ways to get through this crunch period with fewer negative emotions. In healthier families, *everyone's mood during this period was more favorable*. Irrespective of mothers' and fathers' employment situations, they avoided the hostile and explosive feelings that are rife in other families.

Part of the problem, as we have discussed, is that fathers bring home emotional stress from work. The other part of the problem is that, in most families, everything that needs to be done during this period hinges on the mother. This can be especially problematic in dual-earner families, where the mother is coming home tired from work herself. In these families the father often flops down in front of the TV, while the mother, who is equally tired, is forced into labor. The result is often negative feelings all around.

So how did healthier families get through this difficult time? In the Schaak family, it was simply understood that Erik, who usually got home from work around 3:30 P.M., was jointly responsible for the urgent tasks of this period. He reported folding clothes with his wife one late afternoon and changing the baby's diaper on another. On yet another, he cooked dinner for Judy, who had had a particularly rough day.

Unlike most fathers, Erik Schaak refused to see his tiredness as more debilitating than his wife's, and Judy was unambivalent about sharing responsibilities with him. Before the school year started, Judy reported, they "sat down and figured out menus for the week and what days laundry and other housework would be done." Now, whatever needed to be done, Erik pitched right in. At times he would lose his cool with the children—late afternoon could still be a stressful period for all. But the fact that both Erik and Judy were involved made them more flexible to handle whatever combination of pressing needs people brought home.

The Schaak family's solution to the 6 o'clock crunch is more the exception than the rule. Some other families reduced the amount of labor required by making microwave dinners or ordering takeout food. Other families have relaxed the expectation that they share a hot meal at 6 each day; in one, different combinations of family members went to exercise during this time, an activity that was effective in both dissipating the day's stress and giving them a chance to check in with each other. In another, each ate separately; the daily family time was not at 6 over supper, but at 10 when all shared a snack and discussed events of the day.

These findings suggest that the art of cultivating a healthy family resides in finding creative solutions for household work, particularly during the 6 o'clock crunch. Each evening produced its unique vortex of urgencies, but through communication, flexibility, and engagement of all members, these healthier families were *usually* able to get through this challenging period with less conflict and transmission of negative emotion.

In Search of Quality Time

Healthy families, according to some family advocates, require not just the avoidance of destructive emotional exchanges, they require renewing ones. Eating meals or spending other time together is thought to provide the opportunity for a family to replenish themselves and affirm their experience of "we-ness."

But defining what makes for this "quality time" is elusive. Some dysfunctional families eat every breakfast and dinner together and spend enormous amounts of time with each other. Spending time in a dysfunctional family may only make members more dysfunctional. "Togetherness is a grand and wonderful thing," the family therapist Nathan Ackerman has written, "but . . . mere physical togetherness may be worse than none at all."

Clearly, just clocking in hours with each other does not automatically reinvigorate the family. We reported earlier that the amount of time husband and wife spent together is related to better marital adjustment, but the same is not true of shared time between parents and adolescents. You may remember that adolescents often experience family time as slow, boring, and constrained; it is thus easy to see why an increase of this kind of time does not enhance family health. But what kind of time do healthier families share? Is there anything unique about their daily contact that might provide hints about improving families' functioning?

First, we found that *members of these families reported fewer negative states when they were together.* Mothers, fathers, and adolescents in the healthier families we studied reported fewer occasions of feeling irritable and angry in each other's presence. This follows from what we have just discussed above: These families find ways to minimize situations that create and perpetuate negative feelings. They maintain a comfortable, relaxed climate in which sustained anger, hurt, and unhappiness cannot thrive.

Second, we found that *the healthier families spent more time in leisure together.* They were more likely than distressed families to go to the zoo, visit relatives, or, as the Schaaks did frequently, just watch TV together. Part of the reason they had more time for each other is that they apparently limited the net hours of work that family members performed. Families who spent most of their time working were less likely to be healthy; this was true irrespective of family social class or mother's employment, suggesting the pattern is not merely a result of financial pressures. Rather than tying up their weekends working overtime or doing household work, members of healthier families are more likely to be available for shared recreational activities.

The third characteristic is that *these families experienced their time together as more egalitarian.* Fewer of them reported a unilateral power structure among members. For times they were together, they reported no one to be the leader twice as often. This mutuality is evident, for example, on a Sunday night when one family was planning a fishing trip together, and all contributed ideas. It is evident in another when they went out for ice cream cones and shared a calm, low-key mood. In many other instances this mutuality was reported when doing chores together or even watching TV. Parents were able to set aside their impulse to control things. These families appeared more able to relax traditional authority structures and find islands of time when they could interact as equals.

What, then, is quality family time? To define it by any rigid criteria would be mistaken. The activities, topics of conversations, and emotional spirit that rekindle family élan may vary from household to household, occasion to occasion, and even from person to person within a family. The elements we have discussed—shared leisure, egalitarian relationships, and avoidance of negative emotion—are important, but there is surely no simple formula. For some families, quality time might even include fathers and adolescents openly airing negative feelings. What is important, we suspect, is not any singular group activity or mystical state, but a climate of attunement between family members, interactions in which each is able to listen and respond to what others are thinking and feeling, even when there is conflict.

In this and the other properties of healthier families, we see a pattern of relating in which fathers, mothers, and adolescents transcend traditional prescriptions for their behavior. . . .

READING

18

Good Dads–Bad Dads: Two Faces of Fatherhood

Frank F. Furstenberg, Jr.

Bill Cosby's bestselling *Fatherhood* was no fluke. It is one of a growing list of volumes on the rewards of paternity with titles like *The Father's Book*, *The Nurturing Father*, and *The Wonderful Father Book*. Treatises on how to be a good dad are by no means unprecedented but the popularity and profusion of father self-help books in the 1980s are. There is no question about it: fatherhood is in vogue. Men enter fatherhood consciously and perform their fatherly duties self-consciously.

Television, magazines, and movies herald the coming of the modern father—the nurturant, caring, and emotionally attuned parent. Cosby is the prototype. No longer confined to their traditional task of being the good provider, men have broken the mold. The new father is androgynous; he is a full partner in parenthood. Today's father is at least as adept at changing diapers as changing tires.

There is another side to fatherhood, a darker side. More fathers than ever before are absent from the home. A growing proportion of men fathering children deny paternity or shirk their paternal obligations. This darker side of fatherhood has also entered our cultural consciousness through the mass media. We are bombarded with research data detailing the rising number of single mothers, inadequately supported by the men who fathered their children. A TV documentary on the breakdown in the black family, hosted by Bill Moyers, presents a young father boasting about the number of women he has impregnated. The nation is outraged. Deadbeat fathers—men who refuse to support their children—have become a political issue. The level of child support is so low that federal and state laws have been enacted to try to enforce paternal obligations.

Reconciling or at least making sense of these seemingly conflicting trends is the aim of this article. The simultaneous appearance of the good father and the bad father are two sides of the same cultural complex. Both patterns can be traced to the declining division of labor in the family. To advance this argument, the first section of this article briefly recounts the historical change in the role of fathers.

The second part examines varied sources of data that have mapped recent trends in the attitudes and behavior of fathers and points out some of the consequences of change. This examination is intended to uncover some indications of future trends in the paternal role. Is the pattern of polarization that has yielded two distinct paternal styles likely to continue? Answering this question involves considering how current public and private policies affect the distribution of paternal styles. The concluding section speculates about how some of these policies could shape the future of fatherhood.

Lest the reader expect more from this ambitious agenda than will be forthcoming, let me emphasize that this article primarily summarizes and interprets existing research. Evidence on fatherhood, though far more abundant now than a few years ago, is still sparse, especially when it comes to trend data (Lewis 1986; Parke and Tinsley 1984; Stein 1984). In any event, this article is not intended to be a review of existing research on fathers; several excellent reviews and compilations of reviews have already summarized the fragmentary literature (Lamb 1987; Lewis and Sussman 1986; Parke and Tinsley 1984). I draw on these reviews and certain seminal studies to present an impression of the changing character of fatherhood and to render a sociological reading of present trends and possible futures. On this latter matter, I am unabashedly, but I hope not recklessly, speculative.

A BRIEF HISTORY OF FATHERHOOD IN AMERICA

John Demos (1986) begins his recent essay on the social history of fatherhood by commenting, "Fatherhood has a very long history, but virtually no historians." Apparently, family historians and feminist scholars have written much about patriarchy while largely ignoring the role of the patriarch (Bloom-Feshbach 1981). Relying heavily on the work of several of his students, Demos briefly outlines the changing role of fathers over the past several centuries.

The story that Demos tells sounds familiar to readers acquainted with other features of family history. The pattern of change has not been completely linear, and much of the action has occurred in the twentieth century (Filene 1986; Parke and Tinsley 1984). After all, the changing role of fathers is part and parcel of a larger configuration of changes in the American family. (For a succinct summary of these changes, see Cherlin 1981; Thornton and Freedman 1983.)

Fathers played a dominant role in the lives of their children in the Colonial period. Fathers assumed a broad range of responsibilities, defining and supervising the children's development. Domestic control largely resided in the hands of men; wives were expected to defer to their husbands on matters of child rearing. According to E. Anthony Rotundo (1985, p. 9), a student of Demos, who has surveyed the history of fatherhood:

Colonial fathers often showed a keen interest in the infants and toddlers of the household, but it was the mothers who fed the little ones, cared for them, and established intimate bonds with them. When children reached an age where they could understand what their parents told them (probably around age three) the lines of parent-child connection changed. Fathers began to tutor all their children in moral values at this point.

A father's moral role persisted throughout childhood, indeed into adult life; his influence was pervasive, usually exceeding the mother's responsibilities over the child. This was especially true for sons. Demos illustrates this point by noting that typically sons, when serving as apprentices, would write to their fathers, asking only to be remembered to their mothers. Both Demos and Rotundo argue that the dominant position of fathers can be traced to their economic role as landowners. (See also Greven 1970.)

At least one source of the erosion of paternal control over children was a shortage of land in New England and the shift away from an agrarian to an industrial mode of production in the beginning of the nineteenth century. However, European scholars argue that from the late eighteenth century, and perhaps earlier, an increase of affective ties within the family reshaped the nature of parenthood and parent-child relations (Shorter 1975; Stone 1979). A general decline of patriarchy, indeed, of parental authority, initiated the emergence of modern fatherhood. As men's economic roles increasingly drew them outside the home and into the marketplace, women extended their sphere of domestic influence (Filene 1986; Lasch 1977).

In a wonderfully provocative essay on the rise and fall of the "good provider" role, Jessie Bernard (1981) provides a similar account of the shift in the balance of power within the family. She observes that by the time that Tocqueville visited America in the 1830s, the nineteenth century pattern of a sharp family and parental division of labor was plainly evident. Tocqueville (1840, p. 212) portrays, as did scores of other foreign travelers (Furstenberg 1966), the contours of the modern nuclear family when he wrote that the public responsibility of men "obliges a wife to confine herself to the house, in order to watch in person and very closely over the details of domestic economy."

The spatial separation of work and home, the hallmark of an urbanized and industrialized economy, was revising both marriage and parent roles. For fathers, it meant the beginning of an almost exclusive emphasis on economic responsibilities, which curtailed the men's day-to-day contact with their children. Demos (p. 51) tells us that the consequences of the uncoupling of work and family life for men cannot be exaggerated. "Certain key elements of premodern fatherhood dwindled and disappeared (e.g., father as pedagogue, father as moral overseer, father as companion), while others were transformed (father as psychologist, father as example)."

Rotundo reports that men still continued to act as disciplinarians in the family, but their removal from the home meant that they "stood outside the strongest currents of feeling that flowed between generations in a family." The father as "instrumental leader," as he was later dubbed by sociologists, derived his status from the outside world, that is from his position in the marketplace. A man's occupational standing established his authority in the home and his worthiness as a husband and father. This movement from ascription to achievement, which occurred throughout the nineteenth century, signaled a profound erosion in the role of fathers. And this transformation is one source of the good father–bad father complex that becomes more evident in the twentieth century.

The strength of the evidence for this historical account is not great, however. True, as Demos and Rotundo observe, the nineteenth-century advice books reveal a growing tendency to speak to mothers exclusively about child-rearing matters, apparently acknowledging the shrinking role of fathers. A more convincing bit of evidence is provided by changing custody practices. Until the middle of the nineteenth century, custody following marital disruption was typically awarded to fathers, who, after all, were assumed to maintain control over marital property (of which the children were a part). By the end of the century, with the growth of family specialization, children increasingly remained with their mothers when marriages dissolved. Early in the twentieth century, the practice of granting custody to mothers was enshrined in the doctrine of "the tender years," which holds that the children's interests are best served when they are raised by their mothers, who ordinarily possess superior parental skills.

Yet, it is easy to overdraw the picture of change. Most available evidence is derived from the middle class. Then, too, accounts of family life in the nineteenth century, not to mention earlier times, are so sketchy that it is difficult to tell how much confidence to place in the existing evidence. As Demos points out, fathers retained considerable authority throughout the nineteenth century, while some may even have increased their affective involvement in child rearing. We should, therefore, assume only that a change occurred in the modal family type, or perhaps in the degree of cultural support for a more detached and distant style of child rearing. But as is true today, some fathers were unwilling to cede so much of the supervision of their offspring to their wives and became involved in the day-to-day upbringing of their children. It seems likely, however, that the number of these actively involved fathers may well have declined in the nineteenth century (Filene 1986). Jessie Bernard, among others, has contended that the more restrictive role of fathers ("good providers") accompanies the development of the privatized nuclear family, the "haven in a heartless world" (cf. Lasch 1977).

The image of the father as good provider remained securely in place—except, perhaps, during the Depression years, when many men could not make good on their end of the bargain (Benson 1968)—until the middle of the twentieth century. The Great Depression literature contains abundant evidence that the strict division of labor was necessarily violated, as women frequently were forced or permitted to assume a more dominant economic role and men occasionally were compelled to pick up domestic tasks in the wake of these changes (Komarovsky 1940). Women's economic roles were also expanded during the war years, as they demonstrated a capacity to fill positions in the job market. Despite these changes, there is little reason to believe that the legitimacy of the existing domestic order was seriously challenged until the 1960s. Indeed, the early post–World War II era appeared to restore the so-called traditional family by strengthening the gender-based division of labor in the family. Perhaps, participation in war enhanced the relative position of males in society and undermined gender stratification within the family. In any event, the post-war period appears to have been the heyday of the nuclear family.

Yet it was becoming clear that discontents on the part of both sexes were producing fault lines in this family form. Feminist scholars have made a strong case that the domestic accord regulating the division of labor within the family was problematic even before Betty Friedan's proclamation of grievances in 1963 issued in *The Feminine Mystique*. Barbara Ehrenreich (1983), in a fascinating cultural account of the changing male role, forcefully argues that concurrent with, if not prior to, the reawakening of feminist consciousness, men were experiencing their own resentments about the burdens of the good-provider role. She contends that in the 1950s men gradually began to retreat from the bread-winning role because they felt imprisoned both socially and emotionally by the sharply delineated masculine role. (See also Filene 1986.) So men had an independent interest in shucking the exclusive responsibilities of providing for their families. Ehrenreich (1983, p. 116) writes:

> The promise of feminism—that there might be a future in which no adult person was either a "dependent creature" or an overburdened breadwinner—came at a time when the ideological supports for male conformity were already crumbling.

What followed, Ehrenreich argues, was a male revolt that occurred in tandem with the feminist revolution of the 1970s. Both movements helped reorder domestic life, producing a family form singularly different from the traditional model that had emerged in the nineteenth century. The collapse of the breadwinner role and the simultaneous entrance of women into the labor force are twin products of twin discontents, according to Ehrenreich.

Ehrenreich gives far more weight to cultural discontents than do economists who argue that it was the economic expansion of service jobs and the growth of wage rates for female employment that ultimately drew women into the labor force. Similarly, demographers and sociologists might provide other accounts for the disintegration of the strict, gender-based division of labor in the family. Declining fertility and high rates of divorce figured into changing opportunities or requirements for women to assume a larger economic role. And economists, demographers, and sociologists all might argue that rising educational levels of women made work outside the home more attractive than full-time mothering.

It is probably not useful to try to separate the cultural from the structural determinants of family change. They are really part and parcel of the events in the 1960s and 1970s that transformed the family. The decline of the good-provider role and of the father as instrumental leader came about when ideology and social structural change converged. The changes in the family that took place during the past two decades were, in effect, sociologically "overdetermined."

The cultural and structural accounts of change strike a common theme: the strict division of labor in the family that predominated for a century or more was precarious from the start. This family arrangement lasted for a time because gender roles were clear and men and women were mutually dependent, owing to their trained incapacity to share tasks. But its demise was predetermined because it set such rigid conditions for successful performance. Ultimately, neither men nor women were willing to uphold their end of the bargain. Women insisted on a larger role in the outside world, and men, it seems, demanded a larger role inside the family. Or, did they? On this point the evidence is much less clear-cut and consistent.

The next section of this article examines in greater detail the experiences of men over the past decade as they have presumably relinquished their responsibilities as sole providers and presumably taken up more of the slack in the home.

MEN IN THE HOME: CURRENT PATTERNS OF FATHERING

Our consideration of fathers in the home begins on a discordant note. There are two sides to male liberation. As men have escaped from the excessive burdens of the good provider role, they have been freed to participate more fully in the family. They have also been freed from family responsibilities altogether. This contradiction emerges directly from the history of fatherhood just reviewed.

The "flight from commitment," as Barbara Ehrenreich describes the process of male liberation, is the inevitable process of the breakdown of the gender bargain that prevailed until the middle of the twentieth century. Ehrenreich (1983, p. 181), citing statistics of the rising reluctance of males to enter and maintain marital arrangements, is deeply skeptical about men's willingness to support women:

> If we accept the male revolt as a historical fait accompli and begin to act on its economic consequences for women—which I have argued that we must do—are we not in some way giving up on men . . . ? Are we acquiescing to a future in which men will always be transients in the lives of women and never fully members of the human family?

Hedging just a bit on the answer to this unsettling question, Ehrenreich concludes that in all probability men will not change and that women must rely on their own economic power with the support of an expanded welfare state.

Jessie Bernard, analyzing the changing role of the good-provider, arrives at a similar conclusion, although she is less prepared to abandon the possibility that men may find a way back into the family. The good-provider role is on its way out, she tells us, but "its legitimate successor has not yet appeared on the scene." She compares the reconstruction of gender and family roles to the deprogramming of a cult member. It has been far easier to convince husbands to share economic responsibilities with their wives than to assume domestic and child care responsibilities.

Historians Demos and Rotundo, in their individual assessments of the future of fatherhood, express similar apprehensions. Rotundo, in particular, is alarmed about the growing trend toward fathers' absence from families and the apparent unwillingness, when living apart from their children, to assume economic responsibility for their support. Rotundo comments, "Although this failure (of divorced fathers to pay child support) represents a dramatic defiance of the ideas of Modern Fatherhood, it is consistent with an extreme strain of male individualism that reacts to family responsibility as a quiet form of tyranny." He, too, questions whether androgynous fatherhood will emerge as the predominant pattern, even in the middle class where it has been championed, at least in some quarters. In sum, Rotundo expresses many of the same doubts that were voiced by feminists like Ehrenreich and Bernard about the willingness of males to remain involved in the family, now that the gender-based division of labor is no longer in place.

Let us have a closer look at the evidence they find so disturbing—the retreat from paternal obligations. Then we shall turn to the data on the other side: are fathers becoming more involved and, if so, what are the likely consequences for their spouses and their offspring?

In drawing any conclusions about trends in paternal involvement, we must be aware that the time we choose to begin our examination will to some extent affect the results. Most comparisons of demographic changes in the family begin in the 1950s and 1960s, in part because data from that period are abundant and the contrasts are almost invariably dramatic. Yet it is important to recognize, as Cherlin (1981) and others have pointed out, that comparisons between today and the baby boom era invariably exaggerate the amount of change. Even taking into account this tendency to magnify the patterns of change, it is hard to dispute that in some important respects, fathers do indeed seem to be receding from the family.

Eggebeen and Uhlenberg (1985), two demographers, have provided a descriptive overview of the declining involvement of men in families during the period from 1960 to 1980. Using data from the decennial censuses in 1960 and 1970 and the 1980 Current Population Survey, they calculate the amount of time men spend in family environments living with children. Later marriage, a decline in fertility, and increasing rates of marital dissolution all have contributed to a sharp decline—43 percent between 1960 and 1980—in the average number of years that men between ages 20 to 49 spend in families where young children live (falling from 12.34 years on average in 1960 to just 7.0 in 1980).

The decline is most evident for more educated males and is much sharper for blacks than whites. Eggebeen and Uhlenberg interpret these results to mean that the opportunity costs for entering fatherhood may be growing as the social pressure for men to become parents declines. In short, fatherhood is becoming a more voluntary role that requires a greater degree of personal and economic sacrifice.

An interesting corollary of this observation is that as fewer men assume the role, those who do will be selected among the most committed and dedicated. If this is true, one might expect to find that fathers today are fulfilling their paternal obligations more, not less, conscientiously. Fathers may be becoming a more differentiated population, with only more highly committed males entering their ranks.

This reassuring observation is, however, not entirely consistent with much of the available evidence on the entrance to fatherhood. Trends on the resolution of premarital pregnancies show a growing proportion of couples electing not to marry (O'Connell and Rogers 1984). Of course, women may be less eager than formerly to enter marriage. Social pressure and pressure from sexual partners have both declined, freeing males from entering marriage in order to make "honest women" of their partners or to "give their child a name." This more elective response to unplanned parenthood has been accompanied by a widespread reluctance of unmarried males to assume economic responsibility for their offspring. Data are unavailable to document whether or not the proportion of unmarried men who contribute to the support of their children has decreased during the past several decades, but most experts would probably agree that it has.

First, many males today do not report their children in social surveys. Fertility histories from males are notoriously unreliable because many men simply "forget" children living outside the household. My own study of unmarried youth in Baltimore showed strikingly higher reports of offspring among females than males, and recent reports indicate that many males are simply reluctant to acknowledge children they do not see or support.

Of course, it is possible to argue that such findings are not discrepant with a trend toward a more voluntaristic notion of parenthood. After all, men are increasingly selective in their willingness to assume the responsibilities of parenthood. But once they do, they may be counted on for support. Not so. A growing body of evidence suggests that adherence to child support is very undependable, even among men who are under a court agreement.

More than half of all men required to pay child support do not fully comply. Moreover, a substantial number of males leave marriage without a child support agreement. In all, only a third of all children living in fatherless homes receive paternal assistance. Among those receiving economic aid, the level is usually so low that it only rarely lifts children out of poverty. The average amount of child support paid to divorced women was $2,220 in 1981 (this figure excludes women due but not receiving support). The amount of child support measured in real dollars actually dropped from 1979 to 1981 (Weitzman 1985, ch. 9). Several studies show that divorced men typically spend a much lower proportion of their postmarital income on child support than do their ex-wives. According to Weitzman (p. 295):

> Most fathers could comply with court orders and live quite well after doing so. Every study of men's ability to pay arrives at the same conclusion: the money is there. Indeed, there is normally enough to permit payment of significantly higher awards than are currently being made.

Many authorities believe that the main reason why men do not pay child support is limited enforcement. In 1984, Congress enacted legislation empowering and encouraging states to adopt stricter provisions for collecting child support. It is still too soon to tell whether the new procedures will significantly alter the level of compliance.

My own hunch is that the issue cannot be solved merely by stricter enforcement measures, although they are certainly a step in the right direction. The more intractable problem stems from the fact that many, if not most, noncustodial fathers are only weakly attached to their children. Data from the 1981 National Survey of Children revealed some alarming statistics on the amount of contact between noncustodial fathers and their offspring (who were between the ages of 11 and 16 at the time of the interview). Close to half of all children in mother-headed households had not seen their biological father during the 12 months preceding the survey, and another sixth of the sample had seen him only once or twice in the past year. And, only a sixth of the children saw their fathers as often as once a week on the average (Furstenberg et al. 1983).

Contact between children and their noncustodial fathers drops off sharply with the length of time since separation. Only about a third of the children in marriages that broke up 10 years earlier have seen their fathers in the past year. The provision of child support is closely related to the amount of contact maintained, which, in turn, is strongly associated with men's socioeconomic position. Less educated and lower income males are less likely to remain connected to their children than those with more resources. Significantly, the figures for support by and contact with never-married fathers are almost as high as the figures for men who were wed to the mothers. It appears, then, that matrimony confers little advantage in maintaining bonds between noncustodial fathers and their offspring.

In general, these figures, along with the child support statistics, provide a dismal picture of the commitment of fathers to their children—at least to those not living in the home. Of course, we cannot completely dismiss the accounts of some noncustodial fathers who report that they are, in effect, "locked out" of a relationship with their offspring by their former wives, who resist their efforts to play to larger role in child rearing. Such men often say they are unwilling to provide child support when they are not permitted to see their offspring regularly.

Some of these responses, no doubt, are credible. More often, it seems, custodial mothers complain that they cannot interest their former husbands in seeing their children. In the National Survey of Children, 75 percent of the women stated that they thought that the children's fathers were too little involved in child care responsibilities, and most stated that they wished the fathers would play a larger role in the children's upbringing.

Having sifted through evidence from this survey and from a smaller and more qualitative study I carried out with Graham Spanier in Central Pennsylvania, the women's accounts are generally more accurate (Furstenberg and Spanier 1984). Fathers typically are unwilling or unable to remain involved with their children in the aftermath of divorce. Instead, men often assume child-rearing responsibilities in a new household after remarriage. This curious arrangement resembles a pattern of "child swapping," whereby many men relinquish the support of biological children from a first marriage in favor of biological or stepchildren in a successive union.

Interestingly, children in stepfamilies report roughly comparable levels of interaction with parents as children in families with two biological parents. Although they are less content with their stepfather's attentions, most acknowledge that their stepfathers are indeed involved in their upbringing—almost as involved as biological fathers in never-divorced families (Furstenberg 1987). It seems, then, that fatherhood is a transient status for many men. Paternal obligations are dictated largely by residence. This is not to say that some men do not maintain enduring ties with biological children when they move apart, especially with sons (Morgan, Lye and Condran 1987), but a substantial number seem to give equal or greater allegiance to their stepchildren.

This picture of men migrating from one family to the next modifies to some extent the proposition that a growing number of men are retreating from fatherhood. Just as they return to marriage, many men who have abandoned their biological children ultimately assume paternal responsibilities for a new set of offspring. Over their life course, most men will spend time raising children, if not their own, then someone else's . Yet it is clear that, from the children's point of view, this more transient notion of fatherhood may be less secure and satisfying.

Current estimates reveal that more than half of all children growing up today will spend at least part of their childhood in a single-parent household, usually headed by a woman. For many of these children, contact with and support from their biological fathers will be sporadic, at best. Although most will in time acquire stepfathers, these men will often be imperfect surrogates for missing biological fathers. They will be less constant in their attentions and, at least from the children's perspective, less often role models for adulthood. Researchers are divided over the issue of how much permanent emotional damage to children is created by marital disruption, but virtually all studies show that spells of paternal absence inevitably place children at a severe economic disadvantage in later life.

Unquestionably, then, the dark side of fatherhood, which I discussed at the beginning of this chapter, casts a large shadow over the sanguine reports of a rising interest in fatherhood. In the breakdown of the good-provider role, a large number of men, in Jessie Bernard's words, have become "role rejectors," men who retreat from family obligations. As she observes, the retreat from fatherhood is not new. Family desertion has always occurred and appeared to be common during the Depression. Then and now, a disproportionate share of the role rejectors are drawn from the ranks of the economically disadvantaged. What may be new is the number of middle-class men who are reneging on their paternal obligations—men who presumably have the resources but not the commitment to perform their fatherly responsibilities. In the concluding section of this chapter, I return to a consideration of what can or should be done to bolster the involvement of these derelict dads.

Despite the ominous rise in the number of transient fathers, it is impossible not to acknowledge that the decline of the good-provider role has, as so many observers have claimed, also brought about a more felicitous trend—the expansion of fatherhood to permit greater emotional involvement in child care. When I asked my barber, a father of two young children, whether he thought that dads were different today, he said, "They've got to be. They are there right at the beginning, don't you think?" he replied with a question back to me, the expert. When I asked him to elaborate he said, "You are right there when the baby is born. That's got to make a difference, don't you think?" he repeated.

I have not collected any statistics on the presence of men in childbirth classes and the delivery room, but I suspect that my barber is correct. Making childbirth and early infant care an important event for fathers conveys a powerful symbolic message: men are no longer on the outside, looking in; they are now part of the birth process. Whether that early contact has enduring "bonding effects," as some have argued, is a much less interesting and important question than the general impact of permitting, indeed expecting, fathers to be involved (Parke and Tinsley 1984). Unquestionably, as a number of leading developmental psychologists have observed, the shifting emphasis on paternal participation in early child care has created opportunities for a new and expanded definition of fatherhood (Lamb 1987).

The burgeoning developmental literature on fatherhood has focused largely on the consequences of new role responsibilities, especially during infancy and early childhood, for children's relations to their fathers and for their cognitive and emotional gains. Because this research is not central to the theme of this article, I merely note in passing that the seemingly obvious proposition that fathers' involvement in child care consistently and substantially benefits the child has not been well established. Existing evidence suggests that the relationship between paternal involvement and children's well-being is mediated by a number of conditions—the mother's attitude toward paternal participation, her ability to collaborate with the father, the father's skill in establishing a warm relationship to his offspring, and the child's needs, among others. The fact that increasing paternal involvement in child care does not automatically result in improved outcomes for children is not altogether surprising, especially to skeptics of simplistic proposals to enhance family functioning. Nonetheless this discovery has disappointed some of the proponents of the new fatherhood movement (Lamb 1982).

Fathers, it seems, neither matter so much emotionally as some wishful observers claim, nor so little as other skeptics contend. When fathers are strongly committed to playing a major role in their children's upbringing their impact can be large, especially when mothers are a less conspicuous presence in the family. Ordinarily, this is not what happens: mothers are the preeminent figures, and the added impact of paternal involvement in shaping the child's emotional development seems rather small.

But a growing body of research indicates that in certain circumstances fathers do play a central role in child rearing, a role that greatly benefits the cognitive and emotional development of young children. Despite some people's reservations (Rossi 1985), fathers, it seems, can be perfectly capable caretakers of young infants. The notion that mothers possess special or unique talents for child care has not been substantiated (Russell 1986). Fathers do characteristically perform child care duties differently, according to Michael Lamb and others who have investigated infant care by men. In particular, fathers tend to engage in more play and roughhousing. Yet Lamb (1987, p. 13) observes that the emotional tone of the paternal relationship is what matters: "As far as influence on children is concerned, there seems to be little about the gender of the parent that is distinctively important. The characteristics of the father as a parent rather than the characteristics of the father as a man appear to influence child development."

Moreover, it is likely that active paternal participation has broader consequences for family functioning. Lois Hoffman (1983), for example, has assembled evidence showing that greater involvement by fathers in household and child care duties reduces the role strain experienced by working mothers. On the basis of fragmentary data, Hoffman speculates that easing the burdens of employed wives enhances marital well-being, which, in turn, contributes to children's adjustment. If fathers assumed an equal parental role, children would be less likely to acquire gender conceptions that restrict the future family performance of males and occupational performance of females. More immediately, however, conjugal bonds might be strengthened when couples share parental tasks.

Hoffman's assessment of the possible benefits of greater paternal participation is not uniformly rosy, however. She notes that the expansion of fatherhood can and has encroached on the prerogatives of women in the home. A breakdown of the traditional division of labor can erode women's power, create greater conflict when parents do not share similar definitions of desirable parental behavior, and dilute the satisfactions of motherhood for women. Hoffman also observes that as men become more competent parents, they may be more willing to divorce, knowing that they have the skills to claim custodial rights. I arrived at a similar conclusion in a study of divorce and remarriage in Central Pennsylvania. When fathers assumed a more active parental role before divorce, the possibility of postmarital conflict over rights and responsibilities for the children tended to increase.

On balance neither I nor, probably, Hoffman would claim that the costs of greater paternal participation outweigh the potential benefits for children. Most women are only too happy to see their husbands play a greater role in child care and would gladly yield territory in the home to increase their power outside the household. The greater involvement of men in child care probably does more to contribute to marital contentment than it does to increase the risk of conflict and divorce.

What is more open to serious question is the extent to which fathers today actually involve themselves in child care. Here again I turned to my barber for an opinion. How much child care does he, as a liberated father, actually do? "Well, I give my wife some relief, but she naturally does most of it," he volunteered. "I really don't have that much time to help out." He is not unique. The preponderance of data from a variety of sources indicates that most fathers still do very little child care, especially when their children are very young.

The extent to which fathers' roles have changed in recent years cannot easily be measured, for researchers simply did not think to ask about paternal involvement in child care even a decade or so ago. This fact itself might be taken as an index of change. Yet it is possible that fathers in the recent past did more than they got credit for and today do less than we like to think. The consensus of most scholars who have studied the question of role change is that modest change has taken place in both the attitude and the behavior of fathers. The change that has occurred is linked to a general shift in less gender-specific family roles (Thornton and Freedman 1983; Stein 1984). Recent data from the Virginia

Slims Survey of American Women, times-series data on women's issues collected by Roper, reveal similar shifts on a range of gender-related attitudes, although limited information was collected specifically on paternal obligations. From 1974 to 1985, women significantly increased (from 46 to 57 percent) their preference for a marriage in which husband and wife shared responsibility for work, household duties, and child care more equitably. Similarly, the Virginia Slims Survey recorded a sharp rise in wives desire to be paid by their husbands for household work (1985 Virginia Slims American Women's Opinion Poll). Although men were not asked these specific questions, their opinions on other related matters indicated that they, too, had greatly increased their support for more egalitarian marriages.

Whether these attitudinal changes are matched by parallel shifts in behavior is doubtful, though clearly some realignment of marital and child care roles has taken place. Joseph Pleck (1985), who has done the most extensive research on the question, concludes that most of these changes have been relatively modest.

The most recent data on changing patterns of paternal involvement were assembled by Juster and Stafford (1985) of the Institute for Survey Research at the University of Michigan. Juster, in a brief analysis of time spent in family activities, traces changes from 1975 to 1981. Using time diaries, he is able to show that men decreased hours spent at work in favor of home activities while women followed the opposite course. This change was especially marked for younger people. Further evidence of domestic change could be seen in the amount of time men spent in "female" types of activities—household duties that have traditionally been performed by women. Between the mid-1970s and the early 1980s, a distinct realignment in roles occurred, with women relegating more domestic tasks to men. This is further evidence of a movement toward greater equality between the sexes, a movement that Juster believes is likely to accelerate in years to come.

Unfortunately, Juster does not break out the data on child care separately or analyze the changes by the presence or absence of children in the home. Pleck's analysis of time diaries reveals that fathers spend substantially more time in domestic and child care duties in households when mothers are employed, but the men still fall far short of assuming an equal load. Moreover, men in families with young children do less than those in households with no children or older offspring. Clearly, these analyses confound a number of related variables—age, cohort, the number and age of children, and the labor force status of mothers. Unless these separate components of paternal participation in child care are disentangled, it is difficult to get a clear picture of the magnitude of the changes in patterns of child care by men and women.

Lamb and Pleck draw interesting distinctions in paternal child care that involves time spent interacting, time spent being available (being the parent on duty), and time spent being responsible, that is making child care arrangements. Apparently, much of the increase in paternal activity has been in the first realm—fathers as babysitters. The least change has occurred in the sphere as father as orchestrator of the child's activities. In this respect, it appears that fathers are still pinch hitters or part-time players rather than regulars.

Evidence from studies of father's role after divorce or separation shows much the same pattern. Fathers are even more marginal. Despite the considerable attention given to joint-custody arrangements in the mass media, in fact, such agreements are rare and often short-lived. Typically, fathers, even when they remain on the scene, play a recreational rather than instrumental role in their children's lives.

In conclusion, evidence of change is compelling, and some researchers believe that the pace of change may be picking up. But fathers, except in rare circumstances, have not yet become equal partners in parenthood. This is not to say that androgynous fatherhood could not happen, only that it has not happened and is not likely to happen in the near future.

Michael Lamb, Joseph Pleck, and their colleagues have analyzed some of the sources of resistance to change. They mention four in particular: motivation, skills and self-confidence, social support, and institutional practices. Motivation represents the willingness of men to change. (William Goode [1982] has written most cogently on the subtle barriers to changing male prerogatives.) Clearly, further change requires a growing number of men to accept an expanded family role. Unless they acquire the skills to assume a greater scope of parental responsibilities, they are likely to confine their attentions to traditional male tasks. The restructuring of the father role requires support and encouragement from wives. Presumably, some wives are reluctant to give up maternal prerogatives. Finally, a number of institutional practices contribute to the maintenance of the status quo by denying fathers the resources to assume a greater share of child care responsibilities. Entrenched social practices continue to convey the message that parenting is mainly women's work.

Lamb argues that unless there is movement on all four of these fronts, fathers are likely to continue to play a relatively marginal role in the family. Clearly, however, these four components overlap and are interconnected. Although Lamb conceives of them as hierarchical, they are probably better thought of as isomorphic. Change in any one will have ramifications for the others. Shifts at the personal and interpersonal level are likely to create social and political demands for widening opportunities for fathers to become active caretakers, just as changes in women's attitudes and the views of men have created change in the marketplace. But political and economic change—sometimes loosely referred to as structural change—can, by the same token, drastically alter personal and interpersonal expectations. In the next and concluding section, which explores the link between public policy and change in paternal practices, I assume that change may be instituted in a variety of ways. I am primarily interested in the prospects for change, ways that change could come about, and some possible consequences for the future of the family.

PUBLIC POLICY AND PATERNAL PRACTICES

Up to now, I have largely avoided the political question of whether the breakdown of the good-provider role was desirable. But I cannot entirely ignore this issue if I am going to discuss the potential effects of future policy initiatives to further equalize parental responsibilities. After all, many people wish to restore the gender-based division of labor that served as the mainspring of the nuclear family until the middle part of this century.

I suppose that if I believed that the costs involved in this transformation of family form greatly exceeded the benefits derived, I would be obligated to try, at least, to imagine ways of returning to the status quo ante. Some costs may exist, especially for children, who have probably been somewhat ill-served by the rapidity of change. This is not to say that children, girls particularly, have not benefited from the collapse of the gender-based division of labor. But we have not managed to protect children as well as we might have if we regarded their welfare as a collective, rather than merely family-based, obligation.

Change has not been cost-free for women, either. Restrictions on divorce provided social and material protections for women, albeit of a paternalist type. Certainly, the declining economic circumstances of divorced women constitute a serious penalty in the quest for equality. Furthermore, as women have entered the marketplace, they have become susceptible to greater occupational stress, leading in some instances to an increase of mental and physical maladies. Finally, some people have argued that the sexual liberation has placed women at greater, not lesser, risk of sexual exploitation by men. Rises in venereal diseases, pregnancy, abortion, and possibly sexual abuse and rape could be seen as adverse side effects of freer sexual relations.

Yet if one examines the sentiments of both men and women, admittedly imperfectly captured in public opinion surveys, most Americans, men and women alike, seem to endorse the changes that have occurred in recent decades. When asked whether they favored or opposed most of the efforts to strengthen and change women's status in society, only 40 percent of women and 44 percent men were supportive in 1970. Today, 73 percent of women and 69 percent of men sanction continued efforts to improve the status of women. Both men and women anticipate further changes in women's roles, while only a tiny minority believe the traditional roles will be restored. Most important of all, the vast majority of women believe that they have gained respect in the process (1985 Virginia Slims). Possibly these sentiments should be counted as mere rationalizations, but I am inclined to interpret them as strong support for changes that have occurred. Even after experiencing the costs associated with family change, most Americans desired continue movement toward gender equality.

In any event, it is difficult to imagine a scenario that would restore the family form common a generation ago. The collapse of the good-provider role resulted from a combination of economic changes and ideological discontents. What is the possibility of reversing these changes? Engineering the withdrawal of women from the labor force and persuading men to pick up the economic slack would be somewhat like putting Humpty Dumpty together again.

Indeed, there is every reason to believe that we are in for more change of the type that we have seen. The proportion of working mothers with young children continues to climb, putting more pressure on fathers to shoulder more of the child care. Men's attitudes and behavior, whether willingly or grudgingly, may well fall into line, as they are increasingly pressured by their partners and society at large to help out more (Goode 1982). Open support for patriarchal privilege has receded in the middle class and may be on the wane in the working class as well. It is unacceptable to make sexist comments in public arenas and unfashionable to do so in private circles. Sexism, like racism, has been forced underground.

Proponents of change have called for a variety of policies that might hasten the process of accommodation to the new family order: parent education to prepare men for future paternal roles, paternity leave to allow them to accept a fuller measure of care for infants, and flex time to enable them to invest more time in child rearing and domestic duties.

The limited evidence for the efficacy of such programs does not persuade me that any of these measures is likely to substantially increase the level of paternal involvement. Parent education classes may enhance the motivation and skills of young men who want to assume a larger paternal role, but they are not likely to produce many converts to the cause. They are somewhat like watered-down job training programs, which have had little or no effect in increasing occupational prospects. In Sweden, where paternity leave has been available for a number of years, only a small fraction of fathers use the benefit. There is little evidence that Swedish men, who are also exposed to more parent education, have developed more egalitarian child care patterns than American fathers. Finally, experiments to implement more flexible work schedules seem to have had a negligible effect on the participation of fathers in child care.

I do not dismiss these programs out of hand; they may not have had a full and fair chance to show effects. There is some evidence that many parents manage to get by with no outside day care when husbands and wives are able to work separate shifts (Presser and Cain 1983). Possibly, as some have argued, flex-time programs do not go far enough. The same can be said for measures such as education in parenthood or paternity leave. Besides, it might be argued that these provisions convey an important symbolic message to men that they have the right and the obligation to become more involved. Thus, these programs may have important indirect effects on men by changing the normative climate in society at large rather than by directly affecting the men who participate in them.

General family support services such as day care or preschool programs, which relieve the burden of child care for both employed parents, may do as much to foster paternal involvement as do categorical programs directed at fathers alone. Specialized programs can serve only a limited number of fathers—probably, largely the men who are already ideologically receptive. Systems designed to assist parents, regardless of gender, draw from a larger base and attract more public support. Thus, the arena for change may be played out in Parent-Teacher Associations, church groups, professional organizations, and the like. The degree to which these groups welcome or resist gender change within the family is a sensitive barometer to the transformation of family roles.

Enticing fathers in two-parent families to assume a greater share of child care responsibilities may be much less difficult than gaining their involvement when childbearing occurs out-of-wedlock, or retaining their involvement after marriages break up. As we saw earlier, some feminists are prepared to give up on men and turn to a more benign and generous welfare system for support.

Building an economic support system that further weakens paternal obligation is questionable policy on several grounds. First, it is not clear how generous we are prepared to be in providing for the children of single mothers. And even if we raise the economic situation of female heads of families, their children are not going to be on a par with children in two-parent families. Furthermore, policies that let men off the hook are bound to contribute further to the retreat of men from the family. That is bad for women, bad for children, and bad for men as well. It is difficult to argue that black women, children, or even men, for that matter, have benefited from the retreat of males from participation in family life. Everyone seems to have lost as the ability of black males to contribute economically has been eroded over the past two decades. Some might say that the same trends are beginning to occur among poorer whites, as males increasingly offer little economic support to women and children. The rising rates of nonmarital childbearing among young white women may be an ominous harbinger.

As mentioned, vigorous efforts have recently been made to increase the contribution of males to children they have fathered but are not living with. This hardline policy is intended to make men feel responsible for their children, but whether a more aggressive approach to the collection of child support produces a greater sense of paternal obligation remains to be seen.

The "stick" approach is worth trying, but should we not also be conjuring up a few carrots—programs designed to create incentives to paternal participation? In a recent article in the *Public Interest*, Vinovskis and Chase-Lansdale (1987) question whether teenage marriages ought to be discouraged. Citing a mixed bag of evidence, they assert that at least some fathers are capable of supporting their children and young mothers might do better if they were to enter marriage—even if the likelihood of the marriage's survival is low. Without discussing the validity of their claim, it is discouraging to discover that the authors of this provocative thesis suggest no policies for encouraging men to enter marriage other than to say that social scientists have been overly pessimistic about the merits of matrimony. Can we not conceive of ways to make marriage more attractive and to discourage single parenthood?

Previously I have argued, along with Wilson (Wilson and Neckerman 1985) and many others, that marriage is increasingly inaccessible to many low-income youth because males simply do not have the economic prospects to provide females with an incentive for entering marriage. The income-maintenance experiments notwithstanding, I am also persuaded that for many low-income couples, unemployment and poor future earnings weaken conjugal bonds and contribute to the especially high rates of marital instability among poorer Americans. Despite the demise of the good-provider role, men are more likely to move out of a marriage to which they do not contribute and women are less likely to want them to remain even if men are so inclined.

This situation probably could not be immediately remedied even if the unemployment rates were to return to the 1960s levels. With the breakdown of the division of labor within marriage, the value of men's economic contributions probably counts for less today than it once did, and the emotional exchange probably counts for more. Yet material contributions still matter, and a healthier economy would probably reduce, or at least slow down, the retreat from marriage and make remarriage more attractive, especially among disadvantaged populations.

There are probably other ways of making marriage more economically appealing to couples. Eliminating the residual marriage penalty and creating tax incentives for marriage, especially for poor people with children, might have some modest effects by at least reducing the disincentives to marrying. It might also be feasible to devise a program of family assistance linked to Social Security payments. Couples who contribute to the support of children might receive added payments during retirement. Although such a plan might not directly hold couples together, it would certainly encourage fathers to contribute to child support. It might be possible to provide bonus payments to households with two earners or two parents, or both.

Such programs are costly, and, judging from efforts designed to promote pronatalist policies, we should not look for large effects on nuptial behavior from incentive schemes. In some instances, though, even modest results might be cost-effective, given the very real price tag to society associated with single parenthood and the absence of child support. Moreover, as I have contended throughout this chapter, programs tailored to promote paternal involvement bolster the norm that it is desirable for men to participate in the family and support their offspring. As such they may produce indirect effects consistent with the aim of increasing paternal participation in the family.

Finally, it is reasonable to suppose that marital stability may be enhanced, at least slightly, by the diffusion of cultural norms permitting and promoting more child care involvement among fathers. Scattered evidence from a variety of studies, as I mentioned earlier, reveals that marital stress is relieved when men assume a larger burden of child care. Also, greater emotional investment in children by men appears to increase marital stability, reducing the risk that fathers will withdraw from the family (cf. Morgan, Lye, and Condran 1987).

CONCLUSION

Ordinarily it is difficult to predict future family trends. Forecasting changes in the father role is extremely hazardous, as we are witnessing a confluence of conflicting trends. About one thing we can be fairly certain—further attenuation of the good-provider role is likely to take place as fewer women count on their husbands to provide economic support without women's aid and fewer men expect women to manage the household and children without men's assistance. Whether the gender-based division of labor that characterized families until the middle of the twentieth century will disappear altogether is highly questionable. But if I am correct that the breakdown of the good-provider role for men is ultimately responsible for the rise of the good dad–bad dad complex, the bifurcation of fatherhood could continue unabated, creating both more fathers that are closely involved with their children and more that are derelict. Even if two discrete male populations are formed, men, as noted earlier, may migrate from one category to the other during their lifetime.

Some of the conditions that might reduce the number of men who are retreating from fatherhood involve normative shifts that encourage greater participation of fathers in child rearing; these shifts are not easily susceptible to policy manipulation. I nonetheless remain rather sanguine about the prospects of further change if only because the cultural climate appears to be increasingly receptive to this trend.

One set of policies that has been mentioned here involves creating larger incentives to contribute to children and disincentives to withhold support. Experimental programs may provide indications of the results to be expected from the judicious use of the carrot and stick. We probably should not expect too much from policy interventions, if only because we are not prepared to build either a very large carrot or stick. The crux of the problem is that men looking at marriage today may sense that it offers them a less good deal than it once did. This is the inevitable result of reducing male privileges, female deference to men, and a range of services that were customarily provided as part of the conjugal bargain. The loss of these privileges has persuaded some men to opt out of family life altogether.

Those who have not done so now expect more emotional gratification from marriage; more than ever before, intimacy has become the glue of family life. Recently, men have begun to realize a second source of benefits from family life—the gratifications of parenthood and the satisfactions of close ties with their children. These men have become the "new fathers" who are more emotionally invested in parenthood. It is too early to tell whether this new form of fatherhood will enhance stability in family life. Are these more involved fathers more committed to family life, more willing to endure marital discontents in order to remain with their children, and more prepared to sacrifice their own emotional needs in the interests of their offspring? I am not so certain, but time will tell. In the meantime, it may be necessary to devise all the means we can muster to produce more nurturant males, in the hope that they will help to strengthen our present imperfect and tenuous forms of marriage and parenthood.

REFERENCES

Benson, Leonard. 1968. *Fatherhood: A Sociological Perspective.* New York: Random House.

Bernard, Jessie. 1981. "The Good Provider Role: Its Rise and Fall." *American Psychologist* 36: no. 1:1–12.

Bloom-Feshbach, J. 1981. "Historical Perspectives on the Father's Role." In *The Role of the Father in Child Development*, 2nd ed., edited by Michael E. Lamb. New York: John Wiley & Sons.

Cherlin, Andrew J. 1981. *Marriage, Divorce, Remarriage.* Cambridge, Mass.: Harvard University Press.

Demos, John. 1986. *Past, Present and Personal: The Family and the Life Course in American History.* New York: Oxford University Press.

Eggebeen, David, and Peter Uhlenberg. 1985. "Changes in the Organization of Mens' Lives: 1960–1980." *Family Relations* 34, no. 2:251–57.

Ehrenreich, Barbara. 1983. *The Hearts of Men: American Dreams and the Flight from Commitment*. New York: Anchor Press.

Filene, Peter G. 1986. *Him/Her/Self: Sex Roles in Modern America*. Baltimore: The John Hopkins Press.

Friedan, Betty. 1963. *The Feminine Mystique*. W. W. Norton and Company, Inc.

Furstenberg, Frank F., Jr. 1966, "Industrialization and the American Family: A Look Backward." *American Sociological Review* 31:326–37.

Furstenberg, Frank F., Jr. 1987. "The New Extended Family: Experiences in Stepfamilies." In *Remarriage and Step-parenting Today*, edited by Kay Pasley and Marilyn Inhinger-Tallman: 42–61. New York: Guilford Press.

Furstenberg, Frank F., Jr., Christine Winquist Nord, James L. Peterson, and Nicholas Zill. 1983. "The Life Course of Children of Divorce: Marital Disruption and Parental Contact." *American Sociological* Review 48, no. 10: 656–68.

Furstenberg, Frank F., Jr., and Graham B. Spanier. 1984. *Recycling the Family: Remarriage After Divorce*. Beverly Hills: Sage Publications.

Goode, William J. 1982. "Why Men Resist." In *Family in Transition*, edited by Arlene S. Skolnick and Jerome H. Skolnick: 201–18. Boston: Little, Brown and Company.

Greven, Phillip. 1970. *Four Generations: Population, Land and Family in Colonial Andover, Massachusetts*. Ithaca, N.Y.: Cornell University Press.

Hoffman, Lois Wladis. 1983. "Increasing Fathering: Effects on the Mother." In *Fatherhood and Family Policy*, edited by Michael E. Lamb and Abraham Sagi, 167–90. Hillsdale, N.J.: Lawrence Erlbaum Associates.

Juster, Thomas F., and Frank B. Stafford. 1985. *Time, Goods and Well-Being*. Ann Arbor: Institute for Survey Research.

Komarovsky, Mirra. 1940. *The Unemployed Man and His Family*. New York: Dryden Press.

Lamb, Michael E., ed. 1982. *Nontraditional Families: Parenting and Child Development*. Hillsdale, N.J.: Lawrence Erlbaum Associates.

Lamb, Michael E. ed. 1987. *The Father's Role: Cross Cultural Perspectives*. Hillsdale, N.J.: Lawrence Erlbaum Associates.

Lasch, Christopher. 1977. *Haven in a Heartless World: The Family Besieged*. New York: Basic Books.

Lewis, Robert A. 1986. "Men's Changing Roles in Marriage and the Family." In *Men's Changing Roles in the Family*, edited by Robert A. Lewis and Marvin B. Sussman. New York: Haworth Press.

Lewis, Robert A., and Marvin B. Sussman, eds. 1986. *Men's Changing Roles in the Family*. New York: Haworth Press.

Morgan, S. Philip, Diane Lye, and Gretchen Condran. Forthcoming. "Sons, Daughters and Divorce: The Effect of Children's Sex on Their Parent's Risk of Marital Disruption." *American Journal of Sociology*.

O'Connell, Martin, and Carolyn C. Rogers. 1984. "Out-of-Wedlock Births, Premarital Pregnancies, and Their Effect on Family Formation and Dissolution." *Family Planning Perspectives* 16, no. 4:157–62.

Parke, Ross D., and Barbara R. Tinsley. 1984. "Fatherhood: Historical and Contemporary Perspectives." In *Life Span Developmental Psychology:*

Historical and Cohort Effects, edited by K. A. McCluskey and H. W. Reese. New York: Academic Press.

Pleck, Joseph. 1985. *Working Wives Working Husbands*. Beverly Hills: Sage Publications.

Presser, H. B., and V. Cain. 1983. "Shift Work Among Dual-Earner Couples with Children." *Science* 219:876–79.

Rossi, Alice S. 1985. "Gender and Parenthood." In *Gender and the Life Course*, edited by Alice S. Rossi. New York: Aldine Publishing Company.

Rotundo, E. Anthony. 1985. "American Fatherhood: A Historical Perspective." *American Behavioral Scientist*, 29, no. 1:7–25.

Russell, Graeme. 1986. "Primary Caretaking and Role Sharing Fathers." In *The Father's Role: Applied Perspectives*, edited by Michael E. Lamb: 29–57. New York: John Wiley & Sons.

Shorter, Edward. 1975. *The Making of the Modern Family*. New York: Basic Books.

Stein, Peter J. 1984. "Men in Families." *Marriage and Family Review* 7, no. 3:143–62.

Stone, Lawrence. 1979. *The Family, Sex and Marriage in England 1500–1800*. New York: Harper & Row.

Thornton, Arland, and Deborah Freedman. 1983. "The Changing American Family." *Population Bulletin* 38, no. 4:2–44.

Tocqueville, Alexis de. 1954. *Democracy in America*, 2 vols. New York: Vintage Books.

Vinovskis, Maris A. P., and Lindsay Chase-Lansdale. 1987. "Should We Discourage Teenage Marriage?" *Public Interest* 87:23–37.

The 1985 Virginia Slims American Women's Opinion Poll. A Study conducted by the Roper Organization, Inc.

Weitzman, Lenore J. 1985. *The Divorce Revolution: The Unexpected Social and Economic Consequences for Women and Children in America*. New York: Free Press.

Wilson, William Julius, and Kathryn M. Neckerman. 1985. "Poverty and Family Structure: The Widening Gap between Evidence and Public Policy Issues." In *Fighting Poverty: What Works and What Doesn't*, edited by Sheldon H. Danziger and Daniel H. Weinberg: 232–59. Cambridge, Mass.: Harvard University Press.

READING

19

Adoption and Stigma

Elizabeth Bartholet

Adoption has a very bad name. All characters in the adoption story are regularly described as victims, forced by circumstances to live out lives that are significantly diminished in quality. Birth parents and the children they relinquish are said to suffer from the loss of their primal connection. Adoptive parents who have not been able to bear children are said to suffer from the loss of the dream child of procreation.

The stigma surrounding adoption constitutes part of the social conditioning to which we are all subject from birth onward and thus helps shape reality. Birth mothers are conditioned to keep their children; no matter what the circumstances, it is considered "unnatural" to give your child away. Less than one percent of the children born in this society are relinquished for adoption at birth. Indeed, only two percent of the infants born to single mothers are relinquished. The infertile are conditioned to experience their loss as devastation, and they pursue infertility treatment with ever-increasing enthusiasm. It is considered "natural" to want to have your "own" child, even at the cost of years of quite *un*natural treatment at the hands of the high-tech infertility specialists. Adoptive parents and their children are regularly reminded that their families are inferior in important ways to regular families.

This stigma helps shape the priorities for those in charge of regulating adoption. Adoption is set up as a choice of last resort both for birth parents and for the infertile, largely because the regulators think badly of it. This regulatory structure then reinforces the stigma by helping to make adoption an unattractive option.

Despite this universal denigration, the available evidence shows that adoption works extremely well for all those immediately concerned. Why is the success story being suppressed? It may be too threatening. It means, among other things, that women can give away their children or lose their capacity for pregnancy and still function as full human beings. It means that children who are mistreated by their birth parents can be removed for parenting by others. It

---

means that biology is *not* destiny. It raises questions about the goal of self-perpetuation and the value of promoting our own racial, cultural, and national groups. It forces us to think about the appropriate definition of family and community.

THE TRADITION: BLOOD IS THICKER THAN WATER

The stigma surrounding adoption is so pervasive that most people are unaware of its existence; it is part of the air we breathe, part of the atmosphere of our daily existence. But with adoptive parenthood comes a new consciousness, and as time passes you feel successive jars of recognition. You see and hear and feel the stigma because you and your family have become the alien outsiders—the object of the stigma.

We are brought up on stories that illustrate the principle that blood ties are essential to parenting. Fairy tales teach us that stepparents exploit and abuse children, feed them poisoned apples, and cast them out into the forest to starve. Myths involving famous foundlings teach us that children cannot find "real" parents or permanent homes or a community to which they belong in adoption; our biologic origins are central to our destiny. The infant Oedipus, left by his father to die on the mountain, is rescued and adopted by the king of Corinth and grows up thinking, mistakenly, that his adoptive parents are his real parents. But he is compelled by destiny to return to his origins and to fulfill the prophecy that he will kill his father and marry his mother. Moses, saved from the slaughter of male Jewish children by being hidden in the bulrushes of the Nile, is found and brought up by one of Pharaoh's daughters. He fulfills his original destiny by leading "his people," the people of Israel, out of Egypt to the Promised Land.

In raising my adopted children, I am painfully conscious of the prevalence of negative adoption themes in the stories that help shape childhood. The popular *Are You My Mother?* features a baby bird that falls from its nest and then wanders through the world, rushing up to various nonbird creatures to ask eagerly whether they are the missing mother and being told each time that of course they are not. In the end the baby bird is deposited by one of these nonmothers in its original nest, and the mother, who has been off looking for food, reappears. Instant recognition! The absurdity of adoption by any of the nonbirds is patent, and the story turns on this humor and on the rightness of the fact that the bird belongs where he came from. Kipling's story of Mowgli the Jungle Boy is one of many classic children's stories about a child raised by "others," here the jungle animals, with whom he *thinks* he's happy and *feels* he belongs. But in the end Mowgli must go back to live with humankind, and the story teaches that that is where he most surely belongs.

The language surrounding adoption regularly reinforces the message that real parenting is blood-linked. Those struggling with infertility are told, "You should go ahead and adopt, and then you will relax and be able to have one of your own." Adoptive parents are regularly asked, "How much do you know about his *real* parents?" The adopted child's birth parents are described in legislation as well as casual conversation as the "natural" parents. Friends ask of my two adopted children, raised together since birth, "Are they brothers?" And they ask of my biologic child, "How does your *own* child feel about them?" Thus parenting is equated with procreation and kinship with the blood link. It is only genetically linked parents who are truly entitled to possess their children, and to whom children truly belong. Blood strangers who rear and nurture children are unreal, unnatural substitutes for the real thing.

The language surrounding adoption regularly conveys the additional message that adoptive parenting relationships are less powerful, less meaningful, less loving than blood relationships. Adoptive parents are commonly asked, "What made you decide to adopt?" and are commonly told, "What a good thing for you to have done." The clear implication is that people would not adopt for the same reasons that they would produce a child—they would not expect to enjoy the same pleasures or experience the same kind of giving-and-getting relationship. Therefore, some aberrational and perhaps altruistic motive must be involved.

Adoptive relationships are not seen as entitled to the same kind of privacy or respect as birth parenting relationships. Strangers in a supermarket who see me shopping with my children will come up to ask, "Where did you get them?" (Few are questioned in the supermarket about how they happened to get pregnant or whether their husband is of a different race.) When I first adopted, a number of acquaintances told me that they knew others who had adopted and "it had really worked out quite well." A man I had always thought of as a rather sweet and sensitive person launched into an extensive discussion of the troubles that a couple he knew had had with their several adopted children and the negative findings allegedly contained in the literature about adoptees. It was clear that these people assumed that my relationship with my adopted children was far more removed and impersonal than a "normal" parent-child relationship, and that I would therefore be able to discuss with cool detachment the prospects of my children's turning out well or badly.

Some people are quite ready to reveal that they see adoptive parenting as a debased form of parenting and adopted children as inherently inferior to those that you could have produced biologically. "Your children really are very cute, and they seem smart, too": the tone of voice shows how surprising the speaker finds the latter. He goes on. "You're really very lucky, aren't you, because you can't know what you'll get, can you?"

Many people believe they think well of adoption and resist the notion that it is stigmatized generally. "But I think adoption is a *wonderful* thing to do," they protest. They are unaware that when they heap praise on the noble adoptive parent, the implicit message is that adoptive parenting lacks the joyous quality that characterizes true parent-child relationships. They are unaware that when they talk of how lucky the child is to have been adopted, their well-meaning phrases are insulting to the child. Children's reactions are revealing. One study reports that when adoptees first tell their childhood friends of their adoptive status, the most common reaction is a sympathetic "I'm sorry." The friends then tend to avoid discussing the topic or respond to mention of it with embarrassed silence, conveying their sense that being adopted must be so awful that suppression is the best course.

Media coverage reinforces negative stereotypes about adoption. The improper removal of children from birth parents is a favorite topic, and headline status is accorded to stories about alleged kidnapping and baby-buying rings and those that show adoption agents and prospective parents otherwise breaking the law in their efforts to find and place children for adoption. A current hot topic involves the search and reunion theme, emphasizing the centrality of the biologic link. Stories about violent and shocking crimes committed by people who happen to have been adopted tend to highlight their adoptive status, implying that adoption is probably connected in some way to the commission of horrible crimes. "Baby swap" stories, about children who are switched by accident at birth and raised by the "wrong" parents until the accident is discovered, have generated intense media interest. These stories exude sympathy for the "adoptive" as well as the biologic parents, but their basic point is that the switch has created a situation of desperate tragedy for all involved.

The basic vocabulary of families in our society reflects the degree to which we see blood as central to kinship. Family members are identified by terms designed to show who is related by blood and to what degree: mothers-in-law are distinguished from mothers and stepbrothers from half-brothers. The term *family* implies a group linked by blood ties: a married couple are not really a family until they produce the children who provide the blood link trying them all together; when people talk about "starting a family," they refer not to the creation of a marital relationship but to the production of children. Only our blood relationships are permanent: we speak of ex-husbands but not of ex-sisters. David Schneider's classic work *American Kinship* gives this account: "What is out there in nature, say the definitions of American culture, is what kinship is. Kinship is the blood relationship, the fact of shared biogenetic substance. Kinship is the mother's bond of flesh and blood with her child." Schneider points out that while American kinship is typical of modern Western societies, "it is different from the kinds of kinship systems found elsewhere in the world."

The American conception of adoption is also different from that which appears in many other parts of the world. Adoption is both a common and a revered form of family in Pacific island cultures. A study of adoption in Tahiti reports societies in which from 25 to 40 percent of all children are adopted, and the majority of households are involved in either placing or receiving children in adoption. The author speculates that in Polynesian and Micronesian societies, adoption may be at the top of the family hierarchy, and asserts that the goal seems to be to establish "between parents and natural children relationships which coincide as nearly as possible with those between parents and adopted children."

In our society, the law has reflected and reinforced the degraded status of the adoptive family. Judges in earlier times refused to adapt the common law to give legal status to adoptive parenting relationships because blood ties were thought so central to the meaning of family. Legislation was necessary to validate adoptive arrangements in both this country and Great Britain, but even when it was introduced, which was not until the latter half of the nineteenth century, it was strictly construed. In 1891 the Supreme Court of California removed a child from its adoptive parents, ruling that "the right of adoption . . . was unknown to the common law, and as the right when acquired under our statute operates as a permanent transfer of the natural rights of the parent, it is repugnant to the principles of the common law, and one who claims that such a change has occurred must show that every requirement of the statute has been strictly complied with." Legislation giving fully protected parent-child status to the adoptive relationship was not enacted in Europe and Great Britain until the middle of this century.

In formalizing the institution of adoption, the law gave parents and children some important protections. For example, for the first time adoptees had the same entitlement to care and support from their parents and the same inheritance rights as biologic children. But by structuring adoption in imitation of biology, the law reinforced the notion that the adoptive family was an inferior family form.

The sense of shame associated with adoption was intense. Sealed records were designed in part to enable the adoptive family and the birth family to keep their shameful secrets from the world. One goal of placing children with physically similar adoptive parents was to enable the adoptive family to pass as a biologic family. Parents were often advised not to tell anyone, even their children, about the adoption.

Modern adoption orthodoxy emphasizes the importance of acknowledging both the fact of adoption and some of the differences associated with this form of parenting, and today's parents are advised to tell children about their adoptive status as soon as they can understand what that means. But this change in philosophy appears to have occurred largely because it has proven difficult or impossible to keep adoption a secret, particularly when older children and children who look significantly different from their adoptive parents are involved. The secrecy that surrounds the practice of donor insemination reveals that the shame associated with infertility and with parenting that is not biologically linked is still a powerful force. Recent studies show that in families where the wife has become pregnant with sperm from a donor rather than her husband, the parents often keep the child's origins a secret from the outside world and even from the children born of this process.

NEW SOURCES OF STIGMA: OF ROOTS AND THE TRAGIC TRIANGLE

Although some progress was made in the earlier part of this century in upgrading the status of adoptive parenting, powerful forces at work in recent years have revitalized the traditional stigma associated with parenting that is not biologically linked. The search movement, consisting of birth mothers and adoptees, the various advocacy and support groups they have formed, and professionals associated with their cause, represents one such force. The movement has grown apace in the past two decades and exerts a powerful influence. Its basic message is that children "belong" in some primal sense with their family of origin.

The immediate focus of the search movement's efforts is the sealed record system. Movement members advocate opening records so that birth parents and adoptees can identify and connect with each other. The underlying rationale is that biologic links are of fundamental importance.

The long-term goal for many members of the search movement is to eliminate adoption altogether, or at least to limit it to situations of absolute necessity. A recent statement by two search movement leaders argues that the time has come to move beyond the demand for openness to address the "basic issues." It condemns adoption as a "flawed institution," one that "causes pain and lifelong suffering to all the parties involved," and calls for its transformation to a form of guardianship that would permit birth parents to retain some rights over their children even in those "last resort" situations in which it would be necessary physically to remove a child from the birth family.

Search movement activists paint an overwhelmingly negative picture of the impact of adoptive arrangements on all the key parties. They describe a tragic triangle involving the birth parents, the adoptive parents, and the adoptees, with each set of characters doomed to a lifetime of grieving. The birth parents must forever suffer the pain associated with the loss of their child and, if they bear no other children, the loss of genetic continuity into the future. Adoptive parents who are infertile, as is commonly the case, must forever suffer the pain associated with their loss of genetic continuity into the future and of the genetic child of their dreams. Adoptees must forever suffer the loss of their birth parents and the related loss of genetic continuity with the past. In addition, they will suffer the pain of rejection as they become aware of the "original abandonment" involved in their birth parents' decision to give them up, and will struggle with the resulting injury to their sense of self. They will be prone to "genealogical bewilderment" as they struggle to live a life cut off from their genetic origins, in family structures characterized as inherently abusive.

The movement has generated a significant body of literature in recent years whose fundamental message is that the institution of adoption is sick to its core and destructive of the human beings it affects. A news column by Betty Jean Lifton, a leading figure in the movement, gives a sense of the message that is being promoted. She writes about a fourteen-year-old child who killed his adoptive parents by setting fire to their home, allegedly so that he could search for his birth mother, and describes his actions as related to the so-called adopted child syndrome: "The syndrome includes conflict with authority, preoccupation with excessive fantasy, setting fires, pathological lying, stealing, running away from home, learning difficulties, lack of impulse control." Lifton claims that while most adoptees "adjust" to their unfortunate condition, others "cannot control the inchoate rage caused by their feelings of powerlessness and of rejection by the birth parents." Elsewhere she writes that the adoptee, "by being excluded from his own biological clan, forced out of the natural flow of generational continuity, feels as if he or she has been forced out of nature itself. He feels an alien, an outsider, . . . outside the natural realm of being."

Other forces at work in the society at large have helped to make adoption newly suspect in today's world. There has been a new emphasis in recent decades on the importance of "roots" and of group identity. People are supposed to go back to their roots and derive strength from their racial, ethnic, and national communities of origin. This thinking provides fertile ground for theories that children belong with their birth families and that they will suffer a grievous loss if cut off from their prebirth history and their genetic group. And, of course, it helps make transracial and international adoption particularly problematic.

Egalitarian politics have also contributed to the new stigmatization, with critics attacking adoption as one of the ultimate forms of exploitation of the poor by the rich, the black by the white, the Third World by the capitalist West, the struggling single mother by the economically privileged couple. The fact that adoption functions to improve the economic situation of birth mother and child is ignored.

Finally, the current emphasis on the importance of genetic heritage has revived certain classic fears about the viability of adoption—fears rooted in an assumption that parent-child relationships are likely to work only to the degree that parent and child are significantly alike. In the ongoing nature-nurture debate, the voices of genetic theorists have prevailed lately. Their new studies do not show that environment is an unimportant influence. They simply show that biologic heritage is also important and that children do not start life as blank slates on which adoptive parents can write what they will. But those who think that parent-child relationships are threatened by differences in intellect and personality will find it troubling to think that genetic heritage plays a significant part in the child's development. And those who believe that children belong with their birth parents will find confirmation in the evidence of genetic influence.

The last couple of decades have been bad ones for adoption. Its advocates can easily get the sense that they are fighting the tide of history.

THE STUDIES: OF MODERN-DAY MYTHS AND REALITIES

The professional literature on the adoption experience constitutes yet another source of stigma. Much of this literature describes adoptive relationships as inherently problematic, presenting a high risk of damage to all parties involved. But the negative claims are not grounded in evidence that anything actually does go wrong as a result of severing the genetic link between parent and child. The empirical studies discussed at the end of this chapter indicate in fact that as far as anyone can tell, adoption works extremely well from the perspective of everyone involved. It certainly works far better than existing alternatives, such as keeping children with birth parents who are not actually interested in or prepared for parenting. Adoption enables children who have suffered severe neglect and abuse to recover and lead essentially normal lives. Interestingly, when children are placed in adoptive homes in infancy, they apparently do just as well as children raised in birth families.

The negative claims with which the professional literature is filled are based largely on negative *assumptions* about what will happen when birth parents turn their children over for others to raise. Thus the professional literature reflects as it reinforces the adoption stigma.

Much of the literature consists of theoretical work from a psychological perspective. Often it is based on case studies of adoptees referred for treatment and consists of conclusions drawn by clinicians seeking explanations for their patients' pathology. The underlying theory was, of course, developed in a society in which adoption is considered abnormal. This literature conveys an extremely negative message about the nature of adoption. The focus is on identity formation, and the basic argument is that adoptees are necessarily, by virtue of their transfer to an adoptive family, especially susceptible to identity conflicts and especially prone to problems in personality development. Their sense of security is said to be fundamentally damaged by the loss of the original parenting relationship. The theory holds that their ability to resolve developmental conflicts appropriately is complicated because of the existence of two sets of parents, and their identity formation is additionally impaired by the break in genetic and historical connections with the past and the resulting "genealogical bewilderment." One theorist asserts that "the creation of families based on psychological, not blood, ties contains inherent identity problems that practice and law seek to mitigate, but can never eliminate." Another contends, in an article on the "adoption trauma," that adoption puts children at risk for "an 'adopted child' pathology, which can flower into narcissistic character disorder, psychotic episodes, delinquency, homosexuality, fantasized or attempted suicide, incest, homicide, fratricide, murder of one or both adoptive parents, and to patricide or matricide."

While adoption research has generally focused on adoptees, some attention has been devoted more recently to birth and adoptive parents. Again, most of the theoretical literature paints an extremely negative picture, purporting to show birth mothers traumatized by the experience of surrender and adoptive parents traumatized by the experience of infertility.

Search movement advocates have contributed significantly to the negative reports on all parties to the adoption experience. An influential early work is *The Adoption Triangle*, first published in 1978. Since then, books and articles that describe adoptees, birth parents, and adoptive parents as suffering lifelong pain as a result of problems attributed to adoption have poured forth. This literature casts particular blame on the closed and secret nature of the adoption system, but conveys the general impression that opening the system would at best alleviate the pain and suffering caused by separating children from their birth parents. While this literature contributes to the adoption stigma, it provides no sound basis for drawing negative conclusions about adoption. It is written by people who have a powerful bias in demonstrating that adoption is a flawed institution—people whose goal is to eliminate adoption in any form that we know today. It consists largely of anecdotes and speculation. The "studies" that purport to describe characteristics of birth mothers, adoptive parents, and adoptees rely on extremely skewed and misleading samples of these populations. Typically, volunteers are solicited by means of a notice in a search movement newsletter, a method that is quite obviously likely to produce birth mothers and adoptees who are particularly hostile to the institution of adoption or troubled by its effect on their own lives. In addition, no effort is made to compare sampled members of the adoption triangle with appropriate control groups. So, for example, the studies depict birth mothers who testify to the pain they have experienced as a result of having surrendered their children, but provide no basis of comparison with the experience of women in similar circumstances who kept their children and who might have something to say about how they felt about lost opportunities for education or employment or the difficulties of being a single parent without an adequate income.

Much of the negative literature focuses on the entire group of adoptees or on undifferentiated or particularly problematic subgroups. For example, claims about the risk allegedly inherent in adoption are often bolstered by reference to the evidence that adoptees are overrepresented in various clinical populations, such as mental health clinics for troubled children. Also, empirical studies showing that some subgroups of adoptees have adjustment difficulties are used to generalize about the inherently risky nature of adoptive parenting. The fact that some number of adoptions "disrupt," or fall apart, is similarly used.

A major problem with these studies is that they tend to ignore the fact that the adoptee population contains many subgroups whose members are likely to have adjustment difficulties for reasons that have nothing to do with their adoptive status. The literature does not adequately differentiate between those adopted in early infancy and those adopted at older ages, and it does not adequately control for a wide variety of factors likely to influence adjustment, such as pre-adoptive abuse and neglect. By definition, any child placed after infancy will have suffered abuse, neglect, or the disruption of a significant bond with a primary caretaker; many will have suffered all of these. A significant proportion of all adoptees are placed only after many years of what is often severely damaging treatment. Many of these children have significant physical and mental disabilities relating either to their prebirth histories or to their postbirth experiences. As a consequence, studies that focus on undifferentiated groups of adoptees are of essentially no relevance to one of the issues at the heart of the adoption stigma, namely, whether the mere fact of transferring a child from a birth to an adoptive family poses any risk to the child or to the quality of the parent-child relationship. Yet such studies are systematically used to illustrate the alleged problems inherent in the adoptive relationship.

What *is* telling about the studies of undifferentiated groups of adoptees is that these children do so well once adopted, despite the fact that so many of them have suffered very negative preadoptive experiences. There is no evidence that by the time adoptees reach adulthood they are overrepresented in clinical populations. Also, there is reason to think that their apparent overrepresentation in child clinical populations is largely explained by adoptive parents' greater readiness to refer their children for treatment. The vast majority of all adoptive relationships are deemed successful, and the empirical studies reveal that the vast majority of all adoptees function normally in terms of various adjustment measures. Even the studies of children adopted after infancy, including those adopted at older ages and those with traumatic preadoptive histories, show that on the whole the children do very well, and that relatively few of the adoptive relationships disrupt. These studies provide persuasive evidence that many children are able to recover from the adverse effect of disastrous starts in life when placed in nurturing adoptive homes.

The negative claims made in the body of literature described above make a powerful contribution to the adoption stigma. They convey the impression that all sorts of things are likely to go seriously wrong when a child is transferred to a nonbiologic parent for raising. They thereby provide support for the attitudes and policies that give adoption its status as a last resort in our society. Yet when analyzed in any depth, this literature clearly provides no evidence that anything actually *does* go wrong for any of the parties to an adoptive arrangement.

One question that is central in assessing the real effects of adoption has to do with how it compares to existing alternatives for the various parties involved. The available evidence indicates that it compares extremely well. Studies that compare single birth mothers who place their children for adoption with single mothers who keep their children to raise themselves indicate that the decision to place for adoption is likely to have a positive impact on socioeconomic status and is not likely to have any negative psychological effects compared with the decision to keep and parent of the child. For the infertile, adoption provides the opportunity to parent; almost all those who choose to pursue this form of parenting find it enormously satisfying. By contrast, roughly half of those who pursue infertility treatment will be unable to become parents by this route. Finally, studies show that children placed in adoptive homes do far better in terms of standard measures of adjustment and self-esteem than children raised in institutional situations or in foster care, or children returned from foster care to their birth families, or children raised by birth mothers who once considered adoption but decided against it. And the evidence that older children have more trouble adjusting in adoptive homes constitutes a powerful argument against maintaining adoption's status as a last resort—an argument for moving more quickly to remove children from inadequate biologic and foster care situations to permanent adoptive homes. This evidence demonstrates the risks for children in a system that places such a priority on biologic parenting, because it is this priority that is responsible for the reluctance to remove children from damaging homes and legally sever the birth ties so as to free them for adoption.

Another central question has to do with how adoptive parenting compares with biologic parenting when the children are placed at or near birth. This analysis should provide some insight into the question of whether any problems are in fact associated with parenting that is not biologically linked. Only recently have empirical studies focused on nonclinical groups of early-adopted children and compared them with carefully selected control groups of children raised in their birth families. *These studies fail to confirm the negative claims made in the great body of adoption literature. They reveal no significant disadvantages of adoptive as opposed to biologic parenting, and some significant advantages.*

Some of these studies have looked at the quality of "attachment relationships" between adoptive and nonadoptive mother-infant pairs. They have found that adoptive parents and their infants develop warm and secure attachment relationships, which effectively rebuts the claims made in the negative theoretical literature that adoptive bonding is necessarily problematic.

Other studies have looked at the early-adopted children at later stages of development and have found either few or no differences; the general view is that any differences in adjustment that may exist disappear by adolescence. For example, Stein and Hoopes studied a group of adolescents placed in adoptive homes before the age of two and compared them with a closely matched group of adolescents raised in biologic families that were similar in socioeconomic terms. The adopted adolescents looked comparable in terms of various classic measures of identity formation and adjustment. Marquis and Detweiler looked at children aged thirteen to twenty-one who had been placed in adoption during their first year, comparing them to a control group of nonadopted children. In a study designed to test empirically the classic claims in the theoretical literature, they found "not a shred of evidence . . . that indicates any of the previously reported negative characteristics."

The only interesting differences found in the early-adopted adolescents relate to apparent *advantages* in adoptive relationships. Marquis and Detweiler found that adoptees saw themselves as more in control of their lives, had more confidence in their own judgment, and viewed others more positively than did those in the control group. They also rated their parents significantly more favorably, describing them as more nurturing, comforting, and helpful, with more predictable standards and more protective concern. Of course, the research has not generally been designed to assess potentially positive aspects of adoption. The bias has been overwhelmingly in the negative direction. The working assumption of virtually all theoretical and empirical work is that adoptive relationships are somewhere on the spectrum between disastrously and modestly inferior to biologic relationships.

My point is not that adoption is the same as biologic parenting but that it should be recognized as a positive form of family, not ranked as a poor imitation of the real thing on some parenting hierarchy. My attack on the adoption stigma should be understood as an argument for adoption but not against biology. I do not think we should jettison the biologic model of parenting and insist on a universal baby swap at the moment of birth. But I would like to put biology in its place and give appropriate value to nurturing and other social aspects of the parenting relationship.

In my view, there are many good reasons for having some presumption in favor of biologically linked parenthood. Birth parents no doubt do generally feel significant pain at the prospect of severing their relationship to the child they have created and in some sense "known" during pregnancy, and in my view they should; our world would be sadly diminished if relinquishment were a nonevent. I am prepared to think that there are other good things to be said for biologic parenting, and even that there may be some risks inherent in adoptive parenting. The sense that a child is your genetic product, the experience of pregnancy and childbirth, the experience of parenting and nursing a child during its first moments of life—all these things may help create a healthy bond between parent and child, and their absence may create a greater potential for problems. Genetic heritage is an important influence on intellect and personality, and it may be that for many parents some level of likeness is important and too much difference is problematic. Adoption may require parents who are more open to difference, more flexible, and more imaginative than the norm. For these among other reasons, the rule giving biologic parents presumptive parenting rights and the rule forbidding payments to induce birth parents to surrender their children seem to me good rules. But we can recognize the validity of the biology-based family without denigrating adoption.

The adoption stigma helps shape reality in problematic ways. Saying that adoption is a bad thing helps make it a bad thing. In a world in which adoptive status is degraded, it will not feel good to be adopted. While it might feel perfectly all right in some world we can imagine, it will feel problematic in a world in which you and all those around you are conditioned to think that good mothers don't "abandon" their children for others to raise, a world in which others react to the nature of your family situation by saying, "I'm sorry." Thus the adoption stigma necessarily shapes the experience of birth parents who surrender children, of adoptive parents, and of adoptees. Birth parents are conditioned to think that they *should* feel lifelong pain as the result of their "unnatural" act of giving up their "own" child for another to raise. The infertile are conditioned to think that they *should* forever grieve over their inability to reproduce biologically. Adoptive parents and children are conditioned to think that their family relationships are significantly inferior to those enjoyed by "real" families. In fact, they are instructed by the new adoption dogma that they should experience and "acknowledge" the problematic differences between their families and normal families. Claims to normalcy are often treated as evidence of pathology.

The stigma also affects the vision of those doing research on adoption. Conditioned to believe that children "belong" in some essential sense with their birth parents, they are predisposed to look for problems in adoptive parenting situations and to see in such situations the explanation for problematic behavior. It is worth speculating about what they would see if they thought more positively about adoption and designed studies to look for the positive. What if they started with the assumption that the norm and the ideal was the adoptive family, and the question was whether biologic parents should be allowed to raise the children they produce? What might the studies "find" if their starting assumption was that biologic parenting had inherent risks?

Stigma shapes reality in another way, helping to form the policies that in turn help to define the adoption experience. Social regulators translate their suspicion of adoption into screening rules that make the process of becoming an adoptive parent seriously frustrating and unpleasant, so that the infertile have all the more reason to see adoption as a last resort. And the policies designed to protect the biologic tie create the foster care limbo, which in turn produces the damaged children who may well have adjustment difficulties in adoption.

Given the predictable impact of the negative myths about adoption, it is a wonder that the evidence about the actual experience of those involved looks so positive. Given the power of those myths, it is hard to imagine thinking differently. But we should try to free ourselves from the forces that condition us to equate procreation with parenting. We should try to imagine living in a society in which adoption is reversed rather than denigrated. We should focus on what might be the unique benefits of parenting relationships built entirely on social rather than genetic ties. We should come to understand adoption as a uniquely positive form of family—not necessarily better than the biologic family, but not inherently inferior, either. We should make this imaginative leap because adoption is quite obviously a good solution for existing human beings in this world, most particularly the millions of children in need of nurturing homes. But we should also do it because we have a lot to learn about parenting and family and community from adoptive relationships.

Adoption involves the provision of homes to children in need, and thinking well of adoption should involve placing a higher value than we now do on the nurturing aspects of parenting and a lower value on the self-perpetuating and proprietary aspects. Adoption also involves the exercise of conscious choice in matters related to parenting. Thinking well of adoption should be liberating for birth parents and the infertile, giving them far more choice and control over their lives.

The fact that conscious choice is a defining feature of this form of parenting is unnerving for those conditioned to think of biologic inevitability as a part of what parenting is all about, but it can be seen as an enormously positive feature of this form of family. Adoption critics scorn the tradition of referring to the adoptee as a "chosen child," but adoptees *are* chosen children. Adoptive parents may initially have wanted to produce a biologic child, and they are of course limited in the choice of which particular child they will adopt. But all of them consciously choose to become parents, and most of them devote a great deal of effort to becoming adoptive parents. By contrast, it is doubtful that as many as half of all biologic parents initially conceive out of a conscious desire to parent. Many conceive by accident, and many consider abortion or adoptive placement and reject these options not because they actually want to parent but because keeping their child seems the least bad of the various bad options available. The fact that a person has consciously chosen to parent seems as important an indicator of the likely success of the parenting relationship as any factor could be. And indeed, controlled studies comparing wanted with unwanted children have shown a stark contrast; the unwanted do very badly.

Virtually all the aspects of adoptive parenting that are generally understood to be "risk factors" can as easily be understood as opportunities for the development of a particularly good parenting relationship. They can also give us insight into possible problems in our current biologic parenting models. We could view the absence of a genetic connection as liberating. Adoptive parents might, for example, be more able to avoid neurotic forms of overidentification with their children, be more able to let their children develop their own personalities and interests, and feel less driven to relive their own lives through their children. Because of the existence of another set of parents, adoptive parents might have a lessened sense of entitlement to complete control and possession, and this could empower children in healthy ways.

Parents and children could experience a range of special satisfactions in family relationships that cross the various lines of difference involved in adoption. As a parent, I revel in the brown skin and thick black hair and dark eyes and Peruvian features that I could not have produced. I have also felt the shock of seeing myself—my intensity, my gestures, my expressions—as I watch these children. I am enchanted by the tempestuous moods of one child and the laid-back good nature of the other. I am intrigued by the mystery of who they are and will be and what part I will play in this. I am ever conscious of the miracle that these children who possess me to the core of my being are mine and also not mine. I am aware of myriad ways in which my consciousness has been expanded and my life enhanced by these adoptions, and I think of people who have known only biologic parenting as people who are missing a special experience. It is likely that adoptive parents and their children would testify to a wide range of special qualities in their family life if there was an audience for such evidence.

Adoptive parenting may produce parents and children who are unusually open to and tolerant of a wide variety of differences. There is evidence that children raised in transracial adoptive families or by gay or lesbian adoptive parents exhibit these traits. There is also evidence that parents who are initially interested only in adopting a healthy same-race infant, and who in fact adopt such a child are significantly more open at the time of their second adoption to considering an older, handicapped child of a different race.

Adoption creates a family that in important ways is not "nuclear." It creates a family that is *connected* to another family, the birth family, and often to different cultures and to different racial, ethnic, and national groups as well. Adoptive families might teach us something about the value for families of connection with the larger community.

CHAPTER 7

❖

CHILDHOOD

R E A D I N G

20

Revolutions in Children's Lives

Donald Hernandez, with David E. Myers

INTRODUCTION

Revolutionary changes in the life course, the economy, and society have transformed childhood, and the resources available to children, during the past 150 years. A revolutionary decline in the number of siblings in the families of children occurred during the past 100 years. Historically, a substantial minority of children did not spend their entire childhood in a two-parent family, but this will expand to a majority for children born during the past decade. The role of grandparents in the home, as surrogate parents filling the gap left by absent parents, has been important but limited during at least the past half century.

The family economy was revolutionized twice during the past 150 years, first as fathers and then mothers left the home to spend much of the day away at jobs as family breadwinners. With these changes, with instability in fathers' work, and with increasing divorce and out-of-wedlock childbearing, never during the past half century were a majority of children born into "Ozzie and Harriet" families in which the father worked full-time year-round, the mother was a full-time homemaker, and all of the children were born after the parents' only marriage.

Corresponding revolutions in child care occurred first as children over age 5 and then as younger children began to spend increasing amounts of time in formal educational or other settings in the care of someone other than their parents. Since today's children are tomorrow's parents, the spread of universal compulsory education led to revolutionary increases in the educational attainments of parents during the past half century, to the benefit of successive cohorts of children. But as opportunities to complete at least a high school education became substantially more equal for children during the past century, opportunities to go beyond high school and complete at least one year of college became less equal.

The absolute income levels of families increased greatly after the Great Depression and World War II through the 1960s but have changed comparatively little since then. Meanwhile, childhood poverty and economic inequality declined after World War II through the 1960s, then increased mainly during the 1980s. Most poor children throughout the era lived in working-poor families, and only a minority of poor children were fully welfare-dependent.

FAMILY COMPOSITION

Because siblings are the family members who are usually closest in age, needs, and activities, they may be among a child's most important companions and most important competitors for family resources. The typical child born in 1890 lived, as an adolescent, in a family in which there were about 6.6 siblings, but the typical child born in 1994 is expected to live in a family that is only one-third as large—with 1.9 children.

About one-half of this decline in family size had occurred by 1945, and the typical child born during that year lived in a family that had 2.9 siblings. Subsequently, during the postwar baby boom that occurred between 1945 and 1957, the annual number of births jumped by 55 percent (from 2.7 to 4.3 million births per year) and the Total Fertility Rate jumped by 52 percent (from 2.4 to 3.7 births per woman), but the family size of the typical adolescent increased by only 17 percent (from 2.9 to 3.4 siblings).

Changes in the distribution of adolescents by family size tell a similar story. The proportion living in families in which there are 5 or more siblings is expected to decline from 77 percent for children born in 1890 to only 6 percent for children born in 1994. Again, about one-half of the decline had occurred for children born in 1945, 32 percent of whom as adolescents lived in families in which there were 5 or more children, and again the increase during the baby boom was comparatively small at about 6 percentage points. At the opposite extreme, the proportion of adolescents living in families in which there are only 1–2 children is expected to increase from only 7 percent for children born in 1890 to 57 percent for children born in 1994. Among children born in 1945, about 30 percent lived in such small families, and this fell by 10 percentage points to 20 percent during the baby boom.

Historically, black children have tended to live in families in which there were substantially larger numbers of siblings than did white children, but trends in the family sizes of both black and white children were generally similar between the Civil War and 1925. Then for about 20 years, however, the racial gap expanded, apparently because the comparatively large decline in tuberculosis and venereal disease led to increased family sizes among blacks. Since about 1945, the number of siblings in the families of both black and white children have been converging.

Among children born in 1994, family-size differences between blacks and whites, as well as between Hispanic children (of any race) and non-Hispanic children, are expected to essentially vanish. Of the racial convergence in family size that is expected to occur for children born between 1945 and 1994, more than two-thirds had occurred among children born in 1973 who are now about 18 years old and approaching college age.

What are the consequences of this decline for children? First, children with larger numbers of siblings have greater opportunities to experience caring, loving sibling companionship. Hence, the family-size revolution drastically reduced the number of siblings who were available as potential companions during childhood and through adulthood. On the other hand, childhood family size appears to have little effect on psychological well-being later during adulthood. But because children growing up in large families—especially families with 5 or more siblings—tend to complete fewer years of schooling than do children from smaller families, they are less likely to enter high-status occupations with high incomes when they reach adulthood. Hence, the family-size revolution led to greatly improved opportunities for educational, occupational, and economic advancement among successive cohorts of children. . . .

Most children depend mainly on the parents in their homes for financial support and day-to-day care. Hence, it would be surprising if important differences in current welfare and future life chances were not found when children who do spend their entire childhood in a two-parent family are compared with those who do not.

In the short run, for many children the separation or divorce of their parents brings a sharp drop in family income and substantial psychological trauma. When the lone parent in a one-parent family marries to form a stepfamily, however, the children often experience a sharp jump in family income. Still, children in stepfamilies are more likely to have a low family income than are children in intact two-parent families. In addition, since one parent is absent from the home in one-parent families, children in these families may receive substantially less day-to-day care and attention from parents than do children in two-parent families.

Children in one-parent families are more likely, on average, to be exposed to parental stress than are children in two-parent families, more likely to exhibit behavioral problems, more likely to receive or need professional psychological help, more likely to perform poorly in school, and more likely to have health problems. In addition, on average, stepchildren are virtually indistinguishable from children in one-parent families in their chances of having behavioral, psychological, academic, and health problems.

Over the long run, children who do not spend most of their childhood in an intact two-parent family tend, as they reach adulthood, to complete fewer years of schooling, enter lower-status occupations, and earn lower incomes than do adults who did spend most of their childhood in an intact two-parent family. Some children from one-parent families may finish fewer years of school because fathers who can afford to provide financial support in college do not in fact do so when the child reaches college age. Many of the disadvantages associated with living in a one-parent family may result from the low family incomes of many children who live in such families.

In view of the potential disadvantages of not living with two parents, how typical has it become for children not to spend their entire childhood in a two-parent family? Historically, about 90 percent of newborn children under age 1 have lived with both biological parents. Still, between the late 1800s and 1950, a large and nearly stable minority of about 33 percent spent part of their childhood before age 18 with fewer than two parents in the home. Little change occurred during the first half of the twentieth century, despite the rise in parental separation and divorce, because this rise was counterbalanced by declining parental mortality.

Since about 1950 the link between marriage and the bearing and rearing of children has loosened. Because of the rise in out-of-wedlock childbearing that occurred between 1950 and 1980, the proportion of newborn children under age 1 who did not live with two parents doubled, climbing from 9 to 19 percent. Combined with the rise in separation and divorce, the proportion of children who will ever live with fewer than two parents is expected to increase from about 33 percent for the era between the late 1800s and 1950 to about 55–60 percent of children born in 1980.

Since at least the Civil War, white and black children have been quite different in their chances of spending part of their childhood living with fewer than two parents. For example, in 1940 the proportion of newborn children under age 1 who did not live with two parents was about 25 percent for blacks, compared with 7 percent for whites. Historically, it appears that for children born between the late 1800s and 1940, a majority of blacks (55–60 percent) spent part of their childhood in families in which there were fewer than two parents. For whites born between the late 1800s and 1940, a minority (but a large minority of approximately 29–33 percent) spent part of their childhood in families in which there were fewer than two parents. . . .

FAMILY WORK AND EDUCATION

As children were experiencing a revolutionary decline in family size and a large increase in one-parent family living, they also were experiencing two distinct transformations in parents' work and living arrangements. On the family farm, economic production, parenting, and child care were combined, as parents and children worked together to support themselves. This changed with the Industrial Revolution, however. Fathers became breadwinners who took jobs located away from home in order to support the family, and mothers became homemakers who remained at home to personally care for the children as well as to clean, cook, and perform other domestic functions for the family. Following the Great Depression, parents' work and the family economy were again transformed. Today most children live either in dual-earner families in which both parents work at jobs away from home or in one-parent families.

More specifically, between about 1840 and 1920 the proportion of children who lived in two-parent farm families fell from at least two-thirds to about one-third, while the proportion who lived in breadwinner-homemaker families climbed from 15–20 percent to 50 percent. Although a majority of children lived in breadwinner-homemaker families between about 1920 and 1970, this figure never reached 60 percent.

In fact, even during the heyday of the breadwinner-homemaker family, a second transformation in parents' work was under way. Between 1920 and 1970, as the proportion of children living in two-parent farm families continued to fall, the proportion who had breadwinner mothers working at jobs that were located away from home increased, and after 1960 the proportion living in one-parent families with their mothers also increased. The rise in the proportion of children living in dual-earner or one-parent families was extremely rapid, since the increase from 15–20 percent to 50 percent required only 30 years—about one-third as long as the time required for the same rise in the breadwinner-homemaker family to take place.

By 1980, nearly 60 percent of children lived in dual-earner or one-parent families, by 1989 about 70 percent lived in such families, and by the year 2000, only 7 years from now, the proportion of children living in such families may exceed 80 percent. Equally striking is the fact that even between 1920 and 1970, only a minority of children aged 0–17 lived in families that conformed to the mid-twentieth century ideal portrayed, for example, on the "Ozzie and Harriet" television program (that is, a nonfarm breadwinner-homemaker family in which the father works full-time year-round, the mother is a full-time homemaker, and all of the children were born after the parents' only marriage).

In fact, only a minority of newborn children under age 1 lived in such families in any year between 1940 and 1980. During these years a large majority of newborns (75–86 percent) did live with employed fathers, but only 42–49 percent lived with two parents in families in which the father worked full-time year-round and all of the children were born after the parents' only marriage. Still smaller proportions of newborns lived with two parents in families in which the father worked full-time year-round, all of the children were born after the parents' only marriage, and the mother was a full-time homemaker. Between 1940 and 1960, 41–43 percent of newborns lived in such families, and with rising mothers' labor-force participation this fell to only 27 percent in 1980. By age 17, children were even less likely, historically, to live in such families, as the proportion declined from 31 to 15 percent between 1940 and 1980.

These estimates imply that for children born between 1940 and 1960, an average of 65–70 percent of their childhood years were spent in a family situation that did not conform to the mid-twentieth century ideal. Looking ahead, it appears that children born in 1980 may spend an average of 80 percent of their childhood in families that do not conform to this ideal. In addition, children who lived on farms were likely, historically, to experience a parental death or other parental loss, or the economic insecurity associated with drought, crop disease, collapse of commodity prices, and similar catastrophes. Consequently, it is clear that neither historically nor during the industrial era have a majority of children experienced the family stability, the economic stability, and the home-making mother that was idealized in mid-twentieth century America.

For white children, the chances of living in an idealized "Ozzie and Harriet," breadwinner-homemaker family were only slightly larger than for children as a whole. Among newborn black children at least since 1940, however, no more than 25 percent lived in such idealized families, and this figure fell to only 8 percent for black newborns in 1980. By the end of child-hood, among blacks born in 1922, only 15 percent still lived in such families by age 17, and among blacks born in 1962, only 3 percent still lived in such families by age 17. Looking across the entire childhood experience of black children, the average proportion of childhood years not spent in idealized "Ozzie and Harriet" families increased from about 70–80 percent for the 1920s cohort to at least 95 percent for the 1980s cohort.

In 1980 Hispanic children (of any race) were roughly midway between black and white children in their chances of living in an idealized "Ozzie and Harriet" family. Only 10 percent of Hispanic 17-year-olds (of any race) lived in such families in 1980, only 21 percent of Hispanic newborns (of any race) lived in such families in 1980, and among these newborns more than 85 percent of the childhood years will be spent in families that do not conform to the mid-twenti-eth century ideal.

With these two historic transformations in parents' work and living arrangements, children simultaneously experienced two revolutionary increases in nonparental care, first among those over age 5 and then among younger chil-dren.

As farming became overshadowed by an industrial economy in which fathers worked for pay at jobs located away from home, compulsory school attendance and child labor laws were enacted to ensure that children were protected from unsafe and unfair working conditions, that they were excluded from jobs that were needed for adults, and that they received at least a minimal level of education. Also, as time passed increasing affluence allowed families to support themselves without child labor, and higher educational attainments became increasingly necessary in order to obtain jobs that offered higher pay and higher social prestige.

Hence, in 1870 only 50 percent of children aged 5–19 were enrolled in school, and their attendance averaged only 21 percent of the total days in the year. But 70 years later, in 1940, 95 percent of children aged 7–13 were enrolled in school, 79 percent of children aged 14–17 were enrolled in school, and the average attendance amounted to 42 percent of the days in the year. Even as mothers were increasingly viewed as full-time child care providers and home-makers, the need for them to act as full-time child care providers was diminish-ing, both because of the revolutionary decline in family size and because of the quadrupling in the amount of nonparental child care provided by teachers in school.

Since a full adult workday amounted to about 8 hours per day, 5 days per week (plus commuting time) after 1940, a full adult work year amounted to about 65 percent of the days in a year. But by 1940, school days of 5–6 hours (plus commuting time) amounted to about two-thirds of a full workday for about two-thirds of a full work year. As of 1940, then, childhood school attendance had effectively released mothers from personal child care responsibilities for a time period equivalent to about two-thirds of a full-time adult work year, except for the few years before children entered elementary school.

By reducing the time required for a mother's most important homemaker responsibility—the personal care of her children—this first child care revolution contributed to the large increase in mothers' labor-force participation after 1940, not only for school-age children but for preschoolers as well. Increasing mothers' labor-force participation and the rise in one-parent families then ushered in the second child-care revolution for preschool children aged 0–5. Between 1940 and 1989, the proportion of children who had no specific parent at home full-time tripled for school-age children (from roughly 22 to 66 percent) and quadrupled for preschoolers (from about 13 percent to about 52 percent).

Today these proportions are probably fairly typical for children in industrial countries, since by 1980 labor-force participation rates for women who were in main parenting ages in the United States were average when compared with other industrial countries. For example, the labor-force participation rates for women aged 30–39 were 70–90 percent in Sweden, Denmark, and Norway, 60–70 percent in the United States, France, and Canada, and 45–60 percent in the United Kingdom, West Germany, Italy, Belgium, Switzerland, Australia, and Japan.[1]

The increase in the proportion of preschoolers who had no specific parent at home full-time effectively reduced the amount of parental time that was potentially available to care for preschoolers and effectively increased the need for nonparental care. Yet the proportion of preschoolers who had a relative other than a parent in the home who might act as a surrogate parent also declined. For preschoolers living in dual-earner families, the proportion with a potential surrogate parent in the home declined from 19–20 percent in 1940 to only 4–5 percent in 1980. Meanwhile, the proportion of preschoolers living in one-parent families in which there was a potential surrogate parent in the home declined from 51–57 to 20–25 percent.

Time-use studies of nonemployed mothers indicate that the actual time devoted to child care as a primary activity probably increased by about 50–100 percent between 1926–1935 and 1943 and may have increased a bit more during the 20 years that followed. But between the 1960s and the early 1980s, the average amount of time that all mothers of preschoolers devoted to child care as a

---

[1]Data from the U.S. Bureau of the Census for the following years: 1985 (Norway), 1984 (France), 1983 (Sweden), 1982 (U.S.), 1981 (Canada, Denmark, United Kingdom, Italy, Australia), 1980 (Japan, West Germany, Switzerland), 1977 (Belgium).

primary activity declined because an increasing number of mothers were employed outside the home and because employed mothers of preschoolers devote about one-half as much time to child care as a primary activity as do nonemployed mothers (1.2 vs. 2.2 hours per day during the mid-1970s).

By 1989, then, about 48 percent of preschoolers had a specific nonemployed parent at home on a full-time basis (usually the mother), another 12 percent had dual-earner parents who personally provided for their preschoolers' care (often by working different hours or days), and the remaining 40 percent were cared for by someone other than their parents for a large portion of time. Since the proportion of preschoolers who have a specific parent at home full-time declined from about 80 to about 48 percent during the 29 years between 1960 and 1989, we appear to be halfway through the preschool child-care revolution, and we are probably within 30–40 years of its culmination and will then see a very large proportion of preschool children spending increasingly more time in the care of someone other than their parents.

Overall, black children in 1940 were 24 percentage points less likely to have a specific parent at home full-time than were white children, but this racial gap had narrowed to 12 percentage points by 1980. Essentially all of this convergence occurred among older children, since the racial gap among adolescents declined from 27 to 6 percentage points, while the racial gap among preschoolers remained nearly constant at 18–23 percentage points. In 1980, about one-half of the racial gap among preschoolers was accounted for by differences in parental employment, and about one-half was accounted for by differences in the proportion of preschoolers who have no parent in the home.

Also in 1980, Hispanic children (of any race) were generally quite similar to non-Hispanic white children in their parental working and living arrangements, except that Hispanics (of any race) were somewhat more likely to live in one-parent families in which the parent was not employed and somewhat less likely to live in dual-earner families in which at least one parent worked part-time.

The importance of mothers' employment in contributing to family income is discussed below, but what other consequences do mothers' employment and nonparental care have for preschoolers? Past research suggests, broadly, that mothers' employment and nonparental care are neither necessarily nor pervasively harmful to preschoolers. This research also suggests that nonparental care is not a form of maternal deprivation, since children can and do form attachments to multiple caregivers if the number of caregivers is limited, the child-caregiver relationships are long-lasting, and the caregivers are responsive to the individual child.

Available evidence also suggests that the quality of care that children receive is important, and that some children, especially those from low-income families, are in double jeopardy from psychological and economic stress at home as well as exposure to low-quality nonparental child care. Additional potentially beneficial and detrimental effects of mothers' employment and nonparental care for preschoolers have been identified, but most of the results must be viewed as preliminary and tentative. Overall, research on the consequences of nonparental care for preschoolers is itself in its infancy, and much remains to be done.

The first revolution in child care—that is, the advent of nearly universal elementary and high school enrollment between ages 6 and 17—as well as large increases in high school and college graduation, led in due course to a revolutionary increase in parents' education. For example, among children born during the 1920s, the proportions whose fathers completed only 0–8 years of schooling or 4 or more years of high school were 73 and 15 percent, respectively, but these proportions were nearly reversed (at 5 and 85 percent, respectively) among children born only 60 years later during the 1980s. For the same children, those with fathers who had completed 4 or more or 1 or more years of college climbed from 4 and 7 percent, respectively, to 28 and 47 percent. Increases were generally similar for mothers' education, except for a somewhat smaller rise in the proportion with mothers who were college-educated.

Black children, as well as white children, experienced revolutionary increases in parents' education, but blacks continued to lag behind whites, as the black disadvantage effectively shifted higher on the educational ladder but constricted substantially in size. For example, among the 1920s cohort, the maximum racial disadvantages of 38–43 percentage points were in the proportions whose fathers or mothers had completed at least 7–8 years of schooling. But among the 1980s cohort, the maximum racial gaps were only two-fifths as large at 15–16 percentage points, and were in the proportions whose fathers or mothers had completed 13–15 years of schooling.

Measured in terms of the number of decades by which blacks lagged behind whites, the 2–3 decades by which black children born during the 1940s and the 1950s lagged behind whites in having parents who received at least 8 years of education had essentially vanished for the 1970s cohort. But despite a temporary racial convergence among children born during the 1960s and the 1970s, black children born during the 1980s, like black children born during the 1940s and the 1950s, lagged about 2–3 decades behind whites in the proportion whose fathers and mothers had completed at least 4 years of college.

Old-family Hispanic children (of any race) born during the 1960s and the 1970s were fairly similar to non-Hispanic black children in their parents' educational attainments. But first-generation Hispanic children (of any race) were much less likely (by 32–42 percentage points) to have parents who had completed at least 8 years of schooling, presumably because many of their parents had immigrated from countries in which the general educational levels were much lower than those in the United States.

This revolution in parents' education, and continuing differentials by race and Hispanic origin, are important for children both in the short run and throughout their adult years. In the short run, parents with higher educational attainments are more likely to have higher incomes than those with lower educational attainments. In the long run, children whose parents have comparatively high educational attainments also tend, when they reach adulthood, to complete more years of education and thus obtain jobs that offer higher social prestige and income.

Consequently, successive cohorts of children benefited from increasing parents' education both because it contributed to the large increases in family income for children that occurred between World War II and approximately

1970, as described below, and because it contributed to increasing educational levels among children and therefore to higher prestige and income for successive cohorts of children when they reached adulthood. At the same time, the continuing disadvantage of black and Hispanic children (of any race) in their parents' educational attainments tends to limit their current family incomes and their future chances of achieving occupational and economic success during adulthood. . . .

FAMILY INCOME, POVERTY, AND WELFARE DEPENDENCE

Family income, another major feature of family origins, also has important consequences for children's current well-being and future life chances. On a day-to-day basis, whether children live in material deprivation, comfort, or luxury depends mainly on their family's income level. Of particular interest are children in low-income families because they may experience marked deprivation in such areas as nutrition, clothing, housing, or healthcare.

During the 1940s, 1950s, and 1960s, the absolute income levels of American families increased greatly, as real median family income jumped by 35–45 percent per decade, bringing corresponding decreases in absolute want. Associated with this rapid expansion in the ability to purchase consumer products was an unprecedented proliferation in the number and kinds of products that became available, as well as remarkable increases in the quality of these products. By the 1970s the typical American lived in a world of abundance that Americans 30 years earlier could hardly have imagined. Since the beginning of the 1970s, however, real family income has increased comparatively little, despite the ongoing revolution in labor force participation by wives and mothers, and during the 1970s and the 1980s median family income increased by only 5 and 1 percent, respectively.

Despite large improvements in absolute income levels between 1939 and 1969, however, these statistics tell us little about the extent to which children lived in relative deprivation or luxury compared with the standards of the time in which they grew up, because at a specific point in history, the measure of whether a family is judged to be living in deprivation or luxury is that family's income and whether it is especially low or especially high compared with typical families in the same historical period.

Measuring economic deprivation in comparison with median family income in various years, the "relative poverty rate" for children dropped sharply during the 1940s (from 38 to 27 percent) but then much more slowly (to 23 percent in 1969). Subsequently, the relative poverty rate for children increased—mostly during the 1980s—to 27 percent in 1988, reaching the same level experienced almost 40 years earlier in 1949. . . .

CONCLUSION

America's children experienced several interrelated revolutions in their life course, as the family, economy, and society were transformed during the past

150 years. Family size plummeted. One-parent family living jumped. Family farms nearly became extinct, as first fathers and then mothers left the home for much of the day in order to serve as family breadwinners. Formal schooling, nonparental care for children, and parents' educational attainments have increased greatly, although educational opportunities to go beyond high school have become less equal since the turn of the century.

Absolute family incomes multiplied, but the past two decades brought little change in average income and increasing economic inequality among children, despite increasing mothers' labor-force participation. Relative and official poverty rates for children climbed during the past decade. Welfare dependence increased during recent decades, but most poor children historically and today live in working-poor families.

Currently, it appears that many of these revolutionary changes will be most extreme among children born within a decade of this writing. By historical standards, family size can decline comparatively little below the level expected for children born in the mid-1990s. Divorce, the major contributor to one-parent family living, has changed little since the late 1970s. By the year 2000, a large majority of children will live in dual-earner or one-parent families, a majority of preschoolers will receive substantial nonparental care while parents work, and only a small minority, even among newborns, will live in idealized "Ozzie and Harriet" families. Future changes in parents' education, in real income, poverty, and income inequality, and in welfare recipiency appear less certain, partly because they may be more responsive to specific public policies than are family size, divorce, and whether fathers and mothers work outside the home.

Regardless of future public policies, however, it seems likely that the fundamental transformations that have occurred during the past 150 years in the family, the economy, and the society will not be undone. Today, as throughout America's history, most children live with their parents and rely on them to provide for their economic support and day-to-day care. Yet a majority of children—both historically and today—have experienced either the loss of a parent from the home or economic insecurity, or both. Nevertheless, as a result of 150 years of revolutionary change in parents' work, in the family economy, and in the broader economy and society, America's children have entered a new age.

R E A D I N G
21

Children's Adjustment to Divorce

Frank F. Furstenberg and Andrew J. Cherlin

As Helen watched, Sally, then three, walked over to where her six-year-old brother was playing and picked up one of his toy robots. Mickey grabbed the robot out of her hand, shouted "No!" and pushed her away. The little girl fell backward and began to cry. Helen had just finished another frustrating phone call with Herb, who had told her that he could no longer afford to pay as much child support as they had agreed. She was grateful to her parents for allowing her and the kids to live with them temporarily, but the crowded household was beginning to strain everyone's patience. She rushed over to her daughter, picked her up, and shouted at her son, "Don't you hit her like that!" "But it was mine," he said, whereupon he took another robot and threw it on the floor near his mother's feet. She grabbed his arm and dragged him to his room, screaming at him all the way.

Then she sat down in the living room, with Sally in her lap, and reflected on how often scenes such as this were occurring. Ever since the separation eight months earlier, she had had a hard time controlling Mickey. He disobeyed her, was mean to his sister, and fought with friends in school. And when he talked back to her, she lost her temper. But that just made him behave worse, which in turn made her angrier, until he was sent to his room and she sat down, distraught.

Helen's problems with her son fit a pattern familiar to psychologists who study the effects of divorce on children, an escalating cycle of misbehavior and harsh response between mothers and sons. But not all parents and children become caught up in these so-called coercive cycles after the breakup of a marriage. Studies show a wide range of responses to divorce. Some children do very well; others fare poorly. In this chapter we will examine these differences and inquire into why they occur.

We tend to think of divorce as an event that starts when a husband or wife moves out of their home. But it is often more useful to think of divorce as a process that unfolds slowly over time, beginning well before the separation actually occurs. In many cases it is preceded by a lengthy period of conflict between the spouses. It is reasonable to expect that this predisruption conflict, and the corresponding emotional upset on the part of the parents, may cause problems for children.

For example, when things began to heat up between Mickey and his mother, Helen naturally assumed that the problems between them were largely the result of the divorce. Perhaps she was right. But her guilty feelings made Helen conveniently forget that Mickey had had behavioral problems for several years—ever since the quarreling between his parents became severe. Almost two years before the separation, Mickey's preschool teacher had asked Helen if things were going all right at home. Mickey had displayed unusual fits of temper with his classmates and seemed distracted during play periods. If you had asked Mickey's teacher, she would have predicted that Mickey, although bright enough, was going to have adjustment problems in kindergarten. And so he did. True, Mickey's problems did get worse the year that his parents separated, but it is not obvious that his difficulties in school would have been avoided even if his parents had managed to remain together.

In fact, there is evidence that some children show signs of disturbance months, and sometimes even years, before their parents separate. In 1968 a team of psychologists began to study three-year-olds at two nursery schools in Berkeley, California. The psychologists followed these children and their families, conducting detailed personality assessments at ages four, five, seven, eleven, and fourteen. When the study started, 88 children were living with two married parents. Twenty-nine of these children experienced the breakup of their parents marriages by the time they were fourteen. Curious as to what the children were like before the breakup, the psychologists paged backward through their files until they found the descriptions of the children eleven years earlier, when they were age three.

The results were quite dramatic for boys. Years before the breakup, three-year-old boys whose families eventually would disrupt were more likely to have been described as having behavioral problems than were three-year-old boys whose families would remain intact. According to the researchers, Jeanne H. Block, Jack Block, and Per F. Gjerde, three-year-old boys who would eventually experience family disruption already were rated as more "inconsiderate of other children, disorderly in dress and behavior," and "impulsive" and more likely to "take advantage of other children." Moreover, their fathers were more likely to characterize themselves as often angry with their sons, and both fathers and mothers reported more conflict with their sons. Much smaller differences were found among daughters.

Had the Berkeley researchers started their study when the children were age fourteen, they surely would have found some differences between the adolescents from the 29 disrupted families and the adolescents from the 59 intact families. And they probably would have attributed these differences to the aftermath of the disruption, as most other researchers do. But because they could look back eleven years, they saw that some portion of the presumed effects of divorce on children were present well before the families split up.

Why is this so? It is, of course, possible that some children have behavioral problems that put stress on their parents' marriages. In these instances divorce, rather than *causing* children's problems, may be the *result* of them. But it is doubtful that inherently difficult children cause most divorces. The Berkeley researchers suggest, rather, that conflict between parents is a fundamental factor that harms children's development and produces behavioral problems. In many families, this conflict—and the harm it engenders—may precede the separation by many years.

There are many other characteristics of divorce-prone families that might affect children. For example, people who divorce are more likely to have married as teenagers and to have begun their marriages after the wife was pregnant. They also are less religious. It is possible that these families may provide a less stable and secure environment and therefore cause children more problems even while the family is intact. But no researcher would suggest that all of the effects of divorce are determined before the actual separation. Much of the impact depends on how the process unfolds after the separation and how the children cope with it. Nearly all children are extremely upset when they learn of the breakup. For most, it is an unwelcome shock. Judith Wallerstein and Joan Kelly found that young children seemed surprised even in families where the parents were openly quarreling and hostile. Although young children certainly recognize open conflict—and indeed may be drawn into it—they usually can't grasp the long-term significance and don't envisage the separation. Moreover, parents typically don't inform their children of the impending separation until shortly before it occurs.

When children do learn of the breakup, their reactions vary according to their ages. Preschool-age children, whose ability to understand the situation is limited, are usually frightened and bewildered to find that their father or mother has moved out of the house. Preschoolers see the world in a very self-centered way, and so they often assume that the separation must be their fault—that they must have done something terribly wrong to make their parent leave. Three-year-old Sally promised never to leave her room a mess again if only Daddy would come home. Older children comprehend the situation better and can understand that they are not at fault. But they still can be quite anxious about what the breakup will mean for their own lives. And adolescents, characteristically, are more often intensely angry at one or both of their parents for breaking up their families.

SHORT-TERM ADJUSTMENT

The psychologists P. Lindsay Chase-Lansdale and E. Mavis Hetherington have labeled the first two years following a separation as a "crisis period" for adults and children. The crisis begins for children with shock, anxiety, and anger upon learning of the breakup. (But as was noted, the harmful effects on children of marital conflict may begin well before the breakup.) For adults, too, the immediate aftermath is a dismaying and difficult time. It is especially trying for mothers who retain custody of the children, as about nine in ten do.

Helen, for example, faced the task of raising her two children alone. Even when she was married, Helen had taken most of the responsibility for raising the children. But Herb had helped out some and had backed her up when the children were difficult. Now responsibility fell solely on her. What's more, she was working full time in order to compensate for the loss of Herb's income. And all this was occurring at a time when she felt alternately angry at Herb, depressed about the end of her marriage, and anxious about her future. Harried and overburdened, she was sometimes overwhelmed by the task of keeping her family going from day to day. Dinner was frequently served late, and Sally and Mickey often stayed up past their bedtime as Helen tried to complete the household chores.

Children have two special needs during the crisis period. First, they need additional emotional support as they struggle to adapt to the breakup. Second, they need the structure provided by a reasonably predictable daily routine. Unfortunately, many single parents cannot meet both of these needs all the time. Depressed, anxious parents often lack the reserve to comfort emotionally needy children. Overburdened parents let daily schedules slip. As a result, their children lose some of the support they need.

A number of psychological studies suggest that the consequences of the crisis period are worse for boys than for girls; but it may be that boys and girls merely react to stress differently. Developmental psychologists distinguish two general types of behavior problems among children. The first—externalizing disorders—refers to heightened levels of problem behavior directed outward, such as aggression, disobedience, and lying. The second—internalizing disorders—refers to heightened levels of problem behaviors directed inward, such as depression, anxiety, or withdrawal. Boys in high-conflict families, whether disrupted or intact, tend to show more aggressive and antisocial behavior. Hetherington studied a small group of middle-class families, disrupted and intact, for several years. She found coercive cycles between mothers and sons, like the ones between Helen and Mickey, to be prevalent. Distressed mothers responded irritably to the bad behavior of their sons, thus aggravating the very behavior they wished to quell. Even as long as six years after the separation, Hetherington observed this pattern among mothers who hadn't remarried and their sons.

The findings for girls are less consistent, but generally girls appear better behaved than boys in the immediate aftermath of a disruption. There are even reports of overcontrolled, self-consciously "good" behavior. But we should be cautious in concluding that girls are less affected. It may be that they internalize their distress in the form of depression or lowered self-esteem. And some observers suggest that the distress may produce problems that only appear years after the breakup.

It is also possible that boys do worse because they typically live with their opposite-sex parent, their mother. A number of studies report intriguing evidence that children may fare better if they reside with a same-sex parent after a marital disruption. Families in which single fathers become the custodial parent, however, are a small and select group who may be quite different from typical families. Until recently, sole custody was awarded to fathers mainly in cases in which the mother had abandoned the children or was an alcoholic, drug abuser, or otherwise clearly incompetent. Until there is more evidence from studies of broad groups of children, we think it would be premature to generalize about same-sex custody.

To sum up, researchers agree that almost all children are moderately or severely distressed when their parents separate and that most continue to experience confusion, sadness, or anger for a period of months and even years. Nevertheless, the most careful studies show a great deal of variation in the short-term reactions of children—including children in the same family. Most of this variation remains unexplained, although differences in age and gender account for some of it. Part of the explanation, no doubt, has to do with differences in children's temperaments. Some probably are more robust and better able to withstand deprivation and instability. They may be less affected by growing up in a one-parent family, and they may also cope better with a divorce. In addition, clinicians have speculated that some children draw strength from adults or even peers outside of the household, such as grandparents, aunts, or close friends. But we are far from certain just how important each of the sources of resiliency is to the child's ability to cope with divorce.

LONG-TERM ADJUSTMENT

Even less is known about the long-term consequences of divorces than about the short-term consequences. Within two or three years, most single parents and their children recover substantially from the trauma of the crisis period. Parents are able to stabilize their lives as the wounds from the breakup heal. With the exception of some difficulties between single mothers and their sons, parent-child relationships generally improve. And the majority of children, it seems, return to normal development.

But over the long run there is still great variation in how the process of divorce plays out. Without doubt, some children suffer long-term harm. It is easy, however, to exaggerate the extent of these harmful effects. In their widely read book that reports on a clinical study of 60 recently divorced middle-class couples from the San Francisco suburbs and their 131 children, aged two to eighteen, Judith Wallerstein and Sandra Blakeslee paint a picture of a permanently scarred generation. "Almost half of the children," they write, "entered adulthood as worried, underachieving, self-deprecating, and sometimes angry young men and women." Are these difficulties as widespread among children of divorce as the authors suggest? Despite their claim that the families were "representative of the way normal people from a white, middle-class background cope with divorce," it is highly likely that the study exaggerates the prevalence of long-term problems. Its families had volunteered to come to a clinic for counseling, and many of the parents had extensive psychiatric histories. Moreover, there is no comparison group of intact families: instead, all of the problems that emerged after the break-up are blamed on the divorce.

We do not doubt that many young adults retain painful memories of their parents' divorce. But it doesn't necessarily follow that these feelings will impair their functioning as adults. Had their parents not divorced, they might have retained equally painful memories of a conflict-ridden marriage. Imagine that the more troubled families in the Wallerstein study had remained intact and had been observed ten years later. Would their children have fared any better? Certainly they would have been better off economically; but given the strains that would have been evident in the marriages, we doubt that most would have been better off psychologically.

Studies based on nationally representative samples that do include children from intact marriages suggest that the long-term harmful effects of divorce are worthy of concern but occur only to a minority. Evidence for this conclusion comes from the National Survey of Children, which interviewed parents and children in 1976 and again in 1981. For families in which a marital disruption had occurred, the average time elapsed since the disruption was eight years in 1981. James L. Peterson and Nicholas Zill examined parents' 1981 responses to the question, "Since January 1977 . . . has [the child] had any behavior or discipline problems at school resulting in your receiving a note or being asked to come in and talk to the teacher or principal?" Peterson and Zill found that, other things being equal, 34 percent of parents who had separated or divorced answered yes, compared with 20 percent of parents in intact marriages.

Is this a big difference or a small difference? The figures can be interpreted in two ways. First, the percentage of children from maritally disrupted families who had behavior or discipline problems at school is more than half-again as large as the percentage from intact families. That's a substantial difference, suggesting that children from disrupted families have a noticeably higher rate of misbehaving seriously in school. (Although some of these children might have misbehaved even if their parents had not separated.) Second, however, the figures also demonstrate that 66 percent of all children from maritally disrupted homes *did not* misbehave seriously at school. So one also can conclude that most children of divorce don't have behavior problems at school. Both conclusions are equally valid; the glass is either half full or half empty, depending on one's point of view. We think that in order to understand the broad picture of the long-term effects of divorce on children, it's necessary to keep both points of view in mind.

The same half-full and half-empty perspective can be applied to studies of the family histories of adults. Based on information from several national surveys of adults, Sara McLanahan and her colleagues found that persons who reported living as a child in a single-parent family were more likely subsequently to drop out of high school, marry during their teenage years, have a child before marrying, and experience the disruption of their own marriages. For example, the studies imply that, for whites, the probability of dropping out of high school could be as high as 22 percent for those who lived with single parents, compared with about 11 percent for those who lived with both parents, other things being equal. Again, the glass is half-empty; those who lived with a single parent are up to twice as likely to drop out of high school. And it is half-full: the overwhelming majority of those who lived with a single parent graduated from high school.

In addition, the NSC data demonstrate that children in intact families in which the parents fought continually were doing no better, and often worse, than the children of divorce. In 1976 and again in 1981, parents in intact marriages were asked whether they and their spouses ever had arguments about any of nine topics: chores and responsibilities, the children, money, sex, religion, leisure time, drinking, other women or men, and in-laws. Peterson and Zill classified an intact marriage as having "high conflict" if arguments were reported on five or more topics or if the parent said that the marriage, taking things all together, was "not too happy." They found that in 1981, children whose parents had divorced or separated were doing no worse than children whose parents were in intact, high-conflict homes. And children whose parents' marriages were intact but highly conflicted in both 1976 and 1981 were doing the worst of all; these children were more depressed, impulsive, and hyperactive, and misbehaved more often.

To be sure, even if only a minority of children experience long-term negative effects, that is nothing to cheer about. But the more fundamental point—one that all experts agree upon—is that children's responses to the breakup of their parents' marriages vary greatly. There is no ineluctable path down which children of divorce progress. What becomes important, then, is to identify the circumstances under which children seem to do well.

WHAT MAKES A DIFFERENCE?

A critical factor in both short-term and long-term adjustment is how effectively the custodial parent, who usually is the mother, functions as a parent. We have noted how difficult it can be for a recently separated mother to function well. The first year or two after the separation is a difficult time for many mothers, who may feel angry, depressed, irritable, or sad. Their own distress may make it more difficult to cope with their children's distress, leading in some cases to a disorganized household, lax supervision, inconsistent discipline, and the coercive cycles between mothers and preschool-aged sons that have been identified by Hetherington and others. Mothers who can cope better with the disruption can be more effective parents. They can keep their work and home lives going from day to day and can better provide love, nurturing, consistent discipline, and a predictable routine.

Quite often their distress is rooted in, or at least intensified by, financial problems. Loss of the father's income can cause a disruptive, downward spiral in which children must adjust to a declining standard of living, a mother who is less psychologically available and is home less often, an apartment in an unfamiliar neighborhood, a different school, and new friends. This sequence of events occurs at a time when children are greatly upset about the separation and need love, support, and a familiar daily routine.

A second key factor in children's well-being is a low level of conflict between their mother and father. This principle applies, in fact, to intact as well as disrupted families. Recall the finding from the NSC that children who live with two parents who persistently quarrel over important areas of family life show higher levels of distress and behavior problems than do children from disrupted marriages. Some observers take this finding to imply that children are better off if their parents divorce than if they remain in an unhappy marriage. We think this is true in some cases but not in others. It is probably true that most children who live in a household filled with continual conflict between angry, embittered spouses would be better off if their parents split up—assuming that the level of conflict is lowered by the separation. And there is no doubt that the rise in divorce has liberated some children (and their custodial parents) from families marked by physical abuse, alcoholism, drugs, and violence. But we doubt that such clearly pathological descriptions apply to most families that disrupt. Rather, we think there are many more cases in which there is little open conflict, but one or both partners finds the marriage personally unsatisfying. The unhappy partner may feel unfulfilled, distant from his or her spouse, bored, or constrained. Under these circumstances, the family may limp along from day to day without much holding it together or pulling it apart. A generation ago, when marriage was thought of as a moral and social obligation, most husbands and wives in families such as this stayed together. Today, when marriage is thought of increasingly as a means of achieving personal fulfillment, many more will divorce. Under these circumstances, divorce may well make one or both spouses happier; but we strongly doubt that it improves the psychological well-being of the children.

A possible third key factor in children's successful adjustment is the maintenance of a continuing relationship with the noncustodial parent, who is usually the father. But direct evidence that lack of contact with the father inhibits the adjustment of children to divorce is less than satisfactory. A number of experts have stressed the importance of a continuing relationship, yet research findings are inconsistent. The main evidence comes from both the Hetherington and Wallerstein studies, each of which found that children were better adjusted when they saw their fathers regularly. More recently, however, other observational studies have not found this relationship.

And in the NSC, the amount of contact that children had with their fathers seemed to make little difference for their well-being. Teenagers who saw their fathers regularly were just as likely as were those with infrequent contact to have problems in school or engage in delinquent acts and precocious sexual behavior. Furthermore, the children's behavioral adjustment was also unrelated to the level of intimacy and identification with the nonresidential father. No differences were observed even among the children who had both regular contact and close relations with their father outside the home. Moreover, when the children in the NSC were reinterviewed in 1987 at ages 18 to 23, those who had retained stable, close ties to their fathers were neither more nor less successful than those who had had low or inconsistent levels of contact and intimacy with their fathers.

Another common argument is that fathers who maintain regular contact with their children also may keep paying child support to their children's mothers. Studies do show that fathers who visit more regularly pay more in child support. But it's not clear that they pay more *because* they visit more. Rather, it may be that fathers who have a greater commitment to their children both visit and pay more. If so, then the problem is to increase the level of commitment most fathers feel, not simply to increase the amount of visiting.

These puzzling findings make us cautious about drawing any firm conclusions about the psychological benefits of contact with noncustodial parents for children's adjustment in later life. Yet despite the mixed evidence, the idea that continuing contact with fathers makes a difference to a child's psychological well-being is so plausible and so seemingly grounded in theories of child development that one is reluctant to discount it. It may be that evidence is difficult to obtain because so few fathers living outside the home are intimately involved in child-rearing. It is also likely that, even when fathers remain involved, most formerly married parents have difficulty establishing a collaborative style of child-rearing. We remain convinced that when parents are able to cooperate in child-rearing after a divorce and when fathers are able to maintain an active and supportive role, children will be better off in the long run. But we are certain that such families are rare at present and unlikely to become common in the near future.

DOES CUSTODY MAKE A DIFFERENCE FOR CHILDREN?

The belief that the father's involvement is beneficial to children was an important reason why many states recently adopted joint-custody statutes. Supporters argued that children adjust better when they maintain a continuing relationship with both parents. They also argued that fathers would be more likely to meet child-support obligations if they retained responsibility for the children's upbringing. Were they correct? Joint custody is so recent that no definitive evidence exists. But the information to date is disappointing.

Joint *legal* custody seems to be hardly distinguishable in practice from maternal sole custody. A recent study of court records in Wisconsin showed no difference in child-support payments in joint-legal-custody versus mother-sole-custody families, once income and other factors were taken into account. The Stanford study found little difference, three and one-half years after separation, between joint-legal-custody (but not joint-physical-custody) families and mother-sole-custody families. Once income and education were taken into account, fathers who had joint legal custody were no more likely to comply with court-ordered child-support awards than were fathers whose former wives had sole legal and physical custody. They did not visit their children more often; they did not cooperate and communicate more with their former wives; and they didn't even participate more in decisions about the children's lives. The investigators concluded that joint legal custody "appears to mean very little in practice."

The handful of other small-scale studies of joint legal custody show modest effects, at most. It appears that joint legal custody does not substantially increase the father's decision-making authority, his involvement in childrearing, or the amount of child support he pays. Why is it so hard to increase fathers' involvement after divorce? For one thing . . . many men don't seem to know how to relate to their children except through their wives. Typically, when married, they were present but passive—not much involved in childrearing. When they separate, they carry this pattern of limited involvement with them; and it is reinforced by the modest contact most have with their children. Uncomfortable and unskilled at being an active parent, marginalized by infrequent contact, focused on building a new family life, many fathers fade from their children's lives.

Less is known about joint physical custody. But a few recent studies suggest that it isn't necessarily better for children's adjustment than the alternatives. Among all families in the Stanford Study in which children still were seeing both parents about two years after the separation, parents in dual-residence families talked and coordinated rules more; but they quarreled about the children just as much as did parents in single-residence families. Several colleagues of Wallerstein followed 58 mother-physical-custody families and 35 joint-physical-custody families for two years after the families had been referred to counseling centers in the San Francisco area. Many of the parents were disputing custody and visitation arrangements. Children from the joint-physical-custody families were no better adjusted than children from the mother-physical-custody families: their levels of behavioral problems, their self-esteem, their ease at making friends were very similar. What did make a difference for the children was the depression and anxiety levels of their parents and the amount of continuing verbal and physical aggression between them, regardless of the custody arrangement. The authors suggest that children whose parents are having serious disputes may have more behavior problems, lower self-esteem, and less acceptance by friends if they shuttle between homes. They are exposed to more conflict, and their movement back and forth may even generate it.

The admittedly limited evidence so far suggests to us that custody arrangements may matter less for the well-being of children than had been thought. It is, of course, possible that when more evidence is available, joint custody will be shown to have important benefits for some families. As with father involvement, the rationale for joint custody is so plausible and attractive that one is tempted to disregard the disappointing evidence and support it anyway. But based on what is known now, we think custody and visitation matter less for children than the two factors we noted earlier: how much conflict there is between the parents and how effectively the parent (or parents) the child lives with functions. It is likely that a child who alternates between the homes of a distraught mother and an angry father will be more troubled than a child who lives with a mother who is coping well and who once a fortnight sees a father who has disengaged from his family. Even the frequency of visits with a father seems to matter less than the climate in which they take place.

For now, we would draw two conclusions. First, joint physical custody should be encouraged only in cases where both parents voluntarily agree to it. Among families in which both parents shared the childrearing while they were married, a voluntary agreement to maintain joint physical custody probably will work and benefit the children. Even among families in which one parent did most of the childrearing prior to the divorce, a voluntary agreement won't do any harm—although we think the agreement likely will break down to sole physical custody over time. But only very rarely should joint physical custody be imposed if one or both parents do not want it. There may be a few cases in which the father and mother truly shared the childrearing before the divorce but one of them won't agree to share physical custody afterward. These difficult

cases call for mediation or counseling, and they may require special consideration. But among the vastly larger number of families in which little sharing
occurred beforehand and one or both parents doesn't want to share physical
custody afterward, imposing joint physical custody would invite continuing
conflict without any clear benefits. Even joint legal custody may matter more as
a symbol of fathers' ties to their children than in any concrete sense. But
symbols can be important, and joint legal custody seems, at worst, to do no
harm. A legal preference for it may send a message to fathers that society
respects their rights to and responsibilities for their children.

Our second conclusion is that in weighing alternative public policies
concerning divorce, the thin empirical evidence of the benefits of joint custody
and frequent visits with fathers must be acknowledged. All of the findings in
this chapter have implications for the way in which we as a society confront the
effects of divorce on children. A question we will examine later is: Which
public policies should have priority? What outcomes are most important for
society to encourage and support? In some cases, such as the economic slide of
mothers and children, the problem is clear, and alternative remedies readily
come to mind. In other cases, the problems are complex and the remedies
unclear. . . .

. . . [H]owever, we must note that a divorce does not necessarily mark the
end of change in the family lives of children. A majority will see a new partner
move into their home. A remarriage, or even a cohabiting relationship, brings
with it the potential both to improve children's lives and to complicate further
their adjustment . . . .

R E A D I N G

22

The Changing Meanings of Spanking

Phillip W. Davis

The general consensus is that adults in the past treated children in ways that seem especially harsh by today's standards (e.g., deMause 1974; but see also Pollock 1983). In fact, "whipping" children with buggy whips, cat-o'-nine-tails, riding crops, plough lines, sticks, switches and rods, as well as hair brushes and the "maternal slipper," did not generally lose favor in the United States until the 1830s, when "spanking" became more popular (Pleck 1987). Since then, the topic of spanking has arisen repeatedly in public and private arenas, with ministers, popular childrearing experts, researchers, parents, media representatives, and even politicians debating whether spanking is too harsh.

Some critics argue for national legislation such as that found in Sweden and a few other European countries banning all physical punishment of children, but the issue has not led to much activity among policymakers. Even though many critics link spanking and physical punishment with child abuse, policymakers have generally resisted treating physical discipline as abuse (Nelson 1984:127). As a columnist wrote decades ago, "Despite years of debate on the matter, 'spanking' remains a fighting word" (D. Barclay 1962).

Why examine the debate over spanking? Like the other authors in this book, I am interested in the links between children and social problems. By looking at this particular debate, I think that we can better understand how seemingly simple matters of childrearing often involve complex, changing, and competing ideas about the essential nature of children and their appropriate place in society. I also think that we can see how the social meanings of a seemingly simple practice such as spanking can emerge, develop, and shift as one kind of social issue transforms into another.

There have always been controversies over how best to deal with children (Elkin and Handel 1989). As those controversies develop, the key themes, issues, and definitions associated with the problem frequently change. Take child care. The debate in the popular press over daycare shifted in its key concerns over time (Cahill and Loseke 1993), and issues of institutional sponsorship arose only after attention shifted from the desirability of daycare to its availability (Klein

From *Troubling Children: Studies of Children and Social Problems.* Edited by Joel Best. Copyright © 1994 Walter de Gruyter, Inc., New York. pp. 133–149. (Chapter 7. References and notes have been omitted.)

1992). Or take child abuse. First "discovered" and publicized by medical experts, its meanings have changed since the 1960s in response to claims by a widespread child-protection movement (Best 1990; Johnson 1985; Nelson 1984).

Researchers usually ignore the spanking controversy, focusing instead on spanking behavior. Most define spanking as a kind of physical punishment, perhaps the "prototypical" punishment (Sears, MacCoby, and Levin 1957), although Straus (1991a:134) recently defined physical punishment as a "legally permissible physical attack." Sociologists have focused on spanking's developmental effects for the child's conscience and aggressive behavior (Steinmetz 1979), its uneven distribution by social class (Duvall and Booth 1979; Erlanger 1974), the widespread cultural approval for the practice (Straus, Gelles, and Steinmetz 1980), how often people spank (Wauchope and Straus 1990), the influence of religious fundamentalism on attitudes towards physical punishment (Ellison and Sherkat 1993; Wiehe 1990), and the role of physical punishment in shaping juvenile and adult deviance (Erlanger 1979; Straus 1991a).

Spanking, however, is more than mild physical punishment to make children behave. It is also the focus of competing ideas, beliefs, and vocabularies put forth by critics and advocates in a debate over spanking's definition, appropriateness, and implications. There is a long history of religious and secular justifications for spanking (Grevens 1991). Beliefs that spanking is natural, normal, and necessary form a "spare the rod ideology" that may perpetuate the practice (Straus, Gelles, and Steinmetz 1980). Trivializing terms such as "smack," "spank," and "whack" are at the heart of a rhetoric of punishment that presupposes the legitimacy of parental authority and makes assumptions about the impersonality of adult motivation (Harding and Ireland 1989; Maurer 1974). Spanking is a socially constructed reality; it means what people say it means.

Controversial topics such as spanking cause people to trade competing images and moral vocabularies. They look selectively at certain parts of the "problem" and not at others. They also name and characterize the problem in the course of making claims and counterclaims about its essential nature, typical features, and social implications (Best 1990; Miller and Holstein 1993; Spector and Kitsuse 1987). Sometimes, they identify types of people with certain characteristics and moral qualities as part of the problem (Loseke 1993).

My purpose in this chapter is to compare the traditional defense of spanking with the emergent criticism of spanking, identifying the claims and counterclaims spanking's advocates and critics have made in the popular press since midcentury. I also want to link both formulations to wider cultural influences. I will limit my focus to the debate over spanking by parents, recognizing that there is a parallel debate about spanking in schools. In general I argue that the debate over spanking has become more complex in its themes and vocabularies. New definitions of spanking supplement older ones, and what was once primarily a childrearing issue has become a child-protection issue as well.

DATA AND MATERIALS

My research strategy involves an ethnographic content analysis (Altheide 1987) of newspaper and popular magazine articles that either focus on spanking or consider spanking in the course of discussing something else. This kind of analysis is appropriate when the research goal is to document and understand social meanings. First, I examined articles indexed in *The Reader's Guide to Periodical Literature* (RGPL) between 1945 and 1993. I chose articles spanning nearly half a century because I wanted to compare more recent statements about spanking with older arguments. The RGPL listed "spanking" as a subject category for those years and also referred readers to "corporal punishment" for specific articles. Most of the 142 articles listed under "corporal punishment" dealt with paddling in the schools; only 47 (33 percent) focused on spanking by parents. The RGPL excludes most religious periodicals, although it indexes a few (e.g., *Christianity Today* and *U.S. Catholic*). I also searched RGPL for the same years under "children—behavior and training," collecting more items on spanking and screening many pieces on discipline to see if they addressed spanking in any way.

To sample newspaper coverage of spanking, I searched the *New York Times Index* from 1945 to 1993, collecting articles and columns listed under "corporal punishment" or "children—care and training." I also searched a computerized index of seven major newspapers from 1985 to 1993 under the subject "spanking." I collected over 100 magazine articles and over 80 newspaper articles and columns about spanking.

Not all of these articles are by self-identified advocates or critics. Many summarize the debate, often presenting what are described as the "pros" and "cons" of spanking. Others are news reports about conference activities or research reports having to do with spanking. The reactions and opinions of pediatricians, sociologists, psychologists, childrearing "experts," and others are incorporated into many articles, usually couched in terms of their support or rejection of spanking. Occasionally, a magazine or newspaper article inspired letters to the editor criticizing or applauding the article, and I collected these as well.

Large-city newspapers and mainstream magazines are but one arena or claimsmaking setting in which contrasting ideas and images of spanking appear. Of course, these materials do not reveal what is written in small-city newspapers, religious magazines and pamphlets, childrearing manuals, parent-education texts, and abolitionist pamphlets. We also miss what is said on radio and television shows and in other popular cultural sources. Debates over spanking also occur in semipublic arenas such as churches and parent-education classes and in private arenas where parents, children, and others formulate their own claims about spanking as an issue in their everyday lives.

My materials represent a mix of primary and secondary claims (Best 1990:19). Most newspaper articles present the secondary claims of reporters, recasting the claims of the "experts" interviewed for the story. Editorial and letter writers, however, as well as family columnists, take sides and write as primary claimsmakers—champions or critics of spanking. Most magazine articles also present primary claimsmaking by advocates or critics exhorting readers to support or condemn spanking. They also tend to rely heavily on the opinions of experts and the findings of researchers in making their case. Written to sway an audience, these materials are an example of what Lofland (1976:113) calls "mediated exhortatory encounters." The readily available data are "frozen in print."

This paper begins by identifying themes associated with traditional defenses of spanking and noting how critics traditionally respond to those defenses. I take up the newer critiques of spanking that have appeared since the early 1970s, arguing that spanking is compulsive, violent, and abusive. Finally, I identify some of the likely influences on the development of these newer meanings and discuss the implications of these changes for understanding spanking and the social transformation of social issues.

TRADITIONAL DEFENSES OF SPANKING

Spanking's advocates traditionally use a rhetoric and vocabulary that paints spanking as the reasonable reaction of responsible parents to their wayward children. They claim that spanking is (1) the sign of nonpermissiveness; (2) anticipatory socialization; (3) God's will; (4) a morally neutral childrearing tool; and (5) a psychic release.

The Sign of Nonpermissiveness

Advocates often present spanking as an answer to the problem of permissive parents who are responsible for much of the "youth problem." The argument is that parents' lax attitudes result in the "undercontrol" of their children who go on to become delinquents, hippies, political activists, liars, cheaters, and thieves who lack respect for authority. In this view, failure to spank becomes the standard or benchmark of nonpermissiveness. The close association of nonspanking and the "permissive" label is clear in an interview with Dr. Benjamin Spock:

> He laughs when the subject of permissive child-raising is brought up, and how he is often blamed for the recent youth rebellions in this country: "In the first place, as anybody who has read my books knows, I was never permissive," he said. "I never said that parents shouldn't spank their children. To some parents, spanking is a natural way of making children behave. I would never tell them not to spank," he added. (Klemesrud 1970)

Advocates also argue that character flaws lie behind the permissiveness of parents who do not spank; they lack the courage and responsibility that spanking is said to require. Parents who don't spank have neglected their responsibilities, taken the easy way out, or let themselves be duped by experts into taking a scientifically progressive but unwittingly troubled path. One father wrote how he and his wife started out permissive, despite his "itching palm." Finally they decided to try some real "action":

> More than once, the palm of my hand itched, but our textbook made it plain that the ultimate parental weapon, physical discipline, was arbitrary and old-fashioned. . . . Eight years of "permissiveness" had made my boy a liar, and an unrepentant and defiant one at that. "All right," I said heavily, realizing there was no alternative, "over

my knee!" . . . George is 13 now and in the intervening five years, I don't think I have had to spank him more than three or four times. Once my wife and I steeled ourselves to substitute action for pleading words, we had no hesitations about spanking Linda, or Johnny as he grew older. (Conway 1955) . . .

Anticipatory Socialization

A second claim is that spanking effectively prepares children for the tribulations of life and the vagaries of adulthood. Some advocates argue that children will profit from spankings once they enter the real world, a world that is characteristically more difficult and demanding than family life. Although the idea that physically harsh treatment somehow hardens and toughens children, especially boys, is centuries old (deMause 1974; Grevens 1991), it is the hard realities of an industrialized world that these modern advocates care about. One father described spanking as a sign of caring:

> To have rules for behavior without the threat of physical punishment is like having laws without jails. . . . Better to punish children than to be indifferent to them, since it is the neglected child who is more likely to grow up to be a problem. A father who spanks can at least be said to care. . . . may I say that life spanks us all for mistakes which, had they been caught in time by a parent who cared enough to correct them, need never have happened? (Dempsey 1958)

Another advocate wrote that going "back to the hairbrush" prepares children for life's "booby-traps":

> The "permissive" parents have to suffer through the uncurbed tantrums and general hell-raising of their offspring. . . . And the poor kids, when they eventually break out of the cocoon of an undisciplined childhood, are completely unprepared for the fenced-in and booby-trapped pattern of conventional adult life. (*Colliers* 1951)

This statement appeals to the idea that modernity and nonspanking are an unfortunate combination and that old-fashioned approaches better prepare children for the confinements of adult life.

God's Will

When religious themes appear in the materials I examined, it is usually when authors mention "biblical sanctions" as a traditional argument for spanking. Some ministers are quoted in support of spanking, but they are just as likely to emphasize effectiveness as divine sanction. James Dobson, author of *Dare to Discipline* and *James Dobson's New Dare to Discipline*, writes from the standpoint of Christian fundamentalism and is notorious among critics for his advocacy of spanking and switching: "I think we should not eliminate a biblically sanctioned approach to raising children because it is abused in some cases" (Neff 1993).

Although the definition of spanking as a "biblically sanctioned approach" figures prominently in the fundamentalist Christian press (Grevens 1991), it is relatively uncommon in the materials I examined. More often, articles make passing mention of religious themes or mention them in setting up a more secular discussion. Most people probably believe that the phrase, "spare the rod and spoil the child" comes from the Bible, but it first appeared in a poem by Samuel Butler published in 1664 (Gibson 1978:49).

A Morally Neutral Childrearing Tool

Advocates often refer to spanking as a tool, technique, or method, writing about it as if its "use" were but the impersonal and mechanical application of a morally neutral procedure. The virtues of this technique are said to include speed, efficiency, and efficacy. Spanking creates obedience and respect with minimum effort and without long, "dragged-out" discussions. These claims contend that the good child is an obedient child and that faster techniques are superior to slower ones. Defining spanking as a tool or method suggests that spankers are purposive rather than aimless and depicts spanking as a logical activity rather than an emotional outburst. The overall image of parents who spank is that their "applications" are part of a method that is reasonable, systematic, and even merciful:

> Why spank? Simply because there are times when spanking is the easiest, best method of correction—best for the children, easiest for me. I believe in spanking because it works! (Bramer 1948)
> A spanking is concrete enough to be effective, soon over, and more merciful than a prolonged bout or clash of wills. (English and Foster 1950)

The definition of spanking as a childrearing tool or technique is especially clear in the widespread claim by advocates in the popular press that spanking should be used as a "last resort," only after other, presumably less harsh, efforts have failed. The rhetoric of "last resorts" implies that spankers possess the knowledge and ability to mete out penalties of varying severity in the proper sequence.

A Psychic Release

Another common contention is that spanking resolves particular conflicts by somehow allowing parents and their children to start over, because it "clears the air." The popularity of this phrase no doubt derives from its use in Spock's popular *Baby and Child Care*, first published in 1945. Some authors elaborate on the phrase, claiming that spanking frees children from guilt by providing them with an opportunity for repentance or offers a cathartic release of the parent's tension and anger. One parent wrote:

> One salubrious effect of spanking, which is often overlooked by those who hold out for other methods of punishment, is the resulting feeling of expiation. . . . A child likes to feel that "it's all over now," that he's paid the price for his bad behavior, the slate's clean, the air clear, and the fresh start made. (Bramer 1948)

Advocates also contend that parents who don't spank will find other, less healthy, ways of expressing their anger:

> This is frequently the best reason for doing it—tensions that might otherwise remain bottled up are given a therapeutic release. While it is true that the child is not happy about this, he might be far less happy with a father who restrains his temper at the cost of continued irritability. (Dempsey 1958)

If they don't become neurotically guilty, insecure, or repressed, parents may erupt later and do greater harm to the child, for all their progressive efforts to conform to the new psychology.

The Critics Respond

Critics of spanking claim that these traditional defenses are flawed for a variety of reasons. They argue that, rather than preventing youth problems, spanking creates them. For one thing, spanking makes children untrustworthy:

> Few children feel as kindly toward a parent after a spanking as they did before. In time, bitter resentment, antagonism and strained child-parent relationships develop. To escape spankings, many a child develops into a sneak, a cheat or a liar. (Hurlock 1949)

Critics also claim that, although spanking may "work" in the immediate situation, its effects are highly limited: "It's true that a spanking can, very occasionally, work wonders with the child who has gotten a bit frisky, but it usually causes rebellion and resentment instead, especially in a preteen" (Kelly 1989). They also argue that, while it may be effective, it is effective for the wrong reason. Instead of complying voluntarily out of respect based on reason, children who are spanked comply out of fear. Critics claim that spankers are irresponsible, because they are avoiding the harder but superior alternatives. Spankers worry too much about teaching the values of respect and authority, oblivious to the fact that spanking really teaches the legitimacy of aggression, brute strength, and revenge. Critics also contend that spanking can easily escalate. A physician answered questions about spanking in his *McCall's* column:

> Q: *Should I hit my child back when he hits me?*
> A: No, you should not. If you strike him back, you are simply teaching him that the only way to respond in anger is by physical blows, and it may turn into a fist fight. (Senn 1957)

Critics argue that the true meaning of discipline involves teaching children the lesson of self-control, whereas "physical discipline" only teaches them "might makes right."

In sum, since mid-century advocates and critics in the popular press have been invoking several different meanings of spanking. Advocates claim that children are "underdisciplined," that they need to be spanked, that parents who do not spank are mollycoddling their children, that being spanked doesn't harm children, and that nonspanking parents are irresponsible. Critics respond that spanking is futile at best and counterproductive at worst. In this traditional debate, advocates emphasize the drawbacks of permissiveness as a cause of delinquency and rebellion, and critics argue that discipline should involve teaching and self-control.

EMERGENT MEANINGS

The traditional claims about spanking persist. Popular experts, columnists, researchers, professionals, and parents still argue for or against spanking by talking about effectiveness, lessons, psychic release, preparation, and permissiveness. Spanking is still said to work or not work, to counter permissiveness or encourage aggression, to reflect concern for the child's well-being or indicate a lack of self-control, to clear the air or breed resentment. Although claims about delinquency prevention and rhetoric about the woodshed have generally faded from view, along with worries about hippies and the youth rebellion, most of the other claims appear routinely in contemporary materials. One recent letter to a magazine, for example, echoes older claims: "Spanking is immediate, sharply focused, and lets everyone get on with their lives. It should be used sparingly and only as a last resort. But believe me, it can be effective." (*U.S. Catholic* 1993). But spanking's critics bring newer, supplementary meanings to the debate, meanings that coincide with changing concerns and arguments borrowed from debates over other issues.

Spanking Is Compulsive

The critics' first new claim is that spanking is compulsive, habit-forming, or addictive. This claim depicts parents as people who have lost their autonomy by becoming dependent on a highly satisfying behavior that they can abandon only with considerable difficulty. Critics compare spanking to smoking, because both practices are legal, harmful, and habitual. A mother described the day she decided to "kick the habit": "It was akin to the evening I found myself digging through a trash basket for a half-smoked cigarette butt and decided to quit smoking. And like the days that followed that decision, kicking the spanking habit proved to be tough" (Hyde 1980). A psychologist extended the analogy:

> People who smoke claim that it makes them feel better and helps them to relax; parents who spank their children also feel better by getting out their anger . . . there is liberal evidence that both are fraught with potential harm. Of course, most people who smoke never get cancer, and most children who are excessively spanked do not become delinquent. Yet for those who are affected, it is a serious matter indeed. (Welsh 1985) . . .

Spanking is a Demeaning, Violent Act

Critics in the popular press routinely echo the view of most family violence researchers that spanking is a form of violence. Critics frequently quote researchers such as Murray Straus and Richard Gelles in their articles. They describe spanking as an act of violence that models violent behavior for the child and teaches children that violence is socially acceptable. Penelope Leach, an extremely popular British author, argues for no spankings and fewer time outs in the name of clear thinking and nonviolence: "a spanking humiliates and devalues the whole child, overwhelms thought with anger, and demonstrates that physical violence is a good way to solve problems" (Leach 1992). A newspaper columnist points to the lessons in violence that spanking teaches: "Spanking demeans parents as well as children by presenting violence as an acceptable way to solve problems" (Ashkinase 1985). Other critics define spanking as an assault. In a *Psychology Today* reader survey on spanking and physical punishment, "one woman said that hitting a child should be considered assault: 'It gives the message that size and power make abusive behavior acceptable' " (Stark 1985). For critics, spanking is a prime example of minor violence that later causes adult violence, especially by those who experience frequent, severe spankings as children.

Spanking Is Abusive

With increasing frequency, newspaper and magazine articles interweave references to spanking and abuse, although the nature of the claimed connection varies considerably. I found no flat statements that "spanking is child abuse," but one article noted: "Parents Anonymous, a group for parents who want to avoid abusing their children, recently declared that any physical punishment is emotionally abusive and should not be sanctioned" (Lehman 1989). Some critics argue that spanking is associated with future abuse by the spanked child:

> Clearing the air with a quick spank sometimes *seems* to halt the progress of a deteriorating situation. . . . Nevertheless, the short-term utility must be weighed against the real possibility, gleaned from clinical evidence, that corporal punishment is not associated, in the long run, with self-discipline; rather, it is associated with the abuse of the child of the next generation. (Katz 1980—emphasis in original)

Others emphasize that a "fine line" separates spanking and abuse, a line that is too easily crossed. The notion of fine lines appears frequently in professional writings, and its popularization has been successful:

> You should never hit your children, even when you've reached the end of your rope because that's exactly when you are the least in control of yourself. Lines can blur and a hitting can turn into real, if unintentional, child abuse. (Schlaerth 1993)

In discussing "The Three Cardinal Rules of Good Discipline" (don't insult or demean your child, don't forget that you are a role model, and "spare the rod, period"), a psychologist concludes: "Worst of all, for many grown-ups, the line between physical punishment and child abuse can become blurred with frightening ease" (Segal 1986).

The Advocates Respond

Advocates have had little say about the idea that spanking is a compulsion, but they take issue with critics who claim it is violent or abusive. They go about this in various ways. Some claim that critics are less concerned about raising children than they are about social appearances. One professor emeritus of English wrote in a *Wall Street Journal* commentary (with the headline, "The Bottom Line on Spanking"):

> My wife recalls that when she misbehaved as a child, her mother cut a switch from a tree in the backyard and whaled her with it then and there. Any mother so thwacking today would be condemned. . . . Joan Beck, a nationally syndicated columnist, equates corporal punishment in schools with child abuse. Thus has political correctness befogged one of civilization's most useful ways to raise the young. . . . I do not recommend beating children. . . . Spanking a child is but a single act—among many—that supports civilized behavior against the natural barbarism of the American brat." (Tibbetts 1992) . . .

In his syndicated column William Raspberry reacted to the publicity given a 1989 conference on physical punishment. After a disclaimer, he ridiculed the idea that spanking and abuse are different points on the same continuum:

> Well, it's time to confess. My parents, for all their surface warmth and respectability, were into physical cruelty—child abuse, to put it plainly. You see, they spanked their children. I'm no advocate of child abuse, but it strikes me that the experts at Wingspread . . . are guilty of what might be called the fallacy of the false continuum . . . child abuse—the depressingly frequent incidents of child battering—is, for these experts, just another point on a continuum that begins with spanking. . . . Ordinary fanny dusting, to which some parents resort when more intelligent approaches fail, teaches children that violence is an acceptable way of settling disputes. . . . I think these experts are nuts. (Raspberry 1989)

The columnist notes that other approaches are more intelligent but also normalizes spankings by calling them "ordinary." His vocabulary pits "fanny dustings" against abuse, making light of what the critics take too seriously—spankings, after all, are only a light brushing of an unimportant part of the child's body. He also claims that people who confuse something inconsequential with something as important as violence are irrational and not to be taken seriously. A letter to the editor complained:

> I object to Columnist William Raspberry's characterization that we are "nuts" to link spanking to child abuse. . . . Without love, hitting children—no matter how euphemistically described—very easily becomes severe child abuse. (Hare 1989)

Some writers make increasingly sharp distinctions between spanking and abuse, between "an occasional swat" and spankings, or between rare swats and corporal punishment. They then discuss the differences these distinctions represent, emphasizing how rare swats are more defensible and less incriminating than the other things. One columnist reporting on a conference noted, for example: "Several specialists left the door open for that rare swat of a child who repeatedly endangers himself" (Lehman 1989). The occasional swat was also the topic of a syndicated column after Lady Di spanked Prince William, age 8, when he wouldn't stay at her side during his school's sports day in 1990. The writer wondered whether such a swat is the same as corporal punishment:

> The incident has revived debate over how parents should respond when their children misbehave and whether there is a difference between corporal punishment and a rare swat from a loving parent. . . . "She sounds pretty human," said Dr. T. Berry Brazelton. . . . "What Princess Di did, and what I probably would have done too, is to react in a way that lets the boy know that you really mean it," he said. "All of my kids will tell you that I've swatted them on the bottom when I've been upset with them." He added that he sees this as different from unacceptable physical punishments like planned or protracted spankings. (Kutner 1990)

DISCUSSION

I have examined spanking as a controversial topic rather than a behavior. Spanking remains a fighting word, and what people are fighting about is both complex and changing. I have identified arrays of older and newer meanings of spanking in a long-lived controversy filled with fluid, shifting claims by spanking's advocates and critics. In the course of formulating, defining, and characterizing spanking over time, a topic traditionally approached as a childrearing issue in a debate over "what works" is now also a child-protection issue in a debate over whether spanking is violent and abusive.

I have shown that advocates and critics employ rhetorical formulations that define and characterize spanking in ways meant to resonate deeply among readers, exhorting them to accept or reject "good old-fashioned" spankings. Advocates of spanking extol its virtues in the name of tradition, effectiveness, efficiency, and responsibility, defining it essentially as a tool, technique, or method for making children behave. Spanking is said to offer an antidote to the youth problem, release tension for both parent and child, and prepare children for life's hardships. Advocates generally ignore or trivialize children's suffering, portray nonspankers as irresponsible, and cite their own positive personal histories as spanked children. Critics counter that spanking ironically promotes, rather than deters, misbehavior. They contend that it is usually an expression of the parent's anger and frustration and teaches children that violence and aggression are acceptable. More recent critics also define spanking as a bad habit, an act of violence, and a form of abuse. All too often, they argue, spanking leads to abuse later in life or is closely linked to the abuse of the spanked child.

In the context of increasingly broad definitions of child abuse, some advocates argue for narrow definitions of spanking (e.g., bottom-only). Narrow definitions, as well as distinctions between planned spankings and the occasional smack, are ways of maintaining a "place" for spanking on the list of what parents can rightfully do to their children without lapsing into a new category of "putative person" (Loseke 1993). Otherwise, the moral character of spankers is vulnerable to allegations of being "old-fashioned" if not sadistic. To look at their rhetoric, advocates seem to embrace the notion of being old-fashioned, but they ridicule the idea that there is something incriminating about a normal form of discipline.

Activities in wider professional, scientific, religious, and political contexts have no doubt prompted and shaped these changing meanings for spanking. Psychological research and popular writings on aggression in the 1950s and 1960s challenged behaviorist assumptions about the role of punishment. Some well-publicized studies provided dramatic ironies such as the finding by Sears, Maccoby, and Levin (1957) that physical punishment for aggressive behavior is associated with more, not less, aggression by children. Many of these scholarly ideas and facts made their way into articles and stories in the popular press.

Moreover, in the 1960s and early 1970s, the development of a modern child-protection movement, the discovery of child abuse, and the continuing emergence of violence as a major policy issue led to a series of controversies associated with the idea that children are increasingly "at risk" (Wollons 1993). As these issues developed, spanking was mentioned, and sometimes its importance was highlighted. Working for the National Commission on the Causes and Prevention of Violence, for example, Stark and McEvoy (1970) wrote about spanking alongside fist fights, vigilantism, police violence, assassination, and military violence. In his influential book on child abuse, David Gil (1970) stressed how approval of physical punishment creates a cultural climate in which abuse can flourish. Both studies received national media attention.

There has also been a convergence of interests and activities among anticorporal punishment and antiabuse organizations. Organizations such as the National Coalition to Abolish Corporal Punishment in Schools, the National Center for the Study of Corporal Punishment and Alternatives, and End Violence against the Next Generation, although they focus on educational settings, regularly point to spanking and physical punishment by parents as an analogous issue (Hyman 1990). The National Committee for the Prevention of Child Abuse (NCPCA) has been actively seeking the primary prevention of child abuse through pamphlets, surveys, and press releases about physical punishment and spanking since the mid-1980s.

We cannot make a flat statement that the newer meanings of spanking are now dominant. The themes in the newer debate suggest only a partial transformation of the traditional childrearing issue into a contemporary child-protection controversy. There is certainly the potential for definitions related to abuse to become dominant. Whether the transformation proceeds further depends in part on the discourse, resources, and activities of advocates and critics in organizational, political, media, and movement contexts.

Activities in medical settings will have an impact. The Centers for the Study of Disease Control instituted a division for the study of domestic violence in 1992. The June 1992 issue of the *Journal of the American Medical Association* was devoted to family violence and included an article on spanking as a form of corporal punishment. Some physicians now claim that "corporal punishment is child abuse" (Leung, Robson, and Lim 1993:42). These medical developments, if they are recognized by the press, policymakers, and agency officials, should encourage spanking's association with child abuse.

Other activities are likely to inhibit the ascendance of abuse meanings. Religious action groups are sensitive and alert to any move to broaden definitions of abuse to include spanking, or to remove existing legal protections of parents who use "reasonable physical discipline." We may see other spanking-related controversies develop as groups organize to resist further involvement by the state in family matters (Johnson 1986). In addition, some critics promote the idea that spanking is really a civil rights issue, and civil rights organizations may make spanking part of their agenda. Their constructions of the problem might easily bypass the issue of abuse or make it secondary to the issue of discrimination on the basis of age. Similarly, critics campaigning for state and national legislation comparable to that in Sweden may successfully promote the association of spanking with the violation of human or children's rights rather than child abuse. Finally, it is likely that child-protection officials will continue to warn that their limited resources should be reserved for "truly" abused children. Whether spanking ever fully becomes a child-protection issue, these emergent meanings challenge the assumptions that spanking is natural, normal, and necessary on a fundamental level.

PART FOUR

◈

FAMILIES
IN
SOCIETY

◈

INTRODUCTION

During the 1950s and 1960s, family scholars and the mass media presented an image of the typical, normal, or model American family. It included a father, a mother, and two or three children living a middle-class existence in a single-family home in an area neither rural nor urban. Father was the breadwinner, and mother was a full-time homemaker. Both were, by implication, white.

No one denied that many families and individuals fell outside the standard nuclear model. Single persons, one-parent families, two-parent families in which both parents worked, three-generation families, and childless couples abounded. Three- or four-parent families were not uncommon, as one or both divorced spouses often remarried. Many families, moreover, neither white nor well-off, varied from the dominant image. White and seemingly middle-class families of particular ethnic, cultural, or sexual styles also differed from the model. The image scarcely reflected the increasing ratio of older people in the empty nest and retirement parts of the life cycle. But like poverty before its "rediscovery" in the mid-1960s, family complexity and variety existed on some dim fringe of semi-awareness.

When discussed, individuals or families departing from the standard model were analyzed in a context of pathology. Studies of one-parent families or working mothers, for example, focused on the harmful effects to children of such situations. Couples childless by choice were assumed to possess some basic personality inadequacy. Single persons were similarly interpreted, or else thought to be homosexual. Homosexuals symbolized evil, depravity, and degradation.

Curiously, although social scientists have always emphasized the pluralism of American society in terms of ethnic groups, religion, and geographic region, the concept of pluralism had rarely been applied to the family.

In the wake of the social upheavals of the 1960s and 1970s, middle-class "mainstream" attitudes toward women's roles, sexuality, and the family were transformed. Despite the conservative backlash that peaked in the 1980s, the traditional family did not return. American families became increasingly diverse, and Americans were increasingly willing to extend the notion of pluralism to family life.

The selections in this part of the book discuss not only diversity in families, but also the reality that families are both embedded in and sensitive to changes in the social structure and economics of American life. As Lillian B. Rubin writes in "Families on the Fault Line," words like "downsizing," "restructuring," and "reengineering" have become all too familiar and even terrifying to workers and their families who worry about paying the rent or the next mortgage payment. Through evocative case studies, the selection by Rubin develops three major themes: the impact of downsizing on all families who experience it; the differential outcomes by social class; and, finally, the corrosive effects downsizing has had on relations among racial and ethnic communities in the United States.

In a selection that complements Rubin's, Maxine Baca Zinn focuses specifically on the chronic problems of unemployment that prevail in America's inner cities, and their impact on families. Why over the past two decades have we witnessed the growth of a seemingly permanent "underclass" in America—a population of unmarried mothers, "illegitimate" children, and jobless men? Baca Zinn summarizes and evaluates the leading explanations. Many commentators blame the swelling underclass on a self-perpetuating "culture of poverty"—a value system that rejects hard work and achievement and accepts female-headed families. Cultural explanations come in a number of versions, but they all see family disintegration as the source of poverty.

There is, however, a different causal view. This interpretation, rooted in a large body of theory and research, stresses the importance of transformations in the American economy and its opportunity structure, rather than culture, as the foundation of the poverty of the underclass. Baca Zinn concludes that the evidence best supports the structural explanation. But she also contends that most writers who present the structural view, in emphasizing the need to increase employment opportunities for inner city males, overlook the changes in women's roles in recent years.

The other articles in this chapter discuss the revolution in women's roles that has taken place during the past two decades. The two-parent family in which both parents work is the form that now comes closest to being the "typical American family." In the 1950s, the working mother was considered deviant, even though many women were employed in the labor force. It was taken for granted that maternal employment must be harmful to children; much current research on working mothers still takes this "social problem" approach to the subject.

What happens inside the family as women routinely are expected to contribute to family income? Arlie Hochschild and Anne Machung take a close look at the emotional dynamics inside the family when both parents work full-time and the "second shift"—the work of caring for children and maintaining the home—is not shared equitably. The selection from their book portrays a painful dilemma shared by many couples in their study: The men saw themselves as having equal marriages; they were doing more work around the house than their fathers had done and more than they thought other men did. The women, whose lives were different from their own mothers', saw their husbands' contributions as falling far short of true equality. They resented having to carry more than their share of the "second shift," yet stifled their angry feelings in order to preserve their marriages. Still, this strategy took its toll on love and intimacy.

Chapter nine addresses family diversity along a number of dimensions, including race, ethnicity, life span, and lifestyles. Five authors—Paulette Moore Hines, Nydia Garcia-Preto, Monica McGoldrick, and Susan Weltman—examine intergenerational relations in a variety of ethnic and cultural groups, including African Americans and Latinos, Irish and Italians, Asian Indians and Jews. They make the important point that different groups have different expectations about how children are expected to care for aging parents, and about how different responsibilities accrue to women and men. The authors, who are family therapists, argue that although the push to assimilate and acculturate is strong, family therapists need to understand, appreciate, and integrate the distinctive cultural properties of ethnic groups into their thinking and practice.

In 1992, President and candidate George Bush said that "children should have the benefit of being born into a family with a mother and father." But, as Laura Benkov suggests, although Bush spoke in the nineties, his voice was of an earlier decade. As we approach a new century, Americans are facing a tension between the remembered past when "family" was defined by heterosexual procreative unions sanctioned by the law, and families as defined by the quality of relationships—even when these encompass lesbians and gay men choosing to have children. America, Benkov argues, should not grant more privileges to children raised in traditional family forms than to those reared in families formed with nontraditional structures and gender ties.

African Americans are currently the largest minority group in the United States, but they won't be for long. The twenty-first century will see Latinos and their families occupying that position. Like African-American families, those of Hispanic origin differ from white families in a number of ways. But like white families, Hispanic families also reflect a great deal of cultural diversity, says Catherine Street Chilman. Simply because they speak a common language does not mean that Puerto Ricans, Mexican Americans, Cuban Americans, and South and Central American immigrants are culturally unified. Understanding diversity in family life means that we must recognize variation within as well between ethnic, racial, and religious groups.

Of course, that understanding holds for African-American families as well. William P. O'Hare, Kelvin M. Pollard, Tanyia L. Mann, and Mary M. Kent explore some of that variation for African-American households, which have undergone rather dramatic changes in recent decades. These include an increase in single-parent families and a decline in the proportion of children who live with two parents. Their article also discusses how larger social and economic forces have had an impact on the family life of African Americans.

Chapter ten discusses another major change in family life occasioned by the fact that people, especially Americans, are living longer than ever before. In the first article in this chapter, Matilda White Riley discusses the new variations of family life resulting from the "revolution in longevity." During this century, life expectancy has risen from under 50 to over 70 years of age—and it continues to rise. This sharp increase in life expectancy has been accompanied by a greatly expanded kinship structure persisting through time. People used to have lots of relatives, but they didn't live very long. Now people begin with smaller families, but these persist and grow through marriage, procreation, and remarriage. Kinship structures used to look like short, stubby, ephemeral bushes. Now they have sprouted into long, slender trees, with many branches. Riley argues optimistically that the new kinship structure offers more choice for selecting relationships that can provide emotional support.

In earlier years—the so-called good old days—when death took family members at relatively young ages, grandparents were a rare family species. Young people today, even adolescents and twenty- and thirty-somethings, grow up knowing grandparents, a phenomenon that has developed largely since World War II, as a result of medical advances. The grandfather of one of the editors of this volume had his life saved by the then–miracle drug, penicillin, and he went on to live to 98 years of age. Because grandparenthood is so common today, it should not, as Andrew J. Cherlin and Frank. J. Furstenberg observe, be taken for granted. Widespread grandparenthood is a phenomenon of the last half-century, and as they show, it is having a significant effect on contemporary family relations.

Scientific progress is usually positive, but, as with most things in life, there can be unanticipated and unwanted outcomes. As gender and family roles have changed, and as modern methods of contraception have become available, society has experienced a sexual revolution. Part of it, perhaps the most dramatic part, has been the increasing sexual activity of teenagers, especially of girls. Teenage girls who are having sex are also experiencing more pregnancies. In the first reading in Chapter eleven on family troubles, Kristin Luker argues that, while teenage pregnancy is indeed a problem, its causes are often misinterpreted. It is not, she argues, simply an issue of immorality, of young women out of control. Rather, she argues, it makes far more sense to understand that teenage pregnancy reflects limited opportunities for realizing personal achievement, fulfillment, and enhancement of self-esteem.

Where Lillian Rubin's article (Chapter eight) focuses on working-class and ethnic families, Katherine Newman discusses the dark side of the American Dream—the slide down the economic ladder—for white-middle class families. What happens when a successful breadwinner loses his job and the family must suffer the loss of a formerly comfortable, middle-class lifestyle? The result is often a severe loss of status and self-respect for the father, a radical change in family emotional bonds, and the withdrawal of the family from the rest of the community. For middle-class families, the pain of downward social mobility is not just the loss of status and material comfort; it is also, Newman argues, a broken covenant. It is a profound violation of American cultural expectations that if we work hard we will succeed; that we, not economic forces beyond our control shape our fate and that the future will be rosier than the past.

Whatever the gnawing hurts of downward social mobility, the most dramatic, painful, and pronounced of family troubles is violence within the family, whether between partners or against children. Richard J. Gelles and Murray A. Straus provide us with a "profile" of violent families in three dimensions: first, the social organizational features of home and family that contribute to violence; second, the particular characteristics that put certain families at high risk for violence; and third, where and when violence in the home is likely to occur.

CHAPTER 8

WORK
AND
FAMILY

R E A D I N G
23

Families on the Fault Line

Lillian B. Rubin

THE BARDOLINOS

It has been more than three years since I first met the Bardolino family, three years in which to grow accustomed to words like *downsizing, restructuring,* or the most recent one, *reengineering;* three years in which to learn to integrate them into the language so that they now fall easily from our lips. But these are no ordinary words, at least not for Marianne and Tony Bardolino.

The last time we talked, Tony had been unemployed for about three months and Marianne was working nights at the telephone company and dreaming about the day they could afford a new kitchen. They seemed like a stable couple then—a house, two children doing well in school, Marianne working without

---

From Lillian B. Rubin. 1994. *Families on the Fault Line*. New York: HarperCollins Publishers. pp. 217–43. (Reference notes have been omitted.)

complaint, Tony taking on a reasonable share of the family work. Tony, who had been laid off from the chemical plant where he had worked for ten years, was still hoping he'd be called back and trying to convince himself their lives were on a short hold, not on a catastrophic downhill slide. But instead of calling workers back, the company kept cutting its work force. Shortly after our first meeting, it became clear: There would be no recall. Now, as I sit in the little cottage Marianne shares with her seventeen-year-old daughter, she tells the story of these last three years.

"When we got the word that they wouldn't be calling Tony back, that's when we really panicked; I mean *really* panicked. We didn't know what to do. Where was Tony going to find another job, with the recession and all that? It was like the bottom really dropped out. Before that, we really hoped he'd be called back any day. It wasn't just crazy; they told the guys when they laid them off, you know, that it would be three, four months at most. So we hoped. I mean, sure we worried; in these times, you'd be crazy not to worry. But he'd been laid off for a couple of months before and called back, so we thought maybe it's the same thing. Besides, Tony's boss was so sure the guys would be coming back in a couple of months; so you tried to believe it was true."

She stops speaking, takes a few sips of coffee from the mug she holds in her hand, then says with a sigh, "I don't really know where to start. So much happened, and sometimes you can't even keep track. Mostly what I remember is how scared we were. Tony started to look for a job, but there was nowhere to look. The union couldn't help; there were no jobs in the industry. So he looked in the papers, and he made the rounds of all the places around here. He even went all the way to San Francisco and some of the places down near the airport there. But there was nothing.

"At first, I kept thinking, *Don't panic; he'll find something*. But after his unemployment ran out, we couldn't pay the bills, so then you can't help getting panicked, can you?"

She stops again, this time staring directly at me, as if wanting something. But I'm not sure what, so I sit quietly and wait for her to continue. Finally, she demands, "Well, can you?"

I understand now; she wants reassurance that her anxiety wasn't out of line, that it's not she who's responsible for the rupture in the family. So I say, "It sounds as if you feel guilty because you were anxious about how the family would manage."

"Yeah, that's right," she replies as she fights her tears. "I keep thinking maybe if I hadn't been so awful, I wouldn't have driven Tony away." But as soon as the words are spoken, she wants to take them back. "I mean, I don't know, maybe I wasn't that bad. We were both so depressed and scared, maybe there's nothing I could have done. But I think about it a lot, and I didn't have to blame him so much and keep nagging at him about how worried I was. It wasn't his fault; he was trying.

"It was just that we looked at it so different. I kept thinking he should take anything, but he only wanted a job like the one he had. We fought about that a lot. I mean, what difference does it make what kind of job it is? No, I don't mean that; I know it makes a difference. But when you have to support a family, that should come first, shouldn't it?"

As I listen, I recall my meeting with Tony a few days earlier and how guiltily he, too, spoke about his behavior during that time. "I wasn't thinking about her at all," he explained. "I was just so mad about what happened; it was like the world came crashing down on me. I did a little too much drinking, and then I'd just crawl into a hole, wouldn't even know whether Marianne or the kids were there or not. She kept saying it was like I wasn't there. I guess she was right, because I sure didn't want to be there, not if I couldn't support them."

"Is that the only thing you were good for in the family?" I asked him.

"Good point," he replied laughing. "Maybe not, but it's hard to know what else you're good for when you can't do that."

I push these thoughts aside and turn my attention back to Marianne. "Tony told me that he did get a job after about a year," I remark.

"Yeah, did he tell you what kind of job it was?"

"Not exactly, only that it didn't work out."

"Sure, he didn't tell you because he's still so ashamed about it. He was out of work so long that even he finally got it that he didn't have a choice. So he took this job as a dishwasher in this restaurant. It's one of those new kind of places with an open kitchen, so there he was, standing there washing dishes in front of every-body. I mean, we used to go there to eat sometimes, and now he's washing the dishes and the whole town sees him doing it. He felt so ashamed, like it was such a comedown, that he'd come home even worse than when he wasn't working.

"That's when the drinking really started heavy. Before that he'd drink, but it wasn't so bad. After he went to work there, he'd come home and drink himself into a coma. I was working days by then, and I'd try to wait up until he came home. But it didn't matter; all he wanted to do was go for that bottle. He drank a lot during the day, too, so sometimes I'd come home and find him passed out on the couch and he never got to work that day. That's when I was maddest of all. I mean, I felt sorry for him having to do that work. But I was afraid he'd get fired."

"Did he?"

"No, he quit after a couple of months. He heard there was a chemical plant down near L.A. where he might get a job. So he left. I mean, we didn't exactly separate, but we didn't exactly not. He didn't ask me and the kids to go with him; he just went. It didn't make any difference. I didn't trust him by then, so why would I leave my job and pick up the kids and move when we didn't even know if he'd find work down there?

"I think he went because he had to get away. Anyway, he never found any decent work there either. I know he had some jobs, but I never knew exactly what he was doing. He'd call once in awhile, but we didn't have much to say to each other then. I always figured he wasn't making out so well because he didn't send much money the whole time he was gone."

As Tony tells it, he was in Los Angeles for nearly a year, every day an agony of guilt and shame. "I lived like a bum when I was down there. I had a room in a place that wasn't much better than a flop house, but it was like I couldn't get it together to go find something else. I wasn't making much money, but I had enough to live decent. I felt like what difference did it make how I lived?"

He sighs—a deep, sad sound—then continues, "I couldn't believe what I did, I mean that I really walked out on my family. My folks were mad as hell at me. When I told them what I was going to do, my father went nuts, said I shouldn't come back to his house until I got some sense again. But I couldn't stay around with Marianne blaming me all the time."

He stops abruptly, withdraws to someplace inside himself for a few moments, then turns back to me. "That's not fair. She wasn't the only one doing the blaming. I kept beating myself up, too, you know, blaming myself, like I did something wrong.

"Anyhow, I hated to see what it was doing to the kids; they were like caught in the middle with us fighting and hollering, or else I was passed out drunk. I didn't want them to have to see me like that, and I couldn't help it. So I got out."

For Marianne, Tony's departure was both a relief and a source of anguish. "At first I was glad he left; at least there was some peace in the house. But then I got so scared; I didn't know if I could make it alone with the kids. That's when I sold the house. We were behind in our payments, and I knew we'd never catch up. The bank was okay; they said they'd give us a little more time. But there was no point.

"That was really hard. It was our home; we worked so hard to get it. God, I hated to give it up. We were lucky, though. We found this place here. It's near where we used to live, so the kids didn't have to change schools, or anything like that. It's small, but at least it's a separate little house, not one of those grungy apartments." She interrupts herself with a laugh, "Well, 'house' makes it sound a lot more than it is, doesn't it?"

"How did your children manage all this?"

"It was real hard on them. My son had just turned thirteen when it all happened, and he was really attached to his father. He couldn't understand why Tony left us, and he was real angry for a long time. At first, I thought he'd be okay, you know, that he'd get over it. But then he got into some bad company. I think he was doing some drugs, although he still won't admit that. Anyway, one night he and some of his friends stole a car. I think they just wanted to go for a joyride; they didn't mean to really steal it forever. But they got caught, and he got sent to juvenile hall.

"I called Tony down in L.A. and told him what happened. It really shocked him; he started to cry on the phone. I never saw him cry before, not with all our trouble. But he just cried and cried. When he got off the phone, he took the first plane he could get, and he's been back up here ever since.

"Jimmy's trouble really changed everything around. When Tony came back, he didn't want to do anything to get Jimmy out of juvy right away. He thought he ought to stay there for a while; you know, like to teach him a lesson. I was mad at first because Jimmy wanted to come home so bad; he was so scared. But now I see Tony was right.

"Anyhow, we let Jimmy stay there for five whole days, then Tony's parents lent us the money to bail him out and get him a lawyer. He made a deal so that if Jimmy pleaded guilty, he'd get a suspended sentence. And that's what happened. But the judge laid down the law, told him if he got in one little bit of trouble again, he'd go to jail. It put the fear of God into the boy."

For Tony, his son's brush with the law was like a shot in the arm. "It was like I had something really important to do, to get that kid back on track. We talked it over and Marianne agreed it would be better if Jimmy came to live with me. She's too soft with the kids; I've got better control. And I wanted to make it up to him, too, to show him he could count on me again. I figured the whole trouble came because I left them, and I wanted to set it right.

"So when he got out of juvy, he went with me to my folks' house where I was staying. We lived there for awhile until I got this job. It's no great shakes, a kind of general handyman. But it's a job, and right from the start I made enough so we could move into this here apartment. So things are going pretty good right now."

"Pretty good" means that Jimmy, now sixteen, has settled down and is doing well enough in school to talk about going to college. For Tony, too, things have turned around. He set up his own business as an independent handyman several months ago and, although the work isn't yet regular enough to allow him to quit his job, his reputation as a man who can fix just about anything is growing. Last month the business actually made enough money to pay his bills. "I'll hang onto the job for a while, even if the business gets going real good, because we've got a lot of catching up to do. I don't mind working hard; I like it. And being my own boss, boy, that's really great," he concludes exultantly.

"Do you think you and Marianne will get together again?"

"I sure hope so; it's what I'm working for right now. She says she's not sure, but she's never made a move to get a divorce. That's a good sign, isn't it?"

When I ask Marianne the same question, she says, "Tony wants to, but I still feel a little scared. You know, I never thought I could manage without him, but then when I was forced to, I did. Now, I don't know what would happen if we got together again. It wouldn't be like it was before. I just got promoted to supervisor, so I have a lot of responsibility on my job. I'm a different person, and I don't know how Tony would like that. He says he likes it fine, but I figure we should wait a while and see what happens. I mean, what if things get tough again for him? I don't ever want to live through anything like these last few years."

"Yet you've never considered divorce."

She laughs, "You sound like Tony." Then more seriously, "I don't want a divorce if I can help it. Right now, I figure if we got through these last few years and still kind of like each other, maybe we've got a chance."

* * *

In the opening pages of this book, I wrote that when the economy falters, families tremble. The Bardolinos not only trembled, they cracked. Whether they can patch up the cracks and put the family back together again remains an open question. But the experience of families like those on the pages of this book provides undeniable evidence of the fundamental link between the public and private arenas of modern life.

No one has to tell the Bardolinos or their children about the many ways the structural changes in the economy affect family life. In the past, a worker like Tony Bardolino didn't need a high level of skill or literacy to hold down a well-paying semiskilled job in a steel mill or an automobile plant. A high school education, often even less, was enough. But an economy that relies most heavily on its service sector needs highly skilled and educated workers to fill its better-paying jobs, leaving people like Tony scrambling for jobs at the bottom of the economic order.

The shift from the manufacturing to the service sector, the restructuring of the corporate world, the competition from low-wage workers in underdeveloped countries that entices American corporations to produce their goods abroad, all have been going on for decades; all are expected to accelerate through the 1990s. The manufacturing sector, which employed just over 26 percent of American workers in 1970, already had fallen to nearly 18 percent by 1991. And experts predict a further drop to 12.5 percent by the year 2000. "This is the end of the post–World War boom era. We are never going back to what we knew," says employment analyst Dan Lacey, publisher of the newsletter *Workplace Trends*.

Yet the federal government has not only failed to offer the help working-class families need, but as a sponsor of a program to nurture capitalism elsewhere in the world it has become party to the exodus of American factories to foreign lands. Under the auspices of the U.S. Agency for International Development (AID), for example, Decaturville Sportswear, a company that used to be based in Tennessee, has moved to El Salvador. AID not only gave grants to trade organizations in El Salvador to recruit Decaturville but also subsidized the move by picking up the $5 million tab for the construction of a new plant, footing the bill for over $1 million worth of insurance, and providing low-interest loans for other expenses involved in the move.

It's a sweetheart deal for Decaturville Sportswear and the other companies that have been lured to move south of the border under this program. They build new factories at minimal cost to themselves, while their operating expenses drop dramatically. In El Salvador, Decaturville is exempted from corporate taxes and shipping duties. And best of all, the hourly wage for factory workers there is forty-five cents an hour; in the United States the minimum starting wage for workers doing the same job is $4.25.

True, like Tony Bardolino, many of the workers displaced by downsizing, restructuring, and corporate moves like these will eventually find other work. But like him also, they'll probably have to give up what little security they knew in the past. For the forty-hour-a-week steady job that pays a decent wage and provides good benefits is quickly becoming a thing of the past. Instead, as part of the new lean, clean, mean look of corporate America, we now have what the federal government and employment agencies call "contingent" workers—a more benign name for what some labor economists refer to as "disposable" or "throwaway" workers.

It's a labor strategy that comes in several forms. Generally, disposable workers are hired in part-time or temporary jobs to fill an organizational need and are released as soon as the work load lightens. But when union contracts call for employees to join the union after thirty days on the job, some unscrupulous employers fire contingent workers on the twenty-ninth day and bring in a new crew. However it's done, disposable workers earn less than those on the regular payroll and their jobs rarely come with benefits of any kind. Worse yet, they set off to work each morning fearful and uncertain, not knowing how the day will end, worrying that by nightfall they'll be out of a job.

The government's statistics on these workers are sketchy, but Labor Secretary Robert Reich estimates that they now make up nearly one-third of the existing work force. This means that about thirty-four million men and women, most of whom want steady, full-time work, start each day as contingent and/or part-time workers. Indeed, so widespread is this practice now that in some places temporary employment agencies are displacing the old ones that sought permanent placements for their clients.

Here again, class makes a difference. For while it's true that managers and professionals now also are finding themselves disposable, most of the workers who have become so easily expendable are in the lower reaches of the work order. And it's they who are likely to have the fewest options. These are the workers, the unskilled and the semiskilled—the welders, the forklift operators, the assemblers, the clerical workers, and the like—who are most likely to seem to management to be interchangeable. Their skills are limited; their job tasks are relatively simple and require little training. Therefore, they're able to move in and perform with reasonable efficiency soon after they come on the job. Whatever lost time or productivity a company may suffer by not having a steady crew of workers is compensated by the savings in wages and benefits the employment of throwaway workers permits. A resolution that brings short-term gains for the company at the long-term expense of both the workers and the nation. For when a person can't count on a permanent job, a critical element binding him or her to society is lost.

THE TOMALSONS

When I last met the Tomalsons, Gwen was working as a clerk in the office of a large Manhattan company and was also a student at a local college where she was studying nursing. George Tomalson, who had worked for three years in a furniture factory, where he laminated plastic to wooden frames, had been thrown out of a job when the company went bankrupt. He seemed a gentle man then, unhappy over the turn his life had taken but still wanting to believe that it would come out all right.

Now, as he sits before me in the still nearly bare apartment, George is angry. "If you're a black man in this country, you don't have a chance, that's all, not a chance. It's like no matter how hard you try, you're nothing but trash. I've been looking for work for over two years now, and there's nothing. White people are complaining all the time that black folks are getting a break. Yeah, well, I don't know who those people are, because it's not me or anybody else I know. People see a black man coming, they run the other way, that's what I know."

"You haven't found any work at all for two years?" I ask.

"Some temporary jobs, a few weeks sometimes, a couple of months once, mostly doing shit work for peanuts. Nothing I could count on."

"If you could do any kind of work you want, what would you do?"

He smiles, "That's easy; I'd be a carpenter. I'm good with my hands, and I know a lot about it," he says, holding his hands out, palms up, and looking at them proudly. But his mood shifts quickly; the smile disappears; his voice turns harsh. "But that's not going to happen. I tried to get into the union, but there's no room there for a black guy. And in this city, without being in the union, you don't have a chance at a construction job. They've got it all locked up, and they're making sure they keep it for themselves."

When I talk with Gwen later, she worries about the intensity of her husband's resentment. "It's not like George; he's always been a real even guy. But he's moody now, and he's so angry, I sometimes wonder what he might do. This place is a hell hole," she says, referring to the housing project they live in. "It's getting worse all the time; kids with guns, all the drugs, grown men out of work all around. I'll bet there's hardly a man in this whole place who's got a job, leave alone a good one."

"Just what is it you worry about?"

She hesitates, clearly wondering whether to speak, how much to tell me about her fears, then says with a shrug, "I don't know, everything, I guess. There's so much crime and drugs and stuff out there. You can't help wondering whether he'll get tempted." She stops herself, looks at me intently, and says, "Look, don't get me wrong; I know it's crazy to think like that. He's not that kind of person. But when you live in times like these, you can't help worrying about everything.

"We both worry a lot about the kids at school. Every time I hear about another kid shot while they're at school, I get like a raving lunatic. What's going on in this world that kids are killing kids? Doesn't anybody care that so many black kids are dying like that? It's like a black child's life doesn't count for anything. How do they expect our kids to grow up to be good citizens when nobody cares about them?

"It's one of the things that drives George crazy, worrying about the kids. There's no way you can keep them safe around here. Sometimes I wonder why we send them to school. They're not getting much of an education there. Michelle just started, but Julia's in the fifth grade, and believe me she's not learning much.

"We sit over her every night to make sure she does her homework and gets it right. But what good is it if the people at school aren't doing their job. Most of the teachers there don't give a damn. They just want the paycheck and the hell with the kids. Everybody knows it's not like that in the white schools; white people wouldn't stand for it.

"I keep thinking we've got to get out of here for the sake of the kids. I'd love to move someplace, anyplace out of the city where the schools aren't such a cesspool. But," she says dejectedly, "we'll never get out if George can't find a decent job. I'm just beginning my nursing career, and I know I've got a future now. But still, no matter what I do or how long I work at it, I can't make enough for that by myself."

George, too, has dreams of moving away, somewhere far from the city streets, away from the grime and the crime. "Look at this place," he says, his sweeping gesture taking in the whole landscape. "Is this any place to raise kids? Do you know what my little girls see every day they walk out the door? Filth, drugs, guys hanging on the corner waiting for trouble.

"If I could get any kind of a decent job, anything, we'd be out of here, far away, someplace outside the city where the kids could breathe clean and see a different life. It's so bad here, I take them over to my mother's a lot after school; it's a better neighborhood. Then we stay over there and eat sometimes. Mom likes it; she's lonely, and it helps us out. Not that she's got that much, but there's a little pension my father left."

"What about Gwen's family? Do they help out, too?"

"Her mother doesn't have anything to help with since her father died. He's long gone; he was killed by the cops when Gwen was a teenager," he says as calmly as if reporting the time of day.

"Killed by the cops." The words leap out at me and jangle my brain. But why do they startle me so? Surely with all the discussion of police violence in the black community in recent years, I can't be surprised to hear that a black man was "killed by the cops."

It's the calmness with which the news is relayed that gets to me. And it's the realization once again of the distance between the lives and experiences of blacks and others, even poor others. Not one white person in this study reported a violent death in the family. Nor did any of the Latino and Asian families, although the Latinos spoke of a difficult and often antagonistic relationship with Anglo authorities, especially the police. But four black families (13 percent) told of relatives who had been murdered, one of the families with two victims—a teenage son and a twenty-two-year-old daughter, both killed in violent street crimes.

But I'm also struck by the fact that Gwen never told me how her father died. True, I didn't ask. But I wonder now why she didn't offer the information. "Gwen didn't tell me," I say, as if trying to explain my surprise.

"She doesn't like to talk about it. Would you?" he replies somewhat curtly.

It's a moment or two before I can collect myself to speak again. Then I comment, "You talk about all this so calmly."

He leans forward, looks directly at me, and shakes his head. When he finally speaks, his voice is tight with the effort to control his rage. "What do you want? Should I rant and rave? You want me to say I want to go out and kill those mothers? Well, yeah, I do. They killed a good man just because he was black. He wasn't a criminal; he was a hard-working guy who just happened to be in the wrong place when the cops were looking for someone to shoot," he says, then sits back and stares stonily at the wall in front of him.

We both sit locked in silence until finally I break it. "How did it happen?"

He rouses himself at the sound of my voice. "They were after some dude who robbed a liquor store, and when they saw Gwen's dad, they didn't ask questions; they shot. The bastards. Then they said it was self-defense, that they saw a gun in his hand. That man never held a gun in his life, and nobody ever found one either. But nothing happens to them; it's no big deal, just another dead nigger," he concludes, his eyes blazing.

It's quiet again for a few moments, then, with a sardonic half smile, he says, "What would a nice, white middle-class lady like you know about any of that? You got all those degrees, writing books and all that. How are you going to write about people like us?"

"I was poor like you once, very poor," I say somewhat defensively.

He looks surprised, then retorts, "Poor and white; it's a big difference."

* * *

Thirty years before the beginning of the Civil War, Alexis de Tocqueville wrote: "If ever America undergoes great revolutions, they will be brought about by the presence of the black race on the soil of the United States; that is to say they will owe their origin, not to the equality, but to the inequality of condition." One hundred and sixty years later, relations between blacks and whites remain one of the great unresolved issues in American life, and "the inequality of condition" that de Tocqueville observed is still a primary part of the experience of black Americans.

I thought about de Tocqueville's words as I listened to George Tomalson and about how the years of unemployment had changed him from, as Gwen said, "a real even guy" to an angry and embittered one. And I was reminded, too, of de Tocqueville's observation that "the danger of conflict between the white and black inhabitants perpetually haunts the imagination of the [white] Americans, like a painful dream." Fifteen generations later we're still paying the cost of those years when Americans held slaves—whites still living in fear, blacks in rage. "People see a black man coming, they run the other way," says George Tomalson.

Yet however deep the cancer our racial history has left on the body of the nation, most Americans, including many blacks, believe that things are better today than they were a few decades ago–a belief that's both true and not true. There's no doubt that in ending the legal basis for discrimination and segregation, the nation took an important step toward fulfilling the promise of equality for all Americans. As more people meet as equals in the workplace, stereotypes begin to fall away and caricatures are transformed into real people. But it's also true that the economic problems of recent decades have raised the level of anxiety in American life to a new high. So although virtually all whites today give verbal assent to the need for racial justice and equality, they also find ways to resist the implementation of the belief when it seems to threaten their own status or economic well-being.

Our schizophrenia about race, our capacity to believe one thing and do another, is not new. Indeed, it is perhaps epitomized by Thomas Jefferson, the great liberator. For surely, as Gordon Wood writes in an essay in the *New York Review of Books*, "there is no greater irony in American history than the fact that

America's supreme spokesman for liberty and equality was a lifelong aristocratic owner of slaves."

Jefferson spoke compellingly about the evils of slavery, but he bought, sold, bred, and flogged slaves. He wrote eloquently about equality but he was convinced that blacks were an inferior race and endorsed the racial stereotypes that have characterized African-Americans since their earliest days on this continent. He believed passionately in individual liberty, but he couldn't imagine free blacks living in America, maintaining instead that if the nation considered emancipating the slaves, it must also prepare for their expulsion.

No one talks seriously about expulsion anymore. Nor do many use the kind of language to describe African-Americans that was so common in Jefferson's day. But the duality he embodied—his belief in justice, liberty, and equality alongside his conviction of black inferiority—still lives.

THE RIVERAS

Once again Ana Rivera and I sit at the table in her bright and cheerful kitchen. She's sipping coffee; I'm drinking some bubbly water while we make small talk and get reacquainted. After a while, we begin to talk about the years since we last met. "I'm a grandmother now," she says, her face wreathed in a smile. "My daughter Karen got married and had a baby, and he's the sweetest little boy, smart, too. He's only two and a half, but you should hear him. He sounds like five."

"When I talked to her the last time I was here, Karen was planning to go to college. What happened?" I ask.

She flushes uncomfortably. "She got pregnant, so she had to get married. I was heartbroken at first. She was only nineteen, and I wanted her to get an education so bad. It was awful; she had been working for a whole year to save money for college, then she got pregnant and couldn't go."

"You say she had to get married. Did she ever consider an abortion?"

"I don't know; we never talked about it. We're Catholic," she says by way of explanation. "I mean, I don't believe in abortion." She hesitates, seeming uncertain about what more she wants to say, then adds, "I have to admit, at a time like that, you have to ask yourself what you really believe. I don't think anybody's got the right to take a child's life. But when I thought about what having that baby would do to Karen's life, I couldn't help thinking, *What if . . . ?*" She stops, unable to bring herself to finish the sentence.

"Did you ever say that to Karen?"

"No, I would *never* do that. I didn't even tell my husband I thought such things. But, you know," she adds, her voice dropping to nearly a whisper, "if she had done it, I don't think I would have said a word."

"What about the rest of the kids?"

"Paul's going to be nineteen soon; he's a problem," she sighs. "I mean, he's got a good head, but he won't use it. I don't know what's the matter with kids these days; it's like they want everything but they're not willing to work for anything. He hardly finished high school, so you can't talk to him about going to college. But what's he going to do? These days if you don't have a good education, you don't have a chance. No matter what we say, he doesn't listen, just goes on his smart-alecky way, hanging around the neighborhood with a bunch of no-good kids looking for trouble.

"Rick's so mad, he wants to throw him out of the house. But I say no, we can't do that because then what'll become of him? So we fight about that a lot, and I don't know what's going to happen."

"Does Paul work at all?"

"Sometimes, but mostly not. I'm afraid to think about where he gets money from. His father won't give him a dime. He borrows from me sometimes, but I don't have much to give him. And anyway, Rick would kill me if he knew."

I remember Paul as a gangly, shy sixteen-year-old, no macho posturing, none of the rage that shook his older brother, not a boy I would have thought would be heading for trouble. But then, Karen, too, had seemed so determined to grasp at a life that was different from the one her parents were living. What happens to these kids?

When I talk with Rick about these years, he, too, asks in bewilderment: What happened? "I don't know; we tried so hard to give the kids everything they needed. I mean, sure, we're not rich, and there's a lot of things we couldn't give them. But we were always here for them; we listened; we talked. What happened? First my daughter gets pregnant and has to get married; now my son is becoming a bum."

"Roberto—that's what we have to call him now," explains Rick, "he says it's what happens when people don't feel they've got respect. He says we'll keep losing our kids until they really believe they really have an equal chance. I don't know; I knew I had to *make* the Anglos respect me, and I had to make my chance. Why don't my kids see it like that?" he asks wearily, his shoulders seeming to sag lower with each sentence he speaks.

"I guess it's really different today, isn't it?" he sighs. "When I was coming up, you could still make your chance. I mean, I only went to high school, but I got a job and worked myself up. You can't do that anymore. Now you need to have some kind of special skills just to get a job that pays more than the minimum wage.

"And the schools, they don't teach kids anything anymore. I went to the same public schools my kids went to, but what a difference. It's like nobody cares anymore."

"How is Roberto doing?" I ask, remembering the hostile eighteen-year-old I interviewed several years earlier.

"He's still mad; he's always talking about injustice and things like that. But he's different than Paul. Roberto always had some goals. I used to worry about him because he's so angry all the time. But I see now that his anger helps him. He wants to fight for his people, to make things better for everybody. Paul, he's like the wind; nothing matters to him.

"Right now, Roberto has a job as an electrician's helper, learning the trade. He's been working there for a couple of years; he's pretty good at it. But I think—I hope—he's going to go to college. He heard that they're trying to get Chicano students to go to the university, so he applied. If he gets some aid, I think he'll go," Rick says, his face radiant at the thought that at least one of his children will fulfill his dream. "Ana and me, we tell him even if he doesn't get aid, he should go. We can't do a lot because we have to help Ana's parents and that takes a big hunk every month. But we'll help him, and he could work to make up the rest. I know it's hard to work and go to school, but people do it all the time, and he's smart; he could do it."

His gaze turns inward; then, as if talking to himself, he says, "I never thought I'd say this but I think Roberto's right. We've got something to learn from some of these kids. I told that to Roberto just the other day. He says Ana and me have been trying to pretend we're one of them all of our lives. I told him, 'I think you're right.' I kept thinking if I did everything right, I wouldn't be a 'greaser.' But after all these years, I'm still a 'greaser' in their eyes. It took my son to make me see it. Now I know. If I weren't I'd be head of the shipping department by now, not just one of the supervisors, and maybe Paul wouldn't be wasting his life on the corner."

* * *

We keep saying that family matters, that with a stable family and two caring parents children will grow to a satisfactory adulthood. But I've rarely met a family that's more constant or more concerned than the Riveras. Or one where both parents are so involved with their children. Ana was a full-time homemaker until Paul, their youngest, was twelve. Rick has been with the same company for more than twenty-five years, having worked his way up from clerk to shift supervisor in its shipping department. Whatever the conflicts in their marriage, theirs is clearly a warm, respectful, and caring relationship. Yet their daughter got pregnant and gave up her plans for college, and a son is idling his youth away on a street corner.

Obviously, then, something more than family matters. Growing up in a world where opportunities are available makes a difference. As does being able to afford to take advantage of an opportunity when it comes by. Getting an education that broadens horizons and prepares a child for a productive adulthood makes a difference. As does being able to find work that nourishes self-respect and pays a living wage. Living in a world that doesn't judge you by the color of your skin makes a difference. As does feeling the respect of the people around you.

This is not to suggest that there aren't also real problems inside American families that deserve our serious and sustained attention. But the constant focus on the failure of family life as the locus of both our personal and social difficulties has become a mindless litany, a dangerous diversion from the economic and social realities that make family life so difficult today and that so often destroy it.

THE KWANS

It's rare sunny day in Seattle, so Andy Kwan and I are in his backyard, a lovely showcase for his talents as a landscape gardener. Although it has been only a few years since we first met, most of the people to whom I've returned in this round of interviews seem older, grayer, more careworn. Andy Kwan is no exception. The brilliant afternoon sunshine is cruel as it searches out every line of worry and age in his angular face. Since I interviewed his wife the day before, I already know that the recession has hurt his business. So I begin by saying, "Carol says that your business has been slow for the last couple of years."

"Yes," he sighs. "At first when the recession came, it didn't hurt me. I think Seattle didn't really get hit at the beginning. But the summer of 1991, that's when I began to feel it. It's as if everybody zipped up their wallets when it came to landscaping.

"A lot of my business has always been when people buy a new house. You know, they want to fix up the outside just like they like it. But nobody's been buying houses lately, and even if they do, they're not putting any money into landscaping. So it's been tight, real tight."

"How have you managed financially?"

"We get by, but it's hard. We have to cut back on a lot of stuff we used to take for granted, like going out to eat once in a while, or going to the movies, things like that. Clothes, nobody gets any new clothes anymore.

"I do a lot of regular gardening now—you know, the maintenance stuff. It helps; it takes up some of the slack, but it's not enough because it doesn't pay much. And the competition's pretty stiff, so you've got to keep your prices down. I mean, everybody knows that it's one of the things people can cut out when things get tough, so the gardeners around here try to hold on by cutting their prices. It gets pretty hairy, real cutthroat."

He gets up, walks over to a flower bed, and stands looking at it. Then, after a few quiet moments, he turns back to me and says, "It's a damned shame. I built my business like you build a house, brick by brick, and it was going real good. I finally got to the point where I wasn't doing much regular gardening anymore. I could concentrate on landscaping, and I was making a pretty good living. With Carol working, too, we were doing all right. I even hired two people and was keeping them busy most of the time. Then all of a sudden, it all came tumbling down.

"I felt real bad when I had to lay off my workers. They have families to feed, too. But what could I do? Now it's like I'm back where I started, an ordinary gardener again and even worrying about how long that'll last," he says disconsolately.

He walks back to his seat, sits down, and continues somewhat more philosophically, "Carol says I shouldn't complain because, with all the problems, we're lucky. She still has her job, and I'm making out. I mean, it's not great, but it could be a lot worse." He pauses, looks around blankly for a moment, sighs, and says, "I guess she's right. Her sister worked at Boeing for seven years and she got laid off a couple of months ago. No notice, nothing; just the pink slip. I mean, everybody knew there'd be layoffs there, but you know how it is. You don't think it's really going to happen to you.

"I try not to let it get me down. But it's hard to be thankful for not having bigger trouble than you've already got," he says ruefully. Then, a smile brightening his face for the first time, he adds, "But there's one thing I can be thankful for, and that's the kids; they're doing fine. I worry a little bit about what's going to happen, though. I guess you can't help it if you're a parent. Eric's the oldest; he's fifteen now, and you never know. Kids get into all kinds of trouble these days. But so far, he's okay. The girls, they're good kids. Carol worries about what'll happen when they get to those teenage years. But I think they'll be okay. We teach them decent values; they go to church every week. I have to believe that makes a difference."

"You say that you worry about Eric but that the girls will be fine because of the values of your family. Hasn't he been taught the same values?"

He thinks a moment, then says, "Did I say that? Yeah, I guess I did. I think maybe there's more ways for a boy to get in trouble than a girl." He laughs and says again, "Did I say *that?*" Then, more thoughtfully, "I don't know. I guess I worry about them all, but if you don't tell yourself that things'll work out okay, you go nuts. I mean, so much can go wrong with kids today.

"It used to be the Chinese family could really control the kids. When I was a kid, the family was law. My father was Chinese-born; he came here as a kid. My mother was born right here in this city. But the grandparents were all immigrants; everybody spoke Chinese at home; and we never lived more than a couple of blocks from both sides of the family. My parents were pretty Americanized everywhere but at home, at least while their parents were alive. My mother would go clean her mother's house for her because that's what a Chinese daughter did."

"Was that because your grandmother was old or sick?"

"No," he replies, shaking his head at the memory. "It's because that's what her mother expected her to do; that's the way Chinese families were then. We talk about that, Carol and me, and how things have changed. It's hard to imagine it, but that's the kind of control families had then.

"It's all changed now. Not that I'd want it that way. I want my kids to know respect for the family, but they shouldn't be servants. That's what my mother was, a servant for her mother.

"By the time my generation came along, things were already different. I couldn't wait to get away from all that family stuff. I mean, it was nice in some ways; there was always this big, noisy bunch of people around, and you knew you were part of something. That felt good. But Chinese families, boy, they don't let go. You felt like they were choking you.

"Now it's *really* different; it's like the kids aren't hardly Chinese any more. I mean, my kids are just like any other American kids. They never lived in a Chinese neighborhood like the one I grew up in, you know, the kind where the only Americans you see are the people who come to buy Chinese food or eat at the restaurants."

"You say they're ordinary American kids. What about the Chinese side? What kind of connection do they have to that?"

"It's funny," he muses. "We sent them to Chinese school because we wanted them to know about their history, and we thought they should know the language, at least a little bit. But they weren't really interested; they wanted to be like everybody else and eat peanut butter and jelly sandwiches. Lately it's a little different, but that's because they feel like they're picked on because they're Chinese. I mean, everybody's worrying about the Chinese kids being so smart and winning all the prizes at school, and the kids are angry about that, especially

Eric. He says there's a lot of bad feelings about Chinese kids at school and that everybody's picking on them—the white kids and the black kids, all of them.

"So all of a sudden, he's becoming Chinese. It's like they're making him think about it because there's all this resentment about Asian kids all around. Until a couple of years ago, he had lots of white friends. Now he hangs out mostly with other Asian kids. I guess that's because they feel safer when they're together."

"How do you feel about this?"

The color rises in his face; his voice takes on an edge of agitation. "It's too bad. It's not the way I wanted it to be. I wanted my kids to know they're Chinese and be proud of it, but that's not what's going on now. It's more like . . . , " he stops, trying to find the words, then starts again. "It's like they have to defend themselves *because* they're Chinese. Know what I mean?" he asks. Then without waiting for an answer, he explains, "There's all this prejudice now, so then you can't forget you're Chinese.

"It makes me damn mad. You grow up here and they tell you everybody's equal and that any boy can grow up to be president. Not that I ever thought a Chinese kid could ever be president; any Chinese kid knows that's fairy tale. But I did believe the rest of it, you know, that if you're smart and work hard and do well, people will respect you and you'll be successful. Now, it looks like the smarter Chinese kids are, the more trouble they get."

"Do you think that prejudice against Chinese is different now than when you were growing up?"

"Yeah, I do. When I was a kid like Eric, nobody paid much attention to the Chinese. They left us alone, and we left them alone. But now all these Chinese kids are getting in the way of the white kids because there's so many of them, and they're getting better grades, and things like that. So then everybody gets mad because they think our kids are taking something from them."

He stops, weighs his last words, then says, "I guess they're right, too. When I was growing up, Chinese kids were lucky to graduate from high school, and we didn't get in anybody's way. Now so many Chinese kids are going to college that they're taking over places white kids used to have. I can understand that they don't like that. But that's not our problem; it's theirs. Why don't they work hard like Chinese kids do?

"It's not fair that they've got quotas for Asian kids because the people who run the colleges decided there's too many of them and not enough room for white kids. Nobody ever worried that there were too many white kids, did they?"

* * *

"It's not fair"— a cry from the heart, one I heard from nearly everyone in this study. For indeed, life has not been fair to the working-class people of America, no matter what their color or ethnic background. And it's precisely this sense that it's not fair, that there isn't enough to go around, that has stirred the racial and ethnic tensions that are so prevalent today.

In the face of such clear class disparities, how is it that our national discourse continues to focus on the middle class, denying the existence of a working class and rendering them invisible?

Whether a family or a nation, we all have myths that play tag with reality—myths that frame our thoughts, structure our beliefs, and organize our systems of denial. A myth encircles reality, encapsulates it, controls it. It allows us to know some things and to avoid knowing others, even when somewhere deep inside we really know what we don't want to know. Every parent has experienced this clash between myth and reality. We see signals that tell us a child is lying and explain them away. It isn't that we can't know; it's that we won't, that knowing is too difficult or painful, too discordant with the myth that defines the relationship, the one that says: *My child wouldn't lie to me.*

The same is true about a nation and its citizens. Myths are part of our national heritage, giving definition to the national character, offering guidance for both public and private behavior, comforting us in our moments of doubt. Not infrequently our myths trip over each other, providing a window into our often contradictory and ambivalently held beliefs. The myth that we are a nation of equals lives side-by-side in these United States with the belief in white supremacy. And, unlikely as it seems, it's quite possible to believe both at the same time. Sometimes we manage the conflict by shifting from one side to the other. More often, we simply redefine reality. The inequality of condition between whites and blacks isn't born in prejudice and discrimination, we insist; it's black inferiority that's the problem. Class distinctions have nothing to do with privilege, we say; it's merit that makes the difference.

It's not the outcome that counts, we maintain; it's the rules of the game. And since the rules say that everyone comes to the starting line equal, the different results are merely products of individual will and wit. The fact that working-class children usually grow up to be working-class parents doesn't make a dent in the belief system, nor does it lead to questions about why the written rule and the lived reality are at odds. Instead, with perfect circularity, the outcome reinforces the reasoning that says they're deficient, leaving those so labeled doubly wounded—first by the real problems in living they face, second by internalizing the blame for their estate.

Two decades ago, when I began the research for *Worlds of Pain*, we were living in the immediate aftermath of the civil rights revolution that had convulsed the nation since the mid-1950s. Significant gains had been won. And despite the tenacity with which this headway had been resisted by some, most white Americans were feeling good about themselves. No one expected the nation's racial problems and conflicts to dissolve easily or quickly. But there was also a sense that we were moving in the right direction, that there was a national commitment to redressing at least some of the worst aspects of black-white inequality.

In the intervening years, however, the national economy buckled under the weight of three recessions, while the nation's industrial base was undergoing a massive restructuring. At the same time, government policies requiring preferential treatment were enabling African-Americans and other minorities to make small but visible inroads into what had been, until then, largely white terrain. The sense of scarcity, always a part of American life but intensified sharply by the history of these economic upheavals, made minority gains seem particularly threatening to white working-class families.

It isn't, of course, just working-class whites who feel threatened by minority progress. Wherever racial minorities make inroads into formerly all-white territory, tensions increase. But it's working-class families who feel the fluctuations in the economy most quickly and most keenly. For them, these last decades have been like a bumpy roller coaster ride. "Every time we think we might be able to get ahead, it seems like we get knocked down again," declares Tom Ahmundsen, a forty-two-year-old white construction worker. "Things look a little better; there's a little more work; then all of a sudden, boom, the economy falls apart and it's gone. You can't count on anything; it really gets you down."

This is the story I heard repeatedly: Each small climb was followed by a fall, each glimmer of hope replaced by despair. As the economic vise tightened, despair turned to anger. But partly because we have so little concept of class resentment and conflict in America, this anger isn't directed so much at those above as at those below. And when whites at or near the bottom of the ladder look down in this nation, they generally see blacks and other minorities.

True, during all of the 1980s and into the 1990s, white ire was fostered by national administrations that fanned racial discord as a way of fending off white discontent—of diverting anger about the state of the economy and the declining quality of urban life to the foreigners and racial others in our midst. But our history of racial animosity coupled with our lack of class consciousness made this easier to accomplish than it might otherwise have been.

The difficult realities of white working-class life not withstanding, however, their whiteness has accorded them significant advantages—both materially and psychologically—over people of color. Racial discrimination and segregation in the workplace have kept competition for the best jobs at a minimum. They do, obviously, have to compete with each other for the resources available. But that's different. It's a competition among equals; they're all white. They don't think such things consciously, of course; they don't have to. It's understood, rooted in the culture and supported by the social contract that says they are the superior ones, the worthy ones. Indeed, this is precisely why, when the courts or the legislatures act in ways that seem to contravene that belief, whites experience themselves as victims.

From the earliest days of the republic, whiteness has been the ideal, and freedom and independence have been linked to being white. "Republicanism," writes labor historian David Roediger, "had long emphasized that the strength, virtue and resolve of a people guarded them from enslavement." And it was whites who had these qualities in abundance, as was evident, in the peculiarly circuitous reasoning of the time, in the fact that they were not slaves.

By this logic, the enslavement of blacks could be seen as stemming from their "slavishness" rather than from the institution of slavery. Slavery is gone now, but the reasoning lingers on in white America, which still insists that the lowly estate of people of color is due to their deficits, whether personal or cultural, rather than to the prejudice, discrimination, and institutionalized racism that has barred them from full participation in the society.

This is not to say that culture is irrelevant, whether among black Americans or any other group in our society. The lifeways of a people develop out of their experiences—out of the daily events, large and small, that define their lives; out of the resources that are available to them to meet both individual and group needs; out of the place in the social, cultural, and political systems within which group life is embedded. In the case of a significant proportion of blacks in America's inner cities, centuries of racism and economic discrimination have produced a subculture that is both personally and socially destructive. But to fault culture or the failure of individual responsibility without understanding the larger context within which such behaviors occur is to miss a vital piece of the picture. Nor does acknowledging the existence of certain destructive subcultural forms among some African-Americans disavow or diminish the causal connections between the structural inequalities at the social, political, and economic levels and the serious social problems at the community level.

In his study of "working-class lads" in Birmingham, England, for example, Paul Willis observes that their very acts of resistance to middle-class norms—the defiance with which these young men express their anger at class inequalities—help to reinforce the class structure by further entrenching them in their working-class status. The same can be said for some of the young men in the African-American community, whose active rejection of white norms and "in your face" behavior consigns them to the bottom of the American economic order.

To understand this doesn't make such behavior, whether in England or the United States, any more palatable. But it helps to explain the structural sources of cultural forms and to apprehend the social processes that undergird them. Like Willis's white "working-class lads," the hip-hoppers and rappers in the black community who are so determinedly "not white" are not just making a statement about black culture. They're also expressing their rage at white society for offering a promise of equality, then refusing to fulfill it. In the process, they're finding their own way to some accommodation and to a place in the world they can call their own, albeit one that ultimately reinforces their outsider status.

But, some might argue, white immigrants also suffered prejudice and discrimination in the years after they first arrived, but they found more socially acceptable ways to accommodate. It's true—and so do most of today's people of color, both immigrant and native born. Nevertheless, there's another truth as well. For wrenching as their early experiences were for white ethnics, they had an out. Writing about the Irish, for example, Roediger shows how they were able to insist upon their whiteness and to prove it by adopting the racist attitudes and behaviors of other whites, in the process often becoming leaders in the assault against blacks. With time and their growing political power, they won the prize they sought—recognition as whites. "The imperative to define themselves as white," writes Roediger, "came from the particular 'public and psychological wages' whiteness offered to a desperate rural and often preindustrial Irish population coming to labor in industrializing American cities."

Thus does whiteness bestow its psychological as well as material blessings on even the most demeaned. For no matter how far down the socioeconomic ladder whites may fall, the one thing they can't lose is their whiteness. No small matter because, as W. E. B. DuBois observed decades ago, the compensation of white workers includes a psychological wage, a bonus that enables them to believe in their inherent superiority over nonwhites.

It's also true, however, that this same psychological bonus that white workers prize so highly has cost them dearly. For along with the importation of an immigrant population, the separation of black and white workers has given American capital a reserve labor force to call upon whenever white workers seemed to them to get too "uppity." Thus, while racist ideology enables white workers to maintain the belief in their superiority, they have paid for that conviction by becoming far more vulnerable in the struggle for decent wages and working conditions than they might otherwise have been. . . .

R E A D I N G

24

Family, Race, and Poverty

Maxine Baca Zinn

The 1960s Civil Rights movement overturned segregation laws, opened voting booths, created new job opportunities, and brought hope to Black Americans. As long as it could be said that conditions were improving, Black family structure and life-style remained private matters. The promises of the 1960s faded,

From *Signs: Journal of Women in Culture and Society* 1989, vol. 14, no. 4 © 1989 by The University of Chicago. Reprinted by permission.

however, as the income gap between whites and Blacks widened. Since the middle 1970s, the Black underclass has expanded rather than contracted, and along with this expansion emerged a public debate about the Black family. Two distinct models of the underclass now prevail—one that is cultural and one that is structural. Both of them focus on issues of family structure and poverty.

THE CULTURAL DEFICIENCY MODEL

The 1980s ushered in a revival of old ideas about poverty, race, and family. Many theories and opinions about the urban underclass rest on the culture-of-poverty debate of the 1960s. In brief, proponents of the culture-of-poverty thesis contend that the poor have a different way of life than the rest of society and that these cultural differences explain continued poverty. Within the current national discussion are three distinct approaches that form the latest wave of deficiency theories.

The first approach—culture as villain—places the cause of the swelling underclass in a value system characterized by low aspirations, excessive masculinity, and the acceptance of female-headed families as a way of life.

The second approach—family as villain—assigns the cause of the growing underclass to the structure of the family. While unemployment is often addressed, this argument always returns to the causal connections between poverty and the disintegration of traditional family structure.

The third approach—welfare as villain—treats welfare and antipoverty programs as the cause of illegitimate births, female-headed families, and low motivation to work. In short, welfare transfer payments to the poor create disincentives to work and incentives to have children out of wedlock—a self-defeating trap of poverty.

Culture as Villain

Public discussions of urban poverty have made the "disintegrating" Black family the force most responsible for the growth of the underclass. This category, by definition poor, is overwhelmingly Black and disproportionately composed of female-headed households. The members are perceived as different from striving, upwardly mobile whites. The rising number of people in the underclass has provided the catalyst for reporters' and scholars' attention to this disadvantaged category. The typical interpretation given by these social commentators is that the underclass is permanent, being locked in by its own unique but maladaptive culture. This thinking, though flawed, provides the popular rationale for treating the poor as the problem.

The logic of the culture-of-poverty argument is that poor people have distinctive values, aspirations, and psychological characteristics that inhibit their achievement and produce behavioral deficiencies likely to keep them poor not only within generations but also across generations, through socialization of the young.[1] In this argument, poverty is more a function of thought processes than of physical environment.[2] As a result of this logic, current discussions of ghetto poverty, family structure, welfare, unemployment, and out-of-wedlock births connect these conditions in ways similar to the 1965 Moynihan Report.[3] Because Moynihan maintained that the pathological problem within Black ghettos was the deterioration of the Negro family, his report became the generative example of blaming the victim.[4] Furthermore, Moynihan dismissed racism as a salient force in the perpetuation of poverty by arguing that the tangle of pathology was "capable of perpetuating itself without assistance from the white world."[5]

The reaction of scholars to Moynihan's cultural-deficiency model was swift and extensive although not as well publicized as the model itself. Research in the sixties and seventies by Andrew Billingsley, Robert Hill, Herbert Gutman, Joyce Ladner, Elliot Leibow, and Carol Stack, to name a few, documented the many strengths of Black families, strengths that allowed them to survive slavery, the enclosures of the South, and the depression of the North.[6] Such work revealed that many patterns of family life were not created by a deficient culture but were instead "a rational adaptational response to conditions of deprivation."[7]

A rapidly growing literature in the eighties documents the disproportionate representation of Black female-headed families in poverty. Yet, recent studies on Black female-headed families are largely unconcerned with questions about adaptation. Rather, they study the strong association between female-headed families and poverty, the effects of family disorganization on children, the demographic and socioeconomic factors that are correlated with single-parent status, and the connection between the economic status of men and the rise in Black female-headed families.[8] While most of these studies do not advance a social-pathology explanation, they do signal a regressive shift in analytic focus. Many well-meaning academics who intend to call attention to the dangerously high level of poverty in Black female-headed households have begun to emphasize the family structure and the Black ghetto way of life as contributors to the perpetuation of the underclass.

The population press, on the other hand, openly and enthusiastically embraced the Moynihan thesis both in its original version and in Moynihan's restatement of the thesis in his book *Family and Nation*.[9] Here Moynihan repeats his assertion that poverty and family structure are associated, but now he contends that the association holds for Blacks and whites alike. This modification does not critique his earlier assumptions; indeed, it validates them. A profoundly disturbing example of this is revealed in the widely publicized television documentary, CBS Reports' "The Vanishing Family."[10] According to this refurbished version of the old Moynihan Report, a breakdown in family values has allowed Black men to renounce their traditional breadwinner role, leaving Black women to bear the economic responsibility for children.[11] The argument that the Black community is devastating itself fits neatly with the resurgent conservatism that is manifested among Black and white intellectuals and policymakers.

Another contemporary example of the use of the culture of poverty is Nicholas Lemann's two-part 1986 *Atlantic Monthly* article about the Black underclass in Chicago.[12] According to Lemann, family structure is the most visible manifestation of Black America's bifurcation into a middle class that has escaped the ghetto and an underclass that is irrevocably trapped in the ghetto.

He explains the rapid growth of the underclass in the seventies by pointing to two mass migrations of Black Americans. The first was from the rural South to the urban North and numbered in the millions during the forties, fifties, and sixties; the second, a migration out of the ghettos by members of the Black working and middle classes, who had been freed from housing discrimination by the civil rights movement. As a result of the exodus, the indices of disorganization in the urban ghettos of the North (crime, illegitimate births) have risen, and the underclass has flourished.[13] Loose attitudes toward marriage, high illegitimacy rates, and family disintegration are said to be a heritage of the rural South. In Lemann's words, they represent the power of culture to produce poverty:

> The argument is anthropological, not economic; it emphasizes the power over people's behavior that culture, as opposed to economic incentives, can have. Ascribing a society's condition in part to the culture that prevails there seems benign when the society under discussion is England or California. But as a way of thinking about black ghettos it has become unpopular. Twenty years ago ghettos were often said to have a self-generating, destructive culture of poverty (the term has an impeccable source, the anthropologist Oscar Lewis). But then the left equated cultural discussions of the ghetto with accusing poor blacks of being in a bad situation that was of their own making. . . . The left succeeded in limiting the terms of the debate to purely economic ones, and today the right also discusses the ghetto in terms of economic "incentives to fail," provided by the welfare system. . . . In the ghettos, though, it appears that the distinctive culture is now the greatest barrier to progress by the black underclass, rather than either unemployment or welfare.[14]

Lemann's essay, his "misreading of left economic analysis, and cultural anthropology itself"[15] might be dismissed if it were atypical in the debate about the culture of poverty and the underclass. Unfortunately, it shares with other studies the problems of working "with neither the benefit of a well-articulated theory about the impact of personality and motivation on behavior nor adequate data from a representative sample of the low-income population."[16]

The idea that poverty is caused by psychological factors and that poverty is passed on from one generation to the next has been called into question by the University of Michigan's Panel Study of Income Dynamics (PSID), a large-scale data collection project conceived, in part, to test many of the assumptions about the psychological and demographic aspects of poverty. This study has gathered annual information from a representative sample of the U.S. population. Two striking discoveries contradict the stereotypes stemming from the culture-of-poverty argument. The first is the high turnover of individual families in poverty and the second is the finding that motivation cannot be linked to poverty. Each year the number of people below the poverty line remains about the same, but the poor in one year are not necessarily the poor in the following year. "Blacks from welfare dependent families were no more likely to become welfare dependent than similar Blacks from families who had never received welfare. Further, measures of parental sense of efficacy, future orientation, and achievement motivation had no effects on welfare dependency for either group."[17] This research has found no evidence that highly motivated people are more successful at escaping from poverty than those with lower scores on tests.[18] Thus, cultural deficiency is an inappropriate model for explaining the underclass.

The Family as Villain

A central notion within culture-of-poverty arguments is that family disintegration is the source and sustaining feature of poverty. Today, nearly six out of ten Black children are born out of wedlock, compared to roughly three out of ten in 1970. In the 25–34-year age bracket, today the probability of separation and divorce for Black women is twice that of white women. The result is a high probability that an individual Black woman and her children will live alone. The so-called "deviant" mother-only family, common among Blacks, is a product of "the feminization of poverty," a shorthand reference to women living alone and being disproportionately represented among the poor. The attention given to increased marital breakups, to births to unmarried women, and to the household patterns that accompany these changes would suggest that the bulk of contemporary poverty is a family-structure phenomenon. Common knowledge—whether true or not—has it that family-structure changes cause most poverty, or changes in family structure have led to current poverty rates that are much higher than they would have been if family composition had remained stable.[19]

Despite the growing concentration of poverty among Black female-headed households in the past two decades, there is reason to question the conventional thinking. Research by Mary Jo Bane finds that changes in family structure have less causal influence on poverty than is commonly thought.[20] Assumptions about the correlation and association between poverty and family breakdown avoid harder questions about the character and direction of causal relations between the two phenomena.[21] Bane's longitudinal research on household composition and poverty suggests that much poverty, especially among Blacks, is the result of already-poor, two-parent households that break up, producing poor female-headed households. This differs from the event transition to poverty that is more common for whites: "Three-quarters of whites who were poor in the first year after moving into a female-headed or single person household became poor simultaneously with the transition; in contrast, of the blacks who were poor after the transition, about two-thirds had also been poor before. Reshuffled poverty as opposed to event-caused poverty for blacks challenges the assumption that changes in family structure have created ghetto poverty. This underscores the importance of considering the ways in which race produces different paths to poverty."[22]

A two-parent family is no guarantee against poverty for racial minorities. Analyzing data from the PSID, Martha Hill concluded that the long-term income of Black children in two-parent families throughout the decade was even lower than the long-term income of non-Black children who spent most of the decade in mother-only families: "Thus, increasing the proportion of Black children growing up in two-parent families would not by itself eliminate very much of the racial gap in the economic well-being of children; changes in the economic circumstances of the parents are needed most to bring the economic status of Black children up to the higher status of non-Black children."[23]

Further studies are required if we are to understand the ways in which poverty, family structure, and race are related.

Welfare as Villain

An important variant of the family-structure and deficient-culture explanations, one especially popular among political conservatives, is the argument that welfare causes poverty. This explanation proposes that welfare undermines incentives to work and causes families to break up by allowing Black women to have babies and encouraging Black men to escape family responsibilities. This position has been widely publicized by Charles Murray's influential book, *Losing Ground*.[24] According to Murray, liberal welfare policies squelch work incentives and thus are the major cause of the breakup of the Black family. In effect, increased AFDC benefits make it desirable to forgo marriage and live on the dole.

Research has refuted this explanation for the changes in the structure of families in the underclass. Numerous studies have shown that variations in welfare across time and in different states have not produced systematic variation in family structure.[25] Research conducted at the University of Wisconsin's Institute for Research on Poverty found that poverty increased after the late sixties due to a weakening economy through the seventies. No support was found for Murray's assertion that spending growth did more harm than good for Blacks because it increased the percentage of families headed by women. Trends in welfare spending increased between 1960 and 1972, and declined between 1970 and 1984; yet there were no reversals in family-composition trends during this period. The percentage of these households headed by women increased steadily from 10.7 percent to 20.8 percent between 1968 and 1983.[26]

Further evidence against the "welfare-dependency" motivation for the dramatic rise in the proportion of Black families headed by females is provided by William Darity and Samuel Meyers. Using statistical causality tests, they found no short-term effects of variations in welfare payments on female headship in Black families.[27]

Other research draws similar conclusions about the impact of welfare policies on family structure. Using a variety of tests, David Ellwood and Lawrence Summers dispute the adverse effects of AFDC.[28] They highlight two facts that raise questions about the role of welfare policies in producing female-headed households. First, the real value of welfare payments has declined since the early 1970s, while family dissolution has continued to rise. Family-structure changes do not mirror benefit-level changes. Second, variations in benefit levels across states do not lead to corresponding variations in divorce rates or numbers of children in single-parent families. Their comparison of groups collecting AFDC with groups that were not, found that the effects of welfare benefits on family structures were small.[29] In sum, the systematic research on welfare and family structure indicates that AFDC has far less effect on changes in family structure than has been assumed.

OPPORTUNITY STRUCTURES IN DECLINE

A very different view of the underclass has emerged alongside the popularized cultural-deficiency model. This view is rooted in a substantial body of theory and research. Focusing on the opportunity structure of society, these concrete studies reveal that culture is not responsible for the underclass.

Within the structural framework there are three distinct strands. The first deals with transformations of the economy and the labor force that affect Americans in general and Blacks and Hispanics in particular. The second is the transformation of marriage and family life among minorities. The third is the changing class composition of inner cities and their increasing isolation of residents from mainstream social institutions.

All three are informed by new research that examines the macrostructural forces that shape family trends and demographic patterns that expand the analysis to include Hispanics.

Employment

Massive economic changes since the end of World War II are causing the social marginalization of Black people throughout the United States. The shift from an economy based on the manufacture of goods to one based on information and services has redistributed work in global, national, and local economies. While these major economic shifts affect all workers, they have more serious consequences for Blacks than whites, a condition that scholars call "structural racism."[30] Major economic trends and patterns, even those that appear race neutral, have significant racial implications. Blacks and other minorities are profoundly affected by (1) the decline of industrial manufacturing sectors and the growth of service sectors of the economy; and (2) shifts in the geographical location of jobs from central cities to the suburbs and from the traditional manufacturing cities (the rustbelt) to the sunbelt and to other countries.

In their classic work *The Deindustrialization of America*, Barry Bluestone and Bennett Harrison revealed that "minorities tend to be concentrated in industries that have borne the brunt of recent closing. This is particularly true in the automobile, steel, and rubber industries."[31] In a follow-up study, Bluestone, Harrison, and Lucy Gorham have shown that people of Color, particularly Black men, are more likely than whites to lose their jobs due to the restructuring of the U.S. economy and that young Black men are especially hard hit.[32] Further evidence of the consequences of economic transformation for minority males is provided by Richard Hill and Cynthia Negrey.[33] They studied deindustrialization in the Great Lakes region and found that the race-gender group that was hardest hit by the industrial slumps was Black male production workers. Fully 50 percent of this group in five Great Lakes cities studied lost their jobs in durable-goods manufacturing between 1979 and 1984. They found that Black male production workers also suffered the greatest rate of job loss in the region and in the nation as a whole.

The decline of manufacturing jobs has altered the cities' roles as opportunity ladders for the disadvantaged. Since the start of World War II, well-paying blue-collar jobs in manufacturing have been a main avenue of job security and mobility for Blacks and Hispanics. Movement into higher-level blue-collar jobs was one of the most important components of Black occupational advancement in the 1970s. The current restructuring of industries creates the threat of downward mobility for middle-class minorities.[34]

Rather than offering opportunities to minorities, the cities have become centers of poverty. Large concentrations of Blacks and Hispanics are trapped in cities in which the urban employment base is shifting. Today inner cities are shifting away from being centers of production and distribution of physical goods toward being centers of administration, information, exchange, trade, finance, and government service. Conversely, these changes in local employment structures have been accompanied by a shift in the demographic composition of large central cities away from European white to predominantly Black and Hispanic, with rising unemployment. The transfer of jobs away from central cities to the suburbs has created a residential job opportunity mismatch that literally leaves minorities behind in the inner city. Without adequate training or credentials, they are relegated to low-paying, nonadvancing exploitative service work or they are unemployed. Thus, Blacks have become, for the most part, superfluous people in cities that once provided them with opportunities.

The composition and size of cities' overall employment bases have also changed. During the past two decades most older, larger cities have experienced substantial job growth in occupations associated with knowledge-intensive service industries. However, job growth in these high-skill, predominantly white-collar industries has not compensated for employment declines in manufacturing, wholesale trade, and other predominantly blue-collar industries that once constituted the economic backbone of Black urban employment.[35]

While cities once sustained large numbers of less skilled persons, today's service industries typically have high educational requisites for entry. Knowledge and information jobs in the central cities are virtually closed to minorities given the required technological education and skill level. Commuting between central cities and outlying areas is increasingly common; white-collar workers commute daily from their suburban residences to the central business districts while streams of inner-city residents are commuting to their blue-collar jobs in outlying nodes.[36]

An additional structural impediment inner-city minorities face is their increased distance from current sources of blue-collar and other entry-level jobs. Because the industries that provide these jobs have moved to the suburbs and nonmetropolitan peripheries, racial discrimination and inadequate incomes of inner-city minorities now have the additional impact of preventing many from moving out of the inner city in order to maintain their access to traditional sources of employment. The dispersed nature of job growth makes public transportation from inner-city neighborhoods impractical, requiring virtually all city residents who work in peripheral areas to commute by personally owned automobiles. The severity of this mismatch is documented by John Kasarda: "More than one half of the minority households in Philadelphia and Boston are without a means of personal transportation. New York City's proportions are even higher with only three of ten black or Hispanic households having a vehicle available."[37]

This economic restructuring is characterized by an overall pattern of uneven development. Manufacturing industries have declined in the North and Midwest while new growth industries, such as computers and communications equipment, are locating in the southern and southwestern part of the nation. This regional shift has produced some gains for Blacks in the South, where Black poverty rates have declined. Given the large minority populations in the sunbelt, it is conceivable that industrial restructuring could offset the economic threats to racial equality. However, the sunbelt expansion has been based largely on low-wage, labor-intensive enterprises that use large numbers of underpaid minority workers, and a decline in the northern industrial sector continues to leave large numbers of Blacks and Hispanics without work.

Marriage

The connection between declining Black employment opportunities (especially male joblessness) and the explosive growth of Black families headed by single women is the basis of William J. Wilson's analysis of the underclass. Several recent studies conducted by Wilson and his colleagues at the University of Chicago have established this link.[38] Wilson and Kathryn Neckerman have documented the relationship between increased male joblessness and female-headed households. By devising an indicator called "the index of marriageable males," they reveal a long-term decline in the proportion of Black men, and particularly young Black men, who are in a position to support a family. Their indicators include mortality and incarceration rates, as well as labor-force participation rates, and they reveal that the proportion of Black men in unstable economic situations is much higher than indicated in current unemployment figures.[39]

Wilson's analysis treats marriage as an opportunity structure that no longer exists for large numbers of Black people. Consider, for example, why the majority of pregnant Black teenagers do not marry. In 1960, 42 percent of Black teenagers who had babies were unmarried; by 1970 the rate jumped to 63 percent and by 1983 it was 89 percent.[40] According to Wilson, the increase is tied directly to the changing labor-market status of young Black males. He cites the well-established relationship between joblessness and marital instability in support of his argument that "pregnant teenagers are more likely to marry if their boyfriends are working."[41] Out-of-wedlock births are sometimes encouraged by families and absorbed into the kinship system because marrying the suspected father would mean adding someone who was unemployed to the family's financial burden.[42] Adaptation to structural conditions leaves Black women disproportionately separated, divorced, and solely responsible for their children. The mother-only family structure is thus the consequence, not the cause, of poverty.

Community

These changes in employment and marriage patterns have been accompanied by changes in the social fabric of cities. "The Kerner Report Twenty Years Later," a conference of the 1988 Commission on the Cities, highlighted the growing isolation of Blacks and Hispanics.[43] Not only is inner-city poverty worse and more persistent than it was twenty years ago, but ghettos and barrios have become isolated and deteriorating societies with their own economies and with increasingly isolated social institutions, including schools, families, businesses, churches, and hospitals. According to Wilson, this profound social transformation is reflected not only in the high rates of joblessness, crime, and poverty but also in a changing socioeconomic class structure. As Black middle-class professionals left the central city, so too did working-class Blacks. Wilson uses the term "concentration effects" to capture the experiences of low-income families who now make up the majority of those who live in inner cities. The most disadvantaged families are disproportionately concentrated in the sections of the inner city that are plagued by joblessness, lawlessness, and a general milieu of desperation. Without working-class or middle-class role models these families have little in common with mainstream society.[44]

The departure of the Black working and middle classes means more than a loss of role models, however. As David Ellwood has observed, the flight of Black professionals has meant the loss of connections and networks. If successfully employed persons do not live nearby, then the informal methods of finding a job, by which one worker tells someone else of an opening and recommends her or him to the employer, are lost.[45] Concentration and isolation describe the processes that systematically entrench a lack of opportunities in inner cities. Individuals and families are thus left to acquire life's necessities though they are far removed from the channels of social opportunity.

THE CHANGING DEMOGRAPHY OF RACE AND POVERTY

Hispanic poverty, virtually ignored for nearly a quarter of a century, has recently captured the attention of the media and scholars alike. Recent demographic and economic patterns have made "the flow of Hispanics to urban America among the most significant changes occurring in the 1980s."[46]

As the Hispanic presence in the United States has increased in the last decade, Hispanic poverty rates have risen alarmingly. Between 1979 and 1985, the percentage of Latinos who were poor grew from 21.8 percent to 29.0 percent. Nationwide, the poverty rate for all Hispanics was 27.3 percent in 1986. By comparison, the white poverty rate in 1986 was 11 percent; the Black poverty rate was 31.1 percent.[47] Not only have Hispanic poverty rates risen alarmingly, but like Black poverty, Hispanic poverty has become increasingly concentrated in inner cities. Hispanics fall well behind the general population on all measures of social and economic well-being: jobs, income, educational attainment, housing, and health care. Poverty among Hispanics has become so persistent that, if current patterns continue, Hispanics will emerge in the 1990s as the nation's poorest racial-ethnic group.[48] Hispanic poverty has thus become a trend to watch in national discussions of urban poverty and the underclass.

While Hispanics are emerging as the poorest minority group, poverty rates and other socioeconomic indicators vary widely among Hispanic groups. Among Puerto Ricans, 39.9 percent of the population lived below the poverty level in 1986. For Mexicans, 28.4 percent were living in poverty in 1986. For Cubans and Central and South Americans, the poverty rate was much lower: 18.7 percent.[49] Such diversity has led scholars to question the usefulness of this racial-ethnic category that includes all people of Latin American descent.[50] Nevertheless, the labels Hispanic or Latino are useful in general terms in describing the changing racial composition of poverty populations. In spite of the great diversity among Hispanic nationalities, they face common obstacles to becoming incorporated into the economic mainstream of society.

Researchers are debating whether trends of rising Hispanic poverty are irreversible and if those trends point to a permanent underclass among Hispanics. Do macrostructural shifts in the economy and the labor force have the same effects on Blacks and Latinos? According to Joan W. Moore, national economic changes do affect Latinos, but they affect subgroups of Latinos in different ways:

> The movement of jobs and investments out of Rustbelt cities has left many Puerto Ricans living in a bleak ghetto economy. This same movement has had a different effect on Mexican Americans living in the Southwest. As in the North, many factories with job ladders have disappeared. Most of the newer Sunbelt industries offer either high paying jobs for which few Hispanics are trained or low paying ones that provide few opportunities for advancement. Those industries that depend on immigrant labor (such as clothing manufacturing in Los Angeles) often seriously exploit their workers, so the benefits to Hispanics in the Southwest of this influx of industries and investments are mixed. Another subgroup, Cubans in Miami, work and live in an enclave economy that appears to be unaffected by this shift in the national economy.[51]

Because shifts in the subregional economies seem more important to Hispanics than changes in the national economy, Moore is cautious about applying William Wilson's analysis of how the underclass is created.

Opportunity structures have not declined in a uniform manner for Latinos. Yet Hispanic poverty, welfare dependence, and unemployment rates are greatest in regions that have been transformed by macrostructural economic changes. In some cities, Puerto Rican poverty and unemployment rates are steadily converging with, and in some cases exceeding, the rates of Blacks. In 1986, 40 percent of Puerto Ricans in the United States lived below the poverty level and 70 percent of Puerto Rican children lived in poverty.[52]

Family structure is also affected by economic dislocation. Among Latinos, the incidence of female-headed households is highest for Puerto Ricans—43.3 percent—compared to 19.2 percent for Mexicans, 17.7 for Cubans, and 25.5 percent for Central and South Americans.[53] The association between national economic shifts and high rates of social dislocation among Hispanics provides further evidence for the structural argument that economic conditions rather than culture create distinctive forms of racial poverty. . . .

NOTES

1. Mary Corcoran, Greg J. Duncan, Gerald Gurin, and Patricia Gurin, "Myth and Reality: The Causes and Persistence of Poverty," *Journal of Policy*

Analysis and Management 4, no. 4 (1985): 516–36.

2. Mary Corcoran, Greg J. Duncan, and Martha S. Hill, "The Economic Fortunes of Women and Children: Lessons from the Panel Study of Income Dynamics," *Signs: Journal of Women in Culture and Society* 10, no. 2 (Winter 1984): 232–48.

3. Daniel P. Moynihan, "The Negro Family: The Case for National Action," in *The Moynihan Report and the Politics of Controversy*, ed. L. Rainwater and W. L. Yancy (Cambridge, Mass.: MIT Press, 1967), 39–132.

4. Margaret Cerullo and Marla Erlien, "Beyond the 'Normal Family': A Cultural Critique of Women's Poverty," in *For Crying Out Loud*, ed. Rochelle Lefkowitz and Ann Withorn (New York: Pilgrim Press, 1986), 246–60.

5. Moynihan, 47.

6. Leith Mullings, "Anthropological Perspectives on the Afro-American Family," *American Journal of Social Psychiatry* 6, no. 1 (Winter 1986): 11–16; see the following revisionist works on the Black family: Andrew Billingsley, *Black Families in White America* (Englewood Cliffs, N.J.: Prentice-Hall, 1968); Robert Hill, *The Strengths of Black Families* (New York: Emerson-Hall, 1972); Herbert Gutman, *The Black Family in Slavery and Freedom* (New York: Pantheon, 1976); Joyce Ladner, *Tomorrow's Tomorrow: The Black Woman* (New York: Doubleday, 1971); Elliot Leibow, *Talley's Corner: A Study of Negro Street Corner Men* (Boston: Little, Brown, 1967); Carol Stack, *All Our Kin* (New York: Harper & Row, 1974).

7. William J. Wilson and Robert Aponte, "Urban Poverty," *Annual Review of Sociology* 11 (1985): 231–58, esp. 241.

8. For a review of recent studies, see ibid.

9. Daniel Patrick Moynihan, *Family and Nation* (San Diego: Harcourt, Brace, Jovanovich, 1986).

10. "The Vanishing Family: Crisis in Black America," narrated by Bill Moyers, Columbia Broadcasting System (CBS) Special Report, January 1986.

11. "Hard Times for Black America," *Dollars and Sense*, no. 115 (April 1986), 5–7.

12. Nicholas Lemann, "The Origins of the Underclass: Part 1," *Atlantic Monthly* (June 1986), 31–55; Nicholas Lemann, "The Origins of the Underclass: Part 2," *Atlantic Monthly* (July 1986), 54–68.

13. Lemann, "Part 1," 35.

14. Ibid.

15. Jim Sleeper, "Overcoming 'Underclass': More Jobs Are Still the Key," *In These Times* (June 11–24, 1986), 16.

16. Corcoran et al. (n. 1 above), 517.

17. Martha S. Hill and Michael Ponza, "Poverty and Welfare Dependence Across Generations," *Economic Outlook U.S.A.* (Summer 1983), 61–64, esp. 64.

18. Anne Rueter, "Myths of Poverty," *Research News* (July–September 1984), 18–19.

19. Mary Jo Bane, "Household Composition and Poverty," in *Fighting Poverty*, ed. Sheldon H. Danziger and Daniel H. Weinberg (Cambridge, Mass.: Harvard University Press, 1986), 209–31.

20. Ibid.

21. Betsy Dworkin, "40% of the Poor Are Children," *New York Times Book Review* (March 2, 1986), 9.

22. Bane, 277.

23. Martha Hill, "Trends in the Economic Situation of U.S. Families and Children, 1970–1980," in *American Families and the Economy*, ed. Richard R. Nelson and Felicity Skidmore (Washington, D.C.: National Academy Press, 1983), 9–53, esp. 38.

24. Charles Murray, *Losing Ground* (New York: Basic, 1984).

25. David T. Ellwood, *Poor Support* (New York: Basic, 1988).

26. Sheldon Danziger and Peter Gottschalk, "The Poverty of *Losing Ground*," *Challenge* 28 (May/June 1985): 32–38.

27. William A. Darity and Samuel L. Meyers, "Does Welfare Dependency Cause Female Headship? The Case of the Black Family," *Journal of Marriage and the Family* 46, no. 4 (November 1984): 765–79.

28. David T. Ellwood and Lawrence H. Summers, "Poverty in America: Is Welfare the Answer or the Problem?" in *Fighting Poverty* (n. 19 above), 78–105.

29. Ibid., 96.

30. "The Costs of Being Black," *Research News* 38, nos. 11–12 (November–December 1987): 8–10.

31. Barry Bluestone and Bennett Harrison, *The Deindustrialization of America* (New York: Basic, 1982), 54.

32. Barry Bluestone, Bennett Harrison, and Lucy Gorham, "Storm Clouds on the Horizon: Labor Market Crisis and Industrial Policy," 68, as cited in "Hard Times for Black America" (n. 11 above).

33. Richard Child Hill and Cynthia Negrey, "Deindustrialization and Racial Minorities in the Great Lakes Region, U.S.A.," in *The Reshaping of America: Social Consequences of the Changing Economy*, ed. D. Stanley Eitzen and Maxine Baca Zinn (Englewood Cliffs, N.J.: Prentice-Hall, 1989), 168–77.

34. Elliot Currie and Jerome H. Skolnick, *America's Problems: Social Issues and Public Policy* (Boston: Little, Brown, 1984), 82.

35. John D. Kasarda, "Caught in a Web of Change," *Society* 21 (November–December 1983): 41–47.

36. Ibid., 45–47.

37. John D. Kasarda, "Urban Change and Minority Opportunities," in *The New Urban Reality*, ed. Paul. E. Peterson (Washington, D.C.: Brookings Institution, 1985), 33–68, esp. 55.

38. William J. Wilson with Kathryn Neckerman, "Poverty and Family Structure: The Widening Gap between Evidence and Public Policy Issues," in *The Truly Disadvantaged*, by William J. Wilson (Chicago: University of Chicago Press, 1987), 63–92.

39. Ibid.

40. Jerelyn Eddings, "Children Having Children," *Baltimore Sun* (March 2, 1986), 71.

41. As quoted in ibid., 71.

42. Noel A. Cazenave, "Alternate Intimacy, Marriage, and Family Lifestyles among Low-Income Black Americans," *Alternative Lifestyles* 3, no. 4 (November 1980): 425–44.

43. "The Kerner Report Updated" (Racine, Wis.: Report of the 1988 Commission on the Cities, March 1, 1988).

44. Wilson, *The Truly Disadvantaged* (n. 38 above), 62.

45. Ellwood (n. 25 above), 204.

46. Paul E. Peterson, "Introduction: Technology, Race, and Urban Policy," in *The New Urban Reality*, ed. Paul E. Peterson (Washington, D.C.: Brookings Institution, 1985), 1–35, esp. 22.

47. Jennifer Juarez Robles, "Hispanics Emerging as Nation's Poorest Minority Group," *Chicago Reporter* 17, no. 6 (June 1988): 1–3.

48. Ibid., 2–3.

49. Ibid., 3.

50. Alejandro Portes and Cynthia Truelove, "Making Sense of Diversity: Recent Research on Hispanic Minorities in the United States," *Annual Review of Sociology* 13 (1987): 359–85.

51. Joan W. Moore, "An Assessment of Hispanic Poverty: Does a Hispanic Underclass Exist?" *Tomás Rivera Center Report* 2, no. 1 (Fall 1988): 8–9.

52. Robles, 3.

53. U.S. Bureau of the Census, *Current Population Reports*, Series P-20, nos. 416, 422 (Washington, D.C.: Government Printing Office, March 1987).

25

The Second Shift: Working Parents and the Revolution at Home

Arlie Hochschild, with Anne Machung

Between 8:05 A.M. and 6:05 P.M., both Nancy and Evan are away from home, working a "first shift" at full-time jobs. The rest of the time they deal with the varied tasks of the second shift: shopping, cooking, paying bills; taking care of the car, the garden, and yard; keeping harmony with Evan's mother who drops over quite a bit, "concerned" about Joey, with neighbors, their voluble baby-sitter, and each other. And Nancy's talk reflects a series of second-shift thoughts: "We're out of barbecue sauce. . . . Joey needs a Halloween costume. . . . The car needs a wash. . . ." and so on. She reflects a certain "second-shift sensibility," a continual attunement to the task of striking and restriking the right emotional balance between child, spouse, home, and outside job.

When I first met the Holts, Nancy was absorbing far more of the second shift than Evan. She said she was doing 80 percent of the housework and 90 percent of the childcare. Evan said she did 60 percent of the housework, 70 percent of the childcare. Joey said, "I vacuum the rug, and fold the dinner napkins," finally concluding, "Mom and I do it all." A neighbor agreed with Joey. Clearly, between Nancy and Evan, there was a "leisure gap": Evan had more than Nancy. I asked both of them, in separate interviews, to explain to me how they had dealt with housework and childcare since their marriage began.

One evening in the fifth year of their marriage, Nancy told me, when Joey was two months old and almost four years before I met the Holts, she first seriously raised the issue with Evan. "I told him: 'Look, Evan, it's not working. I do the housework, I take the major care of Joey, *and* I work a full-time job. I get pissed. This is *your* house too. Joey is *your* child too. It's not all *my* job to care for them.' When I cooled down I put to him, 'Look, how about this: I'll cook Mondays, Wednesdays, and Fridays. You cook Tuesdays, Thursdays, and Saturdays. And we'll share or go out Sundays.' "

According to Nancy, Evan said he didn't like "rigid schedules." He said he didn't necessarily agree with her standards of housekeeping, and didn't like that standard "imposed" on him, especially if she was "sluffing off" tasks on him, which from time to time he felt she was. But he went along with the idea in principle. Nancy said the first week of the new plan went as follows: On Monday, she cooked. For Tuesday, Evan planned a meal that required shopping for a few ingredients, but on his way home he forgot to shop for them. He came home, saw nothing he could use in the refrigerator or in the cupboard, and suggested to Nancy that they go out for Chinese food. On Wednesday, Nancy cooked. On Thursday morning, Nancy reminded Evan, "Tonight it's your turn." That night Evan fixed hamburgers and french fries and Nancy was quick to praise him. On Friday, Nancy cooked. On Saturday, Evan forgot again.

As this pattern continued, Nancy's reminders became sharper. The sharper they became, the more actively Evan forgot—perhaps anticipating even sharper reprimands if he resisted more directly. This cycle of passive refusal followed by disappointment and anger gradually tightened, and before long the struggle had spread to the task of doing the laundry. Nancy said it was only fair that Evan share the laundry. He agreed in principle, but anxious that Evan would not share, Nancy wanted a clear, explicit agreement. "You ought to wash and fold every other load," she had told him. Evan experienced this "plan" as a yoke around his neck. On many weekdays, at this point, a huge pile of laundry sat like a disheveled guest on the living-room couch.

In her frustration, Nancy began to make subtle emotional jabs at Evan. "I don't know *what's* for dinner," she would say with a sigh. Or "I can't cook now, I've got to deal with this pile of laundry." She tensed at the slightest criticism about household disorder; if Evan wouldn't do the housework, he had absolutely *no* right to criticize how she did it. She would burst out angrily at Evan. She recalled telling him: "After work *my* feet are just as tired as *your* feet. I'm just as wound up as you are. I come home. I cook dinner. I wash and I clean. Here we are, planning a second child, and I can't cope with the one we have."

About two years after I first began visiting the Holts, I began to see their problem in a certain light: as a conflict between their two gender ideologies. Nancy wanted to be the sort of woman who was needed and appreciated both at home and at work—like Lacey, she told me, on the television show "Cagney and Lacey." She wanted Evan to appreciate her for being a caring social worker, a committed wife, and a wonderful mother. But she cared just as much that she be able to appreciate *Evan* for what *he* contributed at home, not just for how he supported the family. She would feel proud to explain to women friends that she was married to one of these rare "new men."

A gender ideology is often rooted in early experience, and fueled by motives formed early on and such motives can often be traced to some cautionary tale in early life. So it was for Nancy. Nancy described her mother:

> My mom was wonderful, a real aristocrat, but she was also terribly depressed being a housewife. My dad treated her like a doormat. She didn't have any self-confidence. And growing up, I can remember her being really depressed. I grew up bound and

determined not to be like her and not to marry a man like my father. As long as Evan doesn't do the housework, I feel it means he's going to be like my father—coming home, putting his feet up, and hollering at my mom to serve him. That's my biggest fear. I've had *bad* dreams about that.

Nancy thought that women friends her age, also in traditional marriages, had come to similarly bad ends. She described a high school friend: "Martha barely made it through City College. She had no interest in learning anything. She spent nine years trailing around behind her husband [a salesman]. It's a miserable marriage. She hand washes all his shirts. The high point of her life was when she was eighteen and the two of us were running around Miami Beach in a Mustang convertible. She's gained seventy pounds and she hates her life." To Nancy, Martha was a younger version of her mother, depressed, lacking in self-esteem, a cautionary tale whose moral was "if you want to be happy, develop a career and get your husband to share at home." Asking Evan to help again and again felt like "hard work" but it was essential to establishing her role as a career woman.

For his own reasons, Evan imagined things very differently. He loved Nancy and if Nancy loved being a social worker, he was happy and proud to support her in it. He knew that because she took her caseload so seriously, it was draining work. But at the same time, he did not see why, just because she chose this demanding career, *he* had to change *his own* life. Why should her personal decision to work outside the home require him to do more inside it? Nancy earned about two-thirds as much as Evan, and her salary was a big help, but as Nancy confided, "If push came to shove, we could do without it." Nancy was a social worker because she loved it. Doing daily chores at home was thankless work, and certainly not something Evan needed her to appreciate about him. Equality in the second shift meant a loss in his standard of living, and despite all the high-flown talk, he felt he hadn't *really* bargained for it. He was happy to help Nancy at home if she needed help; that was fine. That was only decent. But it was too sticky a matter "committing" himself to sharing.

Two other beliefs probably fueled his resistance as well. The first was his suspicion that if he shared the second shift with Nancy, she would "dominate him." Nancy would ask him to do this, ask him to do that. It felt to Evan as if Nancy had won so many small victories that he had to draw the line somewhere. Nancy had a declarative personality; and as Nancy said, "Evan's mother sat me down and told me once that I was too forceful, that Evan needed to take more authority." Both Nancy and Evan agreed that Evan's sense of career and self was in fact shakier than Nancy's. He had been unemployed. She never had. He had had some bouts of drinking in the past. Drinking was foreign to her. Evan thought that sharing housework would upset a certain balance of power that felt culturally "right." He held the purse strings and made the major decisions about large purchases (like their house) because he "knew more about finances" and because he'd chipped in more inheritance than she when they married. His job difficulties had lowered his self-respect, and now as a couple they had achieved some ineffable "balance"—tilted in his favor, she thought—which, if corrected to equalize the burden of chores, would result in his giving in "too much." A certain driving anxiety behind Nancy's strategy of actively renegotiating roles had made Evan see agreement as "giving in." When he wasn't feeling good about work, he dreaded the idea of being under his wife's thumb at home.

Underneath these feelings, Evan perhaps also feared that Nancy was avoiding taking care of *him*. His own mother, a mild-mannered alcoholic, had by imperceptible steps phased herself out of a mother's role, leaving him very much on his own. Perhaps a personal motive to prevent that happening in his marriage—a guess on my part, and unarticulated on his—underlay his strategy of passive resistance. And he wasn't altogether wrong to fear this. Meanwhile, he felt he was "offering" Nancy the chance to stay home, or cut back her hours, and that she was refusing his "gift," while Nancy felt that, given her feelings about work, this offer was hardly a gift.

In the sixth year of her marriage, when Nancy again intensified her pressure on Evan to commit himself to equal sharing, Evan recalled saying, "Nancy, why don't you cut back to half time, that way you can fit everything in." At first Nancy was baffled: "We've been married all this time, and you *still* don't get it. Work is important to me. I worked *hard* to get my MSW. Why *should* I give it up?" Nancy also explained to Evan and later to me, "I think my degree and my job has been my way of reassuring myself that I won't end up like my mother." Yet she'd received little emotional support in getting her degree from either her parents or in-laws. (Her mother had avoided asking about her thesis, and her in-laws, though invited, did not attend her graduation, later claiming they'd never been invited.)

In addition, Nancy was more excited about seeing her elderly clients in tenderloin hotels than Evan was about selling couches to furniture salesmen with greased-back hair. Why shouldn't Evan make as many compromises with his career ambitions and his leisure as she'd made with hers? She couldn't see it Evan's way, and Evan couldn't see it hers.

In years of alternating struggle and compromise, Nancy had seen only fleeting mirages of cooperation, visions that appeared when she got sick or withdrew, and disappeared when she got better or came forward.

After seven years of loving marriage, Nancy and Evan had finally come to a terrible impasse. Their emotional standard of living had drastically declined: they began to snap at each other, to criticize, to carp. Each felt taken advantage of: Evan, because his offering of a good arrangement was deemed unacceptable, and Nancy, because Evan wouldn't do what she deeply felt was "fair."

This struggle made its way into their sexual life—first through Nancy directly, and then through Joey. Nancy had always disdained any form of feminine wiliness or manipulation. Her family saw her as "a flaming feminist" and that was how she saw herself. As such, she felt above the underhanded ways traditional women used to get around men. She mused, "When I was a teenager, I vowed I would *never* use sex to get my way with a man. It is not self-respecting; it's demeaning. But when Evan refused to carry his load at home, I did, I used sex, I said, 'Look, Evan, I would not be this exhausted and asexual every night if I didn't have so much to face every morning.' " She felt reduced to an old "strategy," and her modern ideas made her ashamed of it. At the same time, she'd run out of other, modern ways.

The idea of a separation arose, and they became frightened. Nancy looked at the deteriorating marriages and fresh divorces of couples with young children around them. One unhappy husband they knew had become so uninvolved in family life (they didn't know whether his unhappiness made him uninvolved, or whether his lack of involvement had caused his wife to be unhappy) that his wife left him. In another case, Nancy felt the wife had "nagged" her husband so much that he abandoned her for another woman. In both cases, the couple was less happy after the divorce than before, and both wives took the children and struggled desperately to survive financially. Nancy took stock. She asked herself, "Why wreck a marriage over a dirty frying pan?" Is it really worth it?

UPSTAIRS-DOWNSTAIRS: A FAMILY MYTH AS "SOLUTION"

Not long after this crisis in the Holts' marriage, there was a dramatic lessening of tension over the issue of the second shift. It was as if the issue was closed. Evan had won. Nancy would do the second shift. Evan expressed vague guilt but beyond that he had nothing to say. Nancy had wearied of continually raising the topic, wearied of the lack of resolution. Now in the exhaustion of defeat, she wanted the struggle to be over too. Evan was "so good" in *other* ways, why debilitate their marriage by continual quarreling. Besides, she told me, "Women always adjust more, don't they?"

One day, when I asked Nancy to tell me who did which tasks from a long list of household chores, she interrupted me with a broad wave of her hand and said, "I do the upstairs, Evan does the downstairs." What does that mean? I asked. Matter-of-factly, she explained that the upstairs included the living room, the dining room, the kitchen, two bedrooms, and two baths. The downstairs meant the garage, a place for storage and hobbies—Evan's hobbies. She explained this as a "sharing" arrangement, without humor or irony—just as Evan did later. Both said they had agreed it was the best solution to their dispute. Evan would take care of the car, the garage, and Max, the family dog. As Nancy explained, "The dog is all Evan's problem. I don't have to deal with the dog." Nancy took care of the rest.

For purposes of accommodating the second shift, then, the Holts' garage was elevated to the full moral and practical equivalent of the rest of the house. For Nancy and Evan, "upstairs and downstairs," "inside and outside," was vaguely described like "half and half," a fair division of labor based on a natural division of their house.

The Holts presented their upstairs-downstairs agreement as a perfectly equitable solution to a problem they "once had." This belief is what we might call a "family myth," even a modest delusional system. Why did they believe it? I think they believed it because they needed to believe it, because it solved a terrible problem. It allowed Nancy to continue thinking of herself as the sort of woman whose husband didn't abuse her—a self-conception that mattered a great deal to her. And it avoided the hard truth that, in his stolid, passive way,

Evan had refused to share. It avoided the truth, too, that in their showdown, Nancy was more afraid of divorce than Evan was. This outer cover to their family life, this family myth, was jointly devised. It was an attempt to agree that there was no conflict over the second shift, no tension between their versions of manhood and womanhood, and that the powerful crisis that had arisen was temporary and minor.

The wish to avoid such a conflict is natural enough. But their avoidance was tacitly supported by the surrounding culture, especially the image of the woman with the flying hair. After all, this admirable woman also proudly does the "upstairs" each day without a husband's help and without conflict.

After Nancy and Evan reached their upstairs-downstairs agreement, their confrontations ended. They were nearly forgotten. Yet, as she described their daily life months after the agreement, Nancy's resentment still seemed alive and well. For example, she said:

> Evan and I eventually divided the labor so that I do the upstairs and Evan does the downstairs and the dog. So the dog is my husband's problem. But when I was getting the dog outside and getting Joey ready for childcare, and cleaning up the mess of feeding the cat, and getting the lunches together, and having my son wipe his nose on my outfit so I would have to change—then I was pissed! I felt that I was doing *every-thing*. All Evan was doing was getting up, having coffee, reading the paper, and saying, "Well, I have to go now," and often forgetting the lunch I'd bothered to make.

She also mentioned that she had fallen into the habit of putting Joey to bed in a certain way: he asked to be swung around by the arms, dropped on the bed, nuzzled and hugged, whispered to in his ear. Joey waited for her attention. He didn't go to sleep without it. But, increasingly, when Nancy tried it at eight or nine, the ritual didn't put Joey to sleep. On the contrary, it woke him up. It was then that Joey began to say he could only go to sleep in his parents' bed, that he began to sleep in their bed and to encroach on their sexual life.

Near the end of my visits, it struck me that Nancy was putting Joey to bed in an "exciting" way, later and later at night, in order to tell Evan something important: "You win, I'll go on doing all the work at home, but I'm angry about it and I'll make you pay." Evan had won the battle but lost the war. According to the family myth, all was well: the struggle had been resolved by the upstairs-downstairs agreement. But suppressed in one area of their marriage, this struggle lived on in another—as Joey's Problem, and as theirs.

NANCY'S "PROGRAM" TO SUSTAIN THE MYTH

There was a moment, I believe, when Nancy seemed to *decide* to give up on this one. She decided to try not to resent Evan. Whether or not other women face a moment just like this, at the very least they face the need to deal with all the feelings that naturally arise from a clash between a treasured ideal and an incompatible reality. In the age of a stalled revolution, it is a problem a great many women face.

Emotionally, Nancy's compromise from time to time slipped; she would forget and grow resentful again. Her new resolve needed maintenance. Only half aware that she was doing so, Nancy went to extraordinary lengths to maintain it. She could tell me now, a year or so after her "decision," in a matter-of-fact and noncritical way: "Evan likes to come home to a hot meal. He doesn't like to clear the table. He doesn't like to do the dishes. He likes to go watch TV. He likes to play with his son when he feels like it and not feel like he should be with him more." She seemed resigned.

Everything was "fine." But it had taken an extraordinary amount of complex "emotion work"—the work of *trying* to feel the "right" feeling, the feeling she wanted to feel—to make and keep everything "fine." Across the nation at this particular time in history, this emotion work is often all that stands between the stalled revolution on the one hand, and broken marriages on the other.

HOW MANY HOLTS?

In one key way the Holts were typical of the vast majority of two-job couples: their family life had become the shock absorber for a stalled revolution whose origin lay far outside it—in economic and cultural trends that bear very differently on men and women. Nancy was reading books, newspaper articles, and watching TV programs on the changing role of women. Evan wasn't. Nancy felt benefited by these changes; Evan didn't. In her ideals and in reality, Nancy was more different from her mother than Evan was from his father, for the culture and economy were in general pressing change faster upon women like her than upon men like Evan. Nancy had gone to college; her mother hadn't. Nancy had a professional job; her mother never had. Nancy had the idea that she should be equal with her husband; her mother hadn't been much exposed to that idea in her day. Nancy felt she should share the job of earning money, and that Evan should share the work at home; her mother hadn't imagined that was possible. Evan went to college, his father (and the other boys in his family, though not the girls) had gone too. Work was important to Evan's identity as a man as it had been for his father before him. Indeed, Evan felt the same way about family roles as his father had felt in his day. The new job opportunities and the feminist movement of the 1960s and '70s had transformed Nancy but left Evan pretty much the same. And the friction created by this difference between them moved to the issue of second shift as metal to a magnet. By the end, Evan did less housework and childcare than most men married to working women—but not much less. Evan and Nancy were also typical of nearly 40 percent of the marriages I studied in their clash of gender ideologies and their corresponding difference in notion about what constituted a "sacrifice" and what did not. By far the most common form of mismatch was like that between Nancy, an egalitarian, and Evan, a transitional.

But for most couples, the tensions between strategies did not move so quickly and powerfully to issues of housework and childcare. Nancy pushed harder than most women to get her husband to share the work at home, and she also lost more overwhelmingly than the few other women who fought that hard. Evan pursued his strategy of passive resistance with more quiet tenacity than most men, and he allowed himself to become far more marginal to his son's life than most other fathers. The myth of the Holts' "equal" arrangement seemed slightly more odd than other family myths that encapsulated equally powerful conflicts.

Beyond their upstairs-downstairs myth, the Holts tell us a great deal about the subtle ways a couple can encapsulate the tension caused by a struggle over the second shift without resolving the problem or divorcing. Like Nancy Holt, many women struggle to avoid, suppress, obscure, or mystify a frightening conflict over the second shift. They do not struggle like this because they started off wanting to, or because such struggle is inevitable or because women inevitably lose, but because they are forced to choose between equality and marriage. And they choose marriage. When asked about "ideal" relations between men and women in general, about what they want for their daughters, about what "ideally" they'd like in their own marriage, most working mothers "wished" their men would share the work at home.

But many "wish" it instead of "want" it. Other goals—like keeping peace at home—come first. Nancy Holt did some extraordinary behind-the-scenes emotion work to prevent her ideals from clashing with her marriage. In the end, she had confined and miniaturized her ideas of equality successfully enough to do two things she badly wanted to do: feel like a feminist, and live at peace with a man who was not. Her program had "worked." Evan won on the reality of the situation, because Nancy did the second shift. Nancy won on the cover story; they would talk about it as if they shared.

Nancy wore the upstairs-downstairs myth as an ideological cloak to protect her from the contradictions in her marriage and from the cultural and economic forces that press upon it. Nancy and Evan Holt were caught on opposite sides of the gender revolution occurring all around them. Through the 1960s, 1970s, and 1980s masses of women entered the public world of work—but went only so far up the occupational ladder. They tried for "equal" marriages, but got only so far in achieving it. They married men who liked them to work at the office but who wouldn't share the extra month a year at home. When confusion about the identity of the working woman created a cultural vacuum in the 1970s and 1980s, the image of the supermom quietly glided in. She made the "stall" seem normal and happy. But beneath the happy image of the woman with the flying hair are modern marriages like the Holts', reflecting intricate webs of tension, and the huge, hidden emotional cost to women, men, and children of having to "manage" inequality. Yet on the surface, all we might see would be Nancy Holt bounding confidently out the door at 8:30 A.M. briefcase in one hand, Joey in the other. All we might hear would be Nancy's and Evan's talk about their marriage as happy, normal, even "equal"—because equality was so important to Nancy.

CHAPTER 9

❖

FAMILY DIVERSITY

READING

26

Intergenerational Relationships
Across Cultures

Paulette Moore Hines, Nydia Garcia-Preto, Monica McGoldrick,
Rhea Almeida, and Susan Weltman

The powerful influence of ethnicity on how individuals think, feel, and behave has only recently begun to be considered in family therapy training and practice as well as in the larger human services delivery system.

In our efforts to promote the melting-pot myth and the notion that all individuals are equal, we tend to perpetuate the notion that to be different is to be deficient or bad. Although similarities exist across individuals and groups in this country and the push for acculturation is strong, differences among groups need to be recognized, valued, and integrated into our thinking and practice of family therapy. Human behavior cannot be understood properly in isolation from the context in which an individual is embedded.

Ethnicity is a critical, but not sufficient, consideration for understanding personal development and family life throughout the life cycle. McGoldrick (1982) defined ethnicity as a sense of commonality transmitted over genera-

---

tions by the family and reinforced by the surrounding community. Our cultural values and assumptions, often unconscious, influence every aspect of our being, including what we label as a problem, how we communicate, beliefs about the cause of a problem, whom we prefer as a helper, and what kind of solutions we prefer.

The rules governing intergenerational relationships in families throughout the life cycle vary across cultures. For instance, considerable differences exist among ethnic groups as to the degree of intergenerational dependence and sharing expected between adult children and their aging parents. Whereas Italians or Greeks are likely to grow up with the expectation that eventually they will take care of their parents, white Anglo-Saxon Protestant (WASP) parents' worst nightmare might be that eventually they will have to depend on their child for support. Minimal interdependence is expected or fostered so that adult children feel relatively guilt free when they have to put their parents in a nursing home. Conversely, adult children avoid asking their parents for support beyond paying for their education.

Another significant difference among groups is the way in which cultures define responsibilities and obligations according to gender roles. Groups differ profoundly in their expectations of motherhood and fatherhood as well as in their treatment of sons and daughters. Families evolve through the life cycle and encounter conflicts at different developmental phases. Marriage, child rearing, leaving home, and caring for the elderly demand changes in relationships that are inherently stressful, especially when ascribed cultural rules for dealing with these stages are challenged or cease to be functional. When conflict erupts, families usually attempt resolution by drawing on the strengths and legacies passed from one generation to the next.

Needless to say, it is difficult to share personal and clinical observations about our respective ethnic groups without generalizing. Thus, readers should understand that, among other variables, the following portraits of ethnic groups are affected by gender, generation, residence, education, socioeconomic status, and migration as well as by the life experience of the authors. We acknowledge that significant variations exist within groups and that ethnic values and practices are constantly evolving.

Clinicians need to remain open to what families tell us about themselves and take care to enter the therapeutic process without predetermined conclusions about families based merely on ethnic generalizations. Equally important is the fact that clinicians neither formulate theories nor conduct interventions in a vacuum. Our cultural lenses dictate our world view and what we consider "normal." It is also useful to have a point of departure in one's work that is larger than one's own limited experiences; hypotheses are simply starting points from which one proceeds to look for data that support or contradict one's initial notions. In the interests of offering that starting point for practitioners, this article addresses rules for relationships, common conflicts, resources and/or legacies that promote or hinder conflict resolution, and implications for assessment and intervention with African American, Hispanic, Irish, Asian Indian, and Jewish families.

AFRICAN AMERICAN FAMILIES

African traditions, the experience of slavery, assimilation into the American mainstream, the psychological scars of past and current discrimination, age, education, religion, and geographic origins allow for great heterogeneity within African American culture. However, survival issues based on interdependence and oppression due to racism are commonalities that transcend individual and group differences.

Despite conscious and consistent efforts by members of the dominant culture to erase all remnants of African culture from the memories and practices of African slaves and their descendants, a sense of "oneness," as exemplified in the practice of greeting one another as "sister" or "brother," is critical to understanding the dynamics of relationships among African Americans. A general assumption exists among African Americans that regardless of the educational or economic advantages of individuals, the legacy of slavery, racism, and oppression is a common bond.

Family relationships, more so than bank accounts, represent "wealth" and guarantee emotional and concrete support in the face of negative feedback from the larger society. The emotional significance of relationships is not determined solely by the immediacy of blood ties. In fact, "family" is an extended system of blood-related kin and persons informally adopted into this system (Hines & Boyd-Franklin, 1982; Boyd-Franklin, 1989). Extended-family systems tend to be large and constantly expanding as new individuals and their families are incorporated through marriage. Commonly, three or four generations live in proximity, sometimes residing in the same household.

Strong value is placed on loyalty and responsibility to others. This value is reinforced through the belief that everything one does in the public domain reflects on one's family and other African Americans. Similarly, African Americans often believe that one does not succeed just for oneself but for one's family and race as well. In essence, African Americans believe that "you are your brother's keeper."

Among African Americans, respect is shown to others because of their intrinsic worth and character, not for their status or what they have accumulated in material wealth. Personal accomplishments are considered the dual consequence of individual effort and, importantly, also due to the sacrifice of others. Success is to be acknowledged and celebrated but not overemphasized, as positive outcomes cannot be guaranteed despite one's efforts in a racist environment. Furthermore, even when success is achieved, it may be short lived. Intelligence and education without character and "common sense" have little value. Good character involves respect for those who helped one succeed and survive difficult circumstances. Family members are expected to stay connected and to reach out and assist others who are in need (McGoldrick, Garcia-Preto, Hines, & Lee, 1989).

The elderly are held in reverence. Older women, more than men, are called upon to impart wisdom as well as to provide functional support to younger family members. Older adults are testimony to the fact that one not only can survive but can transcend difficult circumstances as well. They serve as models for self-sacrifice, personal strength, and integrity. By example, they show that although suffering is inevitable, one can grow from hardship and adversity. Children and adults are expected to show verbal and nonverbal "respect" to the elderly. Titles such as Mr., Mrs., Aunt, and Uncle are used to convey respect, deriving from the slavery and post-slavery eras during which African American men and women, irrespective of their age, were treated and referred to as objects or children.

Children and adolescents may express their feelings and opinions but are not allowed to argue with adults after a final decision has been made. Although adults have the liberty to voice dissenting opinions to those who are older, younger adults are expected to acknowledge respectfully the older adult's opinion and perspective. To fail to do so shows disrespect for the life experience of the older person. Use of profanity in an intergenerational context is generally not acceptable.

Young adulthood for African Americans is a critical period during which poor decisions and impulsive behavior can have life-long consequences (Hines, 1989). The usual stressors on intergenerational relationships during this phase of the family life cycle can be both eased and complicated by the numerous adults who may be intensely concerned about a young adult's well-being. Young adults with few employment possibilities and who find it difficult to achieve adult status while living at home may move in with relatives until they become economically self-sufficient. They remain subject, however, to older family members' collective efforts to protect them from life hardships that might be avoided.

Some young African American adults fear failure and disappointing significant others. Others fear success as a result of internalizing the older generation's concerns about losing one's cultural connectedness. Some young adults are ambivalent about personal success because they are materially comfortable while significant others, especially parental figures, are struggling for basic survival. Conflicts may arise when younger adults believe that the advice of older adults is not appropriate to the context in which the young adult operates. Sometimes older adults may minimize the concerns and distress of younger people because they feel that such concerns are trivial compared with their difficult life experiences. Consequently, some young adults find it difficult to seek help within their families for fear of being perceived as weak; others are afraid that they will overwhelm family members who are already burdened by other life stresses. Young adults may be reluctant to pursue help from appropriate professionals in the work setting for fear of being negatively labeled as well as adversely affecting opportunities for other African Americans. The consequence of these scenarios is over- or underfunctioning, which may result in or exacerbate internal and intergenerational conflicts.

Similar intergenerational issues may surface in families with young children and adolescents. The role flexibility (exchange of responsibilities) characteristic of African American families allows adults to help children thrive in environments with many "mine fields" (Hines, 1990). The proverb "It takes a village to raise a child" works well as long as roles are clearly defined, rules are consistent, and ultimate authority is clearly established. However, boundaries may not be clearly delineated, which creates confusion. Intergenerational conflicts are most likely to arise as a result of a child's "disrespectful" behavior at home or school, poor academic functioning, and behaviors that may put the youth at risk of compromising his or her personal freedom. The primary concerns are that male adolescents will get into trouble with legal authorities and that female adolescents will act out sexually or, worse, become pregnant. Parents may resort to overfunctioning (i.e., become inflexible) and turn to relatives for help. Male adolescents from female-headed households are particularly inclined to rebel against the power and influence of their mothers and other females in positions of authority (Hines, 1990).

Although African Americans have the capacity to be openly expressive of their feelings, such expression may be held in check in an effort to minimize intergenerational conflicts. Such conflicts threaten unity and diminish energy needed to deal with everyday life. Conflict often occurs when individuals are perceived to have lost hope, self-respect, and/or self-responsibility; when they are perceived to be wallowing in sorrow, engaging in self-destructive behaviors, or pursuing individual interests without concern for significant others, particularly children and older adults.

Intergenerational conflicts may revolve around whether children are being taught traditional values basic to the survival of African American people. Parents who invest in providing material things and opportunities to their children that were not available to them while growing up may be perceived by other family members as "spoiling" their children. Conflicts are likely to focus on how to teach children survival skills without depriving them of the fruits of the previous generation's labor. . . .

American clients are uncomfortable in groups in which, as the sole African American participant, their problems might seem to be "exceptional" or different from everyone else's. Clients should be offered the opportunity to discuss such concerns, and alternatives should be made available. Young adults should also be encouraged to develop and use natural support groups within their work and social environments if they are struggling under the weight of unrealistic family- or self-imposed expectations as well as challenged by the inherent stress of working in a bicultural setting.

HISPANIC FAMILIES

The web of relationships that extends across generations in Hispanic families provides a support network sustained by rules of mutual obligation. These rules are perpetuated by patterns of caretaking that fulfill expectations of emotional, physical, and economic support for those who need it from those capable of providing it. Rules of respect also play an important role in preserving this intergenerational network of close personal relationships. Children, for example, learn to relate to others according to their age, sex, and social class. When the system works, that is, if sacrifices do not border on martyrdom, the support and emotional acceptance provided can be very healthy and nurturing as well as reassuring and validating.

The sense of responsibility and mutual obligation can be so ingrained among Hispanics that individuals with few resources run the risk of self-sacrifice. Women, in particular, are expected to assume caretaking roles in the family and tend to experience more pressure than do men to devote their lives to the welfare of others. Becoming martyrs gives them special status, in that family members often see their sacrifice as exemplary. However, the price they pay for "carrying this cross" is often too high (Garcia-Preto, 1990). This behavior is reinforced by the cultural concepts of *marianismo* and *hembrismo*, which contribute to the complexity of Hispanic gender roles.

Marianismo stems from the cult of the Virgin Mary, whereby women are considered morally superior to men and, therefore, capable of enduring the suffering inflicted by men (Stevens, 1973). *Hembrismo*, which literally means femaleness, has been described as a cultural revenge to *machismo* (Habach, 1972) and as a frustrated attempt to imitate a male. *Hembrismo*, within a historical context, shares common elements with the women's movement in the areas of social and political goals (Gomez, 1982). *Hembrismo*, according to Comas-Diaz (1989), connotes strength, perseverance, flexibility, and the ability to survive. However, she adds that it can also translate into a woman's attempt to fulfill her multiple-role expectations as a mother, wife, worker, daughter, and community member—in other words, the "superwoman" working a double shift at home and on the job. In therapy, many Hispanic women present symptoms related to *marianista* behavior at home and *hembrista* behavior at work (Comas-Diaz, 1989).

Men, on the other hand, are more likely to assume financial responsibility for elderly parents, younger siblings, and nephews and nieces. This behavior, too, is admired and respected. Grandparents and other elderly relatives, although not expected to contribute financially to the family, often do so indirectly by caring for grandchildren and thus enabling parents to work or go to school. In return for this assistance and by virtue of their being in need, it is expected that the elderly will be cared for by their adult children. If such expectations are not met, intergenerational conflicts are likely to occur throughout the family system.

A common source of intergenerational conflict in Hispanic families who enter therapy is the struggle between parents and children who have grown apart while trying to adapt to American culture. Traditionally, Hispanic children tend to have closer relationships with their mothers than with their fathers. Perhaps because women are responsible for holding the family together, they tend to develop very strong relationships with their children and other family members. This central position in the family system gives them a measure of power, which is reflected in their alliances with children against authoritarian fathers, who are perceived as lacking understanding with regard to emotional issues. Relationships between sons and mothers are close and dependent; it is not uncommon for a son to protect his mother against an abusive husband.

Mothers and daughters also have close relationships, but these are more reciprocal in nature. Mothers teach their daughters how to be good women who deserve the respect of others, especially males, and who will make good wives and mothers. Daughters usually care for their elderly parents, often taking them into their homes when they are widowed. Relationships between Hispanic women and their fathers vary according to family structure. In families in which fathers assume an authoritarian position, the father-daughter relationship may be marked by distance and conflict. While attempting to be protective, fathers may become unreasonable, unapproachable, and highly critical of their daughters' behavior and friends. On the other hand, in families in which men are more submissive and dependent on their wife to make decisions, fathers may develop special alliances with their daughters, who in turn may assume a nurturing role toward them.

When Hispanic families arrive in the United States, the children usually find it easier to learn English and adapt to the new culture than do parents. The parents, on the other hand, may find English too difficult to learn and the new culture unwelcoming and dangerous. They may react by taking refuge in the old culture, expecting their children to do the same. When this occurs, children typically rebel against their parents' rigidity by rejecting parental customs, which are viewed as inferior to the American way of life.

Children may become emotionally distanced from their parents, who often feel they have lost control. Parents usually react by imposing stricter rules; corporal punishment may be used. Commonly, parents will demand respect and obedience, cultural values that are traditionally seen as a solution to misbehavior. Parents may become very strict and overprotective of adolescents, especially if the family lives in a high-crime community where drugs are prevalent. Daughters, especially, may be overprotected because they are viewed as being more vulnerable than males in a society with loose sexual mores. Such patterns of overprotection are more characteristic of families who are isolated or alienated from support systems in the community and when extended-family members are not available (Garcia-Preto, 1982).

Children who are caught in the conflict of cultures and loyalties may develop a negative self-image, which can inhibit their chances for growth and accomplishment. Parents, then, may feel thwarted at every turn and consequently give up on their children. In therapy, it may be useful to see adolescents alone if they are unable to speak freely in front of their parents. Issues of respect and fear about their parents' reactions may inhibit adolescents from speaking about sex, drugs, incest, problems at school, or cultural conflicts at home and in the community. In such instances, obvious goals include helping adolescents define and share with their parents personal issues that affect their relationship in an effort to find compromises. Discussing a family's migratory history and acculturation process may help clarify conflicts over cultural values. The therapist can also encourage parents to redefine privileges and responsibilities and to discuss their genuine concern for the child. By encouraging parents to express their love, concern, and fear to their children, therapists help parents and children relate in a more positive manner (Garcia-Preto, 1982). . . .

As stated earlier, intergenerational conflict is often caused by the inability of one generation to provide care for another. Adult children who are unable to care for their elderly parents, especially if the parents are ill, may experience stress and guilt. Conflicts with siblings and other family members may result.

Practitioners need to encourage communication among family members in order to help them find ways to contribute to the care of elderly parents. Women who devote themselves to caring for elderly parents may express their stress and resentment through somatic complaints and/or depression. Therapists can help these women express their resentments openly as well as assist them in finding support from other family members or community resources.

Leaving the family system (e.g., through divorce or separation) is extremely risky for both men and women because it implies loss of control, support, and protection. For couples who are still adjusting to American culture, the loss of the family system can be devastating. For example, women usually depend on other women in the extended family for help with child-rearing and domestic tasks, because men are not expected to share these responsibilities. Without the help of their mother, mother-in-law, grandmothers, aunts, or sisters, Hispanic women may become overburdened and begin demanding assistance from their husband. The husband may, in turn, resent these demands and become argumentative and distant, perhaps turning to alcohol, gambling, or extramarital affairs. The extended family can provide a measure of control for aggression and violence by intervening in arguments and providing advice to couples. Helping couples make connections with relatives, friends, or community supports may be the therapist's most crucial task.

IRISH FAMILIES

Intergenerational relationships among the Irish are not generally characterized by intimacy. Unlike many other groups, such as African Americans, Italians, or Hispanics, who tend to view the extended family as a resource in times of trouble, the Irish tend to take the attitude that having a problem is bad enough, but if your family finds out, you have two problems: the problem and your embarrassment in front of your family. It is said of the Irish that they suffer alone. They do not like others to see them when they are in pain. It is not so much a fear of dependence, as with WASPs, but a sense of embarrassment and humiliation at not being able to keep up appearances. Intergenerational secrets are common. The Irish would often rather tell almost anything to a stranger than to a family member, but if they do share it with a family member it is usually told to someone of the same sex and generation as the teller. . . .

Within the family, intergenerational relationships throughout the life cycle are handled primarily by the mother. She cares for both the old and the young. She views caretaking as her responsibility, as does everyone else in the family. Her main supporters are her daughters, though she might also call on her sisters.

The Irish sense of duty is a wonderful resource. Parents want to "do the right thing" for their children; it is not a lack of care, but a lack of attention to detail that most often interferes with appropriate nurturing of their children. The Irish tend to focus more on their children's conformity to rules than on other aspects of their child's development, such as emotional expression, self-assertiveness, or creativity. Should a child be brought to the school principal for misbehavior, a traditional Irish mother's reaction to the child might be: "I don't want to hear your explanations or excuses. Just never let it happen that the principal has to contact me again." Traditionally, the Irish have believed that children should be seen and not heard. They should not bring outside notoriety to the family, especially for bad behavior. Less emphasis is placed on being a star student than on not standing out from the group for misbehavior. Irish parents tend to have a superficial sense of child psychology, hoping that keeping their children clean, out of trouble, and teaching them right from wrong will get them through. When children develop psychological symptoms, Irish parents are often mystified. When children act out, parents tend to blame outside influences, although privately they blame themselves.

During the child-rearing phase, the biggest problem in Irish families occurs if a child gets in trouble with outside authorities such as the school system. When the adults have problems at home during this phase, for example, if the father is an alcoholic, Irish children can be remarkably inventive in developing strategies to obey family rules of denial while appearing to function well. However, they may later pay a high price emotionally for having learned at an early age to suppress unacceptable feelings.

During the adolescent phase and the launching years, heavy drinking may become a major, often unidentified, problem that the parents—primarily the mother—do not know how to handle. It therefore may be ignored, often with disastrous consequences.

Irish fathers play a peripheral role in intergenerational family relationships, whereas Irish mothers are at the center. They are indomitable. But the stereotype of the "sainted Irish mother" is not totally positive (McGoldrick, 1991; Rudd, 1984; McGoldrick, 1982; Diner, 1983; McKenna, 1979; Scheper-Hughes, 1979); she can also be critical, distant, and lacking in affection, less concerned about nurturing her children than about control and discipline. She may worry about their dirty underwear lest they be in an accident and she be called in to claim the body. She can be sanctimonious, preoccupied with categories of right and wrong and about what the neighbors think, consciously withholding praise of her children for fear it will give them "a swelled head." Such attitudes and behaviors make sense in a culture with such a long history of foreign domination, in which Irish mothers sought control over "something" through whatever means were available to them and felt a need to keep their family in line to minimize the risk of members being singled out for further oppression.

Sons and daughters rarely voice resentment toward their mothers. To do so is to risk guilt and to undermine their admiration for her stoic self-sacrifice. For generations, Irish women have held rule in their families, including control of the family money. Children tend to speak of "my mother's house," dismissing the role of the father (Diner, 1983). Irish mothers often fail to recognize their own strength or ability to intimidate their children, whether through teasing, ridicule, a disapproving glance, or a quick hand. One Irish mother in therapy described her son's arrest for a drunken escapade as follows:

Joey's afraid of me. I know he is, because when he got arrested and I went down there to pick him up, the policeman expected when I walked in there that he'd see a big witch of a woman coming through the door, because Joey had said to him, "Just promise me one thing, just protect me from my mother." But I didn't do anything. When I went in there, I just gave him a smack across the face, because I didn't need that nonsense.

Implicit in her comment are ridicule for her son's fear of her and a bold assertion of her own righteousness.

Perhaps because of their history of oppression, the Irish tend to communicate indirectly, often believing that putting feelings into words only makes things worse. They can also be uncomfortable with physical affection (Rudd, 1984; McGoldrick, 1982; Barrabe & von Mering, 1953) and tend to relate to their children through fixed labels: "Bold Kathleen," "Poor Paddy," and "That Joey." Children are loved, but not intimately known (Rudd, 1984).

As a result of her need for ambiguous communication and ambivalence with regard to self-assertion, a mother may indirectly belittle her child for "putting himself ahead" while in the same breath chide him for not being more aggressive and achievement oriented. Irish mothers tend to dote on their sons, overprotecting them and drawing them into powerful bonds more intense than their marital tie. Conversely, Irish parents tend to underprotect their daughters, treating them like sisters and often not allowing them much of a childhood by raising them to be overresponsible and self-sufficient, just like the mothers (Byrne & McCarthy, 1986). This failure to protect daughters teaches them to repress personal needs and contributes to an ongoing fatalism, emotional repression, and stoicism in the next generation of women.

Irish women have little expectation of or interest in being taken care of by a man. Their hopes are articulated less often in romantic terms than in aspirations for self-sufficiency. They are often reluctant to give up their freedom and economic independence for marriage and family responsibilities.

What about Irish fathers and daughters? One pattern involves the "dutiful daughter," especially if the mother is absent, who becomes the caretaker for her father without much real intimacy in the relationship. In other families, the daughter may become "Daddy's girl," even his companion, who is sent to bring him home from the bar or chosen to work with him, especially if there is no son in the family. Generally, however, father-daughter relationships are distant, possibly because the father fears that closeness will be confused with trespass of sexual boundaries. Moreover, Irish families are not very good at differentiating among anger, sexuality, and intimacy. A father may maintain distance from his daughter, or perhaps be sarcastic and teasing, not because such behavior reflects his true feelings but because he is unsure how to approach her.

With sons a father may share sports, work, and jokes, although the teasing and ridicule that are so common in Irish parent-child relationships may be very painful to a son. Some Irish fathers remain silent, almost invisible, in the family. Another common pattern is the father who is jovial or silent, except when drinking, at which time he becomes a fearsome, intimidating, larger-than-life antagonist, who returns to his gentler self when sober with no acknowledgment of this transformation. Children are kept off guard in such relationships. They may be drawn to the humor and fun, yet terrified of the unpredictable and violent moods. In cultures with less dissociation of self from negative behaviors (such as among Italians or Puerto Ricans), children may fear a parent who drinks, but they will not be as mystified by parents' denial of an out-of-control situation.

Resentment over class differences may surface when Irish children marry. The Irish tend to measure others hierarchically as being "better than" or "inferior to" themselves. Thus, parents may criticize children for "marrying up" and putting on airs (which usually means marrying a WASP) or may criticize them for "marrying down." Both of these parental reactions are deeply rooted in tensions stemming from the Irish history of oppression by the British, which left the Irish with a deep sense of inferiority.

When Irish children reach their mid-20s or more, they may begin to resent the denial and emotional suppression of their childhood. Such resentments may be evident in their young-adult relationships with others. Irish communication patterns are generally characterized by a high degree of ambiguity and confusion. Because Irish parents often control their children via indirect communication, such as humor, teasing, sarcasm, and ridicule, outsiders may not understand why children become so frustrated dealing with their parents and feel a need to distance themselves from the family in order to feel "sane." The resentments that Irish children have buried since childhood often continue into adulthood without realization that resolution is possible.

Resentments and distancing may become more intense throughout the adults' life, especially if parents' subtle disapproval continues or if adult children assume caretaking responsibilities for their parents. Unlike other children—such as African American, Greek, Italian, or Jewish—who are freer to express their resentments, Irish children may be extremely sensitive to perceived slights, such as favors shown to siblings, or other imagined wrongs. They may never confront the parent or the sibling with their feelings, dutifully continuing their caretaking responsibilities while maintaining tense silence with regard to their emotional wounds.

As parents age, intimacy typically does not increase. The mother may maintain her matriarchal role within the family. She may be seen as intimidating and indomitable. She may be unaware of the hold she has on her family because inwardly she feels that hold slipping.

Although unmarried children may continue to be emotionally dependent on their parents (and outwardly deny this dependence), they have no strong sense of filial responsibility. For example, placing a parent in a nursing home when the time comes may be acceptable to both children and parents, who prefer to "suffer alone" and never become a burden to their children. . . .

ASIAN INDIAN FAMILIES

In the past 10 years, Asian Indian immigration to the United States has been opened to nonprofessional classes. Twenty years ago, families immigrating here were primarily of the professional class. Today, however, the influx of uneducated families settling into menial jobs has created many problems similar to those experienced by earlier groups of immigrants from other countries.

Despite the intersecting influences of caste, region, and religion, predictable intergenerational conflicts emerge among family members. Relationships within and across generations are influenced by beliefs in caste and karma. These beliefs are pervasive despite the diversity among Asian Indians in the "old country" and in the United States (Malyala, Kamaraju, & Ramana, 1984). However, the degree to which these beliefs affect adaptation to life in Western society is influenced by level of education and acculturation (Segal, 1991; Matsuoka, 1990). For example, an educated family living in this country for 10 to 20 years will adapt to Western values around education and socialization for their children. However, they frequently revert back to Indian values as the marriage of a child approaches.

The caste system is a stratified social system into which one is born as a result of one's fate or karma. Karma can be changed only through death and subsequent rebirth. It is believed that with each rebirth a person moves from a lower caste (pollution) to a higher caste (purity) until "nirvana" (eternal afterlife) is achieved. These beliefs perpetuate values of passivity and tolerance, suffering and sacrifice. The more accepting one is of one's karma (passivity), the greater assurance one has of achieving spiritual afterlife (tolerance).

Hindu culture portrays women in paradoxical positions. Women are sacred (pure) in the afterlife yet they are devalued (polluted) in present life (Bumiller, 1990; Almeida, 1990; Wadley, 1977). Although men share power with women in the scriptures, in present life the male-centered family system exerts enormous social and economic power over women and children. With its concepts of "purity" and "pollution," the caste system shapes both intragenerational and intergenerational relationships. Prejudices related to lighter vs. darker shades of skin color are deeply embedded within the culture, with light skin symbolizing "purity" and dark skin symbolizing "pollution." These "ideals" are carried into the acculturation process in that Asian Indian immigrants find it easier to connect with white Americans than with non-whites, including other Asians. Asian Indian experiences of racism are generally not talked about, as though acknowledgment of racism might connect them with others who are similarly discriminated against. Although work and educational opportunities are available to all, women and lower-caste men have fewer choices regarding marriage partners. Such contradictions are pervasive and are explained in terms of karma.

Karma focuses on past and future life space. Current life dilemmas are explained in terms of karma. For example, a wife who is mistreated by her in-laws might say, "I must deserve this for something bad I did in a past life. If I endure my current life, I know I will be taken care of by God in a future life." Making choices to alter current life struggles is possible within this belief system. Sacrificial actions may alter one's current life and thus are meaningful. Fasting, praying, somatic complaints, head shaving, and suicide alter "karma" and move one toward a better life. In working with Asian Indian clients, therapists might suggest culturally appropriate constructions of less destructive "solutions" such as limited fasting, praying, meditating, or even haircutting.

Intergenerational patterns are embedded and negotiated within a collective consciousness. Relationships are other-directed rather than self-centered. Spirituality and simplicity are applauded, and family-centered decisions take priority over individual preferences. Within the family of origin, older men assume decision-making authority over all members of the family. Fathers are responsible for the education of their male children and for the care of their elderly parents. Emotional connectedness between sons and fathers, as well as among other extended family members, is not expected. However, intimacy between the son and mother is emphasized. Fathers are responsible for the dowry and marriage of their daughters; uncles or older male siblings take on this responsibility in the event of a father's death. Mothers expect their sons to control their wives with regard to money, work, and social activities. Older women gain status and power through the mother-in-law role. Younger women are socialized by their mothers and sisters to idealize the role of "mother-in-law." The cultural system (i.e., caste and karma with their values of tolerance and passivity) supported by the male-family lineage (endorsing tolerance and passivity) enables this process. In this system, women realize power by exerting control over women of lesser status. Caretaking of grandchildren and food preparation are used as "covert" means of gaining power in family relations. A mother-in-law, in charge of preparing food while the daughter-in-law works, might cook only according to her son's desires. Young children are generally overprotected by grandparents, while being taught to respect their elders. Children are taught to avoid direct eye contact with their elders and to avoid disagreeing with them. Older sisters-in-law assume a degree of power over younger women entering into the male-centered family system.

Education of male children is considered necessary for the economic needs of the entire family, whereas education for female children increases their marketability as brides. Aging parents are cared for within the family by adult married male children and, in rare instances, by female children who have families of their own.

Child rearing is a shared responsibility of the women in the male-extended-family system. These women can be aunts or friends of the family from India who visit for extended periods during the family's initial years of child rearing. When young mothers are forced to parent without this extended-kinship system, children are more at risk, because family conflicts tend to be expressed in the mother-child dyad rather than in the marital dyad.

Power in Western marriages is directly connected to the economic resources of each partner. This notion of power and relationships is less applicable to Asian Indian families, because a couple's economic resources are distributed across the extended male-oriented family system (Conklin, 1988). Unlike the white, American, middle-class nuclear family, in which marriage stands at the center of the family system, men and their mothers are at the center of the Asian Indian family system. The mother-son tie is prominent in both Hindu and Christian Asian Indian families (Almeida, 1990; de Souza, 1975). Sons provide their mothers and grandmothers with the ultimate pride and status afforded women in "this" life (Issmer, 1989). Young wives do not participate in this system of power, even when they contribute economically to the family unit (Chakrabortty, 1978). Marriage is complicated by overarching problems of caste, dowry, and expensive weddings.

Arranged marriages are the norm in the adopted country as well as in India. When the family chooses to emphasize college education over marriage, or if the child asserts his or her personal rights over the parents' choice of mates or chooses career and money over marriage, major conflicts within the family system arise. Parents expect daughters to be married between 18 and 22 years of age and sons between the ages of 22 and 26. When this does not occur, parents lack a clear role in their adult child's life. The process of differentiation of self from family, which has various implications for Asian Indians as a result of their cultural norms, is particularly problematic at this stage. Despite their efforts to create choices for their sons and daughters, cultural expectations for "arranged" marriages take precedence.

> An Asian Indian family entered therapy because of their 21-year-old daughter's difficulty completing her last semester of college. They expressed their helplessness in dealing with her launching. The mother said, "Shiva is very immature and irresponsible; it worries me that she does not know the meaning of money or getting a job, and yet she is about to graduate. I think of her as a selfish brat sometimes. She says she is not ready to think about marriage, and I believe it sometimes, but all of our friends and relatives think I am being neglectful in my responsibility to find her a nice man. If she waits until she is 30, then by the time she is 40, when she should be taking care of us, she and her husband will still have the responsibility of young children. I might be too old to be the kind of grandparent I have to be. Of course, I know that if Shiva gets married, then I will be pushing her to give me grandchildren, so I suppose I have to trust that my husband's and my choice to allow her to be independent will turn out OK."

An Asian Indian woman's status within the family is determined by the gender order of her children. First-born males are preferred. First-born females are vulnerable to conflict between the mother and her in-laws and are perceived as diminishing the father's status with the deities. However, a second-born male child helps normalize the situation. A second-born female child following a first-born female child is at risk for premature death through malnutrition and abuse, even in the United States, if the family does not have sufficient social and economic support. Male children offer the family greater economic support and thereby afford better marital opportunities for the female children in the family. A woman's relationship with her mother-in-law may become strained and the marriage may suffer if she is infertile and thus does not meet the family's role expectations. Sons who are unable to support the elderly family members, widowed mothers, or unmarried sisters extort large dowries from their brides as solutions to this intergenerational legacy (Ramu, 1987).

These intergenerational patterns often conflict with Asian Indian acculturation (Słuzki, 1979). Although most Asian Indians accommodate to the work ethic and value of education, they maintain strong cultural ties to Asian Indian concepts of marriage, child rearing, parenting, and the sharing and allocation of economic resources.

Western values of privacy and individualism conflict with Indian values of collectivity and family-centerdness. In the context of separation, less acculturated families view adolescents' and young adults' struggles with independence as disrespect. When Asian Indians speak of *respect*, they mean *obedience* to the family and culture. Similarly, it is difficult for these family members to understand that the Western ideal of love includes separation and independence from the family of origin. Consequently, the Asian Indian concept of love includes control (Mukherjee, 1991). . . .

JEWISH FAMILIES

Judaism has the unusual distinction of being both a religion and an ethnic identity (Farber, Mindel, & Lazerwitz, 1988). Jews, who have a long tradition of intellectual debate and dialogue, carry on a never-ending discussion about who is a Jew and what it means to be a Jew. This debate has been engendered in part by the Jewish history of exclusion, discrimination, and wandering, culminating in the Holocaust and the founding of Israel. As waves of Jewish immigrants entered the United States, including early settlers from Germany who were relatively wealthy, the poor and less assimilated Eastern Europeans before and after World War I, Holocaust survivors, and, most recently, Russian and Israeli Jews, the question of essential Jewishness has continued to be debated—a legacy that has led to sensitivity over issues of discrimination and a sense of being "other." Although "Jewishness" may not be apparent to the outsider, most Jews are sensitive to interactions that might be perceived as anti-Semitic and thus may adopt a defensive posture that seems inexplicable to non-Jews.

Jews in the United States have been both fearful of and fascinated by assimilation into the mainstream culture (Herz & Rosen, 1982). Many families are overwhelmingly concerned that family members marry within the faith, or, if members marry outside the faith, that they maintain their Jewish traditions. A primary concern for many parents who move to a new community is whether their children will have other Jewish children with whom to play and date. The issue is further complicated by the diversity of Jewish religious practice; acceptable "Jewishness" in one family may be considered "too assimilated" in another.

Families often enter treatment to deal with conflicting feelings with regard to intermarriage, which may be perceived as destroying the integrity of the family and the faith. Generally, the families' most immediate concerns revolve around who, if anyone, will be expected to convert, who will perform the wedding, and how the grandchildren will be raised. Intermarriage is often felt to be a failure on the part of the parents, who, somehow, should have prevented this from happening. Such feelings exist even in families that are "culturally" rather than religiously observant Jews and are not affiliated with a synagogue.

When intermarriage is an issue, it is important that therapists attempt to gather concerned family members together. The parent or grandparent who is most upset may be difficult to engage. Because Jews traditionally have had a high regard for discourse and the transmission of cultural tradition and history, it can be helpful to review family history and to engage the family in searching for other families for whom intermarriage did not result in leaving the faith. Jewish families respond well to information and the sharing of stories; thus, referrals to a support group and/or interfaith classes run by Reform synagogues can be effective.

Regardless of geographic distance among family members, maintaining close family ties is important to Jewish families. It is important that the therapist identify family members who are critical to the treatment process but who are not immediately available. Soliciting these persons' involvement as consultants (through inclusion in family sessions, a joint phone call, or a letter) can help promote change.

Jewish families' focus on children, particularly their education and nurturing, can be a mixed blessing. Children are expected to be a source of pride and pleasure for parents and grandparents. However, children may find it difficult to be the focus of so much attention, with so many people having an expressed point of view. Young people may find it difficult to operate independently in their own interests (Farber et al., 1988). Separation and individuation are difficult to achieve if the family has rigid definitions of acceptable and successful behaviors. Young Jewish men and women often enter treatment because they are having difficulty dealing with enmeshment issues. Parents may perceive themselves as being generous and supportive and feel hurt by their children's efforts to become more independent. Reframing and relabeling their adult children's need to separate as "successful" and productive behavior can be an effective treatment approach.

The changing mores of late 20th century American life have been stressful for Jewish families. Traditionally, Jewish women stayed home, complying with the dictum to "be fruitful and multiply." Jewish law has rigidly defined rules for men's and women's behavior, with women having a minor function in religious ritual. Such traditions are less rigidly observed in Reform and Conservative congregations, where women now can be ordained as rabbis and participate in religious ritual. Despite the fact that many Jewish laws concerning gender roles are neglected in all but Orthodox families, these laws still have a subtle influence on role definition and expectations.

In Jewish families, women have traditionally held power at home while the husband faced the work world. Jewish mothers have been responsible for maintaining traditions and culture. However, because many Jewish women were employed outside the home during the Great Depression in the 1930s, many families remember grandmothers or other female relatives who worked out of necessity. Their daughters were primarily homemakers, and their granddaughters now expect themselves to be "supermoms" (Hyman, 1991). The dilemma faced by all three generations has been how to reconcile social expectations with cultural expectations. Women who saw their mothers helping support the family during the Depression came to value their homemaker role. The granddaughters have aspired to raise their family while participating in the educational and professional world. Issues faced by American women in the 1980s and 1990s have been especially complicated for Jewish women due to the emphasis Jewish culture places on education, social consciousness, and tradition. In such situations, the grandmother may serve as a role model for both working and maintaining a family.

Significant shifts in the role of the Jewish husband/father have also occurred. Jewish men have experienced discrimination and violence in the community. Traditionally, their home has been the place where they achieve respect and authority. Because both spouses may work, the father may be called upon or may wish to be a more active parent. But when he does take an active role, he risks the scorn of his own parents, who see him in an unconventional role. The extended family may not be supportive of these changes.

Religion is another source of intergenerational conflict. The majority of Jews in the United States are affiliated with Reform congregations, which do not follow many of the commandments that Orthodox and Conservative Jews follow. Intergenerational conflict may arise over the perceived religious laxity or conservatism of family members. Parents may be disappointed if their child chooses not to be affiliated with a synagogue and not to have a bar mitzvah for their grandson or a bas mitzvah for their granddaughter.

Conversely, some young people have become more observant of the Jewish faith than their families, perhaps joining an Orthodox congregation and living a life-style that is foreign to their families (keeping a kosher home, not traveling on the Sabbath, not practicing birth control). Conflicts in some families may occur if younger family members emigrate to Israel, thus separating parents from their children and grandchildren. Families may enter treatment to deal with feelings of loss and may need help in understanding that their needs are acceptable even if they differ from those of their parents.

Jewish families tend to seek expert opinions and may ask a therapist many questions about professional degrees and competence. Although such inquiries may make practitioners feel uncomfortable and challenged, they may help clients feel more comfortable in therapy. Directing Jewish families to appropriate reading materials about their problems can be helpful, because many Jewish persons place value on being well-informed. Referrals to self-help groups can also be helpful.

Jews are avid consumers of psychotherapy, in part as a result of their comfort with discourse, their search for solutions, and expectation that family life should follow predefined rules (Herz & Rosen, 1982). However, extensive analysis does not always lead to resolution of problems. . . . Families may need to be reminded that the goal of therapy is not to tell a good story or to be "right" in the eyes of the therapist, but to resolve the conflict or assuage the pain that brought the family to therapy.

REFERENCES

Almeida, R. V. (1990). Asian Indian mothers, *Journal of Feminist Family Therapy*, 2(2), 33–39.

Barrabe, P., & von Mering, O. (1953). Ethnic variations in mental stress in families with psychotic children. *Social Problems, 1*, 48–53.

Boyd-Franklin, N. (1989). *Black families in therapy*. New York: Guilford.

Bumiller, E. (1990). *May you be the mother of a hundred sons: A journey among the women of India*. New York: Random House.

Byrne, N., & McCarthy, I. (1986, September 15). *Irish women*. Family Therapy Training Program Conference, Robert Wood Johnson Medical School,

Piscataway, NJ.

Chakrabortty, K. (1978). *The conflicting worlds of working mothers.* Calcutta, India: Progressive Publishers.

Comas-Diaz, L. (1989). Culturally relevant issues for Hispanics. In V. R. Koslow & E. Salett (Eds.), *Crossing cultures in mental health.* Washington, DC: Society for International Education, Training and Research.

Conklin, G. H. (1988). The influence of economic development and patterns of conjugal power and extended family residence in India. *Journal of comparative family studies, 19,* 187–205.

de Souza, A. (1975). *Women in contemporary India.* New Delhi, India: Manohar.

Diner, H. R. (1983). *Erin's daughters in America.* Baltimore, MD: Johns Hopkins University Press.

Farber, B., Mindel, C. H., & Lazerwitz, B. (1988). In C. H. Mindel & R. W. Habenstein (Eds.), *Ethnic families in America: Patterns and variations.* New York: Elsevier.

Garcia-Preto, N. (1982). Puerto Rican families. In M. McGoldrick, J. K. Pearce, & J. Giordano (Eds.), *Ethnicity and family therapy.* New York: Guilford.

Garcia-Preto, N. (1990). Hispanic mothers. *Journal of feminist family therapy, 2* (2), 15–21.

Gomez, A. G. (1982). Puerto Rican Americans. In A. Gaw (Ed.), *Cross cultural psychiatry* (pp. 109–136). Boston: John Wright.

Habach, E. (1972). Ni machismo, ni hembriso. In *Coleccion: Protesta.* Caracas, Venezuela: Publicaciones EPLA.

Herz, F. M., & Rosen, E. J. (1982). Jewish families. In M. McGoldrick, J. K. Pearce, & J. Giordano (Eds.), *Ethnicity and family therapy.* New York: Guilford.

Hines, P. (1989). The family life cycle of poor black families. In B. Carter & M. McGoldrick (Eds.), *The changing family life cycle: A framework for family therapy* (2nd ed.). New York: Gardner Press.

Hines, P. (1990). African American mothers. *Journal of Feminist Family Therapy, 2*(2), 23–32.

Hines, P., & Boyd-Franklin, N. (1982). Black families. In M. McGoldrick, J. K. Pearce, & J. Giordano (Eds.), *Ethnicity and family therapy.* New York: Guilford.

Hyman, P. (1991). Gender and the immigrant Jewish experience, J. R. Baskin (Ed.), *Jewish women in historical perspective.* Detroit, MI: Wayne State University Press.

Issmer, S. D. (1989). The special function of out-of-home care in India, *Child Welfare, 68,* 228–232.

Malyala, S., Kamaraju, S., & Ramana, K. V. (1984). Untouchability—need for a new approach. *Indian Journal of Social Work, 45,* 361–369.

Matsuoka, J. K. (1990). Differential acculturation among Vietnamese refugees. *Social Work, 35,* 341–345.

McGoldrick, M. (1982). Irish Americans. In M. McGoldrick, J. K. Pearce, & J. Giordano (Eds.), *Ethnicity and family therapy.* New York: Guilford.

McGoldrick, M. (1991). Irish mothers. *Journal of Feminist Family Therapy. 2*(2), 3–8.

McGoldrick, M., Garcia-Preto, N., Hines, P., & Lee, E. (1989). Ethnicity and women. In M. McGoldrick, C. Anderson, & F. Walsh (Eds.), *Women in families,* New York: W. W. Norton.

McGoldrick, M., Garcia-Preto, N., Hines, P., & Lee, E. (1991). Ethnicity and family therapy. In A. Gurman & D. Kniskern (Eds.), *The handbook of family therapy* (2nd ed.) (pp. 546–582). New York: Guilford.

McKenna, A. (1979). Attitudes of Irish mothers to child rearing. *Journal of Comparative Family Studies, 10,* 227–251.

Mukherjee, B. (1991). *Jasmine.* New York: Fawcett Crest.

Ramu, G. N. (1987). Indian husbands: Their role perceptions and performance in single- and dual-earner families. *Journal of Marriage and the Family, 49,* 903–915.

Rudd, J. M. (1984). *Irish American families: The mother-child dyad.* Thesis, Smith College School of Social Work.

Scheper-Hughs, N. (1979). *Saints, scholars, and schizophrenics.* Berkeley, CA: University of California Press.

Segal, U. A. (1991). Cultural variables in Asian Indian families. *Families in Society, 72,* 233–241.

Sluzki, C. (1979). Migration and family conflict. *Family Process, 18,* 379–390.

Stevens, E. (1973). Machismo and marianismo. *Transaction Society, 10*(6), 57–63.

Wadley, S. (1977). Women and the Hindu tradition, *Journal of Women in Culture and Society, 3*(1), 113–128.

R E A D I N G

27

Reinventing the Family

Laura Benkov

There is a certain distortion that occurs when we look back at the past through the lens of the present. When what once seemed impossible has become reality, it is easy to forget the groping in the dark along an untrodden and sometimes treacherous path. It was with this in mind that in March 1988 I read the clipping a friend had sent me from the *Hartford Advocate.* Underneath the headline "The Lesbian Baby Boom," it said "Even Geraldo's covered it—but the women who

---

"Choosing Children" from *Reinventing the Family: Lesbian and Gay Parents.* Laura Benkov, Ph.D. New York: Crown Trade Paperbacks. 1994.

are doing it say it's no big deal." Almost a decade had passed since I first dared to ask myself if I, a lesbian, could choose to have children. Now as I read the words "No big deal" I flashed back to those sleepless nights clouded with confusion, shame, trepidation, grief, and longing.

One's perspective on the lesbian baby boom is clearly a matter of whom you talk to. When I finally broke through my isolation and began to speak to lesbians who had chosen to raise children, some— like the women described in the *Hartford Advocate*—told me they had never viewed their desire for parenthood as incompatible with their lesbianism. Andrea, a mother of two, said, "I always knew that I was going to be a mother, and being a lesbian never felt like I was making a choice not to have children. That probably had a lot to do with the fact that I came out during the seventies, amid a sense of all sorts of opportunities for women." Yet Andrea's ease with her status as lesbian mother was only one story. There were many other lesbians who had come to be mothers only after significant personal struggle. It is no wonder that I found myself drawn to their descriptions of arduous journeys. Susan lived years of ambivalence about her sexuality, not because she was uncertain of whom she loved but because she believed that choosing a woman meant giving up her lifelong dream of being a parent. Esther talked of being suddenly overcome by grief on an otherwise ordinary evening as she watched her lover washing her hair, when she recognized for the first time a yearning she could not imagine would ever come to fruition: to raise a child with this person she loved so deeply.

If we were indeed in the midst of a lesbian baby boom, then it *was* a big deal, for it was a painful and often lonely journey past grief that had brought us here.

Somewhere along the way these lesbians stopped assuming they couldn't be parents and began figuring out how to bring children into their lives. As I listened to their tales of transformation, each marked by a unique moment of revelation, the "boom" seemed the social equivalent of spontaneous combustion. So many lesbians struggled to become parents at precisely the same historical moment, yet each experienced herself as unique and alone. Of course, no one was as alone as she might have felt, and the movement certainly hadn't appeared out of the blue. Many social forces had laid the groundwork for its emergence.

As women influenced by second-wave feminism questioned their roles in the traditional family, they discovered possibility where before there had been only closed doors. Raising children without being married emerged as a potentially positive decision, not an unwanted circumstance. It is no accident that the rise of lesbian parenting has coincided with the burgeoning of single heterosexual women choosing to have children. The idea that women could shape their intimate lives according to their own standards and values rather than conform to constricting social norms was powerful in its own right. But the feminist movement was significant beyond the realm of ideas. On a very practical level, women's fight for control over their reproductive capacities created a context in which the choice to bear a child was as significantly opened up as the choice not to bear one; abortion rights and access to reproductive technology such as donor insemination are flip sides of the same coin.

The gay rights movement also contributed greatly to the parenting boom, enabling people to take a less fearful, more assertive stance toward society and yielding more visible communities, with the support and social dialogue that implies. From that supportive base, many began to define the kinds of lives they wanted to live, and to pursue their wish to be parents.

Perhaps most significant of all to what has become known in some circles as the choosing children movement, were the lesbian and gay parents who'd come out of heterosexual marriages. They had stepped out of the shadows, transforming the notion of lesbian and gay parents from a contradiction in terms to a visible reality that society had to contend with.

The fact that in our society women tend more than men to be intensely involved with raising children was reflected in the choosing children movement, just as it had been in the battles of parents coming out of heterosexual marriages. During the late 1970s, the first signs of lesbians choosing to have children were evident. By the mid-1980s, the trend had expanded from its initial West Coast and urban-center origins to throughout the nation. It was not until the late 1980s that a similar movement, smaller in scope, emerged among gay men. Though gay men's efforts overlap in some ways with lesbian endeavors, they are also distinctive. Often societal taboos against homosexuals more strongly burden gay men. And homosexuality aside, the notion of men as primary nurturing parental figures is ill defined in our culture. Many gay men seeking to become fathers, and perhaps to raise children without significant female input, feel out of place simply by virtue of their gender.

Initially, gay men participated in the lesbian baby boom as fathers sought by lesbians who chose to bear children. The advent of AIDS profoundly curtailed the move toward joint parenting arrangements. But in many communities it also brought gay men and lesbians together; and in more recent years, with growing consciousness about HIV prevention and testing available, joint parenting arrangements seem to be on the rise again.

Taking on secondary parenting roles in families headed by lesbians does suit some gay men, but others want, as do their lesbian counterparts, to have a more intensive, primary parental relationship. Increasingly, gay men are choosing to become parents through adoption, surrogacy, or joint parenting arrangements.

Within a decade, the unimaginable became commonplace. This remarkable shift occurred against a backdrop of skepticism and hostility. Society remained fixed on the question of whether homosexuals should be allowed to raise children, even as they were becoming parents in record numbers. The fierce debates that began in the early 1970s only continued as openly gay men and women chose parenthood. By the mid-1980s, a multitude of new controversies clamored for attention. Lesbian and gay parents had pushed Americans to look more closely than ever before at a deceptively simple question: What is a family? If the family is not defined by heterosexual procreative union, then what indeed is it? Perhaps it was the fear of this very question that underlay the hostility toward lesbian and gay parents to begin with. If the capacity to have and raise children does not distinguish heterosexuals from homosexuals, then what does?

In a recent *New York Times* book review, Margaret O'Brien Steinfels posed the following question: Does a married heterosexual couple's "capacity to have children [represent] a differentiating quality in heterosexual relationships?" According to Steinfels:

> Our legislatures and our religious faiths may come up with new ways to regulate or recognize erotically bound relationships beyond the traditional form of marriage: the state may devise practical solutions to problems like insurance and shared property, and religious bodies may try to encourage lasting and exclusive intimacy in a monogamous setting. Nonetheless society has a legitimate interest in privileging those heterosexual unions that are oriented toward the generation and rearing of children. That, at any rate, is the widely held conviction that remains to be debated. . . ."

Steinfels's suggestion that heterosexual unions are uniquely bound to childrearing rings false at this historical moment. Heterosexual procreation is only one of many means of family making. This is underscored not only by the fact that lesbian and gay unions can include childrearing but also because heterosexual unions often do not. Many heterosexual couples choose not to raise children, and many others, despite their heterosexuality, cannot procreate. Divorce, adoption, and reproductive technology mean that children often aren't raised by their birth parents, and likewise many parents aren't genetically connected to their kids. Steinfels's query embodies a myth our society clings to despite its distance from reality: that heterosexual unions, by virtue of their potential link to procreation, are somehow necessary to the survival of the species and therefore morally superior. Lesbians and gay men choosing to parent are not unique in challenging this myth, but they do so most explicitly, often sparking heated backlash.

During his 1992 campaign for reelection, George Bush said that "children should have the benefit of being born into a family with a mother and a father," thus citing the number and gender of parents as a pivotal aspect of optimal family life and implicitly privileging biological connection between parents and children by the phrase "born into." In short, he held up as the ideal the traditional family, characterized by heterosexual procreative unions and legal sanction.

Eight-year-old Danielle, the daughter of lesbian and gay parents, vehemently disagreed. "I have two moms and two dads," she said. "A family is people who all love each other, care for each other, help out and understand each other."

In defining the ideal family, Bush emphasized structural characteristics while Danielle, in contrast, highlighted emotions and relationships. Their disagreement aptly reflects this moment in American society: the tension between idealization of the traditional family and the reality of families that don't fit that mold is strongly emerging as a key issue of our times. As lesbians and gay men choose to raise children, the many different kinds of families they create reveal the inadequacy of a definition of family that rests on one particular structure. Increasingly, our society must heed Danielle's idea that family is defined by the quality of relationships, which can exist in many forms.

DONOR INSEMINATION: A MIMICRY OF PROCREATIVE UNION

In 1884, according to one of the earliest accounts of donor insemination in America, a woman lay unconscious on an examining table while, without her knowledge much less her consent, a doctor inseminated her with sperm from the "handsomest medical student" in his class. It was only after the insemination that the doctor informed the woman's infertile husband, who, pleased by the news, asked that his wife never be told what had occurred. The insemination resulted in the birth of a baby boy, who, presumably along with his mother, wasn't informed of the circumstances of his conception. A little over a century later, though women who are inseminated are neither unconscious nor uninformed, much of this early account remains salient. Donor insemination has evolved as a medically controlled practice, largely restricted to infertile heterosexual couples and shrouded in secrecy. Where then do lesbians fit in?

In the beginning of its use in this country, donor insemination was seen solely as a solution to infertility among married heterosexual couples. As such, donor insemination practices were structured to produce families that mimicked in every way possible the traditional heterosexual family. Both medical practitioners and the law geared donor insemination toward creating families that looked like, and had the legal status of, a family consisting of a married man and woman and their biological offspring.

This attempt to mimic the traditional heterosexual family included an effort to hide the very fact that donor insemination was used. The appearance of a biological connection was painstakingly constructed by matching the donor's physical traits with the husband's. By and large, the fact that a child had been conceived through donor insemination was rarely disclosed within families and was barely discussed in the larger cultural arena. In one major text of the 1960s, a doctor noted that one of the advantages of donor insemination, as compared to adoption, was that its use need never be revealed. He further suggested that screening criteria for couples receiving donor insemination include an assessment of how well they could keep a secret. Now, thirty years later, donor characteristics are still most often matched to that of the husband and secrecy continues.

The effort to hide the use of donor insemination parallels past approaches to adoption. There, too, great pains were taken to match the physical characteristics of children with those of their adoptive parents, and adoption was held as a secret around which much anxiety revolved. More recently, adoption practices have shifted: there is much less emphasis on matching physical characteristics, and experts encourage parents to speak openly about adoption, with the idea that talking to children about their origins from an early age is key to their overall well-being. Unlike earlier practices, this way values honesty in family life over the appearance of a biological family unit. Along with more honesty within adoptive families has come more open discussion of adoption in society. While much thinking about adoption continues to reflect a cultural bias that elevates biological families over all others, adoption practices have begun to move beyond this ideology by coming out of the closet. In contrast, the secrecy surrounding donor insemination points up the continuing emphasis on the appearance of a biological family unit.

The painstaking attention to appearance and the secrecy surrounding donor insemination stem from an insidious ideology: heterosexual procreation is the ideal basis of a family, one which if not achieved in actuality should at least be aspired to in appearance. With this as an undercurrent, donor insemination is characterized by a contradictory view of genetics. On the one hand, the practice distinguishes genetic and social parent roles, relegating genetics to an inconsequential position by severing all ties between donors and their offspring, and by recognizing those who take on the social role of parenthood as fathers of those children. On the other hand, hiding the fact that this process has occurred reveals an almost superstitious belief in the power of genetics. The implication is that biological connection is such a crucial aspect of parenting that its absence is shameful and should be hidden. The social role of a nonbiological parent is not highly valued in its own right, and instead must be bolstered by the illusion of a genetic connection. In this pervasive view, a "real" parent is the biological parent. If you have to, donor insemination is okay to do, but it's not okay to talk about.

THE LEGAL CONSTRUCTIONS OF FAMILY IN DONOR INSEMINATION PRACTICES

As with the secrecy and matching practices, the laws surrounding donor insemination reinforce efforts to make these families look like the standard nuclear model. Children conceived through donor insemination in the context of a heterosexual marriage are deemed the legal children of the recipient and her husband. Donors, on the other hand, waive all parental rights and responsibilities. The complex reality of such families—that there are both a biological and a social father involved—is set aside in favor of a simpler one. Severing the donor tie and sanctioning the husband's parental relationship serve the purpose of delineating one—and only one—father.

As donor insemination was more widely practiced in this country, legal parameters developed that, like the practices themselves, value the traditional family over all others. Among the first legal questions posed about donor insemination was whether it constituted adultery and, along with that, whether the child so conceived was "illegitimate." As the courts decided these initial cases they exhibited a strong conviction that children need to be "legitimate"— that is, to have fathers. From this premise the law constructed the husbands of inseminated women as the legal fathers of the resulting children. Father status thus hinged on marriage— that is, children were considered to be the "issue of the marriage." This was automatic, with no mediating process such as adoption needed to complete the arrangement. Initially these parameters were outlined only when disputes arose, but as the use of donor insemination grew more widespread, legislation was enacted that explicitly delineated what the courts had implicitly held all along: families that, in fact, were not created through the procreative union of a married heterosexual couple were given the legal status of this traditional unit. The state threw a safety net around the families created through donor insemination when, and only when, those families were headed by married heterosexual couples. On a state-by-state basis, the law carved out a distinction between donors and fathers: donors, in surrendering their sperm to doctors, waived parental rights and responsibilities, while the men married to inseminating women took on the legal rights and responsibilities of father-hood.

Significantly, in many states, the donors' lack of parental status hinges on medical mediation. That is, donors who directly give sperm to women can be, and often are, legally considered parents. Thus, not only is heterosexuality a prerequisite to the legal delineation of families constituted through donor insemination but medical control of the process is built into the law. People creating families through donor insemination do so most safely—that is, with least threat to their integrity as a family unit—if they utilize medical help.

LESBIANS AND SINGLE WOMEN SEEK DONOR INSEMINATION

The extent to which donor insemination practices emphasize the appearance of a procreative heterosexual union has, of course, great implications for lesbians and unmarried heterosexual women—most especially with respect to access to the technology. In conceiving through donor insemination, these women have little possibility of creating "pretend father" relationships that would obscure the fact that donor insemination has occurred. Indeed, when lesbians and single heterosexual women use donor insemination, they bring the practice out of the closet, revealing it to be a way that women can bear children in the absence of any relationship to men. It is no wonder that unmarried women, regardless of their sexual orientation, have been barred from using donor insemination, given the challenge their access poses to deeply held beliefs. To be inseminated as a single straight woman or lesbian is to boldly acknowledge that the resulting child has no father and that women can parent without input from men beyond the single contribution of genetic material. Such inseminations also highlight the separation between social and genetic parenting roles. This last aspect is especially obvious when lesbian couples use donor insemination: a nonbiological mother, clearly not a father, becomes the child's other parent.

For many years, the medical profession would not grant unmarried women access to insemination. A study done in 1979 found that over 90 percent of doctors wouldn't inseminate unmarried women. The doctors gave several reasons for their decision, the most central being their beliefs that lesbians and single women are unfit parents and that all children need fathers. However, some doctors refused to inseminate unmarried women, not out of deep personal conviction, but because they mistakenly believed that it was illegal. Though the statutory language about donor insemination often includes mention of marriage, it does not require it. A number of doctors also feared future wrong-ful-life suits, assuming that children raised by lesbians or single women would ultimately be unhappy enough to sue those responsible for their existence.

In the late 1970s, into the context of medically controlled, heterosexual-marriage–oriented donor insemination practices, came single heterosexual women and lesbians wanting to have children. The technology was an obvious choice for these women, not only in its most basic sense as a source of sperm, but also as a way of forming families whose integrity would be legally protected. Many want to establish families as couples or individuals without having to negotiate parenting responsibilities with an outside adult. Lesbians choosing to have children are much more vulnerable than married heterosexual couples to disputes about the boundaries of their families. Homophobia in the legal system renders them generally more subject to custody problems. Furthermore, since lesbians are unable to marry, and the female partners of inseminating women by and large can't adopt the resulting children, nonbiological lesbian mothers have no protected legal parent status. In this social context, creating families through known donors poses tremendous legal risks if those donors ever make custody claims. For lesbians, therefore, the legal protection of a family unit created through anonymous donor insemination is crucial.

But since access to the most legally safe source of insemination—that is, medically controlled— was highly restricted in the early days of the lesbian baby boom, many of the first lesbians to have children did so on the margins of mainstream donor insemination practices. Some women created their own alternatives. They inseminated themselves and, in an effort to protect the integrity of their families, created their own systems of anonymity, using go-betweens to conceal the identity of the sperm donors. However, this means of anonymity didn't provide firm protection against the possibility of custody disputes. In practice, the anonymity of donors would often be hard to maintain in small communities, and legally—especially in the absence of medical mediation—an identified donor would have parental rights. Matters became more complicated with the advent of AIDS, which made this way of inseminating a highly risky business. Ultimately, the self-created system gave way to another approach.

Some lesbians moved in a different direction, attempting to change the exclusionary practices themselves. During the late 1970s and early 1980s, as the feminist health-care movement grew and women fought to gain reproductive freedom, unmarried women made headway with demands for access to medically controlled donor insemination. The Sperm Bank of California in Oakland was established in 1982 by women running the Oakland Feminist Women's Health Center in response to the rising number of unmarried women seeking advice about insemination. The Sperm Bank of California led the way in establishing an insemination program that didn't screen out women on the basis of sexual orientation or marital status. Currently there are several such sperm banks throughout the country, and increasingly doctors are willing to inseminate unmarried women. However, access remains restricted in certain areas, and many insurance companies will cover insemination expenses only for married women.

During the last fifteen years, lesbians choosing to be parents have been charting a course through society that began on the margins and has increasingly moved into the mainstream, yielding social changes along the way.

In the realm of donor insemination, the reciprocal influence of heterosexual, nuclear family ideology and lesbian parenthood is strikingly apparent.

Lesbians choosing to have children shape their families along parameters stemming from the idealization of the traditional nuclear family, but by the same token they significantly transform many of those parameters. Donor insemination has shifted from a completely medically dominated, heterosexually defined technology to a practice that serves unmarried women, both straight and gay, and thereby yields many different sorts of families. As lesbians and single heterosexual women make more use of donor insemination, the practice itself is changing: by necessity, donor insemination is coming out of the closet. In our culture there are few stories of conception through donor insemination. Despite the fact that approximately a million Americans have been conceived this way, we continue to behave as though conception occurs only through heterosexual union. Ultimately, lesbians will write the stories of donor insemination, as they speak openly to their children about another way that people come into the world.

Choices: Known or Unknown Donors

As the doors to donor insemination opened for lesbians, a new era began. Having access to the technology is not synonymous with wanting to use it. Most lesbian mothers-to-be spend considerable time deciding whether to do so through a known or unknown donor. The complexity of this decision was a theme in many of my talks with lesbian mothers. In December 1991, as I was trying to sort through the many layers of this decision, both for myself and in relation to this book, I decided to visit the sperm bank in Oakland. I was not prepared for the intensity of my response. Barbara Raboy, the director, explained the process of freezing and storing sperm as I stared at hundreds upon hundreds of specimens neatly ordered in dozens of large metal tanks. It was about what I'd expected to see, except for the names scribbled in marker across the outside of the tanks and in smaller letters on the compartments within each tank. In front of me was the Artist tank, with Fuchsia, Chartreuse, and Amber as its subdivisions. Next to it was the Universe tank, with Mars, Pluto, and Jupiter; and behind that, the Landscape tank, with Rocky Mountain, Grand Canyon, and Yellowstone. Barbara noticed my puzzlement and explained: "We thought names would be more fun than a strict number and letter filing system, so the staff take turns naming the tanks and the subdivisions within them—it's how we locate any particular specimen—you know donor number 5003 is in the A row in the Fuschia section of the Artist tank." I was disappointed that the tank names had no more salient correspondence to the sperm inside, but the knowledge freed me from the mind-boggling task of imagining what distinguished a Rocky Mountain sperm specimen from a Jupiter one.

Instead, I began to imagine the people who dreamed up these names: huddled among the slides and test tubes, who had been most pleased by colors, who by mountain vistas or thoughts of intergalactic travel? As the namers became more real to me, so too did the men whose sperm was sequestered in the tiny vials. Several pages listed donor characteristics—no. 2017, Dutch descent, blue eyes, brown wavy hair, 6 feet tall, athletic student of computer technology.

If you wanted to know more about a particular donor, there were additional sheets—medical history and some personal information. But when all was said and done, the wish to know would remain just that. To see these vials was to glimpse the unknown. Throughout the country women were waiting—some whose male partners were infertile, some who were single, some who were lesbian. What they had in common was a strong yearning for children. This is what I was thinking as I looked at vial no. 2017. Then my ears rang with the voices of children, and I knew that I was standing in a place of beginnings, surrounded by mystery.

My initial puzzlement about the tank labels was a clue to my state of mind. I'd entered the sperm bank as I would a foreign country, imagining the tank names held some crucial meaning as unintelligible to me as a street sign in China. It struck me as odd that I could feel this way despite the fact that for years I'd thought about becoming a mother through this very process. Donor insemination was potentially a key element of my future, one that would involve my body and my most intimate relationships; yet simultaneously, I experienced it as a strange, foreign, and mystifying process.

I was not alone in this contradictory place. Though donor insemination has been practiced in this country for over a century, as a culture we have barely begun to grapple with the meaning it holds for us. Standing amid the vials of semen at the sperm bank, I could not help but be aware of the unique historical moment in which we are living. The very fact that I, a lesbian, could consider insemination is remarkable. Just ten years earlier I would have been shut out of any insemination program. But choices bring great complexity. Layers of thinking make up the decision about whether to become pregnant through a donor, known or unknown. How do lesbians aspiring to be mothers respond to society's constraints? What ways of forming a family will be safe in a culture that doesn't recognize our primary intimate connections? Because society as yet barely acknowledges donor insemination, an air of mysteriousness pervades the practice. How then do lesbians sort out the meanings donor insemination has for us and may have for our children?

From the language of "illegitimacy" and "bastards" to the tales of adopts searching for their birth parents, we are inundated with ideas that a father's absence is always problematic and knowledge of our genetic roots always essential. What do we accept of these stories? What do we reject? All of this is filtered through our most intensely personal experiences and histories. Ultimately it is from these many layers that lesbians create their families. Self-consciously exploring the meaning of family, each woman writes her own story. But no one writes it alone: each family is shaped by the culture it is embedded in, and in turn, the culture is changed by these emerging families.

The Role of the State

After twelve years together, Jasmine and Barbara agreed they were ready to raise children. Other than the gender of their partners, they envisioned family life in rather traditional terms. Their household would define the boundaries of their family; as a couple, they would jointly share parenting. Jasmine saw their decision to inseminate with an unknown donor as stemming clearly from the surrounding social context.

Jasmine explains: "We were very stuck on the method of conception—a known versus an unknown donor. One of the things that happened around the time we were thinking about this question was the foster-care issue in Massachusetts. We knew women who had adopted young children through foreign adoptions, and I listened to their descriptions of the home-study process. I felt very uncomfortable with the idea that somebody was judging you, and that you in a sense had to give them this little drama that 'I'm the one who's adopting and this woman is my roommate.'

"Not only did we feel angry about the injustice of it, but we also felt frustrated by the fact that as a couple we had so much more to offer in terms of the structure of our lives than this fallacy would indicate. When the foster-care uproar happened, we were very indignant about the idea that we could be judged that way. If we had gone along with the little drama of who we were supposed to be, it wouldn't have barred us from adopting, so it was really our decision that we wanted as few external people as possible out there judging us or making decisions about our lives.

"We didn't want that interference. That spilled over into the issue of the donor. We really needed to feel in control. The thing was, we were the parents and we wanted to make the decisions as the child grew up about other adults in the child's life. It's not that we wanted to shelter the child from other people, but we certainly didn't want an obligation ready-set. So given that we wanted integrity as a family unit, we decided to go with an unknown donor."

The influence of homophobia and heterosexist constructions of the family is apparent in Jasmine's explanation for their decision to use an anonymous donor. Jasmine and Barbara shied away from adoption because they didn't want to be subjected to state scrutiny that would have failed to recognize the value of their relationship. The homophobia unleashed during the Massachusetts foster-care battle was a bitter reminder of their vulnerability. A known donor was also someone who could potentially bring the state to bear on their family life—someone who in the eyes of the law would have parental rights in contrast to the nonbiological mother. Protecting the integrity of their family unit as they defined it meant using an unknown donor.

Though all prospective lesbian parents face the same legal constraint—a definition of family that gives privilege to genetic connection and heterosexual parenting—people see the state's potential role in their lives quite differently. Unlike Jasmine and Barbara, Susan and Dana chose to have a child with a man they knew who would be involved as a parent but in a secondary role. Each had a close relationship with her own father, and they wanted the same for their children. Though concerned about how legally vulnerable the nonbiological mother would be, Susan and Dana proceeded on the assumption that they could work out a trusting relationship with the father, one which would not ultimately bring them face-to-face with the state's ill-fitting definition of family.

Susan, explaining their decision, says: "The legal line obviously is 'don't take risks, therefore don't use a known father who would then have the possibility of having rights.' I agree that that's one way to avoid the particular risk of a custody fight and control issues over the child. But I think it's one of the most personal choices in the world—anything about reproductive issues and how one wants to raise one's children are very intimate and individual, and I think you shouldn't make decisions frankly just on the legal basis.

"You should make them on your whole world view and your values and what you want for your child. Maybe the risk of a custody fight could be minimized by choosing a person carefully and by choosing a gay man rather than a person who would have the gay issue to use against you."

Jasmine and Barbara's thinking diverges from Susan and Dana's along several lines. First, the two couples position themselves very differently in relation to the state. Jasmine and Barbara are acutely focused on the threat the state poses to the integrity of their family unit. Susan and Dana, on the other hand, feel that threat less acutely because they believe that recourse to the state's definition can most likely be avoided through establishing trustworthy relationships. Marie, another lesbian who chose a known donor, explains the position:

> I don't have the kind of fears around the legal stuff that some people do. You have to pick really carefully. Obviously there are certainly men out there whom you could enter into this kind of relationship with and it would be a disaster. But I don't think it's impossible to find a situation where you can have some confidence that this guy will do what he says he'll do. I understand legally you leave yourself open. I think it would be dangerous to do this with a man who is conflicted and who's doing this because he wishes he had kids. Then, ten years down the line he might turn around and say, "I want the child."

These women are grappling with the question of whether you can create a family that defies the state's definition and feel safe that its boundaries will remain as you intended them to be. In part, the different choices lesbians make about family structure stem from different perspectives on the state's ultimate power in their lives.

What Makes a Family?

There is another important dimension to the decision of choosing between known and unknown donors: what should constitute the boundaries of a family? Many women, like Marie and her lover, Jana, choose a donor who will be known to the child but won't take on a parental role. Essentially, except for the fact that the child can know the donor, these families closely resemble families like Jasmine and Barbara's, where the women are the child's sole parents. However, often lesbians choosing known donors draw the boundaries around their families a little differently. Though frequently the men aren't primary parents, they do have a parental role. Susan and Dana created this type of family. While they define their family primarily within the bounds of their own household, their arrangement with their children's father is similar to an extended family. Though at first they were most concerned about maintaining their status as primary parents, as the family became securely established, Susan and Dana wanted the father to be more rather than less involved. They encouraged him to develop a strong relationship with the children. Susan says, "You realize that there are so many things to do. There's never enough time in a day. So additional people to help out is wonderful. We should all have bigger extended families, especially when we're all working. We've been lucky that not just our children's biological father but his choice of partners and his family have been a very rich source of additional good people in the kids' lives."

Opening boundaries in this way can be challenging, however. For a while, Dana, who was to be the nonbiological mother struggled with her lack of society-recognized parent status. "I think for a lot of Susan's pregnancy I was obsessed that this child might be born and this father would have more rights than I would. I had this image that he would never be doing the dirty work of everyday parenting. He'd show up as this knight on a white horse and get all this affection and admiration."

Susan and Dana were deeply committed to the idea that Dana was as much a mother as Susan, and Dana's feelings of doubt dissipated soon after their daughter's birth. "Once Danielle was born it was bizarre to think that. Her father is an important part of her life, but there's a whole 'nother ball game in terms of who her parents are who raise her. My fears were so far from reality. Before Danielle and I had this bond I imagined, in the naiveté of someone who's not a parent, that someone who shows up once a week could be an equal parent to someone who's with you twenty-four hours a day."

Deciding who will be part of one's family is, of course, a highly personal endeavor. The decision regarding a known or unknown donor is partly a decision about what kind of intimate relationships to create. Some are comfortable sharing parenting with people outside a romantic relationship, while others find this a complicated and unrewarding situation.

The Ties that Bind?—the Meaning of Genetic Connections

Beyond thinking about the relationships they want for themselves, lesbians choosing between known and unknown donors must consider how their choice will affect their children. As lesbians think about this, beliefs about the importance of genetic connections take center stage. These beliefs come partly from personal history and partly from ideas that dominate our culture. When women consider whether to use a known or unknown donor, complex, intense, and often conflicting feelings arise. Esther, for instance, originally tried to find a man who would be willing to be a sperm donor but maintain a minimal role in the child's life. The men she approached either wanted more involvement or were worried that they would be asked to take on more responsibility than they bargained for. Esther reconciled herself to conceiving with an anonymous donor, but her feelings about her son Ian's origins intensely color her relationship with him. She says, "I'm consumed by the connections. I look at Ian and see my grandmother's hands. He's an incredible dancer and my father was, too. I don't know if there's a dancing gene.

That's why I wanted a Jewish donor. I wanted the history and culture. A known donor would have embodied more of that. Ian's relation to the donor has been a presence for me since he was born. It's hard to sort out my own sadness about my father's death and my sadness for Ian in not having that relationship."

It is hard also to separate Esther's personal history from the culture we are immersed in. As a society, we tend to emphasize intergenerational biological connections and pay scant attention to nonbiological relationships. For example, we continually hear stories about adopted children who feel an absence in their lives and need to search for their birth parents. We rarely hear about the adopted children—of whom there are also many—who don't feel a need for this contact. Hearing these stories of searches for genetic roots, many lesbians are uncomfortable with anonymous donor insemination. As Marie put it, "I don't think an anonymous donor is the best thing for a kid. I'm sure that kids conceived that way will manage and will be okay if their parents handle it levelly and matter-of-factly. But we don't really know. We haven't had a generation of kids growing up without knowing anything about half of their genetic material. What we do know about is kids who were adopted and don't have that kind of information. Most of them go through something about it whether they end up searching or not. It just makes sense to me that if you can provide a child with that basic information, then you should."

While many like Marie see children as better off with access to genetic information, even if the donor is uninvolved as a parent, a good case can be made for the opposite decision. Jenny, for instance, chose a sperm bank, in part to protect her child from possibly feeling rejected by a known but uninvolved donor. "I'd rather take responsibility for my choice to have him this way," she said. "He can be angry at me for my decision, rather than feel hurt because there's a man he can identify who doesn't behave as a father."

As important as it is for lesbians to think through their decisions, the reality all ultimately may have to come to terms with is not a singular model. Instead, we must come to recognize and appreciate pluralism: children who are loved and given opportunities to grow can thrive in many different family contexts. Knowing this, we can discard a determination of which family structure is "best" in favor of finding ways to make all the different structures work.

GAY MEN HAVE A DIFFERENT SET OF DECISIONS

Gay men are often in the position of parenting children who are primarily raised by lesbians. This family model fits in a culture in which women are socialized toward primary childrearing and men toward a secondary role. While there are many gay men for whom this arrangement works well, there are also those who, like their lesbian counterparts, want more involvement with their children. But men do not have the same options as lesbians. There is no equivalent of donor insemination. Surrogacy comes the closest, but it is a much more biologically, ethically, legally, financially, and psychologically complex process. Similarly, gay men are considerably less likely to find women willing to be the equivalent of a known donor—that is, to have babies with whom they will be minimally involved (though on occasion people do make such arrangements). For gay men who want to be primary parents, adoption is often a more feasible option than biological parenting. Given all this, the issues faced by gay men who choose to become fathers through biological conception are quite distinct from lesbians' concerns.

Becoming a Father Through Surrogacy

Eric and Jeff were college sweethearts who came out together. Though each had imagined they would get married and have children, it was clear early on in their relationship that their futures were bound together. Jeff never gave up the idea of having children, though he didn't actively pursue it until he hit his thirties. At that point, he approached Eric with the idea of advertising for a surrogate mother. Though he thought about adoption, he wanted to have a child who was biologically connected to him. Eric was doubtful that they would find someone willing to be a surrogate. "Everything you read about surrogacy is these women who are married who have several kids, who want to give this to another couple who can't have kids—it's all portrayed in a straight, heterosexual way."

They discussed the possibility of co-parenting with lesbians, but that wasn't an appealing arrangement. Jeff says, "I wanted this to be our child—for this to be a family of three." Eric says, "We've structured a life for ourselves that we feel very comfortable with, that we like a lot, and we set the parameters for that. We don't let others set the parameters, and that's important to us. A co-parenting relationship would just be way too complicated, and too many people who we know don't approach life the way we do." Jeff adds, "Being dependent on someone else would be very frustrating." They placed an ad that specified they were two gay men wanting to raise a child. They got one response, which they pursued.

Paid surrogacy is a complicated social and personal step. It is fundamentally a financial arrangement through which a child comes into the world. The biological parameters, including a woman's efforts to conceive and nine months of carrying a child, are much more extensive than for donor insemination. For these reasons, the social and psychological issues that surround the process are complex.

One of the most troubling aspects of surrogacy is the class imbalance: Eric and Jeff wanted a child and were well off financially; Donna, who responded to their ad, did not want a child, but needed money. Eric and Jeff hoped that they could work out a friendly arrangement, one that would benefit all concerned. At first it seemed they were on their way to doing just that. An agreement was hammered out with lawyers, and the insemination and pregnancy went smoothly. In less than two years since Jeff first proposed parenting, he and Eric had a baby girl, Leah.

Eric, Jeff, and Donna were on friendly terms and had agreed on limited visitation, but this eventually became a source of strife. Jeff and Eric wanted the visits to be supervised and to occur in their home; Donna wanted to take the baby on her own. Communication broke down when Eric and Jeff refused Donna's request. There was a series of exchanges in letters, through which Jeff and Eric tried to establish ground rules for Donna's visitation. Ultimately, Donna didn't respond and contact ceased.

Despite the problems that arose, Eric feels that, "If there wasn't a whole lot of emotional baggage involved on the part of the mother, contact would be preferable. It would be easier for Leah to understand more of her background and her heritage, and who she is as a person if she had that contact, but I could be wrong."

Jeff doesn't quite agree. "I've changed my opinion. Now I feel that other than curiosity, it would be a lot easier for them to have next to no involvement with each other. We have very little in common with her mother. . . . I think those relationships where a gay man helps out two women and stays involved and all are friends are wonderful, but they're unrealistic in these circumstances. Surrogacy is just this bizarre thing where you're dealing with different financial statuses. Because there's such disparity, there's so little in common to base that kind of friendship on."

Like some women who conceive through unknown donors, Jeff is ambivalent about his wish that there be no contact between his child and her biological mother. "I do worry sometimes, like when I see people on television who've been adopted and haven't seen their biological parents, and are freaked out. But I think that doesn't have to happen—that often those people have a lot of other emotional baggage." Eric points out the different positions of gay men and lesbians. "I feel kind of envious of women who go to sperm banks. Once they make that decision, it's over. They may still agonize over not being able to provide that connection for their child, but it's done." In contrast, surrogacy often involves a process of negotiation and the formation of a relationship. As it was for Eric, Jeff, and Donna, surrogacy can be an intense and complex undertaking. What it will ultimately mean to children like Leah is yet to be seen.

As the nonbiological parent, Eric was in a vulnerable position. Like most lesbian and gay couples raising children, Eric and Jeff had to rely on mutual trust. Jeff says, "We can't conceive of ourselves breaking up. If for some unknown reason we ever did, it would have to be amicable—it's just we can't not be that way. We have a relationship where we talk and communicate better than almost anyone we know." Eric adds, "If you can't work out your differences, I believe you have no right to take this kind of adventure. Because we are trailblazing, we take the responsibility very seriously."

Legally, the surrogacy process is not complete until an adoption has occurred. In the case of heterosexual couples, the biological mother terminates her parental rights, and the spouse of the biological father adopts the child, making the couple the child's only legal parents. In their attempt to "close the circle" of the surrogacy arrangement, Jeff and Eric attempted a second-parent adoption. When Donna agreed to terminate her parental rights, it was Eric who would adopt Leah. The legal question revolved around whether he could do that without Jeff giving up his parental rights. If he had not been able to, the couple considered having Eric become the sole legal parent, as a source of balance.

However, shortly before Leah's second birthday, Eric and Jeff were successful in their adoption attempt—their particular circumstances making them a first in the country. When Leah was two years old, Jeff and Eric initiated another surrogacy arrangement through which they had a son.

For the most part, access to surrogacy—like access to other alternative modes of bringing children into one's life—is much more available to heterosexual infertile couples than to gay men. However, surrogacy is much like independent adoption, with access strongly related to financial resources. Surrogacy is far less popular among gay men than donor insemination is among lesbians. Its high cost, along with the social complexity it involves, render it a less frequent approach than adoption or joint-family arrangements.

Surrogacy has been practiced since biblical times—in some informal sense, there have always been women bearing children for friends or family members. But formal, paid contracts for surrogacy arrangements first emerged in this country around 1976, and have been on the rise ever since. Though in any given case surrogacy can work well for all involved, it poses major ethical issues not just for its participants but for society as well. It involves much more than a separation between genetic and social parenting roles, since gestation and birth are processes involving not only a woman's body but also her relation to the child she bears. For the most part, these arrangements involve large sums of money, and bring wealthy people who want children together with poor women in need of money. Out of these issues—the psychological ramifications and the financial exchange—arise many crucial questions.

The major societal quandaries about surrogacy fall into two categories: is it baby selling? and is it exploitative of women? These questions came most vividly to public attention in 1987, when Mary Beth Whitehead, having given birth to the child the courts would refer to as Baby M after signing a surrogacy contract for William and Betsy Stem, changed her mind and wanted to keep the baby. Was she bound by the contract she'd signed? Was the contract, in which there was an exchange of money and an exchange of human life, legal? Was it ethical? And, most important, who should get the child? Mary Beth Whitehead argued that the contract was invalid; she captured the complexity of the surrogacy issue in her statement that she'd "signed on an egg, not on a baby." After a much publicized trial, the Stems were awarded full custody of the one-year-old child. However, along with that decision came a ruling that made surrogacy illegal in the state of New Jersey, where the case had occurred.

While there is little legislation explicitly applying to surrogacy, after the Whitehead case, seventeen states enacted some form of applicable legislation. For the most part, these laws make surrogacy contracts unenforceable. The legal reasoning is drawn from several other areas of law. One argument is that a woman cannot consent to adoption before the birth of a child, and hence cannot be bound by a surrogacy contract drawn up at the time of conception. Another is that in every state baby selling is illegal. Here though, much of surrogacy bypasses this idea, treating compensation not as money in exchange for a human life but as payment for the mother's expenses or for her work in gestation—akin to rent. Some of the laws have focused on money as the key issue, strictly forbidding any exchange other than expenses; a few states prohibit mediators (that is, brokers) from accepting fees. Even with the contracts legally unenforceable, many of the problems that arise when mothers change their minds remain unresolved. Since surrogacy arrangements by and large involve men with substantial resources and women in need of money, if a child is born from such an arrangement and the surrogate changes her mind, most often a typical custody battle ensues, with the best-interests-of-the-child standard applied by the courts. Here, surrogate mothers are at a considerable disadvantage, often not well off enough to pursue a court battle. Surrogacy practices contain a major potential for the exploitation of women in desperate financial circumstances. The guidelines that minimize the risk of such exploitation include making contracts unenforceable (that is, permanently decided only after birth, as in adoption) and giving, as only New York does, the woman custody without a court battle in the event that she changes her mind.

Another Kind of Extended Family

Not all surrogacy arrangements involve a financial exchange. At the other end of the spectrum from the tradition of women as primary and men as secondary parents are the more rare arrangements of women who bear children for men to raise. Such was the case with Kevin, John, and Toni. Kevin had always wanted to be a father and had thought seriously about adopting a child, but he was ultimately discouraged by the foster-care debate in Massachusetts. He was a publicly gay man who would neither have nor want the option of passing as straight in order to adopt a child, so he worried that his chances of getting a child were minimal. Over many years, Kevin had become very close friends with Toni, a single bisexual mother. Kevin had been present at the birth of Toni's second child, and he and John were now like uncles to the children. A close-knit extended-family relation was well established by the time Toni shocked Kevin with the offer to bear a child for him and John to raise. Toni felt she could offer a child no better parents than Kevin and John. For his part, Kevin was overwhelmed by Toni's offer. "I would never have asked a woman to have a baby for me—it's way too much to ask. But I was thrilled."

John was skeptical, feeling strongly still that adopting an existing child was a better way to go. But as the foster-care battle raged, "biological parenting began to seem more appealing because of the legal protection it provided." The three carefully hammered out an agreement, one that included a clear commitment on John and Kevin's part not to challenge Toni if she changed her mind and wanted the baby. For her part, however, Toni was far more worried about the opposite occurrence; she did not want to raise another child, and wanted John and Kevin to have primary responsibility. Her involvement with now two-year-old Amber is substantial, and the group does function as an extended family, with Toni's other children clearly Amber's siblings. Though the arrangement thus bears some resemblance to the familiar family, it is also highly unusual, especially because, simultaneously to being Amber's mother, Toni is not her parent; both the power and the responsibility of parenting fall equally on John and Kevin's shoulders.

JOINT PARENTING—LESBIANS AND GAY MEN TOGETHER

Arrangements such as Kevin and John's with Toni, or Susan and Dana's with their children's father, bring lesbians and gay men together to form families. Most commonly these arrangements involve a division into primary and secondary parenting centered in one household, most often the woman or women involved. These setups resemble amicable custody arrangements in cases of divorce, but they are in reality quite different because they are planned this way and from the outset fall outside of the law's definitions.

Lesbians and gay men also come together in a different family form, that of equally shared parenting. Though it has much in common with the arrangement described above, this particular version deserves separate consideration. Joint-parenting arrangements bring lesbians and gay men together in ways that push even further beyond the nuclear family model, creating an altogether new family form. Truly joint-parenting arrangements decenter family life, creating strong bonds between lesbians and gay men established around parenting itself and independent of primary erotic and romantic unions. Such was the family Barry and Adria established.

"I always say this is the longest pregnancy in the world because it took thirteen years of actively trying to become a dad 'til the time Ari was born," Barry said. He had always seen himself as someone who would have children and, though he didn't know how it would happen, that vision didn't change when he came out at age twenty-two. In his late twenties, he began to discuss the possibility of shared parenting with a heterosexual female friend. But over the course of their conversations, it became clear to Barry that the relationship wouldn't work; much as he wanted a child, he decided not to pursue that possibility.

Then he began to look into adoption as a single man, getting as far as the home-study stage. But at that point he backed away from the process. "It was not a time I wanted to invite the state into my home to scrutinize the way I lived. Also I didn't really want to raise a child alone. I really did want to have another parent."

Shortly after that, he was approached by an acquaintance. "She had had a child when she was really young and felt both trapped in her life and not able to figure out how she could get out of the trap in terms of getting more money and some skills. She had seen me interact with her son who was three at the time, and she knew I was trying to become a father and thought it was really unfair that gay men had such a hard time doing it. She offered to be a surrogate mom if I would help her get some kind of training so that she could get a better kind of job. She still wanted to be friends, and thought maybe an appropriate arrangement would be that she would relate to this child like a distant relative. We hadn't worked out the details, but it was '81 and AIDS was happening. There were no tests, and I didn't feel like I could responsibly inseminate so I decided not to do it."

With his third attempt to become a father failing to pan out, and AIDS on the horizon, Barry put the question of children on the back burner for the next four years. Once the HIV test was available and he tested negative, he decided he could continue his quest.

On New Year's Eve, 1986, Barry was introduced by a mutual friend to Adria, a lesbian who was looking for someone with whom to raise a child. In her early adulthood, Adria had assumed she would adopt children. But as she became focused on her work and community, the idea of becoming a parent faded into the background. Unlike Barry, Adria hadn't spent years engrossed in the pursuit of parenthood. At age forty-two, her world view shifted dramatically when a close friend was diagnosed with AIDS and moved into her home. During the process of caring for him while he was dying, Adria became possessed with an intense desire to be pregnant. What had previously been a source of ambivalence and questioning became definitive. Living through her friend's illness, Adria felt, "If I can do this, I can do anything," The catch was, that Adria had been in a relationship with Marilyn for eight years and Marilyn was not keen on the idea of raising a child. Adria, for her part, wanted her child to have an involved father. This proved to be a good fit, since from Marilyn's perspective it would be more comfortable if Adria had a co-parent other than herself.

Barry describes the tumble of feelings and questions he encountered during their first meetings: "We'd been part of overlapping communities with the same kind of political history, so we knew things about each other and felt very familiar when we actually met, but we had never met before we sat down to ask questions like, 'Would you like to make a commitment for the rest of your life with this stranger and have a very intimate relationship—not sexual, but as close as you can be?' It was very awkward, like going through a series of courting behaviors—checking each other out, putting your best foot forward, and there are these flirtations going on. Our process was that we couldn't say, 'Yes, this is working, let's do it.' It was more like looking for why it wouldn't work until we could find nothing more, then saying, 'Is there any reason why we couldn't do this?' " Adria, on the other hand, immediately impressed by Barry's integrity and level of commitment to parenting, knew at their first encounter that she and Barry would become family.

During the next five months, they let each other into their lives. "It became clear that our sensibility around child-rearing was very similar even though we're very different people," Barry remembers. "Our personalities and backgrounds are very different. Starting this process at an older age, we were both clear about what we wanted and what we didn't want. We wanted to build family with each other. I think we both hoped that ideally that could happen, but if we could find someone close enough, with a similar enough world-view, we knew enough not to expect everything on our list. We introduced each other to our circle of friends, celebrated our birthdays together, gradually doing some of those kinds of family things."

A month after Barry and Adria decided to go ahead with the plan, Barry met Michael. "Here I am, not looking for a relationship, because I'm clear I want kids. You know, if a relationship happens that's fine, that can come later. And then, here's Michael to integrate into this picture. Part of his attraction to me was that I was building a family and he loves children—so we have this dynamic of Michael who is outside wanting in as much as he could, and Marilyn, who is inside wanting to have boundaries as much as she could. And there's Adria and me in the middle, trying to make this happen."

During the next two years, Barry and Adria went through a very intense period that included difficulty conceiving and four miscarriages. The process was particularly discouraging, given Adria's age. One doctor dismissed them completely, chalking up the difficulties to approaching menopause. Adria feared that Barry would abandon the effort to have a baby with her since he so badly wanted a child. But there was never any question in Barry's mind. "We were clear that we really wanted to parent together. That had already been born in this process. We were already really close friends and had this thing that was starting to cross all the traditional lines between gay men and lesbians—building the most physical, intimate relationship you can. Being in the medical part of this process, which was very unpleasant, was really one of the things that pulled us together. Those miscarriages, though I don't recommend this as a strategy, turned out to be a way to find out how you are together. Going through hard times, what we learned is that our instincts pull us together—that's how we deal with hardship. And so that brought us even closer." Barry and Adria supported each other through each episode and were very much partners in the effort. Eventually they saw a fertility specialist, who prescribed Clomid and took over the insemination process. Barry became an expert at assisting the doctor in ultrasound and follicle measuring. At age forty-four, Adria became pregnant and carried to term.

Throughout this process a complicated dynamic developed among the four adults. In many ways Adria and Barry developed a primary intimate relationship, one that had to be balanced with their respective partner relationships. It was the beginning of what was to be their particular sort of family—not a uniform, single entity but more like concentric circles, with four overlapping intimate adult relationships. Though Barry and Adria were at the center of this parenting unit, their approach was inclusive, embracing Michael and Marilyn. This was evident as they moved about the world. Barry remembers the day Adria was late for her first Lamaze class: "So in this room are all these straight couples with very pregnant women, and in walk Barry, Michael, and Marilyn, who is an Olympic athlete, with a very slender toned body—I mean, this woman is not pregnant. It's an awkward threesome. The teacher looks at us and says, "This is the birthing class." And we say, "Great, we're in the right place." Now they're really confused, and we go around the room to introduce ourselves. You have to say your name and the magic due date, so I say 'My name is Barry and I'm the father of this child that Adria, who's not here, is carrying,' and then Michael says, 'My name is Michael and I'm Barry's partner, and I'm going to help parent this child that Adria, who's not here, is carrying,' and then Marilyn, 'I'm Marilyn and I'm Adria's partner.' Their eyes are getting bigger and their mouths are falling open, and finally Adria comes, not having a clue what she was walking into."

Ari was delivered through cesarean section in 1989—Marilyn, Barry, and Michael were all present at his birth. Adria and Barry had agreed to share parenting equally. This is difficult to achieve in the context of two separate households. Each can be with Ari whenever he or she wants and also whenever he is needing one of them. Though they have free access to each other's homes, separation is a key issue in this family. From the very beginning of his life, Ari has gone back and forth between the households almost every other day. Barry and Adria also do a lot of traveling. In the first couple of months, before Ari began to travel back and forth, Barry slept at Adria's house. After that, while Adria was nursing Ari, she would come to Barry's house on the days he wasn't with her. At six months of age, Ari began to take a bottle as well, which somewhat eased the stress.

As they look toward the future, both Barry and Adria have some trepidation about their own feelings regarding separations. They are beginning to feel that Ari, now a preschooler, needs longer stretches in each household. Barry anticipates this. "It's hard for me to imagine him not being home for three days in a row. I just can't—not that I'm not totally comfortable and happy with where he is, because he's at home being loved by his wonderful mother and other parent, and nothing could please me more, but he's not home with me. I find myself wandering into his room a lot when he's not there, looking for him."

Adria has been known to appear at Barry's house in the middle of the night, needing to check in with Ari. Speculating about Ari's responses to the constant comings and goings, Adria says, "I think he suffers as any being would suffer from everything changing all the time. It's the same two houses, it's the same people, and he has everything at both places. He always has his little shopping bag and he carries his blanket with him wherever he goes. I think he'll either grow up to be a person who will only be in one place and will be kind of rigid about it because he's had enough of this, or he'll be someone who any place he hangs his hat will be his home. I think he'll have a certain kind of autonomy and confidence, because he seems to now, but I think he'll also have some issues about being left—people always come back , but they also always leave." One of the issues Barry and Adria are currently trying to address is their desire to have more time together with Ari rather than being on separate shifts.

The complexities of the four-way relationship take a lot of energy to navigate. Though decisions are essentially a matter of consensus, the family's communication about Ari is primarily channeled through Barry and Adria. In a sense, Michael and Marilyn have become the keepers of their respective couple relationships. As Adria sees it, "they watch over the intimacy of the couples— and they help each couple to separate from the other." For Marilyn, Barry's and Michael's involvements with Ari have freed her to be his parent. "The fact that she's not the only other parent besides me, the fact that there's someone else who's fifty percent responsible for him has allowed her a lot of room, to in fact be a very important parent. In our family, because she doesn't want to be a mother, there's not much competition like you'll see in some lesbian couples. And she doesn't want to be his father; there's not competition with Michael and

Barry, either. She has her place with Ari. She's the only athlete among us. He's a little talking boy—he's not very athletic. She teaches him how to jump. That's where they live together, in this sort of playful world and he's very close to her."

Michael, unlike Marilyn, has much more interest in a primary parenting role, and has had to grapple with that in the context of a family unit that is clearly centered on Barry and Adria as primary parents. He and Barry think about expanding the family—through having Michael father a child. "When Ari's at our house he's there with both of us and it's fairly equal in terms of day-to-day doing things," Barry says. "Michael has stepped in as the cook. He likes to do it and he cooks for Ari all the time, so he's Ari's best cook and when he's hungry he looks to Michael. I know Michael has felt unseen and unrecognized but not by me or our family. My father, for instance, was watching Michael put Ari to bed one night and he just said 'it's so amazing—he is a father to this child.' But even though Michael gets recognition from our family and community, there's so much in this culture that in basic ways doesn't recognize his role. We try to be especially conscious of it and name it when it's happening."

As with the Lamaze class, as they move about the world this family shakes people's attitudes. Once, Ari closed a car door on his hand. In the emergency room, Barry and Michael met Adria and Ari at the hospital. Barry remembers that day vividly; "So I'm holding Ari and he's telling me the story, saying 'Daddy, I cried a little but it's okay now,' and we go together but they keep trying to separate us all. Then we get to the point of registering, and I'm holding Ari and the clerk is asking me all these questions that I'm answering while Michael and Adria stand behind me. Then the clerk says to me, 'Okay, Michael, so you're the father,' and Michael says 'No, I'm Michael and he's on my plan.' Meanwhile, Ari is pointing to me saying, 'This is the father.' So, okay, this is the father, but Michael learned that in order to get his work to pay these bills—to not raise red flags—he says he's the stepfather. And the clerk must be thinking—well, okay, this is a very friendly divorce—here's the mom, dad, stepfather, and kid. Then he asks Michael for his address. I'd already given him my address as the father and, of course, it's the same address. At this point we're all fidgeting, and Adria says, 'I bet you want to know my address next.' So we have these funny experiences, but we make it work."

Of his family life, Barry says, "It's made us all look at how we do relationships. I think our mode of operating now is basically to act out of the basic goodness that's there in all of these relationships and to let go of a lot of the petty stuff about each other that drives each of us crazy. We pick and choose what we have to deal with. It works incredibly well, and it's also complicated trying to manage these multiple needs." Looking back at his original decision to become a parent in this way, Barry says, "It's important to try to imagine every situation you can before you do something like this, 'cause it gets you thinking, but there's no way to know what the reality will be. No matter how much we talked, there was no way I could be prepared for the instant of Ari's birth, when I went from one primary relationship with Michael to three. And of course it doesn't matter what the adults decide in advance; once the child is born, their needs are going to determine—and should determine—what happens. Sometimes that can bear no relation to all these plans."

Amid all the complexity, Ari seems to thrive. He makes families out of everything, one of his favorites being clothes hangers. The blue one is always himself, and then there is a Mommy, a Daddy, a Marilyn, and a Michael. He wonders why his best friend has no Marilyn or Michael.

THE REINVENTED FAMILY

Lesbian and gay parents essentially reinvent the family as a pluralistic phenomenon. They self-consciously build from the ground up a variety of family types that don't conform to the traditional structure. In so doing, they encourage society to ask, "What is a family?" The question has profound meaning in both the culture at large and the very heart of each of our intimate lives. It is like a tree trunk from which many branches extend: What is a mother, a father, a parent, a sibling? Can a child have two or more mothers or fathers? Is one more "real" by virtue of biological or legal parent status? How does society's recognition (or its absence) foster or impede parent-child relationships? To what extent does the state shape family life? To what extent can nontraditional families alter the state's definition of family?

These questions go well beyond the issue of whether families headed by lesbians and gay men should exist. There emerges a complex reciprocal tension between lesbian and gay family life on the one hand and homophobia and the idealization of the traditional family on the other. Clearly, lesbian and gay parents don't create their families in a vacuum. Their choices are shaped by the institutions that mediate family formation, most notably the legal and medical systems, and adoption agencies. Lesbian and gay parents vary with respect to how they view the state. While some let legal definitions inform their choices, others feel they can probably keep the state out of their lives by relying on trust and goodwill. Sometimes families who've taken this route end up, to their dismay, in the courts, challenging prevailing legal thought.

However they choose to form their families, lesbians and gay men do so in the context of the idealization of the traditional model; their families are inevitably shaped by this fact. Yet at the same time, over the past decade, many changes have been wrought by lesbian and gay family formation itself—ranging from unmarried women's increased access to donor insemination to the particular challenges that lesbian and gay families bring to the law. Though our society is a long way from embracing eight-year-old Danielle's deceptively simple statement that a "family is people who all love each other, care for each other, help out, and understand each other," her words may yet prove to be our most crucial guide to the future.

READING

28

Hispanic Families in the United States: Research Perspectives

Catherine Street Chilman

The impact of the Hispanic population on American society is enormous and diverse, having many implications for family research, professional practice, and public policies. Scholars and professionals need a deeper understanding of the variety of Hispanic individuals and families in this country.

Although it is common to view all Hispanic families in this country as being similar in values, beliefs, behaviors, resources, and concerns, such sweeping assumptions are seriously erroneous (Andrade, 1982; Cortes, 1980; de Silva, 1981; Frisbie, 1986; Mirandé, 1977; Staples and Mirandé, 1980). These families are far from homogeneous; they represent a number of different national and ethnic origins, vary by social class, speak a variety of dialects, have differing histories, differ in immigration and citizenship status, and live in various regions of this country. . . .

The first part of this chapter provides general immigration and demographic facts about each of the major Hispanic groups in the United States. The second section discusses some of the chief social and psychological research findings regarding these families. . . .

SOME CURRENT ISSUES IN IMMIGRATION

Until 1945, legal immigration to the United States was mainly governed by an act of Congress of 1924, which was amended in 1952. This used the national origin system, which favored Western Europeans over Asians and Pacific peoples. In general, there was a ratio for each nation in the world that limited immigrants to numbers proportional to the population makeup of the United

From Catherine Street Chilman, "Hispanic Families in the United States: Research Perspectives," in *Family Ethnicity: Strength in Diversity*, ed. by Harriette Pipes McAdoo (Newbury Park, CA: Sage, 1993), pp. 141–163

States in 1920 (for example, about one-fourth of immigrants granted entry were from Great Britain). However, the independent countries of the Western Hemisphere were afforded unlimited entry under this act.

In 1965, new legislation abolished restrictions against Asian and Pacific peoples. However, it imposed limits on immigration from the Western Hemisphere, with a quota of 120,000 persons a year being established. Preference was given to those with occupational skills judged to be needed in this country (LaPorte, 1977).

Because of severe economic and political problems in their own countries, larger numbers of Hispanics have sought to enter the United States than provided for under immigration laws. Thus many illegal aliens have recently entered this country, particularly from Mexico and Central and South America. Portes (1979) holds that the current large waves of illegal immigrants, most of whom are Mexicans, could be prevented from entering the United States, but that business and industry do not want this to occur. These workers are a cheap source of labor, and the fact that they are illegal creates an advantage for their employers, because they are highly vulnerable employees.

The Immigration Reform and Control Act of 1986 offered legal status in the United States or amnesty to illegal aliens who could prove they had resided continuously in this country since before January 1, 1982. More liberal amnesty provisions were developed for agricultural workers. The amnesty program includes sanctions against employers who hire illegal aliens and provisions for stepped-up border patrol and immigration service enforcement agents. The goal is to deter further illegal immigration while offering the protection of legal status to aliens who have lived here since before January 1, 1982 (Applebome, 1988).

Aliens applying for jobs had to apply for amnesty by the end of August 1987 to be hired for work that year, but applications were low and only about half of the estimated 2 million illegal aliens in this country had applied for amnesty by January 1, 1988, even though the deadline for such application was May 1, 1988. Most observers agree that the major impediment to this application was fear that families would be broken up, because some members of a number of families lacked documentary proof that they had lived continuously in the United States since before January 1, 1982. In fact, it is probable that many family members did not live in this country before 1982 and that of those who were here at that early date, a number probably had moved back and forth across the border. Attempts were made in Congress in 1987 to amend the legislation to protect family unity and grant amnesty to all family members if some members had gained amnesty or were eligible for it, but these amendments failed to pass.

The family issue is but one difficult aspect of the immigration problem. There are powerful economic and political pressures in countries of origin inducing immigrants to cross the border, whether these immigrants can gain legal entry or not. At the same time, many Hispanics south of the United States yearn to enter this country because of the relative economic gains and personal freedoms it appears to offer. Moreover, the long border between the countries is very difficult to police adequately, and a number of U.S. employers desire the cheap labor provided by illegal immigrants who fear discovery and deportation.

It is essential for family researchers, policy and program personnel, and practitioners to recognize the severe problems families face when they have immigrated to this country illegally. As suggested earlier, they are extremely vulnerable to employer exploitation. They also live in constant fear of discovery and are therefore difficult to reach if they need assistance. Further, they are ineligible for public aid and must rely on private sources for help. Immigration, in and of itself, poses a number of problems for families; illegal immigration severely escalates these problems.

POPULATION CHARACTERISTICS

There are difficulties in defining the term *Spanish origin*. Recognizing that census reports do contain some errors, it is helpful, nonetheless, to consider the data they present. According to these reports, there were more than 12 million persons of Spanish origin in the United States in 1979: 7.3 million Chicanos, 1.7 million Puerto Ricans, 800,000 Cubans, 900,000 Central or South Americans, and more than 1 million persons of other Spanish backgrounds. The total number of Hispanic-origin people in the United States increased by 33 percent between 1970 and 1979, with the fastest-growing group being Mexican—which grew by 62 percent. The majority of Hispanic families live in Arizona, California, Colorado, New Mexico, Texas, Florida, and New York. These families are largely concentrated in 10 of the nation's 305 metropolitan areas, with especially large numbers in New York and Los Angeles.

Age

The median age of the Hispanic population is fairly young when compared with the remainder of the population. This difference in age level is both a result and a cause of the higher fertility rate of Hispanic families. This comparatively youthful age has a number of other implications for public policy, including the likelihood that programs for children and adolescents will have a disproportionate number of Hispanics in them.

Educational Levels

On the average, members of Hispanic families, particularly the elderly, have lower educational levels than any other population group in the United States (U.S. Bureau of the Census, 1980). These lower levels of education for most Hispanics are partly a result of the recent migration of many of them, as well as the poverty and low levels of public education in their former countries. Continuing problems of low educational achievement for many Hispanic-Americans, including children and youth, is a matter of intense concern, especially because it adversely affects their future employment opportunities.

Employment and Income

Racial discrimination is apt to be another important factor in the high rates of unemployment of those Puerto Ricans who have dark skins and are classed as nonwhites—an effect of the African, Indian, and Spanish mix of their native land. Racial discrimination, still present in the United States, often comes as a shock to immigrants who have experienced much less of this in Puerto Rico (M. Delgado, 1987).

Spanish-American men and women are more apt than the rest of the population to be in blue-collar and service occupations. This is especially true for people of Mexican and Puerto Rican origin. Women are more apt than men to be in white-collar occupations. The great majority of Hispanic families live in urban areas today. There has been a massive shift away from farm employment, mostly because of the industrialization of agriculture. However, on average, there has been little advancement in occupational level.

Hispanic women are generally paid at a lower wage level than either white or African-American women. This is also true for those Hispanic men who are in clerical occupations or who are factory operatives. On the other hand, Hispanic men who are in professional or managerial fields earn more, on average, than black men in these occupations but considerably less than white males.

As of the 1980 census, more than 50 percent of all female-headed Hispanic families were below the poverty line, including 72 percent of Puerto Rican families, 49 percent of Chicanos, and 38 percent of other Hispanic families. For all groups, two-parent families with the wife in the labor force had the highest income, and one-parent families had the lowest annual income: about $25,000 for white one-parent families, $15,000 for African-Americans, and $18,000 for Hispanics (U.S. Bureau of the Census, 1983). In general, families with young children had the lowest average annual income in the nation. Overall, a large percentage of the children lived in impoverished families—a shocking and tragic fact. Minority children were in particularly adverse situations: 46 percent of black families with children had incomes below the poverty line. This was the case for 39 percent of Hispanic families and 16 percent of white families. . . .

Marital Stability

The 1980 census data for five southwestern states show that rates of marital stability are about the same for Mexican-Americans, Cuban-Americans, and Anglo-Americans, with divorce and separation rates of about 25 percent for these groups (U.S. Bureau of the Census, 1980). However, both blacks and Puerto Ricans experienced rates of about 40 percent. Mexican-Americans and Cuban-Americans had a far lower remarriage rate than did Anglos, but the reasons for this are unknown. Interestingly, Mexican-American divorce rates rise with higher levels of education for women, though the reverse tends to be true for Anglos (except for those women with graduate educations). Frisbie (1986) speculates that Mexican-American women with higher levels of education tend to become more acculturated to American patterns and are, therefore, more accepting of separation and divorce; however, this may be an overtly simple explanation.

Precise data regarding unmarried parenthood among Hispanic-Americans tend to be missing. However, studies of unmarried adolescent mothers reveal that Hispanic girls are fairly similar to other adolescent women (*Family Planning Perspectives*, 1983). Although premarital chastity has been emphasized within the culture, this norm has been drastically eroded in recent years. Thus nonmarital intercourse and pregnancy have become increasingly common. Although the parents of pregnant teenage girls usually consider illegitimate childbearing a serious problem, they tend to welcome the baby into the family if the young woman decides to keep her child and not get married—a decision she frequently makes.

Fertility

According to the 1980 census, Hispanic women had higher birth rates than did either blacks or Anglos; however, those rates have been declining somewhat in more recent years. For example, only a little more than one-third of the women aged 15 to 44 had three or more children in 1980, compared with almost half of this group in 1970. Estrada (1987) notes that these high rates are caused by a number of factors: the youthful age structure of the Hispanic-American population, large families and high fertility rates of incoming immigrants, and traditional, though fading, negative attitudes toward birth control. These attitudes are partly associated with the fact that the huge majority of Hispanic-Americans are Catholic.

Large families are most likely to be characterized by low levels of employment, education, and income. This is found for such families in most parts of the world. Therefore, although these data can be interpreted as the consequence of high fertility, analyses also show that high fertility is a result of little education, unemployment, and poverty and the hopelessness, alienation, and lack of medical care they often engender (Chilman, 1968, 1983). High fertility also tends to go with low levels of modernization and a predominantly agricultural society (Chilman, 1968). There is evidence that the birth rate for Hispanic-American families is currently declining in association with rising levels of education, urbanization, and employment of Hispanic women. Increased availability of low-cost, high-quality family planning services also has been helpful, although addition of Spanish-speaking personnel to the professional staffs of such service agencies is frequently needed (J. Jones, 1985).

Language

The vast majority of Hispanics in this country are bilingual. Two-thirds of those who speak Spanish report that they also speak English well or very well (Estrada, 1987). A recent Institute of Social Research survey of Mexican-American households in the Southwest and Midwest revealed that the majority of adults interviewed spoke both English and Spanish. There was general consensus among the respondents that the speaking of Spanish was very important. Most thought there ought to be bilingual education in the schools. There was a generally strong feeling of ethnic identity, with many of the younger members of the population showing a particularly enthusiastic movement in this direction (Arce, 1982).

Many of the elderly and recent immigrants speak only Spanish, and many Hispanics, in general, chiefly speak Spanish within the family. As with other immigrant groups, it is common for the children to learn English before the parents do and for family members who are mainly confined to the home (often the elderly and mothers of young children) to speak English far less well than those who are in school or employed. This can create a number of disruptive family problems and is another indication that professionals who seek to work with Hispanic families should be bilingual, so that they can converse directly with all family members (Bernal, 1982; Falicov, 1982; Garcia-Preto, 1982).

Variations by National Origin

In the discussion that follows, emphasis is placed on the family-related cultural patterns of various Hispanic-American groups. There are two reasons for this emphasis: (a) most of the associated research and clinical observations reported in the literature emphasize cultural patterns and (b) these patterns are important in affecting individual and family behaviors, although not as important as much of the literature, including the following discussion, would suggest.

It is essential to recognize that cultural patterns by themselves do not determine an individual's behavior, although they may strongly affect his or her values, attitudes, and norms. Each person's behavior is also strongly affected by her or his temperament, special abilities and limitations, physical condition, age, life situation, and total developmental experience within the family and elsewhere. Moreover, the behavior of families is an outcome of the interaction of the individuals within them, plus the family's size, structure, history, developmental stage, and total situation—as well as cultural patterns.

Thus these patterns constitute one of a number of complex factors that affect familial behaviors and those of family members. For instance, Baca Zinn (1980) perceptively wrote that cultural values are important in family life, but should be studied in social context. They become fully meaningful only when they are related to historical, economic, residential, and other structural factors. Although they are important dimensions of families, they do not by themselves determine, or fully explain, family organization. Rather, one needs to study actual behaviors of families as well as their expressed beliefs (Baca Zinn, 1980, pp. 68–69). One also needs to take into account the economic resources of a family. For instance, members of an extended family may live together out of economic need rather than preference. Younger relatives may provide support for aging kin—again, more because of necessity than because of cultural norms.

The historical background of a people also influences the behavior of its members in a number of subtle and not-so-subtle ways. Among other things, history, including legends, affects the self-image of group members as well as their perceptions of people of other national origins. Thus brief historical sketches of various Hispanic groups are provided below.

Puerto Ricans

Puerto Rico was a Spanish colony from the time of its discovery by Columbus in 1493 until the United States invaded and annexed it in 1898 during the Spanish-American War (Fitzpatrick, 1981; Garcia-Preto, 1982). Although Puerto Rico gained increasing control over its own affairs during the next half century, becoming a commonwealth in 1952, real political control over the island remains in the United States today. This fact has spawned understandable resentment among Puerto Ricans, with some groups agitating for complete independence, some for statehood, and others for continued collaboration with the United States and the resulting benefits of this partnership, perceived by some as outweighing the costs. These varying positions naturally affect the attitudes of Puerto Ricans who come to the United States; it can be expected that a number would continue to harbor antipathy toward this country, with resulting barriers to acculturation.

As a people, Puerto Ricans are of many colors, from completely Negroid to completely Caucasian, and they must face the difficult problem of racial prejudice in the United States (Fitzpatrick, 1981). Poverty has been widespread in Puerto Rico, a central reason for the large migration to the continental United States. Cultural patterns are highly variable, affected by the kind of occupation pursued, the region of the island (such as isolated rural areas, farm villages, or urban areas), and social class status. Fitzpatrick (1981) cites a number of studies of family life and socialization in Puerto Rico, but most of them were carried out during the 1950s and 1960s and are therefore now rather out of date. There seems to be almost no research regarding Puerto Rican family life in this country. Thus in their discussions of the topic, both Garcia-Preto (1982) and Fitzpatrick (1981) tend to rely chiefly on clinical observations.

According to Garcia-Preto (1982), the dignity of the individual and respect for each person, regardless of her or his status, is of basic importance to most Puerto Ricans. This also pertains to respect for authority within the family as well as elsewhere. "The rules for respect are complex. For instance, Puerto Ricans think that a child who calls an adult by his or her first name is disrespectful. To make direct eye contact with strangers, especially women and children, is also unacceptable" (Garcia-Preto, 1982, p. 172). Garcia-Preto writes further that Puerto Ricans strongly favor self-control and an appearance of calm; they tend to attribute stressful situations to external factors and to express stress indirectly through somatic complaints.

Traditionally, Puerto Ricans place a high value on the family's unity, welfare, and honor. Emphasis is on commitment to the group, rather than the individual, and on familial responsibilities, including obligations to and from the extended family.

The double standard of sexual morality has been instilled as a basic value, with emphasis on modesty and virginity in women, sexual freedom among men, and, simultaneously, the obligation of men to protect the honor of the women in the family. This double standard has been considerably eroded in recent years, owing to the impact of changing cultural patterns in the United States and in

Puerto Rico itself. Clearly defined sex roles have been common, but this pattern is changing, especially as more and more women find employment outside the home.

Parent-youth conflicts are observed by clinicians to be common among Puerto Rican families in the United States, especially among recent immigrants. As often happens with immigrants, traditional family values and roles are frequently challenged by children and adolescents as they seek to become completely "Americanized" in our highly individualistic, competitive society. As parents feel they are losing control, they often become more authoritarian, emphasizing responsibility, obedience, and respect toward the family. This tends to escalate the conflict, which may become particularly intense and harmful because the support of a homogeneous neighborhood and extensive family network is generally lacking—aids that had been of important assistance in their former island home (for further details, see Fitzpatrick, 1981; Garcia-Preto, 1982).

The above observations concerning Puerto Rican cultural patterns should be viewed with a certain amount of skepticism, especially with regard to Puerto Rican families in this country. As noted earlier, cultural patterns vary from group to group within Puerto Rico and also within the United States. The latter variation is strongly affected by the reasons, timing, and conditions of immigration and the region of the United States to which the immigrants came. For instance, the existence of large Puerto Rican communities within New York City and the constant movement back and forth, to and from the island, tend to reduce ready acculturation and shifts from more traditional family roles. This movement has a deep impact on the family, as it reinforces many links to the island and fosters continuous dismantling and reconstruction of family life (Rodriguez, Sanchez, and Alers, 1980). Puerto Ricans who have moved to other regions, such as in the Midwest, less readily find compatriots and may, therefore, take on American ways, including egalitarian family patterns and individualism, more quickly. However, they may also suffer more from a sense of loneliness and isolation.

As indicated earlier, Puerto Ricans, on the average, tend to have more economic, occupational, familial, and educational problems than other Hispanic groups in this country. The reasons are unclear, but such problems are probably a result of such factors as the poverty in Puerto Rico, from which they have fled; poor economic and social conditions in New York City, where most of them live; racism; lack of facility in the English language; perhaps, in some cases, a search for the more generous public assistance grants in New York as against Puerto Rico; and slow acculturation to this country because of frequent travel back and forth to the homeland.

A large percentage of Puerto Ricans in this country receive public assistance. This is partly a result of their ready eligibility for this aid because they are citizens of the United States, an outcome of Puerto Rico's status as a commonwealth of this country. This status also makes it possible for them to move readily to the U.S. mainland without immigration restrictions. Their citizenship status, in sum, confers certain privileges on them and makes them different from other Hispanic groups seeking entry to, and citizenship in, this country.

Mexican-Americans

Most Mexicans are of mixed Spanish and Indian descent. Their national heritage goes back many centuries to Indian civilizations that existed before the arrival of the Spanish explorers in the early 1500s. During the seventeenth, eighteenth, and nineteenth centuries, Spain extended its rule over the region that is now Mexico, California, and the southwestern United States. Mexico finally obtained its independence from Spain in 1821, but it was a weak country with little control over its vast territory (Kraus, 1959).

The rule by the United States over what is now the American Southwest and was previously part of Mexico dates only from the Mexican War of 1848—a war that ended in victory for the United States and the acquisition of lands that now include Arizona, California, Nevada, Utah, and Wyoming. Texas, which had recently (1835) won its independence from Mexico, was annexed by the United States in 1844. Thus, for a number of Mexicans in this country, their roots in what is now American soil far predate the arrival of the Anglos (Falicov, 1982). It is natural that Indian-Spanish heritage remains strong and that many continue to have feelings of resentment toward the United States. Although some Mexican-Americans have been in this country for many generations, the majority are either first- or second-generation immigrants.

Resentment toward this country has been perpetuated and, at times, strengthened by discriminatory and often exploitative behaviors by some Anglo-Americans toward many Mexicans in the United States and toward Mexico itself (Alvirez, Bean, and Williams, 1981). However, this resentment is mixed with admiration and envy of this country, which, potentially at least, offers many more opportunities than Mexico does for economic advancement.

At different time periods there have been large waves of Mexican immigration to the United States for political reasons (for example, flight from the violence of the Mexican Revolution of 1910) and for economic reasons (for example, the flight from crushing poverty and unemployment in Mexico in recent years). Most Mexican-Americans in the United States continue to suffer discrimination today, with limited access to good housing, education, and jobs. They are often exploited by employers, especially if they are illegal immigrants. They also have high rates of both unemployment and early school leaving.

Although most Mexican-Americans live in the Southwest, some have migrated to other parts of the country. For instance, some have lived in midwestern cities for three generations or more. As in the case of other immigrant groups, those who live near the borders of their "mother" country are less likely to acculturate readily than those who live far from their native land. For example, Mexicans who live in Chicago are more apt to become Americanized quickly than are those who live in southern Texas.

Much more has been studied and written about the family patterns of Chicanos (the appellation that many of today's Mexican-Americans prefer) than any other Hispanic group in the United States. Earlier research tended to assume that Mexican and Mexican-American life family patterns were essentially the same. It was generally believed that Hispanics were all highly familistic, with authoritarian, patriarchal patterns, including machismo for males and submissiveness for females. It was also held that premarital virginity and high fertility norms were characteristic of these families.

Andrade (1982) has summarized numerous studies and reports that an exaggerated supermother figure emerges from a summary of impressions of Mexican-American women: the unceasingly self-sacrificing, ever-fertile woman without aspirations for herself other than to reproduce. Andrade comments that several of the investigations from which this interpretation emerged were carried out in rural settings by Anglos, many of whom were males, unfamiliar with the culture or the situation they were investigating. Notably, almost all of these studies investigated lower-class samples, thus confounding ethnicity with socioeconomic status. Moreover, samples tended to be small and nonrandom (Andrade, 1982, p. 229).

Both Andrade (1982) and Mirandé (1977, 1979) emphasize that early writings about Hispanic family patterns (especially those about the Chicanos) were quite erroneous in stressing lack of egalitarian behaviors between husbands and wives. Mirandé (1979, p. 474) proposes that the concept of the all-dominant and controlling Chicano male is largely mythical. He criticizes unfounded psychoanalytic interpretations that interpret the machismo concept as a pathological defense against the Mexican-American male's feelings of inadequacy engendered by the adverse effects of discrimination and poverty. Mirandé also stresses that there are many kinds of Mexican-American families, with differing culture patterns. These patterns vary in accordance with recency of immigration, place of residence, socioeconomic status, degree of intermarriage with other ethnic groups, age, urbanization, and employment of women outside the home.

According to Mirandé (1979), more recent studies have shown an egalitarian family pattern in the behaviors of urban as well as rural Chicano families. One Mexican-American study project found, in both Los Angeles and San Antonio, that the families were not patriarchal, as had been frequently assumed (Grebler, Moore, and Guzman, 1973). Rigid differentiation of sex role tasks was lacking, and both men and women shared in homemaking and child rearing as needed. However, fathers tended to have a stronger role outside the family, and mothers were usually the dominant persons in the day-to-day matters of child rearing and homemaking—a point also made by Baca Zinn (1980). See also Cromwell and Cromwell (1978), Hawkes and Taylor (1975), and Staton (1972) for generally similar findings.

Mirandé (1977) describes the Chicano woman as the center of the family and the mainstay of the culture. As with many other ethnic groups, the mother tends to perpetuate the language and values of the "old country" and is usually a source of warmth and nurturance within the home.

The father is seen as the authority figure in many Chicano families. He is usually warm in his relationships with younger children, but more controlling as they get older. He often appears to be aloof and uninvolved in the details of family matters. Although he is seen by himself and others as the family leader who has power, the culture also includes a strong sense of related paternal responsibility.

Children are taught to carry family responsibilities, to prize family unity, and to respect their elders. However, the peer group becomes very important to adolescent boys as they grow older. Traditionally, girls stay at home with their mothers until marriage, but Chicanas (Mexican-American females) today are struggling for greater equality with both men and Anglos. They wish to keep their ethnic identity, but they also desire more flexibility in family and other roles.

The culture also emphasizes the family as a basic source of emotional support, especially for children. Support is provided not only by the parents, but also by grandparents, uncles, aunts, cousins, and friends. For example, although there has been a great deal of rural-urban migration among Hispanic populations, it appears that many Chicanos continue to live in comparatively large, intact kinship units where there are extensive networks of relatives who are helpful and supportive (Arce, 1982). No sharp distinction is made between relatives and friends, with the latter being considered as virtually kin if a close relationship has been formed. The term *compadrazo* is often used for this relationship. However, the pattern of close extended family relationships tends to fade among third- and fourth-generation families and among those who are upwardly mobile (Alvirez et al., 1981).

Bean, Curtis, and Marcum (1977) carried out an analysis of 1969 data from 325 Mexican-American couples who were members of a stratified sample in the Southwest. They found, among other things, that couples with egalitarian relationships were highest in their marital satisfaction—hardly a surprise. In general, the authors found little to support the concept that Mexican-American families have cultural patterns that are different from those of Anglo families and unique, culturally related sources of marital satisfaction. This point is also made by Zapata and Jaramillo (1981), who compared a small sample of Anglo families to Mexican-American ones in two southwestern cities. They found that differences in perceived family roles and alliances pertained far more to differences in socioeconomic status than to ethnicity.

Vega, Patterson, et al. (1986) provided helpful information regarding selected family patterns of a group of southwestern urban Mexican-American and Anglo parents with fifth- and sixth-grade children ($N = 147$ in each group). Using the Family Adaptability and Cohesion Scale II (Olsen, Russell, and Sprenkel, 1982), observers rated these families for the above characteristics. They also used an acculturation scale developed by Cuellar, Harris, and Jasso (1980). As might be expected, Vega, Patterson, et al. (1986) found that levels of acculturation varied for the Mexican-Americans according to their length of residence in the United States and their socioeconomic status.

Cuban-Americans

Cuban-Americans have a rather different background and immigration history than either Puerto Ricans or Mexican-Americans. . . . Cuba had been a colony of Spain for hundreds of years before the intervention of the United States in 1898, following an insurrection of some Cuban groups against oppressive Spanish domination. American motivations for intervention were mixed: Some liberal groups supported the Cuban cause of independence from Spain, but more powerful groups were swayed by their economic and political interests in this strategic island (Dulles, 1959).

After victory in the Spanish-American War, the United States established a strong political hold on Cuba, inducing rebellions, especially on the part of those people who were victims of the one-crop sugar economy and land owner-ship by the very few. The Cuban revolution of 1959 brought Castro and a predominantly socialist government into power and created fear and resistance in the United States, especially among those who, correctly or incorrectly, equated the Castro government with Soviet intrusion into the Western Hemisphere. At the present time, barely contained conflict between the United States and Cuba continues. One result of this conflict has been differing waves of immigration from Cuba to this country (Bernal, 1982; Dulles, 1959).

Many of the first wave of Cuban immigrants made a poor adjustment to the United States, partly because of their own troubled and disadvantaged back-grounds (Bernal, 1982). A serious public policy issue has arisen concerning government plans to deport some of those Cubans who have criminal records and the resistance of many to being deported. Cuban immigrants have settled chiefly in metropolitan areas such as Miami, New York, and Chicago. Although the different immigrant groups vary enormously in a number of ways, they also share a general cultural heritage.

Although formal research regarding Cuban-American families seems to be lacking, Bernal (1982) presents a summary of largely clinical observations. The traditional Cuban emphasis on familism, including the extended family, appears to be much like that found in other Hispanic countries. According to Bernal, the double standard of sexual morality, along with the concept of male dominance has prevailed in Cuban culture as well. However, as shown above concerning Mexican and Puerto Rican families in the United States, when women work outside the home, egalitarian values and behaviors tend to emerge.

Bernal cites several small studies from the 1970s to the effect that younger and second-generation Cubans become acculturated to the United States more quickly than older or first-generation immigrants. As in reports regarding Puerto Rican families and immigrant families from many countries, the cultural differences between children and their parents often lead to youthful rebellions, authoritarian parental reactions, and considerable family stress. Bernal observes further that Cubans tend to regard themselves as a special people, perhaps because of their homeland's strategic political and economic importance to other nations over the centuries. This sense of being special may lend a feeling of superiority to some Cubans, with allied attitudes of chauvinism, racism, and classism, which may be viewed by some observers as arrogance and grandiosity. However, as in the case of Puerto-Rican Americans, more research about Cuban-American families is needed before much can be said about the ways in which they are like or different from other families in this country.

Immigrants from Central and South America

Very little has been written about the family patterns of other Hispanic immigrants. According to L. Cohen (1977), two-thirds of the immigrants from Central and South America during the 1970s were women. Most had children whom they left behind with their maternal grandmothers. These women often came on student or tourist visas or crossed the border illegally. They frequently had kin and friends who helped them come into this country and find work. They were afraid to bring their young children with them, and often dreaded returns home to visit for fear they could not reenter the United States.

These women were usually never married, separated, divorced, or widowed. They had a harder time than men in getting employment because of both sex and ethnic discrimination (L. Cohen, 1977). Despite low wages, most sent money home to help their families. They found it hard to bring their children to this country because it is difficult to gain permission for immigration of whole families to the United States. Much more needs to be learned about immigrant families in the United States from many parts of Central and South America, but there appears to be limited research about them. . . .

SOME IMPLICATIONS FOR RESEARCH

As we have seen, there has been relatively little research devoted to Hispanic-American families. Most studies have focused on selected marital attitudes and behaviors of Mexican-American couples. The majority of these studies have looked at what significant differences, if any, are to be found between these couples and their Anglo counterparts, especially in matters pertaining to traditional male-dominant behaviors and segregated, rigidly defined sex roles. No significant differences between groups have been found, and it seems that these particular questions do not need further general exploration with respect to Mexican-Americans. However, they might well be asked in studies of particularly problem-laden subgroups, as well as Puerto Rican, Cuban, and other Hispanic families in this country, with the appropriate use of demographic controls.

Research has far from answered a number of other questions that might be raised about Hispanic family relationships, including further exploration of the impact on marital and parent-child relationships of recent immigration, extended families, unmarried parenthood, divorce, remarriage, unemployment, substance abuse, and family violence.

Much more needs to be known about Hispanic child-rearing beliefs, attitudes, goals, and behaviors with respect to the various ethnic and social class groups and in association with child development outcomes in such areas as school achievement, parent and child satisfaction, crime and delinquency, and youth employment. . . .

REFERENCES

Alvirez, D., Bean, F., & Williams, D. (1981). "The Mexican-American Family." In C. H. Mindel and R. W. Habenstein (eds.), *Ethnic families in America: Patterns and variations* (2nd ed., pp. 269–292). New York: Elsevier.

Andrade, S. (1982). "Social science stereotypes of the Mexican American woman: Policy implications for research." *Hispanic Journal of Behavioral Science*, 4, 223–243.

Applebome, P. (1988, January 3). "Amnesty requests by aliens decline." *New York Times*, pp. 11, 12Y.

Arce, C. (1982, March). "Maintaining a group culture." *ISR Newsletter*.

Baca Zinn, M. (1980). "Employment and education of Mexican-American women: The interplay of modernity and ethnicity in eight families." *Harvard Educational Review*, 50, 47–62.

Bean, F. D., Curtis, R., and Marcum, J. (1977). "Families and marital status among Mexican Americans." *Journal of Marriage and the Family*, 39, 759–767.

Bernal, G. (1982). "Cuban families." In M. McGoldrick, J. K. Pearce, and J. Giordano (eds.), *Ethnicity and family therapy* (pp. 186–207), New York: Guilford.

Chilman, C. (1968). "Fertility and poverty in the United States." *Journal of Marriage and the Family*, 30, 207–227.

Chilman, C. (1983). *Adolescent sexuality in a changing american society: Social and psychological perspectives for human services professions.* New York: John Wiley.

Cohen, L. (1977). "The female factor in resettlement." *Society*, 14(6), 27–30.

Cortes, C. (1980). *The Cuban experience in the United States.* New York: Arno.

Cromwell, V. L., and Cromwell, R. E. (1978). "Perceived dominance in decision making and conflict resolution among Anglo, Black, and Chicano couples." *Journal of Marriage and the Family*, 40, 749–759.

Cuellar, I., Harris, L., and Jasso, R. (1980). "An acculturation scale for Mexican American normal and clinical populations." *Hispanic Journal of the Behavioral Sciences*, 2, 199–217.

Delgado, M. (1987). "Puerto Ricans." In *Encyclopedia of social work* (vol. 2, pp. 427–432). Silver Spring, MD: National Association of Social Workers.

de Silva, E. (1981). *Survival and adjustment skills to the new culture: Working with Hispanic women who have settled in the United States.* Paper presented at the National Conference on Social Welfare, San Francisco.

Dulles, F. (1959). *The United States since 1865.* Ann Arbor: University of Michigan Press.

Estrada, L. (1987). "Hispanics." In *Encyclopedia of social work* (vol. 1, pp. 730–739). Silver Spring, MD: National Association of Social Workers.

Falicov C. (1982). "Mexican families." In M. McGoldrick, J. K. Pearce, and J. Giordano (eds.), *Ethnicity and family therapy* (pp. 134–163). New York: Guilford.

Family Planning Perspectives. (1983). vol. 15(4), 197.

Fitzpatrick, J. (1981). "The Puerto Rican family." In C. H. Mindel and R. W. Habenstein (eds.), *Ethnic families in America: Patterns and variations* (2nd ed., pp. 189–214). New York: Elsevier.

Frisbie, W. (1986). "Variations in patterns of marital instability among Hispanics." *Journal of Marriage and Family Therapy*, 48, 99–106.

Garcia-Preto, N. (1982). "Puerto Rican families." In M. McGoldrick, J. K. Pearce, and J. Giordano (eds.), *Ethnicity and family therapy* (pp. 164–186). New York: Guilford.

Grebler, L., Moore, J. W., and Guzman, R. (1973). "The family: Variations in time and space." In L. Duran and H. Bernal (eds.), *Introduction to Chicano studies: A reader.* New York: Macmillan.

Hawkes, G., and Taylor, M. (1975). "Power structure in Mexican and Mexican-American farm labor families." *Journal of Marriage and the Family*, 37, 806–811.

Hetherington, M., Cox, M., and Cox, R. (1978). "The aftermath of divorce." In J. Stevens and M. Mathews (eds.), *Mother-child, father-child relationships.* Washington, DC; National Association for the Education of Young Children.

Jones, J. (1985). "Fertility-related care." In H. P. McAdoo and T. Parkam (eds.), *Services to young families* (pp. 167–206). Washington, DC: American Public Welfare Association.

Kraus, M. (1959). *The United States to 1865.* Ann Arbor: University of Michigan Press.

LaPorte, B. (1977). "Visibility of the new immigrants." *Society*, 14(6), 18–22.

Mirandé, A. (1977). "The Chicano family: A reanalysis of conflicting views." *Journal of Marriage and the Family*, 39, 747–756.

Mirandé, A. (1979). "Machismo: A reinterpretation of male dominance in the Chicano family." *Family Coordinator*, 28, 473–479.

Olsen, D., Russell, C., and Sprenkel, D. (1982). "The circumplex model of marital and family systems: VI. Theoretical update." *Family Process*, 22, 69–83.

Portes, A. (1979). "Labor functions of illegal aliens." *Society*, 14(6), 31–37.

Rodriguez, C., Sanchez-Korrol, V., and Alers, J. (1980). *The Puerto Rican struggle: Essays on survival.* New York: Puerto Rican Migration Research Consortium.

Staples, R. & Mirandé, A. (1980). "Racial and cultural variations among American families: An analytic review of the literature on minority families." *Journal of Marriage and the Family*, 42, 887–904.

Staton, R. (1972). "A comparison of Mexican and Mexican-American families." *Family Coordinator*, 21, 325–329.

U.S. Bureau of the Census. (1980). *Persons of Spanish Origin in the United States: March 1979* (Current Population Reports, Series P-20, no. 354). Washington, DC: Government Printing Office.

U.S. Bureau of the Census. (1983). *Characteristics of the population below the poverty level* (Current Population Reports, Series P-60, no. 138). Washington, DC: Government Printing Office.

Vasquez, M., and Gonzalez, A. (1981). "Sex roles among Chicanos." In A. Baron, Jr. (ed.), *Explorations in Chicano psychology* (pp. 50–70). New York: Praeger.

Vega, W. A., Kolody, B., and Valle, J. (1986). "The relationship of marital status, confidant support, and depression among Mexican immigrant women." *Journal of Marriage and the Family*, 48, 597–605.

Vega, W. A., Patterson, T., Sallis, J., Nader, P., Atkins, C., and Abramson, I. (1986). "Cohesion and adaptability in the Mexican American and Anglo families." *Journal of Marriage and the Family*, 48, 857–867.

Wallerstein, J. (1985). "The over-burdened child: Some long-term consequences of divorce." *Social Work*, 30, 116–123.

Ybarra, L. (1982). "When wives work." *Journal of Marriage and the Family*, 44, 169–177.

Zapata, J., and Jaramillo, P. (1981). "Research on the Mexican-American family." *Journal of Individual Psychology*, 37, 72–85.

R E A D I N G

29

African-Americans in the 1990s

William P. O'Hare, Kelvin M. Pollard, Taynia L. Mann, and Mary M. Kent

African-Americans—30 million in number in 1991—are the largest and most visible minority group in the United States.[1] Because of their population size, along with their legacy of slavery and legal subjugation, blacks occupy a special niche in U.S. society. We often view the progress of blacks as a litmus test of how open our society really is. Furthermore, as African-Americans become a larger share of the U.S. population, the black experience assumes a greater part of our national character.

From William P. O'Hare, Kelvin M. Pollard, Taynia L. Mann, and Mary M. Kent, "African-Americans in the 1990s," *Population Bulletin*, 46, no. 1 (July, 1991).

Blacks have made significant progress on many fronts since the 1950s and 1960s, when major civil rights legislation was enacted. In general, the education, health, living conditions, and incomes of African-Americans have improved. Many more blacks vote in elections and get elected to public office. But the remarkable progress of the post–World War II era appears to have slowed during the 1980s, even regressed in some areas. And African-American still rank below whites on nearly every measure of socioeconomic status.

The gap between the well-being of blacks and whites is continuing evidence of the second-class status of African-Americans. Black infants are twice as likely to die as are white infants. Black children are nearly three times more likely to live in a single-parent family or to live in poverty than are white children. Blacks are only half as likely to go to college; those who earn college degrees have incomes one-third less than do whites with the same education. And, while the number of affluent blacks has skyrocketed over the past decade, the net wealth of black households is only one-tenth that of whites.

Why has the progress of African-Americans slowed? Many observers feel that Ronald Reagan's presidential administration, which dominated national politics during most of the 1980s, was particularly harmful to black socioeconomic advancement, erasing civil rights gains and promoting a general antiminority climate. Others see a myriad of factors that combined to thwart the progress of blacks. Some of these factors have polarized American society in general, widening the gap between rich and poor and chipping away at the middle class. Among African-Americans, opportunities continue to open up for the educated middle class while the urban poor appear stuck in a quagmire of unstable families, intermittent employment, welfare dependence, and the temptations of crime.

This view of black Americans as living within two increasingly separate worlds gained wide acceptance during the 1980s. William Julius Wilson, a sociologist at the University of Chicago who emerged as a major analyst of U.S. blacks in the past decade, argues that economic changes, combined with social and demographic forces within the black community, produced these countervailing trends.[2] Wilson contends that the urban poor became more impoverished and more isolated because the decline of manufacturing and the movement of many blue-collar jobs to suburban areas eliminated a source of relatively well-paying, secure jobs for blacks. Joblessness increased among urban blacks, reducing the pool of marriageable men and undermining the strength of the family. Poverty increased as the number of female-headed households grew.

At the same time, new opportunities for middle-class blacks were generated by the expansion of civil rights. But the movement of the middle class out of the ghettos left "behind an isolated and very poor community without the institutions, resources and values necessary for success in modern society."[3]

This interpretation of the origins of urban poverty drew attention away from racial discrimination as the major barrier to the progress of African-Americans and toward the effects of broad economic, demographic, and social welfare trends. But recent studies provide new evidence that racial discrimination continues to undermine the progress of blacks.

Assessing the well-being of blacks is more difficult now than in the past. Only a few generations ago, 90 percent of African-Americans lived in poverty and racial inequities seemed obvious. Today, the root of the disparities between blacks and whites is harder to discern. Is racism dying, or is it still the primary reason for black underachievement? Why are some blacks moving into the middle and upper classes while others remain in poverty? There is no consensus about the answers to these complex questions. We can, however, sketch a portrait of African-Americans in the 1990s using demographic and socioeconomic data, and shed some light on these complex relationships.

AFRICAN-AMERICAN FAMILIES

No change in the black community has been more dramatic or more fundamental than the reordering of families and family relationships. In recent years, these changes have prompted many observers to proclaim a crisis in the black family, generally characterized by the growing numbers of poor, female-headed families.

While the vast majority of the 10 million African-American households are family households (that is, the household members are related by birth, marriage, or adoption), only about half the families were headed by a married couple in 1990, down from 68 percent in 1970 and 56 percent in 1980. A much higher percentage (83 percent) of white families are headed by married couples, although this percentage also has slipped over the past two decades.[4]

African-American households are larger than white households, but are slightly smaller than Hispanic households. The average black household contained 2.9 persons in 1990, compared with 2.6 persons for all whites and 3.5 persons for Hispanics. Both African-American and Hispanic female-headed households have one more person, on average, than households headed by whites females. Black households also are more likely than white to include adults in addition to a married couple or household head. In 1990, about a third of all black households included other adults, compared with only a fourth of white households.[5]

Changing Marriage Patterns

Marriage and divorce statistics since the 1960s record major shifts in the African-American family. In 1960, 65 percent of black women age 30 to 34 were in an intact marriage. In 1990, only 39 percent were married and living with their husbands. Over the same period, the percentage divorced grew from 8 to 12 percent, and the percentage who had never married grew from 10 to 35 percent. While a similar movement away from marriage occurred among white women, the change was much more dramatic among blacks.

Some analysts explain the decline in marriage among blacks in economic and demographic terms, while others cite more fundamental societal changes that have affected all Americans. The rising divorce rates and increase in the number of persons who choose not to marry may indicate that the institution of marriage itself is weakening. The marketplace and public institutions provide many of the goods and services that previously were the domain of the family. Low fertility rates have curtailed the number of years parents have dependent children living at home. The increased job opportunities for women make marriage less of an economic necessity, and, in the more tolerant climate of modern society, less of a social necessity for women. With a fourth of all children born to unmarried women, even childbearing is no longer confined to marriage. The movement away from marriage can also be seen as a consequence of modernization and urbanization, which has fostered individualism, weakening the family.[6]

Many social scientists focus on the relationship between marriage rates and the relative number of men and women. Women are more likely to marry when the ratio of men to women is high than when there is a relative shortage of men. The rapid rise in the number of births during the baby boom created a "marriage squeeze" in the 1970s and 1980s because there were more women than men in the marrying ages. This caused many young Americans to delay or forego marriage and childbearing.[7] This imbalance of the sexes was more extreme for the black than for the white population: On average, the ratio of males to females at birth is lower among blacks than whites,[8] and black male mortality is relatively high in the young adult ages. Even allowing for an undercount of black men in the census, black women outnumber men in the ages when most people marry and start families, age 20 to 49. Following this reasoning, fewer black women are getting married because there are not enough eligible men available.

In addition to demographic and social factors, economic changes—which eliminated many jobs held by black men in central city areas—and racial discrimination in hiring and firing have pushed many black men to the margins, or completely out, of the labor force. The deteriorating economic position of black men has been blamed for further discouraging the formation of married-couple families. Black men, with low wages and little job security, have difficulty fulfilling the traditional role as the major breadwinner for a family. The rise in female-headed families, whether formed through divorce, separation, or out-of-wedlock childbearing, has been linked to the decline in the ratio of employed black men per black woman.

Several analysts claim that welfare programs designed to aid single-parent families were a disincentive for low-income blacks to marry, although statistical analysis has failed to find a strong association between welfare payment levels and family composition.[9]

Many analysts argue that the modern African-American family has always differed from European-American families and should not be expected to conform to the married-couple pattern. Modern black family structure can be viewed as a legacy of slavery, when marriage among blacks was not recognized legally. Slave families tended to be consanguineal (organized around blood relatives) rather than conjugal (built around a married couple). Some trace this family structure back to the social structure in the African countries from which the ancestors of American blacks came.[10]

There is an ongoing debate as to whether the retreat from marriage among black Americans resulted directly from the disruptive effects of slavery; whether it is only indirectly associated with slavery through the continuing economic marginalization of blacks; or whether black culture and social structure, emanating from African roots, lead to different marriage and family patterns. Recently, social scientists have focused on issues related to the social and economic marginalization of black men to explain the low marriage rates among African-Americans.

Overwhelmingly, blacks still marry other blacks, despite opinion polls showing that interracial marriage has become socially acceptable to a growing percentage of Americans. The percentage of married African-Americans whose spouse is not black has not changed over the past decade. In 1987, only 3 percent of married blacks had a nonblack spouse. In contrast, about 16 percent of married Asians and Hispanics had a non-Asian or non-Hispanic spouse. When African-Americans do marry a nonblack, it is usually the wife who is white, Asian, or of another race.

The Children

African-American children have been most affected by the changes in marital status and family composition that have occurred over the past few decades. The share of black children living with two parents declined from 58 percent in 1970 to 38 percent in 1990.[11] Just over half (55 percent) of black children lived in a single-parent household in 1990, 51 percent with their mother. In contrast, 19 percent of white children lived in single-parent households in 1989—a significant share, but minor compared with the statistic for blacks (see Table 29.1).

TABLE 29.1   Living Arrangements of Children Under 18 by Race and Ethnic Group, 1990 (numbers in thousands)

	BLACKS		WHITES		HISPANICS[a]	
	Number	Percent	Number	Percent	Number	Percent
Total children	10,018	100.0	51,390	100.0	7,174	100.0
Living with						
Two parents	3,781	37.7	40,593	79.0	4,789	66.8
One parent	5,485	54.8	9,870	192.	2,154	30.0
Mother only	5,132	51.2	8,321	16.2	1,943	27.1
Father only	353	3.5	1,549	3.0	211	2.9
Other relative[b]	654	6.5	708	1.4	177	2.5
Nonrelative	98	1.0	220	0.4	54	0.8

[a]Hispanics may be of any race.

[b]463,000 black children and 452,000 white children lived with a grandparent with neither parent present.

Source: Bureau of the Census, *Current Population Reports* P-20, no. 447 (Washington, D.C.: GPO, 1990), table 4.

Black children are more likely to live with a grandparent than are white or Hispanic children. In 1990, 12 percent of black children lived in households that included their grandparents, compared with only 4 percent of whites and 6 percent of Hispanics.[12]

More than a fourth (27 percent) of all African-American children live with mothers who have never married. The percentage is highest among young children: 39 percent for children under age six.[13] One of the major consequences of living in a female-headed family is that such families generally have fewer economic resources than married-couple families. Nearly two-thirds are poor and live in central cities; over one-quarter live in public housing (see Table 29.2). The 3.8 million black children living in two-parent families appear privileged in comparison. Their parents are more educated, earn nearly four times as much money, and are more than twice as likely to own their own home. These stark differences highlight the two separate worlds inhabited by poor and middle-class black children, and suggest that the African-American population will become more polarized as these children mature.

FERTILITY

Black Americans have had higher fertility than white Americans for the past two centuries. At the height of the baby boom in the mid-1950s, blacks were having an average of 4.4 children per woman, compared with 3.6 among whites. Because of their higher birth rates and younger age structure, a disproportionately high share of U.S. births are black. In 1988, the National Center for Health Statistics registered 671,976 African-American births—17 percent of all births that year.[14] The total fertility rate (TFR), or total number of lifetime births per woman, has remained higher for blacks. The TFR, which provides a good barometer of fertility independent of age structure, was 32 percent higher for blacks than for whites in 1988—2.4 children per woman compared with 1.8 per woman for whites.

TABLE 29.2   Characteristics of Black Children and Their Families, 1990

	CHILDREN LIVING IN	
	Two-Parent Households	Female-Headed Households
Median family income (1989)	$31,757	$9,590
Percent of children whose families:		
Are headed by a high school graduate	79.2	66.0
Own their home	55.3	22.3
Live in central cities	49.7	63.6
Live in public housing	6.3	29.8
Have incomes below poverty	18.1	61.1

Source: Bureau of the Census, *Current Population Reports* P-20, no. 450 (Washington, D.C.: GPO, 1991), table 6.

There has been remarkable stability in the ratio of black to white fertility rates since 1960: the TFR for blacks has remained one-quarter to one-third higher than the TFR for whites. Fertility levels for blacks and whites fell in tandem during the 1960s and 1970s and have fluctuated similarly during the 1980s. The TFRs for both groups have risen slightly in recent years.[15]

Socioeconomic differences between blacks and whites explain much of the difference in their fertility levels. Birth rates are similar among black and white women with the same level of educational attainment, for example. In 1988, the completed fertility rate of black women age 35 to 44 with some college education was only 4 percent higher than that of their white counterparts. The black rate was 11 percent higher among women with less than a college education.[16] And among low-income families in 1985, white women were more likely to have had a child in the previous year than were black women.[17]

Regardless of the reasons, black fertility remains slightly higher than white fertility. In addition, two glaring disparities in the childbearing patterns of blacks and whites are cause for concern: compared with whites, black babies are nearly four times more likely to be born to a single mother, and three times more likely to be born to a young teenage mother.

In 1988, 64 percent of black babies were born out-of-wedlock, compared with 18 percent of white babies. Birth rates for unmarried women have soared in the 1980s, as shown in Figure 29.1. In fact, the rates have increased faster among whites than blacks. Still, single black women of every age are more likely to have a child than single white women. The disparity is greatest among teenagers. In 1988, unmarried white teenagers age 15 to 17 bore 17 births per 1,000 girls, while unmarried black teenagers bore 74 births per 1,000.

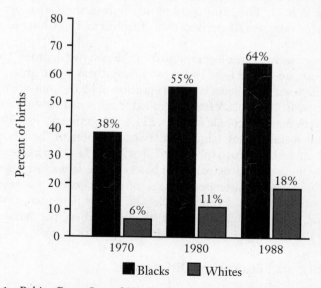

FIGURE 29.1 Babies Born Out-of-Wedlock, by Race, 1970, 1980, and 1988. *Source:* National Center for Health Statistics, *Monthly Vital Statistics Report* 39, no. 4, supplement (1990), table 18, and *Vital Statistics of the United States* 1987 (Washington, D.C.: GPO, 1989), table 1–31.

Birth rates for all teenagers have fallen over the past two decades. Between 1970 and 1985, the fertility rate for teenage black girls age 15 to 17, whether married or single, declined from 101 to 70 births per 1,000 girls; for white teenagers, the rate fell from 29 to 24. In the past several years, however, teenage fertility has edged upward. By 1988, birth rates had increased to 77 for black teenagers and to 26 for white teenagers. Throughout the 1980s, however, the gap between black and white teenage fertility remained fairly constant.

The disproportionately high rate of teen childbearing in the African-American community exacerbates many social problems. Health problems, high infant mortality, educational deficiencies, long-term welfare dependency, and poverty are among the consequences risked by teens who have babies. Teenage mothers are more likely to be unmarried, and therefore without the potential income and support a husband could provide. Many analysts also fear that a "cycle" of teenage childbearing may continue into succeeding generations.[18]

INCOME, WEALTH, AND POVERTY

Black family incomes increased during the 1950s and 1960s, but beginning with the recession in the early 1970s, the income levels for blacks have stagnated. In 1989, the median annual income for black families was $20,200, a 6 percent improvement over 1980 after adjusting for inflation, but slightly below the comparable figure for 1969.[19]

White families, in contrast, continued to increase their incomes during the 1970s and 1980s, albeit at a lower rate than during the expansionary years just after World War II. The ratio of black to white earnings has actually fallen. Black family income was 61 percent that of whites in 1969, but only 56 percent as high as in 1989.

Why have black families lost ground over the past two decades? Demographic factors explain part of the loss. Foremost among them is the growth in female-headed families, which pulled a larger proportion of black families into the lowest income groups. In 1989, black female-headed families had only a third the annual income of black married-couple families, $11,600 compared with $30,700.

Also, the average black family has fewer members in the labor force than white families, 1.51 compared with 1.67 in 1989. This 10 percent difference is explained by the lower participation of blacks in the labor force, higher unemployment rates, and greater percentages of single-parent households among black than white families. Even if blacks and whites held comparable jobs and earned equal pay, the higher number of wage-earners per family for whites would keep their average family income above that for blacks.

Age, Family, and Education Differences

Average income figures also fail to show the vast diversity within the African-American population. While the percentage of low-income families is much greater among blacks, there is also a solid middle class. The plethora of studies on blacks in poverty may give a distorted view of the African-American population.[20] Only a few writers have focused on the middle-class and affluent blacks, yet these groups have increased significantly.[21]

In 1989, 26 percent of black families had incomes below $10,000, 32 percent earned between $10,000 and $25,000, and 42 percent received $25,000 or more per year. Among whites, however, only 8 percent of families had incomes under $10,000, while 69 percent were in the $25,000 or over category.

Income levels differ markedly by educational level, age, and family type. Black married-couple families, for example, increased their earnings during the 1970s and 1980s. By 1989, the median income for blacks had grown to 82 percent that of whites for families in which both husband and wife worked.

In families headed by younger blacks, especially those with a college degree, average income is almost as high for blacks as it is for whites. Among married-couple families where the head of household is 25 to 44 years old and a college graduate, the median income of blacks ($54,400) is 93 percent that of whites ($58,800).[22]

Female-headed families rank at the bottom of the income distribution, but there is considerable diversity even within this group. The extremely low median income of black female-headed households—less than $12,000, compared with nearly $19,000 for white female-headed households—is partially attributable to the lower educational levels and the lower percentages of divorced women among blacks. White women are more likely to obtain a legal divorce, and therefore to receive alimony or child support, an important source of additional income. Among white and black women with similar marital and educational characteristics and who head their families, however, the income differences diminish. Average incomes for families headed by single women who are college graduates are no higher for white than for black families.

While a college education erases some of the income difference between whites and blacks, blacks do not reap the same financial rewards from education as do whites. The average incomes for blacks invariably are lower than for whites, regardless of educational level or geographic area (see Table 29.3). Race differences are somewhat smaller in the South than in the North, especially in nonmetropolitan areas where all incomes are lower.

THE FUTURE OF AFRICAN-AMERICANS

The history of the black population in the United States is fairly well documented, but what does the future hold for these Americans? Many of the forces that will shape the advancement of black Americans have been described above, but it is not clear what the sum of these forces portends.

Many of the trends outlined here suggest that the black population will be more diverse as America moves into the twenty-first century. The economic gap between rich and poor blacks is growing. Many black scholars argue that *race* will lose significance while *class* divisions gain importance. Already, many young

TABLE 29.3 Median Income and Poverty Rates by Education in Three Geographic Areas: Blacks and Whites Age 25–44, 1989

	METROPOLITAN NORTH		METROPOLITAN SOUTH		NONMETROPOLITAN SOUTH	
	Black	White	Black	White	Black	White
Median personal income (dollars per year)						
Less than high school	$5,700	$9,800	$6,000	$8,300	$4,900	$8,200
High school only	13,000	17,000	12,500	15,100	10,000	13,000
Some college	18,100	21,800	17,000	19,000	12,600	16,900
College graduate	26,000	30,100	24,000	29,000	20,000	22,500
Poverty rate (percent)						
Less than high school	51	23	41	26	52	25
High school only	24	6	18	8	24	10
Some college	13	3	13	4	23	6
College graduate	4	2	3	1	6	4

Source: Authors analysis of the March 1990 Current Population Survey.

blacks who spent most of their lives in post-1960s America see issues differently than their parents, who grew up enduring overt racial oppression.

The middle-class blacks of the future may feel little in common with poor blacks because their experiences will have been dramatically different in so many ways. By the year 2000, every black under age 40 (nearly 60 percent of the black population) will have grown up in the more hospitable post-1960 racial climate.

Yet racism—one of the major forces that led blacks to rely so heavily on one another—is still very much evident. While the attitudes of whites toward blacks have softened a great deal over the past few decades, many still harbor discriminatory attitudes. Indeed, efforts to promote fuller participation of blacks in colleges and the work force have generated claims of reverse discrimination by some whites. Furthermore, the actions of many whites in the voting booth, in hiring, and in decisions of where to live are at odds with the benign attitudes expressed in opinion polls. To confound matters, the rapid growth of Hispanics and Asians may imperil black economic advancement, heighten group tensions, and lead to stronger black cohesiveness. While the future of America's black population is uncertain, it is clear that African-Americans will continue to be a highly visible feature of the American social and political landscape.

NOTES

1. The terms "African-American" and "black" are used interchangeably in this report. The term "white" refers to all whites, including Hispanics, unless specifically stated otherwise. Hispanics may be of any race, but the majority are white.

2. William J. Wilson, *The Truly Disadvantaged: The Inner City, the Underclass, and Public Policy* (Chicago: University of Chicago Press, 1987); and William J. Wilson, *The Declining Significance of Race: Blacks and Changing American Institutions* (Chicago: University of Chicago Press, 1978).

3. Douglas Massey and Mitchell L. Eggers, "The Ecology of Inequality: Minorities and the Concentration of Poverty, 1970–1980," *American Journal of Sociology* 95 (March 1990)): 1153–1188.

4. Paul C. Glick, "A Demographic Picture of Black Families," in *Black Families*, ed. Harriette P. McAdoo (Beverly Hills, Calif.: Sage Publications, 1981), p. 108; and Bureau of the Census, "Household and Family Characteristics: March 1990 and 1989," *Current Population Reports* P-20, no. 447 (Washington, D.C.: GPO, 1990), table 1.

5. Bureau of the Census, P-20, no. 447, 1990, op. cit., table 16.

6. Thomas J. Espenshade, "Marriage Trends in America: Estimates, Implications, and Underlying Causes," *Population and Development Review* 11, no. 2 (1985): 193–245; and Charles Westoff, "Fertility Decline in the West: Causes and Prospects," *Population and Development Review* 9, no. 1 (1983): 99–104.

7. Espenshade, op. cit., pp. 232–234.

8. Among white Americans, nearly 106 male babies are born for every 100 female babies, on average. Among African-Americans, 103 males are born for every 100 females. Male mortality is higher than female at every age, further depleting the number of African-American men relative to women. For the 20 to 49 age group, there are only 89 black men for every 100 black women.

9. Wilson 1987, op. cit., pp. 95–100; Jaynes and Williams, op cit., p. 531; see also Reynolds Farley and Walter R. Allen, *The Color Line and the Quality of Life in America* (New York: Russell Sage Foundation, 1987), p. 170.

10. Farley and Allen, op. cit., p. 171; and Floretta Dukes McKenzie, "Education Strategies for the '90s," in *The State of Black America 1991*, ed. Janet Dewart (New York: National Urban League, Inc., 1991), pp. 95–110.

11. Glick, op. cit., p. 110; and Bureau of the Census, "Marital Status and Living Arrangements: March 1990," *Current Population Reports* P-20, no. 450 (Washington, D.C.: GPO, 1991), table 4.

12. Bureau of the Census, P-20 no. 450, 1991, op. cit., table 4.

13. Ibid., tables 4 and 6.

14. National Center for Health Statistics, "Advance Report of Final Natality Statistics 1988," *Monthly Vital Statistics Report* 39, no. 4, supplement (15 August 1990), table 1.

15. Ibid., table 4.

16. Bureau of the Census, "Fertility of American Women: June 1988," *Current Population Reports* P-20, no. 436 (Washington, D.C.: GPO, 1989), table 2.

17. O'Hare 1987, op. cit., p. 46.

18. Reid, op. cit., pp. 12–13.

19. Bureau of the Census, P-60, no. 168, 1990. op. cit., table 8.

20. Wilson 1987, op. cit.; Jencks and Peterson, op. cit.; Ken Auletta, *The Underclass* (New York: Random House, 1982); Fred Harris and Roger W. Wilkins, eds., *Quiet Riots: Race and Poverty in the United States* (New York: Pantheon Books, 1988); and Nicholas Lemann, *Promised Land: the Great Black Migration and How it Changed America* (New York: Alfred A. Knopf, 1991).

21. Bart Landry, *The New Black Middle Class* (Berkeley, Calif.: University of California Press, 1987); and William P. O'Hare, "In the Black," *American Demographics* 11 (November 1989): 25–29.

22. Bureau of the Census, P-60, no. 168, 1990, op. cit., table 4.

CHAPTER 10

❖

THE AGE
REVOLUTION

READING
30

The Family in an Aging Society: A
Matrix of Latent Relationships

Matilda White Riley

I am going to talk about families and the revolution in longevity. This revolution has produced configurations in kinship structure and in the internal dynamics of family life at every age that have never existed before.

Over two-thirds of the total improvement in longevity from prehistoric times until the present has taken place in the brief period since 1900 (Preston, 1976). In the United States, life expectancy at birth has risen from less than 50 in 1900 to well over 70 today. Whereas at the start of the century most deaths occurred in infancy and young adulthood, today the vast majority of deaths are postponed to old age. Indeed we are approaching the "squared" mortality curve,

From *Journal of Family Issues*, Vol. 4, No. 3, September 1983, pp. 439–454. Copyright © 1983 by Sage Publications, Inc. By permission of Sage Publications, Inc.

in which relatively few die before the end of the full life span. For the first time in all history, we are living in a society in which most people live to be old.[1]

Though many facts of life extension are familiar, their meanings for the personal lives of family members are elusive. Just how is increasing longevity transforming the kinship structure? Most problematic of all, how is the impact of longevity affecting those sorely needed close relationships that provide emotional support and socialization for family members (see Parsons and Bales, 1955)? To answer such questions, I must agree with other scholars in the conclusion that we need a whole new way of looking at the family, researching it, living in it, and dealing with it in professional practice and public policy.

Indeed, an exciting new family literature is beginning to map and interpret these unparalleled changes: it is beginning to probe beneath the surface for the subjective implications of the protracted and intricate interplay of family relationships. As the kinship structure is transformed, many studies are beginning to ask new questions about how particular relationships and particular social conditions can foster or inhibit emotional support and socialization—that is, the willingness to learn from one another. They are asking how today's family can fill people's pressing need for close human relationships.

From this developing literature, four topics emerge as particularly thought-provoking: (1) the dramatic extension of the kinship structure; (2) the new opportunities this extension brings for close family relationship; (3) the special approaches needed for understanding these complex relationships; and (4) the still unknown family relationship of older people in the future. I shall touch briefly on each of these topics. From time to time I shall also suggest a few general propositions—principles from the sociology of age (see M. W. Riley, 1976; forthcoming) that seem clearly applicable to changing family relationships. Perhaps they will aid our understanding of increasing longevity and the concomitant changes about us. The propositions may guide us in applying our new understanding in research, policy, and practice.

THE CHANGING CONFIGURATIONS OF THE KINSHIP STRUCTURE

I shall begin with the kinship structure as influenced by longevity. The extent and configurations of this structure have been so altered that we must rethink our traditional view of kinship. As four (even five) generations of many families are now alive at the same time, we can no longer concentrate primary attention on nuclear families of young parents and their children who occasionally visit or provide material assistance to grandparents or other relatives. I have come to think of today's large and complex kinship structure as a matrix of latent relationships—father with son, child with great-grandparent, sister with sister-in-law, ex-husband with ex-wife, and so on—relationships that are latent because they might or might not become close and significant during a lifetime. Thus I am proposing a definition of the kinship structure as a latent web of continually shifting linkages that provide the *potential* for activating and intensifying close family relationships.

The family literature describes two kinds of transformations in this structure that result from increasing longevity: (1) The linkages among family members have been prolonged, and (2) the surviving generations in a family have increased in number and complexity.

Prolongation of Family Relationships

Consider how longevity has prolonged family relationships. For example, in married couples a century ago, one or both partners were likely to have died before the children were reared. Today, though it may seem surprising, couples marrying at the customary ages can anticipate surviving together (apart from divorce) as long as 40 or 50 years on the average (Uhlenberg, 1969, 1980). As Glick and Norton (1977:14) have shown, one out of every five married couples can expect to celebrate their fiftieth wedding anniversary. Because the current intricacy of kinship structures surpasses even the language available to describe it (our step-in-laws might not like to be called "outlaws"), it sometimes helps to do "thought experiments" from one's own life. As marital partners, my husband and I have survived together for over 50 years. What can be said about the form (as distinct from the content) of such a prolonged relationship?

For one thing, we share over half a century of experience. Because we are similar in age, we have shared the experience of aging—biologically, psychologically, and socially—from young adulthood to old age. Because we were born at approximately the same time (and thus belong to the same cohort), we have shared much the same historical experiences—the same fluctuations between economic prosperity and depression, between periods of pacifism and of war, between political liberalism and reactionism, and between low and high rates of fertility. We have also shared our own personal family experiences. We shared the bearing and raising of young children during our first-quarter century together; during our second quarter century we adjusted our couplehood to our added roles as parents-in-law and grandparents. The third quarter-century of our married life, by the laws of probability, should convert us additionally into grandparents-in-law and great-grandparents as well. In sum, prolonged marriages like ours afford extensive common experiences with aging, with historical change, and with changing family relationships.

Such marriages also provide a home—an abiding meeting place for two individuals whose separate lives are engrossed in varied extrafamilial roles. Just as longevity has prolonged the average duration of marriage, it has extended many other roles (such as continuing education, women's years of work outside the home, or retirement). For example, Barbara Torrey (1982) has estimated that people spend at least a quarter of their adult lives in retirement. Married couples, as they move through the role complexes of their individual lives, have many evening or weekend opportunities either to share their respective extrafamilial experiences, to escape from them, or (though certainly not in my own case) to vent their boredom or frustration on one another (see Kelley, 1981).

Thus two features of protracted marriages become apparent. First, these marriages provide increasing opportunity to accumulate shared experiences and meanings and perhaps to build from these a "crescive" relationship, as suggested by Ralph Turner (1970) and Gunhild Hagestad (1981). But second, they also present shifting exigencies and role conflicts that require continual mutual accommodation and recommendation. As Richard Lazarus (DeLongis, et al., 1982) has shown, "daily hassles" can be more destructive of well-being than traumatic family events. And Erving Goffman (1959:132) warns that the home can become a "backstage area" in which "it is safe to lapse into an asociable mood of sullen, silent irritability."

Many marriages, not ended by death, are ended by divorce. The very extension of marriage may increase the likelihood of divorce, as Samuel Preston (1976:176–177) has shown. Returning to my personal experience, I was the only one of four sisters who did not divorce and remarry. But as long as their ex-husbands were alive none of my sisters could ever entirely discount the remaining potential linkages between them. These were not only ceremonial or instrumental linkages, but also affective linkages that could be hostile and vindictive, or (as time passes and need arises) could renew concern for one another's well-being. Whatever the nature of the relationship, latent linkages to ex-spouses persist. Thus, a prolonged marriage (even an ex-marriage) provides a continuing potential for a close relationship that can be activated in manifold ways.

The traditional match-making question—"Will this marriage succeed or fail?"—must be replaced and oft-repeated as the couple grows older by a different question: "Regardless of our past, can we—do we want [to]—make the fresh effort to succeed, or shall we fail in this marriage?"

Here I will state as my first proposition: *Family relationships are never fixed:* they change as the self and the significant other family members grow older, and as the changing society influences their respective lives. Clearly, the longer the relationship endures (because of longevity) the greater the opportunity for relational changes.

If, as lives are prolonged, marital relationships extend far beyond the original nuclear household, parent-offspring relationships also take on entirely new forms. For example, my daughter and I have survived together so far for 45 years of which only 18 were in the traditional relationship of parent and child. Unlike our shorter-lived forebearers, my daughter and I have been able to share many common experiences although at different stages of our respective lives. She shares a major portion of the historical changes that I have experienced. She also shares my earlier experience of sending a daughter off to college, and will perhaps share my experience of having a daughter marry and raise children. Of course, she and I differ in age. (In Alice Rossi's study of biological age differences, 1980, the consequences for parent-offspring relationships of the reciprocal tensions between a pubescent daughter and her older mother who is looking ahead to the menopausal changes of midlife were explored.)[2] Although the relational age between me and my daughter—the 26 years that separate us—remains the same throughout our lives, the implications of this difference change drastically from infancy to my old age.

Number and Stability of Generations

I have dwelt at length on the prolongation of particular relationships to suggest the consequent dramatic changes in the family structure. Longevity has, in addition, increased the stability and the number of generations in a family. A poignant example of this instability (Imhof, 1982) can be found in an eighteenth century parish where a father could spawn twenty-four offspring of whom only three survived to adulthood—a time in which "it took two babies to make one adult." With increased longevity each generation becomes more stable because more of its members survive. For the young nuclear family in the United States, for example, though the number of children born in each family has been declining over this century, increased longevity has produced a new stability in the family structure. In an important quantitative analysis, Peter Uhlenberg (1980) has shown how the probability of losing a parent or a sibling through death before a child reaches age 15 [has] decreased from .51 in 1900 to .09 in 1976. Compared with children born a century ago, children born today are almost entirely protected against death of close family members (except for elderly relatives). To be sure, while mortality has been declining, divorce rates have been increasing but less rapidly. Thus, perhaps surprisingly, Uhlenberg demonstrates that disruptions of marriage up through the completion of child rearing have been declining since 1900. In other words, many marriages have been broken by divorce, but overall more have remained intact because of fewer deaths! Thus the young family as well as each of the older generations becomes more stable through survival.

At the same time, the number of older generations has been increasing. Looking up the generational ladder, increasing numbers of a child's four grandparents survive. Among middle-aged couples, whereas back in 1900 more than half had no surviving elderly parents, today half have two or more parents still alive (Uhlenberg, 1980:318). Conversely looking down the generational ladder, each set of elderly parents has adult children with spouses and children of their own. Meanwhile, the increase in divorce and remarriage (four out of five divorced people remarry) compounds the complexity of this elaborate structure, as Andrew Cherlin (1981) has shown. In my own family, for example, each of our two middle-aged children have their own children, and they also have us as two elderly parents; my daughter's husband also has two parents; and my son (who has married twice) has his ex-wife's parents and his current wife's mother, father, and step-mother in addition to us. A complex array!

Of course, as these surviving generations proliferate and overlap, each generation is continually growing older and moving up the generational ladder to replace its predecessor until ultimately the members of the oldest generation die. Because of longevity, every generation—the oldest as well as the youngest—is increasingly stable and more likely to include its full complement of surviving members.

CHANGING DYNAMICS OF CLOSE FAMILY RELATIONSHIPS

What, then, are the implications of this greatly expanded kinship structure for the dynamics of close family relationships? How does the matrix of latent kinship linkages provide for close ties between particular individual lives, as these lives weave in and out of the intricate and continually shifting kinship network? Under what conditions do some family members provide (or fail to provide) recognition, advice, esteem, love, and tension release for other family members?

The answer, it seems to me, lies in the enlarged kinship structure: It provides many new opportunities for people at different points in their lives to select and activate the relationships they deem most significant. That is, the options for close family bonds have multiplied. Over the century, increased longevity has given flexibility to the kinship structure, relaxing both the temporal and the spatial boundaries of optional relationships.

Temporally, new options have arisen over the course of people's lives because, as we have seen, particular relationships have become more enduring. Particular relationships (even following divorce) are bounded only by the birth and death of members. Now that the experience of losing family members by death is no longer a pervasive aspect of the full life course (and is in fact rare except in old age), people have greater opportunity to plan their family lives. They have time to make mutual adjustments to personal crises or to external threats such as unemployment or the fear of nuclear war. Here we are reminded of my first proposition: Family relationships are never fixed, but are continually in process and subject to change. As family members grow older, they move across time—across history and through their own lives—and they also move upward through the generations in their own families and the age strata of society.[3] As individual family members who each pursue a separate life course, thoughts and feelings for one another are developed; their lives weave together or apart so as to activate, intensify, disregard, or disrupt particular close relationships. Thus the relationship between a mother and daughter can, for example, become close in the daughter's early childhood, her first years of marriage, and again after her children have left home although there may be interim lapses. Or, as current norms permit, couples can try each other out through cohabitation, before deciding whether or not to embark upon marriage.

Just as such new options for close ties have emerged from the prolongation of family relationships, other options have arisen because the number and variety of latent linkages has multiplied across the entire kinship structure. Spatially, close relationships are not bounded by the nuclear households that family members share during their younger lives. Given the intricacy of current kin networks, a wide range of linkages can be activated—between grandchild and grandparent, between distantly related cousins, between the ex-husbands of sisters, or between a child and his or her new step-parent. (Only in Grimm's fairy tales, which reflected the earlier frequency of maternal deaths and successive remarriages, were step-mothers always "wicked.") Aided by modern communication and transportation, affection and interaction can persist even during long periods of separation. On occasion, long-separated relatives or those not closely related may arrange to live together or to join in congregate housing or communes.

Given these options, let me now state a second general proposition: As active agents in directing the course of their own lives, *individuals have a degree of control over their close family relationships.* This control, I submit, has been enhanced because longevity has widened the opportunities for selecting and activating relationships that can provide emotional support and advice when needed.

This part of my discussion suggests a new view of the family. Perhaps we need now to think of a family less as the members of one household with incidental linkages to kin in other households and more as a continuing interplay among intertwined lives within the entire changing kinship structure. The closeness of these intertwined lives and the mutual support they provide depend on many factors (including the predispositions of each individual and the continuing motivation to negotiate and renegotiate their joint lives) but the enlarged kinship structure provides the potential.

NEW APPROACHES TO FAMILY RESEARCH AND PRACTICE

Before considering how the oldest family members—those in the added generation—fit into these intertwined lives, let me pause to ask how we can approach these complex and changing family relationships. If the tidy concept of the nuclear family is no longer sufficient, how can we deal in research and in professional practice with the newly emerging concepts? Clearly, special approaches are required for mapping and understanding the centrifugal and centripetal processes of family relationships within the increasing complexity of the kinship matrix. Such approaches must not only take into account my first two propositions (that relationships continually change, and that family members themselves have some control over this change) but must also consider a third proposition: *The lives of family members are interdependent* such that each person's family life continually interacts with the lives of significant relatives. Though long-recognized by students of the family, this proposition takes on fresh significance in the matrix of prolonged relationships.

As case examples, I shall describe two or three studies that illustrate how we can deal with the family as a system of interdependent lives. These studies are also important as they add to our understanding of emotional support and socialization under current family conditions.

In one study of socialization outcomes, Mavis Hetherington et al. (1977) have shown how parental disruption through divorce has a complex impact on the still-intertwined lives of the spouses and on the socialization of their children. Over a two-year period, detailed investigations were made of nursery school boys and girls and their parents, half of whom were divorced and the other half married. Differences were detected: Divorced parents showed comparatively less affection for their children, had less control over them, and elicited more dependent, disobedient, and aggressive child behavior—particularly in mother-son interactions. But relations between the parents also made a difference in these parent-child relationships: If divorced couples kept conflict low and agreed about child rearing, their ineffectiveness in dealing with children could be somewhat offset. This two-year tracing of the three-way interrelationships among spouses and children in disrupted families yields many insights into the interdependence of life course processes.

As family relationships are prolonged, socialization is more frequently recognized as a reciprocal process that potentially extends throughout the lives of parents and children as well as of marital partners. How can socialization operate across generations that belong to differing periods of historical change? One key mechanism, as Marilyn Johnson (1976) has demonstrated, is normative expectations. Parents can influence offspring by expecting behavior that is appropriate to social change, and can in turn be guided by offspring in formulating these expectations. Such subtleties to intergenerational influence are illustrated in a small study which Johnson and I made of high school students in the early 1960s (see Riley, 1982). Just as women's careers were burgeoning, we found that most girls looked forward to combining a career with marriage, whereas most boys did not anticipate marrying wives who worked. How had these young people been socialized to such sharply conflicting norms? We questioned their mothers and fathers to find out. Indeed we learned that, on the whole, parents wanted self-fulfillment for their daughters both in marriage and in work outside the home, while for their sons they wanted wives who would devote themselves fully to home and children. These slight yet provocative findings did presage the future impact of the women's movement on family lives, but I note them here as another instance of research that fits together the differing perspectives of the several interdependent family members.

Analyzing such studies of close relationships impresses one with the problem of studying families from what is often called the "life course" or "lifespan perspective" (see Dannefer, forthcoming). We are indeed concerned with people moving through life. Yet we are concerned not with a single life or a statistical aggregate of lives, but with the dynamic family systems of interdependent lives. An example I often use in teaching comes from the early work of Cottrell and Burgess in predicting success or failure in marriage. Starting with a case study, Cottrell (1933) saw each partner in a marriage as reenacting his or her childhood roles. He showed how the outcome of the marriage depended upon the mesh between these two different sets of early-life experiences—that is, how nearly they would fit together so that each partner met the role expectations of the other. Unfortunately, however, these researchers subsequently departed from this admirable model by questioning large samples of men and women as individuals and then analyzing the data for separate aggregates of men and women rather than for male-female pairs. Each individual was given a score of likely success in marriage, but without considering the success of a marriage between a particular man and a particular woman! Because the interdependent lives were not examined jointly, the central objective of the project was lost.

This difficulty, which I now call "life-course reductionism," still persists. Although many studies purport to study families as systems, they in fact either aggregate individual lives (as Cottrell and Burgess did) or reason erroneously from the lives of single members about the lives of other family members significant to the relationship. The danger of not considering a key family member is highlighted, for example, in Frank Furstenberg's (1981) review of the literature on kinship relations after divorce. Some studies had suggested that divorce disrupts the relations with parents-in-law (that is, with the parents of the ex-spouse) but these studies failed to include the children of the broken marriage. Only after examining the children's generation was it learned that they, by retaining contact with both sets of their grandparents, could help to link divorced spouses to their former in-laws. Supporting this clue from a small study of his own, Furstenberg found that the ties between grandparents and grandchildren did continue to exist in most cases, even though for the divorced parents (the middle generation) the former in-law relationships were largely attenuated or broken. In reconstituted families, then, grandparents can perhaps serve as "kinkeepers."

Among the studies that pursue close relationships across three generations is a national survey of divorce and remarriage now being conducted by Frank Furstenberg, Andrew Cherlin, Nicholas Zill, and James Peterson. In this era of widespread divorce and remarriage, this study is examining the important hypothesis that new intergenerational ties created by remarriage will balance—or more than balance—the losses incurred as a result of divorce. Step-relationships may replace disrupted natural relationships. The intricacy of interdependent lives within our proliferating kinship structure is dramatized by the design of this study. Starting with a sample of children aged 11 to 16 and their parents (who were originally interviewed five years earlier) the research team will now also question these children's grandparents; note that there can be two sets of grandparents where the parents are in intact first marriages or have been divorced, three sets if one parent has remarried after divorce, and four sets (no less than eight grandparents) if both have remarried. Thus, as surviving generations proliferate, their part in the family system will be explored in this study by questioning the many members of the grandparent generation. Surviving generations cannot be fully understood (as many studies of three generations have attempted) by examining a simple chain of single individuals from each of the generations.

These studies, as models for research, reflect the complex family relationships within which people of all ages today can seek or can give affection, encouragement, companionship, or advice.

OLDER GENERATIONS OF THE FUTURE

About the fourth generation (great-grandparents) that is being contributed by longevity, I want to make three final points.

First, it is too early to tell how an enlarged great-grandparent generation will fit into the kinship structure, or what close family relationships it may form. It is too early because the marked increase in longevity among the old began only in recent decades and are still continuing at a rate far exceeding earlier predictions (Preston, 1976; Manton, 1982; Brody and Brock, n.d.). Will this added generation be regarded as the more familiar generation of grandparents has been regarded—either as a threat to the young adult generation's independence, or as a "social problem" for family and community, requiring care from the mid-generation that is "squeezed" between caring for both young children and aging parents? Or will an added fourth generation mean new coalitions and new forms of personal relationships? And what of five-generation families in which a grandmother can be also a granddaughter (see Hagestad, 1981)? It is still too early to tell what new family norms will develop (see Riley, 1978).

Second, while we do not know how a fourth or even a fifth generation may fit in, we do know that most older family members are not dependent or disabled (some 5 percent of those 65 and over are in nursing homes). For those requiring care or instrumental support, families generally make extraordinary efforts to provide it (see Shanas, 1979). Yet most of the elderly, and especially those who are better educated and more active, are stronger, wiser, more competent, and more independent than is generally supposed. Public stereotypes of old people are far more negative than old people's assessments of themselves (National Council on the Aging, 1981). Healthy members of this generation, like their descendants, must earn their own places in the family and create their own personal ties. They cannot expect obligatory warmth or emotional support.

Third, at the close of their lives, however, old people will need advice and emotional support from kin. This need is not new in the annals of family history. What is new is the fact that terminal illness and death are no longer scattered across all generations but are concentrated in the oldest one. Today two-thirds of all deaths occur after age 65, and 30 percent after age 80 (Brody and Brock, n.d.). And, although most deaths occur outside the home, programs such as the hospice movement are being developed for care of the dying in the home where the family can take part (see J. W. Riley, forthcoming).

In conclusion, I have attempted to trace the impact of the unprecedented increases in longevity on the family and its relationships. In our own time the kinship structure has become more extensive and more complex, the temporal and spatial boundaries of the family have been altered, and the opportunities for close family relationships have proliferated. These relationships are no longer prescribed as strict obligations. They must rather be earned—created and recreated by family members throughout their long lives. Each of us is in continuing need of advice and emotional support from one another, as we contend with personal challenges and troubles, and with the compelling effects of societal changes in the economy, in technology, in culture, and in values. We all must agree with Mary Jo Bane (1976) that the family is here to stay, but in forms that we are beginning to comprehend only now. As members of families and students of the family—whether we are theorists, researchers, counselors, or policy makers—we must begin to realign our thinking and our practice to incorporate the new realities that are being engendered by increasing longevity.

NOTES

1. Note that increasing longevity in a society is not necessarily the same as increasing proportions of old people in the population, a proportion influenced in the long-term more by fertility than by mortality. Longevity affects individual lives and family structures, while population composition affects the total society.

2. Gunhild Hagestad (1982) talks even of menopausal grandmothers with pubescent granddaughters.

3. Of course, divisions between generations are only loosely coterminous with age divisions (see the discussion of the difference between "generations" and "cohorts" in the classic piece by Duncan, 1966, and a definitive formulation of this distinction in Kertzer, forthcoming). As Gunhild Hagestad (1981) puts it, "people do not file into generations by cohorts." There are wide ranges in the ages at which particular individuals marry and have children. In addition to the recognized differences by sex, there are important differences by social class. For example, Graham Spanier (Spanier and Glick, 1980) shows how the later marriage age in upper as compared with lower socioeconomic classes postpones many subsequent events in the lives of family members, thus slowing the proliferation in numbers of surviving generations.

REFERENCES

Bane, M. J. 1976. *Here to Stay: American Families in the 20th Century*. New York: Basic Books.

Brody, J. A., and D. B. Brock, n.d. "Epidemiologic and statistical characteristics of the United States elderly population." (unpublished)

Cherlin, A. J. 1981. *Marriage, Divorce, Remarriage*. Cambridge, MA: Harvard University Press.

Cottrell, L. S., Jr. 1933. "Roles and marital adjustment." *American Sociological Society*, 27, 107–115.

Dannefer, D. Forthcoming. "The sociology of the life course." *Annual Review of Sociology*.

DeLongis, A., J. C. Coyne, G. Dakof, S. Folkman, and R. S. Lazarus. 1982. "Relationship of daily hassles, uplifts, and major life events to health status." *Health Psychology*, 1, 119–136.

Duncan, O. D. 1966. "Methodological issues in the analysis of social mobility," pp. 51–97 in N. J. Smelser and S. M. Lipsett (eds.), *Social Structure and Mobility in Economic Development*. Chicago, IL: Aldine.

Furstenberg, F. F., Jr. 1981. "Remarriage and intergenerational relations," pp. 115–142 in R. W. Fogel et al. (eds.), *Aging: Stability and Change in the Family*. New York: Academic Press.

Glick, P. C., and A. J. Norton. 1977, "Marrying, divorcing, and living together in the U.S. today." Population Bulletin 32. Washington, D.C. Population Reference Bureau.

Goffman, E. 1959. *The Presentation of Self in Everyday Life*. Garden City, NY: Doubleday.

Hagested, G. O. 1982. "Older women in intergenerational relations." Presented at the Physical and Mental Health of Aged Women Conference, October 21–22, Case Western University, Cleveland, OH.

———. 1981, "Problems and promises in the social psychology of intergenerational relations," pp. 11–46 in R. W. Fogel et al. (eds.), *Aging: Stability and Change in the Family*. New York: Academic Press.

Hetherington, E. M., M. Cox, and R. Cox. 1977. "The aftermath of divorce," in J. H. Stevens, Jr. and M. Matthews (eds.), *Mother-Child, Father-Child Relations*. Washington, D.C.: National Association for the Education of Young Children.

Imhof, A. E. 1982. "Life course patterns of women and their husbands—16th to 20th century." Presented at the International Conference on Life Course Research on Human Development, September 17, Berlin, Germany.

Johnson, M. 1976. "The role of perceived parental models, expectations and socializing behaviors in the self-expectations of adolescents, from the U.S. and West Germany." Dissertation, Rutgers University.

Kelley, H. H. 1981. "Marriage relationships and aging," pp. 275–300 in R. W. Fogel et al. (eds.), *Aging: Stability and Change in the Family*. New York: Academic Press.

Kertzer, D. I. Forthcoming. "Generations as a sociological problem." *Annual Review of Sociology*.

Manton, K. G. 1982. "Changing concepts of morbidity and mortality in the elderly population." Milbank Memorial Fund Q. 60: 183–244.

National Council on the Aging. 1981. *Aging in the Eighties: America in Transition*. Washington, D.C.: Author.

Parsons, T., and R. F. Bales. 1955. *Family, Socialization and Interaction Process*. New York: Free Press.

Preston, S. H. 1976. *Mortality Patterns in National Population: With Special References to Recorded Causes of Death*. New York: Academic Press.

Riley, J. W., Jr. Forthcoming. "Dying and the meanings of death: sociological inquiries." Annual Review of Sociology.

Riley, M. W. 1976. "Age strata in social systems," pp. 189–217 in R. H. Binstock and E. Shanas (eds.), *Handbook of Aging and the Social Sciences*. New York: Van Nostrand Reinhold.

———. 1978. "Aging, social change, and the power of ideas." Daedalus 107, 4: 39–52.

———. 1982. "Implications for the middle and later years," pp. 399–405 in P. W. Berman and E. R. Ramey (eds.), *Women: A Development Perspective NIH Publication* No. 82-2298. Washington, DC: Dept. of Health and Human Services.

———. Forthcoming. "Age strata in social systems," in R. H. Binstock and E. Shanas (eds.), *The New Handbook of Aging and the Social Sciences*.

Rossi, A. S. 1980. "Aging and parenthood in the middle years," in P. B. Baltes and O. G. Brim, Jr. (eds.), *Life-Span Development and Behavior 3*. New York: Academic Press.

Shanas, E. 1979. "Social myth as hypothesis: the case of the family relations of old people." *The Gerontologist* 19: 3–9.

Spanier, G. B., and P. C. Glick. 1980. "The life cycle of American families: an expanded analysis," J. of Family History: 97–111.

Torrey, B. B. 1982. "The lengthening of retirement," pp. 181–196 in M. W. Riley et al. (eds.), *Aging from Birth to Death, vol. II: Sociotemporal Perspectives*. Boulder, CO: Westview.

Turner, R. H. 1970. *Family Interaction*. New York: John Wiley.

Uhlenberg, P. R. 1969. "A study of cohort life cycles: cohorts of native born Massachusetts women. 1830–1920," Population Studies 23, 3: 407–420.

———. 1980. "Death and the family." J. of Family History (Fall): 313–320.

R E A D I N G

31

The Modernization of Grandparenthood

Andrew J. Cherlin and Frank F. Furstenberg, Jr.

Writing a book about grandparents may seem an exercise in nostalgia, like writing about the family farm. We tend to associate grandparents with old-fashioned families—the rural, extended, multigenerational kind much celebrated in American mythology. Many think that grandparents have become less important as the nation has become more modern. According to this view, the shift to factory and office work meant that grandparents no longer could teach their children and grandchildren the skills needed to make a living: the fall in fertility and the rise in divorce weakened family ties; and the growth of social welfare programs meant that older people and their families were less dependent on each other for support. There is some truth to this perspective, but it ignores a powerful set of historical facts that suggest that grandparenthood—as a distinct and nearly universal stage of family life—is a post–World War II phenomenon.

Consider first the effect of falling rates of death. Much of the decline in mortality from the high preindustrial levels has occurred in this century. According to calculations by demographer Peter Uhlenberg, only about 37 percent of all males and 42 percent of all females born in 1870 survived to age sixty-five; but for those born in 1930 the comparable projections were 63 percent for males and 77 percent for females. The greatest declines in adult mortality have occurred in the last few decades, especially for women. The average number of years that a forty-year-old white woman could expect to live increased by four between 1900 and 1940; but between 1940 and 1980 it increased by seven. For men the increases have been smaller, though still substantial: a two-year increase for forty-year-old whites between 1900 and 1940 and a four-year increase between 1940 and 1980. (The trends for nonwhites are similar.) Consequently, both men and women can expect to live much longer lives than was the case a few decades ago, and more and more women are outliving men. In 1980, the average forty-year-old white woman could expect to live to age eighty, whereas the average forty-year-old white man could expect to live only to age seventy-four. As a result, 60 percent of all the people sixty-five and over in the United States in 1980 were women. Thus, there are many more grandparents around today than just a few decades ago simply because people are living longer—and a majority of them are grandmothers.

This decline in mortality has caused a profound change in the relationship between grandparents and grandchildren. For the first time in history, most adults live long enough to get to know most of their grandchildren, and most children have the opportunity to know most of their grandparents. A child born in 1900, according to Uhlenberg, had a better than nine-out-of-ten chance that two or more of his grandparents would be alive. But by the time that child reached age fifteen, the chances were only about one out of two that two or more of his grandparents would still be alive. Thus, some children were fortunate enough to establish relationships with grandparents, but in many other families the remaining grandparents must have died while the grandchild was quite young. Moreover, it was unusual for grandchildren at the turn of the century to know all their grandparents: only one in four children born in 1900 had four grandparents alive, and a mere one in fifty still had four grandparents alive by the time they were fifteen. In contrast, the typical fifteen-year-old in 1976 had a nearly nine-out-of-ten chance of having two or more grandparents still alive, a better than one-out-of-two chance of having three still alive, and a one-out-of-six chance of having all four still alive. Currently, then, nearly all grandchildren have an extended relationship with two or more grandparents, and substantial minorities have the opportunity for extended relationships with three or even all four.

Indeed, Americans take survival to the grandparental years pretty much for granted. The grandparents we spoke to rarely mentioned longer life when discussing the changes since they were children. *Of course* they were still alive and reasonably healthy; that went without saying. But this taken-for-granted-ness is a new phenomenon; before World War II early death was a much greater threat, and far fewer people lived long enough to watch their grandchildren grow up.

Most people are in their forties or fifties when they first become grandparents. Some observers have mistakenly taken this as an indication that grandparents are younger today than in the past. According to one respected textbook:

> Grandparenting has become a phenomenon of middle age rather than old age. Earlier marriage, earlier childbirth, and longer life expectancy are producing grandparents in their forties.

But since the end of the nineteenth century (the earliest period for which we have reliable statistics) there has been little change in the average age at marriage. The only exception was in the 1950s, when ages at marriage and first birth did decline markedly but only temporarily. With the exception of the unusual 1950s, then, it is likely that the age when people become grandparents has stayed relatively constant over the past century. What has changed is the amount of time a person spends as a grandparent: increases in adult life expectancy mean that grandparenthood extends into old age much more often. In our national sample of the grandparents of teenagers, six out of ten had become grandparents while in their forties. When we interviewed them, however, their average age was sixty-six. Grandparenting has been a phenomenon of middle age for at least the past one hundred years. The difference today is that it is now a phenomenon of middle age *and* old age for a greater proportion of the population. To be sure, our notions of what constitutes old age also may have changed, as one woman in our study implied when discussing her grandmother:

> She stayed home more, you know. And I get out into everything I can. That's the difference. That is, I think I'm younger than she was at my age.

Moreover, earlier in the century some middle-aged women may have been too busy raising the last of their own children to think of themselves as grandmothers. Nevertheless, in biological terms, the average grandparent alive today is older, not younger, than the average grandparent at the turn of the century.

Consider also the effects of falling birth rates on grandparenthood. As recently as the late 1800s, American women gave birth to more than four children, on average. Many parents still were raising their younger children after their older children had left home and married. Under these conditions, being a grandparent often overlapped with being a parent. One would imagine that grandparenthood took a back seat to the day-to-day tasks of raising the children who were still at home. Today, in contrast, the birth rate is much lower; and parents are much more likely to be finished raising their children before any of their grandchildren are born. In 1900, about half of all fifty-year-old women still had children under eighteen; but by 1980 the proportion had dropped to one-fourth. When a person becomes a grandparent now, there are fewer family roles competing for his or her time and attention. Grandparenthood is more of a separate stage of family life, unfettered by child care obligations—one that carries its own distinct identification. It was not always so.

The fall of fertility and the rise of life expectancy have thus greatly increased the supply of older persons for whom grandparenthood is a primary intergenerational role. To be sure, there always have been enough grandparents alive so that everyone in American society (and nearly all other societies, for that matter) was familiar with the role. But until quite recently, an individual faced a considerable risk of dying before, or soon after, becoming a grandparent. And even if one was fortunate enough to become a grandparent, lingering parental obligations often took precedence. In past times, when birth and death rates were high, grandparents were in relatively short supply. Today, as any number of impatient older parents will attest, grandchildren are in short supply. Census data bear this out: in 1900 there were only twenty-seven persons aged fifty-five and over for every one hundred children fourteen and under; but by 1984 the ratio had risen to nearly one-to-one. In fact, the Bureau of the Census projects that by the year 2000, for the first time in our nation's history, there will be more persons aged fifty-five and over than children fourteen and under.

Moreover, technological advances in travel and long-distance communication have made it easier for grandparents and grandchildren to *see* or talk to each other. . . . [T]he grandparents at one senior citizen center had to remind us that there was a time within their memories when telephone service was not universal. We tend to forget that only fifty years ago the *Literary Digest* predicted a Landon victory over Roosevelt on the basis of responses from people listed in telephone directories—ignoring the crucial fact that telephones were to be found disproportionately in wealthier, and therefore more often Republican, homes. As late as the end of World War II, only half the homes in the United States had a telephone. The proportion rose quickly to two-thirds by the early 1950s and three-fourths by the late 1950s. Today, more than 97 percent of all homes have telephones. About one-third of the grandparents in our survey reported that they had spoken to the study child on the telephone once a week or more during the previous year.

Nor did most families own automobiles until after World War II, as several grandparents reminded us:

> I could be wrong, but I don't feel grandparents felt as close to grandchildren during that time as they do now. . . . Really back there, let's say during the twenties, transportation was not as good, so many people did not have cars. Fortunately, I can say that as far back as I remember my father always had a car, but there were many other people who did not. They traveled by horse and buggy and some even by wagons. And going a distance, it did take quite some time. . . .

Only about half of all families owned automobiles at the end of the war. Even if a family owned an automobile, long trips still could take quite some time:

> Well, I didn't see my grandmother that often. They just lived one hundred miles from us, but back then one hundred miles was like four hundred now, it's the truth. It just seemed like clear across the country. It'd take us five hours to get there, it's the truth. It was an all-day trip.

But in the 1950s, the Federal government began to construct the interstate highway system, which cut distances and increased the speed of travel. The total number of miles driven by passenger vehicles increased from about 200 million miles in the mid-1930s to about 500 million miles in the mid-1950s to over a billion miles in the 1980s. Not all of this increase represents trips to Grandma's house, of course; but with more cars and better highways, it became much easier to visit relatives in the next county or state.

But weren't grandparents and grandchildren more likely to be living in the same household at the turn of the century? After all, we do have a nostalgic image of the three-generation family of the past, sharing a household and solving their problems together. Surprisingly, the difference between then and now is much less than this image would lead us to believe. To be sure, there has been a drastic decline since 1900 in the proportion of older persons who live with their adult children. In 1900 the proportion was more than three out of five, according to historian Daniel Scott Smith; in 1962 it was one out of four; and by 1975 it had dropped to one in seven. What has occurred is a great increase in the proportion of older people who live alone or only with their spouses. Yet the high rates of co-residence in 1900 do not imply that most grandparents were living with their grandchildren—much less that most grandchildren were living with their grandparents. As Smith's data show, older persons who were married tended to live with unmarried children only; children usually moved out when they married. It was mainly widows unable to maintain their own households who moved in with married children. Consequently, according to Smith's estimates, only about three in ten persons sixty-five and over in 1900 lived with a grandchild, despite the great amount of co-residence between older parents and their adult children. What is more, because of the relative shortage of grandparents, an even lower percentage of grandchildren lived with their grandparents. Smith estimates that about one in six children under age ten in 1900 lived in the same household with someone aged fifty-five or over. Even this figure overestimates the number of children living with their grandparents, because some of these elderly residents were more distant kin, boarders, or servants.

There were just too many grandchildren and too few grandparents for co-residence to be more common. In the absence of more detailed analyses of historical censuses, however, the exact amount of change since 1900 cannot be assessed. Nor was our study designed to provide precise estimates of changes in co-residence. But it is still worth nothing that just 30 percent of the grandparents in our sample reported that at least one of their grandparents ever lived with them while they were growing up. And 19 percent reported that the teenaged grandchild in the study had lived with them for at least three months. Undoubtedly, some of the grandparents in our study had shared a household with some of their own grandchildren, although we unfortunately did not obtain this information. Thus, although our study provides only imperfect and incomplete data on this topic, the responses are consistent with our claim that the change in the proportion of grandparents and grandchildren who share a household has been more modest than the change in the proportion of elderly persons who share a household with an adult child.

Grandparents also have more leisure time today, although the trend is more pronounced for men than for women. The average male can now expect to spend fifteen years of his adult life out of the labor force, most of it during retirement. (The labor force comprises all persons who are working for pay or looking for work.) The comparable expected time was ten years in 1970, seven years in 1940, and only four years in 1900. Clearly, a long retirement was rare early in this century and still relatively rare just before World War II. But since the 1960s, workers have begun to leave the labor force at younger ages. In 1961, Congress lowered the age of eligibility for Social Security benefits from sixty-five to sixty-two. Now more than half of all persons applying for Social Security benefits are under sixty-five. Granted, some of the early retirees are suffering from poor health, and other retirees may have difficulty adjusting to their new status. Still, when earlier retirement is combined with a longer life span, the result is a greatly extended period during which one can, among other things, get to know and enjoy one's grandchildren.

The changes in leisure time for women are not as clear because women have always had lower levels of labor force participation than men. To be sure, women workers also are retiring earlier and, as has been noted, living much longer. And most women in their fifties and sixties are neither employed nor raising children. But young grandmothers are much more likely to be employed today than was the case a generation ago; they are also more likely to have aged parents to care for. Young working grandmothers, a growing minority, may have less time to devote to their grandchildren.

Most employed grandparents, however, work no more than forty hours per week. This, too, is a recent development. The forty-hour work week did not become the norm in the United States until after World War II. At the turn of the century, production workers in manufacturing jobs worked an average of fifty hours per week. Average hours dropped below forty during the depression, rose above forty during the war, and then settled at forty after the war. Moreover, at the turn of the century, 38 percent of the civilian labor force worked on farms, where long hours were commonplace. Even in 1940, about 17 percent of the civilian labor force worked on farms; but currently only about 3 percent work on farms. So even if they are employed, grandparents have more leisure time during the work week than was the case a few decades ago.

They also have more money. Living standards have risen in general since World War II, and the rise has been sharpest for the elderly. As recently as 1960, older Americans were an economically deprived group; now they are on the verge of becoming an economically advantaged group. The reason is the Social Security system. Since the 1950s and 1960s, Congress has expanded Social Security coverage, so that by 1970 nearly all nongovernment workers, except those in nonprofit organizations, were covered. And since the 1960s, Congress has increased Social Security benefits far faster than the increase in the cost of living. As a result, the average monthly benefit (in constant 1980 dollars, adjusted for changes in consumer prices) rose from $167 in 1960, to $214 in 1970, to $297 in 1980. Because of the broader coverage and higher benefits, the proportion of the elderly who are poor has plummeted. In 1959, 35 percent of persons sixty-five and over had incomes below the official poverty line, compared to 22 percent of the total population. By 1982 the disparity had disappeared: 15 percent of those sixty-five and over were poor, as were 15 percent of the total population. The elderly no longer were disproportionately poor, although many of them have incomes not too far above the poverty line. Grandparents, then, have benefitted from the general rise in economic welfare and, as they reach retirement, from the improvement in the economic welfare of the elderly.

Because of the postwar prosperity and the rise of social welfare institutions, older parents and their adult children are less dependent on each other economically. Family life in the early decades of the century was precarious; lower wages, the absence of social welfare programs, and crises of unemployment, illness, and death forced people to rely on their kin for support to a much greater extent than is true today. There were no welfare checks, unemployment compensation, food stamps, Medicare payments, Social Security benefits, or government loans to students. Often there was only one's family. Some older people provided assistance to their kin, such as finding a job for a relative, caring for the sick, or tending to the grandchildren while the parents worked. Sometimes grandparents, their children, and their grandchildren pooled their resources into a single family fund so that all could subsist. Exactly how common these three-generational economic units were we do not know; it would be a mistake to assume that all older adults were cooperating with their children and grandchildren at all times. In fact, studies of turn-of-the-century working-class families suggest that widowed older men—past their peak earning capacity and unfamiliar with domestic tasks as they were—could be a burden to the households of their children, while older women—who could help out domestically—were a potential source of household assistance. Nevertheless, these historical accounts suggest that intensive intergenerational cooperation and assistance was more common than it is today. Tamara Hareven, for example, studied the families of workers at the Amoskeag Mills in Manchester, New Hampshire, at the turn of the century. She found that the day-to-day cooperation of kin was necessary to secure a job at the mill, find housing, and accumulate enough money to get by. Cooperation has declined because it is not needed as often: social welfare programs now provide services that only the family formerly provided; declining rates of illness, death, and unemployment have reduced the frequency of family crises; and the rising standard of living—particularly of the elderly—has reduced the need for financial assistance.

The structure of the Social Security system also has lessened the feelings of obligation older parents and their adult children have toward each other. Social Security is an income transfer system in which some of the earnings of workers are transferred to the elderly. But we have constructed a fiction about Social Security, a myth that the recipients are only drawing out money that they put into the fund earlier in their lives. This myth allows both the younger contributors and the older recipients to ignore the economic dependency of the latter. The elderly are free to believe that they are just receiving that to which they are entitled by virtue of their own hard work. The tenacity of this myth—it is only now breaking down under the tremendous payment burden of our older age structure—demonstrates its importance. It allows the elderly to accept financial assistance without compromising their independence, and it allows children to support their parents without either generation openly acknowledging as much.

All of these trends taken together—changes in mortality, fertility, transportation, communications, the work day, retirement, Social Security, and standards of living—have transformed grandparenthood from its pre–World War II state. More people are living long enough to become grandparents and to enjoy a lengthy period of life as grandparents. They can keep in touch more easily with their grandchildren; they have more time to devote to them; they have more money to spend on them; and they are less likely still to be raising their own children.

⬖

CHAPTER 11

TROUBLE IN THE FAMILY

Dubious Conceptions: The Controversy Over Teen Pregnancy

Kristin Luker

The conventional wisdom has it that an epidemic of teen pregnancy is today ruining the lives of young women and their children and perpetuating poverty in America. In polite circles, people speak regretfully of "babies having babies." Other Americans are more blunt. "I don't mind paying to help people in need," one angry radio talk show host told Michael Katz, a historian of poverty, "but I don't want my tax dollars to pay for the sexual pleasure of adolescents who won't use birth control."

By framing the issue in these terms, Americans have imagined that the persistence of poverty and other social problems can be traced to youngsters who are too impulsive or too ignorant to postpone sexual activity, to use contraception, to seek an abortion, or failing all that, especially if they are white, to give their babies up for adoption to "better" parents. Defining the problem this

From *The American Prospect*, No. 5, Spring 1991, pp. 73–83. Copyright © 1991 by New Prospect, Inc. Reprinted by permission.

way, many Americans, including those in a position to influence public policy, have come to believe that one attractive avenue to reducing poverty and other social ills is to reduce teen birth rates. Their remedy is to persuade teenagers to postpone childbearing, either by convincing them of the virtues of chastity (a strategy conservatives prefer) or by making abortion, sex education, and contraception more freely available (the strategy liberals prefer).

Reducing teen pregnancy would almost certainly be a good thing. After all, the rate of teen childbearing in the United States is more similar to the rates prevailing in the poor countries of the world than in the modern, industrial nations we think of as our peers. However, neither the problem of teen pregnancy nor the remedies for it are as simple as most people think.

In particular, the link between poverty and teen pregnancy is a complicated one. We do know that teen mothers are poorer than women who wait past their twentieth birthday to have a child. But stereotypes to the contrary, it is not clear whether early motherhood causes poverty or the reverse. Worse yet, even if teen pregnancy does have some independent force in making teen parents poorer than they would otherwise be, it remains to be seen whether any policies in effect or under discussion can do much to reduce teen birth rates.

These uncertainties raise questions about our political culture as well as our public choices. How did Americans become convinced that teen pregnancy is a major cause of poverty and that reducing one would reduce the other? The answer is a tale of good intentions, rising cultural anxieties about teen sex and family breakdown, and the uses—and misuses—of social science.

HOW TEEN PREGNANCY BECAME AN ISSUE

Prior to the mid-1970s, few people talked about "teen pregnancy." Pregnancy was defined as a social problem primarily when a woman was unmarried; no one thought anything amiss when an 18- or 19-year-olds got married and had children. And concern about pregnancies among unmarried women certainly did not stop when the woman turned twenty.

But in 1975, when Congress held the first of many hearings on the issue of adolescent fertility, expert witnesses began to speak of an "epidemic" of a "million pregnant teenagers" a year. Most of these witnesses were drawing on statistics supplied by the Alan Guttmacher Institute, which a year later published the data in an influential booklet, *Eleven Million Teenagers*. Data from that document were later cited—often down to the decimal point—in most discussions of the teenage pregnancy "epidemic."

Many people hearing these statistics must have assumed that the "million pregnant teenagers" a year were all unmarried. The Guttmacher Institute's figures, however, included married 19-year-olds along with younger, unmarried teenage girls. In fact, almost two-thirds of the "million pregnant teenagers" were 18- and 19-year-olds; about 40 percent of them were married, and about two-thirds of the married women were married prior to the pregnancy.

Moreover, despite the language of epidemic, pregnancy rates among teenagers were not dramatically increasing. From the turn of the century until the end of World War II, birth rates among teenagers were reasonably stable at approximately 50 to 60 births per thousand women. Teen birth rates, like all American birth rates, increased dramatically in the period after World War II, doubling in the baby boom years to a peak of about 97 births per thousand teenaged women in 1957. Subsequently, teen birth rates declined, and by 1975 they had gone back down to their traditional levels, where, for the most part, they have stayed (see Figure 32.1).

Were teen births declining in recent decades only because of higher rates of abortion? Here, too, trends are different from what many people suppose. The legalization of abortion in January of 1973 made it possible for the first time to get reliable statistics on abortions for women, teenagers and older. The rate among teenagers rose from about 27.0 to 42.9 abortions per 1,000 women between 1974 and 1980. Since 1980 teen abortion rates have stabilized, and may even have declined somewhat. Moreover, teenagers account for a declining proportion of all abortions: in the years just after *Roe v. Wade*, teenagers obtained almost a third of all abortions in the country; now they obtain about a quarter. A stable teen birth rate and a stabilizing teen abortion rate means that pregnancy rates, which rose modestly in the 1970s, have in recent years leveled off.

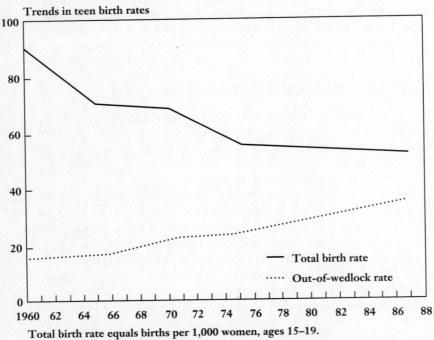

Total birth rate equals births per 1,000 women, ages 15–19.
Out-of-wedlock rate equals births per 1,000 unmarried women, ages 15–19.

FIGURE 32.1 Total birth rate equals births per 1,000 women, ages 15–19. Out-of-wedlock rate equals births per 1,000 unmarried women, ages 15–19. *Sources:* National Center for Health Statistics, *Annual Vital Statistics*, and *Monthly Vital Statistics Reports*; U.S. DHEW, Vital and Health Statistics, "Trends in Illegitimacy, U.S. 1940–1965."

What has been increasing—and increasing dramatically—is the percentage of teen births that are out-of-wedlock (Figure 32.1). In 1970 babies born out of wedlock represented about a third of all babies born to teen mothers. By 1980 out-of-wedlock births were about half; and by 1986 almost two-thirds. Beneath these overall figures lie important racial variations. Between 1955 and 1988 the out-of-wedlock rate rose from 6 to 24.8 per thousand unmarried, teenage, white women, while for unmarried, nonwhite teenagers the rate rose from 77.6 to 98.3 per thousand. In other words, while the out-of-wedlock birth rate was rising 25 percent among nonwhite teens, it was actually quadrupling among white teens.

The immediate source for this rise in out-of-wedlock teen pregnancy might seem to be obvious. Since 1970 young women have increasingly postponed marriage without rediscovering the virtues of chastity. Only about 6 percent of teenagers were married in 1984, compared to 12 percent in 1970. And although estimates vary, sexual activity among single teenagers has increased sharply, probably doubling. By 1984 almost half of all American teenage women were both unmarried and sexually active, up from only one in four in 1970.

Yet the growth of out-of-wedlock births has not occurred only among teens; in fact, the increase has been more rapid among older women. In 1970 teens made up almost half of all out-of-wedlock births in America; at present they account for a little less than a third. On the other hand, out-of-wedlock births represent a much larger percentage of births to teens than of births to older women. Perhaps for that reason, teenagers have become the symbol of a problem that, to many Americans, is "out of control."

Whatever misunderstandings may have been encouraged by reports of a "million pregnant teenagers" a year, the new concept of "teen pregnancy" had a remarkable impact. By the mid-1980s, Congress had created a new federal office on adolescent pregnancy and parenting; 23 states had set up task forces; the media had published over 200 articles, including cover stories in both *Time* and *Newsweek;* American philanthropy had moved teen pregnancy into a high priority funding item; and a 1985 Harris poll showed that 80 percent of Americans thought teen pregnancy was a "serious problem" facing the nation, a concern shared across racial, geographic, and economic boundaries.

But while this public consensus has been taking shape, a debate has emerged about many of its premises. A growing number of social scientists have come to question whether teen pregnancy causes the social problems linked to it. Yet these criticisms have a times been interpreted as either an ivory-tower indifference to the fate of teen parents and their babies or a Panglossian optimism that teen childbearing is just one more alternate lifestyle. As a result, clarity on these issues has gotten lost in clouds of ideological mistrust. To straighten out these matters, we need to understand what is known, and not known, about the relation of teen pregnancy to poverty and other social problems.[1]

DISTINGUISHING CAUSES FROM CORRELATIONS

As the Guttmacher Institute's report made clear, numerous studies have documented an association between births to teenagers and a host of bad medical and social outcomes. Compared to women who have babies later in life, teen mothers are in poorer health, have more medically treacherous pregnancies, more stillbirths and newborn deaths, and more low-birthweight and medically compromised babies.

Later in life, women who have babies as teenagers are also worse off than other women. By their late 20s, women who gave birth as teenagers are less likely to have finished high school and thus not to have received any subsequent higher education. They are more likely to have routine, unsatisfying, and dead-end jobs, to be on welfare, and to be single parents either because they were never married or their marriage ended in divorce. In short, they often lead what the writer Mike Rose has called "lives on the boundary."

Yet an interesting thing has happened over the last twenty years. A description of the lives of teenage mothers and their children was transmuted into a causal sequence, and the often-blighted lives of young mothers were assumed to flow from their early childbearing. Indeed, this is what the data would show, if the women who gave birth as teenagers were the same in every way as women who give birth later. But they are not.

Although there is little published data on the social origins of teen parents, studies have documented the effects of social disadvantage at every step along the path to teenage motherhood. First, since poor and minority youth tend to become sexually active at an earlier age than more advantaged youngsters, they are "at risk" for a longer period of time, including years when they are less cognitively mature. Young teens are also less likely to use contraceptives than older teenagers. Second, the use of contraception is more common among teens who are white, come from more affluent homes, have higher educational aspirations, and who are doing well in school. And, finally, among youngsters who become pregnant, abortions are more common if they are affluent, white, urban, of higher socio-economic status, get good grades, come from two-parent families, and aspire to higher education. Thus, more advantaged youth get filtered out of the pool of young women at risk of teen parenthood.

Two kinds of background factors influence which teens are likely to become pregnant and give birth outside of marriage. First is inherited disadvantage. Young women from families that are poor, or rural, or from a disadvantaged minority, or headed by a single parent are more likely to be teen mothers than are their counterparts from more privileged backgrounds. Yet young mothers are not just disadvantaged; they are also discouraged. Studies suggest that a young woman who has other troubles—who is not doing well in school, has lower "measured ability," and lacks high aspirations for herself—is also at risk of becoming a teenaged mother.

Race plays an independent part in the route to teen motherhood. Within each racial group, according to Linda Waite and her colleagues at the Rand Corporation, teen birth rates are highest for those who have the greatest economic disadvantage and lowest academic ability. The effects of disadvantage, however, vary depending on the group. The Rand study found that among young high-ability, affluent black women from homes with two parents, only about one in a hundred become single, teenage mothers. For comparable whites, the risk was one in a thousand. By contrast, a poor, black teenager from a female-headed household who scores low on standardized tests has an astonishing one in four chance of becoming an unwed mother in her teens. Her white counterpart has one chance in twelve. Unwed motherhood thus reflects the intersecting influences of race, class, and gender; race and class each has a distinct impact on the life histories of young women.

Since many, if not most, teenage unwed mothers are already both disadvantaged and discouraged before they get pregnant, the poor outcomes of their pregnancies as well as their later difficulties in life are not surprising. Consider the health issues. As the demographer Jane Menken pointed out some time ago (and as many other studies have corroborated), the medical complications associated with teen pregnancy are largely due not to age but to the poverty of young mothers. As poor people, they suffer not from some biological risk due to youth, but from restricted access to medical care, particularly to prenatal care. (To be fair, some research suggests that there may be special biological risks for the very youngest mothers, those under age 15 when they give birth, who constitute about 2 percent of all teen mothers.)

Or, to take a more complicated example, consider whether bearing a child blocks teenagers from getting an education. In the aggregate, teen mothers do get less education than women who do not have babies at an early age. But teen mothers are different from their childless peers along exactly those dimensions we would expect independently to contribute to reduced schooling. More of them are poor, come from single-parent households, and have lower aspirations for themselves, lower measured ability, and more problems with school absenteeism and discipline. Given the nature of the available data, it is difficult to sort out the effects of a teen birth apart from the personal and social factors that predispose young women to both teen motherhood and less education. Few would argue that having a baby as a teenager enhances educational opportunities, but the exact effect of teen birth is a matter of debate.

Educational differences between teen mothers and other women may also be declining, at least in terms of graduating from high school. Legislation that took effect in 1975 forbade schools to expel pregnant teens. Contrary to current skepticism about federal intervention, this regulation seems to have worked. According to a study by Dawn Upchurch and James McCarthy, only 18.6 percent of teenagers who had a baby in 1958 subsequently graduated from high school. Graduation rates among teen mothers reached 29.2 percent in 1975; by 1986 they climbed to 55 percent. Teen mothers were still not graduating at a rate equal to other women (as of 1985, about 87 percent of women ages 25 to 29 had a high school diploma or its equivalent). But over the decade prior to 1986, graduation rates had increased more quickly for teen mothers than for other women, suggesting that federal policies tailored to their special circumstances may have made a difference.

Since education is so closely tied to later status, teasing out the relationship between teen pregnancy and schooling is critical. The matter is complicated, however, because young people do many things simultaneously, and sorting out the order is no easy task. In 1984 Peter Morrison of the Rand team reported that between a half and a third of teen mothers in high school and beyond dropped out before they got pregnant. Upchurch and McCarthy, using a different and more recent sample, found that the majority of female dropouts in their study left school before they got pregnant and that teens who got pregnant while still in school were not particularly likely to drop out. On the other hand, those teens who first drop out and then get pregnant are significantly less likely to return to school than other dropouts who do not get pregnant. Thus the conventional causal view that teens get pregnant, drop out of school, and as a result end up educationally and occupationally disadvantaged simply does not match the order of events in many people's lives.

THE SEXUAL ROOTS OF PUBLIC ANXIETY

Teen pregnancy probably would not have "taken off" as a public issue quite so dramatically, were it not for the fact it intersects with other recent social changes in America, particularly the emergence of widespread, anxiety-producing shifts in teen sex. Academics debate whether there has been a genuine "sexual revolution" among adults, but there is no doubt in regard to teenagers. Today, by the time American teenagers reach age 20, an estimated 70 percent of the girls and 80 percent of the boys have had sexual experiences outside of marriage. Virtually all studies confirm that this is a dramatic historical change, particularly for young women. (As usual, much less is known about the historical experience of young men.) For example, Sandra Hofferth and her colleagues, using nationally representative data from the 1982 National Survey of Family Growth, found that women navigating adolescence in the late 1950s had a 38.9 percent chance of being sexually active before marriage during their teenage years. Women who reached their twentieth birthday between 1979 and 1981, in contrast, had a 68.3 percent likelihood.

Yet even these statistics do not capture how profoundly different this teen sexuality is from that of earlier eras. As sources such as the Kinsey Report (1953) suggest, premarital sex for many American women before the 1960s was "engagement" sex. The woman's involvement, at least, was exclusive, and she generally went on to marry her partner in a relatively short period of time. Almost half of the women in the Kinsey data who had premarital sex had it only with their fiancés.

But as the age at first marriage has risen and the age at first intercourse has dropped, teen sexuality has changed. Not surprisingly, what scattered data we have about numbers of partners suggest that as the period of sexual activity before marriage has increased, so has the number of partners. In 1971, for example, almost two-thirds of sexually active teenaged women in metropolitan areas had had only one sexual partner; by 1979 fewer than half did. Data from the 1988 National Survey of Family Growth confirm this pattern for the nation as a whole, where about 60 percent of teens have had two or more partners. Similarly, for metropolitan teens, only a small fraction (about 10 percent) were engaged at the time of their first sexual experience, although about half described themselves as "going steady."

Profound changes in other aspects of American life have complicated the problem. Recent figures suggest that the average age at first marriage has increased to almost 24 years for women and over 25 years for men, the oldest since reliable data have been collected. Moreover, the age of sexual maturity over the last century has decreased by a little under six months each decade owing to nutritional and other changes. Today the average American girl has her first menstrual period at age 12½, although there are wide individual variations. (There is less research on the sexual maturity of young men.) On average, consequently, American girls and their boyfriends face over a decade of their lives when they are sexually mature and single.

As teenagers pass through this reproductive minefield, the instructions they receive on how to conduct themselves sexually are at best mixed. At least according to public opinion polls, most Americans have come, however, reluctantly, to accept premarital sex. Yet one suspects that what they approve is something closer to Kinsey-era sex: sexual relations en route to a marriage. Present-day teenage sex however, starts for many young people not when they move out of the family and into the orbit of what will be a new family or couple, but while they are still defined primarily as children.

When young people, particularly young women, are still living at home (or even at school) under the control, however nominal, of parents, sexual activity raises profound questions for adults. Many Americans feel troubled about "casual" sex, that is, sex which is not intimately tied to the process by which people form couples and settle down. Yet many teenagers are almost by definition disqualified as too young to "get serious." Thus the kinds of sexuality for which they are socially eligible—sex based in pleasure, not procreation, and in short-term relationships rather than as a prelude to marriage—challenge fundamental values about sexuality held by many adults. These ambiguities and uncertainties have given rise to broad anxieties about teen sexuality that have found expression in the recent alarm about teen pregnancy.

RAISING CHILDREN WITHOUT FATHERS

While Americans have had to confront the meaning and purpose of sexuality in the lives of teenagers, a second revolution is forcing them to think about the role—and boundaries—of marriage and family. Increasingly, for Americans, childbearing and, more dramatically, childrearing have been severed from marriage. The demographer Larry Bumpass and his colleagues have estimated that under present trends, half or more of all American children will spend at least part of their childhood in a single-parent (mainly mother-only) family, due to the fact that an estimated 60 percent of recent marriages will end in divorce.

At the same time, as I indicated earlier, out-of-wedlock births are on the rise. At present, 26 percent of all births are to single women. If present trends continue, Bumpass and others estimate, almost one out of every six white women and seven out of ten black women will give birth to a child without being married. In short, single childbearing is becoming a common pattern of family formation for all American women, teenagers and older.

This reality intersects with still another fact of American life. The real value of inflation-adjusted wages, which grew 2.5 to 3.0 percent a year from the end of World War II to at least 1973, has now begun to stagnate and for certain groups decline; some recent studies point to greater polarization of economic well-being. Americans increasingly worry about their own standard of living and their taxes, and much of that worry has focused on the "underclass." Along with the elderly and the disabled, single women and their children have been the traditional recipients of public aid in America. In recent years, however, they have become especially visible among the dependent poor for at least two reasons. First, the incomes of the elderly have improved, leaving behind single mothers as a higher percentage of the poor; and second, the number of female-headed households has increased sharply. Between 1960 and 1984, households headed by women went from 9.0 percent to 12.0 percent of all white households, and from 22.0 percent to 43 percent of all black households. The incomes of about half of all families headed by women, as of 1984, fell below federal poverty levels.

Raising children as a single mother presents economic problems for women of all ages, but the problem is especially severe for teenagers with limited education and job experience. Partly for that reason, teenagers became a focus of public concern about the impact of illegitimacy and single parenthood on welfare costs. Data published in the 1970s and replicated in the 1980s suggested that about half of all families supported by Aid to Families with Dependent Children (AFDC) were started while the mother was still a teenager. One estimate calculated that in 1975 the costs for these families of public assistance alone (not including Medicaid or food stamps) amounted to $5 billion; by 1985, that figure increased to $8.3 billion.

Yet other findings—and caveats—have been ignored. For example, while about half of all AFDC cases may be families begun while the woman was still a teenager, teens represent only about 7 percent of the caseload at any one time. Moreover, the studies assessing the welfare costs of families started by teens counted any welfare family as being the result of a teen birth if the woman first had a child when under age 20. But, of course, that same woman—given her prior circumstances—might have been no less likely to draw welfare assistance if, let us say, she had a baby at age 20 instead of 19. Richard Wertheimer and Kristin Moore, the source of much of what we know about this area, have been careful to note that the relevant costs are the marginal costs—namely, how much less in welfare costs society would pay if teen mothers postponed their first births, rather than foregoing them entirely.

It turns out, not surprisingly, that calculated this way, the savings are more modest. Wertheimer and Moore have estimated that if by some miracle we could cut the teen birth rate in half, welfare costs would be reduced by 20 percent, rather than 50 percent, because many of these young women would still need welfare for children born to them when they were no longer teens.

Still other research suggests that most young women spend a transitional period on welfare, while finishing school and entering the job market. Other data also suggest that teen mothers may both enter and leave the welfare ranks earlier than poor women who postpone childbearing. Thus teen births by themselves may have more of an effect on the timing of welfare in the chain of life events than on the extent of welfare dependency. In a study of 300 teen mothers and their children originally interviewed in the mid-1960s, Frank Furstenberg and his colleagues found seventeen years later that two-thirds of those followed up had received no welfare in the previous five years, although some 70 percent of them had received public assistance at some point after the birth of their child. A quarter had achieved middle-class incomes, despite their poverty at the time of the child's birth.

None of this is to deny that teen mothers have a higher probability of being on welfare in the first place than women who begin their families at a later age, or that teen mothers may be disproportionately represented among those who find themselves chronically dependent on welfare. Given the disproportionate number of teen mothers who come from socially disadvantaged origins (and who are less motivated and perhaps less able students), it would be surprising if they were not overrepresented among those needing public assistance, whenever they had their children. Only if we are prepared to argue that these kinds of women should never have children—which is the implicit alternative at the heart of much public debate—could we be confident that they would never enter the AFDC rolls.

RETHINKING TEEN PREGNANCY

The original formulation of the teen pregnancy crisis seductively glossed over some of these hard realities. Teen motherhood is largely the province of those youngsters who are already disadvantaged by their position in our society. The major institutions of American life—families, schools, job markets, the medical system—are not working for them. But by framing the issue as teenage pregnancy, Americans could turn this reality around and ascribe the persistence of poverty and other social ills to the failure of individual teenagers to control their sexual impulses.

Framing the problem as teen pregnancy, curiously enough, also made it appear universal. Everyone is a teenager once. In fact, the rhetoric has sometimes claimed that the risk of teen pregnancy is universal, respecting no boundaries of class or race. But clearly, while teenage pregnancies do occur in virtually all walks of life, they do not occur with equal frequency. The concept of "teen pregnancy" has the advantage, therefore, of appearing neutral and universal while, in fact, being directed at people disadvantaged by class, race, and gender.

If focusing on teen pregnancy cast the problem as deceptively universal, it also cast the solution as deceptively simple. Teens just have to wait. In fact, the tacit subtext of at least some of the debate on teen pregnancy is not that young women should wait until they are past their teens, but until they are "ready." Yet in the terms that many Americans have in mind, large numbers of these youngsters will never be "ready." They have already dropped out of school and will face a marginal future in the labor market whether or not they have a baby. And as William J. Wilson has noted, many young black women in inner-city communities will not have the option of marrying because of the dearth of eligible men their age as a result of high rates of unemployment, underemployment, imprisonment, and early death.

Not long ago, Arline Geronimous, an assistant professor of public health at the University of Michigan, caused a stir when she argued that teens, especially black teens, had little to gain (and perhaps something to lose) in postponing pregnancy. The longer teenagers wait, she noted, the more they risk ill health and infertility, and the less likely their mothers are to be alive and able to help rear a child of theirs. Some observers quickly took Geronimous to mean that teen mothers are "rational," affirmatively choosing their pregnancies.

Yet, as Geronimous herself has emphasized, what sort of choices do these young women have? While teen mothers typically report knowing about contraception (which they often say they have used) and knowing about abortion, they tell researchers that their pregnancies were unplanned. In the 1988 National Survey of Family Growth, for example, a little over 70 percent of the pregnancies to teens were reported as unplanned; the teenagers described the bulk of these pregnancies as wanted, just arriving sooner than they had planned.

Researchers typically layer their own views on these data. Those who see teens as victims point to the data indicating most teen pregnancies are unplanned. Those who see teens as acting rationally look at their decisions not to use contraceptives or seek an abortion. According to Frank Furstenberg, however, the very indecisiveness of these young people is the critical finding. Youngsters often drift into pregnancy and then into parenthood, not because they affirmatively choose pregnancy as a first choice among many options, but rather because they see so few satisfying alternatives. As Laurie Zabin, a Johns Hopkins researcher on teen pregnancy, puts it, "As long as people don't have a vision of the future which having a baby at a very early age will jeopardize, they won't go to all the lengths necessary to prevent pregnancy."

Many people talk about teen pregnancy as if there were an implicit social contract in America. They seem to suggest that if poor women would just postpone having babies until they were past their teens, they could have better lives for themselves and their children. But for teenagers already at the margins of American life, this is a contract that American society may be hard put to honor. What if, in fact, they are acting reasonably? What can public policy do about teen pregnancy if many teenagers drift into childbearing as the only vaguely promising option in a life whose options are already constrained by gender, poverty, race, and failure?

The trouble is that there is little reason to think any of the "quick fixes" currently being proposed will resolve the fundamental issues involved. Liberals, for example, argue that the answer is more access to contraception, more readily available abortion, and more sex education. Some combination of these strategies probably has had some effect on teen births, particularly in keeping the teen pregnancy rate from soaring as the number of sexually active teens increased. But the inner logic of this approach is that teens and adults have the same goal: keeping teens from pregnancies they do not want. Some teens, however, do want their pregnancies, while others drift into pregnancy and parenthood without ever actively deciding what they want. Consequently, increased access to contraceptives, sex education, and abortion services are unlikely to have a big impact in reducing their pregnancies.

Conservatives, on the other hand, often long for what they imagine was the traditional nuclear family, where people had children only in marriage, married only when they could prudently afford children, and then continued to provide support for their children if the marriage ended. Although no one fully understands the complex of social, economic, and cultural factors that brought us to the present situation, it is probably safe to predict that we shall not turn the clock back to that vision, which in any event is highly colored by nostalgia.

This is not to say that there is nothing public policy can do. Increased job opportunities for both young men and young women; meaningful job training programs (which do not slot young women into traditional low-paying women's jobs); and child support programs[2] would all serve either to make marriage more feasible for those who wish to marry or to support children whose parents are not married. But older ages at first marriage, high rates of sex outside of marriage, a significant portion of all births out of wedlock, and problems with absent fathers tend to be common patterns in Western, industrialized nations.

In their attempts to undo these patterns, many conservatives propose punitive policies to sanction unmarried parents, especially unmarried mothers, by changing the "incentive structure" young people face. The new welfare reform bill of 1988, for example, made it more difficult for teens to set up their own households, at least in part because legislators were worried about the effects of welfare on the willingness to have a child out of wedlock. Other, more draconian writers have called for the children of unwed teen parents to be forcibly removed and placed into foster care, or for the reduction of welfare benefits for women who have more than one child out of wedlock.

Leave aside, for the moment, that these policies would single out only the most vulnerable in this population. The more troublesome issue is such policies often fall most heavily on the children. Americans, as the legal historian Michael Grossberg has shown, have traditionally and justifiably been leery of policies that regulate adult behavior at children's expense.

The things that public policy could do for these young people are unfortunately neither easy to implement nor inexpensive. However, if teens become parents because they lack options, public policy towards teen pregnancy and teenage childbearing will have to focus on enlarging the array of perceived options these young people face. And these must be changes in their real alternatives. Programs that seek to teach teens "future planning," while doing nothing about the futures they can expect, are probably doomed to failure.

We live in a society that continues to idealize marriage and family as expected lifetime roles for women, even as it adds on the expectation that women will also work and be self-supporting. Planning for the trade-offs entailed in a lifetime of paid employment in the labor market and raising a family taxes the skills of our most advantaged young women. We should not be surprised that women who face discrimination by race and class in addition to that of gender are often even less adept at coping with these large and contradictory demands.

Those who worry about teenagers should probably worry about three different dangers as Americans debate policies on teen pregnancy. First, we should worry that things will continue as they have and that public policy will continue to see teens as unwitting victims, albeit victims who themselves cause a whole host of social ills. The working assumption here will be that teens genuinely do not want the children that they are having and that the task of public policy is to meet the needs of both society and the women involved by helping them not to have babies. What is good for society, therefore, is good for the individual woman.

This vision, for all the reasons already considered, distorts current reality, and as such, is unlikely to lower the teen birth rate significantly, though it may be effective in keeping the teen birth rate from further increasing. To the extent that it is ineffective, it sets the stage for another risk.

This second risk is that the ineffectiveness of programs to lower teen pregnancy dramatically may inadvertently give legitimacy to those who want more punitive control over teenagers, particularly minority and poor teens. If incentives and persuasion do not lead teenagers to conduct their sexual and reproductive lives in ways that adults would prefer, more coercive remedies may be advocated. The youth of teen mothers may make intrusive social control seem more acceptable than it would for older women.

Finally, the most subtle danger is that the new work on teen pregnancy will be used to argue that because teen pregnancy is not the linchpin that holds together myriad other social ills, it is not a problem at all. Concern about teen pregnancy has at least directed attention and resources to young, poor, and minority women; it has awakened many Americans to their diminished life chances. If measures aimed at reducing teen pregnancy are not the quick fix for much of what ails American society, there is the powerful temptation to forget these young women altogether and allow them to slip back to their traditional invisible place in American public debate.

Teen pregnancy is less about young women and their sex lives than it is about restricted horizons and the boundaries of hope. It is about race and class and how those realities limit opportunities for young people. Most centrally, however, it is typically about being young, female, poor, and non-white and about how having a child seems to be one of the few avenues of satisfaction, fulfillment, and self-esteem. It would be a tragedy to stop worrying about these young women—and their partners—because their behavior is the measure rather than the cause of their blighted hopes.

NOTES

1. Teen pregnancy affects both young men and young women, but few data are gathered on young men. The availability of data leads me to speak of "teen mothers" throughout this article, but it is important to realize that this reflects an underlying, gendered definition of the situation.

2. Theda Skocpol, "Sustainable Social Policy: Fighting Poverty Without Poverty Programs" *TAP,* Summer 1990.

READING

33

The Downwardly Mobile Family

Katherine S. Newman

Brutal though it can be, the damage downward mobility does to a displaced manager is only the beginning of a longer story. Like a storm gathering force, failure in the work world engenders further havoc, first buffeting relations between breadwinner and spouse, then spreading to the children. Economic foundations are wrenched out from under the family, and emotional bonds are stretched to the breaking point. In the end, even children's values and plans for the future are drawn into the maelstrom as they struggle to reconcile the teachings of meritocratic individualism with their parents' glaring inability to prove their worth in the world.

As unwilling refugees from the middle class, children of downwardly mobile managers offer a unique window into the world they have left behind. Most had taken their old affluent life-style for granted and did not understand the significance of what they had had until after it was gone.

For Penny Ellerby, who was fifteen when the great crash came, the most immediate and troubling impact was the change it wrought upon the father she looked up to:

> The pressure on my Dad was intense. From my point of view he just seemed to be getting irrational. He would walk around the house talking to himself and stay up all night, smoking cigarettes in the dark.
>
> When things started to fall apart no one would tell my sister or me anything about what was happening. So all I perceived is that somebody who used to be a figure of strength was behaving strangely: starting to cry at odd times . . . hanging around the house unshaven in his underwear when I would bring dates home from high school. In the absence of any understanding of what was going on, my attitude was one of anger and disgust, like "Why don't you get your act together? What's the matter with you?"

Penny's father had been a successful show business promoter. He had invested most of the family's assets in a talent show that ran successfully for four years until its sponsors pulled the plug and sent his career into a tailspin. Penny remembers the spectacular crash that followed:

> We went from one day in which we owned a business that was worth probably four or five million dollars in assets and woke up the next day to find that we were personally probably a half million in debt. Creditors called at the house and started to send threatening notes.
>
> First he started a novel, but that didn't last more than two months. Then he went back into a public relations project, which also didn't work out. Then he tried to put together a series of college film festivals. Nothing worked.

Penny's adolescence came to an abrupt end at that point. Her father was unable to find a professional position of any kind. Tension between her parents rose to unbearable heights. Her dad finally left home, one step ahead of the bill collectors. She had not seen him for nearly ten years; for most of that time he has lived on the streets in San Francisco. Penny's mother managed to find a low-level clerical job but it could not begin to sustain the life-style she had known as the wife of a promoter. Today she lives in one of New York's tougher public housing projects and faces problems familiar to many a marginal wage earner: how to make ends meet and how to face the prospect of poverty-level retirement.

* * *

Downward mobility can occur as the result of a precipitous crash whose effects are felt immediately. Indeed, Penny's story demonstrates how rapidly, and how completely, downward mobility can undermine a family. But for most managerial families, the process is one of gradual erosion. Occupational dislocation may occur suddenly, but its consequences can take six or seven years to become fully evident, depending upon the resources the families can tap.

When occupational disaster strikes, the first impulse is typically to contain the damage to the work world, and to continue as far as possible to maintain a sense of normalcy in the family realm. Hence families continue to pay the mortgage and send the kids off to school. But as months elapse without reemployment, and bank balances plummet, the attempt to maintain a normal life-style falters. What begins as a principled commitment to avoid defeatism and get on with life takes on a new character—the family starts to dissemble and hide its problems from the outside world, starting with small cover stories. Paul Armand instructed his son on how to describe his Dad's unemployment to his friends at boarding school: "In his school, everybody's father is the head of this and that. So I said, 'You just tell them your Dad was VP of a company and he just refused to go on an overseas assignment. . . .' I told him if anybody asks, tell them I started my own firm." This was, at best, a shading of the truth. Paul had created a "firm" on paper, but it was not engaged in any money-making enterprises.

The impetus to conceal, if not lie, sometimes comes from adolescent children. The world of the middle-class adolescent is consumerist, elitist, and exceptionally unforgiving of divergence from the norm. Teenagers want to look like, act like, and think like their friends. The paradox of middle-class adolescents is that they must achieve individuality first and foremost by learning to look and sound just like "everyone else" their own age. Dress style and musical taste are only part of the cultural baggage American adolescents bring to the task of peer consolidation. Children of affluence—the sons and daughters of the managerial middle class—also rely upon their families' social position in seeking peer acceptance. Their fathers' occupation, and the life-style that it makes possible, is part and parcel of a cultural image they attempt to project.

When David Patterson moved his wife and two teenage children from California to Long Island, his children complained at first that they were looked upon, with some degree of suspicion, as "transients." To overcome the ill-will and cultivate new friends, Patterson's son boasted his father's status as an executive. The scheme worked, for local families were highly attuned to occupational prestige. Consequently, when Patterson received his pink slip, it threatened to undermine his teenagers' public identity and put their social acceptance by peers at risk. The children reacted with shame and with secrecy: They stopped bringing acquaintances home; they avoided discussing the family crisis with peers or school counselors. They became overwhelmed by the feeling that if their father's downward mobility became public knowledge, their own social standing would be destroyed.

The downwardly mobile managerial family jealously guards its public face, even if this means that everyone must eat a dreary diet so that the children can have some stylish clothes for school. They cherish central symbols of belonging, like the family home, and families make considerable sacrifices in other domains to hold on to these valued possessions. Large houses are rarely traded in for something more modest until there is no other alternative.

Families avoid bankruptcy, both because they look upon it as the coward's way out of a disaster and as a too-public admission of failure and surrender. Dierdre Miller's father inherited a family firm that ran aground in the late 1960s. By the time Dierdre was a teenager, the firm was near collapse and the creditors began to hound Mr. Miller to pay up on his bills. It was clear to Dierdre's mother that they needed to declare bankruptcy to protect the family's remaining assets. But as Dierdre tells it, this was unthinkable:

> My dad wouldn't hear of the idea of declaring bankruptcy or of selling the family business. He felt he had a reputation to protect and that if he went bankrupt it would be destroyed. He used to tell me that you just have to meet your obligations, that you can just walk out on people and companies you owe money to. I think he felt that if he declared bankruptcy he'd never be able to recover. It would be the end because no one would respect him.

Joan deLancy, a Wall Street lawyer, remembers that her father—whose career as an engineer bit the dust in the wake of defense department cutbacks in the early 1970s—felt the same way:

> My father did earn money through various consulting jobs and short-term positions of one kind or another, but we didn't see much of it. It went toward paying off their debts. He could have walked away from them by declaring bankruptcy, but he thought that would really seal his fate. Bankruptcy was too final, too much an admission of failure. Besides, it is not part of his character to walk away from responsibilities. As bad as things were financially, I think my parents were proud of the fact that they didn't take the easy way out.

As the financial slide worsens, the task of keeping up appearances becomes more difficult. Dierdre Miller's family lived in one of California's wealthiest suburbs before their troubles and continued to hold on after the crisis. She remembers that her mother would drive miles out of her way to spend the family allotment of food stamps in neighborhoods where her face was unknown. Though the Miller family was in serious financial trouble, with no money coming in to speak of, the mother's primary concern was maintaining face: "My mother wouldn't go down and apply for the food stamps. She made my father do all of that. She wouldn't have anything to do with [it]. She was real ashamed." Mrs. Miller's strategy worked. For many years, outward appearances provided no clue that her family was poor enough to qualify for public assistance. The Miller children stopped bringing their friends home and virtually never talked about their family troubles to anyone.

Eventually however, most downwardly mobile families find themselves in such financial straits that they can no longer camouflage their situation. Children begin to feel uncomfortable about the increasing visibility of the material differences between themselves and their peers, a problem that exacerbates the stigma of their fathers ending up in low status jobs.

The Boeing company was Seattle's largest employer up until the late 1960s. In 1968, it shut down a large part of its operations, throwing thousands of engineers, draftsmen, and technicians onto a weak labor market. The Boeing slump spread like a wave through the supplier industries in the area, compounding the disaster. Alice Pendergast's father was a sales manager in a firm that made precision tools; their biggest client was Boeing. By the time Alice was thirteen, five years after the crash, the depth of the Pendergast family disaster had become clear, especially by comparison to her more fortunate friends:

> My junior high school was situated right under this big hill where all the Seattle executives lived, and so I started going to school with their kids. It ended up that my best friend's father was the vice president of the biggest bank in town. She lived in this house that seemed like the most beautiful place I'd ever seen. I remember feeling really awful because she had so much stuff.
>
> I guess our standard of living was all right, given the bad money situation. But I always felt we were quite poor because I couldn't go out and buy new clothes like all my friends at school. Instead of shopping at Nordstrom's, the high-class department store, we used to go to K-Mart or Penney's. When I was a kid, trying to impress my peers, it was awful. I remember going to school every day and thinking. "Well, I got this new shirt but I got it because it was on sale at K-Mart."

Alice's dilemma is shared, in part, by all poor kids who rub shoulders with the more affluent. But she suffered an additional humiliation: She used to shop in exclusive stores, and therefore fully understood the disdain the Benetton set have for K-Mart kids.

It took a number of years before John Steinberg's family sank under the weight of prolonged income loss. In the good old days, John had enjoyed summers at the local country club, winter vacations in the Caribbean, and family outings to fancy restaurants. The Steinbergs lived in a magnificent three-story house atop a hill, a stately place fronted by a circular drive. Five years into the disaster, and with no maintenance budget to speak of, it was becoming visibly run down.

John remembers that by the time he was a college sophomore, the paint was peeling badly on the outside. The massive garden, long since bereft of a professional landscaper, was so overgrown he could no longer walk to the back of it. The inside of the house was a study in contrasts. Appliances that were standard issue for the managerial middle class—dishwashers, washing machines, dryers, televisions—stood broken and unrepaired. The wallpaper grew dingy, and the carpet on the stairs became threadworn. The antique chairs in the dining room were stained, the silk seat cushions torn. Chandeliers looked vaguely out of place in the midst of this declining splendor. The whole household had the look of a Southern mansion in the aftermath of the Civil War—its structure reflected a glorious past, but its condition told of years of neglect.

The family car was a regulation station wagon, the kind designed to haul a mob of kids. It aged well, but as John neared the end of high school the car developed signs of terminal mechanical failure. By this time, John's mother had taken a factory job in a nearby town and was dependent on the old wagon to travel to work. The starter motor went out at a particularly bad moment and, for nearly six months, the car could only function by being pushed out of the driveway and rolled down the hill until it picked up enough speed to jump-start in second gear. John remembers being grateful they lived on such a steep incline.

The Steinberg children had, in years past, accompanied their mother on her weekly shopping trips, for the fun of the outing and to make sure special treats found their way home. They would walk up and down the main street of their Connecticut town, stopping at the various specialty stores lining the prosperous commercial strip. Meat came from a butcher shop, bread from a fancy bakery, treats from the handmade candy shop, and staples from an independent, small grocery store. By the time John was in his late teens, the specialty stores were a thing of the past:

> I remember the first time I went with my mother to a big supermarket, a chain store we hadn't been to much before. She went to the meat counter and there were these precut packages of meat in plastic wrap. I had never seen meat set out of that way before. We had always gone to the butcher and he cut the meat to order for us and wrapped it in small white packages.

There are many people in the United States and around the world who would be more than satisfied to eat at the table of the downwardly mobile managerial family. None of these people were hungry or malnourished. But food has greater significance than the vitamins it provides. That middle-class families can open the refrigerator and eat their fill is a demonstration of their freedom from want. The recent proliferation of "designer" foods and fancy delicatessens reveals the additional role of food as fashion and of gastronomy as tourism. And not least, food is a symbol of social status.

For affluent adolescents wolfing down pizza, the connection between diet and fortune is obscure. They devote little energy to thinking about how the food they see on their own tables compares to the fare consumed by other, less fortunate families. Downwardly mobile children *do* learn about how high income underwrites a refrigerator stocked with goodies—when these items disappear. John Steinberg again:

> My family was the real meat and potatoes type. We used to have roast beef and steak all the time. After a few years we couldn't afford it and it was just hamburger and more hamburger. That didn't bother me or my sisters. We were teenagers and we were perfectly happy with it. But I can remember one time my mother went out and splurged on what must have been a fairly cheap roast. It wouldn't hold up under my Dad's carving knife. It just fell apart. He was so disgusted he just walked out of the dining room, leaving my mother to face the kids. He was mad about having to eat that way.

Food, appliances, vacations, clothes, and cars—these basics of middle-class existence are transformed under the brunt of downward mobility. The loss of these items is not just a matter of inconvenience or discomfort. The lack of wheels whittles down each family member's freedom of movement and underlines a new dependency upon others. Dietary changes symbolize a shrinkage in the family's realm of choice. In a culture that lionizes independence, discretion, and autonomy, these material transformations become dramatic emblems of the family's powerlessness to affect its own fate.

But it is the loss of the home, the most tangible symbol of a family's social status, that is the watershed event in the life cycle of downward mobility. In one act, years of attachment to a neighborhood and a way of life are abruptly terminated. The blow is a hard one to withstand, for at least since the era of the GI mortgage, owning a house has defined membership in the middle class. Home ownership is America's most visible measure of economic achievement. Adults who have lost their homes—to foreclosure or distress sales—have truly lost their membership card in the middle class.

It took nearly eight years from the time John Steinberg's father lost his job to the time they lost the house. But when it finally happened, the family was grief-stricken:

> Letting go of that house was one of the hardest things we ever had to do. We felt like we were pushed out of the place we had grown up in. None of the rental houses my family lived in after that ever felt like home. You know, we had a roof over our heads, but losing that house made us feel a little like gypsies.

Distress sales can free up capital and provide some cash reserves to draw on, but the financial relief is often short lived. The house is usually the last thing to go and debts have ordinarily piled high before that occurs. Hence the profits are already earmarked for debt relief. Moreover, the need to relocate finds the downwardly mobile family facing the same escalating housing costs that enabled them to pull a profit from their own home. Rental accommodations anywhere near the family's original homestead are frequently costly. Indeed, rents can be much higher than the house payments on the old home, simply because it was purchased years ago, in the days of low mortgages and reasonable prices. These market factors ultimately lead the downwardly mobile in the direction of lower-income neighborhoods, where their dollars go farther but where the atmosphere is comparatively déclassé.

The sliding standard of living the downwardly mobile endure constitutes a drift away from normal middle-class expectations and behavior. The family is growing more deviant over time—its resemblance to the "precrisis" era becomes increasingly faint. Some of the slide can be hidden through dissembling, lies, or cover-ups. The whole family goes "into the closet"—hiding the real situation from the outside world, trying to appear "straight" to their neighbors—while behind the scenes its life steadily draws farther and farther away from the middle-class norm. But there is a psychological cost to living in the closet: Relations between family members grow more intense, and new, sometimes arduous, demands are placed upon children.

R E A D I N G

34

Profiling Violent Families

Richard J. Gelles and Murray A. Straus

Each incident of family violence seems to be unique—an uncontrolled explosion of rage, a random expression of anger, an impulse, a volcanic eruption of sadism. Each abuser seems a bit different. The circumstances never seem to be the same. In one home a child may be attacked for talking back to a parent, in another the precipitating incident may be a broken lamp. Wives have been beaten because the food was cold, because the house was cold, because they were cold.

If we reject the notion that violence and abuse are the products of mental illness or intraindividual pathologies, then we implicitly accept the assumption that there is a social pattern that underlies intimate abuse.[1] The public and the media recognize this underlying pattern. Perhaps the most frequently asked question by the press, public, and clinicians who treat cases of domestic abuse is, "what is the profile of a violent parent, husband, wife, family?" . . . [H]umans have an innate desire for social order. They want to live in a predictable world.

From pp. 77–97 in *Intimate Violence*. New York: Simon & Schuster Copyright © 1988 by Richard J. Gelles and Murray A. Straus. Reprinted by permission of Simon & Schuster, In

Even though violence in the home is more socially acceptable than violence in the street and thus, to a degree, more orderly, people still want to know what to look for. What are the signs, indicators, predictors, of a battering parent, an abusive husband?

A profile of intimate violence must include at least three dimensions. First, we need to examine the social organization of families in general that contributes to the risk of violence in the home. Second, we review the characteristics of families in particular that make certain families high risk for violence. Third, we discuss the temporal and spatial patterns of intimate violence—where and when violence is most likely to occur.

VIOLENCE AND THE SOCIAL ORGANIZATION OF THE FAMILY

The myth that violence and love do not coexist in families disguises a great irony about intimacy and violence. There are a number of distinct organizational characteristics of the family that promote intimacy, but at the very same time contribute to the escalation of conflict to violence and injury.[2] Sometimes, the very characteristics that make the family a warm, supportive, and intimate environment also lead to conflict and violence.

The time we spend with our family almost always exceeds the time we spend at work or with nonfamily members. This is particularly true for young children, men and women who are not in the work force, and the very old. From a strictly quantitative point of view, we are at greater risk in the home simply because we spend so much time there. But, time together is not sufficient to lead to violence. What goes on during these times is much more important than simply the minutes, hours, days, weeks, or years spent together.

Not only are we with our parents, partners, and children, but we interact with them over a wide range of activities and interests. Unless you live (and love) with someone, the total range of activities and interests you share are much narrower than intimate, family involvements. While the range of intimate interactions is great, so is the intensity. When the nature of intimate involvement is deep, the stakes of the involvement rise. Failures are more important. Slights, insults, and affronts hurt more. The pain of injury runs deeper. A cutting remark by a family member is likely to hurt more than the same remark in another setting.

We know more about members of our family than we know about any other individuals we ever deal with. We know their fears, wants, desires, frailties. We know what makes them happy, mad, frustrated, content. Likewise, they know the same about us. The depth of knowledge that makes intimacy possible also reveals the vulnerabilities and frailties that make it possible to escalate conflict. If, for instance, our spouse insults us, we know in an instant what to say to get even. We know enough to quickly support a family member, or to damage him. In no other setting is there a greater potential to support and help, or hurt and harm, with a gesture, a phrase, or a cutting remark. Over and over again, the people we talk to point to an attack on their partner's vulnerabilities as precipitating violence:

If I want to make her feel real bad, I tell her how stupid she is. She can't deal with this, and she hits me.

We tear each other down all the time. He says things just to hurt me—like how I clean the house. I complain about his work—about how he doesn't make enough money to support us. He gets upset, I get upset, we hit each other.

If I really want to get her, I call her dirty names or call her trash.

We found, in many of our interviews with members of violent families, that squabbles, arguments, and confrontations escalate rapidly to violence when one partner focused on the other's vulnerabilities. Jane, a 32-year-old mother, found that criticizing her husband's child-care skills often moved an argument to violence:

Well, we would argue about something, anything. If it was about our kids I would say, "But you shouldn't talk, because you don't even know how to take care of them." If I wanted to hurt him I would use that. We use the kids in our fights and it really gets bad. He [her husband] doesn't think the baby loves him. I guess I contribute to that a bit. When the baby start's fussin' my husband will say "Go to your mom." When I throw it up to him that the baby is afraid of him, that's when the fights really get goin'.

It is perhaps the greatest irony of family relations that the quality that allows intimacy—intimate knowledge of social biographies, is also a potential explosive, ready to be set off with the smallest fuse.

The range of family activities includes deciding what television program to watch, who uses the bathroom first, what house to buy, what job to take, how to raise and discipline the children, or what to have for dinner. Whether the activities are sublime or ridiculous, the outcome is often "zero-sum" for the participants. Decisions and decision making across the range of family activities often mean that one person (or group) will win, while another will lose. If a husband takes a new job in another city, his wife may have to give up her job, while the children may have to leave their friends. If her job and the children's friends are more important, then the husband will lose a chance for job advancement or a higher income. While the stakes over which television station to watch or which movie to go to may be smaller, the notion of winning and losing is still there. In fact, some of the most intense family conflicts are over what seem to be the most trivial choices. Joanne, a 25-year-old mother of two toddlers, remembers violent fights over whether she and her husband would talk or watch television:

When I was pregnant the violence was pretty regular. John would come home from work. I would want to talk with him, 'cause I had been cooped up in the house with the baby and being pregnant. He would just want to watch the TV. So he would have the TV on and he didn't want to listen to me. We'd have these big fights. He pushed me out of the way. I would get in front of the TV and he would just throw me on the floor.

We talked to one wife who, after a fight over the television, picked the TV up and threw it at her husband. For a short time at least, they did not have a television to fight over.

Zero-sum activities are not just those that require decisions or choices. Less obvious than choices or decisions, but equally or sometimes more important, are infringements of personal space or personal habits. The messy wife and the neat husband may engage in perpetual zero-sum conflict over the house, the bedroom, and even closet space. How should meals be served? When should the dishes be washed? Who left the hairbrush in the sink? How the toothpaste should be squeezed from the tube, and a million other daily conflicts and confrontations end with a winner and a loser.

Imagine you have a co-worker who wears checkered ties with striped shirts, who cannot spell, whose personal hygiene leaves much to be desired. How likely are you to (1) tell him that he should change his habits; (2) order him to change; (3) spank him, send him to his room, or cut off his paycheck until he does change? Probably never. Yet, were this person your partner, child, or even parent, you would think nothing of getting involved and trying to influence his behavior. While the odd behavior of a friend or co-worker may be cause for some embarrassment, we typically would not think of trying to influence this person unless we had a close relationship with him. Yet, family membership carries with it not only the right, but sometimes the obligation, to influence other members of the family. Consequently, we almost always get involved in interactions in the home that we would certainly ignore or make light of in other settings.

Few people notice that the social structure of the family is unique. First, the family has a balance of both males and females. Other settings have this quality—coeducational schools, for instance. But many of the social institutions we are involved in have an imbalance of males and females. Some settings—automobile assembly lines, for instance—may be predominantly male, while other groups—a typing pool, for instance—may be almost exclusively female. In addition to the fact that intimate settings almost always include males and females, families also typically include a range of ages. Half of all households have children under 18 years of age in them.[3] Thus the family, more so than almost any other social group or social setting, has the potential for both generational and sex differences and conflicts. The battle between the sexes and the generation gap have long been the source of intimate conflict.

Not only is the family made up of males and females with ages ranging from newborn to elderly, but the family is unique in how it assigns tasks and responsibilities. No other social group expects its members to take on jobs simply on the basis of their age or their sex. In the workplace, at school, and in virtually every other social setting, roles and responsibilities are primarily based on interest, experience, and ability. In the home, duties and responsibilities are primarily tied to age and gender. There are those who argue that there is a biological link between gender and task—that women make better parents than men. Also, the developmental abilities of children certainly preclude their taking on tasks or responsibilities that they are not ready for. But, by and large, the fact that roles and responsibilities are age- and gender-linked is a product of social organization and not biological determinism.

When someone is blocked from doing something that he or she is both interested in and capable of doing, this can be intensely frustrating.[4] When the inequality is socially structured and sanctioned within a society that at the same time espouses equal opportunity and egalitarianism, it can lead to intense conflict and confrontation. Thus, we find that the potential for conflict and violence is especially high in a democratic and egalitarian society that sanctions and supports a male-dominated family system. Even if we did not have values that supported democracy and egalitarianism, the linking of task to gender would produce considerable conflict, since not every man is capable of taking on the socially prescribed leadership role in the home; and not every woman is interested in and capable of assuming the primary responsibility for child care.

The greater the inequality, the more one person makes all the decisions and has all the power, the greater the risk of violence. Power, power confrontations, and perceived threats to domination, in fact, are underlying issues in almost all acts of family violence. One incident of nearly deadly family violence captures the meaning of power and power confrontations:

> My husband wanted to think of himself as the head of the household. He thought that the man should wear the pants in the family. Trouble was, he couldn't seem to get his pants on. He had trouble getting a job and almost never could keep one. If I didn't have my job as a waitress, we would have starved. Even though he didn't make no money, he still wanted to control the house and the kids. But it was my money, and I wasn't about to let him spend it on booze or gambling. This really used to tee him off. But he would get the maddest when the kids showed him no respect. He and I argued a lot. One day we argued in the kitchen and my little girl came in. She wanted to watch TV. My husband told her to go to her room. She said, "No, I don't have to listen to you!" Well, my husband was red. He picked up a knife and threw it at my little girl. He missed. Then he threw a fork at her and it caught her in the chin. She was bloody and crying, and he was still mad and ran after her. I had to hit him with a chair to get him to stop. He ran out of the house and didn't come back for a week. My little girl still has a scar on her cheek.

You can choose whom to marry, and to a certain extent you may choose to end the marital relationship. Ending a marital relationship, even in the age of no-fault divorce, is not neat and simple. There are social expectations that marriage is a long-term commitment—"until death do us part." There are social pressures that one should "work on a relationship" or "keep the family together for the sake of the children." There are also emotional and financial constraints that keep families together or entrap one partner who would like to leave.

You can be an ex-husband or an ex-wife, but not an ex-parent or an ex-child.[5] Birth relationships are quite obviously involuntary. You cannot choose your parents or your children (with the exception of adoption, and here your choices are still limited).

Faced with conflict, one can fight or flee. Because of the nature of family relations, it is not easy to choose the flight option when conflict erupts. Fighting, then, becomes a main option for resolving intimate conflict.

The organization of the family makes for stress. Some stress is simply developmental—the birth of a child, the maturation of children, the increasing costs of raising children as they grow older, illness, old age, and death. There are also voluntary transitions—taking a new job, a promotion, or moving. Stress occurring outside of the home is often brought into the home—unemployment, trouble with the police, trouble with friends at school, trouble with people at work.

We expect a great deal from our families: love, warmth, understanding, nurturing, intimacy, and financial support. These expectations, when they cannot be fulfilled, add to the already high level of stress with which families must cope.

Privacy is the final structural element of modern families that makes them vulnerable to conflict, which can escalate into violence. . . . The nuclear structure of the modern family, and the fact that it is the accepted norm that family relations are private relations, reduces the likelihood that someone will be available to prevent the escalation of family conflict to intimate violence.

We have identified the factors that contribute to the high level of conflict in families. These factors also allow conflicts to become violent and abusive interchanges. By phrasing the discussion differently, we could have presented these factors as also contributing to the closeness and intimacy that people seek in family relations. People who marry and have families seek to spend large amounts of time together, to have deep and long-lasting emotional involvement, to have an intimate and detailed knowledge of another person, and to be able to create some distance between their intimate private lives and the interventions of the outside world.

There are a number of conclusions one can draw from the analysis of the structural factors that raise the risk of conflict and violence in the family. First, there is a link between intimacy and violence. Second is the classic sociological truism—structures affect people. Implicit in the discussion of these factors is that one can explain part of the problem of violence in the home without focusing on the individual psychological status of the perpetrators of violence and abuse. Violence occurs, not just because it is committed by weird, bad, different, or alien people, but because the structure of the modern household is conductive to violent exchanges.

FAMILY AND INDIVIDUAL CHARACTERISTICS RELATED TO INTIMATE VIOLENCE

The structural arrangement of the family makes it possible for violence to occur in all households. However, not all homes are violent. A profile of intimate violence needs to analyze the characteristics of violent individuals and their families.

Volumes could be written inventorying the characteristics that are thought to be related to family violence. The earliest students of child and wife abuse focused on individual personality characteristics.[6] Abusers were described as sadomasochistic, having poor emotional control, self-centered, hypersensitive, dependent, egocentric, narcissistic, and so on. Later, those who studied violence and abuse examined social and social psychological factors such as income, education, age, social stress, and social isolation.[7] Other investigators focused on experience with and exposure to violence. Still others chose to study violence from the point of view of the family level of analysis, examining family size, family power, and family structure.[8]

Sometimes investigators agree on specific characteristics that are believed to be associated with violence; other times the findings are contradictory. There is one thing that researchers agree on—there are a multitude of factors associated with violence in the home.[9] Despite public clamor for a single-factor explanation, no one factor—not mental illness, not experience with violence, not poverty, not stress, and not alcohol or drugs—explains all or most acts of intimate violence.

Abusive Violence Toward Children

Most people who try to explain and understand individual acts of deviant or aberrant behavior such as child abuse immediately turn their focus on the perpetrator. Our culture has a definite "individual level" bias when it comes to trying to explain seemingly unexplainable acts. When someone does something outrageous, weird, or bizarre, our immediate reaction is to look for the answer within that individual. A full understanding of abusive violence, however, requires an examination of not only the violent parent, but the child and family situation.

If one had to come up with a profile of the prototypical abusive parent, it would be a single parent who was young (under 30), had been married for less than ten years, had his or her first child before the age of 18, and was unemployed or employed part time.[10] If he or she worked, it would be at a manual labor job. Studies show that women are slightly more likely to abuse their children than men. The reason is rather obvious: Women typically spend more time with children. But, even if mothers and fathers spend equal time with children (and this is rare), it is the woman who is typically given the responsibility of caring for and dealing with the children.

Economic adversity and worries about money pervade the typical violent home. Alicia, the 34-year-old wife of an assembly-line worker, has beaten, kicked, and punched both her children. So has her husband Fred. She spoke about the economic problems that hung over their heads:

> He worries about what kind of a job he's going to get, or if he's going to get a job at all. He always worries about supporting the family. I think I worry about it more than he does. . . . It gets him angry and frustrated. He gets angry a lot. I think he gets angry at himself for not providing what he feels we need. He has to take it out on someone, and the kids and me are the most available ones.

We witnessed a more graphic example of the impact of economic stress during one of our in-home interviews with a violent couple. When we entered the living room to begin the interview we could not help but notice the holes in the living room walls. During the course of the interview, Jane, the 24-year-old mother of three children, told us that her husband had been laid off from his job at a local shipyard and had come home, taken out his shotgun, and shot up the living room. Violence had not yet been directed at the children, but as we left and considered the family, we could not help but worry about the future targets of violent outbursts.

Stressful life circumstances are the hallmark of the violent family. The greater the stress individuals are under, the more likely they are to be violent toward their children. Our 1976 survey of violence in the American family included a measure of life stress.[11] Subjects were asked if they had experienced any of a list of 18 stressful events in the last year, ranging from problems at work, to death of a family member, to problems with children. Experience with stress ranged from households that experienced no stressful event to homes that had experienced 13 of the 18 items we discussed. The average experience with stress, however, was modest—about two stressful life events each year. Not surprisingly, the greater the number of stressful events experienced, the greater the rate of abusive violence toward children in the home. More than one out of three families that were unfortunate enough to encounter ten or more stressful events reported using abusive violence toward a child in the previous year. This rate was 100 percent greater than the rate for households experiencing only one stressful incident.

Violent parents are likely to have experienced or been exposed to violence as children. Although this does not predetermine that they will be violent (and likewise, some abusive parents grew up in nonviolent homes), there is the heightened risk that a violent past will lead to a violent future.

One of the more surprising outcomes of our first national survey of family violence was that there was no difference between blacks and whites in the rates of abusive violence toward children. This should not have been the case. First, most official reports of child abuse indicate that blacks are overrepresented in the reports. Also, blacks in the United States have higher rates of unemployment than whites and lower annual incomes—two factors that we know lead to higher risk of abuse. That blacks and whites had the same rate of abusive violence was one of the great mysteries of the survey. A careful examination of the data collected unraveled the apparent mystery. While blacks did indeed encounter economic problems and life stresses at greater rates than whites, they also were more involved in family and community activities than white families. Blacks reported more contact with their relatives and more use of their relatives for financial support and child care. It was apparent that the extensive social networks that black families develop and maintain insulate them from the severe economic stresses they also experience, and thus reduce what otherwise would have been a higher rate of parental violence.[12]

Most of the cases of child abuse we hear about involve very young children. There is nothing that provokes greater sadness and outrage than seeing the battered body of a defenseless infant. The youngest victims evoke the most sympathy and anger, best fit the stereotype of the innocent victim, and are more likely to be publicly identified as victims of abuse. The youngest children are indeed the most likely to be beaten and hurt.

However, the myth that only innocents are victims of abuse hides the teenage victim. Teenagers are equally likely to be abused as children under three years of age. Why are the youngest children and teenagers at the greatest risk of abusive violence? When we explain why the youngest children are likely victims the answer seems to be that they are demanding, produce considerable stress, and cannot be reasoned with verbally. Parents of teenagers offer the same explanation for why they think teenagers as a group are at equally high risk.

Among the younger victims of violence and abuse, there are a number of factors that make them at risk. Low birth weight babies, premature children, handicapped, retarded, and developmentally disabled children run a high life-long risk of violence and abuse.[13] In fact, the risk is great for any child who is considered different.

If you want to prevent violence and abuse, either have no children or eight or nine. This was the somewhat common-sense outcome of our research on family factors related to violence toward children. It is rather obvious that more children create more stress. Why then did we find no violence in the families with eight or nine children? Perhaps people who have the largest families are the kindest, most loving parents. Perhaps they are simply exhausted. A more realistic explanation is that at a certain point, children become resources that insulate a family from stress. A family with eight or nine children probably did not have them all at once. With a two- or three-year gap between children, a family with eight or more children has older children at home to help care for and raise the infants, babies, and toddlers. If there is a truly extended family form in our society, it is the large family with children ranging from newborn to 20 living in the home.

A final characteristic of violent parents is that they are almost always cut off from the community they live in. Our survey of family violence found that the most violent parents have lived in their community for less than two years. They tend to belong to few, if any, community organizations, and have little contact with friends and relatives. This social isolation cuts them off from any possible source of help to deal with the stresses of intimate living or economic adversity. These parents are not only more vulnerable to stress, their lack of social involvement also means that they are less likely to abandon their violent behavior and conform to community values and standards. Not only are they particularly vulnerable to responding violently to stress, they tend not to see this behavior as inappropriate.

Abusive Violence Between Partners

Dale, wife of a Fortune 500 executive, wrote us so that we would know that wife beating is not confined to only poor households. Her husband beats her regularly. He has hurled dishes at her, thrown her down stairs, and blackened her eyes. When her husband drinks, she often spends the night huddled in the backseat of their Lincoln Continental. Marion lives so far on the other side of the tracks, she might as well be on another planet. She and her husband live five stories up in a run-down tenement. Heat is a luxury that they often cannot afford, and when they can afford it, the heat rarely works. Marion's husband has broken her jaw and ribs, and has shot at her on two occasions. The range of homes where wife beating occurs seems to defy categorization. One can pick up a newspaper and read of wife beating in a lower-class neighborhood and then turn the page and read that the wife of a famous rock musician has filed for divorce claiming she was beaten.

If there is a typical wife beater, he is not a rock musician, actor, football player, or business executive.[14] The typical beater is employed part-time or not at all. His total income is poverty level. He worries about economic security, and he is very dissatisfied with his standard of living. He is young, between the ages of 18 and 24—the prime age for violent behavior in and out of the home—and has been married for less than ten years. While he tries to dominate the family and hold down what he sees as the husband's position of power, he has few of the economic or social resources that allow for such dominance; not only does his neighbor have a better job and earn more money than he does, but often so does his wife.

Researchers have found that status inconsistency is an important component of the profile of the battering husband.[15] An example of status inconsistency occurs when a man's educational background is much higher than his occupational attainment—a Ph.D. who drives a taxicab for a living. Status inconsistency can also result when a husband does not have as much occupational or educational status as his wife. Researchers Carton Hornung, Claire McCullough, and Taichi Sugimoto report that contrary to what is generally believed, violence is less common when the wife is at home than when she works. They suggest that status inconsistency explains this finding. Husbands, they note, can be more threatened when their wives work and have an independent source of income and prestige than when they are home and dependent. Conflict and verbal aggression are frequent occurrences in the wife beater's home. Verbal violence and mental abuse are also directed at his spouse. Perhaps the most telling of all attributes of the battering man is that he feels inadequate and sees violence as a culturally acceptable way to be both dominant and powerful.

There is a great tendency to blame the victim in cases of family violence. Battered women have frequently been described as masochistic. The debate over such presumed masochism has raged to the point where a substantial group of psychologists have called for elimination of the diagnostic category "masochist" from the revision of DSM-III, the official description of psychological diagnostic groupings.

There is not much evidence that battered women as a group are more masochistic than other women. There are, however, some distinct psychological attributes found among battered women. Victims of wife beating are often found to be dependent, having low self-esteem, and feeling inadequate or helpless.[16] On the other hand, battered wives have been found to be aggressive, masculine, and frigid. In all likelihood these contradictory findings are the result of the fact that there is precious little research on the consequence of being battered, and the research that has been conducted frequently uses small samples, without comparison groups. This makes generalizing from such research difficult and contradictory findings inevitable.

Another problem with assessing the psychological traits of battered women is the difficulty in determining whether the personalities were present before the battering or were the result of the victimization. . . .

Pregnant women often report being beaten.[17] Pregnancy, however, does not make women vulnerable to violence and battering.[18] When we analyzed the results of the Second National Family Violence Survey we found that age, not pregnancy, is the best predictor of risk of wife beating. Women between the ages of 18 and 24 are more likely to be beaten, whether they are pregnant or not. Women older than 24 years of age are less likely to be beaten.

Although pregnant women are not more vulnerable to violence, the nature of the violent attack does appear to change when a woman is pregnant. One of the first interviews we ever conducted still stands out in our minds. The subject was a 30-year-old woman who had been beaten severely throughout her marriage. The beatings were more severe, and took on a different tone, when she was pregnant: "Oh, yeah, he hit me when I was pregnant. It was weird. Usually he just hit me in the face with his fist, but when I was pregnant he used to hit me in the belly."

Perhaps the most controversial finding from our 1975 National Family Violence Survey was the report that a substantial number of women hit and beat their husbands. Since 1975 at least ten additional investigations have confirmed the fact that women hit and beat their husbands.[19] Unfortunately, the data on wife-to-husband violence have been misreported, misinterpreted, and misunderstood. Research uniformly shows that about as many women hit men as men hit women. However, those who report that husband abuse is a common as wife abuse overlook two important facts. First, the greater average size and strength of men and their greater aggressiveness means that a man's punch will probably produce more pain, injury, and harm than a punch by a woman. Second, nearly three-fourths of the violence committed by women is done in self-defense. While violence by women should not be dismissed, neither should it be overlooked or hidden. On occasion, legislators and spokespersons like Phyllis Schlafly have used the data on violence by wives to minimize the need for services for battered women. Such arguments do a great injustice to the victimization of women.

As we said, more often than not a wife who beats her husband has herself been beaten. Her violence is the violence of self-defense. On some occasions she will strike back to protect herself; on others she will strike first, believing that if she does not, she will be badly beaten. Sally, a 44-year-old woman married for 25 years, recounted how she used violence to protect herself:

> When he hits me, I retaliate. Maybe I don't have the same strength as he does, but I know how to hold my own. I could get hurt, but I am going to go down trying. You know, it's not like there is anyone else here who is going to help me. So . . . I hit him back . . . I pick something up and I hit him.

Marianne does not wait until she is hit. She says she has learned the cues that her husband is about to hit her:

> I know that look he gets when he gets ready to hit me. We've been married for ten years, and I've seen that look of his. So he gets that look, and I get something to hit him with. Once I hit him with a lamp. Another time I stabbed him. Usually I don't get so bad, but I was real fearful that time.

The violence in Marianne's home is not just one way. She has been hospitalized four times as a result of her husband's beatings. Her fears are very real.

The profile of those who engage in violence with their partners is quite similar to the profile of the parents who are abusive toward their children. The greater the stress, the lower the income, the more violence. Also, there is a direct relationship between violence in childhood and the likelihood of becoming a violent adult. Again, we add the caution that although there is a relationship, this does not predetermine that all those who experience violence will grow up to be abusers.

One of the more interesting aspects of the relationship between childhood and adult violence is that *observing* your parents hit one another is a more powerful contributor to the probability of becoming a violent adult than being a victim of violence. The learning experience of seeing your mother and father strike one another is more significant than being hit yourself. Experiencing, and more importantly observing, violence as a child teaches three lessons:

1. Those who love you are also those who hit you, and those you love are people you can hit.

2. Seeing and experiencing violence in your home establishes the moral rightness of hitting those you love.

3. If other means of getting your way, dealing with stress, or expressing yourself do not work, violence is permissible.

The latter lesson ties in well with our finding that stress also leads to an increased risk of violence in the home. One theory holds that people learn to use violence to cope with stress. If this is correct, then stress would be a necessary, but not sufficient, precondition for family violence. In other words, stress alone does not cause violence unless the family members have learned that being violent is both appropriate and also will not meet with negative sanctions. Another theory is that learning to be violent and stress are two independent contributors to intimate violence and abuse.

The sociologists Debra Kalmuss and Judith Seltzer tested these two theories using the data collected for the First National Family Violence Survey.[20] They found that stress and learning are independent contributions to the risk of abusive violence. Moreover, observing and experiencing violence while growing up was a more powerful contributor to the later risk of intimate violence than was life stress.

Lurking beneath the surface of all intimate violence are confrontations and controversies over power. Our statistical evidence shows that the risk of intimate violence is the greatest when all the decision making in a home is concentrated in the hands of one of the partners. Couples who report the most sharing of decisions report the lowest rates of violence. Our evidence goes beyond the statistics. Over and over again, case after case, interview after interview, we hear batterers and victims discuss how power and control were at the core of the events that led up to the use of violence. Violent husbands report that they "need to" hit their wives to show them who is in charge. Some of the victimized wives struggle against domination and precipitate further violence. Other wives tell us that they will actually provoke their husband to violence because they want him to be more dominant. This is not so much a case of the wife being a masochist as it is another example of the conflicts and struggles that occur as couples confront the traditional cultural expectation that the male should be the dominant person in the household. Some couples fight against this prescription, while others fight to preserve it.

NO PLACE TO RUN, NO PLACE TO HIDE

Eleanor began to prepare dinner for her two children and her husband. It was evening on a Saturday night in January. While she grilled hamburgers, her husband Albert walked in. An argument began over whether Eleanor had taken Albert's shirts to the cleaners. Eleanor protested she had. Albert said she was lying. Eleanor protested, yelled, and finally said that Albert was drunk so often he never remembered whether his shirts were clean or dirty. Albert lunged at his wife. He pushed her against the stove, grabbed the sizzling burgers, and threw them across the room. He stalked out, slamming the front door behind him. Quiet tension reigned in the house through a dinner of tuna fish sandwiches and some television, and then the children were put to bed. Eleanor went to bed at 11:00 P.M., but could not fall asleep. At around 1:00 A.M. Albert returned home. He was quiet as he removed his clothes and got into bed. Eleanor turned over, her back to Albert. This signaled that she was awake, and another argument began to brew. This time it was over sex. Eleanor resisted. She always resisted when Albert was drunk. Tonight she resisted because she was still angry over the dinnertime argument. Albert lay his heavy arms around Eleanor and she struggled to get free. The quiet, almost silent struggle began to build. Angry whispers, angry gestures, and finally yelling ensued. Eleanor knew that Albert kept a gun in his night table drawer. Once, after a fight, Albert had gone to bed by putting the bullets on Eleanor's nightstand and the gun under his pillow. As the midnight fight escalated, Albert made a gesture toward the night table. For whatever reason, Eleanor thought that this would be the time that Albert would try to shoot her. She dove across the bed, pulled the drawer out of the night table, clawed for the gun as it rattled to the floor, and came to her feet with the gun in her hand. The first shot tore through Albert's right arm, the second slammed into the wall, the third tore away the top of his head. Eleanor stopped firing only after she heard three of four clicks as the hammer struck the now empty cylinders.

This could be a story out of a soap opera or a supermarket newsstand magazine. It is, unfortunately, a story repeated 2,000 times a year. We have focused on the family structure and the individual and family characteristics that increase the risk of violence in specific households. Eleanor's and Albert's story illustrates the situational structure of intimate violence.

It goes without saying that intimate violence is most likely to occur in intimate settings. Occasionally couples will strike one another in the car. Husbands sometimes grab their wives at a party or on the street. Husbands or wives rarely slap their partners in public. The majority of domestic combat takes place in private, behind closed doors. We have known men and women to stifle their anger and see the while guests are in the home. As the last guest leaves and the door closes, the fight and the violence erupt.

Eleanor and Albert began their path to their lethal confrontation in the kitchen. When we interviewed couples about the location of violence between partners and toward children, more than half said that the violence occurs in the kitchen. The living room and bedroom were the next most likely scenes. Only the bathroom seemed free from conflict and violence—perhaps because most bathrooms are small, have locks, or most likely because bathrooms are places of individual privacy.

Students of domestic homicide report that the bedroom is the most lethal room in the home. The criminologist Marvin Wolfgang reported that 20 percent of *all* victims of criminal homicide are killed in the bedroom.[21] The kitchen and dining room are the other frequent scenes of lethal violence between family members.

After 8:00 P.M. the risk for family violence increases.[22] This is almost self-evident, since this is also the time when family members are most likely to be together in the home. We found that four out of ten cases of domestic violence occur between 8:00 P.M. and midnight. Eight out of ten domestic fights take place between 5:00 P.M. and 7:00 A.M. Early evening fights occur in the kitchen. The living room becomes the likely setting for evening disputes, and the most violent and most lethal altercations break out in the bedroom, late at night.

The temporal and spatial patterns of intimate violence support our notion that privacy is a key underlying factor that leads to violence. Time and space constrain the options of both the offender and the victim. As the evening wears on, there are fewer places to run to, fewer places to hide. When the first fight broke out between Eleanor and Albert, it was about 5:00 P.M. Albert rushed out of the house in a huff—most likely heading for the neighborhood bar. The bar closed at 1:00 A.M., and that was when Albert went home to his final conflict.

A fight that erupts in the bedroom, in the early morning, constrains both parties. It is too late to stalk out of the home to a bar and too late to run to a friend or family member. The bed and the bedroom offer no protection and precious few places to flee or take cover. It is not surprising that so many of the most violent family fights end there.

Common sense would argue that weekends are the most violent time of the week for families. Common sense would not lead one to assume that the most violent times of the year are Christmas and Easter. When we looked at which day of the week violence was most likely to occur, we found that the empirical evidence was in full support of common sense. Weekends are when families spent the most time together and when the potential for conflicts and conflicts of interest is greatest. Not surprisingly, seven out of ten violent episodes we talked about with family members took place on either Saturday or Sunday. Weekends after a payday can be especially violent. Janice, the mother of an infant daughter, told us about the typical weekend fight:

> It starts over money. He gets paid on Friday. So he comes home on Fridays and I ask him for money. I am usually at the stove cooking when he comes home. And I have no money left. So I ask. This last Friday he said he didn't have no money. I got real mad. I mean, its payday and he has no money? He said he borrowed money and had to pay it back. I said he just must be lyin'. He spends it on booze or gambles it. Other

times we fight because he gives me only fifty dollars. I can't feed him and the baby with just fifty dollars. So I got mad and started to yell.

Thus, the days of the week that are the most violent are those that combine the most conflict and violence-producing structural components of family life—time together, privacy, and stress.

Common sense would not suggest that violence is most likely to erupt at times of the year when families celebrate holidays and the spirit of family togetherness. Yet, contrary to common sense, it is the time from Thanksgiving to New Year's Day and again at Easter that violence in the home peaks.

As we conducted our interviews with members of violent homes we heard again and again about violence that occurred around the Christmas tree. Even the Christmas tree became a weapon in some homes:

I remember one particularly violent time. When we were first married. He was out drinking and he came home stinking drunk. I suppose I must have said something. Well, he took a fit. He started putting his first through the walls. Finally, he just picked up the Christmas tree and threw it at me.

Another woman recalled her most violent experience:

He hit me just before New Year's Day. I don't really recall what went on. We argue a lot. This time it might have been about money, or maybe the kids. Anyway, he got fierce. He punched me again and again. I was bleeding real bad. He had to take me to the hospital. It was the worst time of the year I ever had.

Perhaps people have a clearer memory of a violent event if it happens around a holiday. While this is a plausible explanation for our findings, it is not the complete answer. We have examined weekly reports of hospital admissions for child abuse and neglect, and found that the peak times of year for admissions were the period from Christmas to New Year's Day, and again in the spring around Easter Sunday.

A number of factors may contribute to the likelihood of domestic violence and abuse during the Christmas season. This is a time when families can assume tremendous financial burdens. Purchasing Christmas gifts can either take a toll on a family's resources or plunge a family into debt. Stress can also come from *not* buying gifts and presents. If a family cannot afford gifts expected by children, loved ones, and others, this can be extremely frustrating. The holiday season offers a stark contrast between what is expected and what a family can afford.

Holidays also create nonfinancial stress. Christmas and Easter holidays project images of family harmony, love, and togetherness. Songs, advertisements, and television specials all play up the image of the caring, loving, and even affluent family. A family with deep conflict and trouble may see these images in sad and frustrating contrast with their own lives. We know that prison riots are more likely to occur during holiday seasons, as prisoners apparently become stressed about being separated from family and friends during times of the year when such closeness is expected. Clearly, being with family and friends, but having unmet expectations for love and warmth, can also be extremely frustrating.

Time of day and time of year analysis supports the notion that privacy and stress are important structural contributors to domestic violence. Conflict frequently erupts over a stressful event, during a stressful time of the day, or around a stressful time of year. If the eruption takes place in a private setting, and at a time and place where it is difficult to flee or back down, the conflict can escalate into violence. The more privacy, the greater the power difference, and the fewer options the victim has in terms of getting help or finding protection, the more the violence can escalate.

The saddest and most frustrating aspect of our analysis of the structural, personal, familial, temporal, and spatial dynamics of intimate violence is that our results seem to say that violence in the home is inevitable. Lessons learned as a child set the stage for using violence as an adult. The structural makeup of the modern family is like a pressure cooker containing and escalating stress and conflict. If violence breaks out late at night, on a weekend, or a holiday, victims often have no place to run, no place to hide.

Our profile of violent families is not quite as bleak as it might seem. First, no one structural factor, personal experience, or situation predetermines that all or any family will be violent. Second, families do not live in a vacuum. Family members and people outside of the home can intervene to turn down the heat under the pressure cooker. We have found that friends, relatives, and neighbors can successfully intervene and reduce the pressure that could lead to violence.

NOTES

1. Two articles that critique the theory that abuse is the product of mental illness or psychopathology are Richard J. Gelles, "Child Abuse as Psychopathology: A Sociological Critique and Reformulation," *American Journal of Orthopsychiatry* 43 (July 1973): 611–21; and J. Spinetta and D. Rigler, "The Child-Abusing Parent: A Psychological Review," *Psychological Bulletin* 77 (April 1972): 296–304.

2. The organizational characteristics of the family that promote both intimacy and conflict were first described in Richard J. Gelles and Murray A. Straus, "Determinants of Violence in the Family: Towards an Integrated Theory," in Wesley Burr, Reuben Hill, F. Ivan Nye, and Ira I. Reiss, eds., *Contemporary Theories About the Family* vol. 1. (New York: Free Press, 1979), 549–81. These ideas were further developed in Murray A. Straus and Gerald T. Hotaling, eds., *The Social Causes of Husband-Wife Violence* (Minneapolis: University of Minnesota Press, 1980); and Richard J. Gelles and Claire Pedrick-Cornell, *Intimate Violence in Families* (Beverly Hills, Calif.: Sage, 1985).

3. U.S. Bureau of the Census, *Statistical Abstract of the United States: 1987*, 107th ed. (Washington, D.C.: Government Printing Office, 1986), chart 45; U.S. Bureau of the Census, *Current Population Report*, ser. P-20, no. 411.

4. This is the classic statement of psychological frustration/aggression theory. The theory has been articulated by J. C. Dollard, L. Doob, N. Miller, O.

Mowrer, and R. Sears, *Frustration and Aggression* (New Haven, Conn.: Yale University Press, 1939); and N. E. Miller, "The Frustration-Aggression Hypothesis," *Psychological Review* 48, no. 4 (1941): 337–42. A sociological formulation of the notion that blocked goals can be frustrating can be found in Robert K. Merton, "Social Structure and Anomie," *American Sociological Review* 3 (October 1938): 672–82.

5. This idea was first presented by Alice Rossi in her article, "Transition to Parenthood," *Journal of Marriage and the Family* 30 (February 1968): 26–39.

6. See, for example: Vincent J. Fontana, *The Maltreated Child: The Maltreatment Syndrome in Children* (Springfield, Ill.: Charles C. Thomas, 1971); Richard Galdston, "Observations on Children Who Have Been Physically Abused and Their Parents," *American Journal of Psychiatry* 122, no. 4 (1965): 440–43; Leroy G. Schultz, "The Wife Assaulter," *Journal of Social Therapy* 6, no. 2 (1960): 103–12; Brandt F. Steele and Carl B. Pollock, "A Psychiatric Study of Parents Who Abuse Infants and Small Children," in R. Helfer and C. Henry Kempe, eds., *The Battered Child* (Chicago: University of Chicago Press, 1968), 103–47; and S. R. Zalba, "Battered Children," *Transaction* 8 (July–August 1971): 58–61.

7. See Gelles, "Child Abuse"; and David Gil, "Violence Against Children," *Journal of Marriage and the Family* 33 (November 1971): 637–48.

8. See R. Emerson Dobash and Russell Dobash, *Violence Against Wives: The Case Against Patriarchy* (New York: Free Press, 1979).

9. For a review of the factors related to family violence, see Richard J. Gelles, "Family Violence," in Ralph H. Turner and James F. Short, eds., *Annual Review of Sociology*, vol. 11 (Palo Alto, Calif.: Annual Reviews, Inc. 1985), 347–67; Marc F. Maden and D. F. Wrench, "Significant Findings in Child Abuse Research," *Victimology* 2 (1977): 196–224; and Suzanne K. Steinmetz, "Violence Between Family Members," *Marriage and Family Review* 1 (1978): 1–16.

10. The profile that is presented is a statistical profile. It would be incorrect to assume that someone who does not fit this profile would not be an abuser. Similarly, someone who fit the profile is likely to abuse, but is not always an abuser. The profile was developed in Murray A. Straus, Richard J. Gelles, and Suzanne K. Steinmetz. *Behind Closed Doors: Violence in the American Family* (Garden City, N.Y.: Anchor Books, 1980).

11. The survey is reported in Straus, Gelles, and Steinmetz, *Behind Closed Doors*. The measure of stress was adapted from T. H. Holmes and R. H. Rahe, "The Social Readjustment Rating Scale," *Journal of Psychosomatic Research* 11 (1967): 213–18.

12. Straus, Gelles, and Steinmetz, *Behind Closed Doors;* and Noel Cazenave and Murray A. Straus, "Race, Class, Network Embeddedness and Family Violence: A Search for Potent Support Systems," *Journal of Comparative Family Studies* 10 (Autumn 1979): 281–300.

13. A review of child factors that are related to physical abuse can be found in W. N. Friedrich and J. A. Boriskin, "The Role of the Child in Abuse: A

Review of the Literature," *American Journal of Orthopsychiatry* 46 (October 1976): 580–90.

14. The profile of wife beaters is a statistical profile and was first presented in Straus, Gelles, and Steinmetz, *Behind Closed Doors*.

15. C. A. Hornung, B. C. McCullough, and T. Sugimoto, "Status Relationships in Marriage: Risk Factors in Spouse Abuse," *Journal of Marriage and the Family* 43 (August 1981): 675–92.

16. Lenore Walker, *The Battered Woman* (New York: Harper & Row, 1979).

17. Richard J. Gelles, "Violence and Pregnancy: A Note on the Extent of the Problem and Needed Services," *Family Coordinator* 24 (January 1975): 81–86.

18. When we analyzed the results of the Second National Family Violence Survey, we did find that the rates of violence and abuse were higher among pregnant women than women who were not pregnant. However, when we controlled for age, the differences disappeared. Women under the age of 24 years old experienced high rates of violence and abuse, but the rates were the same for pregnant and nonpregnant women. Women over 24 years old experienced lower rates of violence, and again, there were no differences between pregnant and nonpregnant women. Thus, the relationship between violence and pregnancy which we first reported in 1975 (Gelles, "Violence and Pregnancy") and which others have reported, turns out to be spurious.

19. Michael David Allan Freeman. *Violence in the Home: A Socio-legal Study* (Farnborough, England: Saxon House, 1979); Richard J. Gelles, *The Violent Home: A Study of Physical Aggression Between Husbands and Wives* (Beverly Hills, Calif.: Sage, 1974); Morgan E. Scott, "The Battered Spouse Syndrome," *Virginia Medical* 107 (January 1980): 41–43; Suzanne Sedge, "Spouse Abuse," in Marilyn R. Block and Jan D. Sinnott, eds., *The Battered Elder Syndrome: An Exploratory Study* (College Park, Md.: Center on Aging, 1979), 33–48; Suzanne K. Steinmetz, "The Battered Husband Syndrome," *Victimology* 2 (1978): 499–509; Straus, Gelles, and Steinmetz, *Behind Closed Doors;* Mary Warren, "Battered Husbands," in Margaret E. Ankeney, ed., *Family Violence: A Cycle of Abuse* (Laramie, Wyo.: College of Education, University of Wyoming, 1979), 76–78.

20. Debra Kalmuss and Judith A. Seltzer, "A Test of Social Learning and Stress Models of Family Violence." (Paper presented at the annual meetings of the American Sociological Association, New York, 1986).

21. Marvin Wolfgang, *Patterns in Criminal Homicide* (Philadelphia: University of Pennsylvania Press, 1958).

22. This analysis was first presented in Gelles, *Violent Home*, chapter 4.